HUMAN RELATIONS
IN ORGANIZATIONS

APPLICATIONS AND SKILL BUILDING

ELEVENTH EDITION

HUMAN RELATIONS IN ORGANIZATIONS

APPLICATIONS AND SKILL BUILDING

ELEVENTH EDITION

Robert N. Lussier, Ph.D.
Springfield College

Mc
Graw
Hill
Education

HUMAN RELATIONS IN ORGANIZATIONS: APPLICATIONS AND SKILL BUILDING,
ELEVENTH EDITION

Published by McGraw-Hill Education, 2 Penn Plaza, New York, NY 10121. Copyright © 2019 by McGraw-Hill Education. All rights reserved. Printed in the United States of America. Previous editions © 2017, 2013, and 2010. No part of this publication may be reproduced or distributed in any form or by any means, or stored in a database or retrieval system, without the prior written consent of McGraw-Hill Education, including, but not limited to, in any network or other electronic storage or transmission, or broadcast for distance learning.

Some ancillaries, including electronic and print components, may not be available to customers outside the United States.

This book is printed on acid-free paper.

4 5 6 7 8 9 LKV 21 20 19 18

ISBN 978-1-260-04367-9 (bound edition)
MHID 1-260-04367-3 (bound edition)
ISBN 978-1-260-30882-2 (loose-leaf edition)
MHID 1-260-30882-0 (loose-leaf edition)

Portfolio Manager: *Laura Spell*
Marketing Manager: *Debbie Clare*
Content Project Managers: *Ryan Warczynski, Katie Reuter, Karen Jozefowicz*
Senior Buyer: *Sandy Ludovissy*
Design: *Jessica Cuevas*
Content Licensing Specialist: *Jacob Sullivan*
Cover Image: *©Shutterstock/dotshock*
Compositor: *MPS Limited*

All credits appearing on page or at the end of the book are considered to be an extension of the copyright page.

Library of Congress Cataloging-in-Publication Data

Lussier, Robert N., author.
 Human relations in organizations: applications and skill building /
 Robert N. Lussier, Ph.D., Springfield College.
 Human relations in organisations
 Eleventh Edition. | Dubuque: McGraw-Hill Education, [2018] |
 Revised edition of the author's Human relations in organizations, [2017] |
 Includes index.
 LCCN 2017058661 | ISBN 9781260043679 (alk. paper)
 LCSH: Organizational behavior. | Interpersonal relations.
 LCC HD58.7 .L86 2018 | DDC 658.3—dc23 LC record available
 at https://lccn.loc.gov/2017058661

The Internet addresses listed in the text were accurate at the time of publication. The inclusion of a website does not indicate an endorsement by the authors or McGraw-Hill Education, and McGraw-Hill Education does not guarantee the accuracy of the information presented at these sites.

mheducation.com/highered

I would like to dedicate this book to my wife, Marie, and our children, Jesse, Justin, Danielle, Nicole, Brian, and Renee, for their loving support.

CONTENTS IN BRIEF

In his book *Power Tools,* John Nirenberg asks: "Why are so many well-intended students learning so much and yet able to apply so little in their personal and professional lives?" Is it surprising that students can neither apply what they read nor develop skills when most textbooks continue to focus on reading about concepts and examples, rather than taking the next step and teaching them how to apply what they read and develop the skills required for using the concepts? I wrote this book to give students the opportunity to apply the concepts and develop skills used in their personal and professional lives.

I wrote the first edition back in 1988, prior to AACSB calls for skill development and outcomes assessment, to help professors develop their students' ability to apply the concepts and develop organizational behavior/human relations skills. Unlike competitors, I don't just tell you about the concepts. With networking, for instance—the way most people get jobs and promotions today—I tell you step-by-step how to network and provide you with self-assessment exercises, application exercises, skill development exercises, and, often, videos. So, rather than simply knowing the concepts, you can actually develop skills.

But is the skills approach any good? John Bigelow compared skills texts in his article, "Managerial Skills Texts: How Do They Stack Up?" in the *Journal of Management Education,* and he gave *Human Relations in Organizations* a top rating for a general OB course. Reviewers continue to say it is the best "how to work with people" textbook on the market. Although competing texts now include exercises, reviewers continue to say that no competitor offers the quality and quantity of application and skill-building material.

ENGAGING NETGEN STUDENTS

Today's traditional students are being called Digital Millennial or NetGen learners. Being brought up on the Internet, they have different preferred learning styles than students in prior generations. NetGens prefer active, collaborative, and team-based learning. *Human Relations in Organizations,* Eleventh Edition, is designed to be flexible enough to be used with the traditional lecture method while offering a wide range of engaging activities to select from that best meet students' and professors' educational goals and preferred teaching/learning styles. Below is a list of learning preferences of NetGens and how this text can be used to engage them both in and out of the classroom.

INTEGRATION WITH FLEXIBILITY

This book continues to have a balanced three-pronged approach:

- A clear, concise understanding of human relations/organizational behavior (HR/OB) concepts (second to none);

- The application of HR/OB concepts for critical thinking in the business world (there are nine types of applications, including videos and the Test Bank and Instructor's Manual); and

- The development of HR/OB skills (there are eight types of skills-activities, including videos and the Test Bank and Instructor's Manual).

In addition to this text and its ancillary package to support these distinct but integrated parts, there are tests to

NetGen Learning Preference	How *Human Relations in Organizations* Engages NetGens
Reading: Students prefer active learning to reading.	Students find the text easy to read and understand.
Attention and variety through applications and skill-building exercises: Breaking reading and class time into "chunks" helps keep their attention and improve learning.	The text is broken into "chunks," with concepts, followed by interactive applications and skill-building exercises (see below). Each section consists of a major heading with concepts and application material. Unlike many books with exercises that are simply discussion-based, *Human Relations* develops actual skills that can be used immediately.
Directions: Students benefit from checklists, formulas, and recipes for learning and for life.	*Human Relations* is the most "how to" textbook available, including behavioral model steps for handling common human relations issues, such as conflict, and exercises to develop skills.
Internet: NetGens are comfortable with online environments.	Connect (connect.mheducation.com) provides chapter review material and interactive exercises.

Source: Erika Matulich, Raymond Papp, and Diana Haytko, "Continuous Improvement Through Teaching Innovations: A Requirement for Today's Learners," *Marketing Education Review* 18(1) 2008: 1–7.

assess student performance in all three areas. I wrote almost every application and skill exercise in this text and the Instructor's Manual to ensure complete integration and a seamless course experience.

The concepts, applications, and skill-building material are clearly identified and delineated in this preface, text, and IM/test bank. Our package offers more quality and quantity of application and skill-building material to allow professors to create their unique courses using only the features that will achieve their objectives in the classroom or online. Thus, it is the most flexible package on the market. Next is an explanation of features to choose from for concepts, applications, and skill building.

CONCEPTS

- *Research-based and current.* The book is based on research, not opinion. The eleventh edition has been completely updated. There are more than 925 new references, for an average of 78 per chapter, resulting in 91 percent new references. This is from 30 to 50 percent more references per chapter than major competitors. Earlier references are primarily classics, such as the motivation (Maslow) and leadership (Fiedler) theories.

- *Comprehensive coverage.* The text includes more topics than most competing texts.

- *Systems orientation.* The text is organized in two ways. First, the parts of the book are based on the competency model of managerial education, building from intrapersonal skills, to interpersonal skills, to leadership skills. Second, it also follows the levels of behavior approach, going from individual, to group, to organizational levels of behavior. The systems effect is discussed throughout the book. Cases from Chapters 2 through 12 have questions based on previous chapters to integrate the concepts of multiple chapters.

- *Recurring themes.* Chapters 2 through 12 begin with a discussion of how the chapter concepts affect behavior, human relations, happiness, and performance. Chapters include a discussion of how the concepts differ globally.

- *Pedagogy.* Each chapter contains the following: (1) Learning outcomes at the beginning and in the body of the chapter where the objective can be met. A summary of each learning outcome is given in the Review section at the end of the chapter. (2) Key terms at the beginning of each chapter and again at the end of the Review. The key terms appear in **boldface** and *are defined within the chapter in italic* so they are easy to find. (3) Exhibits, some of which contain multiple concepts or theories. (4) Review. The unique feature of the Review is that it is active in two ways. Students first

answer true/false questions. Then they must fill in the blanks with the appropriate key terms in one of three ways: from memory, from a list of key terms at the end of the review, or from the key terms at the beginning of the chapter.

- *Test bank assessment of concepts.* The test bank includes true/false and multiple-choice questions for the concepts, including the key terms, presented in each chapter. The test bank also includes the learning outcomes from each chapter, which can be used as short-answer questions to test concept understanding. A summary of the learning outcomes appears in the Review, the Instructor's Manual, and the test bank.

APPLICATIONS

1. *Opening Case.* Each chapter opens with a case. Throughout the chapter, the ways the text concepts apply to the case are presented so that students can understand the application of the concepts to actual people in organizations.

2. *Work Applications.* Throughout each chapter there are approximately 11 questions (more than 140 total) that require the students to apply the concepts to their own work experience. Work experience can be present or past and may include part-time, summer, or full-time employment. Work applications require the students to think critically and bridge the gap between the concepts and their world.

3. *Application Situations.* Each chapter contains two to six boxes, each with 5 to 10 questions (300 total) that require students to apply the concept illustrated in a specific, short example. The questions develop critical thinking skills through the application process.

4. *Cases—with Internet video and cumulative questions; plus role-play exercises.* Each chapter has a case study from a real-world organization. At the end of the case, the organization's Web site is given so that students can visit the Web to get updated information on the case. Some of the cases also include Web sites to view case manager interviews/talks. Chapters 2 through 12 include cumulative questions. Cumulative questions include concepts from previous chapters. Thus, students continually review and integrate concepts from earlier chapters. Following each case is a role-play exercise to develop skills based on the concepts illustrated in the case.

5. *Objective Cases.* At the end of each chapter there is a short objective case. The unique feature is the "objective" part, with 10 multiple-choice questions, followed by one or more open-ended questions. These cases require students to apply the concepts to people and organizations.

6. *Communication Skills Questions.* There are more than 125 communication skills questions, an average of approximately nine per chapter, which can be used for class discussion and/or written assignments.

7. *Test Bank Assessment of Applications and Instructor's Manual.* The test bank includes the work applications from the text as well as multiple-choice questions, similar to the Application Situations and case questions, to evaluate critical thinking skills. The Instructor's Manual includes the recommended answers for all the application features above, except the opening case, which is illustrated throughout the chapter text.

SKILL BUILDING

1. *Self-Assessment Exercises.* Each chapter has between one and five (more than 45 total, an average of three per chapter) self-assessment exercises to enable students to gain personal knowledge. Some of the exercises are tied to skill-building exercises to enhance the impact of the self-assessment. All information for completing and scoring, and self-assessment, is contained within each exercise. A unique new feature includes determining a personality profile (in Chapter 3); in all other chapters, students find out how their personality relates to their use of the chapter concepts.

2. *Skill-Building Exercises.* There are more than 50 exercise (average of 4 per chapter). Each exercise states if it is individual or group focused, and if it is appropriate for *in-class and/or online class activitie*s.

3. *Individual and Group Skill-Building Exercises.* Around 60 percent of the skill-building exercises focus primarily on individual skill building, most of which is done outside class as preparation for the exercise. However, in-class and/or online work in groups or as a class using the concepts and sharing answers can enhance skill building. Thus, the instructor has the flexibility to (1) simply have students complete the preparations outside class and during class or online discussion, and then go over the answers, giving concluding remarks and/or leading a class discussion without using any small-group time, or (2) spend group class time as directed in the exercise.

4. *Role-Play Skill-Building Exercises.* Around 10 percent of the skill-building exercises focus primarily on developing skills through behavior modeling, as discussed next. Thus, breaking into groups and role-playing is required. Again, all 12 cases include a role-play exercise.

5. *Models, Behavior Model Videos, and Skill-Building Exercises.* Throughout the book are more than 25 models with step-by-step instructions for handling day-to-day human relations situations. How to use several of the models is illustrated in the behavior-modeling videos. For example, students read the model in the book and watch people send messages, give praise, resolve conflicts, handle complaints, and coach an employee, following the steps in the model. After viewing the video, students role-play how they would handle these human relations situations. Students may also give each other feedback on the effectiveness of their role-plays. Videos can also be used as stand-alone activities.

6. *Test Bank Assessment of Skill-Building and Instructor's Manual.* The test bank includes skill-building questions to assess skill building. The Instructor's Manual gives detailed instructions on using all skill-building exercises and answers to skill-building exercises. It also states how students can be tested on the exercises and provides instructions to give to students.

7. *Skill-Building Objectives and AACSB Competencies.* Each skill-building exercise states its objective and the Association to Advance Collegiate Schools of Business (AACSB) competencies developed through the exercise.

SUMMARY OF INNOVATIONS

- The three-pronged approach to the text: concepts, applications, skills.

- The three-pronged test bank: concepts, applications, skills.

- Eight types of applications, clearly marked in the text, for developing critical thinking skills.

- Eight types of skill-building exercises, clearly marked in the text, that truly develop skills that can be used in one's personal and professional lives.

- Flexibility—use all or only some of the features; select the ones that work for you.

OVERALL REVISIONS

Reorganization and Title Changes

- Chapter 4, Time and Career Management, from the tenth edition has been moved to a new Appendix A. The new Appendix also includes the etiquette section from Chapter 9 in the tenth edition. The new combined Appendix A is "Time, Career, and Etiquette Management."

- Chapter 1 title now includes "Being Happy." How to be happy is presented in Chapter 1 and discussed throughout the rest of the book.

- Chapters 5–13 are now 4–12, as the first part loses a chapter to Appendix A.

- The title of Part 3 has been changed to "Leadership Skills: Influencing to Help Yourself and Others Succeed."

- Chapter 8 title has been changed by dropping Etiquette, which has been moved to Appendix A.

- Chapter 12 title is now "Valuing Diversity and Inclusion Globally," to emphasize the increased coverage of inclusion.

- Chapter 12 has been reorganized to include more coverage of the various types of diversity groups and global differences.

- In Chapter 1, the Assessing Your HR Abilities and Skills 43 questions have been changed to reflect the revised contents. The assessment now has 12 questions. In Appendix B, the same assessment appears for a pretest and posttest comparison. However, there is also a new, longer 36 question assessment.

Updated and New

- The book is completely updated with more than 825 new current references, for a total of more than 925 references; over 91 percent of the references are new to this edition. References include a balance of scholarly journals (including the *Academy of Management Journal, Academy of Management Review, Academy of Management Perspectives,* and *Academy of Management Learning & Education*) to provide research support for the text concepts and business publications (including *Business Week, Forbes, Fortune,* and *The Wall Street Journal*) to provide advice and examples of how the concepts are used in all types of organizations.

- There are more than 100 new people and organization examples of how they use the text concepts.

- There is a new, shorter 12 question pretest and posttest assessment, and a longer 36 question assessment for course learning comparisons.

- Five (42 percent) of the end-of-chapter cases are new to this edition, and the other cases have been updated.

- Most of the new cases, and some of the updated cases, now have suggested video links and new questions related to the case.

- There are three new Application Situation boxes, adding 15 new questions.

- There is a new Skill Building Exercise, Developing New Habits, stating in Chapter 1 and repeated continuing through Appendix A. Based on the chapter concepts, the exercise requires selecting any one habit to change following the three step model.

- AACSB standards have been updated using the 2016 AACSB Business Accreditation Standards, General Skills Areas. The listing of AACSB skills developed in

- each of the Skill Building Exercises throughout the book has also been updated.

- ACBSP (Accreditation Council for Business Schools and Programs), and IACBE (International Assembly for Collegiate Business Education) are now included in Chapter 1.

- New concepts discussed in the new edition include Five-Factor Model, OCEAN (openness, conscientiousness, extraversion, agreeableness, and neuroticism), Human-Metrics, Test Your Stress Smarts, relativism ethics, bullying, idea and personal conflict, authentic leadership, LMX leadership, altercast, networks of teams, multi-team systems, healthy and unhealthy cultures.

- There is less of a management focus so that everyone can clearly understand how to improve human relations and happiness in their personal and professional lives, regardless of their position in the organization.

- Virtually all of the major chapter sections have minor updates, most have revisions, and some sections have been rewritten, as described below.

CHANGES BY CHAPTER

Chapter 1
- The entire chapter has been updated with 62 (88 percent) new references to this new edition, keeping the 6 classic historic references, for a total of 76 references.

- There are 18 new people and company/brand examples: Zappos, Fortune Editor Alan Murray, Wells Fargo, Yahoo, Home Depot, Sonja Lyubomirsky, Booker T. Washington, B.C. Forbes, Neil Pasricha, Facebook's Sheryl Sandberg, Sealed Air, Kirk Douglas, Nike, ACBSP (Accreditation Council for Business Schools and Programs), IACBE (International Assembly for Collegiate Business Education).

- The major change to this chapter is the addition of a new title including Being Happy. There is a new section "Happiness and Relationships" that explains the importance of how relationships affect happiness.

- There is a new subsection "New Habits" that discusses how to make positive habits to improve relationships. Plus, there is a new Skill Building Exercise 1-4, Developing a New Habit to develop this skill.

- Another major change is "Assessing Your HR Abilities and Skills." There is now a short version in Chapter 1 and a longer version in Appendix B. The assessment in Chapter 1 now only has 12 questions, one per chapter and Appendix A (down from 43 questions). The longer version now has 36 questions, three per chapter and Appendix B (down from 43 questions).

- A short paragraph before the opening case now includes an explanation of why we open with a case and how to use the case.

- The section "What's in It for Me?" has been expanded to include how readers can benefit from the book in their personal and professional lives with all new references.

- In the Myths and Reality section, Myth 2 now includes the importance of developing relationships, which is the focus of the book.

- The section "Human Relations: Past, Present, and Future" subsection "Current and Future Challenges in the 21st Century," has been rewritten with all new updated references.

- In addition to AACSB, this section now also states the it meets the core professional components of **ACBSP** (Accreditation Council for Business Schools and Programs), and **IACBE** (International Assembly for Collegiate Business Education) standards.

- The end of chapter case has been updated.

- The format of all Skill Building Exercises has been changed to better indicate if the exercise is individual focused and answers are shared in-class or online in groups. AACSB competencies are updated and clearly listed.

- Skill Building Exercise 1-3 has revised questions to focus more on the positives of human relations content.

Chapter 2

- The entire chapter has been updated with 53 (82 percent) new references to this new edition, for a total of 65 references.

- There are 13 new people and company/brand examples: Google, Lowe's, McDonald's, RadioShack, Xerox, OCEAN, Bill Gates, Steve Jobs, Human Metrics, APA (American Psychological Association) "Test Your Stress Smarts!," PepsiCo CEO Indra Nooyi.

- The "Big Five Model of Personality" states that is it commonly called the Five-Factor Model by academics, and that it is also known as OCEAN (openness, conscientiousness, extraversion, agreeableness, and neuroticism).

- In the "Myers-Briggs Type Indicator (MBTI), it now states that you can also take a free 64 question survey at the **HumanMetrics** website link (http://www .humanmetrics.com/cgi-win/jtypes2.asp).

- The key term stressors has been moved from the "What Is Stress?" section introduction to the subsection "Problems Associated with Too Much Stress."

- The "Signs of Stress" section now states that the **APA** (American Psychological Association) has the "Test Your Stress Smarts!" you can take for free at http:// www.apa.org/helpcenter/stress-smarts.aspx to assess how much you know about stress.

- Work Application 2-3 now includes the question, "How does your stress personality type enhance and/ or hurt your performance?"

- The section "The Learning Organization" has been rewritten with two new subsections "The Need for Individual Learning" and "Group and Organizational Learning" to separate and expand on these topics.

- In the "Perception" section, there is a new description of why we have perception differences and how to improve obtaining perceptual congruence.

- The section "Developing Positive First Impressions" now includes Image Management to stress the importance of a continuing positive impression.

- The subsection "Nonverbal Communications" now has level 3 heading to identify "Facial expressions," "Eye contact," and "Handshake" discussions.

- The end of chapter case has been updated.

- The format of all Skill Building Exercises has been changed to better indicate if the exercise is individual focused and answers are shared in-class or online in groups. AACSB competencies are updated and clearly listed.

- There is a new Skill Building Exercise "New Habits" to develop skills related to the chapter topics.

Chapter 3

- The entire chapter has been updated with 88 (94 percent) new references to this new edition, for a total of 94 references.

- There are 15 new people and company/brand examples: Jessica Herrin, Founder of Stella & Dot, Intel, IBM, Twitter, Google, Steve Jobs Apple, Pixar, Countrywide Financial, Wells Fargo Bank, Indra Nooyi CEO of PepsiCo, Royal Dutch Shell,

- The first section title now includes Happiness—How Attitudes, Job Satisfaction, Self-Concept, Values and Ethics Affect Behavior, Human Relations, Happiness, and Performance.

- The Self-Concept section now discusses the importance of having a positive self-concept in getting a job.

- The Building a Positive Self-Concept section now includes using habits to change behavior.

- The beginning of the Values section has been reorganized and much of it rewritten.

- The entire Ethics section has been expanded as follows:

  - In the Ethics section, the first section has been rewritten with expanded coverage. It is now titled "Why Do People Behave Unethically and Does Ethical Behavior Pay?" The first subsection is "Why Do Good People Do Bad Things," followed by "Individual Ethics," "Organizational Business Ethics," and "Caution Against Escalation of Unethical Behavior, with Relativism Ethics."

- The "How People Justify Unethical Behavior" section now includes key terms for the examples of unethical behavior.

- The "Human Relations Guides to Ethical Decision Making" now includes subheads to clearly identify the prior three guidelines, with two new topics discussing "Discernment and Advice" and "Application of Ethical Guides."

- The "Global Ethics" section is now "Managing Ethics Globally." It now has a section discussing how to manage ethics.

- The end of chapter case is new.

- The format of all Skill Building Exercises has been changed to better indicate if the exercise is individual focused and answers are shared in-class or online in groups. AACSB competencies are updated and clearly listed.

- There is a new Skill Building Exercise "New Habits" to develop skills related to the chapter topics.

Chapter 4

- With the reorganization of the book, Chapter 4 was Chapter 5 in the tenth edition.

- The entire chapter has been updated with 90 (97 percent) new references to this new edition, for a total of 93 references.

- There are new people and company/brand examples: LinkedIn, Broadcom CEO Scott McGregor, Yahoo, Home Depot, Apple Senior Vice President of Retail and Online Stores Angela Ahrendts.

- The Introduction section title now includes Happiness and has been rewritten with all new references.

- The subsection "Social Media," in the Digital Information Technology section, has expanded coverage.

- In the "Cross-Cultural Communications" section, coverage of nonverbal communications has been expanded.

- The introduction to the "Receiving Messages" section has been rewritten with all new references.

- The Emotions subsection "Global Difference" now includes a discussion of crying at work and global differences of its acceptance.

- In the Emotions subsection "Getting Criticism," there are new suggestions on how to get feedback from your boss and better performance reviews.

- The end of chapter case is new.

- The format of all Skill Building Exercises has been changed to better indicate if the exercise is individual

focused and answers are shared in-class or online in groups. AACSB competencies are updated and clearly listed.

- There is a new Skill Building Exercise "New Habits" to develop skills related to the chapter topics.

Chapter 5

- With the reorganization of the book, Chapter 5 was Chapter 6 in the tenth edition.

- The entire chapter has been updated with 44 (90 percent) new references to this new edition, for a total of 49 references.

- There are 3 new people and company/brand examples: Bridgewater Associates, CEO Los Angeles Opera, Christopher Koelsch.

- The Introduction section title now includes Happiness and has all new updated references.

- The "Anger and Violence" section now discussed bullying in the subsections.

- The "Conflict Management Styles" first subsection has been changed to "Reasons for and Types of Conflict." It also has two third level headings "Psychological Contract" and "Idea and Personal Conflict" that explain the difference in positive conflicts of ideas for improvement versus personal conflict that tends to be negative and hurt relationships.

- The "Accommodating Conflict Style" section now includes a discussion of its importance in our personal life.

- The introduction to the "Resolving Conflict" section has been rewritten with all new references improving the integration with the prior section "Conflict Management Styles."

- The end of chapter case is new: Trying Times for Uber's Co-founder & CEO Travis Kalanick.

- The format of all Skill Building Exercises has been changed to better indicate if the exercise is individual focused and answers are shared in-class or online in groups. AACSB competencies are updated and clearly listed.

Chapter 6

- With the reorganization of the book, Chapter 6 was Chapter 7 in the tenth edition.

- The entire chapter has been updated with 70 (86 percent) new references to this new edition, for a total of 81 references.

- There are new people and company/brand examples: General Electric (GE), Integrate CEO Jeremy Boom, New York Times bestselling Author Lewis Howes, Meg Whitman, CEO of IBM, Gene Lee CEO of Darden Restaurants.

- The introduction to the opening section "How Leadership Affects Behavior Human Relations, Happiness, and Performance" has been rewritten with all new references. There is also a new level three heading "Leadership in Your Personal" to make students realize they use leadership skills virtually every day to influence others to get what they want. There is also a new level three head "Participative Leadership" to help students realize the trend is to teamwork and shared leadership, so leadership skills are important to employees too.

- The subsection of "Behavioral Leadership Theories" now includes authentic leadership and LMX leadership.

- The introduction to the "Trust" section has been rewritten with all new references and better ties the topics of leadership and trust.

- The end of chapter case has been updated.

- The format of all Skill Building Exercises has been changed to better indicate if the exercise is individual focused and answers are shared in-class or online in groups. AACSB competencies are updated and clearly listed.

- There is a new Skill Building Exercise "New Habits" to develop skills related to the chapter topics.

Chapter 7

- With the reorganization of the book, Chapter 7 was Chapter 8 in the tenth edition.

- The entire chapter has been updated with 60 (85 percent) new references to this new edition, for a total of 71 references.

- There are 16 new people and company/brand examples, including Acuity insurance, Facebook, Google, Kimberly-Clark, GE, Wells Fargo, Johnson & Johnson, Apple, Tesla, AB InBev, GM CEO Mary Barra, Berkshire Hathaway CEO Warren Buffett, Foot Locker CEO Ken Hicks.

- The section "How Motivation Affects Behavior, Happiness, Human Relations, and Performance" title now includes Happiness, and the section is completely rewritten with all new updated references.

- The "Equity Theory" section now has more discussion of how to treat people fairly and expanded coverage of how to "Motivate with Equity Theory."

- The two sections "Job Enrichment" and "Job Design" have been combined to "Job Enrichment and Design."

- In the "Putting the Motivation Theories Together" section there is a new level two heading "Self-Motivation" with two level three headings "Interpersonal Skills"

and "Career Success" to discuss the importance of interpersonal skills to self-motivation and two major factors to career success. The second level two heading is "The Self-Motivation Model."

- The end of chapter case is updated.

- The format of all Skill Building Exercises has been changed to better indicate if the exercise is individual focused and answers are shared in-class or online in groups. AACSB competencies are updated and clearly listed.

- There is a new Skill Building Exercise "New Habits" to develop skills related to the chapter topics.

Chapter 8

- With the reorganization of the book, Chapter 8 was Chapter 9 in the tenth edition.

- Included in the re-organization of the eleventh edition contents, the material covering Etiquette has been moved to the new Appendix A: Time, Career, and Etiquette Management.

- The entire chapter has been updated with 71 (97 percent) new references to this new edition, for a total of 73 references.

- There are three new people and company/brand examples: Actor Steve Martin, Racecar champion Mario Andretti, Zig Ziglar.

- The opening section has been rewritten with all new references.

- Because the "Business Etiquette" section has been moved to Appendix A, we now state that it is part of organizational politics in the level two heading "Developing Political Skills" as a level three head "Business Etiquette," stating that the topic will be discussed in Appendix A.

- The "Power" section "Influencing Tactics—Ingratiation" now includes how to altercast and ask for a favor.

- The tenth edition section "Customer Satisfaction and Etiquette" is now "Customer Satisfaction and Complaints." There is a new section heading "Dealing with Customer Complaints."

- The tenth edition section "Do Power, Politics, and Etiquette Apply Globally?" is now "Do Power and Politics Apply Globally."

- The format of all Skill Building Exercises has been changed to better indicate if the exercise is individual focused and answers are shared in-class or online in groups. AACSB competencies are updated and clearly listed.

- There is a new Skill Building Exercise "New Habits" to develop skills related to the chapter topics.

Chapter 9

- With the reorganization of the book, Chapter 9 was Chapter 10 in the tenth edition.

- The entire chapter has been updated with 35 (88 percent) new references to this new edition, for a total of 40 references.

- There are 21 new people and company/brand examples, including www.ideed.com, Shark Tank, CEO of Pixel Mobb Christopher Perilli, Microsoft, JPMorgan Chase, Healthcare Business Women's Association, Pricewaterhouse Coopers, The Principal Financial Group, New York State Bar Association, National Association of Women Lawyers, BS MoneyWatch, NPR, Martha Stewart Living Radio, Newsday, Cosmopolitan Magazine, Women's Health, The New York Times, Sheryl Sandberg, COO of Facebook, *Lean In: Women and the Will to Work,* Yahoo.

- The Introduction section has been rewritten with all new references.

- "The Why and Reality of Networking" now has a new level three head "The Networking Process" to identify the steps.

- The "Developing Your Network" section has been expanded. It now has level three heads: "Primary Contacts," "Secondary Contacts," "Using Your Self-Sell," "Expanded Contacts," "Starting Conversations," and "Job Search Networking Form." To extend the how to networking approach, 19 Questions have been added that can be used to start a conversation in any setting, at a networking event, and at a conference.

- The opening section of "Negotiating" has been revised with all new references.

- In the "Negotiating Planning" section BANTA is now clearly defined.

- The case has been renamed "Carol Frohlinger: President of Negotiating Women," and updated, taking out prior discussion of Deborah Kolb who is no longer listed on the website.

- The Objective Case has been revised and now provides more positive information on Amway.

- The format of all Skill Building Exercises has been changed to better indicate if the exercise is individual focused and answers are shared in-class or online in groups. AACSB competencies are updated and clearly listed.

- There is a new Skill Building Exercise "New Habits" to develop skills related to the chapter topics.

Chapter 10

- With the reorganization of the book, Chapter 10 was Chapter 11 in the tenth edition.

- The entire chapter has been updated with 90 (100 percent) new references to this new edition, for a total of 90 references.

- The Introduction section has been rewritten with all new references.

- In the "Types of Teams" "Functional Teams" subsection, the new terms *networks of teams* also called *multiteam systems* has been added.

- There is a new introduction to the "Team Development Stages and Leadership" that states the relationship between team dynamics and development, and that everyone should contribute to team development.

- The "Leadership Skills in Meetings" section subsection "The First Meeting" now includes Setting Ground Rules, emphasizing the need to start and end meetings on time.

- The case has been updated.

- The format of all Skill Building Exercises has been changed to better indicate if the exercise is individual focused and answers are shared in-class or online in groups. AACSB competencies are updated and clearly listed.

- There is a new Skill Building Exercise "New Habits" to develop skills related to change.

Chapter 11

- With the reorganization of the book, Chapter 11 was Chapter 12 in the tenth edition.

- The entire chapter has been updated with 83 (99 percent) new references to this new edition, for a total of 84 references.

- The Introduction section has been updated with twice as many references.

- The "Change Model" section now includes a new third model under the new subheading "Habit Changing Model—Overcoming Your Resistance" to focus on how we can overcome our own resistance to change and develop new habits.

- The "Organizational Culture" subsection "Positive and Negative Cultures" now includes healthy and unhealthy cultures.

- The case is new—Elon Musk.

- The format of all Skill Building Exercises has been changed to better indicate if the exercise is individual focused and answers are shared in-class or online in groups. AACSB competencies are updated and clearly listed.

- There is a new Skill Building Exercise "New Habits" to develop skills related to the chapter topics.

Chapter 12

- With the reorganization of the book, Chapter 12 was Chapter 13 in the tenth edition.

- The title has been changed to include "Inclusion."

- This chapter has major revisions. The material on human relations issues has been decreased, while the coverage of diversity and inclusion and global diversity have been expanded with new coverage discussed below.

- The entire chapter has been updated with 98 (84 percent) new references to this new edition, for a total of 116 references.

- The Introduction section has been updated and now has three level two heads to emphasize the importance of diversity: "Diversity in America, Global Diversity, and Is Diversity and Inclusion Really Important?"

- The second section "Prejudice and Discrimination" now has three subsections: Prejudice, Discrimination, and Common Areas of Employment Discrimination. The prior subsection "Valuing-Diversity/Inclusion Training" has been deleted, with content moved to other sections.

- The third section "Equal Employment Opportunity for All" has an expanded list of those protected under the law enforced by the EEOC. Exhibit 12.1, Federal Employment Laws, has been revised. The laws are now presented in chronological order, and the less relevant laws have been deleted, and the Genetic Information Act of 2008 has been added. The Learning Outcome and answer have been changed to include the seven major diversity laws enforced by the EEOC. Also, the subsection "From AA to Valuing Diversity to Inclusion" has been moved to the end of the fourth section.

  - The fourth section has been remained "Dimension of Diversity and Inclusion" and rewritten with multiple changes to expand coverage of diversity.

  - The prior first subsection has been replaced and expanded with "Diversity Types and Discrimination" and list the EEOC eight protected groups, plus an extended list of other types of diversity. Therefore, prior coverage of alcohol and drug abuse and AIDS has been deleted. There is a new Work Application question 12-5 and a new link to a self-assessment exercise on diversity.

  - The second section is now "Gender, Sexual Orientation, and Sexual Harassment" with increased updated coverage of these topics including discussing the difference between sex and gender, and the long EEOC definition of harassment has been deleted while quid pro quo and hostile work environment sexual harassment have been added.

- The last section is "From Affirmative Action to Valuing Diversity to Inclusion" with expanded coverage focusing on inclusion. Its Work Application question 12-8 now includes valuing diversity and inclusion.

- The fifth section title is the same, but it has major revisions with three subsections, instead of five. Women in the Workforce and Women and Minority Managers is now combined and rewritten, titled: "Women and Minority in the Work Force and Advancement." Work and Family Balance is now a subsection of How Families and Gender Roles Are Changing.

- The sixth section is now "Global Cultural Diversity and Relations." There is a new subsection "National Culture and GLOBE" discussing these two new topics. There is a new Learning Outcome 12-6 and a new Application Situation box 12-5 to apply GLOBE dimensions.

- The prior "Managing Diversity" section has been deleted and is now "Managing Diversity Globally" and has been rewritten replacing U.S. human resource material with inclusion and global coverage. There are two new Work Applications 12-14 and 12-15.

- The case is still Google, but it is new because it has been rewritten with all new questions.

- The format of all Skill Building Exercises has been changed to better indicate if the exercise is individual focused and answers are shared in-class or online in groups. AACSB competencies are updated and clearly listed.

- There is a new Skill Building Exercise "New Habits" to develop skills related to the chapter topics.

Appendix A

- Appendix A Time and Career Management are from Chapter 4 of the tenth edition, and the Etiquette section is from Chapter 9.

- The Appendix has been updated with 25 new references to this new edition, for a total of 58.

- The case Jay-Z is not used in this edition. The appendix does not include a case.

- The Objective Case "Overworked" from prior Chapter 4 has been retained.

- The format of all Skill Building Exercises has been changed to better indicate if the exercise is individual focused and answers are shared in-class or online in groups. AACSB competencies are updated and clearly listed.

- There is a new Skill Building Exercise "New Habits" to develop skills related to the chapter topics.

Appendix B

- This was Appendix A in the tenth edition.

- The Assessment from Chapter 1 is repeated in Appendix B for a direct comparison of pre and post assessment of HR abilities and skills. Plus, there is a new 36 question end of course Assessment.

- Changing behavior through the changing habits guidelines has been added to this Appendix.

SUPPLEMENTS FOR INSTRUCTORS AND STUDENTS

Instructor Library

The Connect Management Instructor Library is your repository for additional resources to improve student engagement in and out of class. You can select and use any asset that enhances your lecture. The Connect Instructor Library includes:

- Instructor Manual
- PowerPoint files
- Test Bank

Manager's Hot Seat Video

Now instructors can put students in the hot seat with access to an interactive program. Students watch real managers apply their years of experience when confronting unscripted issues. As the scenario unfolds, questions about how the manager is handling the situation pop up, forcing the student to make decisions along with the manager. At the end of the scenario, students watch an interview with the manager and view how their responses matched up to the manager's decisions. The Manager's Hot Seat videos are now available as assignments in Connect.

 **connect**®

McGraw-Hill Connect® is a highly reliable, easy-to-use homework and learning management solution that utilizes learning science and award-winning adaptive tools to improve student results.

Homework and Adaptive Learning

- Connect's assignments help students contextualize what they've learned through application, so they can better understand the material and think critically.
- Connect will create a personalized study path customized to individual student needs through SmartBook®.
- SmartBook helps students study more efficiently by delivering an interactive reading experience through adaptive highlighting and review.

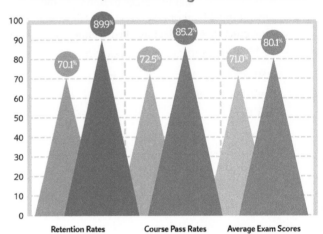

Connect's Impact on Retention Rates, Pass Rates, and Average Exam Scores

without Connect   with Connect

> Over **7 billion questions** have been answered, making McGraw-Hill Education products more intelligent, reliable, and precise.

> Using **Connect** improves retention rates by **19.8** percentage points, passing rates by **12.7** percentage points, and exam scores by **9.1** percentage points.

> 73% of instructors who use **Connect** require it; instructor satisfaction **increases** by 28% when **Connect** is required.

Quality Content and Learning Resources

- Connect content is authored by the world's best subject matter experts, and is available to your class through a simple and intuitive interface.
- The Connect eBook makes it easy for students to access their reading material on smartphones and tablets. They can study on the go and don't need internet access to use the eBook as a reference, with full functionality.
- Multimedia content such as videos, simulations, and games drive student engagement and critical thinking skills.

Robust Analytics and Reporting

- Connect Insight® generates easy-to-read reports on individual students, the class as a whole, and on specific assignments.

- The Connect Insight dashboard delivers data on performance, study behavior, and effort. Instructors can quickly identify students who struggle and focus on material that the class has yet to master.

- Connect automatically grades assignments and quizzes, providing easy-to-read reports on individual and class performance.

©Hero Images/Getty Images

Impact on Final Course Grade Distribution

without Connect		with Connect
22.9%	A	31.0%
27.4%	B	34.3%
22.9%	C	18.7%
11.5%	D	6.1%
15.4%	F	9.9%

More students earn **As** and **Bs** when they use **Connect**.

Trusted Service and Support

- Connect integrates with your LMS to provide single sign-on and automatic syncing of grades. Integration with Blackboard®, D2L®, and Canvas also provides automatic syncing of the course calendar and assignment-level linking.

- Connect offers comprehensive service, support, and training throughout every phase of your implementation.

- If you're looking for some guidance on how to use Connect, or want to learn tips and tricks from super users, you can find tutorials as you work. Our Digital Faculty Consultants and Student Ambassadors offer insight into how to achieve the results you want with Connect.

www.mheducation.com/connect

ACKNOWLEDGMENTS

I want to thank Dr. Christopher Achua, University of Virginia, College at Wise, for writing five new cases and updating the others.

Special thanks to the reviewers of the eleventh edition of my manuscript for their excellent recommendations:

David John Bergen, *High Point University*

Margaret V. Ryan, *Highline College*

Pamela K. Ball, *Clark State Community College*

Teddie Laing, *Miami Dade College*

Philip Mathew, *Olympic College*

Lo-An Tabar-Gaul, *Mesa Community College*

Samira Hussein, *Johnson County Community College*

Frederick Brockmeier, *Northern Kentucky University* and *University of Phoenix*

S. Graham Bourne, *Lake-Sumter State College*

Daniel Bialas, *Muskegon Community College*

Thanks also to reviewers of past editions:

Lydia Anderson, *Fresno City College*

Bonnie Andrys, *Northland Community & Technical College*

Wayne Gawlik, *Joliet Junior College*

Melanie Hilburn, *Lone Star College-North Harris*

Norma Johansen, *Scottsdale Community College*

Joseph Randall, *Bainbridge State College*

Randall Wade, *Rogue Community College*

Teresa R. Campbell, *Clark State Community College*

Shannon Durham, *Middle Georgia Technical College*

Jennifer Susan Malarski, *Minneapolis Community and Technical College*

Keith D. Matthews, *Northeast Community College*

Connie Smejkal, *Centralia Community College*

Mary Hedberg, *Johnson County Community College*

Jane Bowerman, *University of Oklahoma*

Margaret Ryan, *Highline Community College*

Mofidul Islam, *Columbia Southern University*

Marilyn J. Carlson, *Clark State Community College*

John Thiele, *Cañada College*

Rachel Erickson, *National College of Business and Technology*

Cindy Brown, *South Plains College*

Robert Losik, *Southern New Hampshire University*

Daniel Lybrook, *Purdue University*

Thomas McDermott, *Pittsburgh Technical Institute*

Therese Palacios, *Palo Alto College*

Margaret V. Ryan, *Highline Community College*

Thomas J. Shaughnessy, *Illinois Central College*

Mary Alice Smith, *Tarrant County College*

Joseph Wright, *Portland Community College*

Boyd Dallos, *Lake Superior College*

Sally Martin Egge, *Cardinal Stritch University*

Brian E. Perryman, *University of Phoenix*

Glenna Vanderhoof, *Southwest Missouri State University*

Marion Weldon, *Edmonds Community College*

Lee Higgins, *Southeast Community College–Beatrice Campus*

Janet Weber, *McCook Community College*

William Weisgerber, *Saddleback College*

Andy C. Saucedo, *Dona Ana Community College*

Charleen Jaeb, *Cuyahoga Community College*

John J. Heinsius, *Modesto Junior College*

Roger E. Besst, *Muskingum Area Technical College*

Rebecca S. Ross, *Shenango Valley School of Business*

Thomas E. Schillar, *University of Puget Sound*

Rosemary Birkel Wilson, *Washtenaw Community College*

Edward J. LeMay, *Massasoit Community College*

Julie Campbell, *Adams State College*

John Gubbay, *Moraine Valley Community College*

Ruth Dixon, *Diablo Valley College*

John J. Harrington, *New Hampshire College*

Robert Wall Edge, *Commonwealth College*

Abbas Nadim, *University of New Haven*

Steve Kober, *Pierce College*

Dee Dunn, *Commonwealth College*

Marlene Frederick, *New Mexico State University at Carlsbad*

Linda Saarela, *Pierce College*

David Backstrom, *Allan Hancock College*

Rob Taylor, *Indiana Vocational Technical College*

Warren Sargent, *College of the Sequoias*

Jane Binns, *Washtenaw Community College*

Charles W. Beem, *Bucks County Community College*

Robert Nixon, *Prairie State College*

Leo Kiesewetter, *Illinois Central College*

Stephen C. Branz, *Triton College*

William T. Price, Jr., *Virginia Polytechnic Institute and State University*

Jerry F. Gooddard, *Aims Community College*

Rex L. Bishop, *Charles Community College*

Bill Anton, *DeVard Community College*

Stew Rosencrans, *University of Central Florida*

John Magnuson, *Spokane Community College*

Doug Richardson, *Eastfield College*

Thanks to the following students for suggesting improvements:

Doug Nguyen, *Truckee Meadows Community College of Nevada*

Richard Gardner, *New Hampshire College*

Peter Blunt, *New Hampshire College*

Christianne Erwin, *Truckee Meadows Community College*

Robert Neal Chase, *New Hampshire College*

Cheryl Guiff, *Taylor University Online*

CONTACT ME WITH FEEDBACK

I wrote this book for you. Let me know what you think of it. Write to me and tell me what you did and/or didn't like about it. More specifically, how could it be improved? I will be responsive to your feedback. If I use your suggestion for improvement, your name and college will be listed in the acknowledgment section of the next edition. I sincerely hope that you will develop your human relations skills through this book.

Robert N. Lussier
Professor of Management
Management Department
Springfield College
Springfield, MA 01109
413-748-3202
rlussier@springfieldcollege.edu

PART 1

Intrapersonal Skills: Behavior, Human Relations, and Performance Begin with You

CHAPTER 1

Understanding Behavior, Human Relations, and Performance and Being Happy

©Rawpixel.com/Shutterstock

LEARNING OUTCOMES

After completing this chapter, you should be able to:

LO 1-1 Explain why human relations skills are important.

LO 1-2 Discuss the goal of human relations.

LO 1-3 Describe the relationship between individual and group behavior and organizational performance.

LO 1-4 Briefly describe the history of the study of human relations.

LO 1-5 State some of the trends and challenges in the field of human relations.

LO 1-6 List 10 guidelines for effective human relations.

LO 1-7 Identify your personal low and high human relations ability and skill levels.

LO 1-8 Identify five personal human relations goals for the course.

LO 1-9 Define the following 17 key terms (in order of appearance in the chapter):

human relations (HR)	performance
goal of human relations	systems effect
win–win situation	Elton Mayo
total person approach	Hawthorne effect
behavior	Theory Z
levels of behavior	intrapersonal skills
group behavior	interpersonal skill
organization	leadership skill
organizational behavior (OB)	

OPENING CASE WORK SCENARIO

We begin each chapter with an opening short case to give you an overview of the human relations (HR) topics covered in the chapter using a work scenario. Within the chapter, we explain how these HR topics are applied to the opening case with the heading / / / Opening Case Work Scenario. The symbols / / / and / / / identify the beginning and end of the case work scenario.

/ / / When Olin Ready graduated from college, he accepted his first full-time job with IBM. As he drove to work on his first day, he thought: How will I fit in? Will my peers and new boss Nancy Westwood like me? Will I be challenged by my job? Will I be able to get raises and promotions?

At about the same time, Nancy was also driving to work thinking about Olin: Will Olin fit in with his peers? Will he be open to my suggestions and leadership? Will Olin work hard and be a high performer?

What would you do to ensure success if you were Olin? What would you do to ensure Olin's success if you were Nancy? Meeting employees' needs while achieving the organization's objectives is the goal of positive human relations in any organization. / / /

WHY HUMAN RELATIONS SKILLS ARE SO IMPORTANT

Learning Outcome 1-1

Explain why human
relations skills are
important.

We begin by discussing what's in this book for you, followed by a look at some of the major myths about human relations and the realities of why human relations skills are so important. We then discuss the goal of human relations and the total person approach to human relations.

What's in It for Me?

It's natural to be thinking, What can I get from this book? What's in it for me?[1] This are common questions in all human relations, although they are seldom directly asked and answered.[2] Here is the short, bottom-line answer: The better you can work with people—and that is what the course is all about—the more successful you will be in your personal and professional lives.[3] Life is about relationships.[4] This may be one of the few courses you take in which you can actually use what you learn during the course in your personal life.

If you want to be a manager, this course is clearly relevant. But if you aren't or don't want to be a manager, 70% to 90% of all work is done by non-managers.[5] The current trend is participative management, Zappos has even dropped the title "manager,"[6] so organizations are recruiting people with management skills,[7] which you can develop in this course.

You don't need to wait until you graduate to apply what you learn and develop your human relations skills.[8] Now let's expand on what's in it for you by exploring some of the myths and realities surrounding human relations.

Myths and Realities about Human Relations

There are three myths about human relations: (1) technical skills are more important than human relations skills; (2) it's just common sense; and (3) leaders are born, not made.

Myth 1: Technical Skills Are More Important Than Human Relations Skills   Some people believe that a human relations or organizational behavior (OB) course is less important than more technical courses, such as computer science and accounting. Yes, technology is important, but it is people who develop the tech.[9] Fortune editor Alan Murray says, "Today, human capital is the most valuable capital in every company, no matter what industry it is in."[10] The new management model's emphasis is on "soft skills" or people skills.[11] Thus, the job market's most sought-after skills are people skills.[12] People skills will continue to increase in importance in the knowledge-based environment.[13] If you can't work effectively with coworkers, you could be fired.[14] Thus, management education is placing more emphasis on people and leadership skill development,[15] and again this course is all about developing people and leadership skills. /// **In the opening case,** by studying human relations, you will learn soft skills that will help you in situations like Nancy's and Olin's. ///

Myth 2: Human Relations Is Just Common Sense   Some people believe that human relations is simple and just common sense. Do you always get along well with your family and friends and coworkers—no conflicts? If human relations is just common sense, then why don't we all always get along? How do human relations affect your personal and job satisfaction? Developing good relationships is critical to personal and professional success,[16] and that's a skill you can develop through this course.

Myth 3: Leaders Are Born, Not Made   Leadership skills are crucial for success in today's business world.[17] The question "Are leaders born or made?" has been researched over the years. Leadership experts generally agree that some people have more natural leadership ability but that leadership skills can be developed.[18] Regardless of your natural ability, using the material in this book, you can develop your human relations skills.

Communication Skills
Refer to CS Question 1.

WORK APPLICATION **1-1**

In your own words, explain why human relations skills are important to you. How will they help you in your career?

Throughout this book we use many important, or key, terms. To ensure that you have a clear understanding of these terms, when a key term first appears, we present it in **bold letters** with its definition *italicized*.

Goal of Human Relations

Learning Outcome 1-2

Discuss the goal of human relations.

The term **human relations** means *interactions among people*. Organizations can't function without human relations. /// **In the opening case,** when Olin Ready arrives at IBM on his first day of work, he will interact with his new boss, Nancy. Next, a variety of people will help orient and train Olin. Later, as he performs his daily tasks, Olin will interact with Nancy and his coworkers, as well as with people from other departments and with customers. Olin's success at IBM will be based on human relations, and his job satisfaction will affect his personal life.///

WORK APPLICATION **1-2**

Give an example, personal if possible, of a situation in which the goal of human relations was met. Explain how the individual's needs were met and how the organizational objectives were achieved.

The **goal of human relations** is to *create a win–win situation by satisfying employee needs while achieving organizational objectives*. A **win–win situation** occurs when *the organization and the employees both get what they want*. When we wonder, What's in it for me?, we are expressing what we want. When employees' and organizational goals align, performance tends to follow.

When we are not in a win–win situation, we are usually in conflict. In Chapter 5, you will learn how to create win–win situations when facing conflicts.

The Total Person Approach

WORK APPLICATION **1-3**

Give a specific example, personal if possible, that supports the total person approach. Explain how an individual's job performance was affected by off-the-job problems.

The **total person approach** realizes that *an organization employs the whole person, not just his or her job skills*. It is important to understand the whole person. Holistic thinking helps us to better understand and work better with others.[19] People play many roles throughout their lives, indeed, throughout each day. /// **In the opening case scenario,** Olin, therefore, is more than just an employee; he is also a father, a member of the PTA, a scout leader, a jogger, a student, and a fisherman. At work, Olin will not completely discard all his other roles to be a worker only. His off-the-job life will affect his job performance at IBM. Thus, if Olin has a bad day at work, it may not be related to his job, but to another of his life's roles. Also, a bad day at work can affect personal life satisfaction.///

BEHAVIOR, HUMAN RELATIONS, AND ORGANIZATIONAL PERFORMANCE

Levels of Behavior

The study of human relations looks closely at the way people behave, why people behave the way they do, or what makes them and the people around them tick. **Behavior** is *what people do and say*. Human relations fuel behavior. The three **levels of behavior** are *individual, group, and organizational*. Human relations take place at the individual, group, and organizational levels.[20]

Individual- and Group-Level Behavior   It is individuals, not large organizations, that drive progress.[21] ///In the opening case scenario, As Olin types a letter on the computer or fills out requisition forms, he is engaged in individual behavior./// **Group behavior** consists of *the things two or more people do and say as they interact*. Individual behavior influences group behavior. For example, as ///Olin and Mary work on a project together or attend department meetings, their actions are considered group behavior. /// Studying the chapters in this book, particularly Chapters 1 through 3, should help you understand and predict your own behavior, and that of others, in an organizational setting. In addition, Chapter 10 will help you gain a better understanding of how your behavior affects others, and how their behavior affects you in teams.

Organizational-Level Behavior   An **organization** is *a group of people working to achieve one or more objectives*. This book focuses on human relations in both profit and nonprofit organizations in which people work to make a living. Organizations are created to produce goods and services for the larger society. If you have ever worked, you have been a part of an organization. You also come into contact with organizations on a regular basis, such as when you go into a store, school, church, post office, or health club.

As individuals and groups interact, their collective behavior constitutes the organization's behavior. Thus, **organizational behavior (OB)** is *the collective behavior of an organization's individuals and groups.* ///IBM is an organization, and its collective behavior is based on Olin's behavior, the behavior of Nancy's department, and the behavior of all other departments combined.///

This book explores all three levels of behavior. Chapters 2 and 3 focus primarily on individual behavior, Chapters 4 through 9 examine the skills influencing all three levels of behavior, and Chapters 10 through 12 focus on group and organizational behavior.

Exhibit 1.1 illustrates the three levels of behavior. The focus of level three is on the organization as a whole. At this level, the responsibility of the board of directors and the president is to focus on the entire organization. The focus of level two is on the behavior and human relations within and between groups such as the marketing, production, and finance departments. The focus of level one is on the behavior of any one person in the organization.

EXHIBIT 1.1 | Levels of Behavior

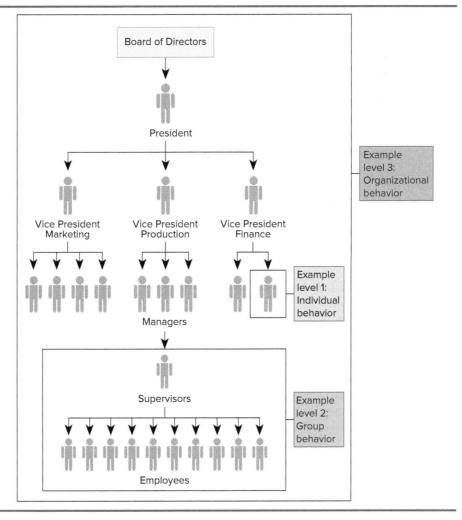

Each manager would have one or more supervisors reporting to him or her, and each supervisor would have several employees reporting to him or her.

WORK APPLICATION 1-4

Give two specific examples of your involvement in human relations—one positive and one negative—and identify the level of behavior for each example.

Exhibit 1.1 is a formal organization structure showing authority and reporting relationships. However, it does not show the multiple possible human relations that exist outside the formal structure. For example, the president could interact with any employee, an employee could interact with a manager, and a supervisor could interact with a vice president's administrative assistant.

The Relationship between Individual and Group Behavior and Organizational Performance

Learning Outcome 1-3

Describe the relationship between individual and group behavior and organizational performance.

Throughout this course you will learn how human relations affects individual and group behavior, and the resulting effects on organizational performance. **Performance** is *the extent to which expectations or objectives have been met. Performance* is a relative term. Performance levels are more meaningful when compared to past performance or the performance of others within and/or outside the organization. Since relationships are the lifeblood of organizations, poor relations impede individual, group, and organizational performance.

APPLICATION SITUATIONS / / /

Understanding Important Terms   AS 1-1

Identify each statement by its key term.

A. Behavior   C. Human relations   E. Performance

B. Goal of human relations   D. Organization   F. Total person approach

_____ 1. It's near quitting time and Karl boxed up the last package to be sent out today.

_____ 2. "I've been working hard to do a good job. I got a raise; now I can buy that new iPhone I've been saving for."

_____ 3. Jack and Wanda are discussing how to complete a project they are working on together.

_____ 4. Julio is quietly working alone on a report.

_____ 5. All the people listed above are members of a(n) _____.

WORK APPLICATION 1-5

Give two specific examples of how human relations affected your performance—one positive and the other negative. Be specific in explaining the effects of human relations in both cases.

The Systems Effect   A system is a set of two or more interactive elements. The systems approach, developed by Russell Ackoff, focuses on the whole system with an emphasis on the relationships between its parts.[22] For our purposes, under the **systems effect** *all people in the organization are affected by at least one other person, and each person affects the whole group or organization.* The organization's performance is based on the combined performance of each individual and group. To have high levels of performance, the organization must have high-performing individuals and groups. Groups are the building blocks of the organization. As a result of the systems effect, the destructive behavior of one individual hurts that group and other departments as well.[23] In addition, the destructive behavior of one department affects other departments and the organization's performance.

The challenge to management is to develop high-performing individuals and groups. In a sense, individuals and groups are the foundation of an organization. If either is ineffective, the organization cannot stand. See Exhibit 1.2 for a graphic illustration.

Just as people are the foundation of the organization, behavior and human relations are the foundation supporting performance. If either is ineffective, performance will fall. Exhibit 1.3 gives a graphic illustration.

EXHIBIT 1.2 | The Relationship between Individual and Group Behavior and Organizational Performance

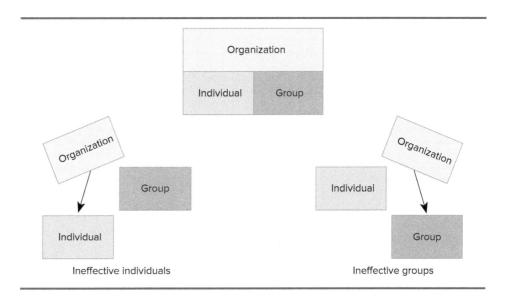

Ineffective individuals   Ineffective groups

APPLICATION SITUATIONS / / /

Focus of Study   AS 1-2

Identify the focus of study in each statement below by selecting two answers. First select the level of behavior:

A. Individual   B. Group   C. Organizational

Then select the scope of study:

A. Behavior   B. Human relations   C. Performance

_____ 6. Apple has just completed its income statement for the year.

_____ 7. The sales department exceeded its sales quota for the year.

_____ 8. Juan and Peg are working on a project together.

_____ 9. The organization chart shows the management hierarchy from the president down to the functional departments to the employee level.

_____10. Latoya is writing a letter to a customer regarding a complaint.

HUMAN RELATIONS: PAST, PRESENT, AND FUTURE

Learning Outcome 1-4

Briefly describe the history of the study of human relations.

Human Relations Is a Multidisciplined Science

Popularly called *organizational behavior* and rooted in the behavioral sciences, the science of human relations was developed in the late 1940s. It is based primarily on psychology (which attempts to determine why individuals behave the way they do) and sociology (which attempts to determine how group dynamics affect organizational performance); social psychology, economics, and political science have also contributed to organizational behavior.

During the 1950s, research in human behavior was conducted in large organizations. By the late 1970s, organizational behavior was recognized as a discipline in its own right, with teachers, researchers, and practitioners being trained in organizational behavior itself. Organizational behavior is a social science that has built its

EXHIBIT 1.3 | The Relationship between Behavior, Human Relations, and Performance

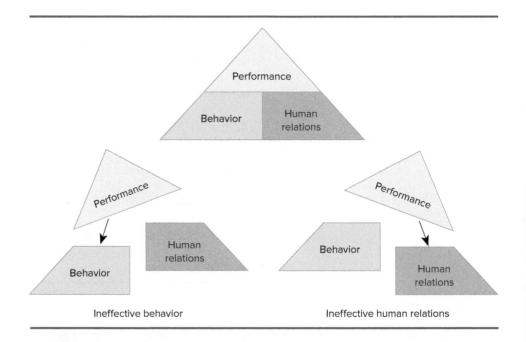

knowledge base on a sound foundation of scientific theory and research. Human relations takes a practical, applied approach. It attempts to anticipate and prevent problems before they occur and to solve existing problems of interpersonal relations in organizations.

The Early Years: Frederick Taylor and Robert Owen

In early America, most people worked on farms or were self-employed tailors, carpenters, shoemakers, or blacksmiths. Then, during the Industrial Revolution, people left the farms to work in factories that were privately owned. These businesses were concerned with profits, not employees, and managers viewed people only as a source of production. Most of the early owner-managers gave little thought to the working conditions, health, or safety of their employees. Working conditions were very poor—people worked from dawn until dusk under intolerable conditions of disease, filth, danger, and scarcity of resources. They had to work this way just to survive; there was no welfare system—you worked or you starved.

Frederick Taylor   Frederick Taylor, an engineer known as the "father of scientific management," focused on analyzing and redesigning jobs more efficiently in the late 1800s and early 1900s, which led to the idea of mass production. Scientific managers focused on production, not people.[24] They assumed that workers always acted rationally and were motivated simply by money. Also, Taylor failed to recognize the social needs of employees and placed them in isolated jobs.

Robert Owen   In 1800, Robert Owen was considered the first manager-entrepreneur to understand the need to improve the work environment and the employee's overall situation. In 1920, Owen was called "the real father" of personnel administration.[25] He believed that profit would be increased if employees worked shorter hours, were paid adequately, and were provided with sufficient food and housing. He refused to employ children under the age of 11. (In the early 1800s, children went to work full-time at the age of 9.) Owen taught his employees cleanliness and temperance and improved their working conditions. Other entrepreneurs of that time did not follow his ideas.

Elton Mayo and the Hawthorne Studies

From the mid-1920s to the early 1930s, Elton Mayo and his associates from *Harvard University* conducted research at the Western Electric Hawthorne Plant near Chicago. The research conducted through the Hawthorne Studies has become a landmark in the human relations field. In fact, **Elton Mayo** is called the *"father of human relations."* As a consequence of these studies, the Hawthorne effect was discovered.[26]

The **Hawthorne effect** refers to *an increase in performance caused by the special attention given to employees, rather than tangible changes in the work.* During the research, Mayo changed the lighting and ventilation. To his surprise, performance went up regardless of the working conditions. Through interviews, Mayo realized that the control group during the research felt important because of all the attention it got; therefore, performance increased because of the special attention given to employees. With the knowledge of the results of the Hawthorne Studies, some managers used human relations as a means of manipulating employees, while others took the attitude that a happy worker is a productive worker. Studies have shown that happy workers are usually, but not always, more productive than unhappy workers.

The 1930s to the 1990s

During the depression of the 1930s, unions gained strength and in many cases literally forced management to look more closely at the human side of the organization and meet employees' needs for better working conditions, higher pay, and shorter hours.

During the 1940s and 1950s, other major research projects were conducted in a number of organizations. Some of the research was conducted by the *University of Michigan,* which conducted studies in leadership and motivation; *Ohio State University,* which also studied leadership and motivation; the *Tavistock Institute of Human Relations* in London, which studied various subjects; and the *National Training Laboratories* in Bethel, Maine, which studied group dynamics. *Peter Drucker's management by objectives* was popular in the 1950s and is still used today.

During the 1960s, *Douglas McGregor* published *Theory X and Theory Y.*[27] A discussion of his theories, which contrast the way managers view employees, appears in Chapter 3. In the same time period, *Eric Berne* introduced *transactional analysis (TA).* (See Chapter 5 for a detailed discussion of TA.) Sensitivity training was popular in the 1960s.

During the 1970s, interest in human relations probably peaked. Quality circles were popular. By the late 1970s, the term *human relations* was primarily replaced with the more commonly used term *organizational behavior.*

In the 1980s, the U.S. rate of productivity was much lower than that of Japan. William Ouchi discovered that a few particularly successful firms did not follow the typical U.S. model. After years of research and investigation, Ouchi developed Theory Z.[28] **Theory Z** *integrates common business practices in the United States and Japan into one middle-ground framework appropriate for use in the United States.*

In their book *In Search of Excellence,* Thomas Peters and Robert Waterman conducted research to determine the characteristics of successful organizations.[29] During the 1980s, their work was criticized as companies identified as excellent began to have problems. Total quality management was popular in the 1980s.

In the 1990s, the trend toward increased participation of employees as a means of improving human relations and organizational performance continued. This trend included greater levels of participation at the lowest level of the organization. As a result, employees have more input into management decisions and how they perform their jobs. The use of groups and teams also became popular in the 1990s and continues today.

WORK APPLICATION 1-6

Give a specific example, personal if possible, of the Hawthorne effect. It could be when a teacher, coach, or boss gave you special attention that resulted in your increased performance.

Communication Skills
Refer to CS Question 2.

APPLICATION SITUATIONS / / /

Human Relations History   AS 1-3

Identify the following people with their contribution to human relations:

A. Eric Berne   C. William Ouchi   E. Tom Peters
B. Elton Mayo   D. Robert Owen   F. Frederick Taylor

_____ 11. Transactional analysis.

_____ 12. The father of personnel administration.

_____ 13. The Hawthorne Studies.

_____ 14. Excellence in American corporations.

_____ 15. Theory Z.

Current and Future Challenges in the 21st Century

Learning Outcome 1-5

State some of the trends and challenges in the field of human relations.

We've discussed the history of human relations; now let's briefly discuss its current and future trends and challenges. In Chapters 2 through 12, we will discuss these topics in detail.

- **Globalization, change, innovation, and speed.** Chief executive officers (CEOs) rate globalization as the top challenge to business leadership in the 21st century.[30] The trend toward globalization has clearly changed the speed at which and the way we do business today.

- **Technology.** The CEOs listed technology (which is moving two to three times faster than management and includes *big data*) as their second major concern.[31] People are using more social media technology to communicate. Are you addicted to your cell phone?

- **Diversity.** With globalization, firms need to adapt to a diversity of cultures.[32] Even domestic companies face a diversity challenge as the American workforce becomes increasingly diversified.[33]

- **Learning and knowledge.** The key to success today is using knowledge effectively to continually innovate to compete in the new mobile global economy.[34]

Communication Skills
Refer to CS Question 3.

- **Ethics.** Trust in business today is low,[35] as media coverage of **Wells Fargo** and other business scandals has heightened awareness of the need for ethical business practices and decisions.[36]

WORK APPLICATION 1-7

Explain how one of the above trends or challenges could personally affect your human relations.

- **Crises.** CEOs also listed cybersecurity (which is based on tech and also includes privacy) that can lead to crises as a top four concern.[37] **Yahoo!**, **Home Depot**, and others had customer data hacked. Safety (including terrorist) and security issues have led to changes in human relations.

As stated, we will talk more about all of these challenges in later chapters.

APPLICATION SITUATIONS / / /

Trends and Challenges of Human Relations   AS 1-4

Identify the factor in each statement as:

A. Global, Change, Innovation, and Speed   C. Diversity   E. Ethics
B. Technology   D. Learning and Knowledge F. Crises

(continued)

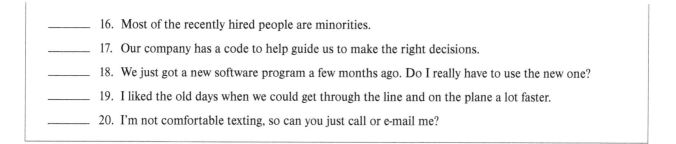

_____ 16. Most of the recently hired people are minorities.

_____ 17. Our company has a code to help guide us to make the right decisions.

_____ 18. We just got a new software program a few months ago. Do I really have to use the new one?

_____ 19. I liked the old days when we could get through the line and on the plane a lot faster.

_____ 20. I'm not comfortable texting, so can you just call or e-mail me?

HAPPINESS AND DEVELOPING HUMAN RELATIONS SKILLS

In this section, we discuss happiness and guidelines that will improve your relationships. We end by discussing how to handle human relations problems. But first let's discuss how this book can help you if you apply what you learn.

This book gives you suggestions, guidelines, and models to follow to improve your people skills. Although these guidelines do not guarantee success, they will increase your probability of being happy with successful human relations in organizations.

Knowing is not enough; we must apply what we learn.[38] Human relations is one of the few courses you can use immediately. Most of the material you will learn can and should be used in your daily personal life with your family, friends, and other people with whom you interact. If you work, use this material on the job to develop your human relations skills.

Happiness and Relationships

Organizations realize that generally happy and engaged workers do a better job,[39] and that work relationships form the foundation of an array of processes, such as how managers and employees lead and how we manage our careers.[40] Organizational performance, perhaps its survival, depends on relationships.[41] Some firms, including **Zappos**, makes employees' happiness a top goal.[42] But let's focus on your happiness here.

Ever wonder why people do stupid things, or why we do the things we do? It's usually because we believe it will make us happy. Are you a happy person? Could you be happier? Where does most of your happiness come from? For most people the answer is relationships—with God, loved ones, family, friends, coaches and teammates, bosses and coworkers, etc. So to be happier, we should develop better relationships, which is the focus of this book. Also, we tend to rise or fall to the level of our relationships.

American society tends to promote two isms that are believed to bring happiness, but they actually tend to lead to unhappiness. First is individualism: being selfish by just looking out for yourself, taking advantage of others, and only doing things that have something in it for you. Second is hedonism: don't do it if you don't feel like doing it; just do what makes you feel good. Do you know any selfish people? Do you like them? Are they really happy? Will they ever be happy?[43]

According to happiness expert **Sonja Lyubomirsky**, happy people are not as self-centered as unhappy people.[44] Booker T. Washington said, "Those who are happiest are those who do the most for others." B.C. Forbes said, to be happy, strive to make others happy.[45] Making sacrifices for others brings true happiness.[46] Author **Neil Pasricha** developed[47] the *Happiness Equation: Want Nothing + Do Anything = Have Everything.*

Pleasure is a feeling, whereas happiness (and love) is a decision. A decision to do what? To do what is right that will make you the best version of yourself by creating win-win situations and by simply helping others. Do you always want to do your work—for the job, school, etc.? If you procrastinate until the last minute or don't do your work, do you really feel happy, especially if you don't do your best and get a poor job review or low grade?

WORK APPLICATION 1-8

Do you believe that you can be happier and will develop your human relations abilities and skills through this course? Explain your answer.

Doing things you don't really want to do to help others goes against individualism and hedonism, but isn't this an important part of true family, friendship, and success? So, to be happy, don't be selfish; be selfless by putting others ahead of yourself, and you will be happier and have better relationships. Easier said than done, but every chapter in the book has material that will help you develop better, more productive relationships that can help make you happier in your personal and professional lives. Let's move on to 10 specific guidelines that improve human relations.

Human Relations Guidelines

Learning Outcome 1-6

List 10 guidelines for effective human relations.

Being likable is important to personal happiness and career success, and it is helpful but not necessary for managers to be liked. Are you the kind of person others enjoy being around? Find out by completing Self-Assessment Exercise 1-1. Then read on.

/ / / Self-Assessment Exercise 1-1 / / /

Likability

Select the number from 1 to 5 that best describes your use of the following behavior, and write it on the line before each statement.

(5) Usually   (4) Frequently   (3) Occasionally   (2) Seldom   (1) Rarely

_____ 1. I'm an optimist. I look for the good in people and situations, rather than the negative.

_____ 2. I avoid complaining about people, things, and situations.

_____ 3. I show a genuine interest in other people. I compliment them on their success.

_____ 4. I smile.

_____ 5. I have a sense of humor. I can laugh at myself.

_____ 6. I make an effort to learn people's names and address them by name during conversations.

_____ 7. I truly listen to others.

_____ 8. I help other people cheerfully.

_____ 9. I think before I act and avoid hurting others with my behavior.

_____ 10. If I were to ask all the people I work/worked with to answer these nine questions for me, they would select the same responses that I did.

To determine your likability, add the 10 numbers you selected as your answers. The total will range from 10 to 50. Place it here _____ and on the continuum below.

Unlikable   10 -------- 20 -------- 30 -------- 40 -------- 50   Likable

If you want to get ahead in an organization, it is important to do a good job. But it is also important that people like you. If people like you, they will forgive just about anything you do wrong. If they don't like you, you can do everything right and it will not matter. Many hardworking, talented people have been bypassed for promotion and fired simply because their bosses or other high-level managers didn't like them.

No one can tell you exactly how to be likable. People who try too hard are usually not well liked. However, in this section you will learn guidelines for being likable through successful human relations. The guidelines are based on the behavior of successful, likable people who possess human relations skills. Although general in nature, these guidelines apply to most situations. Throughout the book, you will learn specific skills for dealing with a wide variety of people issues listed in Exhibit 1.4 and discussed below.

The 10 human relations guidelines are as follows:

Be Optimistic   People who are optimistic and grateful for what they have and focus on the good things in their lives are happier, healthier, and less stressed. Ungrateful people tend to

EXHIBIT 1.4 | Ten Guidelines to Effective Human Relations

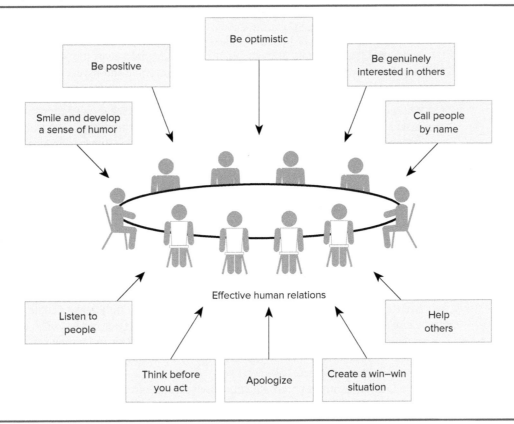

be dissatisfied with what they have and are never happy because no matter how much they get, it is never enough.[48] Former football coach **Lou Holtz** has said that you choose to be optimistic (happy) or pessimistic (sad). Happiness is nothing more than a poor memory for the bad things that happen to you. If you act happy, you can improve your mood and be happier.[49] We usually find what we're looking for. If you look for, and emphasize, the positive, you will find it. Most successful people are optimistic. Do you like being with pessimistic, ungrateful people? Are you optimistic or pessimistic?

Be Positive   Praise and encourage people. People generally don't like to listen to others complain. People often avoid complainers, and you should too. Associating with complainers will only depress you. Don't go around criticizing (putting people down), condemning, or spreading rumors. Do you like negative people who criticize you? To be happier, **Facebook's Sheryl Sandberg** writes down three positive things that happened each day.[50] **Sealed Air CEO Jerome Peribere** says to "Clear your mind so you can see things positively."[51] Are you positive or negative?

Be Genuinely Interested in Other People   Think about your favorite boss and friends. One of the reasons you like them is that they show a genuine interest in you. One of the reasons people fail is the "it's all about me" syndrome. People who feel as though you don't care about them will not come through for you. What is really important is to be able to truly care about other people and to sacrifice for them.[52] Do you care about people? Do you like self-centered people?

Smile and Develop a Sense of Humor   A smile shows interest and caring. It takes fewer muscles to smile than it does to frown. You have probably noticed that frowners are usually unhappy and pessimistic. When we smile, we feel happier; and when we feel angry, we act that way and tend to hurt relationships.[53] Has anyone ever smiled at you and it made you happier? Well, pass it on.

Develop a sense of humor.[54] Relax, laugh, and enjoy yourself. Be willing to laugh at yourself. Likable people do not take their jobs or themselves too seriously. Do you like people who always frown and never laugh? Do you smile and have a sense of humor?

Skill-Building Exercise 1-1 develops this skill.

Call People by Name   Calling people by the name they prefer shows an interest in them and makes them feel important. If you're not good at remembering names, work at it. Like any skill, it takes a conscious effort and some practice to develop. One simple technique you can use to help you remember people's names when you are introduced is to call them by name two or three times while talking to them. Then call them by name the next time you greet them. If you forget a person's name, whenever possible, ask someone else what it is before contacting the person. Remember that in some cultures, however, it is not polite to call a person by his or her first name. In such a culture, use last names, titles, or positions, as expected. Do you like people who don't call you by your name? Do you make an effort to learn people's names?

Listen to People   The ability to listen is an important skill.[55] We learn more by listening than we do by talking. Show respect for the other person's opinions. Don't say "You're wrong" even when the other person is wrong. Such statements only make people defensive and cause arguments, which you should avoid. Saying you disagree has less of an emotional connotation to it. However, when you are wrong, admit it quickly. Admitting you're wrong is not a sign of weakness and is often interpreted as a strength. However, not admitting you are wrong is often interpreted as a weakness.

Encourage others to talk about themselves. This gives you the opportunity to listen and learn while making people feel important. Listening also shows your interest in people. Do you like people who don't listen to you? Are you a good listener?

Help Others   If you want to help yourself, you can do so by helping others. It's a basic law of success. People who use people may be somewhat successful in the short run, but those being used usually catch on. Open and honest relationships in which people help each other meet their needs are usually the best ones. Help others, but don't pry when help is not welcomed. Do you like people who don't help you when you need help? Former actor Kirk Douglas said, "You haven't learned how to live until you've learned how to give."[56] Do you help others?

Think Before You Act   Feel your emotions, but control your behavior. Try not to do and say things you will regret later. Watch your language; don't offend people. It is not always what you say but how you say it that can have a negative impact on human relations. Before you say and do things, think about the possible consequences. Follow a 10-second rule—take 10 seconds before reacting and ask yourself, Would the person I most admire like what I'm about to do or say?[57] Being right is not good enough if it hurts human relations. Conduct your human relations in a positive way. Do you like impulsive people who hurt others? Do you think before you act to avoid hurting others?

Apologize   We all sometimes do or say things (behavior) that offend or hurt others in some way. To truly repair relationships, the best starting point is to admit mistakes and give a "sincere" apology.[58] Even if you don't believe you did anything wrong, you can apologize for offending or hurting the other person. For example, you can say in a sincere voice, "I'm sorry I upset you with my (state the specific behavior, i.e., comment); I will try not to do it again." Just saying you are sorry isn't enough. We need to do our best to not repeat the offense. It takes only a minute to express regret, and apologizing can help develop, maintain, and repair human relations. Think about it: If someone offends or hurts you, are you more willing to forgive and forget and maintain an effective relationship if the person sincerely apologizes? Do you apologize to others when you offend them?

Create Win–Win Situations   Human relations is about how we behave and treat others. The goal of human relations is to create win–win situations. The best way to get what you want is to help other people get what they want and vice versa. Throughout the book you will be given specific examples of how to create win–win situations. Do you like people who win at your expense? Do you help others succeed?

/// **In the opening case scenario,** if Olin follows these 10 human relations guidelines at IBM, he will increase his chances of success. /// If you follow these general guidelines, you too will increase your chances of success in all walks of life. These guidelines are just the starting point of what you will learn in this course. For a review of the 10 guidelines to effective human relations, see Exhibit 1.4.

Remember that what you think about affects how you feel, and how you feel affects your happiness, behavior, human relations, and performance. So think about and actually use these guidelines to improve your human relations.

Handling Human Relations Problems

Even though you follow the human relations guidelines, in any organization there are bound to be times when you disagree with others. And you will more than likely have to interact with people who do not follow the guidelines.

Human relations problems often occur when the psychological contract is not met.[59] The *psychological contract* is the shared expectations between people. At work you have expectations of the things your boss and coworkers should and should not do, and they in turn have expectations of you. As long as expectations are met, things go well. However, if expectations are not met, human relations problems occur. Thus, when people share information and negotiate expectations, have clear roles, and are committed to meeting others' expectations, things go well. We'll focus on sharing information and negotiating expectations throughout this book.

When you encounter a human relations problem, you have to decide whether to avoid the problem or to solve it. In most cases, it is advisable to solve human relations problems rather than ignore them. Problems usually get worse rather than solve themselves. When you decide to resolve a human relations problem, you have at least three alternatives:

1. Change the Other Person   A sure-fire way to become unhappy is to assume that life is fair and that other people will change at your request.[60] Whenever there is a human relations problem, it is easy to blame others and expect them to make the necessary changes in behavior to meet your expectations. In reality, few problems can be blamed entirely on one party. Both parties usually contribute to the problem. Blaming the other party without taking some responsibility usually results in resentment and defensive behavior.

Many self-centered people view themselves as nearly perfect and in no need of personal change. The more you force people to change to meet your expectations, the more difficult it is to maintain effective human relations. Jacob M. Braude says, "Consider how hard it is to change yourself and you'll realize what little chance you have in trying to change others." Do you expect others to change?

2. Change the Situation   If you have a problem getting along with others at work, you can try to change the situation by asking for a change in jobs. There are cases where this is the only solution. However, when you complain to the boss, the boss may decide that you, not the other party, are the problem. Blaming the other party and trying to change the situation enables you to ignore your own behavior, which may be at least part of the problem.

Have you ever noticed that people who have a hard time getting along well with others in one situation, also have trouble in other situations? People who change jobs are often no

Communication Skills
Refer to CS Question 4.

WORK APPLICATION 1-9

Which 2 of the 10 human relations guidelines need the most effort on your part? Which two need the least? Explain your answers.

happier in the new position. The late Zig Ziglar said, "You can't change what's going on around you until you start changing what's going on within you."

Communication Skills
Refer to CS Question 5.

3. Change Yourself   Throughout this book, particularly in Part 1, you will be examining your own behavior. Knowing yourself is important in good human relations through self-assessment. In many situations, your own behavior is the only thing you can control.[61] In most human relations problems, the best alternative is to examine others' behavior and try to understand why they are doing and saying the things they are; then examine your own behavior to determine why you are behaving the way you are.[62]

In most cases, the logical choice is to change your own behavior. But that does not mean doing whatever other people request. In fact, you should be assertive. You will learn how to be assertive in Chapter 5. You are not being forced to change; rather, you are changing your behavior because you elect to do so. When you change your behavior, others may also change. In fact, you can also resolve differences through both of you agreeing to change your behavior, and you will learn how to resolve conflicts in Chapter 5. To increase happiness, we need to change our behavioral habits.[63]

New Habits   Let's face it, we are bound by our habits of routine.[64] If you can't change your mind and embrace change, you cannot change anything.[65] Easier said than done, right? The first step is to realize that we need to take a positive attitude about changing our behavior and actually develop positive habits to improve our relationships. It helps to realize that our brains cling to habit at the exclusion of all else, including common sense. Do you ever do things you know you will regret and make you unhappy later? So we have to change our thoughts and make the change a habit to improve.[66] Change your routine first, and your emotional health and relationships will follow suit.[67] When we change our habits, we change our lives, and successful people have good habits that are the behaviors driving their success.

The reason most people don't keep their New Year's resolution is they don't make it a habit. If you say you will exercise more but don't make a scheduled time to work out (routine habit), you won't work out. Developing a habit takes conscious planning and effort—schedule time to work out, and as Nike say, Just Do It. A habit has three parts, and the following are three examples. Item A is an example of a positive habit to develop, B is a bad habit to break, and C is a behavioral change to improve a relationship.

1. **Cue**. Reminds you to do your new habit (A. Running shoes left near your bed; B. Feel sad; C. Joe yells at you).

2. **Routine**. Do the new habit (A. Run first thing in the morning; B. Eat and/or drink; C. You get upset and yell back at Joe).

3. **Reward—Change**. Positive thing to reinforce new habit (A. Feel good about yourself and healthier, weight loss and more energy, healthy breakfast; B. Temporary escape from sadness, which often doesn't work and can lead to other problems and bad habits—instead, change and get together with family and friends; C. Change by not yelling back at Joe and calming discuss the issue—reward that you don't get upset and stressed—you will learn how to do this in Chapter 5, Dealing with Conflict).

Skill-Building Exercise 1-4
develops this skill.

Think about it. Are there any good habits you should develop, or bad self-destructive ones you should drop or replace? Will you work at being more positive about improving your relationships by developing good habits? Skill Building Exercise 1-4, Developing a New Habit, can help.

WORK APPLICATION 1-10

Give a specific example of a human relations problem in which you elected to change yourself rather than the other person or situation. Be sure to identify your changed behavior.

To finalize the importance of human relations, if you don't like working with people and don't want to improve your people skills, it most likely will hurt your career progression. If you like working with people and think you are good at it, as the standards continue to increase, you will need to continually improve. Changing our behavior and habits is not easy or comfortable, but people skills are critical to personal and professional happiness and success.[68] So make it a new habit to apply what you learn in this book to develop your people skills.

WHAT'S IN THE BOOK

Let's discuss what we are trying to do throughout this book (objectives) and how we are going to do it (organization).

Objectives of the Book

Managers and academics agree that students need to learn relevant people skills,[69] but that students tend to lack the ability to apply what they learn.[70] Therefore, there is a need to focus on applying what you learn.[71] This is the overarching objective of the book. Unlike most other courses that teach you concepts, this course takes you to the next level, as you apply the concepts and develop your human relations skills.

As indicated in the title of the book, it has a three-pronged approach to the objectives:

- To teach you the concepts and theories of human relations.
- To develop your ability to apply the human relations concepts through critical thinking.
- To develop your human relations skills in your personal and professional lives.

This book offers some unique features related to each of the three objectives; these features are listed in Exhibit 1.5. To get the most from this book, turn back to the preface and read the descriptions of these features.

Flexibility   There are so many features that your professor will most likely not use every feature with every chapter. Students have different learning style preferences. There is no one right way of doing things, and you have the flexibility to use your own approach. You may also use features that your professor does not include in the course requirements.

AACSB Learning Standards

It is important to develop human relations competencies.[72] So how do you know what specific competencies will be important to your career success? For the answer, we have turned to the Association to Advance Collegiate Schools of Business (AACSB), which gives accreditation to business schools, that states that "students engage in experiential and active learning designed to improve skills and the application of knowledge in practice is expected." Below is the list of "General Skills Areas" students are expected to develop taken from the 2016 AACSB Accreditation Standards.[73] In addition to AACSB, this book also meets the core professional components of ACBSP (Accreditation Council for Business Schools and Programs)[74] and IACBE (International Assembly for Collegiate Business Education) standards.[75]

EXHIBIT 1.5 | The Three-Pronged Approach: Features of the Book

Learn the Concepts	+	Apply the Concepts	+	Develop Skills	=	Effective Human Relations
• Research-based and current • Comprehensive coverage • Systems-oriented • Learning outcomes • Key terms • Exhibits • Chapter review and glossary		• Opening cases • Work applications • Application situations • Cases • Objective cases		• Self-assessment exercises • Skill-building objectives and AACSB • Skill-building exercises (three types) • Role-playing exercises • Behavior models • Behavior model videos • Manager's hot seat videos		

Analytical and reflective thinking competencies are developed throughout the book. The following competencies are developed in the specific chapter listed. Written and oral *communications* (Chapter 4), *Ethical* understanding and reasoning (Chapter 2), *Interpersonal relations* (all chapters) *teamwork* (Chapter 10), and *Diverse and multicultural* work environments (Chapter 12). The last skill listed is *Application of knowledge*, and you are given the opportunity to apply what you learn in every chapter through the features listed in Exhibit 1.5. Each of the skill-building exercises indicates the AACSB learning standard skill(s) to which the exercise relates.

Organization of the Book

The book is organized in two ways. The first is by the *levels of behavior*. The parts, as well as the chapters within each part, progress from the individual, to the group, to the organizational levels of behavior.

Second, the parts of the book are based on the *domain model of managerial education*. In this model the concept of *skills* has evolved into the concept of competencies. *Competencies* are performance capabilities that distinguish effective from ineffective behavior, human relations, and performance: they are the underlying characteristics of a person that lead to or cause effective and outstanding performance. Every current competency model can be organized in terms of four competency domains: intrapersonal skills, interpersonal skills, leadership skills, and business skills.[76] The first three are human relations skills, and the last is a technical skill.

The three human relations domains, which are discussed below, as well as the levels of behavior are reflected in the table of contents and the profile form on pp. 483–484. This form lists the parts and the chapters within each part.

Part 1. Intrapersonal Skills: Behavior, Human Relations, and Performance Begin with You   *Intra* means "within"; thus, **intrapersonal skills** are *within the individual and include characteristics such as personality, attitudes, self-concept, and integrity.* Intrapersonal skills are the foundation on which careers are built. You will learn about, apply, and develop intrapersonal skills in Chapters 2 to 3. We end the book by coming back to intrapersonal skills in Appendix B, by developing a plan for applying human relations skills.

Part 2. Interpersonal Skills: The Foundation of Human Relations   *Inter* means "between"; thus, interpersonal skills are between people, as are human relations. **Interpersonal skill** is *the ability to work well with a diversity of people.* Clearly, interpersonal skills are based on, and overlap to some extent, intrapersonal skills. You will learn about, apply, and develop interpersonal skills in Chapters 4 and 5.

Part 3. Leadership Skills: Influencing Others and Part 4. Leadership Skills: Team and Organizational Behavior, Human Relations, and Performance   **Leadership skill** is *the ability to influence others and work well in teams.* You will learn about, apply, and develop leadership skills in Chapters 6 through 12. Leadership skills are based on intrapersonal and interpersonal skills. Thus, the sequence of parts in the book, as well as the chapters within each part, constitutes a logical set of building blocks for your competency and skill development.

It's time to assess your intrapersonal skills, interpersonal skills, and leadership skills. Together, these skills are called human relations skills. The following section focuses on self-assessment, an important intrapersonal skill. People with good intrapersonal skills use self-assessment as the basis for improving their human relations skills, which we will be doing throughout the book.

Communication Skills
Refer to CS Question 6.

ASSESSING YOUR HUMAN RELATIONS ABILITIES AND SKILLS

For each of the 12 statements below, record in the blank the number from 1 to 7 that best describes your current level of ability or skill. You are not expected to have all high numbers. This assessment will give you an overview of what you will learn in this course.

Appendix B contains the same assessment and a longer version of this assessment to enable you to compare your skills at the beginning and end of the course.

Low ability/skill   High ability/skill

1	2	3	4	5	6	7

_____ 1. I understand my personality profile, preferred learning style, how to handle stress, and my perception bias.

_____ 2. I know my attitudes and value, how to improve my self-concept, and guidelines to handling ethical dilemmas.

_____ 3. I understand the communications process, how to deal with emotions, and how to give and received criticism to improve performance.

_____ 4. I understand transactional analysis, how to be assertive, and how to resolve conflicts without hurting relationships.

_____ 5. I understand leadership theories, types of trust, and how to develop trust.

_____ 6. I understand the motivation process and the difference among content, process, and reinforcement theories.

_____ 7. I know how to gain and use organizational power and politics.

_____ 8. I know the professional networking process and can negotiate deals that create a win-win situation.

_____ 9. I understand team dynamics and their stages of development, how to conduct a meeting, and how to follow steps in making effective decisions.

10. I know reasons why people resist change and how to overcome the resistance, how employees learn the organization's culture, and how firms use organizational development techniques to make changes.

_____ 11. I understand how important diversity is and can identify legally protected groups; define prejudice, discrimination, sexism, sexual harassment, and racism; and handle complaints.

_____ 12. I can effectively manage my time and career using proper etiquette.

Scoring: Add up the 12 numbers and divide the total by 12 to get your average between 1 and 7. Place your average score on the line below.

_____

Each of the 12 questions gives an overview of the content of the other 11 chapters and Appendix A in the book.

Learning Outcome 1-7

Identify your personal low and high human relations ability and skill levels.

There is no correct score. Review your 12 responses above. Your lower score numbers indicate areas where behavior changes are most warranted. Select the top five areas, abilities, or skills you want to develop through this course. Write them out below. In Chapter 7, we will discuss how to set objectives. At that time you may want to return to write what you wish to learn as objectives.

Skill-Building Exercise 1-2 develops this skill.

1.

2.

3.

4.

Learning Outcome 1-8

Identify five personal human relations goals for the course.

5.

Skill-Building Exercise 1-3 develops this skill.

To improve your human relations skills, be sure to take an active role in your skill development. To do so, learn the concepts in each chapter, then practice applying them every day.[77] As the course progresses, be sure to review your course goals and work toward attaining them.

Don't be too concerned if your scores were not as high as you would like them to be. If you work at it, you will develop your human relations skills through this book.

In this chapter we have discussed how your behavior affects your human relations and performance; why human relations skills are so important; that what you learn in this course can be used immediately in your personal and professional lives; a brief history of human relations; the importance of changing your behavior; and 10 guidelines to follow in developing effective human relations. Next is a chapter review with a glossary and more application and skill-building material to develop your human relations skills based on Chapter 1 concepts.

/ / / R E V I E W / / /

The chapter review is organized to help you master the nine learning outcomes for Chapter 1. First provide your own response to each learning outcome, and then check the summary provided to see how well you understand the material. Next, identify the final statement in each section as either true or false (T/F). Correct each false statement. Answers are given at the end of the chapter.

LO 1-1 Explain why human relations skills are important.
People are an organization's most valuable resource. It is the people who cause the success or failure of an organization. Faulty human relations skill is the most common cause of management failure.

The myths of human relations (HR) are: (1) Technical skills are more important than HR skills; (2) HR is just common sense; (3) global diversity is overemphasized; and (4) leaders are born, not made. T F

LO 1-2 Discuss the goal of human relations.
Organizations that can create a win–win situation for all have a greater chance of succeeding. If the organization offers everyone what they need, all benefit. Satisfying needs is not easy; rather, it is a goal to strive for, which may never be met.

Organizations expect that employees will not let their personal lives affect their work. T F

LO 1-3 Describe the relationship between individual and group behavior and organizational performance.
Through the systems effect, we learn that individuals affect each other's performance and that of the group and organization. The organization is made up of individuals and groups. Its performance is based on individual and group performance.

Human relations takes place only at the group and organizational levels. T F

LO 1-4 Briefly describe the history of the study of human relations.
In the 1800s Frederick Taylor developed scientific management, which focused on redesigning jobs. Also in the 1800s Robert Owen was the first manager-owner to understand the need to improve the work environment and the employee's overall situation. Elton Mayo is called the "father of human relations." In the mid-1920s to the early 1930s he conducted the Hawthorne Studies and thereby identified the Hawthorne effect, an increase in performance due to the special attention given to employees, rather than tangible changes in the work. Through the 1930s to the 1980s much attention was paid to the human side of the organization. Teamwork and increased employee participation became popular during the 1990s.

Thomas Peters and Robert Waterman developed Theory Z. T F

LO 1-5 State some of the trends and challenges in the field of human relations.
Trends and challenges in the field of human relations include: (1) globalization, change, innovation, and speed; (2) technology; (3) diversity; (4) learning and knowledge; (5) ethics; and (6) crisis.

The rate of change and technology is slowing down. T F

LO 1-6 List 10 guidelines for effective human relations.
Guidelines for effective human relations include: (1) be optimistic; (2) be positive; (3) be genuinely interested in other people; (4) smile and develop a sense of humor; (5) call people by name; (6) listen to people; (7) help others; (8) think before you act; (9) apologize; and (10) create win–win situations.

The goal of human relations is within guideline 7: help others. T F

LO 1-7 Identify your personal low and high human relations ability and skill levels.
Answers will vary from student to student.

Most people will have the same score on most abilities and skills. T F

LO 1-8 Identify five personal human relations goals for the course.
Answers will vary from student to student.

The goals you select for this course are neither right nor wrong. T F

LO 1-9 Define the following 17 key terms.
Select one or more methods: (1) fill in the missing key terms for each definition given below from memory; (2) match the key terms from the end of the review with their definitions below; and/or (3) copy the key terms in order from the key terms at the beginning of the chapter.

_____ are interactions among people, while the

_____ is to create a win–win situation by satisfying employee needs while achieving organizational objectives.

A(n) _____ occurs when the organization and employees get what they want.

The _____ realizes that an organization employs the whole person, not just his or her job skills.

_____ is what people do and say.

The _____ are individual, group, and organizational.

_____ is the things two or more people do and say as they interact (human relations).

A(n) _____ is a group of people working to achieve one or more objectives.

_____ is the collective behavior of its individuals and groups.

_____ is the extent to which expectations or objectives have been met.

Under the _____, all people in the organization are affected by at least one other person, and each person affects the whole group or organization.

_____ is called the "father of human relations" and conducted the Hawthorne Studies in the mid-1920s to the early 1930s, considered the first true human relations research.

The _____ refers to an increase in performance due to the special attention given to employees, rather than tangible changes in the work.

_____ integrates common business practices in the United States and Japan into one middle-ground framework.

_____ are within the individual and include characteristics such as personality, attitudes, self-concept, and integrity.

_____ is the ability to work well with a diversity of people.

_____ is the ability to influence others and work well in teams.

KEY TERMS

behavior 4	Hawthorne effect 9	levels of behavior 4	systems effect 6
Elton Mayo 9	human relations 4	organization 4	Theory Z 9
goal of human relations 4	interpersonal skill 18	organizational behavior 5	total person approach 4
group behavior 4	intrapersonal skills 18	performance 6	win–win situation 4
	leadership skill 18		

COMMUNICATION SKILLS

The following critical thinking questions can be used for class discussion and/or as written assignments to develop communication skills. Be sure to give complete explanations for all answers.

1. In your opinion, which myth about human relations holds back the development of human relations skills more than any of the others?

2. Which person's contribution to the history of human relations do you find to be the most impressive?

3. Which one of the trends or challenges do you believe is the most relevant to the field of human relations?

4. Which one of the 10 guidelines for effective human relations do you think is the most important?

5. Of the three ways to handle human relations problems, which ones are the easiest and hardest for you?

6. Of the intrapersonal, interpersonal, and leadership skills, which one is your strongest? Your weakest?

CASE /// **W. L. Gore & Associates: How Employees Relate to One Another Sets Gore Apart.**

Founded in 1958, W. L. Gore & Associates, Inc. has become a modern-day success story as a uniquely managed, privately owned family business that truly understands the connection between behavior, human relations, and performance. Founders Bill and Vieve Gore set out to create a business where innovation was a way of life and not a by-product. Today, Gore is best known for its GORE-TEX range of high-performance fabrics and Elixir Strings for guitars. Gore is the leading manufacturer of thousands of advanced technology products for the medical, electronics, industrial, and fabrics markets. With annual revenues of more than $3 billion, Gore has more than 10,000 employees, called associates, at more than 50 facilities around the world.[i]

Terri Kelly replaced Chuck Carroll as the president and CEO of W. L. Gore & Associates in April 2005. Ms. Kelly attributes the company's success to its unique culture. As she put it, how work is conducted at Gore and how employees relate to one another sets Gore apart. For the 20th consecutive year, Gore has been named among the "100 Best Companies to Work For" in the United States by *Fortune* magazine. In an interview, Kelly was asked what would be the most distinctive elements of the Gore management model to an outsider. She listed four factors: "We don't operate in a hierarchy; we try to resist titles; our associates, who are all owners in the company, self-commit to what they want to do; and our leaders have positions of authority because they have followers." According to Kelly, these four attributes enable Gore to maximize individual potential while cultivating an environment that fosters creativity and also to operate with high integrity. She is quick to remind everyone that all of Gore's practices and ways of doing business reflect the innovative and entrepreneurial spirit of its founders.

Kelly attributes Gore's success to its unique culture. As she put it, how work is conducted at Gore and how employees relate to one another set Gore apart. There are no titles, no bosses, and no formal hierarchy. Compensation and promotion decisions are determined by peer rankings of each other's performance. To avoid dampening employee creativity, the company has an organizational structure and culture that goes against conventional wisdom. Bill Gore (the founder) referred to the company's structure as a "lattice organization." Gore's lattice structure includes the following features:[ii]

- Direct lines of communication—person to person—with no intermediary
- No fixed or assigned authority
- Sponsors, not bosses
- Natural leadership as evidenced by the willingness of others to follow
- Objectives set by those who must "make them happen"
- Tasks and functions organized through commitments
- Complete avoidance of the hierarchical command and control structure

The lattice structure as described by the people at Gore encourages hands-on innovation and discourages bureaucratic red tape by involving those closest to a project in decision making. Instead of a pyramid of bosses and managers, Gore has a flat organizational structure. There are no chains of command, no predetermined channels of communication. It sounds very much like a self-managed team at a much broader scale.

Why has Gore achieved such remarkable success? W. L. Gore & Associates prefers to think of the various people who play key roles in the organization as being leaders, not managers. While Bill Gore did not believe in smothering the company in thick layers of formal management, he also knew that as the company grew, he had to find ways to assist new people and to follow their progress. Thus, W. L. Gore & Associates came up with its "sponsor" program—a human relations partnership between an incumbent, experienced employee and a newly hired, inexperienced employee. Before a candidate is hired, an associate has to agree to be his or her sponsor, or what others refer to as a mentor. The sponsor's role is to take a personal interest in the new associate's contributions, problems, and goals, acting as both a coach and an advocate. The sponsor tracks the new associate's progress, offers help and encouragement, points out weaknesses and suggests ways to correct them, and concentrates on how the associate might better exploit his or her strengths. It's about improving the intrapersonal skills of the new hire.

Sponsoring is not a short-term commitment. All associates have sponsors, and many have more than one. When individuals are hired, at first they are likely to have a sponsor in their immediate work area. As associates' commitments change or grow, it's normal for them to acquire additional sponsors. For instance, if they move to a new job in another area of the company, they typically gain a sponsor there. Sponsors help associates chart a course in the organization that will offer personal fulfillment while maximizing their contribution to the enterprise. Leaders emerge naturally by demonstrating special knowledge, skill, or experience that advances a business objective.

An internal memo describes the three kinds of sponsorship and how they might work:

- **Starting sponsor**–a sponsor who helps a new associate get started on his or her first job at Gore, or helps a present associate get started on a new job.
- **Advocate sponsor**–a sponsor who sees to it that the associate being sponsored gets credit and recognition for contributions and accomplishments.
- **Compensation sponsor**–a sponsor who sees to it that the associate being sponsored is fairly paid for contributions to the success of the enterprise.

An associate can perform any one or all three kinds of sponsorship. Quite frequently, a sponsoring associate is a good friend, and it's not uncommon for two associates to sponsor each other as advocates.

Being an associate is a natural commitment to four basic human relations principles articulated by Bill Gore and still a key belief of the company: fairness to each other and everyone we come in contact with; freedom to encourage, help, and allow other associates to grow in knowledge, skill, and scope of responsibility; the ability to make one's own commitments and keep them; and consultation with other associates before undertaking actions that could affect the reputation of the company. These principles underscore the importance of developing high interpersonal skills for Gore employees.

Commitment is seen as a two-way street at W. L. Gore & Associates–while associates are expected to commit to making a contribution to the company's success, the company is committed to providing a challenging, opportunity-rich work environment, and reasonable job security. The company tries to avoid laying off associates. If a workforce reduction becomes necessary, the company uses a system of temporary transfers within a plant or cluster of plants, and requests voluntary layoffs. According to CEO Kelly, Gore's structure, systems, and culture have continued to yield impressive results for the company. In the more than 50 years that Gore has been in business, it has always made a profit.[iii]

Go to the Internet: To learn more about W. L. Gore & Associates, visit its website (www.gore.com).

Support your answers to the following questions with specific information from the case and text or with other information you get from the web or other sources.

1. What evidence is there that W. L. Gore & Associates aspires to meet the goal of human relations?

2. How does Gore & Associates depict an organization that fully appreciates the "systems effect"?

3. One can argue that W. L. Gore's lattice structure encompasses some of the unexpected discoveries brought out by Elton Mayo and the Hawthorne Studies. Identify some features of the lattice structure that align with some of the unexpected discoveries of the Hawthorne Studies.

4. How does Gore's "sponsorship" program contribute toward meeting some of the 10 human relations guidelines outlined in the chapter?

5. Watch the video (http://www.managementexchange .com/video/terri-kelly-wl-gores-original-management -model-0) of CEO, Terri Kelly, and describe what she believes people would find surprising about management and how they work with their people at W. L. Gore.

Case Exercise and Role-Play

Preparation: You are a manager in an organization that wants to communicate in practical terms the meaning and importance of the systems effect and the total person approach to new employees during the orientation process. The manager is supposed to use examples to make his or her points. Based on your understanding of these two concepts, create a five-minute oral presentation on the meaning and importance of:

a. The systems effect

b. The total person approach

Role-Play: The instructor forms students into manager–new employee pairs and has each pair dramatize exercise a and b in front of the rest of the class. The student playing the role of new employee should then paraphrase the manager's message. After each presentation, the class is to discuss and critique the effectiveness with which the manager clearly communicated the meaning and importance of these two concepts and the effectiveness of the new employee in replaying the message.

OBJECTIVE CASE   /// **Supervisor Susan's Human Relations**

Peter has been working for York Bakery for about three months now. He has been doing an acceptable job until this week. Peter's supervisor, Susan, has called him in to discuss the drop in performance. (*Note:* Susan's meeting with Peter and/or a meeting held by Tim with Susan and Peter can be role-played in class.)

SUSAN: Peter, I called you in here to talk to you about the drop in the amount of work you completed this week. What do you have to say?

PETER: Well, I've been having a personal problem at home.

SUSAN: That's no excuse. You have to keep your personal life separate from your job. Get back to work, and shape up or ship out.

PETER: (Says nothing, just leaves.)

Susan goes to her boss, Tim.

SUSAN: Tim, I want you to know that I've warned Peter to increase his performance or he will be fired.

TIM: Have you tried to resolve this without resorting to firing him?

SUSAN: Of course I have.

TIM: This isn't the first problem you have had with employees. You have fired more employees than any other supervisor at York.

SUSAN: It's not my fault if Peter and others do not want to do a good job. I'm a supervisor, not a babysitter.

TIM: I'm not very comfortable with this situation. I'll get back to you later this afternoon.

SUSAN: See you later. I'm going to lunch.

Answer the following questions. Then in the space next to the questions, state why you selected that answer.

_____ 1. There _____ a human relations problem between Susan and Peter.
   a. is   *b.* is not

_____ 2. Susan has attempted to create a _____ situation.
   a. lose–lose   *b.* win–lose   *c.* win–win

_____ 3. Susan _____ an advocate of the total person approach.
   a. is   *b.* is not

_____ 4. Through the systems effect, Peter's decrease in output affects which level of behavior?
   a. individual   *c.* organizational
   b. group   *d.* all three levels

_____ 5. The scope of study illustrated in this case covers:
   a. behavior   *c.* performance
   b. human relations   *d.* all three

_____ 6. The focus of study by Susan is:
   a. individual/behavior   *c.* group/human relations
   b. individual/performance   *d.* organizational/performance

_____ 7. The focus of study by Tim should be:
   a. individual/behavior   *c.* group/human relations
   b. group/behavior   *d.* organizational/performance

_____ 8. Later that afternoon Tim should:
   a. reprimand Peter
   b. talk to Peter and tell him not to worry about it
   c. bring Susan and Peter together to resolve the problem
   d. do nothing, letting Susan handle the problem herself
   e. fire Susan

_____ 9. The major human relations skill lacking in Susan is:
   a. being optimistic
   b. smiling and developing a sense of humor
   c. thinking before you act
   d. being genuinely interested in other people

_____ 10. Tim _____ work with Susan to develop her human relations skills.
   a. should   *b.* should not

11. Will Peter's performance increase? If you were Peter, would you increase your performance?

12. Have you ever had a supervisor with Susan's attitude? Assume you are in Susan's position. How would you handle Peter's decrease in performance?

13. Assume you are in Tim's position. How would you handle this situation?

/// SKILL-BUILDING EXERCISE 1-1 ///

Getting to Know You by Name

Experience: Groups meet in class, or the professor could meet with groups separately online. You will be involved in a small-group discussion, and one person from each group will ask the instructor questions.

AACSB Competencies: Communications and application of knowledge.

Objectives:

1. *A.* To get acquainted with the members of your permanent group and to name the group.
   B. To get acquainted with some of your classmates.

2. To get to know more about your instructor.

Procedure 1 (2–5 minutes)

A. Your instructor will assign you to your permanent group.

B. Break into groups of three to six, preferably with people you do not know or do not know well.

Procedure 2 (8–12 minutes)

Each group member tells the others his or her name and two or three significant things about himself or herself. After all members have finished, ask each other questions to get to know each other better.

Procedure 3 (2–4 minutes) Permanent groups only

Everyone writes down the names of all group members. Addresses and telephone numbers are also recommended.

Procedure 4 (2–3 minutes) All groups

Each person calls all members by name, without looking at written names. Continue until all members call the others by name. Be sure to use the guidelines for remembering people's names on p. 14.

Procedure 5 (5–10 minutes) Permanent groups only

Members decide on a name for the group; a logo is optional.

Procedure 6 (5–12 minutes)

Elect a spokesperson to record and ask your group's questions. The members select specific questions to ask the instructor under the three categories below. The spokesperson should not identify who asked which questions.

1. Questions about course expectations. Questions about doubts or concerns about this course.

2. Questions about the instructor. (What would you like to know about the instructor to get to know him or her?)

Procedure 7 (10–20 minutes)

Each spokesperson asks the group's question under one category at a time. When all questions from category 1 are asked and answered, proceed to category 2. Spokespersons should not repeat questions asked by other groups.

Questions (2–10 minutes):   For the groups or class.

1. Is it important to know and call people by name? Why or why not?

2. What can you do to improve your ability to remember people's names when you first meet them, and at later times?

Conclusion: The instructor may make concluding remarks.

Application (2–4 minutes):   What have I learned through this exercise? How will I use this knowledge in the future?

Sharing: Volunteers give their answers to the application section.

///   SKILL-BUILDING EXERCISE 1-2   ///

Course Objectives

Experience: Individual may share answers in groups or as a class, in-class or online. You may share your objectives, in-class or online, within a small group or entire class.

AACSB Competencies: Reflective thinking, analytic skills, communication abilities, and application of knowledge.

Objective: To develop HR objectives and share them to get ideas on other objectives you may want to set.

Preparation: You should have completed the Assessing Your HR Abilities and Skills section of this chapter, including five written objectives.

Procedure 1 (5–30 minutes)

Option A: Volunteers state one or more of their course objectives to the class. The instructor may make comments.

Option B: Break into groups of three to six members and share your course objectives.

Option C1:   Same procedure as Option B with the addition of having the group select a member to share five of the group's objectives.

Option C2:   Each group's spokesperson reports its five objectives.

Conclusion: The instructor leads a class discussion and/or makes concluding remarks.

Application (2–4 minutes):   Should I change any of my objectives? If yes, rewrite it/them below.

Sharing: Volunteers give their answers to the application section.

///   SKILL-BUILDING EXERCISE 1-3   ///

Human Relations Overview: OBingo Icebreaker

Experience: Group in-class. You will play an interactive game of bingo related to human relations.

AACSB Competencies: Communications.

Objective: To get an overview of some of the many human relations topics through an icebreaker game of bingo.

Procedure (5–10 minutes)

Go around the room and get signatures of peers who fit the descriptions in the squares on the OBingo card.

Tell the person your name, and sign only if the description really does fit you.

Each person can sign only one square on your card.

Say "bingo" when you get it.

If you get bingo before the time is up, keep getting as many signatures as you can until the time is up.

The number in the square identifies the chapter in which the topic will be covered.

Conclusion: The instructor may make concluding remarks.

Source: This exercise was adapted from Joan Benek-Rivera, Bloomsburg University of Pennsylvania. Dr. Rivera's exercise was presented at the 2002 Organizational Behavior Teaching Conference (OBTC).

HUMAN RELATIONS

OB	I	N	G	O
Has a nice personality [2]	Is a good communicator [4]	Is good at motivating others [7]	Has a good network of people [9]	Is creative [11]
Makes a good first impression [2]	Is assertive, not aggressive [5]	Is a high achiever [7]	Is a good negotiator [9]	Is open to changes [11]
Has a positive attitude [3]	Handles conflict well [5]	Your name	Enjoys working with others [10]	Works well with a diversity of people [12]
Has a positive self-concept [3]	Likes to be in charge [6]	Good at influencing others [8]	Is a good team player [10]	Interested in learning about other cultures [12]
Handles criticisim well [4]	Is trustworthy [6]	Enjoys playing organizational politics [8]	Likes to solve problems [10]	AA Has a career plan [13]

/ / / SKILL-BUILDING EXERCISE 1-4 / / /

Developing a New Habit

Experience: Individual may share answers in groups or entire class, in class or online. You will develop a new habit to improve your human relations. You may also share your habit, in class or online, within a small group or entire class.

AACSB Competencies: Analytic and application of knowledge.

Objective: To develop and share a new habit.

Preparation: Develop a new habit following the guideline below.

It is important to understand the contents of the subsection "New Habits." Realizing the importance of having a positive attitude and thoughts about a change, select a new habit you want to develop, such as A. better study habits or B. losing weight. Now set an objective, for example, To study nine hours a week or To lose five pounds by June 30. Next develop a cue, routine, and reward like the examples below.

1. **Cue.** A. Set a schedule of study in your appointment book/calendar to remind you it's time to study. B. Put a note about diet on fridge.

2. **Routine.** A. Study on Sunday, Monday, and Wednesday from 6:00 to 9:00. B. Drink water (no sugar/diet drinks) and no snacks—eating between meals.

3. **Reward—Change.** A and B. Feel better about yourself. A. Better grades. B. Special snack on Sunday. Lower weight resulting in looking and feeling better.

Let's be honest. We will most likely slip and miss a study session or cheat on our diet. The question is, "How do you handle the slip?" Are you going to give up and go back to your old habits, or will you get back to your new routine? Caution—once you slip, and the more often you slip, the easier it is to go back to your old habits.

Procedure (5–30 minutes)

Option A: Volunteers state their habit to the class. The instructor may make comments.

Option B: Break into groups of three to six members and share your habits.

Option C1: Same procedure as Option B with the addition of having the group select a member to share the group's habits.

Option C2: Each group's spokesperson reports its new habits.

Conclusion: The instructor leads a class discussion and/or makes concluding remarks.

Application (2–4 minutes): Should I change any of my habits? If yes, rewrite it or them below.

Sharing: Volunteers give their answers to the application section.

/ / ANSWERS TO TRUE/FALSE QUESTIONS / /

1. T.
2. F. Organizations employ the total person and realize that personal lives do affect work, so they try to help employees balance their work and personal lives.
3. T.
4. F. William Ouchi developed Theory Z. Peters and Waterman wrote *In Search of Excellence.*
5. F. The rate of change and technology will continue to increase.
6. F. The goal of human relations is (10): create win–win situations.
7. F. People are different and score differently.
8. T.

/ / / NOTES / / /

1. Staff, "4 Questions to Help Build a Purpose-Driven Team," *Inc.* (December 2013/January 2014): 12.
2. R. McCammon, "Do Me a Solid," *Entrepreneur* (March 2014): 32–33.
3. W.L. Bedwell, S.M. Fiore, and E. Salas, "Developing the Future Workforce," Academy of Management Learning & Education 13(2) (2014): 171–186.
4. G. Colvin, "Humans Are Underrated," *Fortune* (August 1, 2015): 100–113.
5. S. Shellenbarager, "Leader? No, Be a Follower," *The Wall Street Journal* (September 30, 2015): D1.
6. V. Harnish, "5 Key Trends to Master in 2016," *Fortune* (December 15, 2015): 52.
7. GE, "Identifying the Leadership Skills That Matter Most," *INC.* (December 2014 / January 2015): 78.
8. T. Ungaretti, K.R. Thompson, A. Miller, and T.O. Peterson, "Problem-Based Learning: Lessons from Medical Education and Challenges for Management Education," *Academy of Management Learning & Education* 14(2) (2015): 173–186.
9. G. Colvin, "Humans Are Underrated," *Fortune* (August 1, 2015): 100–113.
10. A. Murray, "The Pinnacles and Pitfalls of Corporate Culture," *Fortune* (March 15, 2016): 14.
11. A. Murray, "The Pinnacles and Pitfalls of Corporate Culture," *Fortune* (March 15, 2016): 14.
12. K. Davidson, "Hard to Find: Workers with Good Soft Skills," *The Wall Street Journal* (August 31, 2016): B1, B6.
13. S.D. Charlier, "Incorporating Evidence-Based Management Into Management Curricula," *Academy of Management Learning & Education* 13(3) (2015): 467–475.
14. Staff, "The CEO vs. The Chairman," *Fortune* (March 15, 2015): 32–33.
15. T. Ungaretti, K.R. Thompson, A. Miller, and T.O. Peterson, "Problem-Based Learning: Lessons from Medical Education and Challenges for Management Education," *Academy of Management Learning & Education* 14(2) (2015): 173–186.
16. V. Harnish, "5 Crucial Performance Metrics," *Fortune* (August 1, 2016): 32.
17. GE, "Identifying the Leadership Skills That Matter Most," *INC.* (December 2014/January 2015): 78.
18. S.D. Charlier, "Incorporating Evidence-Based Management Into Management Curricula," *Academy of Management Learning & Education* 13(3) (2015): 467–475.
19. Y. Zhang, D.A. Waldman, U.L. Han, and X.B. Li, "Paradoxical Leaders Behaviors in People Management: Antecedents and Consequences," *Academy of Management Journal* 58(2) (2015): 538–566.
20. D.A. Waldman and R.M. Balven, "Responsible Leadership: Theoretical Issues and Research Directions," *Academy of Management Perspectives* 28(3) (2014): 224–234.
21. A. Weir, "The Martian," *Fortune* (December 1, 2015): 22.
22. R. Ackoff, *Creating the Corporate Future* (New York: Wiley, 1981).

23. G. Colvin, "Humans Are Underrated," *Fortune* (August 1, 2015): 100-113.

24. F.W. Taylor, *Principles of Scientific Management* (New York: Harper & Brothers, 1911).

25. L. Frankel and A. Fleisher, *The Human Factor in Industry* (New York: Macmillan, 1920): 8.

26. F. Roethlisberger and W. Dickson, *Management and the Worker* (Boston: Harvard University Press, 1939): 15-86.

27. D. McGregor, *The Human Side of Enterprise* (New York: McGraw-Hill, 1960).

28. W. Ouchi, *Theory Z–How American Business Can Meet the Japanese Challenge* (Reading, MA: Addison-Wesley, 1981).

29. T. Peters and R. Waterman, *In Search of Excellence: Lessons from America's Best Run Companies* (New York: Harper & Row, 1982).

30. G. Colvin, "Four Things That Worry Business," *Fortune* (October 27, 2014): 32.

31. G. Colvin, "Four Things That Worry Business," *Fortune* (October 27, 2014): 32.

32. A. Wolfe, "Jack and Suzy Welch," *The Wall Street Journal* (February 21-22, 2015): C11.

33. L.M. Leslie, D.M. Mayer, and D.A. Kravitz, "The Stigma of Affirmative Action: A Stereotyping-Based Theory and Meta-Analytic Test of the Consequences for Performance," *Academy of Management Journal* 57(4) (2014): 964-989.

34. J.N. Reyt and B.M. Wiesenfeld, "Seeing the Forest for the Trees: Exploratory Learning, Mobile Technology, and Knowledge Workers' Role Integration Behavior," *Academy of Management Journal* 58(3) (2015): 739-762.

35. From the Editors, "Organizations with Purpose," *Academy of Management Journal* 57(5) (2014): 1227-1234.

36. D. Baden, "Look on the Bright Side: A Comparison of Positive and Negative Role Models in Business Ethics Education," *Academy of Management Learning & Education* 13(2) (2014): 154-170.

37. G. Colvin, "Four Things That Worry Business," *Fortune* (October 27, 2014): 32.

38. M. Feldman and M. Worline, "The Practicality of Practice Theory," Academy of Management Learning & Education 15(2) (2016): 304-324.

39. Staff "Optimum Happiness," *INC.* (June 2016): 107.

40. E. Heaphy, J.H. Gittell, C. Leana, D. Sluss, and G. Ballinger, "The Changing Nature of Work Relationships," *Academy of Management Review* 40(4) (2015): 664.

41. D. Korschun, "Boundary-Spanning Employees and Relationships with External Stakeholders: A Social Identity Approach," *Academy of Management Review* 40, no. 4 (2015): 611-629.

42. A. Murray, "The Pinnacles and Pitfalls of Corporate Culture," *Fortune* (March 15, 2016): 14.

43. M. Kelly, *Rediscovering Catholicism* (New York: Beacon, 2010).

44. H. Delehanty, "A Conversation with Sonja Lyubomirsky: Happiness Expert." *AARP Bulletin* (June 2016).

45. Booker T. Washington and B.C. Forbes, quotes from *Forbes* (December 20, 2016): 112.

46. A. Styhre, "What David Foster Wallace Can Teach Management Scholars," *Academy of Management Review* 41(1) (2016): 170-183.

47. N. Pasricha, Happiness Equation taken from his book review in *Fortune* (March 15, 2016): 28.

48. National Public Radio (NPR) aired October 23, 2015.

49. S. Reddy, "Walk This Way: Acting Happy Can Make it So," *Wall Street Journal* (November 18, 2014): D3.

50. S. Sandberg Commencement Speech, UC Berkeley (May 16, 2016).

51. B. O'Keefe, "Tony Robbins," *Fortune* (November 17, 2014): 124-138.

52. A. Styhre, "What David Foster Wallace Can Teach Management Scholars," *Academy of Management Review* 41(1) (2016): 170-183.

53. R. McCammon, "Don't Pop Your Top," *Entrepreneur* (May 2016): 15-16.

54. S. Weems, "It's Funny How Humor Actually Works," *Wall Street Journal* (March 22-23, 2014): C3.

55. K.E. Brink and R.D. Costigan, "Oral Communication Skills: Are the Priorities of Workplace and AACSB-Accredited Business Programs Aligned?" *Academy of Management Learning & Education* 14(2) (2015): 205-221.

56. K. Douglas quote, *Fortune* (November 17, 2014): 126

57. R. McCammon, "Don't Pop Your Top," *Entrepreneur* (May 2016): 15-16.

58. R. McCammon, "A Sorry State of Affairs," *Entrepreneur* (September 2013): 22–23.

59. M. Sytch and A. Tatarynowicz, "Friends and Foes: The Dynamics of Dual Social Structures,"*Academy of Management Journal 57*(2) (2014): 585–613.

60. L. Daska, "4 Pieces of Advice Most People Ignore (but Great Entrepreneurs Don't)," *INC.* (July/August 2015): 8.

61. C. Duhigg, "Habit Forming," *Costco Connection* (January 2014): 61.

62. E. Bernstein, "Spouse, Change Thyself," *Wall Street Journal* (January 7, 2014): D1.

63. N. Pasricha, Happiness information taken from his book review in *Fortune* (March 15, 2016): 28.

64. M. Rosenwald, "Bound by Habit," *BusinessWeek* (March 19–25, 2012): 106–107.

65. "Disrupt This," Adapted from a quote from G.B. Shaw, *Entrepreneur* (November 19, 2015): 10.

66. M. Rosenwald, "Bound by Habit," *BusinessWeek* (March 19–25, 2012): 106–107.

67. N. Pasricha, Happiness Equation information taken from his book review in *Fortune* (March 15, 2016): 28.

68. G. Colvin, "Humans Are Underrated," *Fortune* (August 1, 2015): 100–113.

69. Editors, "From the Guest Editors: Change the World: Teach Evidence-Based Practice!" *Academy of Management Learning & Education* 13(3) (2014): 305–321.

70. J.S. Goodman, M.S. Gary, and R.E. Wood, "Bibliographic Search Training for Evidence-Based Management Education," *Academy of Management Learning & Education* 13(3) (2014): 322–353.

71. S.D. Charlier, "Incorporating Evidence-Based Management Into Management Curricula," *Academy of Management Learning & Education* 13(3) (2014): 467–475.

72. K.J. Lovelace, F. Egger, and L.R. Dyck, "I Do and I Understand: Assessing the Utility of Web-Based Management Simulations," *Academy of Management Learning & Education* 15(1) (2016): 100–121.

73. AACSB Web site, http://www.aacsb.edu/-/media/aacsb/docs/accreditation/standards/businessstds_2013_update -03oct_final_tracked_changes.ashx?la=en, retrieved on March 16, 2017.

74. ACBSP *(*Accreditation Council for Business Schools and Programs). http://www.acbsp.org/ Accessed March 16, 2017.

75. IACBE *(*International Assembly for Collegiate Business Education*).* http://iacbe.org/ Accessed March 16, 2017.

76. R.B. Kaiser and R.B. Kaplan, "The Deeper Work of Executive Development: Outgrowing Sensitivities," *Academy of Management Learning & Education* 5*(*4) (2006): 463–483.

77. R. Reuteman, "Value Lessons," *Entrepreneur* (March 2014): 38–43.

 i. W.L. Gore & Associates Web site, http://www.gore.com, accessed May 24, 2017.

 ii. W.L. Gore & Associates Web site, http://www.gore.com, accessed May 24, 2017.

 iii. G. Hamel, "W.L. Gore: Lessons from a Management Revolutionary," *Wall Street Journal,* March 18, 2010;
 G. Hamel, "W.L. Gore: Lessons from a Management Revolutionary," Part 2, *Wall Street Journal,* April 2, 2010.

Personality, Stress, Learning, and Perception

©Syda Productions/Shutterstock

After completing this chapter, you should be able to:

LO 2-1 Describe the Big Five personality dimensions.

LO 2-2 Explain the benefits of understanding and identifying personality profiles.

LO 2-3 Describe your stress personality type.

LO 2-4 List causes of stress, and describe how to be more effective at controlling stress.

LO 2-5 Describe the four learning styles and know which is your preferred learning style.

LO 2-6 Describe five biases affecting perception.

LO 2-7 Explain the importance of first impressions and how to project a positive image.

LO 2-8 Define the following 15 key terms (in order of appearance in the chapter):

personality	controlling stress plan
Type A personality	intelligence
locus of control	perception
Big Five Model of Personality	stereotyping
stress	perceptual congruence
stressors	primacy effect
burnout	four-minute barrier
	image

OPENING CASE WORK SCENARIO

/ / / June Peterson was walking alone to the lunchroom at PepsiCo. As she walked, she was thinking about her coworker, Rod Wills. June has trouble getting along with Rod because they are complete opposites. As June walked, two general thoughts came to her mind: Why does Rod do the things he does? Why are we so different? More specific questions came to mind: (1) We do the same job—why is he so stressed out and I'm not? (2) Why am I so emotional and interested in people—while Rod isn't? (3) Why am I so eager to get involved and help—while he sits back and watches?

(4) Why is Rod so quiet—while I'm so outgoing? (5) Why do I dislike routine and detail so much—while Rod enjoys it so much? (6) Why does he believe that everything that happens is because of fate—while I don't? (7) When we have to agree on a decision, why is he so slow and analytical—while I'm not? (8) Why is it that we see our jobs so differently when they are the same? (9) When I first met Rod, I thought we would hit it off fine. Why was I so wrong?

Although June's questions have no simple answers, this chapter will give you a better understanding of behavioral differences. / / /

HOW PERSONALITY, STRESS, INTELLIGENCE AND LEARNING, PERCEPTION, AND FIRST IMPRESSIONS AFFECT BEHAVIOR, HUMAN RELATIONS, AND PERFORMANCE

Recall that in Part 1 of the book, in Chapters 2 and 3, we discuss intrapersonal skills that affect behavior, human relations, and performance. In this chapter, we cover several different yet related topics, so let's start with an overview. Your *personality* (patterns of thoughts, feeling, and behaviors[1] affects your behavior and human relations, and your job performance.[2] Your personality also affects your level of *stress*.[3] It is also related to your level of *intelligence* and preferred method of learning, so intelligence also influences your behavior and human relations and is a good predictor of job performance.[4] Finally, your personality and intelligence influence your *perception*,[5] which, in turn, affects your *first impressions* of others, so it also affects human relations and performance.[6]

Throughout this chapter, you will learn how personality, stress, intelligence, perceptions, and first impressions make us similar and different, and how you can better understand yourself and others and work more effectively.

Remember that what you think about affects how you feel, and how you feel affects your behavior, human relations, and performance. So think happy, confident thoughts that you are a winner and you will act and be perceived as a winner and make a good first and lasting image.

PERSONALITY

///In the opening case scenario, As June Peterson's work scenario illustrates, different people behave differently in their everyday lives./// *Personality* is the word commonly used to describe an individual's collection (total person) of such behavioral traits or characteristics. Personal style or **personality** is *a relatively stable set of traits that aids in explaining and predicting individual behavior.* As noted, individuals are all different, yet similar, in many ways.

In this section you will learn about personality and the personality classifications of Type A and Type B; locus of control; the Big Five Model of Personality; and the MBTI. Throughout this chapter and book, you will gain a better understanding of your personality traits, which will help explain why you and others do the things you do (behavior). Employers are checking social media sites, such as **Google**, to get a feel for job candidates personality. Several businesses including **Lowe's**, **McDonald's**, and **Xerox** are giving personality tests to predict job performance.[7]

Personality Development and Classification Methods

Why are some people outgoing and others shy, some loud and others quiet, some aggressive and others passive? This list of behaviors is made up of individual traits. *Traits* are distinguishing personal characteristics. Personality development is based on genetics, experience, and environmental factors.[8] The genes you received before you were born influence your personality traits. Your family, friends, school, and work also influence your personality. In short, personality is the sum of genetics and a lifetime of learning. Personality traits, however, can be changed, with work.[9] For example, people who are shy can change their thoughts and feelings to consciously use more outgoing behaviors.[10]

Type A, Type B, and Locus of Control

Type A and Type B Personalities   Let's begin here with the simple two-dimensional method Type A, Type B. A **Type A personality** is characterized as *fast moving, hard driving, time conscious, competitive, impatient, and preoccupied with work.* Because a *Type B personality* is the opposite of Type A, often it is called laid-back or easygoing.

The Type A personality is commonly associated with a high level of stress, so we discuss it further in the section on causes of stress.

Locus of Control   Another simple two-dimensional personality classification method is locus of control. Before we discuss it, complete Self-Assessment Exercise 2-1 to determine if you are more of an internalizer or externalizer.

/ / / Self-Assessment Exercise 2-1 / / /

Your Locus of Control

Below are five statements. In the blank beside each statement, assign 1 to 5 points based on your agreement with the statement:

Agree		Neutral		Disagree
5	4	3	2	1

_____ 1. Getting ahead in life is a matter of hard work, rather than being in the right place at the right time.

_____ 2. I determine what I do and say, rather than allowing people and situations to upset me and affect how I behave.

_____ 3. Getting a raise and promotion is based on hard work, rather than who you know.

_____ 4. I, rather than other people and situations, determine what happens to my life.

_____ 5. Students earn their grades; teachers don't determine students' grades.

_____ Total. Add the five numbers (1–5). Below, place an X on the continuum that represents your score:

Externalizer 5 - - - - 10 - - - - 15 - - - - 20 - - - - 25 Internalizer

The lower your score, the greater is your belief that you are controlled by external sources such as fate, chance, other people, or environmental situations. The higher your score, the greater is your belief that you are in control of your destiny.

There is no right or wrong score, and a simple five-question instrument may not be totally accurate, but it should be helpful. If you disagree with the score, review the questions and think about why you selected the answers.

Locus of control is _a continuum representing one's belief as to whether external or internal forces control one's destiny._ People with an external locus of control (externalizers) believe that they have little control over their performance and are closed to new experiences. Internalizers believe they are in control and are open to new experiences to improve performance.[11]

Do you believe that you determine your own career success? The importance of an internal locus of control cannot be overstated; it determines your level of satisfaction with self, your stress level, and your career path. Thus, it is absolutely significant that you embrace the message that you control your own destiny and take responsibility for your success.

If you believe that if you try hard, it doesn't matter, that you cannot be successful, you will most likely be unhappy, give up easily, and not have a successful career. Successful people know that they are in control of their lives, and they are happy and successful because they work at it.[12] Successful people have lots of failures, but they keep trying. Internal locus of control can be changed if you work at it.

The Big Five Model of Personality

Learning Outcome 2-1

Describe the Big Five personality dimensions.

Let's begin by completing Self-Assessment Exercise 2-2 to determine your personality profile. The purpose of the Big Five model (commonly called the Five-Factor Model by academics) is to reliably categorize most, if not all, of the traits that you would use to describe someone.[13] The model is organized into five factors or dimensions, and each dimension includes multiple traits. The **Big Five Model of Personality** _categorizes traits into the dimensions of surgency, agreeableness, adjustment, conscientiousness, and openness to experience._ The dimensions are listed in Exhibit 2.1 and described below. Note, however, that the five dimensions are sometimes published with slightly different descriptor names, for example, **OCEAN** (openness, conscientiousness, extraversion, agreeableness, and neuroticism).[14]

/ / / **Self-Assessment Exercise 2-2** / / /

Your Big Five Personality Profile

There are no right or wrong answers, so by being honest you can really increase your self-awareness. We suggest doing this exercise in pencil or making a copy before you write on it. We will explain why later.

Identify each of the 25 statements according to how accurately they describe you. Place a number from 1 to 7 on the line before each statement.

Like me			Somewhat like me			Not like me
7	6	5	4	3	2	1

_____ 1. I step forward and take charge in leaderless situations.

_____ 2. I am concerned about getting along well with others.

_____ 3. I have good self-control; I don't get emotional and get angry and yell.

_____ 4. I'm dependable; when I say I will do something, it's done well and on time.

_____ 5. I try to do things differently to improve my performance.

_____ 6. I enjoy competing and winning; losing bothers me.

_____ 7. I enjoy having lots of friends and going to parties.

_____ 8. I perform well under pressure.

_____ 9. I work hard to be successful.

_____ 10. I go to new places and enjoy traveling.

_____ 11. I am outgoing and willing to confront people when in conflict.

_____ 12. I try to see things from other people's points of view.

_____ 13. I am an optimistic person who sees the positive side of situations (the cup is half full).

_____ 14. I am a well-organized person.

_____ 15. When I go to a new restaurant, I order foods I haven't tried.

_____ 16. I want to climb the corporate ladder to as high a level of management as I can.

_____ 17. I want other people to like me and to be viewed as very friendly.

_____ 18. I give people lots of praise and encouragement; I don't put people down and criticize.

_____ 19. I conform by following the rules of an organization.

_____ 20. I volunteer to be the first to learn or do new tasks at work.

_____ 21. I try to influence other people to get my way.

_____ 22. I enjoy working with others more than working alone.

_____ 23. I view myself as being relaxed and secure, rather than nervous and insecure.

_____ 24. I am considered credible because I do a good job and come through for people.

_____ 25. When people suggest doing things differently, I support them and help bring about change; I don't make statements such as, "It will not work," "We never did it before," "Who else did it?" or "We can't do it."

The columns in the chart below represent specific personality dimensions. To determine *your personality profile,* (1) place the number (1–7) that represents your score for each statement, (2) total each column (5–35), and (3) make a bar chart by marking the total scores on the vertical bars.

Surgency	Agreeableness	Adjustment	Conscientiousness	Openness to experience
_____ 1.	_____ 2.	_____ 3.	_____ 4.	_____ 5.
_____ 6.	_____ 7.	_____ 8.	_____ 9.	_____ 10.
_____ 11.	_____ 12.	_____ 13.	_____ 14.	_____ 15.
_____ 16.	_____ 17.	_____ 18.	_____ 19.	_____ 20.
_____ 21.	_____ 22.	_____ 23.	_____ 24.	_____ 25.
_____ **Total Bar**	_____ **Total Bar**	_____ **Total Bar**	_____ **Total Bar**	_____ **Total Bar**

(Each column has a vertical bar scale marked: 35, 25, 20, 15, 10, 5)

The higher the total number, the stronger is the personality dimension that describes your personality. What are your strongest and weakest dimensions? Continue reading the chapter to find out the specifics of your personality in each of the five dimensions.

EXHIBIT 2.1 | Big Five Dimensions of Traits

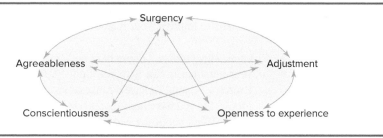

Surgency   The *surgency personality dimension* includes leadership and *extroversion* traits. (1) People strong in leadership, more commonly called dominance, personality traits want to be in charge. They are energetic, assertive, active, and ambitious, with an interest in getting ahead and leading through competing and influencing. **Bill Gates** has a high surgency personality type. People weak in surgency want to be followers, and they don't like to compete or influence. (2) Extroversion is on a continuum between being an extrovert and being an introvert. Extroverts are outgoing, sociable, and gregarious, like to meet new people, and are willing to confront others, whereas introverts are shy. In Self-Assessment Exercise 2-2, review statements 1, 6, 11, 16, and 21 for examples of surgency traits. How strong is your desire to be a leader?

Agreeableness   Unlike the surgency behavior trait of wanting to get ahead of others, the *agreeableness personality dimension* includes traits related to getting along with people. Agreeable personality behavior is strong when someone is called warm, easygoing, courteous, good-natured, cooperative, tolerant, compassionate, friendly, and sociable; it is weak when someone is called cold, difficult, uncompassionate, unfriendly, and unsociable. Strong agreeable personality types are sociable, spend most of their time with other people, and have lots of friends. In Self-Assessment Exercise 2-2, review statements 2, 7, 12, 17, and 22 for examples of agreeableness traits. How important is having good relationships to you?

Adjustment   The *adjustment personality dimension* includes traits related to emotional stability. Adjustment is on a continuum between being emotionally stable and being emotionally unstable.[15] Stability refers to self-control, calmness—good under pressure, relaxed, secure, and positive—and a willingness to praise others. Being emotionally unstable means being out of control—poor under pressure, nervous, insecure, moody, depressed, angry, and negative—and quick to criticize others. People with poor adjustment are often called *narcissists* and tend to be self-centered, looking out only for their self-interest,[16] and cause relationship problems when they get abusive.[17] But they do tend to get promoted to management. **Bill Gates** is said to be more in control of his emotions than **Steve Jobs** was, who was sometimes overly emotional.[18] In Self-Assessment Exercise 2-2, review statements 3, 8, 13, 18, and 23 for examples of adjustment traits. How emotionally stable are you?

Conscientiousness   The *conscientiousness personality dimension* includes traits related to achievement. Conscientiousness is on a continuum between being responsible and dependable and being irresponsible and undependable. Other traits of high conscientiousness include persistence, credibility, conformity, and organization. This trait is characterized as the willingness to work hard and put in extra time and effort to accomplish goals to achieve success. In Self-Assessment Exercise 2-2, review statements 4, 9, 14, 19, and 24 for examples of conscientiousness. Conscientiousness is a good predictor of job success.[19] How strong is your desire to be successful?

Openness to Experience   The *openness to experience personality dimension* includes traits related to being willing to change and try new things. People strong in openness to experience are imaginative, intellectual, open-minded, autonomous, and creative, they seek change, and they are willing to try new things, while those who are weak in this dimension avoid change

WORK APPLICATION 2-1

Describe your Big Five personality profile.

Learning Outcome 2-2

Explain the benefits of understanding and identifying personality profiles.

and new things. In Self-Assessment Exercise 2-2, review statements 5, 10, 15, 20, and 25 for examples of openness to experience. How willing are you to change and try new things, especially to improve your relationships?

Personality Profiles   *Personality profiles* identify individual strong and weak traits. Defining your personality can help you find the right career. Students completing Self-Assessment Exercise 2-2 tend to have a range of scores for the five dimensions. Review your personality profile. Do you have high scores (strong traits) and low scores (weak traits) on some dimensions? Think about the people you enjoy being with the most at school and work. Are their personalities similar to or different from yours?

APPLICATION SITUATIONS / / /

Personality Dimensions   AS 2-1

Identify the personality dimension for each of the five traits or behaviors described below.

A. Surgency   C. Adjustment   E. Openness to experience

B. Agreeableness   D. Conscientiousness

_____ 1. Juan is saying a warm, friendly good morning to others as they arrive at work.

_____ 2. The manager is asking employees for ideas on how to speed up the flow of work.

_____ 3. Ron is yelling at another employee, Susan, about being behind schedule. Susan calmly explains what went wrong.

_____ 4. Tyron is influencing a coworker to do the job the way he wants it done.

_____ 5. The production manager turned in the monthly production report on time as usual.

Communication Skills
Refer to CS Question 1.

The Big Five Model of Personality Has Universal Applications Across Cultures   Studies have shown that people from Asian, Western European, Middle Eastern, Eastern European, and North and South American cultures seem to exhibit the same five personality dimensions.[20] However, some cultures do place varying importance on different personality dimensions. Overall, the best predictor of job success on a global basis is the conscientiousness dimension.

WORK APPLICATION 2-2

Select a present or past boss and describe how his or her personality profile affected behavior, human relations, and performance in your department.

Using Behavior That Matches the Big Five Personality Types

We need to be able to work well with people who have different personalities than ours.[21] To improve our human relations, it is helpful for us to adjust our behavior based on the other person's personality type,[22] especially our bosses, because they evaluate our performance, which affects our career. That subject is what this section is all about.

/// **In the opening case scenario,** recall June's question about why she and Rod are so different. A major reason is that they have different personalities that affect their behavior, human relations, and performance. June has a Type B personality, while Rod has Type A. June is a surgency extrovert, while Rod is an introvert. Not surprisingly, June has a higher agreeableness personality dimension than Rod. They may be similar on the adjustment and conscientiousness personality dimension. June is an internalizer and more open to experience than Rod, who is an externalizer. ///

1. **Determine Personality Type**—First, we have to understand the personality types and determine an individual's personality profile. As you know, people are complex, and identifying a person's personality type is not always easy, especially when he or she is between the two ends of the personality type continuum. However, understanding personality can help you understand and predict behavior, human relations, and performance in a given situation.

2. **Match Personality Type**—Next, we select the behavior we will use to match the other person's personality type. How to deal with each personality type is presented below.

Surgency

Extroverts: They like to talk, so be talkative while showing an interest in them and talking about things they are interested in. If you are not really talkative, ask them questions to get them to do the talking.

Introverts: Take it slow. Be laid-back and don't pressure them, but try to draw them out by asking questions they can easily answer. Ask for ideas and opinions. Don't worry about moments of silence; introverts often like to think before they respond.

Agreeableness

Agreeable: They are easy to get along with, so be friendly and supportive of them. However, remember that they don't tend to disagree with you to your face, so don't assume that just because they don't disagree with you, it means that they actually *do* agree with you. Asking direct questions helps, and be sure to watch for nonverbal behavior that does not match a verbal statement of "I agree with you."

Disagreeable: Try not to do things that will get them upset, but don't put up with mistreatment; be assertive (you will learn how in Chapter 5). Be patient and tolerant, because their behavior is sometimes defensive to keep them from being hurt, but inside, they do want friends. So keep being friendly and trying to win them over.

Adjustment

Emotionally stable: They tend to be easy to get along with.

Emotionally unstable: They tend to be highly emotional and unpredictable, so try to be calm yourself and keep them calm by being supportive while showing concern for them. Also, follow the guidelines of dealing with disagreeable types. You will learn how to deal with emotions and emotional people in Chapter 4.

Conscientiousness

Conscientious: They will come through for you, so don't nag; be supportive and thank them when the task is done.

Unconscientious: They tend to need prompting to complete tasks. Set clear deadlines and follow up regularly; express appreciation for progress and task completion.

Open to Experience

Open: They like change and trying new things. Focus on sharing information, ideas, and creative problem solving.

Closed: They don't want change and tend to focus on the short-term without considering how things will be better in the long-term if they change now. Focus on telling them what they have to lose and how they will benefit from the change, and use facts and figures to support the need for change. You will learn how to overcome resistance to change in Chapter 11.

The Myers-Briggs Type Indicator (MBTI)

Our fourth, and most complex, personality classification method is the Myers-Briggs Type Indicator (MBTI). The MBTI model of personality identifies your personality *preferences.* It is based on your four preferences (or inclinations) for certain ways of thinking and behaving.[23] Complete Self-Assessment Exercise 2-3 to determine your MBTI personality preference.

Your MBTI Personality Preference

Classify yourself on each of the four preferences by selecting the one statement that best describes you:

1. *Where you focus your attention*—**Extrovert or Introvert**

_____ I'm outgoing and prefer to deal with people, things, situations, the outer world. (E)

_____ I'm shy and prefer to deal with ideas, information, explanations, or beliefs, the inner world. (I)

2. *How you take in information*—**Sensing or Intuitive**

_____ I prefer facts to have clarity, to describe what I sense with a focus on the present. (S)

_____ I prefer to deal with ideas, look into unknown possibilities with a focus on the future. (N)

3. *How you make decisions*—**Thinking or Feeling**

_____ I prefer to make decisions based on objective logic, using an analytic and detached approach. (T)

_____ I prefer to make decisions using values and/or personal beliefs, with a concern for others. (F)

4. *How you prefer to organize your life*—**Judging or Perceiving**

_____ I prefer my life to be planned, stable, and organized. (J)

_____ I prefer to go with the flow, to maintain flexibility and to respond to things as they arise. (P)

Place the four letters of preferences here: _____ _____ _____ _____

There are 16 combinations, or personality preferences, often presented in the form of a table. Remember, this indicates *preferences* only. You may also use the other traits that you did not select.

ISTJ	ISFJ	INFJ	INTJ
ISTP	ISFP	INFP	INTP
ESTP	ESFP	ENFP	ENTP
ESTJO	ESFJ	ENFJ	ENTJ

Completing Self-Assessment Exercise 2-3 gives you an idea of the types of questions included in the MBTI; it does not give you an MBTI profile. There are actually multiple forms of the MBTI for various uses. For more information on the MBTI,[24] and to complete a more detailed assessment for a fee, visit its website at www.myersbriggs.org. You can also take a free 64-question survey at the **HumanMetrics** website http://www.humanmetrics .com/cgi-win/jtypes2.asp and find out what famous people have your personality profile.[25] Think about your friends and family and the people you work with. What MBTI type are they? How can you improve your human relations with them based on the MBTI?

Communication Skills
Refer to CS Question 2.

STRESS

Learning Outcome 2-3

Describe your stress personality type.

In this section, we discuss what stress is, problems associated with stress, causes of stress, signs of stress, and how to control stress.

What Is Stress?

People react to external stimuli internally, or it is an intrapersonal skill.[26] **Stress** is *an emotional and/or physical reaction to environmental activities and events.* Stress is an individual matter. In the same situation, one person may be comfortable while the other feels stress.[27] /// **In the opening case,** June and Rod have the same job, but Rod is stressed and June isn't. ///

The Positive Side   Some stress helps improve performance by challenging and motivating us. Many people perform best under some pressure. When deadlines are approaching, their adrenaline flows and they rise to the occasion with top-level performance. To meet deadlines, managers often have to apply pressure to themselves and their employees.[28]

Problems Associated with Too Much Stress Situations in which too much pressure exists are known as stressors. **Stressors** are *situations in which people feel anxiety, tension, and pressure.* Stressors are events and situations to which people must adjust, and the impact of the stressor and how people react depend on the circumstances and on each person's physical and psychological characteristics. Too much stress affects your behavior, human relations, and performance. Stress depletes your energy, weakens your brain and relationships, can cause aging and weight gain, weakens your immune system, can ruin your sleep and make you ill, and can even be a cause of death.[29]

Learning Outcome 2-4

List causes of stress, and describe how to be more effective at controlling stress.

Causes of Stress

There are four common stressors related to work: Complete the questionnaire in Self-Assessment Exercise 2-4 to determine your personality type as it relates to stress.

/ / / Self-Assessment Exercise 2-4 / / /

Your Stress Personality Type

Below are 20 statements. Identify how frequently each item applies to you.

(5) Usually   (4) Often   (3) Occasionally   (2) Seldom   (1) Rarely

Place the number 1, 2, 3, 4, or 5 on the line before each statement.

_____ 1. I work at a fast pace.

_____ 2. I work on days off.

_____ 3. I set short deadlines for myself.

_____ 4. I enjoy work/school more than other activities.

_____ 5. I talk and walk fast.

_____ 6. I set high standards for myself and work hard to meet them.

_____ 7. I enjoy competition, I work/play to win; I do not like to lose.

_____ 8. I skip lunch or eat it fast when there is work to do.

_____ 9. I'm in a hurry.

_____ 10. I do more than one thing at a time.

_____ 11. I'm angry and upset.

_____ 12. I get nervous or anxious when I have to wait.

_____ 13. I measure progress in terms of time and performance.

_____ 14. I push myself to the point of getting tired.

_____ 15. I take on more work when I already have plenty to do.

_____ 16. I take criticism as a personal put-down of my ability.

_____ 17. I try to outperform my coworkers/classmates.

_____ 18. I get upset when my routine has to be changed.

_____ 19. I consistently try to get more done in less time.

_____ 20. I compare my accomplishments with those of others who are highly productive.

Total. Add up the numbers (1–5) you have for all 20 items. Your score will range from 20 to 100. Below place an X on the continuum that represents your score.

Type A 100 _ _ _ _ _ 80 _ _ _ _ _ 60 _ _ _ _ _ 40 _ _ _ _ _ 20 Type B
                     A   -A   B+   B

The higher your score, the more characteristic you are of the Type A stress personality. The lower your score, the more characteristic you are of the Type B stress personality. An explanation of these two stress personality types follows.

WORK APPLICATION 2-3

What was your stress personality type score and letter? How does your stress personality type enhance and/or hurt your performance? Should you work at changing your personality type? Explain why or why not. Will you change?

Personality Type   The degree to which stressors affect us is caused, in part, by our personality type. Since stress comes from within, the things we do can cause us stress. As noted earlier, there are Type A and Type B personalities. The 20 statements of Self-Assessment Exercise 2-4 relate to these personality types. People with Type A personalities have more stress than people with Type B personalities. If you scored 60 or above, you have a Type A personality and could end up with some of the problems associated with stress.

- **Organizational Climate.** The amount of cooperation, the level of motivation, and the overall morale in an organization affect stress levels. The more positive the organizational climate and work culture, the less stress there is.

- **Management Behavior.** Calm, participative management styles produce less stress. Tight control through autocratic management tends to create more stress. Some bosses use awful behavior; some are even abusive and have caused stress to the point of driving employees to quit their jobs.[30]

- **Degree of Job Satisfaction.** People who enjoy their jobs and derive satisfaction from them handle stress better than those who do not. In some cases, a change of jobs is a wise move that can lower or get rid of one of your stressors. People who focus in the positives in their job are happier than those who focus on the negative aspects of the job.

APPLICATION SITUATIONS / / /

Stressors   AS 2-2

Identify the stressor in each statement below.

A. Personality type   C. Organizational climate

B. Management behavior   D. Degree of job satisfaction

_____ 6. "Yes. I like my job."

_____ 7. "I'm always pushing myself to beat deadlines around here."

_____ 8. "I don't need my boss to be constantly checking to see how I'm progressing. I wish he would leave me alone."

_____ 9. "I work at a comfortable pace regardless of how long the line of customers gets."

_____ 10. "The level of morale in our department is one of the best in the company."

Signs of Stress

Some of the immediate signs of stress are an increase in the rate of breathing, sweating, change in appetite, and acne.[31] When you continually look at the clock and/or calendar, feel pressured, and fear that you will not meet a deadline, you are experiencing stress.

People often lose interest in and motivation to do their work because of stress. Stress that is constant, chronic, and severe can lead to burnout over a period of time. **Burnout** is *the constant lack of interest and motivation to perform one's job because of stress.* People sometimes experience temporary burnout during busy periods, as is the case with students studying for exams and retailers trying to cope with a holiday shopping season. The use of stress-controlling techniques can often prevent stress and burnout and increase productivity. The **APA** (American Psychological Association) has the **"Test Your Stress Smarts!"** you can take for free at http://www.apa.org/helpcenter/stress-smarts.aspx to assess how much you know about stress.

Controlling Stress

Controlling stress is the process of adjusting to circumstances that disrupt or threaten to disrupt us. Ideally, we should identify what causes stress in our lives and eliminate or decrease it. You can better control stress by following a three-stage plan. The **controlling stress plan** includes: *step 1, identify stressors; step 2, determine their causes and consequences; and step 3, plan to eliminate or decrease the stress.* Below are five ways you can help eliminate or decrease stress.

Exercise   Physical exercise is an excellent way to release tension and reduce weight. Aerobic exercise that increases the heart rate and maintains that rate for 30 minutes or more for at least three or more days per week is generally considered the best type of exercise. Exercises such as fast walking or jogging, biking, swimming, and aerobic dancing are in this category. Yoga and other exercises that require you to increase your heart rate are also beneficial.

Before starting an exercise program, however, check with a doctor to make sure you are able to do so safely. Start gradually and slowly work your way up to 20 to 30 minutes.

Nutrition   Good health is essential to everyone, and nutrition is a major factor in your health. Watch your waistline. Breakfast is considered the most important meal of the day. A good high-protein (eggs/yogurt), high-fiber (whole-grain bread/fruit) breakfast gets you off to a good start. When you eat, take your time, because rushing is stressful and leads to overeating.

Try to minimize your intake of junk food containing high levels of salt, sugar, and white flour. Consume less fat, salt, caffeine (in coffee, tea, cola), alcohol, and drugs. Eat and drink more natural foods, such as fruits and vegetables, and drink plenty of water (not soda or sports drinks).

Relaxation   Get enough rest and sleep. Most adults require 7 to 8 hours of sleep, but Americans are not getting enough sleep. Our brains don't work effectively without enough sleep and we make poor decisions.[32] Trouble retaining information, irritability, minor illness, poor judgment, increased mistakes, and weight gain are all signs that you may need more sleep.

Slow down and enjoy yourself. Have some off-the-job interests that are relaxing. Have some fun, and laugh. Some of the things you can do to relax include praying, meditating, listening to music, reading, watching TV or movies, and engaging in hobbies.[33]

When you feel stress, you can perform some simple relaxation exercises. One of the most popular and simplest is *deep breathing.* You simply take a deep breath, hold it for a few seconds (you may count to five), and then let it out slowly. If you feel tension in one muscle, you may do a specific relaxation exercise, or you may relax your entire body, going from head to toe or vice versa. For a list of relaxation exercises that can be done almost anywhere, see Exhibit 2.2.

Communication Skills
Refer to CS Question 3.

WORK APPLICATION 2-4

Following the controlling stress plan, (1) identify your major stressor, (2) determine its cause and consequences, and (3) develop a plan to eliminate or decrease the stress. Identify each step in your answer.

Positive Thinking   Be optimistic and stay positive. Optimism can be learned. Make statements to yourself in the affirmative,[34] such as "I will do it." Be patient, honest, and realistic. No one is perfect. Admit your mistakes and learn from them; don't let them get you down. Have self-confidence; develop your time management skills (as discussed in Chapters 3). Positive thinkers are happier than negative thinkers. Stay away from negative thinkers because they can bring you down with them.

Support System   We all need people we can depend on. Have family and friends you can go to for help with your problems. Having someone to talk to can be very helpful, but don't take advantage of others and use stress to get attention or to get out of doing what you should do.

For an illustration of the causes of stress and how to control it, see Exhibit 2.3. If you try all the stress-controlling techniques and none of them work, you should seriously consider getting out of the situation.

EXHIBIT 2.2 | Relaxation Exercises

Muscles	Tensing Method
Forehead	Wrinkle forehead. Try to make your eyebrows touch your hairline for 5 seconds. Relax.
Eyes and nose	Close your eyes as tightly as you can for 5 seconds. Relax.
Lips, cheeks, jaw	Draw corners of your mouth back and grimace for 5 seconds. Relax.
Neck	Drop your chin to your chest; then slowly rotate your head in a complete circle in one direction and then in the other. Relax.
Hands	Extend arms in front of you; clench fists tightly for 5 seconds. Relax.
Forearms	Extend arms out against an invisible wall and push forward with hands for 5 seconds. Relax.
Upper arms	Bend elbows. Tense biceps for 5 seconds. Relax.
Shoulders	Shrug shoulders up to your ears for 5 seconds. Relax.
Back	Arch your back off the floor or bed for 5 seconds. Relax.
Stomach	Tighten your stomach muscles for 5 seconds. Relax.
Hips, buttocks	Tighten buttocks for 5 seconds. Relax.
Thighs	Tighten thigh muscles by pressing legs together as tightly as you can for 5 seconds. Relax.
Feet	Flex your feet up toward your body as far as you can for 5 seconds. Relax.
Toes	Curl toes under as tightly as you can for 5 seconds. Relax.

WORK APPLICATION 2-5

Of the five ways to eliminate or decrease stress, which do you do best? Which needs the most improvement and why? What will you do, if anything, to improve in that area?

Let's end this section with a confirmation of your lifestyle or an incentive to change it. According to a research study, if you exercise, don't smoke (or quit), drink only moderately, and eat right (lots of fruits and vegetables and limited junk food), you can live an average of 14 years longer and you will be happier.[35]

Remember that what you think about affects how you feel, and how you feel affects your behavior, human relations, and performance. So think happy, confident thoughts, and if you feel stress, use these guidelines to reduce your stress.

EXHIBIT 2.3 | Causes of Stress and How to Control Stress

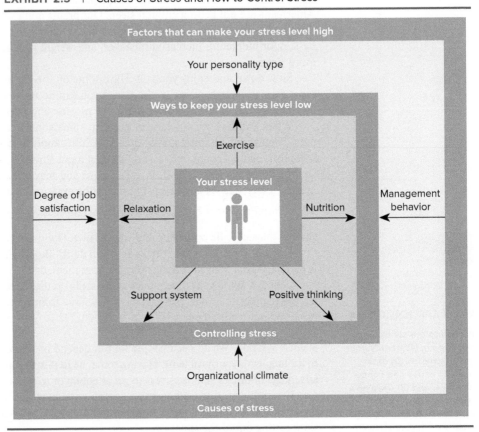

INTELLIGENCE, EMOTIONAL INTELLIGENCE, AND LEARNING

This section discusses the development of intelligence, learning styles, and learning organizations.

Intelligence

Intelligence is also a trait.[36] There are numerous theories of intelligence, many of which view intelligence as the ability to learn and the use of cognitive processes. It is often called general mental ability. For our purposes we will say that **intelligence** is *the level of one's capacity for new learning, problem solving, and decision making.* Today it is generally agreed that intelligence is a product of both genetics and the environment. Most scientists today believe there are at least two and perhaps as many as seven or more different components or kinds of intelligence.

Communication Skills
Refer to CS Question 4.

People often perform at different levels for different tasks. As you know, you are good at doing some things (math, tennis, etc.) and not as good at doing others (biology, writing, etc.). Therefore, people have multiple intelligences.[37] Intelligence is a strong predictor of many important outcomes in life, such as educational and occupational performance.[38]

Emotional Intelligence

Emotions are central to human experience;[39] recall that people are usually more emotional than rational. An offshoot of IQ is EQ (emotional quotient or emotional intelligence [EI]), which is clearly related to the adjustment Big Five personality dimension.[40] EI is all about working well with people. The good news is EI is a learned competence, so you can improve your EI by working at it. That is what this course is all about. So here we list and briefly explain EI components, but you will develop EI skills throughout the course, especially in Chapters 4 and 5. EI is part of multiple intelligences. It has been said, "IQ gets you the job, EQ and I got a clue gets you promoted."

There are five components of EI:

1. Self-awareness (being conscious of your emotions within you; gut feelings)
2. Managing emotions (not letting your emotions get in the way of getting the job done)
3. Motivating yourself (being optimistic despite obstacles, setbacks, and failure)
4. Empathy (putting yourself in someone else's situation and understanding that person's emotions)
5. Social skills (to build relationships, respond to emotions, and influence others)

Remember that what you think about affects how you feel, and how you feel affects your behavior, human relations, and performance. So think happy, confident thoughts to help you stay calm and in control of your emotional behavior. Also, visit the Consortium for Research on Emotional Intelligence in Organizations at www.eiconsortium.org for more information about EI.

/// **In the opening case,** you should now have a better understanding of why June and Rod are different, other than personality. June has greater emotional intelligence. June is more outgoing, in touch with feelings, interested in people, and eager to get involved and help others, while Rod is not.///

Learning Styles

Learning Outcome 2-5

Describe the four learning styles and know which is your preferred learning style.

Our capacity to learn new things is an important aspect of our intelligence. However, we have different preferred learning styles.[41] We will examine four styles people use when learning. Before we describe the four **Kolb** learning styles,[42] determine your preferred learning style. Complete Self-Assessment Exercise 2-5 before reading on. Also, note that the online MBTI assessment at http://www.humanmetrics.com/cgi-win/jtypes2.asp helps you understand your learning style.[43]

/ / / **Self-Assessment Exercise 2-5** / / /

Your Learning Style

Below are 10 statements. For each statement distribute 5 points between the A and B alternatives. If the A statement is very characteristic of you and the B statement is not, place a 5 on the _____ A. line and a 0 on the _____ B. line. If the A statement is characteristic of you and the B statement is occasionally or somewhat characteristic of you, place a 4 on the _____ A. line and a 1 on the _____ B. line. If both statements are characteristic of you, place a 3 on the line that is more characteristic of you and a 2 on the line that is less characteristic of you. Be sure to distribute 5 points between each A and B alternative for each of the 10 statements. When distributing the 5 points, try to recall recent situations on the job or in school.

1. When learning:

_____ A. I watch and listen.

_____ B. I get involved and participate.

2. When learning:

_____ A. I rely on my hunches and feelings.

_____ B. I rely on logical and rational thinking.

3. When making decisions:

_____ A. I take my time.

_____ B. I make them quickly.

4. When making decisions:

_____ A. I rely on my gut feelings about the best alternative course of action.

_____ B. I rely on a logical analysis of the situation.

5. When doing things:

_____ A. I am careful.

_____ B. I am practical.

6. When doing things:

_____ A. I have strong feelings and reactions.

_____ B. I reason things out.

7. I would describe myself in the following way:

_____ A. I am a reflective person.

_____ B. I am an active person.

8. I would describe myself in the following way:

_____ A. I am influenced by my emotions.

_____ B. I am influenced by my thoughts.

9. When interacting in small groups:

_____ A. I listen, watch, and get involved slowly.

_____ B. I am quick to get involved.

10. When interacting in small groups:

_____ A. I express what I am feeling.

_____ B. I say what I am thinking.

Scoring: Place your answer numbers (0–5) on the lines below. Then add the numbers in each column vertically. Each of the four columns should have a total number between 0 and 25. The total of the two A and B columns should equal 25.

(*continued*)

1. _____ A. _____ B.		(5)	2. _____ A. _____ B.		(5)
3. _____ A. _____ B.		(5)	4. _____ A. _____ B.		(5)
5. _____ A. _____ B.		(5)	6. _____ A. _____ B.		(5)
7. _____ A. _____ B.		(5)	8. _____ A. _____ B.		(5)
9. _____ A. _____ B.		(5)	10. _____ A. _____ B.		(5)

Totals _____ A. _____ B. (25)   _____ A. _____ B. (25)

Style   Observing Doing   Feeling Thinking

There is no best or right learning style; each of the four learning styles has its pros and cons. The more evenly distributed your scores are between the As and Bs, the more flexible you are at changing styles. Understanding your preferred learning style can help you get the most from your learning experiences.

Determining your preferred learning style: The five odd-numbered A statements refer to your self-description as being "observing," and the five odd-numbered B statements refer to your self-description as "doing." The column with the highest number is your preferred style of learning. Write it below:

I described myself as preferring to learn by _____.

The five even-numbered A statements refer to your self-description as being a "feeling" person, and the five even-numbered B statements refer to your self-description as being a "thinking" person. The column with the highest number is your preferred style. Write it below:

I described myself as preferring to learn by _____.

Putting the two preferences together gives you your preferred dimension of learning. Check it off below:

_____ Accommodator (combines doing and feeling)

_____ Diverger (combines observing and feeling)

_____ Converger (combines doing and thinking)

_____ Assimilator (combines observing and thinking)

Exhibit 2.4 illustrates the four learning styles.

As stated above, people learn based on two personality dimensions or types—feeling versus thinking and doing versus observing. Even though you have a preferred learning style, you cannot always use it. In this course, you probably don't determine how the instructor will teach it. If the instructor spends more time in class completing and discussing skill-building exercises, the accommodators and convergers will be enjoying their preferred learning style and using their feelings or thoughts when being actively involved.

On the other hand, if the instructor spends more class time lecturing on the material and showing films, the diverger and assimilator will be using their preferred learning style, while emphasizing feelings or thinking.

Your instructor's preferred learning style will most likely influence the way he or she teaches this course. For example, the author of this book is a converger, which influenced his use of a skill-building approach that includes more emphasis on thinking (than feelings) and doing (than observing); however, all four styles of learning are included.

After reading about the four learning styles, you should realize that there is no best learning style; each has its own pros and cons. You probably realize that you have one preferred learning style, but you also have characteristics of other styles as well.

/// **In the opening case,** in addition to having different personalities and levels of emotional intelligence, June and Rod have different learning styles. June combines doing and feeling as an accommodator. Rod combines observing and thinking as an assimilator.

WORK APPLICATION 2-6

What is your preferred learning style? Are the characteristics of the style a good description of you? Explain. Can you change your learning style?

WORK APPLICATION 2-7

Think about the person you enjoy or have enjoyed working with the most. Identify that person's learning style. Is it the same as yours? What is it that you enjoy about the person?

WORK APPLICATION 2-8

Think about the person you dislike or have disliked working with the most. Identify that person's learning style. Is it the same as yours? What is it that you dislike about the person?

EXHIBIT 2.4 | The Four Learning Styles

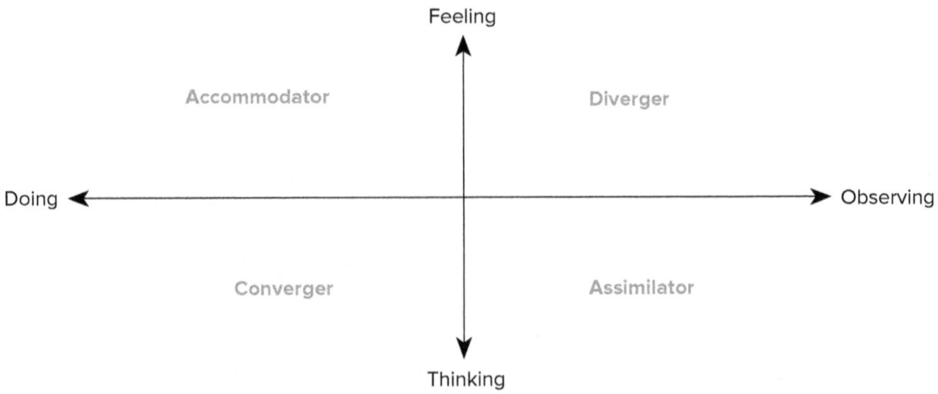

Style	Definition	Characteristics
Accommodators	Prefer learning by doing and feeling.	Tend to learn primarily from hands-on experience. Act on gut feelings, relying more on other people for information than on technical analysis.
Divergers	Prefer learning by observing and feeling.	Have the ability to view concrete situations from many different points of view. Take their time gathering and analyzing many alternatives.
Convergers	Prefer learning by doing and thinking.	Seek practical uses for information focusing on solutions. Prefer dealing with technical tasks and problems rather than with interpersonal issues.
Assimilators	Prefer learning by observing and thinking.	Effective at understanding a wide range of information and putting it into a concise, logical form. Tend to be more concerned with abstract ideas and concepts than with people.

SB

Skill-Building Exercise 2-1 develops this skill.

They make decisions differently. People with similar personalities and learning styles tend to get along better than those who are different. Thus, because June and Rod are different, it is not surprising that they don't hit it off well. /// It takes good intrapersonal skills and interpersonal skills to get along with people who are different from you.

APPLICATION SITUATIONS / / /

Learning Styles AS 2-3

Identify the learning style of the people by the statements made about them.

A. Accommodator B. Diverger C. Converger D. Assimilator

_______ 11. "Harriet says she feels out the customer and then decides her approach, rather than use the standard approach we were taught to use in the sales course."

_______ 12. "I don't want John on the committee because he lives in a fantasy world with impractical ideas."

_______ 13. "Identify which style would be most likely to have made the comment about John in situation 12."

_______ 14. "I'm different from Shannon and it's annoying because she is too slow to make decisions."

_______ 15. "Latoya is a good computer tech because she enjoys fixing things and solving problems."

The Learning Organization

Recall from Chapter 1 that a major challenge today in the global environment is learning and knowledge. Let's discuss the need for individual learning, followed by group and organizational learning, and the learning organization.

The Need for Individual Learning   Probably the most important skill that college provides is the ability to continuously learn. Do not view your education as being over when you get your degree. Graduation commencement actually means the beginning, not the end. Much of what you will do on the job in the future will be learned at work. **PepsiCo CEO Indra Nooyi**'s career advice is, Never stop learning. Admitting you don't know something and asking questions is not a sign of weakness. Successful people are lifelong students.[44] Everyone you meet in your personal and professional lives knows more about something than you do, so get them to pass that knowledge on to you.[45]

Group and Organizational Learning   As we work with individuals and in groups on the job, we are both teaching and learning as we share knowledge. Combined we get organizational learning, and companies that intentionally focus on sharing knowledge are called learning organizations.[46]

Learning organizations cultivate the capacity to learn, adapt, and change with the environment to be innovative with speed. The learning organization focuses on improving learning and determining how knowledge is circulated throughout the organization. Learning from mistakes and failure to continuously improve performance is critical.[47] The learning organization questions old beliefs and ways of doing things, yet it makes the learning and change process as painless as possible.

PERCEPTION

Our personalities, stress, and intelligence affect how we see the world. And our perceptions affect our behavior, human relations, and performance,[48] which in turn affect others.[49] In this section we discuss the nature of perception and bias in perception.

The Nature of Perception

The term **perception** refers to *a person's interpretation of reality.* In the perception process, you select, organize, and interpret stimuli through your senses. Your perception is influenced by heredity and experience. Notice that the definition of perception refers to the "interpretation of reality." In human relations, perception is just as important as reality. People often encounter the same thing and perceive it differently.

Ever hear that there are always two sides to every story? Why? It starts with the way each person perceives the event in the first place, then how and what they remember, so don't assume the other person is lying.[50] So fights often begin with with two versions of events because people perceive the same thing differently.[51]

Bias in Perception

Learning Outcome 2-6

Describe five biases affecting perception.

Some of the biases affecting perception that can hinder communications and lead to conflict include stereotypes, frames of reference, expectations, selective exposure, and interest.

Stereotypes   Consider the bias of **stereotyping**, which is *the process of generalizing the behavior of all members of a group.* Stereotypes are drawn along all kinds of lines, including race, religion, nationality, and sex. Yes, we all stereotype people as a way of quickly perceiving a person's behavior.

Avoid stereotypes. Consciously attempt to get to know people as individuals, rather than to stereotype.

Frame of Reference   Our frame of reference is our tendency to see things from a narrow focus that directly affects us. It is common for employees and management to perceive the same situation from different frames of reference.[52] Do you always see things the same as management or your parents and agree with them?

To be effective in our human relations, we should try to perceive things from the other person's frame of reference and be willing to work together for the benefit of all parties to create a win–win situation.

Expectations   What we expect often influences our perceptions of what we see and experience. For example, read the phrase in the triangle below:

Did you read the word *the* twice? Or, like most people, did you read what you expected, only one *the*? We perceive, select, organize, and interpret information as we expect it to appear.

You have expectations of others in relationships; when they do things you don't expect or like, you have human relations problems. So our preconceived notions and labels can undermine accurate perceptions and effective judgment and decision making.

WORK APPLICATION 2-9

Give an example of when you and another person experienced the same situation but perceived it differently. Which of the six biases affecting perception was responsible for the difference in perception? Explain your answer.

Selective Exposure   We tend to see and hear what we want to. People sometimes selectively pick information they want to hear and ignore information they don't want to hear.[53] How often do you ignore the facts because you don't agree with them?

To ensure effective human relations, we should listen to the entire message, rather than use selective exposure.

Interest   What interests you also affects how you perceive and approach things. Have you ever taken a course and not liked it, while others in the class thought it was great? This difference in perception may be due to different levels of interest in the subject. Interest influences job selection and satisfaction.

APPLICATION SITUATIONS / / /

Bias in Perception   AS 2-4

Identify the particular perception bias in the statements below.

A. Stereotypes   C. Expectations   E. Interest

B. Frame of reference   D. Selective exposure

_____ 16. "A major problem between management and the union is that they only see the issues from their own point of view."

_____ 17. "Joan, you are not really listening to what I'm telling you. Don't ignore the facts."

_____ 18. "George doesn't really listen to others' opinions. He thinks he knows what they want, and he makes decisions without their input."

_____ 19. "Mary doesn't say much when we talk about work, but when we discuss sports she is talkative."

_____ 20. "Why do people keep asking me about basketball? Just because I'm a tall African American doesn't mean I like the game. I play volleyball, but no one ever asks me about it."

EXHIBIT 2.5 | Biases Affecting Perception

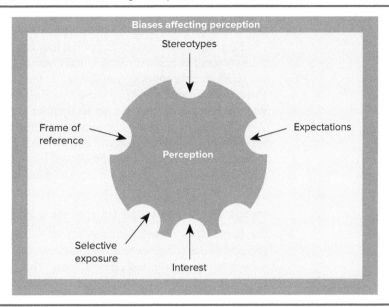

Skill-Building Exercise 2-2 develops this skill.

Communication Skills Refer to CS Question 5.

The term **perceptual congruence** refers to *the degree to which people see things the same way.* When people perceive things the same way, it generally has positive consequences in the organization. However, perception biases also can result in lower performance.[54] Employees who perceive management as supportive are generally happier with their jobs.

What is the reality of any situation? We tend to believe that our perception is reality and the other party's perception is wrong. Remember, people will behave according to their perception, not yours. Thus, it is important to realize that people often see things differently than you do. So we need to look at things from their perspectives and help them remember the facts of the situation, avoid our biases, remember that our memory may be in error, and be willing to admit we misperceived the situation and apologize when we are wrong. Also, accurate communications helps ensure perceptual congruence,[55] and don't forget emotions overtake logic. We'll learn how to communicate, deal with emotions, and resolve conflicts in Chapters 4 and 5. /// **In the opening case,** June and Rod have different perceptions of their jobs./// For a review of the biases affecting perception, see Exhibit 2.5.

DEVELOPING POSITIVE FIRST IMPRESSIONS

Learning Outcome 2.7

Explain the importance of first impressions and how to project a positive image.

In this section we discuss first impressions: the primacy effect and the four-minute barrier. We also examine image projection.

The Primacy Effect and the Four-Minute Barrier

We should realize that it matters how others perceive us.[56] When people meet they form quick impressions of each other. Social psychologists call this process the primacy effect. The **primacy effect** is *the way people perceive one another during their first impressions.* These first impressions establish the mental framework within which people view one another, which affect the development of their relationship, so first impressions do matter, a lot.[57] Employers are searching social media sites to get a first impression of you as a job candidates. A good professional image can lead you to a job, whereas a nonprofessional image tends to take you out of consideration for the job.

The **four-minute barrier** is *the time we have to make a good impression.* It is also called the *four-minute sell* because it is the average time during which people make up their minds to continue the contact or separate during social situations. However, in business and social situations, the time could be less. Some say first impressions are developed between two, yes two, seconds and two minutes, and they are essential for your success.[58] During this short period of time, your relations will be established, denied, or reconfirmed.

First impressions usually linger, but they can be changed. Have you ever disliked someone as a result of first impressions that linger to the present time? On the other hand, can you recall meeting someone you disliked at first, but once you got to know the person, you changed your impression? /// **In the opening case,** recall that June's first impression of Rod was positive, but they did not hit it off for long. ///

If you register negative first impressions in other people, you will have to "prove" yourself to change those impressions,[59] and we will discuss how to do so in Chapter 6. It is easier to begin by projecting an image people will like and maintain it through impression management. Next we discuss how to project and manage a positive image.

Image Projection and Impression Management

Our **image** is *other people's attitudes toward us. Professional image* is the total of others' perceptions of our competence and character in the workplace, which is needed to achieving social approval, power, and career success.[60] Image can be thought of as being on a continuum from positive to negative. *Impression or image management* are techniques used to control how we are perceived by monitoring how you are perceived to develop, control, and maintain positive impressions with others.[61] Our image is developed by our appearance, nonverbal communications, and behavior that we can manage to project a positive image.[62] If you project a positive image during a job interview, you greatly increase your chances of getting the job offer. Each of these three areas is discussed separately below.

Appearance   When people first see you, before you can do or say anything, they begin to develop their first impressions. If people don't like the way you look, your clothes, hairstyle, or grooming, they may not give you the opportunity to show who you really are. If you want to be successful, you should dress appropriately for the situation.[63] A simple rule to follow is to adopt the dress and grooming standards of the organization and, specifically, of the job you want.

You will learn more tips on apparel and grooming in Appendix A in Chapter 4, on career management.

Nonverbal Communication   Your facial expressions, eye contact, and handshake all project your image, as does the tone and the volume of your voice. Your nonverbal and verbal communication are critical to your image.[64] Words have a lasting impact.[65] Perceptions of our intelligence are often based on our communications, so we will develop this skill in Chapter 4.

Facial expressions   After noticing someone's appearance, you tend to look at a person's face. Facial expressions convey feelings more accurately than words. One of the guidelines to human relations is to smile. It is especially important when you first meet someone; you want to project a positive, caring image.

Eye contact   When you first meet someone, eye contact is very important. If you don't look people directly in the eye, they may assume that you do not like them, are not listening, or that you are not a trusting individual. Maintaining eye contact is important, but don't make others uncomfortable by staring at them. Hold eye contact for 7 to 10 seconds one-on-one and 3 to 5 seconds in groups.[66] Look in one eye, then the other; then briefly look away. Be aware, however, that in some cultures eye contact is considered differently than in North America.

Handshake   In many introductions the handshake is used. Your handshake can convey that you are a warm yet strong person. Your handshake is judged on five factors: (1) firmness—people tend to think that a firm handshake communicates a caring attitude, while a weak grip conveys indifference; (2) dryness—people don't like to hold a clammy hand; it sends a message of being nervous; (3) duration—an extended handshake can convey interest; (4) interlock—a

WORK APPLICATION 2-10

Give examples of situations when others formed a positive and a negative first impression of you. Explain the causes (appearance, nonverbal communication, behavior) of those impressions.

WORK APPLICATION 2-11

Which area of projecting a positive image (appearance, nonverbal communication, behavior) is your strongest? Which is your weakest? Explain your answers. What will you do to project a more positive image in the future?

Skill-Building Exercise 2-3 develops this skill.

Communication Skills
Refer to CS Question 6.

Skill-Building Exercise 2-4 develops this skill.

full, deep grip conveys friendship and strength; shallow grips are often interpreted as a weakness; and (5) eye contact—you should maintain eye contact throughout the handshake.

Behavior   After people notice your appearance and nonverbal expressions, they observe your behavior. As stated earlier in the guidelines to effective human relations, while talking to the person, be upbeat and optimistic, don't complain, show a genuine interest in the person, smile, laugh if appropriate, call the person by name, listen, be helpful, and think before you act. Do not do or say anything that is offensive to the person. Be agreeable and complimentary. Watch your manners and be polite. During the four-minute barrier, avoid discussing controversial topics and expressing personal views about them.

Remember that what you think about affects how you feel, and how you feel affects your behavior, human relations, and performance. So think happy, confident thoughts that you are a winner and you will act and be perceived as a winner and make it a habit to make a good first and ongoing image.

As we bring this chapter to a close, you should understand how your *personality* affects your behavior, which in turn affects your human relations and performance, and how to match your behavior to other people's personality type. Your personality type (A vs. B) also affects your behavior, and too much *stress* tends to have a negative effect on behavior, human relations, and performance. Your personality is also related to your level of *intelligence,* and you should know your preferred method of learning. You should realize that people don't see things the same way (*perception*), and understand biases that influence people's perceptions. Finally, you should realize the importance of making a good *first impression* and know how to project and maintain a positive image. Skill-Builder 2-4 gives you the opportunity to create a plan to make new habits to improve your human relations.

/ / / R E V I E W / / /

The chapter review is organized to help you master the eight learning outcomes for Chapter 2. First provide your own response to each learning outcome, and then check the summary provided to see how well you understand the material. Next, identify the final statement in each section as either true or false (T/F). Correct each false statement. Answers are given at the end of the chapter.

LO 2-1   Describe the Big Five personality dimensions.

The *surgency* personality dimension includes leadership and extroversion traits; people high in surgency strive to get ahead of others. In contrast, the *agreeableness* personality dimension includes traits related to getting along with people. The *adjustment* personality dimension includes traits related to emotional stability. The *conscientiousness* personality dimension includes traits related to achievement. The *openness to experience* personality dimension includes traits related to being willing to change and try new things.

The Myers-Briggs Type Indicator (MBTI) is a more complex personality classification method than the Big Five. T F

LO 2-2   Explain the benefits of understanding and identifying personality profiles.

Understanding and identifying personality profiles can help you to understand and predict behavior, human

relations, and performance. One can intentionally change behavior to improve human relations and performance when working with different personality types.

The locus of control is not part of a personality profile. T F

LO 2-3   Describe your stress personality type.

Student answers will vary from Self-Assessment Exercise 2-4: Your Stress Personality Type. People who have a Type A personality are characterized as fast moving, hard driving, time conscious, competitive, impatient, and preoccupied with work; those with a Type B personality are the opposite.

The Type A personality is more prone to stress. T F

LO 2-4   List causes of stress, and describe how to be more effective at controlling stress.

Causes of stress include: personality type, organizational climate, management behavior, and degree of job satisfaction. We can help control stress through exercise, nutrition, relaxation, positive thinking, and support systems. To control stress one should: (1) identify stressors, (2) determine their causes and consequences, and (3) plan to eliminate or decrease stressors.

The five ways recommended to help eliminate or decrease stress are: exercise, nutrition, relaxation, medication, and support systems. T F

LO 2-5 Describe the four learning styles and know which is your preferred learning style.

Accommodators prefer learning by doing and feeling. Divergers prefer learning by observing and feeling. Convergers prefer learning by doing and thinking. Assimilators prefer learning by observing and thinking. Student answers will vary.

The converger learning style is the most effective learning style. T F

LO 2-6 Describe five biases affecting perception.

- *Stereotyping* is the process of generalizing the behavior of all members of a group.

- *Frame of reference* refers to our tendency to see things from a narrow focus that directly affects us.

- *Expectations* refers to how we perceive, select, organize, and interpret information based on how we expect it to appear.

- *Selective exposure* means we tend to see and hear what we want to.

- Our degree of *interest* influences how we perceive things.

Given a good explanation, people perceive things the same way. T F

LO 2-7 Explain the importance of first impressions and how to project a positive image.

We have up to only four minutes to project a positive image. If we present a negative first impression to people, our future human relations with them can suffer. To project a positive first impression, we need to present an appropriate appearance, send positive nonverbal communications, and behave in a manner befitting the occasion.

Our perceptions are the bases for our first impressions. T F

LO 2-8 Define the following 15 key terms.

Select one or more methods: (1) fill in the missing key terms for each definition given below from memory; (2) match the key terms from the end of the review with their definitions below; and/or (3) copy the key terms in order from the key terms at the beginning of the chapter.

_____ is a relatively stable set of traits that aids in explaining and predicting individual behavior.

The _____ is characterized as fast moving, hard driving, time conscious, competitive, impatient, and preoccupied with work.

_____ is a continuum representing one's belief as to whether external or internal forces control one's destiny.

_____ categorizes traits into the dimensions of surgency, agreeableness, adjustment, conscientiousness, and openness to experience.

_____ is an emotional and/or physical reaction to environmental activities and events.

_____ are situations in which people feel anxiety, tension, and pressure.

_____ is the constant lack of interest and motivation to perform one's job because of stress.

The _____ includes step (1) identify stressors; step (2) determine their causes and consequences; and step (3) plan to eliminate or decrease the stress.

_____ is the level of one's capacity for new learning, problem solving, and decision making.

_____ is a person's interpretation of reality.

_____ is the process of generalizing the behavior of all members of a group.

_____ refers to the degree to which people see things the same way.

The _____ is the way people perceive one another during their first impressions.

The _____ is the time we have to make a good impression.

Our _____ is other people's attitudes toward us.

/ / / COMMUNICATION SKILLS / / /

The following critical thinking questions can be used for class discussion and/or as written assignments to develop communication skills. Be sure to give complete explanations for all questions.

1. Which personality traits exhibited by others tend to irritate you? Which of your personality traits tend to irritate others? How can you improve your personality?

2. Do you think that the Big Five Model of Personality or the Myers-Briggs Type Indicator is a more effective measure of personality?

3. Which cause of stress do you think is the major contributor to employee stress in organizations? What can organizations do to help eliminate or reduce employee stress?

4. Do you agree that intelligence (general mental ability) is the most valid predictor of job performance? Should organizations give an IQ test and hire based on the results? Why or why not?

5. How do you know if your perception or that of others is the correct interpretation of reality?

6. Is it ethical to judge and stereotype people based on a few seconds or minutes during first impressions? How do your first impressions help and hinder your human relations?

CASE   / / /   Mark Cuban: Billionaire Entrepreneur with Unique Personality Traits

Mark Cuban is the highly involved and enthusiastic owner of the Dallas Mavericks. On January 14, 2000, Mark Cuban purchased the team, and nothing has been the same since. Almost immediately, Mavericks' games took on a festive atmosphere as the American Airlines Center Arena rocked with jubilant fans. Mavericks' games became more than just ordinary NBA games; they were a total entertainment experience. This transformation is directly attributed to Cuban's energetic personality, positive attitude, and unique leadership style.

In the 20 years before Cuban bought the team, the Mavericks had a winning percentage of 40 percent and playoff record of 21–32. Since his acquisition, the team competed in the NBA Finals for the first time in franchise history in 2006 and became NBA World Champions in 2011. His personality and unorthodox style of motivating the team is frowned on by other NBA executives and loved by the fans and players. Dressed in his jeans and T-shirt, he does not resemble the typical NBA executive. Cuban sits in the front row next to the floor, cheering the team along with thousands of loyal fans. At any other arena, the executives come to the games dressed in suit and tie, and are segregated from the crowds in their luxury skybox seats. It is evident his unorthodoxy is working because today, the Mavericks are the ninth most valuable basketball Franchise in the NBA valued at $1.4 billion. They are currently listed as one of Forbes' most valuable franchises in sports.

Running an NBA team is not the only success Cuban has had in his life. He has been called the "billionaire entrepreneur" for a reason. Prior to his purchase of the Mavericks, Cuban co-founded Broadcast.com in 1995, the leading provider of multimedia and streaming on the Internet, and sold it to Yahoo! in July 1999 for $5.7 billion. Before Broadcast.com, Cuban co-founded MicroSolutions, a leading National Systems Integrator, in 1983, and later sold it to CompuServe. Cuban's other entrepreneurial ventures include cable channel HDNet, Landmark Theatres, and film studio Magnolia Pictures. He appears as a judge on the popular ABC show *Shark Tank*. As of 2017, Cuban is number 564 on Forbes's "World's Richest People" list, with a net worth of $3.4 billion.

Based on the image Cuban projects, especially during Mavericks games, it is possible for some to see him as a self-centered and uncaring individual. However, nothing could be further from the truth. He is a person who cares for others and gives back to help those who are less fortunate.

Cuban started the Fallen Patriot Fund to help families of U.S. military persons killed or injured during the Iraq War, personally matching the first $1 million in contributions with funds from the Mark Cuban Foundation, which is run by his brother Brian Cuban. Cuban financed the movie *Redacted* through his film company, Magnolia Pictures, a documentary based on the Mahmudiyah Killings. The story involves the March 2006 rape, murder, and burning of a 14-year-old Iraqi girl, Abeer Hamza al-Janabi, and the murder of her parents and younger sister by U.S. soldiers. Two of the soldiers were convicted and three pleaded guilty, receiving sentences up to 110 years.

Mark Cuban was born on July 31, 1958, in Pittsburgh, Pennsylvania. He graduated from Indiana University in 1981 with a degree in business. His last name was shortened from "Chabenisky" when his Russian grandparents landed on Ellis Island decades ago. Cuban's father Norton was an automobile upholsterer. Cuban's first attempt at entrepreneurship started at age 12, when he sold garbage bags to pay for a pair of expensive basketball shoes. While in school, he worked in a variety of jobs, including bartender, disco dancing instructor, and party promoter. He paid for college by collecting and selling stamps, and he once earned about $1,100 from starting a chain letter.

Mark Cuban is clearly a person with an internal locus of control and loves his role as a leader. He clearly believes in his ability to lead and effect change. As he puts it, "It doesn't matter if the glass is half-empty or half-full; all that matters is that you are the one pouring."[i] He has a dominant personality, is a positive thinker, is an eternal optimist, and has a high IQ and EQ. It is impossible to know what Mark Cuban will create, produce, buy, or sell next, but no one doubts that he will certainly do something innovative.

Go to the Internet: To learn more about Mark Cuban and the Dallas Mavericks, visit their website at www.nba.com /mavericks/index_main.htm.

Support your answers to the following questions with specific information from the case and text, or with information you get from the web or another source.

1. Personality is a relatively stable set of traits that aids in explaining and predicting individual behavior. What are some of Mark Cuban's traits that can explain his behavior during Mavericks games?

2. Would you describe Mark Cuban as a Type A or Type B personality type?

3. Why is Mark Cuban described as someone with an internal locus of control?

4. The Big Five Model of Personality categorizes traits into the dimensions of surgency, agreeableness, adjustment, conscientiousness, and openness to experience. Which of these dimensions are strongest or clearly evident in Mark Cuban's personality?

5. Is Mark Cuban projecting a positive or negative image with his eccentric behavior during Mavericks games?

Cumulative Case Question

6. Mark Cuban has had several disagreements with the NBA commissioner that have resulted in fines totaling almost a million dollars. Each incident brings a lot of publicity to the team and Cuban himself; most of it is negative. Chapter 1 discusses three alternatives for resolving human relations problems— change the other person, change the situation, or change yourself. Which approach or combination of approaches will you recommend for Mark Cuban, and why?

Case Exercise and Role-Play

Preparation: Return to question 5 above, in which we talked about Mark Cuban projecting a negative or positive image by his appearance, nonverbal communication, and behavior. Using a debate format, divide the class into two teams. One team takes the viewpoint that Cuban's appearance, nonverbal communication, and behavior are projecting a negative image for the Dallas Mavericks, while another team takes the opposite viewpoint. Each team prepares a brief narrative to support its position.

In-Class Groups: Form two groups of four to six members to share ideas and develop the statement supporting their positions.

Role-Play: Each group presents its statement to the entire class, with the class acting as judges of the debate. Each group is given one chance to respond to the other group's points. The judges represented by the rest of the class then decide who has won the debate.

OBJECTIVE CASE /// **Personality Conflict**

Carol is the branch manager of a bank. Two of her employees, Rich and Wonda, came to her and said that they could not work together. Carol asked them why, and they both said, "We have a personality conflict." She asked them to be more specific, and this is what they told her:

RICH: Well, Wonda is very pushy; she tells me what to do all the time, and I let her get away with it because I'm a peace-loving man.

WONDA: That's because Rich is so gullible; he believes anything he is told. I have to look out for him.

RICH: We have different outlooks on life. Wonda believes that if we work hard, we can get ahead in this bank, but I don't agree. I believe you have to be political, and I'm not.

WONDA: That's because I'm motivated and enjoy working.

RICH: Motivated—is that what you call it? She's preoccupied with work. Wonda is rushing all the time, she is impatient, and she always wants to make a contest out of everything.

WONDA: If you were more cooperative, and morale was better, I would not feel stressed the way I do.

RICH: We cannot make decisions together because I am very logical and like to get lots of information, while Wonda wants to make decisions based on what she calls intuition.

WONDA: I thought working here was going to be different. I didn't know I was going to be stuck working with a person who is uncooperative.

RICH: Me? I feel the same way about you.

At this point Carol stopped the discussion.

Answer the following questions. Then in the space between questions, state why you selected that answer.

_____ 1. In Rich's first statement it appears that Wonda has a(n) _____ personality trait, while he has a(n) _____ personality trait.

    a. outgoing, reserved   *c.* conscientious, expedient

    b. aggressive, passive   *d.* imaginative, practical

_____ 2. In statement 2, it appears that Wonda is _____ and Rich is _____ .

    a. shrewd, forthright   *c.* stable, emotional

    b. high, low intelligence   *d.* suspicious, trusting

_____ 3. In statement 3, it appears that Rich has an _____ locus of control while Wonda has an _____ locus of control.

    a. internal, external   *b.* external, internal

_____ 4. In statement 4, Wonda appears to be an:

    a. internalizer   *b.* externalizer

_____ 5. In statement 5, Wonda appears to have a Type _____ personality.

    a. A   *b.* B

_____ 6. In statement 6, Wonda states that _____ is the cause of her stress.

    a. personality   *c.* management effectiveness

    b. organizational climate   *d.* job satisfaction

_____ 7. In statement 7, Rich has described himself as having a(n) _____ learning style.

    a. accommodator   *c.* converger

    b. diverger   *d.* assimilator

_____ 8. In statement 7, Rich has described Wonda as having a(n) _____ learning style.

    a. accommodator   *c.* converger

    b. diverger   *d.* assimilator

_____   9. In statement 8, the perception problem appears to be due to:

      a. stereotyping   *d.* selective exposure

      b. frame of reference   *e.* projection

      c. expectations   *f.* interest

_____   10. Who needs to change their behavior?

      a. Rich   *b.* Wonda   *c.* both

        11. Overall, are your personality, locus of control, stress type, and learning style more like Rich's or Wonda's? If you were Rich or Wonda, what would you do?

        12. If you were Carol, what would you do?

Note: Carol's meeting can be role-played in class.

///   SKILL-BUILDING EXERCISE 2-1   ///

Learning Styles

Experience: Groups by learning style are used for individual learning in class.

AACSB Competencies: Reflective and analytic thinking skills, communication abilities, teamwork, and application of knowledge.

Objectives: To better understand your learning style and how to work more effectively with people with different learning styles.

Preparation: You should have read the chapter and determined your preferred learning style in Self-Assessment Exercise 2-5.

Procedure 1 (2–3 minutes)

The entire class breaks into four groups: The accommodators, divergers, convergers, and assimilators meet in different groups.

Procedure 2 (5–10 minutes)

Each of the four groups elects a spokesperson-recorder. Assume the class was shipwrecked on a deserted island and had to develop an economic system with a division of labor. During this process, what strengths would your group offer each of the other three groups if you were working one-on-one with them? For example, the accommodators state how they would help the divergers if they were the only two styles on the island. Then they assume the convergers and then the assimilators are the only other learning style on the island. Each group does the same. Feel free to refer to the book at any time.

Procedure 3 (5–15 minutes)

The spokesperson for the accommodators tells the other three groups how they would be helpful to that group if they were the only two styles on the island. The divergers go next, followed by the convergers, and then the assimilators.

Procedure 4 (3–7 minutes)

Break into as many discussion groups as there are members of the smallest of the four learning style groups. Each discussion group must have at least one person from all four learning styles; some will have more. For example, if the smallest group is the assimilators with five members, establish five discussion groups. If there are nine convergers, send two members to four groups and one to the remaining group. If there are six divergers, send one to four of the groups and two to one of the groups. Try to make the number of students in each discussion group as even as possible.

Procedure 5 (3–7 minutes)

Elect a spokesperson-recorder. Each group decides which learning style(s) to include in establishing the economic system. During the discussion, the instructor writes the four styles on the board for voting in procedure 6.

Procedure 6 (2–3 minutes)

The instructor records the votes from each group to be included in establishing the economic system.

Conclusion: The instructor leads a class discussion and/or makes concluding remarks.

Application (2-4 minutes):   What have I learned from this exercise? What will I do to be more open to working with people of different learning styles?

Sharing: Volunteers give their answers to the application section.

/ / / S K I L L - B U I L D I N G   E X E R C I S E   2 - 2 / / /

Personality Perceptions

Experience: Groups in class used for individual learning

AACSB Competences: Analytic skills, communication abilities, and application of knowledge.

Objective: To develop your skill at perceiving others' personality traits. With this skill, you can better understand and predict people's behavior, which is helpful to leaders in influencing followers.

Preparation: You should read the sections on personality traits and complete Self-Assessment Exercise 2-2. From this exercise, rank yourself below from highest score (1) to lowest score (5) for each of the Big Five. Do not tell anyone your ranking until told to do so.

_____ Surgency   _____ Agreeableness   _____Adjustment

_____ Conscientiousness   _____ Openness to experience

Procedure 1 (2-4 minutes)

Break into groups of three with people you know the best in the class. You may need some groups of two. If you don't know people in the class and you did Skill-Building Exercise 1-1: Human Relations, get in a group with those people.

Procedure 2 (4-6 minutes)

Each person in the group writes down his or her perception of each of the other two group members. Simply rank which trait you believe to be the highest and lowest (put the Big Five dimension name on the line) for each person. Write a short reason for your perception, which should include some specific behavior you have observed that led you to your perception.

Name _____ Highest personality score _____ Lowest score _____

Reason for ranking _____

Name _____ Highest personality score _____ Lowest score _____

Reason for ranking _____

Procedure 3 (4-6 minutes)

One of the group members volunteers to go first to hear the other group members' perceptions.

1. One person tells the volunteer which Big Five dimensions he or she selected as the person's highest and lowest scores, and why they were selected. Do not discuss them yet.

2. The other person also tells the volunteer the same information.

3. The volunteer tells the two others what his or her actual highest and lowest scores are. The three group members discuss the accuracy of the perceptions.

Procedure 4 (4-6 minutes)

A second group member volunteers to go next to receive perceptions. Follow the same procedure as above.

Procedure 5 (4-6 minutes)

The third group member goes last. Follow the same procedure as above.

Conclusion: The instructor may lead a class discussion and/or make concluding remarks.

Application (2-4 minutes):   What did I learn from this exercise? How will I use this knowledge in the future?

Sharing: Volunteers give their answers to the application section.

///   SKILL-BUILDING EXERCISE 2-3   ///

First Impressions

Experience: Group of two in class access individual first impressions.

AACSB Competencies: Reflective thinking, analytic skills, communication abilities, and application of knowledge.

Objectives: To practice projecting a positive first impression. To receive feedback on the image you project. To develop your ability to project a positive first impression.

Preparation: You should have read and now understand how to project a positive first impression.

Procedure 1 (2-4 minutes)

Pair off with someone you do not know. If you know everyone, select a partner you don't know well. Make one group of three if necessary. Do not begin your discussion until asked to do so.

Procedure 2 (Exactly 4 minutes)

Assume you are meeting for the first time. A mutual friend brought you together but was called to the telephone before introducing you. The mutual friend has asked you to introduce yourselves and get acquainted until he or she returns. When told to begin, introduce yourselves and get acquainted. Be sure to shake hands.

Procedure 3 (7-12 minutes)

Using the Image Feedback sheet below, give each other feedback on the image you projected. To be useful, the feedback must be an honest assessment of the image your partner received of you. So answer the questions with the input of your partner.

///   SKILL-BUILDING EXERCISE 2-4   ///

Developing New Habits

Experience: Individual may share Habits in groups or entire class, in class or online.

AACSB Competencies: Analytic and application of knowledge.

Objective: To develop and share new habits.

Preparation: Select one or more topics from this chapter that will help you improve your human relations, and develop a new habit following the guideline below. You may return to Chapter 1 section Habits and Skill-Building Exercise 1-4 for a discussion and examples of how to develop your cure, routine, and reward-change.

1. **Cue**. What will you do to remind you to engage in the new behavior?

2. **Routine**. Do the new behavior regularly.

3. **Reward—Change**. Positive thing to reinforce new habit.

"How do you handle the slip?" Are you going to give up and go back to your old habits, or will you get back to your new routine? Caution—once you slip, and the more often you slip, the easier it is to go back to your old habits.

Procedure (5-30 minutes)

Follow the procedures from Skill Builder 1-4.

/ / / I M A G E - F E E D B A C K / / /

Human Relations Guidelines

1. I was optimistic _____, neutral _____, pessimistic _____.

2. I did _____, did not _____ complain and criticize.

3. I did _____, did not _____ show genuine interest in the other person.

4. I did _____, did not _____ smile and laugh when appropriate.

5. I did _____, did not _____ call the person by name two or three times.

6. I was a good _____, fair _____, poor _____ listener.

7. I was/tried to be _____, wasn't _____ helpful to the other person.

8. I did _____, did not _____ do or say anything that offended the other person.

Image Projection

Appearance:

9. My appearance projected a positive _____, neutral _____, negative _____ image to the other person.

Nonverbal communication:

10. My facial expressions projected a caring _____, neutral _____, uncaring _____ attitude toward the other person.

11. My eye contact was too little _____, about right _____, too much _____.

12. My handshake was firm _____, weak _____; dry _____, wet _____; long _____, short _____; full grip _____, shallow grip _____; with eye contact _____, without eye contact _____.

13. The behavior the other person liked most was _____.

14. The behavior the other person liked least was _____.

Overall

By receiving this feedback, I realize that I could improve my image projection by:

Perception

It is important to understand both our first impression of others and theirs of us (image). After discussing your images, do you think you made any perception errors? If yes, which one(s)?

Conclusion: The instructor leads a class discussion and/or makes concluding remarks.

Application (2-4 minutes): What did I learn from this exercise? How will I use this knowledge in the future?

Sharing: Volunteers give their answers to the application section.

<hr>

/ / ANSWERS TO TRUE/FALSE QUESTIONS / /

1. T.
2. F. A personality profile includes all types of traits, depending on the personality measurement.
3. T.
4. F. The fourth recommended method is positive thinking, not medication.
5. F. There is no one most effective learning style. We each have a preferred way of learning that works best for us.
6. F. People don't tend to "listen" to an explanation; they perceive based on their bias.
7. T.

/ / / NOTES / / /

1. A.C. Klotz and D.O. Neubaum, "Research on the Dark Side of Personality Traits in Entrepreneurship: Observations from an Organizational Behavior Perspective," *Entrepreneurship Theory and Practice* 40(10) (2016): 7–17.
2. J.C. Molloy and J.B. Barney, "Who Captures the Value Created with Human Capital? A Market-Based View," *Academy of Management Perspectives* 29(3) (2015): 309–325.
3. E. Bernstein, "We Actually Get Nicer with Age," *Wall Street Journal* (April 22, 2014): D1, D2.
4. S.M. Martin, S. Cote, and T. Woodruff, "Ecoes of Our Upbringing: How Growing Up Wealth or Poor Relates to Narcissism, Leader Behavior, and Leader Effectiveness," *Academy of Management Journal* 59(6) (2016): 2157–2177.
5. K. Lanaj and J.R. Hollenbeck, "Leadership Over-Emergence in Self-Managing Teams: The Role of Gender and Countervailing Biases," *Academy of Management Journal* 58(5) (2015): 1476–1494.
6. V. Van Edwards, "You Have Two Seconds to Make a First Impression," *Entrepreneur* (January/February 2017): 38.

7. L. Weber and E. Dwoskin, "As Personality Tests Multiple, Employers are Split," *The Wall Street Journal* (September 30, 2014): A1, A12.

8. F.P. Morgeson, T.R. Mitchell, and D. Liu, "Event System Theory: An Event-Oriented Approach to the Organizational Sciences," *Academy of Management Review* 40(4) (2015): 515-537.

9. Bernstein, "We Actually Get Nicer with Age."

10. A.C. Klotz and D.O. Neubaum, "Research on the Dark Side of Personality Traits in Entrepreneurship: Observations from an Organizational Behavior Perspective," *Entrepreneurship Theory and Practice* 40(10) (2016): 7-17.

11. P. Andruss, "How the Great Ones Got Great," *Entrepreneur* (December 2013): 64.

12. E. Bernstein, "Still Hung Up on Your Past?" *Wall Street Journal* (August 27, 2013): D1, D4.

13. T.A. Judge and C.P. Zapata, "The Person-Situation Debate Revisited: Effect of Situation Strength and Train Activation on the Validity of the Big Five Personality Traits in Predicting Job Performance," *Academy of Management Journal* 58(4) (2015): 1149-1179.

14. B. Antoncic, T.B. Kregar, G. Singh, and A.F. DeNoble, "The Big Five Personality-Entrepreneurship Relationship: Evidence from Slovenia," *Journal of Small Business Management* 53(23) (2015): 819-841.

15. D.V. Caprar, B. Do, S.L. Rynes, and J.M. Bartunek, "It's Personal: An Exploration of Students' (non) Acceptance of Management Research," *Academy of Management Learning & Education* 15(2) (2016): 207-231.

16. B.M. Galvin, D. Lange, and B.E. Ashforth, "Narcissistic Organizational Identification: Seeing Oneself as Central to the Orgnization's Identity,"*Academy of Management Review* 40(2) (2015): 163-181.

17. C.M. Barnes, L. Lucianetti, D.P. Bhave, and M.S. Christian, ""You Wouldn't Like Me When I'm Sleepy: Leaders' Sleep, Daily Abusive Supervision, and Work Unit Engagement," *Academy of Management Journal* 58(5) (2015): 1419-1437.

18. A. Murray, "Should Leaders Be Modest," *Fortune* (September 15, 2015): 28.

19. J.C. Molloy and J.B. Barney, "Who Captures the Value Created with Human Capital? A Market-Based View," *Academy of Management Perspectives* 29(3) (2015): 309-325.

20. S. Nadkarni and P. Herrmann, "CEO Personality, Strategic Flexibility, and Firm Performance: The Case of the Indian Business Process Outsourcing Industry," *Academy of Management Journal 53*(5) (2010): 1050-1073.

21. E. Whitford, "Management Playbook," *Inc.* (April 2014): 46-47.

22. E. Bernstein, "Spouse, Change Thyself," *Wall Street Journal* (January 7, 2014): D1.

23. Myers & Briggs Web site, http://www.myersbriggs.org, retrieved on March 20, 2017.

24. Humanmetrics Inc. http://www.humanmetrics.com/cgi-win/jtypes2.asp retrieved on March 20, 2017.

25. Humanmetrics Inc. http://www.humanmetrics.com/cgi-win/jtypes2.asp retrieved on March 20, 2017.

26. J.E. Bono, T.M. Glomb, W. Shen, E. Kim, A.J. Koch, "Building Positive Resources: Effects of Positive Events and Positive Reflection Work Stress and Health," *Academy of Management Journal* 56(6) (2013): 1601-1627.

27. M.A. LePine, Y. Zhang, E.R. Crawford, and B.L Rich, "Turning Their Pain to Gain: Charismatic Leader Influence on Follower Stress Appraisal and Job Performance," *Academy of Management Journal* 59(3) (2016): 1036-1059.

28. M.A. LePine, Y. Zhang, E.R. Crawford, and B.L Rich, "Turning Their Pain to Gain: Charismatic Leader Influence on Follower Stress Appraisal and Job Performance," *Academy of Management Journal* 59(3) (2016): 1036-1059.

29. American Psychological Association, "Mind/Body Health: Job Stress," www.apa.org/helpcenter/job-stress.aspx retrieved March 20, 2017.

30. C.M. Barnes, L. Lucianetti, D.P. Bhave, and M.S. Christian, "You Wouldn't Like Me When I'm Sleepy: Leaders' Sleep, Daily Abusive Supervision, and Work Unit Engagement," *Academy of Management Journal* 58(5) (2015): 1419-1437.

31. American Psychological Association, "Mind/Body Health: Job Stress," www.apa.org/helpcenter/job-stress.aspx retrieved March 20, 2017.

32. National Public Radio (NPR) Aired December 6, 2015.

33. American Psychological Association, "Mind/Body Health: Job Stress," www.apa.org/helpcenter/job-stress.aspx retrieved March 20, 2017.

34. E. Bernstein, "Train Your Brain to Be Positive, and Feel Happier Every Day," *Wall Street Journal* (January 7, 2014): D1.

35. Exercise, Quitting Smoking," *Wall Street Journal* (January 8, 2008): A1.

36. K. Lanaj and J.R. Hollenbeck, "Leadership Over-Emergence in Self-Managing Teams: The Role of Gender and Countervailing Biases," *Academy of Management Journal* 58(5) (2015): 1476-1494.

37. D.V. Caprar, B. Do, S.L. Rynes, and J.M. Bartunek, "It's Personal: An Exploration of Students' (non) Acceptance of Management Research," *Academy of Management Learning & Education* 15(2) (2016): 207-231.

38. J.C. Molloy and J.B. Barney, "Who Captures the Value Created with Human Capital? A Market-Based View," *Academy of Management Perspectives* 29(3) (2015): 309-325.

39. M. Voronov and K. Weber, "The Heart of Institutions: Emotional Compentence and Institutional Actorhood," *Academy of Management Review* 41(3) (2016): 456-478.

40. D.V. Caprar, B. Do, S.L. Rynes, and J.M. Bartunek, "It's Personal: An Exploration of Students' (non) Acceptance of Management Research," *Academy of Management Learning & Education* 15(2) (2016): 207-231.

41. C. Hardy and D. Tolhurst, "Epistemological Beliefs and Cultural Diversity Matters in Management Education and Learning a Critical Review and Future Directions," *Academy of Management Learning & Education* 13(2) (2014): 265-289.

42. Based on the Kolb Learning Styles Inventory.

43. Humanmetrics Inc. http://www.humanmetrics.com/cgi-win/jtypes2.asp retrieved on March 20, 2017.

44. I. Nooyi, Margin Note, *Fortune* (November 17, 2014): 127.

45. W. Beasley, "Letters to the Editor," 'Listen Up', *Fortune* (November 15, 2015): 21.

46. J.N. Reyt and B.M. Wiesenfeld, "Seeing the Forest for the Trees: Exploratory Learning, Mobile Technology, and Knowledge Workers' Role Integration Behavior," *Academy of Management Journal* 58(3) (2015): 739-762.

47. V. Desai, "Learning Through the Distribution of Failures within an Organization: Evidence from Heart Bypass Surgery Performance," *Academy of Management Journal* 58(4) (2015): 1032-1050.

48. R. Fehr, K.C. Yam, and C. Dang, "Moralized Leadership: The Construction and Consequences of Ethical Leader Perceptions," *Academy of Management Review* 40(2) (2015): 182-209.

49. D.H. Wo, M.L. Ambrose, and M. Schminke, "What Drives Trickle-Down Effects? A Test of Multiple Mediation Processes," *Academy of Management Journal* 58(6) (2015): 1484-1868.

50. E. Bernstein, "Honey, You Never Said...," *The Wall Street Journal* (March 24, 2015): D1, D4.

51. L.R. Weingart, K.J. Behfar, C. Bendersky, G. Todorova, and K.A. Hehn, "The Directness and Oppositional Intensity of Conflict Expression," *Academy of Management Review* 40(2) (2015): 235-262.

52. B.M. Fiorth, J.R. Hollenbeck, J.E. Miles, D.R. Ilgen, and C.M. Barnes, "Same Page, Different Books: Extending Representational Gaps Theory to Enhance Performance in Multiteam Systems," *Academy of Management Journal* 58(3) (2015): 813-835.

53. D.V. Caprar, B. Do, S.L. Rynes, and J.M. Bartunek, "It's Personal: An Exploration of Students' (non) Acceptance of Management Research," *Academy of Management Learning & Education* 15(2) (2016): 207-231.

54. D. Antons and F.T. Piller, "Opening the Black Box of Not Invented Here: Attitudes, Decision Biases, and Behavioral Consequences," *Academy of Management Perspectives* 29(2) (2015): 193-217.

55. M.R. Barrick, G.R. Thurgood, T.A. Smith, and S.H. Courtright, "Collective Organizational Engagement: Linking Motivational Antecedents, Strategic Implementation, and Firm Performance," *Academy of Management Journal* 58(1) (2015): 111-135.

56. A. Meister, K.A. Jehn, and S.M.B. Thatcher, "Feeling Misidentified: The Consequences of Internal Identify Asymmetries for Individuals at Work," *Academy of Management Review* 39(4) (2014): 488-512.

57. R. McCammon, "How to Own the Room," *BusinessWeek* accessed online March 24, 2017.

58. V. Van Edwards, "You Have Two Seconds to Make a First Impression," *Entrepreneur* (January/February 2017): 38.

59. G. O'Brian, "Fixing the First Impression," *Entrepreneur* accessed online March 24, 2017.

60. L.M. Little, V.S. Major, A.S. Hinojosa, D.L. Nelson, "Professional Image Maintenance: How Women Navigate Pregnancy in the Workplace," *Academy of Management Journal* 58(1) (2015): 8-37.

61. A. Meister, K.A. Jehn, S.M.B. Thatcher, "Feeling Misidentified: The Consequences of Internal Identify Asymmetries for Individuals at Work," *Academy of Management Review* 39(4) (2014): 488–512.

62. L.M. Little, V.S. Major, A.S. Hinojosa, D.L. Nelson, "Professional Image Maintenance: How Women Navigate Pregnancy in the Workplace," *Academy of Management Journal* 58(1) (2015): 8–37.

63. L.M. Little, V.S. Major, A.S. Hinojosa, D.L. Nelson, "Professional Image Maintenance: How Women Navigate Pregnancy in the Workplace," *Academy of Management Journal* 58(1) (2015): 8–37.

64. L.M. Little, V.S. Major, A.S. Hinojosa, D.L. Nelson, "Professional Image Maintenance: How Women Navigate Pregnancy in the Workplace," *Academy of Management Journal* 58(1) (2015): 8–37.

65. Staff, "4 Phrases Even Smart People Misuse," *INC.* (June 2015): 12.

66. S. Shellenbarger, "Just Look Me in the Eye Already," *Wall Street Journal* (May 29, 2013): D1–D2.

i. https://www.forbes.com/profile/mark-cuban/ accessed May 24, 2017.

Attitudes, Self-Concept, Values, and Ethics

©LWA/Dann Tardif/Blend Images LLC

After completing this chapter, you should be able to:

LO 3-1 Define attitudes and explain how they affect behavior, human relations, and performance.

LO 3-2 Describe how to change your attitudes.

LO 3-3 List seven job satisfaction determinants.

LO 3-4 Determine whether you have a positive self-concept and how it affects your behavior, human relations, and performance.

LO 3-5 Understand how your manager's and your own expectations affect your performance.

LO 3-6 Demonstrate how to develop a more positive self-concept.

LO 3-7 Identify your personal values.

LO 3-8 Compare the three levels of moral development.

LO 3-9 Define the following 13 key terms (in order of appearance in the chapter):

attitude	self-efficacy
Theory X	self-fulfilling prophecy
Theory Y	attribution
Pygmalion effect	values
job satisfaction	value system
job satisfaction survey	ethics
self-concept	

OPENING CASE WORK SCENARIO

/ / / Rayanne was walking back to work at the Red Cross after a meeting with her supervisor, Kent. Rayanne recalled that Kent had said she had a negative attitude and that it was affecting her performance, which was below standard. Kent had asked Rayanne if she was satisfied with her job. She had said, "No, I really don't like working, and I've messed up on all the jobs I've had. I guess I'm a failure." Kent had tried to explain how her poor attitude and negative self-concept were the cause of her poor performance. But Rayanne hadn't really listened, since work is not important to her. Rayanne has an external locus of control; thus, she believes that her poor performance is not her fault. She doesn't believe Kent knows what he's talking about. Rayanne thinks that Kent is not being ethical, that he is trying to manipulate her to get more work out of her. Is Kent's or Rayanne's analysis correct? Can Rayanne change? / / /

HOW ATTITUDES, JOB SATISFACTION, SELF-CONCEPT, VALUES, AND ETHICS AFFECT BEHAVIOR, HUMAN RELATIONS, HAPPINESS, AND PERFORMANCE

In this chapter, we continue to focus on developing intrapersonal skills. We cover several different yet related topics, so let's start with an overview. *Attitudes* are critical to success.[1] Our attitudes toward others, and their attitudes toward us, clearly affect our behavior, human relations, happiness, and performance.[2] Attitudes are the foundation of our *job satisfaction*.[3] Making employees happy can increase their contributions, effort, and productivity.[4] Our *self-concept* is based on our attitude about ourselves, and our self-confidence also affects our attitudes, values, and ethics.[5] Your work *values* are your standards of behavior, which affect your human relations and performance.[6] *Unethical* behavior hurts human relations, true happiness, and long-run performance.[7]

/// In the opening case, Kent, tries to get Rayanne to understand how her poor attitude and negative self-concept are affecting her job performance, but she does not value work. /// Do you believe Kent is correct? Do you have a positive attitude and self-concept? Are you happy? Would you like to improve your attitude and self-concept? This chapter can help you improve.

ATTITUDES

Learning Outcome 3-1

Define attitudes and explain how they affect behavior, human relations, and performance.

In this section, we examine what an attitude is and the importance of attitudes, how you acquire attitudes, types of management attitudes and how they affect performance, and how to change attitudes.

What Is an Attitude and Are Attitudes Important?

WORK APPLICATION 3-1

Describe your attitude about college in general and the specific college you are attending.

An **attitude** is *a strong belief or feeling toward people, things, and situations.* You have favorable, or positive, attitudes and unfavorable, or negative, attitudes about life, human relations, work, school, and everything else. Attitudes are not quick judgments we change easily but you *can* change your attitudes.[8] People interpret your attitudes by your behavior. Rayanne appears to have a negative attitude toward many things.

Employers place great emphasis on attitude.[9] **Jessica Herrin, Founder of Stella & Dot**, says, "It's All About Attitude."[10] **J. S. Marriott Jr.**, president of **Marriott Corporation**, stated, "We have found that our success depends more upon employee attitudes than any other single factor."

Communication Skills
Refer to CS Question 1.

How We Acquire Attitudes

Attitudes are developed primarily through experiences.[11] As you developed from childhood to adulthood, you interacted with parents, family, teachers, friends, employees, and managers. From all these people, you develop your attitudes.[12]

When encountering new people or situations, you are the most open and impressionable because you usually haven't had time to form an attitude toward them. Recall the importance of first impressions from the last chapter. Before you signed up for this class, you may have asked others questions about it. If they had positive or negative attitudes, you too may have developed a positive or a negative attitude. Getting information from others is fine, but you should develop your own attitudes.

Management's Attitudes and How They Affect Performance

Before reading on, complete Self-Assessment Exercise 3-1 to determine if you have Theory X or Theory Y attitudes.

/ / / **Self-Assessment Exercise 3-1** / / /

Your Management Attitudes

Circle the letter that best describes what you would actually do as a supervisor. There are no right or wrong answers.

Usually (U)   Frequently (F)   Occasionally (O)   Seldom (S)

U   F   O   S   1. I would set the objectives for my department alone (rather than include employee input).

U   F   O   S   2. I would allow employees to develop their own plans (rather than develop them for them).

U   F   O   S   3. I would delegate several tasks I enjoy doing (rather than doing them myself).

U   F   O   S   4. I would allow employees to make decisions (rather than make them for employees).

U   F   O   S   5. I would recruit and select new employees alone (rather than include employees' input).

U   F   O   S   6. I would train new employees myself (rather than have employees do it).

U   F   O   S   7. I would tell employees what they need to know (rather than everything I know).

U   F   O   S   8. I would spend time praising and recognizing my employees' work efforts (rather than not do it).

U   F   O   S   9. I would set several (rather than few) controls to ensure that objectives are met.

U   F   O   S   10. I would closely supervise my employees (rather than leave them on their own) to ensure that they are working.

   To better understand your own attitudes toward human nature, score your answers. For items 1, 5, 6, 7, 9, and 10, give yourself 1 point for each usually (U) answer; 2 points for each frequently (F) answer; 3 points for each occasionally (O) answer; and 4 points for each seldom (S) answer. For items 2, 3, 4, and 8, give yourself 1 point for each seldom (S) answer; 2 points for each occasionally (O) answer; 3 points for each frequently (F) answer; and 4 points for each usually (U) answer. Total all points. Your score should be between 10 and 40. Place your score here _____. Theory X and Theory Y are on opposite ends of a continuum. Most people's attitudes fall somewhere between the two extremes. Place an X on the continuum below at the point that represents your score.

Theory X 10 - - - - - - - - - - - - - - - 20 - - - - - - - - - - - - - - - - 30 - - - - - - - - - - - - - - - 40 Theory Y

   The lower your score, the stronger the Theory X attitude; the higher your score, the stronger the Theory Y attitude. A score of 10 to 19 could be considered a Theory X attitude. A score of 31 to 40 could be considered a Theory Y attitude. A score of 20 to 30 could be considered balanced between the two theories. Your score may not accurately measure how you would behave in an actual job; however, it should help you understand your own attitudes toward people at work.

Communication Skills
Refer to CS Question 2.

Communication Skills
Refer to CS Question 3.

Management Attitudes   Douglas McGregor classified attitudes, which he called *assumptions,* as Theory X and Theory Y. Managers with **Theory X** attitudes hold that *employees dislike work and must be closely supervised to get them to do their work.* **Theory Y** attitudes hold that *employees like to work and do not need to be closely supervised to get them to do their work.* Managers with dominant personalities often do not trust employees. Thus, they have Theory X attitudes and can be abusive.[13]

   Over the years research has shown that managers with Theory Y attitudes tend to have employees with higher levels of job satisfaction than the employees of Theory X managers. However, managers with Theory Y assumptions do not always have higher levels of productivity in their departments.[14]

How Management's Attitudes Affect Employees' Performance   Managers' attitudes and the way they treat employees affect employees' job behavior and performance.[15] Research has supported this theory.[16] It is called the *Pygmalion effect.* The **Pygmalion effect** states that

---

Theory X, Theory Y   AS 3-1

Identify each manager's comments about employees as:

A. Theory X   B. Theory Y

_____ 1. "Yes it is a lousy job, but you still have to do it or get fired."

_____ 2. "Here is a new assignment, but don't mess it up like the last one."

_____ 3. "So you are clear on the assignment. I'm sure you will do a good job."

_____ 4. "I trust you to do the assignment any way you want to get it done."

_____ 5. "Make sure the job gets done on time. I'll be checking up on you regularly."

WORK APPLICATION 3-2

Give two examples of when your attitude affected your performance. One should be a positive effect and the other a negative one. Be sure to fully explain how your attitudes affected performance.

WORK APPLICATION 3-3

Give an example of when you lived up to (or down to) someone else's expectations of your performance (the Pygmalion effect). It could be a parent's, teacher's, coach's, or boss's expectations. Be specific.

Learning Outcome 3-2

Describe how to change your attitudes.

supervisors' attitudes and expectations of employees and how they treat them largely determine their performance. In a study of welding students, the foreperson who was training the group was given the names of students who were quite intelligent and would do well. Actually, the students were selected at random. The only difference was the foreperson's expectations. The so-called intelligent students significantly outperformed the other group members. Why this happened is what this theory is all about. The foreperson's expectations became the foreperson's self-fulfilling prophecy.

In a sense, the Hawthorne effect (Chapter 1) is related to the Pygmalion effect because both affect performance. In the Hawthorne Studies, the special attention and treatment given to the workers by the management resulted in increased performance.

Through the positive expectations of others, people increase their level of performance. Unfortunately, many managers tend to stereotype and see what they expect to see: low performance.[17] And their employees see and do as the managers expect. We all need to expect and treat people as though they are high achievers to get the best from them.

Although others' attitudes can affect your behavior, human relations, and performance, you are responsible for your own actions. Try to ignore negative comments and stay away from people with negative attitudes. Focus on the positives.

Changing Attitudes

Complete Self-Assessment Exercise 3-2. Determine your own job attitude.

/ / / **Self-Assessment Exercise 3-2** / / /

Your Job Attitude

For each of the 10 statements below, identify how often each describes your behavior at work. Place a number from 1 to 5 next to each of the 10 statements.

(5) Always   (4) Usually   (3) Frequently   (2) Occasionally   (1) Seldom

_____ 1. I smile and am friendly and courteous to everyone at work.

_____ 2. I make positive, rather than negative, comments at work.

(continued)

/ / / **Self-Assessment Exercise 3-2** / / / *(continued)*

_____ 3. When my boss asks me to do extra work, I accept it cheerfully.

_____ 4. I avoid making excuses, passing the buck, or blaming others when things go wrong.

_____ 5. I am an active self-starter at getting work done.

_____ 6. I avoid spreading rumors and gossip among employees.

_____ 7. I am a team player willing to make personal sacrifices for the good of the work group.

_____ 8. I accept criticism gracefully and make the necessary changes.

_____ 9. I lift coworkers' spirits and bring them up emotionally.

_____ 10. If I were to ask my boss and coworkers to answer the nine questions for me, they would put the same answers that I did.

_____ Total: Add up the 10 numbers.

Interpreting your score. You can think of your job attitude as being on a continuum from positive to negative. Place an X on the continuum below at the point that represents your score.

Negative attitude 10 - - - - - - - - - - 20 - - - - - - - - - - 30 - - - - - - - - 40 - - - - - - - - - - 50 Positive attitude

Generally, the higher your score, the more positive your job attitude is. You may want to have your boss and trusted coworkers answer the first nine questions, as suggested in question 10, to determine if their perception of your job attitude is the same as your perception.

WORK APPLICATION 3-4

Based on your answers in Self-Assessment Exercise 3–2, what will you do to improve your job attitude? Be specific.

Would you rather work with people who have good or poor job attitudes? You may not be able to change your coworkers' job attitudes and behavior, but you can change your own.[18] Review your answers to the first nine questions in Self-Assessment Exercise 3-2, and think about ways you can improve your job attitude.

Changing Your Attitudes   If you are stuck in an unpleasant situation that you can't change, having a poor negative attitude will only make the situation more unpleasant. You can choose to be and learn to be either optimistic or pessimistic. You can choose to have a positive attitude and be happier and get more out of life. The following hints can help you change your attitudes:

1. Remember that what you think about affects how you feel, and how you feel affects your behavior, human relations, happiness, and performance. Football commentator **Lou Holtz** said, you choose to be happy or sad (or optimistic or pessimistic); happiness comes from having a poor memory for the bad things that happen to us. So if you think about the good things, you will feel happy and have more effective human relations.

2. Be aware of your attitudes. People who are optimistic have higher levels of job satisfaction. Consciously try to have and maintain a positive attitude.

    If you catch yourself complaining or being negative in any way, stop and change to a positive attitude.[19] With time you can become more positive.

3. Realize that there are few, if any, benefits to harboring negative attitudes, such as holding a grudge. They can only hurt your human relations, and hurt yourself in the end.

4. Keep an open mind. Don't have a negative attitude toward people because they look or act differently than you do.

You can gain control of your attitudes and change the direction of your life. Start today. We become what we think about, or "what we think determines what happens to us." So think and act like a winner, and you will become one. /// **In the opening case,** Rayanne does not seem to be interested in changing her attitude. If she doesn't change, Rayanne will never be happy or successful. ///

Shaping and Changing Employee Attitudes   It is difficult to change your own attitudes; it is even more difficult to change other people's attitudes. But it can be done.[20] The following hints can help you, as a manager, change employee attitudes:

1. Give employees feedback and treat them fairly.[21] Employees must be made aware of their negative attitudes if they are to change. The manager must talk to the employee about the negative attitude. The employee must understand that the attitude has negative consequences for her or him and the department. The manager should offer an alternative attitude. /// **In the opening case,** Kent has done this. ///

2. Accentuate positive conditions. Make working conditions as pleasant as possible, and make sure employees have all the necessary resources and training to do a good job.

3. Provide consequences. Employees tend to repeat activities or events followed by positive consequences and to avoid things followed by negative consequences. Try to keep negative attitudes from developing and spreading.

4. Be a positive role model. If you have a positive attitude, employees may also.

See Exhibit 3.1 for a review of how to change your attitudes and those of your employees.

EXHIBIT 3.1 | Changing Attitudes

Changing your attitudes

Be aware of your attitudes

Do not harbor negative thoughts

Keep an open mind

Shaping and changing employee attitudes

Give employees feedback

Accentuate positive conditions

Provide consequences

Be a positive role model

Job Attitudes   AS 3-2

Identify each employee's attitude statement as:

A. Positive   B. Negative

_____ 6. "It's her fault we missed the deadline, not mine."

_____ 7. "I missed it this time, but I'll get it the next time."

_____ 8. "Why am I stuck doing this task; why doesn't he make Hank do it?"

_____ 9. "Sure, I'll have this extra project done by noon for you."

_____ 10. "Can't you see I have to work here? Get out of the way."

JOB SATISFACTION

In this section we discuss the importance and nature of job satisfaction, the determinants of job satisfaction, and facts about job satisfaction globally.

The Importance and Nature of Job Satisfaction

WORK APPLICATION 3-5

Has job or school satisfaction affected your absenteeism? Explain your answer. For example, do you attend a class or job more if you are satisfied with it or if you are dissatisfied with it?

A person's **job satisfaction** is *a set of attitudes toward work.* Work is an important part of life giving us self-worth, and people want to be happy, so naturally people want job satisfaction.[22] Do you? Employees who are more satisfied with their jobs are generally better workers.

A **job satisfaction survey** is *a process of determining employee attitudes about the job and work environment.* Employers, including **Intel, IBM, Twitter,**[23] and **Google** conduct surveys to find out if employees are happy on the job.[24]

Job satisfaction is a part of life satisfaction. As stated in Chapter 1, the total person comes to work.[25] Your off-the-job life also affects your job satisfaction, and in turn your job satisfaction affects your life satisfaction. For example, /// **In the opening case,** Rayanne has brought a negative attitude to work, which in turn has affected her job satisfaction. ///

Determinants of Job Satisfaction

Learning Outcome 3-3

List seven job satisfaction determinants.

Job satisfaction is on a continuum from low to high. It can refer to a single employee, a group or department, or an entire organization. Notice that the definition of job satisfaction identifies an overall attitude toward work. It does so because people usually have positive attitudes about some aspects of work and negative attitudes about other aspects of work.

There are a variety of determinants of job satisfaction. Each of these determinants may be of great importance to some people and of little importance to others.

- **The Work Itself.** Whether you enjoy performing the work itself has a major effect on overall job satisfaction.

- **Pay and Benefits.** Your satisfaction with the pay received affects overall job satisfaction. And the rising cost of health care, along with retirement benefits, make benefits more important than ever.

- **Growth and Upward Mobility.** Whether you are satisfied with personal or company growth and whether the potential for upward mobility exists may affect job satisfaction.

Communication Skills
Refer to CS Question 4.

WORK APPLICATION 3-6

Consider a specific job you hold or have held. Measure your job satisfaction for the job by rating each of the seven determinants of job satisfaction using a scale from 1 (not satisfied) to 5 (satisfied); then add up the total points and divide by seven to get your average, or overall, job satisfaction level. Be sure to write down the seven determinants and your ratings.

WORK APPLICATION 3-7

Has job or school satisfaction affected your performance? Explain your answer. For example, compared to your work in classes or jobs that you are satisfied with, do you work as hard and produce as much for classes or jobs that you are dissatisfied with?

- **Supervision.** Whether you are satisfied with the supervision received affects overall job satisfaction. The personal relationship between you and the boss also affects job satisfaction.[26]

- **Coworkers.** Whether you have positive human relations with coworkers affects overall job satisfaction.[27]

- **Job Security.** Some people are more concerned about not getting laid off than others.

- **Attitude toward Work.** Some people have the attitude that work is fun and interesting, while others do not. Personality is associated with work attitude and behavior.

People differ in the ways they prioritize the above determinants of job satisfaction. You can be highly satisfied in some areas and dissatisfied in others yet have overall job satisfaction. Unfortunately, /// in the opening case, Rayanne doesn't seem happy with any of these determinants of job satisfaction. /// Remember that what you think about affects how you feel, and how you feel affects your behavior, human relations, happiness, and performance. So if you keep thinking about the bad parts of your job, you will feel bad about it. Think about the things you like about the job and you will be happier. For a review of the seven determinants of job satisfaction, see Exhibit 3.2.

Job Satisfaction in the United States and Other Countries

Most people start a new job with high expectations of job satisfaction, but the initial satisfaction often wears off. Companies that work to improve job satisfaction through effective human resource practices have better performance than those that don't. Internationally, education and income do increase job satisfaction. Job satisfaction differences may be driven by the extent to which people in different countries hold jobs that differ in level of interest, promotion prospects, and job security. People in professional and managerial jobs and those performing nonmanual work reported more job satisfaction than those who perform manual work.[28] Also there are different levels of job satisfaction across cultures.[29]

EXHIBIT 3.2 | Determinants of Job Satisfaction

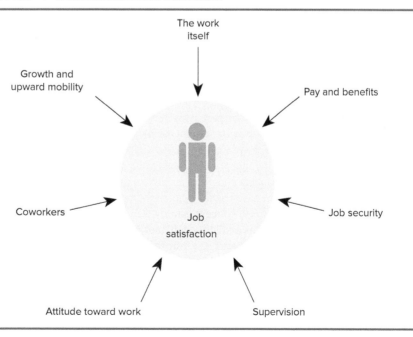

APPLICATION   SITUATIONS / / /

Job Satisfaction   AS 3-3

Identify each statement by its determinant of job satisfaction:

A. Work itself   C. Growth and mobility   E. Coworkers   G. Job security

B. Pay   D. Supervision   F. General work attitude

_____ 11. "I enjoy fixing cars. I wouldn't want to work in an office."

_____ 12. "I think I will be a good manager; that is why I applied for the promotion."

_____ 13. "It is difficult being the only minority at work. The others don't treat me like one of the guys."

_____ 14. "The boss just made another negative comment about me. I wonder if this abuse will stop."

_____ 15. "I like my job and being a woman, but I don't like making less money than the men around here."

SELF-CONCEPT

Learning Outcome 3-4

Determine whether you
have a positive self-concept
and how it affects your
behavior, human relations,
and performance.

In this section, we explain self-concept and how it is formed, self-efficacy, attribution theory and self-concept, and the steps of how to build a positive self-concept. The self-concept is central to understanding human thought, feelings, and behavior.[30]

Self-Concept and How It Is Formed

Your **self-concept** is *your overall attitude about yourself.* Self-concept is also called *self-esteem* and *self-image.*[31] Self-concept can be thought of as being on a continuum from positive to negative, or high to low. Do you like yourself? Are you a valuable person? Are you satisfied with the way you live your life? When faced with a challenge, are your thoughts positive or negative? Do you believe you can meet the challenge or that you're not very good at doing things? If your beliefs and feelings about yourself are positive, you tend to have a high self-concept.[32] Your personality is based, in part, on your self-concept.

Your self-concept includes perceptions about several aspects of yourself. You can have a positive self-concept and still want to change some things about yourself. Self-concept is your perception of yourself, which may not be the way others perceive you. Your thoughts and feelings about yourself have greater influence in determining your self-concept than does your behavior.[33] Even if individuals don't consider themselves likable, others probably do like them.

You develop your self-concept over the years through the messages you receive about yourself from others. Your present self-concept has been strongly influenced by the way others have treated you—the attitudes and expectations others have had of you (Pygmalion effect). Your parents were the first to contribute to your self-concept. Did your parents build you up with statements like, "You're smart—you can do it," or destroy you with "You're dumb—you cannot do it"? If you have siblings, were they positive or negative? Your early self-concept still affects your self-concept today. As you grew through adolescence, your teachers and peers also had a profound impact on your self-concept. Were you popular? Did you have friends who encouraged you? By the time you reach adulthood in your early 20s, your self-concept is fairly well developed. However, when you take on more responsibilities, such as a full-time job, marriage, and children, your self-concept can change.

Apparently, /// **in the opening case,** Rayanne came to work for Kent with a negative self-concept. Rayanne stated that she messed up on all her previous jobs, and she called herself a failure. Her self-concept, like yours, however, is dynamic and capable of changing. Kent is trying to develop a win–win situation by trying to get Rayanne to develop a more positive attitude and self-concept so that she can be happier and more productive. Rayanne can change her attitude and self-concept if she really wants to and is willing to work at it. /// Are you willing to develop a more positive self-concept so that you can be happier and more productive?

APPLICATION SITUATIONS / / /

Self-Concept   AS 3-4

Identify each statement as:

A. Positive   B. Negative

_____ 16. "Yes, I can complete the project by noon."

_____ 17. "It's been a month, but I'm still upset about not getting the assignment."

_____ 18. "I'm a good writer and will get to get a book contract someday."

_____ 19. "I'm not good at doing the math problems."

_____ 20. "This is my third error."

WORK APPLICATION 3-8

Describe your self-concept.

In addition to receiving messages from others, we compare ourselves with others. Such comparisons can have positive or negative influences on your self-concept. Focusing on negative comparisons can cause you to have a negative self-concept and to be unhappy, so don't do it.[34]

Our behavior is consistent with the way we see ourselves, so your self-concept affects your nonverbal and verbal communications behavior projecting a positive or negative level of confidence.[35] A positive self-concept leads to higher levels of performance, even when it is unwarranted.[36] Going into a job interview well prepared and believing you can do the job can help give you a positive self-concept that will increase the odds of getting the job.

Learning Outcome 3-5

Understand how your manager's and your own expectations affect your performance.

Self-Efficacy

Self-efficacy is *your belief in your capability to perform in a specific situation.* Self-efficacy affects your effort, persistence, expressed interest, and the difficulty of goals you select.[37] For example, if your major is business, your self-efficacy may be high for a management course but low for a language or biology course that you may be required to take.

WORK APPLICATION 3-9

Give an example of when you lived up to or down to your own expectations (self-efficacy leading to self-fulfilling prophecy).

Your expectations affect your performance. If you think you will be successful, you will be. If you think you will fail, you will, because you will fulfill your expectations. You will live up to or down to your expectations. This expectation phenomenon is often referred to as the *self-fulfilling prophecy* and the *Galatea effect.* The **self-fulfilling prophecy** occurs when *your expectations affect your success or failure.* /// **In the opening case,** Rayanne stated that she had messed up on all the jobs she had, and she called herself a failure. Is it any surprise to find that Rayanne is having problems in her new job working for Kent? ///

As you can see, self-efficacy and the self-fulfilling prophecy go hand in hand. Your self-efficacy becomes your self-fulfilling prophecy. So you need self-efficacy, or confidence, and believe in yourself to put forth the effort needed to succeed at challenging tasks.[38] There is a lot of truth in the saying, "You can do it if you put your mind to it,"[39] because your thoughts affect your self-efficacy.

Attribution Theory and Self-Concept

Attribution is *one's perception of the reasons for behavior.* When we observe others' behavior, we do not know the reason for it. So we make a judgment as to why people do the things they do.[40] So attribution theory is how we perceive the causes of behavior, which in turn affects our subsequent choices and behaviors.[41] For example, if a person calls you a name in a joking way, why did they do it? Are they being mean or kidding around? How do you respond? As you may have heard, it is not good to assume, so you are better off asking about the behavior and getting it right than guessing and getting in wrong. In Chapter 5 you will learn how to discuss behavior to improve human relations.

/// **In the opening case,** Rayanne is not willing to take responsibility for her poor performance; she says it's not her fault. Nor is she willing to change to improve. Until she takes responsibility and is willing to change, she will not improve. /// Are you willing to change to improve?

Building a Positive Self-Concept

Learning Outcome 3-6

Demonstrate how to develop a more positive self-concept.

You are the ultimate creator of your self-concept, and you can improve your self-concept, even though it is not easy to evaluate yourself and it is even more difficult to change. But it is worth the time and effort to improve your self-concept. The general guidelines below are followed by an action plan that will help you develop a more positive self-concept.

As a manager (coach, parent, teacher, friend), you can work with others using these ideas to help them develop a more positive self-concept. One thing to keep in mind is that you need to be positive and give praise and encouragement. However, real self-esteem is based on achievement, not praise for low performance.[42]

/// **In the opening case,** Kent can teach Rayanne how to improve her self-concept; he should praise her for improvements, but he should not praise her if she does not improve her performance. If Rayanne's performance does not improve and Kent takes no action, her self-concept will not improve and neither will her performance. ///

General Guidelines   The following are general guidelines you can implement in your daily life to improve your self-concept:

1. View mistakes and failures as learning experiences to improve.[43] Realize that we all make mistakes. Talk to any successful businessperson with a positive self-concept and he or she will admit making mistakes. But he or she will tell you that you need to take some risks to be successful. Don't hide in the dugout; go to bat. You get some strike-outs and some hits. That's how life is. Be future-oriented. Don't worry about past mistakes. Dwelling on past mistakes will only have a negative effect on your self-concept.

2. Accept failure and bounce back. Inability to rebound from disappointments is one of the main reasons people fail. Dwelling on failure and disappointment will only have a negative effect on your self-concept. Realize that you will have disappointments but will most likely go on to bigger and better things. Co-founder **Steve Jobs** was fired from **Apple** but went on to start **Pixar** and later returned Apple to success.

3. Control negative behavior and thoughts with self-talk—No Stinking Thinking.[44]

   Thoughts are very important because we become what we think about, and what we think determines what happens to us. If you keep thinking you are a loser and will fail at something, you will, so think about being a winner. Silence the voice that says you can't succeed.

   If you catch yourself thinking negative thoughts, use self-talk with positive affirmations by being aware of what is happening and replace the negative thoughts and beliefs with positive ones, such as "you can do this. It's easy." With time you will have fewer and fewer negative thoughts.[45]

   Always accept a compliment with a thank you. Don't minimize the compliment with a statement such as, "Anyone could have done it" or "It was not a big deal." Never put yourself down in your thoughts, words, or actions; stop and recall your successes.

4. Tap into your spirituality. Use any religious or spiritual beliefs you have that can help you develop a more positive self-concept, for example, "God will help me succeed."

Action Plan for Building a Positive Self-Concept   The three-part action plan for building a positive self-concept is listed in Model 3.1 and discussed below.

Step 1: Identify Your Strengths and Areas That Need Improvement   What are the things about yourself that you like? What can you do well? What do you have to offer other people and organizations?

MODEL 3.1 | Building a Positive Self-Concept Habit

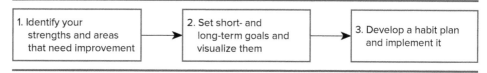

| 1. Identify your strengths and areas that need improvement | → | 2. Set short- and long-term goals and visualize them | → | 3. Develop a habit plan and implement it |

Most of us are in denial of our weaknesses.[46] What are the things about yourself or the behavior that could be improved? No one is good at everything. Know your limitations so you don't try to accomplish something that you can't accomplish—this failure hurts self-concept. Focus on your strengths while working on your weaknesses by changing habits.

Step 2: Set Short- and Long-Term Goals and Visualize Them Before you can get anywhere or get anything out of life, you must first determine where you want to go or what you want. Based on step 1, set some goals for the things about yourself or your behavior that you want to change for the better. Write them down in positive, affirmative language. For example, write:

- "I am calm when talking to others" (not "I don't yell at people").
- "I am a slim _____ pounds [select a weight 5 to 10 pounds less than your current weight]" (not "I must lose weight").
- "I am outgoing and enjoy meeting new people" (not "I must stop being shy").
- "I am smart and get good grades," or "I am good at my job."

Place your goals where you can review them several times each day. Put copies on your mirror, refrigerator, car visor, or desk, or record them so you can play them several times each day. Start and end each day thinking positive thoughts about yourself.

Remember, success comes one step at a time. Reaching one goal helps motivate you to continue, and each success helps you develop a more positive self-concept. Therefore, set short-term goals you can reach. For example, if you presently weigh 150 pounds, start with the goal "I am a slim 110 pounds," but break it up into doable parts: "I will weigh 145 pounds by January 1, 2019," and "I will weigh 140 pounds by March 1, 2019." Compliment and reward yourself regularly as you achieve your short-term goals. As you continue to set and achieve short-term goals, you will continue to build your self-concept as being successful. You will learn about goal setting and motivation in Chapter 8.

Each day, visualize yourself as you want to be, as set forth in your goals. For example, picture yourself being calm when talking to a person you usually yell at. Mentally see yourself at a slim 110 pounds. Picture yourself meeting new people or being successful on the job, and so forth.

Step 3: Develop a Habit Plan and Implement It What specific action will you take to improve your self-concept through changing your thoughts or behavior? Some goals take much planning, while others do not. What will be your plan to lose the weight? Exercise? Diet? What are the specifics? With other goals, such as not yelling at people, making detailed plans is not so easy. However, you can determine what it is that gets you angry and try to eliminate it. What will you do differently?

To change, we need to develop new habits. As presented in Chapter 1, what will be your (1) cue, (2) routine, and (3) reward-change?

Stop comparing yourself with others and downgrading yourself, because this hurts your self-concept. Even the best are eventually topped. Set your goals, develop habit plans, and achieve them. Compare yourself with *you*. Be the best that *you* can be. Continue to improve yourself by setting goals, developing habit plans, and achieving them. Through this process, you will develop your self-concept. You will know and be proud of yourself. See Exhibit 3.3 for a review of how to develop a positive self-concept. Skill-Building Exercise 3–2 gives you the opportunity to develop a plan to improve your self-concept.

Skill Building Exercises 3-2 and 3-3 develop this skill.

Communication Skills
Refer to CS Question 5.

WORK APPLICATION 3-10

Which of the four general guidelines to building a positive self-concept needs the least work? The most work? Explain your answer.

EXHIBIT 3.3 | Developing a Positive Self-Concept

Accept failure
and bounce back

Control negative behavior
and thoughts with self-talk

View mistakes as
learning experiences

Tap into your
spirituality

1. Identify your strengths and areas that need improvement.
2. Set short- and long-term goals and visualize them.
3. Develop a plan and implement it.

/ / / Self-Assessment Exercise 3-3 / / /

Your Personal Values

Below are 16 items. Rate how important each one is to you on a scale of 0 (not important) to 100 (very important). Write a number from 0 to 100 on the line to the left of each item.

Not important				Somewhat important						Very important
0	10	20	30	40	50	60	70	80	90	100

_____   1. An enjoyable, satisfying job.

_____   2. A high-paying job.

_____   3. A good marriage.

_____   4. Meeting new people, social events.

_____   5. Involvement in community activities.

_____   6. My religion.

_____   7. Exercising, playing sports.

_____   8. Intellectual development.

_____   9. A career with challenging opportunities.

_____   10. Nice cars, clothes, home, etc.

_____   11. Spending time with family.

_____   12. Having several close friends.

_____   13. Volunteer work for not-for-profit organizations such as the cancer society.

_____   14. Meditation, quiet time to think, pray, etc.

_____   15. A healthy, balanced diet.

_____   16. Educational reading, self-improvement programs, etc.

Below, transfer the numbers for each of the 16 items to the appropriate column; then add the two numbers in each column.

	Professional	Financial	Family	Social
	1. ____	2. ____	3. ____	4. ____
	9. ____	10. ____	11. ____	12. ____
Totals	____	____	____	____

(continued)

	Community	Spiritual	Physical	Intellectual
	5. ____	6. ____	7. ____	8. ____
	13. ____	14. ____	15. ____	16. ____
Totals	____	____	____	____

The higher the total in any area, the higher the value you place on that particular area. The closer the numbers are in all eight areas, the more well-rounded you are.

Think about the time and effort you put forth in your top three values. Is it sufficient to allow you to achieve the level of success you want in each area? If not, what can you do to change? Is there any area in which you feel you should have a higher value total? If yes, which one? What can you do to change?

VALUES

Learning Outcome 3-7

Identify your personal values.

In this section, we cover individual values and how they are related to, yet different from, attitudes. A person's **values** are *the things that have worth for or are important to the individual,* and a **value system** is *the set of standards by which the individual lives.* An important life question is, What is of value to you?[47] Take time and identify what is truly important to you,[48] at both work and at home.[49] Complete Self-Assessment Exercise 3-3 to help you identify your personal values in eight broad areas of life.

Organizations recruit people with values that match the firm's,[50] and to be happy, choose a place that fits your values.[51] /// **In the opening case,** since work is not important to Rayanne, it is not surprising that she has a negative attitude toward work. ///

Values are developed in much the same way as attitudes. However, values are more stable than attitudes. Attitudes reflect multiple, often changing, opinions. Values about some things do change, but the process is usually slower than a change in attitude. Society influences our value system. What was considered unacceptable in the past may become commonplace in the future, or vice versa. For example, the percentage of smokers and the social acceptance of smoking have decreased over the years. Value changes over the years are often a major part of what is referred to as the *generation gap.*

WORK APPLICATION 3-11

What is your attitude toward your personal values in the eight areas of Self-Assessment Exercise 3-3? Do you plan to work at changing any of your values? Why or why not?

Do you place a high value on relationships? Getting to know people and understanding their values can improve human relations. For example, if Juan knows that Carla has great respect for the president, he can avoid making negative comments about the president in front of her.

Discussions over value issues, such as abortion and homosexuality, rarely lead to changes in others' values. They usually just end in arguments. Therefore, you should try to be open-minded about others' values and avoid arguments that will only hurt human relations.

Skill-Building Exercise 3–1 develops this skill.

Spirituality in the Workplace

People want to be happy, and many people are seeking spirituality as a means of fulfillment in their lives. **Dr. Edward Wilson, Harvard University professor** and two-time Pulitzer Prize-winning expert on human nature, says, "I believe the search for spirituality is going to be one of the major historical episodes of the 21st century."[52]

Judi Neal, Founder and **CEO of Edgewalkers International** at http://edgewalkers.org/, has defined spirituality in the workplace and developed guidelines for leading from a spiritual perspective.[53]

Defining Spirituality in the Workplace   Spirituality in the workplace is about people seeing their work as a spiritual path, as an opportunity to grow personally and to contribute to society in a meaningful way. It is about learning to be more caring and compassionate with fellow employees, with bosses, with subordinates, and with customers. It is about having integrity, being true to oneself, and telling the truth to others. Spirituality in the workplace can refer to an individual's attempts to live his or her values more fully in the workplace. Or it can refer to the ways organizations structure themselves to support the spiritual growth of employees. In the final analysis, your understanding of spirit and of spirituality in the workplace is an individual and personal matter.

Guidelines for Leading from a Spiritual Perspective   Here are five spiritual principles that have been useful in personal and professional development:

1. *Know thyself.* All spiritual growth processes incorporate the principle of self-awareness.
2. *Act with authenticity.* Be yourself.
3. *Respect and honor the beliefs of others.* Be open to other's beliefs and values.
4. *Be as trusting as you can be.* This means trusting yourself and that there is a Higher Power in your life and that if you ask, you will receive guidance on important issues.
5. *Maintain a spiritual practice.* Examples include spending time in nature, attending religious services, meditating, praying, and reading inspirational literature.

Secular institutional research has found that during moments of anger and distress, turning to prayer or meditation, encouraged in nearly all religions, diminishes the harmful effects of negative emotions and stress. Also, people who attend religious services regularly enjoy better-than-average health and live longer, are wealthier, have better marriages, and are happier.[54]

By implementing the ideas presented in this chapter, you can develop positive attitudes and a more positive self-concept, as well as clarify your values. Begin today.

Communication Skills
Refer to CS Question 6.

Communication Skills
Refer to CS Question 7.

ETHICS

As related to values, **ethics** refers to *the moral standard of right and wrong behavior. Honesty* (no lying, stealing, or cheating) is often presented as a minimum moral standard for both society and organizations.[55] In this section, we discuss whether ethical behavior does pay, factors affecting ethical behavior, how people justify unethical behavior, some ethical guidelines, and global ethics. Before we begin, complete Self-Assessment Exercise 3-4 to determine how ethical your behavior is.

/ / / Self-Assessment Exercise 3-4 / / /

How Ethical Is Your Behavior?

For this exercise, you will be using the same set of statements twice. The first time you answer them, focus on your own behavior and the frequency with which you use it. On the line before the question number, place the number from 1 (frequently) to 4 (never) that represents how often you have done the behavior in the past, do the behavior now, or would do the behavior if you had the chance. These numbers will allow you to determine your level of ethics. You can be honest without fear of having to tell others your score in class. *Sharing ethics scores is not part of the exercise.*

Frequently			Never
1	2	3	4

The second time you use the statements, focus on other people in an organization with whom you work or have worked. Place an O on the line after the number if you have observed someone doing this behavior. Also place an R on the line if you have reported (blown the whistle on) this behavior either within the organization or externally.

O = Observed,   R = Reported

1–4   O, R

College

___ / ___   1. ___ / ___   Cheating on homework assignments.
___ / ___   2. ___ / ___   Cheating on exams.
___ / ___   3. ___ / ___   Passing in papers that were completed by someone else as your own work.

(continued)

/ / / **Self-Assessment Exercise 3-4** / / / (*continued*)

1-4   **O, R**

Job

___ / ___ 4. ___ / ___ Lying to others to get what you want or to stay out of trouble.

___ / ___ 5. ___ / ___ Coming to work late, leaving work early, or taking long breaks or lunches and getting paid for it.

___ / ___ 6. ___ / ___ Socializing, goofing off, or doing personal work rather than doing the work that should be done and getting paid for it.

___ / ___ 7. ___ / ___ Calling in sick to get a day off when you are not sick.

___ / ___ 8. ___ / ___ Using the organization's phone, computer, Internet, copier, mail, car, etc. for personal use.

___ / ___ 9. ___ / ___ Taking home company tools or equipment without permission for personal use and returning the items.

___ / ___ 10. ___ / ___ Taking home organizational supplies or merchandise and keeping the items.

___ / ___ 11. ___ / ___ Giving company supplies or merchandise to friends or allowing them to take the items without saying anything.

___ / ___ 12. ___ / ___ Putting in for reimbursement for meals and travel or other expenses that weren't actually eaten or taken.

___ / ___ 13. ___ / ___ Taking your spouse or friends out to eat or on a business trip and charging it to the organizational expense account.

___ / ___ 14. ___ / ___ Accepting gifts from customers or suppliers in exchange for giving them business.

___ / ___ 15. ___ / ___ Cheating on your taxes.

___ / ___ 16. ___ / ___ Misleading customers, such as promising short delivery dates, to make a sale.

___ / ___ 17. ___ / ___ Misleading competitors, such as pretending to be a customer or supplier, to get information to use to compete against them.

___ / ___ 18. ___ / ___ Planting false information to enhance your chances of getting reelected.

___ / ___ 19. ___ / ___ Selling a customer more product than the customer needs just to get the commission.

___ / ___ 20. ___ / ___ Spreading false rumors about coworkers or competitors to make yourself look better for advancement or to make more sales.

___ / ___ 21. ___ / ___ Lying for your boss when asked or told to do so.

___ / ___ 22. ___ / ___ Deleting information that makes you look bad or changing information to look better than the actual results.

___ / ___ 23. ___ / ___ Being pressured, or pressuring others, to sign off on documents that contain false information.

___ / ___ 24. ___ / ___ Being pressured to sign off on documents you haven't read, knowing they may contain information or decisions that may be considered inappropriate, or pressuring others to do so.

___ / ___ 25.   If you were to give this assessment to a person with whom you work and with whom you do not get along very well, would she or he agree with your answers? Use 4 (yes) or 1 (no). Place the appropriate number on the line before the number 25. (No O or R responses are necessary for this question.)

Other Unethical Behavior: On the lines below, add other unethical behaviors you have observed. If you reported the behavior, write an R before the behavior.

26. _____   _____

27. _____   _____

28. _____   _____

Note: This self-assessment is not meant to be a precise measure of your ethical behavior. It is designed to get you thinking about your behavior and that of others from an ethical perspective. There is no right or wrong score; however, each of these actions is considered unethical behavior in most organizations. Another ethical issue in this exercise is your honesty when rating the frequencies of your behavior. How honest were you?

Scoring: To determine your ethics score, add the numbers you recorded. Your total will be between 25 and 100. Place the number here _____ and on the continuum below place an X at the point that represents your score. The higher your score, the more ethical your behavior is; the lower your score, the less ethical your behavior is.

Unethical   25 - - - - 30 -- - - - 40 --- - - 50 - - - - 60 - - - - - 70 - - - - 80 - - - - - 90 - - - - 100   Ethical

Why Do People Behave Unethically, and Does Ethical Behavior Pay?

Why Good People Do Bad Things   Most people understand right and wrong behavior and have a conscience. So why do good people do bad things? Most people aren't simply good or bad; 98 percent of us will be unethical at times, but just a little.[56] We respond to "incentives" and can usually be manipulated to behave ethically or unethically if we find the right incentives.[57] The incentive (or reason we are unethical at times) is usually for personal gain,[58] to avoid getting into trouble, and some people don't believe the rules apply to them.[59] Why did people at **Countrywide Financial** give mortgages to people whose homes would most certainly be repossessed? Why did people at **Wells Fargo Bank** open accounts that customers didn't ask for? There were financial gains for doing so, and some employees feared losing their jobs if they didn't meet high quotas.

Individual Ethics   Does ethics pay? Generally, the answer is yes. Our unethical behavior negatively affects our behavior, happiness, relationships, reputation, and performance.[60] Recall our question "Do you want to be happy?" and that job satisfaction (happiness) comes from strong, rewarding relationships.[61] Relationships are based on trust, and you get and keep friends based on trust.[62] Unethical behavior might give you some type of short-term gain, but in the long run, you've sabotaged yourself.[63] One lie usually leads to another, and the truth usually comes out eventually, and when it does, it usually hurts relationships. Do you trust dishonest people who lie to you? At the end of the day the truth is all that matters.[64] If you are honest during the day, you will sleep well at night.[65] **Indra Nooyi, CEO of PepsiCo**, says that building a strong honest character is a key to personal and career success.[66]

Organizational Business Ethics   Individuals are ethical or unethical, not organizations. But individual unethical behavior affects others and organizational reputation and performance.[67] Unethical decisions can have far-reaching consequences.[68] **Royal Dutch Shell** ignored warning signs and repairs that resulted in an oil spill in the U.S. Gulf of Mexico that killed people and wildlife and damaged the natural environment. Victims of dishonesty often use counterproductive behavior and revenge tactics that can hurt you and the organization.[69] So yes, ethics does matter, or it pays to be ethical.[70]

Caution Against Escalation of Unethical Behavior   It is important to understand the subtlety of how unethical behavior can take hold of you. The first lie is the hardest, and every time after becomes easier.[71] Our memories fade as we repeat unethical behavior.[72] Notice that some people lie regularly, and don't even realize it, even about things that are not important.

Today we live in a time of ethical confusion with *relativism* saying there is no absolute truth or right or wrong—which contradicts itself by using an absolute. It's tempting to change the rules or truth and be unethical for personal gain, and justifying the behavior by telling ourselves it's OK "to do what works for me" or "to do what makes me feel good," which often leads to unethical behavior. The things we do repeatedly determine our character. And as you want people to be ethical with you, its not OK to be dishonest with others.[73]

Did the people at **Enron**, and other companies, start out planning to lie, cheat, and steal? Most didn't. What tends to happen is the company doesn't hit the target numbers, and the employees think, "Let's give inflated numbers this quarter, and we will make it up next quarter, and no one will know or get hurt in any way." The problem is, for several quarters the same thing happens so they get to the point of not being able or willing to admit their unethical/illegal behavior until they get caught. If you are covering up your tracks, you probably realize what you're doing is unethical.[74]

Little white lies are not little.[75] The subtlety creeps up on us because the more we engage in the unethical behavior, and especially if we don't get caught, the easier it is to be unethical. Everything tends to come out in due time anyway, so it's better if it happens early.[76] The moral of the story is: don't take the first step that leads to escalation of unethical behavior. We will give you guidelines to help you make good ethical choices.

How Personality Traits and Attitudes, Moral Development, and the Situation Affect Ethical Behavior

Personality Traits and Attitudes   You probably already realize that because of their personalities, some people have a higher level of ethics than others, as integrity is considered a personality trait. Related to personality is our attitude toward ethics. Unethical people don't care about ethics—"it's all about me and getting what I want." Some people are at the point that they don't even realize they are dishonest and don't see anything wrong with the habit of lying.[77] But don't just assume people are lying. Recall that people perceive the same situation differently and have different memories that are subject to bias.[78]

When you complete Self-Assessment Exercise 3-5 at the end of this section, you will have a better understanding of how your personality affects your ethical behavior.

Learning Outcome 3-8

Compare the three levels of moral development.

Moral Development   *Moral development* refers to understanding right from wrong and choosing to do the right thing.[79] Unfortunately, doing the right thing is rarely easy.[80] There are three levels of personal moral development, as discussed in Exhibit 3.4. Although most of us have the ability to reach this third level, only about 20 percent of people actually do reach it. Most of us behave at the second level, conventional. How do you handle peer pressure? What level of moral development have you attained? What can you do to improve your moral development level?

The Situation   The situational control also affects behavior. People respond to "incentives" and can often be manipulated to do the ethical or unethical thing based on the situation's

EXHIBIT 3.4 | Levels of Moral Development

Level 3: Postconventional

Behavior is motivated by universal principles of right and wrong, regardless of the expectations of the leader or group. One seeks to balance the concerns for self with those of others and the common good. At the risk of social rejection, economic loss, and physical punishment, the individual will follow ethical principles even if they violate the law (Martin Luther King Jr., for example, broke what he considered unjust laws and spent time in jail seeking universal dignity and justice).

"I don't lie to customers because it is wrong."

The common leadership style is visionary and committed to serving others and a higher cause while empowering followers to reach this level.

Level 2: Conventional

Living up to expectations of acceptable behavior defined by others motivates behavior to fulfill duties and obligations. It is common for followers to copy the behavior of the leaders and group. If the group (this could be society, an organization, or a department) accepts lying, cheating, and stealing when dealing with customers, suppliers, the government, or competitors, so will the individual. On the other hand, if these behaviors are not accepted, the individual will not do them either. Peer pressure is used to enforce group norms.

"I lie to customers because the other sales reps do it too."

It is common for lower-level managers to use a leadership style similar to that of the higher-level managers.

Level 1: Preconventional

Self-interest motivates behavior to meet one's own needs and to gain rewards while following rules and being obedient to authority to avoid punishment.

"I lie to customers to sell more products and get higher commission checks."

The common leadership style is autocratic toward others while using one's position for personal advantage.

Source: Based on Lawrence Kohlberg, "Moral Stages and Moralization: The Cognitive-Development Approach," in Moral Development and Behavior: Theory, Research, and Social Issues, ed. Thomas Likona, Austin, TX: Holt, Rinehart and Winston, 1976, 31–53.

WORK APPLICATION 3-12

Give an organizational example of behavior at each of the three levels of moral development.

circumstances.[81] Highly competitive and unsupervised situations increase the odds of unethical behavior. Unethical behavior occurs more often when there is no formal ethics policy or code of ethics and when unethical behavior is not punished. Unethical behavior is especially prevalent when it is rewarded. People are also less likely to report unethical behavior (blow the whistle) when they perceive the violation as not being serious and when the violator is a friend.

How People Justify Unethical Behavior

We all want to view ourselves as good people.[82] Therefore, when we do behave unethically, we usually justify the behavior by *rationalizing* to ourselves that there was a good reason for the behavior.[83] Justification protects our *self-concept* so that we don't have to feel bad about ourselves.[84] If we are only a little dishonest, we can still feel good about our sense of integrity.[85]

WORK APPLICATION 3-13

Give at least two organizational examples of unethical behavior and the process of justification.

Here are some examples of how we justify unethical behavior.[86] *Everyone else does it*—we all cheat in college; everyone takes things home (steals). *I did it for the good of others or the company*—I cooked the books so the company looks good; we are not terrorists, but we are freedom fighters. *I was only following orders*—my boss made me do it. *I'm not as bad as the others*—I only call in sick when I'm not sick once in a while. *Disregard for or distortion of consequences*—No one will be hurt if I inflate the figures, and I will not get caught. And if I do, I'll just get a slap on the wrist anyway.

Human Relations Guide to Ethical Decisions

We continue our discussion of ethics in this section by providing simple guides that will help you make ethical choices.

Communication Skills
Refer to CS Question 8.

The Golden Rule   Most religions have a variation of the Golden Rule: "Do unto others as you want them to do unto you." Or, "Don't do anything to anyone that you would not want them to do to you." Or, "Do to others what they want you to do." If everyone followed this one simple rule, the world would change overnight.

The Stakeholders Approach   Try to meet the goal of human relations by creating a win–win situation for all stakeholders—people you interact with. Some of the relevant stakeholder parties include peers, boss, other department members, and people outside the firm you work for as well. Unfortunately, win–win is not always easy because multiple stakeholders often have conflicting interest.[87]

Skill Building Exercise 3–4
develops this skill.

Four-Way Test   A third guide is the Rotary International four-way test: (1) Is it the truth? (2) Is it fair to all concerned? (3) Will it build goodwill and better friendship? (4) Will it be beneficial to all concerned?

Discernment and Advice   Before you act, use an ethical guide to discern if the behavior is ethical or not. Ask others, if you are unsure whether a decision is ethical, such as your boss, higher-level managers, and other people with high ethical standards. If you are reluctant to ask others for advice because you may not like their answers, the decision may not be ethical.

If you are proud to tell all the relevant parties and hear/read your decision in the media, the decision is probably ethical. If you are embarrassed, if you keep rationalizing the decision, or if you are trying to cover up your behavior, you probably know what you're doing is unethical.[88]

Application of Ethical Guides   Research shows that making quick decisions without using an ethical guide leads to less ethical choices; using ethical guides helps keep you honest.[89] So if you want to maintain or improve your relationships, be ethical and get in the habit of using an ethical guide when making decisions. Are you willing to commit to doing so now?

Remember that what you think about affects your behavior. If you keep thinking about doing something unethical and justifying it, you may give in to the temptation. Remind yourself it is unethical and stop thinking about it.

Managing Ethics Globally

All businesses, and especially multinational corporation (MNCs), should manage ethics. Most MNCs have codes of ethics, also called codes of conduct, to help employees understand what behavior is and is not ethical.[90] When **Google** started, it had the motto, "Don't be evil." But a simple code is not enough. To help ensure ethical behavior, employees should have ethics training, top level managers need to support the code and lead by example with ethical behavior,[91] ethical codes must be enforced, and violators should be punished.[92]

A difficult challenge to MNC managers is the fact that different countries have different levels of ethical standards. For example, it is unethical to give bribes in America, but it is the way in which business is conducted in some countries. Managers typically have two choices. According to *universalism,* managers should make the same ethical decisions across countries, whereas *relativism* calls for decisions to be made based on the ethical standards of the particular country. Thus, the MNC manager using universalism would not give any bribes, whereas the manager using relativism would give bribes in some countries.

WORK APPLICATION 3-14

Give an example, preferably from an organization for which you work or have worked, of an individual creating a win–win situation for all parties involved. Identify all parties involved and how they were winners. Use Exhibit 8.2, Human Relations Guide to Ethical Decision Making (page 266), to help you answer the question.

Although the United States has the Foreign Corrupt Practices Act that defines illegal behavior, it is considered vague and confusing. So there are often no simple answers to what is ethical and not ethical and fair.[93] For more information on the FCPA visit www .foreign-corrupt-practices-act.org. Think of the complexity of conducting business in 100 to 200 countries.

The increasing concern for global managerial ethics calls for a better understanding through cross-national comparisons and the need for a global mindset.[94] To this end, and getting back to justification of unethical behavior, researchers have found that the same justifications presented earlier are used globally.

The global business world is increasingly emphasizing responsible leadership. There is a ranking of the World's Most Ethical Companies, which can be found at www.ethisphere.com.

/// **In the opening case,** Rayanne accused Kent of being unethical by trying to manipulate her into doing more work. /// Was Kent unethical? Before we end the discussion of ethics, complete Self-Assessment Exercise 3-5 to better understand how your personality and attitudes affect your ethical behavior, your moral development, and your justifications for using unethical behavior.

/ / / **Self-Assessment Exercise 3-5** / / /

Your Personality Profile and Ethics

Return to Self-Assessment Exercise 2-2, Your Big Five Personality Profile, on page 34 and place your personality profile scores below:

Surgency _____ Agreeableness _____ Adjustment _____ Conscientiousness _____ Openness to experience _____

Review the discussion of ethics above as it relates to your personality profile. How does your personality affect your ethical behavior? Which guides for ethical decisions will you use?

_____

_____

_____

Which level of moral development have you attained? How can you improve?

_____

_____

_____

Which justifications have you used? How can you improve your ethical behavior by not using justifications?

_____

_____

_____

As we bring this chapter to a close, you should understand the importance of *attitude* and that it affects your behavior, human relations, performance, and *job satisfaction* and how to change your attitudes to be more positive. Your attitude about yourself forms your *self-concept,* and you should understand how to build a more positive self-concept. You should know what is important to you (*values*). You should realize that it does pay to be ethical, as using unethical behavior hurts human relations. You should also understand your level of moral development and how you justify unethical behavior, and be able to use guides to help you use ethical behavior.

/ / / REVIEW / / /

The chapter review is organized to help you master the 9 learning outcomes for Chapter 3. First provide your own response to each learning outcome, and then check the summary provided to see how well you understand the material. Next, identify the final statement in each section as either true or false (T/F). Correct each false statement. Answers are given at the end of the chapter.

LO 3-1 Define attitudes and explain how they affect behavior, human relations, and performance.

Attitudes are strong beliefs or feelings toward people, things, and situations. If we have a positive attitude toward a person, our behavior and interactions with them will be different than our behavior with a person toward whom we have a negative attitude. A supervisor's attitude and expectations of an employee largely determine his or her performance. This is referred to as the Pygmalion effect. Positive attitudes tend to lead to higher levels of performance than negative attitudes, but not always.

Theory Y attitudes are outdated. T F

LO 3-2 Describe how to change your attitudes.

The first thing we must do is be aware of our attitudes, and make a conscious effort to change negative attitudes into positive ones. When we catch ourselves being negative, we must stop and change to a more positive attitude. We should think for ourselves, let negative attitudes go, and keep an open mind.

To change employee attitudes: (1) give them feedback, (2) accentuate positive conditions, (3) provide consequences, and (4) be a positive role model. T F

LO 3-3 List seven job satisfaction determinants.

Seven determinants of job satisfaction are: (1) satisfaction with the work itself, (2) pay and benefits, (3) growth and upward mobility, (4) supervision, (5) coworkers, (6) job security, and (7) attitude toward work.

Most American workers are dissatisfied with their jobs. T F

LO 3-4 Determine whether you have a positive self-concept and how it affects your behavior, human relations, and performance.

Answers will vary from positive to negative self-concepts. Generally, people with positive self-concepts are more outgoing and have more friends than people with negative self-concepts. They also tend to have higher levels of performance.

Your self-concept is influenced by how others treat you—their attitudes and expectations. T F

LO 3-5 Understand how your manager's and your own expectations affect your performance.

When supervisors and coworkers believe and act like employees will be successful, those employees usually are high performers. On the other hand, when supervisors and coworkers believe and act like employees will not be successful, they usually are not high performers. The Pygmalion effect, self-efficacy, and the self-fulfilling prophecy all hold true.

The Pygmalion effect tends to be based on the specific situation, whereas self-efficacy and the self-fulfilling prophecy are more constant. T F

LO 3-6 Demonstrate how to develop a more positive self-concept.

General guidelines for developing a more positive self-concept are: (1) view mistakes as a learning experience, (2) accept failure and bounce back, (3) control negative behavior and thoughts, and (4) tap into your spirituality. An action plan for building a positive self-concept includes the following steps: (1) identify your strengths and areas that need improvement, (2) set goals and visualize them, and (3) develop a plan and implement it.

Having a more positive self-concept can help you succeed in your personal and professional lives. T F

LO 3-7 Identify your personal values.

Answers will vary among students. Some personal values include professional, financial, family, social, community, spiritual, physical, and intellectual.

Spirituality in the workplace is a fad that is decreasing in popularity. T F

LO 3-8 Compare the three levels of moral development.

At the lowest level of moral development, preconventional, behavior is motivated by self-interest; one seeks to gain rewards and avoid punishment. At the second level, conventional, behavior is motivated by meeting the group's expectations to fit in by copying others' behavior. At the highest level, postconventional, behavior is motivated by the desire to do the right thing, even at the risk of alienating the group. The higher the level of moral development, the more ethical the behavior.

Most people are on the preconventional level of moral development. T F

LO 3-9 Define the following 13 key terms.

Select one or more methods: (1) fill in the missing key terms for each definition given below from memory, (2) match the key terms from the end of the review with their definitions below, and/or (3) copy the key terms in order from the key terms at the beginning of the chapter.

A(n) _____ is a strong belief or feeling toward people, things, and situations.

_____ attitudes hold that employees dislike work and must be closely supervised to get them to do their work.

_____ attitudes hold that employees like to work and do not need to be closely supervised to get them to do their work.

The _____ states that management's attitudes and expectations of employees, and how they treat them, largely determine their employees' performance.

_____ is a set of attitudes toward work.

A(n) _____ is a process of determining employee attitudes about the job and work environment.

Our _____ is our overall attitude about ourselves.

_____ is our belief in our capability to perform in a specific situation.

A(n) _____ occurs when your expectations affect your successes or failures.

_____ is one's perception of the reasons for behavior.

_____ are the things that have worth or are important to the individual.

A(n) _____ is the set of standards by which the individual lives.

_____ is the moral standard of right and wrong behavior.

/ / / KEY TERMS / / /

attitude 65	job satisfaction	self-efficacy 73	Theory Y 66
attribution 73	survey 70	self-fulfilling	values 77
ethics 78	Pygmalion effect 66	prophecy 73	value system 77
job satisfaction 70	self-concept 72	Theory X 66	

/ / / COMMUNICATION SKILLS / / /

The following critical thinking questions can be used for class discussion and/or as written assignments to develop communication skills. Be sure to give complete explanations for all questions.

1. What is your attitude toward life? Do you agree with the statement, "Life sucks, then you die"?

2. Do more managers have Theory X or Theory Y attitudes today? Be sure to give examples to back up your statements.

3. Do you really believe that you can get better results with people using the Pygmalion effect—being positive and encouraging, rather than negative and

threatening? Be sure to give examples to back up your statements.

4. Do you believe that most organizations really try to provide employees with job satisfaction? Give examples of what firms do to increase job satisfaction.

5. Is having a positive self-concept really all that important?

6. What is your view of spirituality in the workplace?

7. Do most people behave ethically at work, or do they lie, cheat, and steal?

8. Which method of justifying unethical behavior do you think is most commonly used?

CASE   / / /   **Sheryl Sandberg—Chief Operating Officer of Facebook**

Anyone who is familiar with Silicon Valley or kept up with the tech industry will no doubt recognize the name "Sheryl Sandberg." She is arguably the most influential woman in Silicon Valley. She is a much sought-after speaker on effective leadership, specifically on issues of women in the tech industry. She is an unabashed feminist who believes that women can play a more active role in eliminating sexism by being more assertive. Rather than spending too much time blaming men for the issues of inequality and pay disparity facing women, Sandberg believes women should start taking responsibility for themselves. This is the thesis of her book, *Lean In*. In it, she implores women to act in their own behalf to break down institutional and personal barriers to success.[i]

Sandberg released her most recent book on April 24, 2017, titled *Option B: Facing Adversity, Building Resilience and Finding Joy*. Two weeks after losing her husband, Sheryl said she was preparing for a father-child activity. "I want Dave," she cried. Her friend replied, "Option A is not available," and then promised to help her make the most of *Option B*. As the title suggests, this planted the seed for her latest book. It is a powerful, inspiring, and instructional guide on building resilience and moving forward after life's inevitable tragedies. As Sandberg points out, "We are not born with a fixed amount of resilience. It is a muscle that everyone can build."[ii]

Her high profile and outspokenness have led some to wonder aloud if she is the one who can "upend Silicon Valley's male-dominated culture."[iii] Ms. Sandberg has demonstrated her effectiveness as a leader not only in the way she has transformed Facebook into a highly profitable enterprise but also how she has gone about it.

Sheryl Sandberg joined Facebook in 2008 after Mark Zuckerberg, the founder, spend the better part of 2007 trying to persuade her to join him in running the company. Before joining Facebook, Sandberg was Google's vice president for global online sales and operations. Upon her arrival at Facebook, Sandberg proactively set out to present a sight of her that will immediately calm her peers and subordinates alike. It was clear her attitude was more very positive toward people and not just those in

top management. She showed an innate belief in people and their work ethic. Sandberg employs a participative, team-centered leadership style in how she runs Facebook. She is the type that will walk up to each person and introduce herself rather than waiting for people to come up to her. She wants her subordinates to let their guard down and form strong positive social relationships with her.

To transform Facebook into a profitable enterprise, Sandberg engaged in extensive debate with key employees on the best way to go about it. She did not issue orders. Facebook's business model had a compelling value proposition but a weak profit formula. In other words, it was not clear how it was going to monetize itself. Sandberg asked a series of probing questions: Should the company rely on advertising? On e-commerce? Should it charge a subscription fee? She then convened regular meetings with senior executives. During these meetings, Sandberg said she would go around the room and ask people, "What do you think?" She welcomed debate, particularly on the issues of advertising and revenue. Out of this consultative process developed a consensus that advertising was the best way to monetize Facebook. Sandberg and her team were convinced that with Facebook's growing subscription base, more and more companies would see it as an attractive advertising medium over traditional media such as TV. They were right; by 2010, a company that was bleeding cash when Sandberg arrived had become profitable. Within three years, Facebook grew from 130 employees to 2,500, and from 70 million worldwide users to nearly 700 million.

Another aspect of Sandberg that her peers and followers will agree on is that she has a real sense of self-concept, what others refer to as your "true self." She exudes self-confidence, positivity, and a high level of self-efficacy, qualities that endear her to many. As Sandberg puts it, "I believe in bringing your whole self to work. We are who we are." Being open with your employees, she believes, means that nothing is a surprise to them—even if you fire them.[iv] She shares her life, both happy and sad times, with her friends and coworkers. Sandberg disagrees with the perception that leaders who get too close to their subordinates by being their true self risk their objectivity and ability to make difficult decisions involving those same employees. Sandberg did not shy away from sharing her pain with the public when her husband Dave Goldberg died of heart-related causes on May 1, 2015. Before her husband's death, Sandberg let her audiences know what a wonderful husband, father, and friend he was to her and their children. She described her marriage as a true partnership of equals.

Today, Facebook is over a billion users, beating analysts' revenue and earnings expectations quarter after quarter and year after year. In her eighth year of running the company as COO, Sandberg has seen Facebook's revenues grow by more than 65 times, gone from a $56 million annual loss to a nearly $3.7 billion profit, and it now ranks as the fourth-most valuable tech company in the world (after Apple, Google, and Microsoft) with a market value of more than $320 billion.[v]

Go to the Internet: To learn more about Ms. Sandberg and Facebook, visit its website at www.facebook.com.

Support your answers to the following questions with specific information from the case and text or with information you get from the web or another source.

1. What seemed to be Sandberg's attitude toward her coworkers when she joined the Facebook team?

2. Using Theory X and Theory Y, describe Sandberg's management attitude.

3. What is your sense of Sandberg's self-concept, and how does it influence her leadership style?

4. How are values illustrated in the case?

5. Facebook is a multinational corporation (MNC). Which level of moral development and global corporate social responsibility (GCSR) does Facebook seem to be operating on?

Cumulative Questions

6. How has a company like Facebook influenced communication in the 21st century (Chapter 5)?

Case Exercise and Role Play

Preparation: Sheryl Sandberg wants to see more women in Silicon Valley. There are those who believe that Silicon Valley's male-dominated culture is almost impossible for women to overcome. Sandberg is of a different opinion. She believes that women can play a more active role in eliminating sexism by being more assertive. Rather than spending too much time blaming men for the issues of inequality and pay disparity facing women, Sandberg believes women should start taking responsibility for themselves. She wants women to be seen and to be heard. Sandberg wants women to have a different attitude on this issue—an assertive self-concept and self-efficacy.

Assume you are Sheryl Sandberg. Prepare a 2 to 3 minute motivational speech to a group of women that will inspire them to seek opportunities in Silicon Valley. Remind them of the importance of their attitude, self-concept, and self-efficacy as they seek opportunities in Silicon Valley. Be sure to use the text information and answers to the case questions when developing your speech.

Role-Play: Individuals (or at least one representative of a group) present their motivational talk to the class (the class represents the target audience—women), followed by a question and answer period.

OBJECTIVE CASE   / / /   Job Satisfaction

Kathy Barns was the first woman hired by Kelly Construction Co. to perform a "man's job." When Kathy was interviewed for the job by Jean Rossi, the personnel director, Kathy was excited to get the opportunity to prove a woman could do a man's job. During the first month Kathy never missed a day. However, in the second month she missed four days of work, and by the end of the month she came to tell Rossi she was quitting. Jean was surprised and wanted to find out what happened, so she asked Kathy some questions.

JEAN: How did your orientation for the job go?

KATHY: Well, the boss, Jack, started things off by telling me that he was against my being hired. He told me that a woman couldn't do the job and that I would not last very long.

JEAN: Did Jack teach you the job?

KATHY: He taught me the different parts of the job by beginning with a statement about how difficult it was. Jack made comments like "I'm watching you—don't mess up." He was constantly looking over my shoulder waiting for me to make a mistake, and when I did, he would give me the old "I told you so" speech. A couple of the guys gave me some help, but for the most part they ignored me.

JEAN: Is your job performance satisfactory?

KATHY: It's not as good as it could be, but it cannot be too bad because Jack hasn't fired me. I enjoy the work when Jack leaves me alone, and I do better work, too. But it seems he's always around.

JEAN: Are you really sure you want to quit?

KATHY: *Pauses and thinks.*

Answer the following questions. Then in the space between questions, state why you selected that answer.

_____   1. Jack had Theory _____ attitudes toward Kathy.

        a. X   *b.* Y

_____   2. Kathy started at Kelly with a _____ job attitude.

        a. positive   *b.* negative

_____   3. Most likely there _____ a relationship between Kathy's job satisfaction and her absenteeism.

        a. is   *b.* is not

_____   4. The major determinant of Kathy's job dissatisfaction is:

        a. the work itself   *c.* growth and mobility   *e.* coworkers

        b. pay   *d.* supervision   *f.* general work attitude

_____   5. Job satisfaction _____ the major reason for Kathy's performance being below her potential.

        a. is   *b.* is not

_____   6. Jack's behavior contributed to the _____ of Kathy's self-efficacy.

        a. development   *b.* deterioration

_____   7. The attribution cause for Kathy's lack of success at Kelly is:

        a. internal   *b.* external

_____   8. There _____ a relationship between Kathy's job satisfaction and her quitting (turnover).

        a. is   *b.* is not

_____   9. Kathy's _____ changed over the two months at Kelly Construction.

        a. attitude   *b.* job satisfaction   *c.* values

_____   10. This case best illustrates:

        a. Theory X   *c.* Pygmalion effect   *e.* self-fulfilling prophecy

        b. value system   *d.* self-efficacy

11. How could Jean have prevented this situation?

12. What would you do if you were in Kathy's situation?

Note: Jean's meeting with Kathy can be role-played in class.

/ / / SKILL-BUILDING EXERCISE 3-1 / / /

Self-Learning

Experience: Individual may share answers in groups or entire class, in class or online.

AACSB Competencies: Reflective thinking and analytic skills, and application of knowledge.

Objective: To better understand human behavior.

Preparation: You should have completed Self-Assessment Exercises 3-1, 3-2, and 3-3 in this chapter.

Procedure 1 (5–15 minutes)

Break into groups of two or three members, and share the answers you feel comfortable sharing in Self-Assessment Exercises 3-1, 3-2, and/or 3-3. Do not pressure anyone to share anything that makes him or her uncomfortable. Focus on your similarities and differences and the reasons for them. Your instructor will tell you if you will be doing the sharing in the next section of this exercise.

Sharing: Volunteers state the similarities and differences within their group.

Conclusion: The instructor leads a class discussion and/or makes concluding remarks.

Application: What have I learned from this exercise? How will I use this knowledge in the future?

/ / / SKILL-BUILDING EXERCISE 3-2 / / /

Building a More Positive Self-Concept

Experience: Individual may share answers in groups of 2 or 3 or entire class, in class or online.

AACSB Competences: Reflective thinking and analytic skills and application of knowledge.

Objective: To build a more positive self-concept.

Preparation: This may not be an easy exercise for you, but it could result in improving your self-concept, which has a major impact on your success in life. Below, follow the three-step plan for building a positive self-concept.

You may be asked to share your plan with a person of your choice in class. Your instructor should tell you if you will be asked to share during class. If you will share during class, do not include anything you do not wish to share. Write in the space provided, using additional pages if needed. Write a separate personal plan for yourself if you do not want to share it.

Step 1. Identify your strengths and areas for improvement.

What do I like about myself?

What can I do well? (Reflect on some of your accomplishments.)

What skills and abilities do I have to offer people and organizations?

What are the things about myself or behaviors that could be improved to help me build a more positive self-concept?

Step 2. Set goals and visualize them.

Based on your area(s) for improvement, write down some goals in a positive, affirmative format. Three to five goals are recommended as a start. Once you achieve them, go on to others.

For example:

1. I am positive and successful (not: I need to stop thinking/worrying about failure).

2. I enjoy listening to others (not: I need to stop dominating the conversation).

Visualize yourself achieving your goals. For example, imagine yourself succeeding without worrying, or visualize having a conversation you know you will have, without dominating it.

Optional. If you have a negative attitude toward yourself or others—or you would like to improve your behavior with others (family, coworkers), things, or issues (disliking school or work)—try follow the internationally known motivational speaker and trainer Zig Ziglar's system. Thousands of people have used this system successfully. This system can be used for changing personality traits as well.

Here are the steps to follow, with an example plan for a person who has a negative self-concept and also wants to be more sensitive to others. Use this example as a guide for developing your own plan.

1. *Self-concept.* Write down everything you like about yourself. List all your strengths. Then go on and list all your weaknesses. Get a good friend to help you.

2. *Make a clean new list, and using positive affirmations, write down all your strengths.* Example: "I am sensitive to others' needs."

3. *On another sheet of paper, again using positive affirmations, list all your weaknesses.* For example, don't write, "I need to lose weight." Write, "I am a slim (whatever you realistically can weigh in 30 days) pounds." Don't write, "I have to stop criticizing myself." Write, "I positively praise myself often every day." Write, "I have good communications skills," not "I am a weak communicator." The following list gives example affirmations for improving sensitivity to others. Note the repetition; you can use a thesaurus to help.

I am sensitive to others.

My behavior with others conveys my warmth for them.

I convey my concern for others.

My behavior conveys kindness toward others.

My behavior helps others build their self-esteem.

People find me easy to talk to.

I give others my full attention.

I patiently listen to others talk.

I answer others in a polite manner.

I answer questions and make comments with useful information.

My comments to others help them feel good about themselves.

I compliment others regularly.

4. *Practice.* Every morning and night for at least the next 30 days, look at yourself in the mirror and read your list of positive affirmations. Be sure to look at yourself between each affirmation as you read. Or record the list on a tape recorder and listen to it while looking at yourself in the mirror. If you are really motivated, you can repeat this step at other times of the day. Start with your areas for improvement. If it takes five minutes or more, don't bother with the list of your strengths. Or stop at five minutes; this exercise is effective in short sessions. Although miracles won't happen overnight, you may become more aware of your behavior in the first week. In the second or third week, you may become aware of yourself using new behavior successfully. You may still see some negatives, but the number will decrease in time as the positive increases.

Psychological research has shown that if a person hears something believable repeated for 30 days, they will tend to believe it. Ziglar says that you cannot consistently perform in a manner that is inconsistent with the way you see yourself. So, as you listen to your positive affirmations, you will believe them, and you will behave in a manner that is consistent with your belief. Put simply, your behavior will change with your thoughts without a lot of hard work. For example, if you listen to the affirmation, "I am an honest person" (not, "I have to stop lying"), in time—without having to work at it—you will tell the truth. At first you may feel uncomfortable reading or listening to positive affirmations that you don't really believe you have. But keep looking at yourself in the mirror and reading or listening, and with time you will feel comfortable and believe it and live it.

Are you thinking you don't need to improve, or that this method will not work? Yes, this system often does work. Zig Ziglar has trained thousands of satisfied people. I tried the system myself, and within two or three weeks, I could see improvement in my behavior. The question isn't, Will the system work for you? but rather, Will you work the system to improve?

5. *When you slip, and we all do, don't get down on yourself.* In the sensitivity-to-others example, if you are rude to someone and catch yourself, apologize and change to a positive tone. Effective leaders admit when they are wrong and apologize. If you have a hard time admitting you are wrong and saying you are sorry, at least be obviously nice so that the other person realizes you are saying you are sorry indirectly. Then forget about it and keep trying. Focus on your successes, not your slips. Don't let 10 good discussions be ruined by one insensitive comment. If you were a baseball player and got 9 out of 10 hits, you'd be the best in the world.

6. *Set another goal.* After 30 days, select a new topic, such as developing a positive attitude toward work or school, or trying a specific leadership style that you want to develop. You can also include more than one area to work on.

Step 3. Develop a plan and implement it.

For each of your goals, state what you will do to achieve it. What specific action will you take to improve your self-concept through changing your thoughts or behavior? Number your plans to correspond with your goals.

Procedure 1 (2-4 minutes)

Break into teams of two. You may make a group of three if you prefer. Try to work with someone with whom you feel comfortable sharing your plan.

Procedure 2 (10-20 minutes)

Using your preparation plan, share your answers one at a time. It is recommended that you both share on each step and question before proceeding to the next. The choice is yours, but be sure you get equal time. For example, one person states, "what I like about myself." The other person follows with his or her response. After both share, go on to cover "what I do well," and so on. During your sharing, you may offer each other helpful suggestions, but do so in a positive way; remember you are helping one another build a more positive self-concept. Avoid saying anything that could be considered a put-down.

Conclusion: The instructor may lead a class discussion and/or make concluding remarks.

Application (2-4 minutes): Will I implement my plan? If so, will I succeed at developing a more positive self-concept? What have I learned through this experience?

/ / / SKILL-BUILDING EXERCISE 3-3 / / /

Giving and Accepting Compliments

Experience: Small groups in class

AACSB Competencies: Analytic skills and communication abilities and application of knowledge.

Objective: To give and accept compliments as a means to improving self-concept.

Preparation: Recall that one of the human relations guidelines is to help others. One way to help others is to give them compliments that will help them develop and maintain a positive self-concept. Also, as stated in this chapter, never minimize compliments, but accept them with a thank you. This exercise is based on these two points.

Procedure 1 (2 minutes)

Break into groups of four to six, preferably with people you know.

Procedure 2 (4–8 minutes)

Each person in the group thinks of a sincere, positive compliment to give to each group member (for instance, make a comment on why you like the person). When everyone is ready, one person volunteers to receive first. All the other members give that person a compliment. Proceed until everyone, one at a time, has received a compliment from everyone else.

Procedure 3 (3–6 minutes)

Each group discusses the following questions:

1. How did it feel to receive the compliments? Were you tempted to—or did you—minimize a compliment?
2. How do you feel about people who give you compliments versus those who give you criticism? Is there a difference in your human relations between people in these two groups?
3. How did it feel to give the compliments?
4. What is the value of giving compliments?
5. Will you make an effort to compliment yourself and others?

Conclusion: The instructor may lead a class discussion and/or make concluding remarks. In Chapter 7, Skill-Building Exercise 7-2, Giving Praise (page 246), you can develop the skill of giving compliments.

Application: Write out your answer to question 5 above as the application question.

/ / / SKILL-BUILDING EXERCISE 3-4 / / /

Ethics and Whistle-Blowing

Experience: Individual may share answers in groups or entire class, in class or online.

AACSB Competencies: Reflective thinking and ethical understanding and reasoning, and application of knowledge.

Objective: To better understand ethics and whistle-blowing.

Preparation: You should have completed Self-Assessment Exercise 3-4, How Ethical Is Your Behavior?

Procedure 1 (5 minutes)

Briefly answer the following questions related to Self-Assessment Exercise 3-4:

1. For "College" items 1 through 3, who is harmed and who benefits from these unethical behaviors?
2. For "Job" items 4 through 24, select the three (circle their numbers) that you consider the most severe unethical behavior. Who is harmed and who benefits by these unethical behaviors?
3. If you observed unethical behavior but didn't report it, why didn't you blow the whistle? If you did, why did you report the unethical behavior? What was the result?
4. As a manager, it is your responsibility to uphold ethical behavior. If you know employees are using unethical behavior, will you take action to enforce compliance with ethical standards?
5. What can you do to prevent unethical behavior?
6. As part of the class discussion, share the "Other Unethical Behavior" you have observed. If you didn't add any, try to do so until the time is up.

Procedure 2 (15–30 minutes)

Option A: Break into groups of five or six, and share your answers to the questions. The instructor will tell the group if they should select a spokesperson to report to the entire class.

Option B: The instructor leads a discussion in which students share their answers to the questions. (The instructor may begin by going over the statements and have students who have observed the behavior raise their hands.) Then the instructor will have them raise their hands if they reported the behavior.

Conclusion: The instructor may lead a class discussion and/or make concluding remarks.

Application (2–4 minutes):   What did I learn from this exercise? How will I use this knowledge in the future?

Sharing: Volunteers give their answers to the application section.

/ / / SKILL-BUILDING EXERCISE 3-5 / / /

Developing New Habits

Experience: Individual may share Habits in groups or entire class, in class or online.

AACSB Competencies: Analytic and application of knowledge.

Objective: To develop and share new habits.

Preparation: Select one or more topics from this chapter that will help you improve your human relations. Develop a new habit following the guideline from Chapter 1, section Habits and Skill-Building Exercise 1-4, on how to develop your cure, routine, and reward-change.

Procedure (5–30 minutes)

Follow the procedures from Skill Builder 1-4.

/ / ANSWERS TO TRUE/FALSE QUESTIONS / /

1. F. Theory X attitudes are outdated and being replaced with Theory Y attitudes.
2. T.
3. F. Two-thirds of Americans would take the same job again and 90 percent are at least somewhat satisfied with their jobs.
4. T.
5. F. Self-efficacy is your belief in your ability to perform in a specific situation. The Pygmalion effect and self-fulfilling prophecy are more constant.
6. T.
7. F. This was not stated in the book, and it is not true.
8. F. Most people are on the conventional level of moral development.

/ / / N O T E S / / /

1. D.H. Wo, M.L. Ambrose, and M. Schminke, "What Drives Trickle-Down Effects? A Test of Multiple Mediation Processes," *Academy of Management Journal* 58(6) (2015): 1484–1868.

2. R.C. Liden, S.J. Wayne, C. Liao, J.D. Meuser, "Servant Leadership and Serving Culture: Influence on Individual and Unit Performance, *Academy of Management Journal* 57(5) (2014): 1434–1452.

3. S. Diestel, J. Wegge, and K.H. Schmidt, "The Impact of Social Context on the Relationship between Individual Job Satisfaction and Absenteeism: The Roles of Different Foci of Job Satisfaction and Work-Unit Absenteeism," *Academy of Management Journal* 57(2) (2014): 353–382.

4. R.C. Liden, S.J. Wayne, C. Liao, J.D. Meuser, "Servant Leadership and Serving Culture: Influence on Individual and Unit Performance, *Academy of Management Journal* 57(5) (2014): 1434–1452.

5. D.L. Ferris, H. Lian, D.J. Brown, and R. Morrison, "Ostracism, Self-Esteem and Job Performance" When Do We Self-Verify and When Do We Self-Enhance?" *Academy of Management Journal* 58(1) (2015): 279–297.

6. G. O'Brien, "Questions and Answers," *Entrepreneur* (September 2015): 36.

7. J.A. Clair, "Procedural Injustice in the System of Peer Review and Scientific Misconduct," *Academy of Management Learning & Education* 14(2) (2015): 159–172.

8. R.C. Liden, S.J. Wayne, C. Liao, J.D. Meuser, "Servant Leadership and Serving Culture: Influence on Individual and Unit Performance," *Academy of Management Journal* 57(5) (2014): 1434–1452.

9. L. Gellman, "When a Job Offer Comes Without a Job," *The Wall Street Journal* (December 2, 2015): B1, B7.

10. A. Kirkman, "It's All About Attitude," *Fortune* (November 17, 2014): 34.

11. F.P. Morgeson, T.R. Mitchell, and D. Liu, "Event System Theory: An Event-Oriented Approach to the Organizational Sciences," *Academy of Management Review* 40(4) (2015): 515–537.

12. D. Antons and F.T. Piller, "Opening the Black Box of Not Invented Here: Attitudes, Decision Biases, and Behavioral Consequences," *Academy of Management Perspectives* 29(2) (2015): 193–217.

13. D.H. Wo, M.L. Ambrose, and M. Schminke, "What Drives Trickle-Down Effects? A Test of Multiple Mediation Processes," *Academy of Management Journal* 58(6) (2015): 1484–1868.

14. M. Cording, J.S. Harrison, R.E. Hoskisson, and K. Jonsen, "Walking the Talk: A Multistakeholder Exploration of Organizational Authenticity, Employee Productivity, and Post-Merger Performance," *Academy of Management Perspectives* 28(1) (2014): 38–56.

15. A.C. Peng, J.M. Schaubroeck, and L. Li, "Social Exchange Implications of Own and Coworkers' Experiences of Supervisor Abuse," *Academy of Management Journal* 57(5) (2014): 1385–1405.

16. D. Liu, H. Liao, and R. Loi, "The Dark Side of Leadership: A Three-Level Investigation of the Cascading Effect of Abusive Supervision Employee Creativity," *Academy of Management Journal* 55(5) (2012): 1187–1212.

17. A.C. Peng, J.M. Schaubroeck, and L. Li, "Social Exchange Implications of Own and Coworkers' Experiences of Supervisor Abuse," *Academy of Management Journal* 57(5) (2014): 1385–1405.

18. R.C. Liden, S.J. Wayne, C. Liao, J.D. Meuser, "Servant Leadership and Serving Culture: Influence on Individual and Unit Performance," *Academy of Management Journal* 57(5) (2014): 1434–1452.

19. E. Bernstein, "You Can Do IT! Be a Motivator," *The Wall Street Journal* (June 16, 2016): D1, D3.

20. R.C. Liden, S.J. Wayne, C. Liao, J.D. Meuser, "Servant Leadership and Serving Culture: Influence on Individual and Unit Performance," *Academy of Management Journal* 57(5) (2014): 1434–1452.

21. B.A. Scott, A.S. Garza, D.E. Conlong and Y.J. Kim, "Why Do Managers Act Fairly in the First Place? A Daily Investigation of Hot and Cold Motives and Discretion," *Academy of Management Journal* 57(6) (2014): 1571–1591.

22. D.L. Ferris, H. Lian, D.J. Brown, and R. Morrison, "Ostracism, Self-Esteem and Job Performance" When Do We Self-Verify and When Do We Self-Enhance?" *Academy of Management Journal* 58(1) (2015): 279–297.

23. R. King, "Companies Want to Know: How Do Workers Feel?" *The Wall Street Journal* (October 14, 2015): R3.

24. R.E. Silverman, "Are You Happy in Your Job? Bosses Push Weekly Surveys," *The Wall Street Journal* (December 3, 2014): B1, B4.

25. A.Meister, K.A. Jehn, S.M.B. Thatcher, "Feeling Misidentified: The Consequences of Internal Identify Asymmetries for Individuals at Work," *Academy of Management Review* 39(4) (2014): 488–512.

26. B.A. Scott, A.S. Garza, D.E. Conlong and Y.J. Kim, "Why Do Managers Act Fairly in the First Place? A Daily Investigation of Hot and Cold Motives and Discretion," *Academy of Management Journal* 57(6) (2014): 1571–1591.

27. A. Meister, K.A. Jehn, S.M.B. Thatcher, "Feeling Misidentified: The Consequences of Internal Identify Asymmetries for Individuals at Work," *Academy of Management Review* 39(4) (2014): 488–512.

28. O. Obodaru, "The Self Not Taken: How Alternative Selves Develop and How They Influence Our Professional Lives," *Academy of Management Review* 37(1) (2010): 34–57.

29. M.S. Christian and A.P.J. Ellis, "Examing the Effects of Sleep Deprivation Workplace Deviance: A Self-Regulatory Perspective," *Academy of Management Journal* 54(5) (2010): 913–934.

30. D.L. Ferris, H. Lian, D.J. Brown, and R. Morrison, "Ostracism, Self-Esteem and Job Performance" When Do We Self-Verify and When Do We Self-Enhance?" *Academy of Management Journal* 58(1) (2015): 279–297.

31. D.L. Ferris, H. Lian, D.J. Brown, and R. Morrison, "Ostracism, Self-Esteem and Job Performance" When Do We Self-Verify and When Do We Self-Enhance?" *Academy of Management Journal* 58(1) (2015): 279–297.

32. A. Meister, K.A. Jehn, S.M.B. Thatcher, "Feeling Misidentified: The Consequences of Internal Identify Asymmetries for Individuals at Work," *Academy of Management Review* 39(4) (2014): 488–512.

33. D.V. Caprar, B. Do, S.L. Rynes, and J.M. Bartunek, "It's Personal: An Exploration of Students' (non) Acceptance of Management Research," *Academy of Management Learning & Education* 15(2) (2016): 207–231.

34. D. Sterling, "Best Advice," *Fortune* (October 1, 2015): 116.

35. R. McCammon, "How to Own the Room," *BusinessWeek* accessed online March 24, 2017.

36. A. Murray, "Should Leaders Be Modest," *Fortune* (September 15, 2015): 28.

37. M. Javidan, A. Bullough, and R. Dibble, "Mind the Gap: Gender Differences in Global Leadership Self-Efficacies," *Academy of Management Perspectives* 30(1) (2016): 59–73.

38. D. Sterling, "Best Advice," *Fortune* (October 1, 2015): 116.

39. M. Whelan, "Best Advice," *Fortune* (October 1, 2015): 114.

40. V. Desai, "Learning Through the Distribution of Failures within an Organization: Evidence from Heart Bypass Surgery Performance," *Academy of Management Journal* 58(4) (2015): 1032–1050.

41. P. Jacquart and J. Antonakis, "When Does Charism Matter for Top-Level Leaders? Effect of Attributional Ambiguity," *Academy of Management Journal* 58(4) (2015): 1051–1074.

42. D.L. Ferris, H. Lian, D.J. Brown, and R. Morrison, "Ostracism, Self-Esteem and Job Performance" When Do We Self-Verify and When Do We Self-Enhance?" *Academy of Management Journal* 58(1) (2015): 279–297.

43. V. Desai, "Learning Through the Distribution of Failures within an Organization: Evidence from Heart Bypass Surgery Performance," *Academy of Management Journal* 58(4) (2015): 1032–1050.

44. Zig Ziglar www.ziglar.com Retrieved April 3, 2017.

45. E. Bernstein, "Self Talk, or a Heart-to-Heart With Your Closest Friend," *The Wall Street Journal* (May 6, 2014): D1, D2.

46. Zig Ziglar www.ziglar.com Retrieved April 3, 2017.

47. T. Robbins, "Questions Are the Answer," *Fortune* (November 17, 2014): 140.

48. Editors, "Organizations With Purpose," *Academy of Management Journal* 57(5) (2014): 1227–1234.

49. J. Strober, "Prioritize," *Entrepreneur* (January 2016): 49.

50. G. O'Brien, "Questions and Answers," *Entrepreneur* (September 2015): 36.

51. B. Barron, "Margin note," *Fortune* (November 17, 2014): 138.

52. Edgewalkers International http://edgewalkers.org/ Retrieved April 3, 2017.

53. Edgewalkers International http://edgewalkers.org/ Retrieved April 3, 2017.

54. Marripedia! marripedia.org Retrieved April 3, 2017.

55. K. Leavitt and D.M. Sluss, "Lying for Who We Are: An Identity-Based Model of Workplace Dishonesty," *Academy of Management Review* 40(4) (2014): 587–610.

56. D. Ariely, "Why We Lie," *The Wall Street Journal* (May 26-27, 2012): C1-C2.

57. S.D. Levitt and S.J. Dubner, "SuperFreakonomics: Global Cooling, Patriotic Prostitutes, and Why Suicide Bombers Should Buy Life Insurance," *Academy of Management Perspectives* 25(2) (2011): 86-87.

58. K. Leavitt and D.M. Sluss, "Lying for Who We Are: An Identity-Based Model of Workplace Dishonesty," *Academy of Management Review* 40(4) (2015): 587-610.

59. G. O'Brien, "Sparring Partners," *Entrepreneur* (August 2015): 32.

60. K. Leavitt and D.M. Sluss, "Lying for Who We Are: An Identity-Based Model of Workplace Dishonesty," *Academy of Management Review* 40(4) (2015): 587-610.

61. G. Colvin, "Personal Bests," *Fortune* (March 15, 2015): 106-110.

62. C. Carr, "Stress to Impress," *Costco Connection* (February 2015): 13.

63. Bonanos, "The Lies We Tell at Work," *BusinessWeek* (February 4-10, 2013): 71-73.

64. A.C. Cosper, "Meet Fear's Antidote: Hope," *Entrepreneur* (January 2016): 10.

65. O. Hindawi, "margin note," *Fortune* (October 1, 2015): 114.

66. I. Nooyi, "Reviewer of The Road to Character," *Fortune* (December 1, 2015): 22.

67. K. Leavitt and D.M. Sluss, "Lying for Who We Are: An Identity-Based Model of Workplace Dishonesty," *Academy of Management Review* 40(4) (2015): 587-610.

68. G. O'Brien, "Points of Difference," *Entrepreneur* (January 2016): 20.

69. G.K. Stahl and M.S. De Luque, "Antecedents of Responsible Leader Behavior: A Research Synthesis Conceptual Framework, and Agenda for Future Research," *Academy of Management Perspectives* 28(3) (2014): 235-254.

70. S. Bing, "Does the Truth Matter?" *Fortune* (May 1, 2016): 136.

71. *National Public Radio* (NPR) aired March 28, 2017.

72. *National Public Radio* (NPR) aired September 7, 2016.

73. M. Kelly, *Rediscovering Catholicism* (New York: Beacon, 2010).

74. Contents, "Adapted from a quote," *BusinessWeek* (September 7-13, 2015): 3.

75. R. McCammon, "So, Here's the Bad News ..." *Entrepreneur* (July 2015): 24-25.

76. C. Hann, "Truth Time," *Entrepreneur* (March 2016): 24.

77. C. Bonanos, "The Lies We Tell at Work," *BusinessWeek* (February 4-10, 2013): 71-73.

78. E. Bernstein, "Honey, You Never Said...," *The Wall Street Journal* (March 24, 2015): D1,D4.

79. R. Fehr, K.C. Yam, and C. Dang, "Moralized Leadership: The Construction and Consequences of Ethical Leader Perceptions," *Academy of Management Review* 40(2) (2015): 182-209.

80. L. Daska, "4 Pieces of Advice Most People Ignore (but Great Entrepreneurs Don't)," *INC.* (July/August 2015): 8.

81. S.D. Levitt and S.J. Dubner, "SuperFreakonomics: Global Cooling, Patriotic Prostitutes, and Why Suicide Bombers Should Buy Life Insurance," *Academy of Management Perspectives* 25(2) (2011): 86-87.

82. R. Fehr, K.C. Yam, and C. Dang, "Moralized Leadership: The Construction and Consequences of Ethical Leader Perceptions," *Academy of Management Review* 40(2) (2015): 182-209.

83. K.Y. Hsieh, W. Tsai, and M.J. Chen, "If They Can Do It, Why Not Us? Competitors as Reference Points for Justifying Escalation of Commitment," *Academy of Management Journal* 56(1) (2015): 38-58.

84. H. Willmott, "Reflections on the Darker Side of Conventional Power Analytics," *Academy of Management Perspectives* 27(4) (2013): 281-286.

85. D. Ariely, "Why We Lie," *The Wall Street Journal* (May 26-27, 2012): C1, C2.

86. D. Baden, "Look on the Bright Side: A Comparison of Positive and Negative Role Models in Business Ethics Education," *Academy of Management Learning & Education* 13(2) (2014): 154-170.

87. D. Crilly, M. Hansen, M. Zollo, "The Grammar of Decoupling: A Cognitive-Linguistic Perspective on Firms' Sustainability Claims and Stakeholder' Interpretation," *Academy of Management Journal* 59(2) (2016): 705-729.

88. Contents, "Adapted from a quote," *BusinessWeek* (September 7-13, 2015): 3.

89. D. Ariely, "Why We Lie," *The Wall Street Journal* (May 26-27, 2012): C1-C2.

90. D.T. Welsh and L.D. Ordonez, "Conscience Without Cognition: The Effects of Subconscious Priming on Ethical Behavior," *Academy of Management Journal* 57(5) (2014): 723–1109.

91. R. Fehr, K.C. Yam, and C. Dang, "Moralized Leadership: The Construction and Consequences of Ethical Leader Perceptions," *Academy of Management Review* 40(2) (2015): 182–209.

92. S.S. Wiltermuth, "Power, Moral Clarity, and Punishment in the Workplace," *Academy of Management Journal* 57(3) (2014): 849–868.

93. B.A. Scott, A.S. Garza, D.E. Conlong and Y.J. Kim, "Why Do Managers Act Fairly in the First Place? A Daily Investigation of Hot and Cold Motives and Discretion," *Academy of Management Journal* 57(6) (2014): 1571–1591.

94. M. Javidan, A. Bullough, and R. Dibble, "Mind the Gap: Gender Differences in Global Leadership Self-Efficacies," *Academy of Management Perspectives* 30(1) (2016): 59–73.

 i. J. Bercovici, "Inside the Mind of Facebook's Sheryl Sandberg," *Inc Magazine* (2015).

 ii. http://www.audible.com/pd/Bios-Memoirs/Option-B-Audiobook/B06WRSP9B1/ref=a_search__c4_1_1_srTtl/134-6075244-6908945?qid=1494025406&sr=1-1

iii. K. Auletta, "A Woman's Place: Can Sheryl Sandberg upend Silicon Valley's male-dominated culture?" *The New York Times* (2011).

iv. K. Auletta, "A Woman's Place: Can Sheryl Sandberg upend Silicon Valley's male-dominated culture?" *The New York Times* (2011).

 v. M. Rosoff, "Look at how much Sheryl Sandberg has done for Facebook," *Business Insider* (March 23, 2016).

PART 2

Interpersonal Skills:
The Foundation of Human Relations

Communications, Emotions, and Criticism

©John Lund/Nevada Wier/Getty Images

After completing this chapter, you should be able to:

LO 4-1   Describe how communication flows through organizations.

LO 4-2   List and explain the four steps in the communication process.

LO 4-3   List the five steps in the message-sending process.

LO 4-4   Describe how to get feedback.

LO 4-5   List the three steps in the message-receiving process.

LO 4-6   Define five response styles.

LO 4-7   List the four situational supervisory styles and the four variables to consider in selecting the appropriate communication style.

LO 4-8   Discuss what should and should not be done to calm an emotional person.

LO 4-9   Describe how to get criticism effectively.

LO 4-10   Define the following 14 key terms (in order of appearance in the chapter):

organizational structure	message
organizational communication	decoding
	paraphrasing
vertical communication	feedback
horizontal communication	emotional labor
grapevine	empathic listening
communication process	reflecting statements
encoding	

OPENING CASE WORK SCENARIO

/ / / Janet Low was driving to her new job at the Ford Assembly Plant, thinking about Ford's organizational structure and how she would fit in and communicate with her boss and peers. Would people talk to her and be willing to listen to her and get to know her personally, and would she make new friends? Janet is sensitive, and on her last job the boss was very critical. She was dedicated to doing her best in the hopes that her new boss wouldn't have to criticize her too often. Janet was feeling emotionally excited and wondered how she would like the job. / / /

HOW COMMUNICATIONS, EMOTIONS, AND CRITICISM AFFECT BEHAVIOR, HUMAN RELATIONS, HAPPINESS, AND PERFORMANCE

In this chapter, we take the intrapersonal skills foundation from the first three chapters and start building interpersonal skills in this second section of the book. We present communications from two levels. We start with the organizational level in the next section and proceed to interpersonal communications in sections three to six. In the last section we discuss how emotions and criticism affect communications.

Communication skills are the foundation of human relations, as we initiate, build, and maintain relationships through communications to make us happy.[1] Recall that behavior is what we do and say. Thus, communication skills are a transferable competency between your personal and professional lives.[2] Communication is vital for the success of organizations, both within and outside the organization,[3] because it affects performance.[4] That is why communication and interpersonal skills are ranked as the most important attributes recruiters look for in job candidates,[5] and why AACSB accreditation requires teaching and assessing communication abilities.[6] When communicating, if people get too emotional, such as when being criticized, it can negatively affect their behavior, human relations, happiness, and performance.[7]

ORGANIZATIONAL STRUCTURE AND COMMUNICATION

In this section, we describe how communications flow through organizations. We begin by identifying how organizations are structured, which influences the flow of communications.

Organizational Structure

Organizational structure refers to *the way managers design their firm to achieve the organization's mission and goals.* Managers design formal structures to organize its resources.[8] The organization's structure determines who works together, and organizational communication flows through this structure.[9] In the development of an organizational structure, there are five important questions to be answered. See Exhibit 4.1 for the questions and the principles used to find the answers. See Exhibit 4.2 for an illustration of an organization chart.

WORK APPLICATION 4-1

Give a specific example in which communication affected your behavior, human relations, and performance.

WORK APPLICATION 4-2

Select an organization for which you work or have worked. Is the division of labor specialized? Identify the chain of command from your job to the top of the organization. How many people are in your boss's span of management? Is authority centralized or decentralized? How is work coordinated?

EXHIBIT 4.1 | Designing Organizational Structure

Question	Organization Principle Used to Answer Question
1. How should we subdivide the work?	**Division of labor** (the degree to which tasks are subdivided into separate jobs) **Departmentalization** (grouping of related activities into units)
2. To whom should departments and individuals report?	**Chain of command** (the line of authority from the top to the bottom of the organization, which is shown in an organization chart)
3. How many individuals should report to each manager?	**Span of management** (number of subordinates)
4. At what level should decisions be made?	**Centralized or decentralized authority** (With centralized authority, top managers make important decisions. With decentralized authority, lower-level managers make important decisions.)
5. How do we get everyone to work together as a system?	**Coordination** (implementing the other four principles to achieve organizational mission and goals)

EXHIBIT 4.2 | Organization Chart

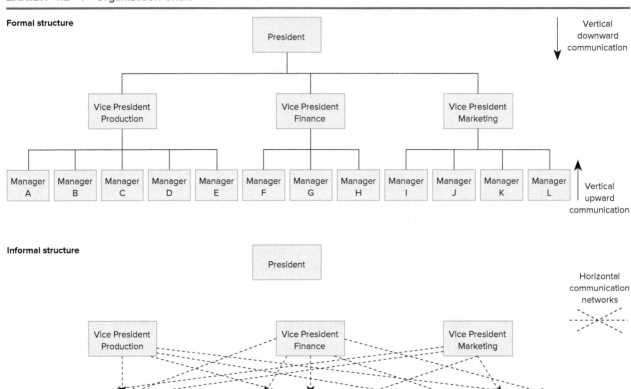

WORK APPLICATION 4-3

Draw an organization chart illustrating the departments in the organization for which you work or have worked.

Some of the organizational structure trends are as follows. Top managers are streamlining structures by getting rid of layers of management. Organizations are increasingly using a team-based structure. Large multinational companies (MNCs) tend to have multibusinesses (companies within one company) and refer to them as business units (BUs), and these BUs create what is called an M-form structure.

Learning Outcome 4-1

Describe how communication flows through organizations.

Organizational Communication

In general, **organizational communication** is *the compounded interpersonal communication process across an organization.* Communication within an organization flows in a vertical, horizontal, or lateral way throughout the firm.[10] It may also be conveyed through the grapevine, which goes in all directions.

Vertical Communication   **Vertical communication** is *the flow of information both up and down the chain of command.* It is often called *formal communication* because it follows the chain of command and is recognized as official. It flows both upward and downward.[11]

WORK APPLICATION 4-4

Give a specific example of when you used vertical communication. Identify it as upward or downward.

When your boss tells you what to do, the manager is using downward communication. When you communicate with your boss or higher-level managers, you are using upward communication.

For an illustration of downward and upward vertical communication, see Exhibit 4.2.

WORK APPLICATION 4-5

Give a specific example of when you used horizontal communication.

Horizontal Communication   **Horizontal communication** is *the flow of information between colleagues and peers.* It is often called *informal and lateral communication* because it does not follow the chain of command, and you may also communicate with people outside the organization.[12] Most messages processed by an organization are carried via informal channels. As an employee, you may find it necessary to communicate with your peers, employees in other departments, and people outside the organization, such as customers, to meet your objectives.

Communication Skills
Refer to CS Question 1.

Grapevine Communication   The **grapevine** is *the informal vehicle through which messages flow throughout the organization.* The grapevine will always exist. It should be considered a communication vehicle.

> Rather than ignore or try to repress the grapevine, tune in to it. Identify the key people in the organization's grapevine and feed them information. To help prevent incorrect rumors, keep the information flowing through the grapevine as accurate and rumor-free as possible. Share all nonconfidential information with employees; tell them of changes as far in advance as possible. Encourage employees to ask questions about rumors they hear.

Gossiping about people can really hurt your human relations with them when they find out about it. In a diverse workplace, it is even more important to be careful about what you say about those who are different from you. The adage "If you can't say anything good about someone, don't say anything at all" is a good human relations rule to follow.

WORK APPLICATION 4-6

Give a specific example of a message you heard through the grapevine. How accurate was it? Was it the same message that management sent?

APPLICATION   SITUATIONS / / /

Communication Flow   AS 4-1

Identify the communication flow as:

A. Vertical–downward   B. Vertical–upward

C. Horizontal   D. Grapevine

_____ 1. "Juan, here is the report you asked me to complete. Let me know if I need to make any changes."

_____ 2. "Jackson, I just closed a larger sales order with Tyson, but I had to guarantee delivery by next Tuesday. Can you produce 100 units on time?"

_____ 3. "Hi Tyler, please take this over to the mail room right away for me."

_____ 4. "Jamal, have you heard that President Flynn is using the company jet to take his mistress out on dates?"

_____ 5. "Judy, will you please hold this so I can put it together–the way I help you all the time?"

Digital Information Technology

Some people prefer personal face-to-face communication, whereas others prefer electronic communications.[13] Either way, digital information technology has clearly changed the way we communicate in our personal and professional lives.[14] Although ability to use technology is a predictor of performance, interpersonal skills remain the key to effective communications.[15] In **Appendix A** we will discuss *digital etiquette* to follow when communicating digitally.

Communication Skills
Refer to CS Question 2.

The Internet, E-Mail, Texting, Skyping, and Wireless Communications   The Internet is a global collection of computer networks linked together to exchange data and information, and the World Wide Web (WWW) is a segment of the Internet in which information is presented in the form of web pages. Three key information technologies used to access the Internet are computers, phones, and handheld devices. E-mail is now the most common way people communicate at work.[16] We went from using hardwired computers to wireless laptops, to notebooks, tablets, and smartphones. And we moved from talking on the phone to Facetiming and Skypeing.[17]

E-Commerce, Mobile Workers, and M-Commerce   *E-commerce* or *e-business* (E = electronic) is work done by using electronic linkages (including the Internet) between employees, partners, suppliers, and customers. A new trend is machine-to-machine (M2M) to connect all our digital devices.

Today, many employees don't have to come to the office to work, as more business is conducted using mobile devices. In 2014, business spending on mobile devices overtook spending on fixed devices. More people are shopping using mobile (*m-commerce*) devices. Are you a m-commerce buyer?

Communication Skills
Refer to CS Question 3.

Social Media   The social networking sites are not only being used by individuals as a way to communicate with friends. Social media, such as **LinkedIn**, are commonly used for networking to get a job. Social media work well to foster in-person meetings.[18]

To better connect with younger workers and customers, many companies are increasing their presence on social media, such as **Facebook, LinkedIn,** and others. Organizations are also using social media to screen job applicants. If they find nonprofessional pictures of candidates, they will not hire them. **Broadcom CEO Scott McGregor** advises that you should never post anything on social media that you wouldn't want your parents (or employer) to see.[19]

WORK APPLICATION 4-7

Give specific examples of how you use digital information technology to communicate.

Cloud Computing   *Cloud computing,* broadly speaking, is any service or program sent over an Internet connection. Cloud computing enables a company and individuals to tap into raw computing power, storage, software applications, and data from large data centers over the Internet. Using the cloud lets businesses avoid building their own data centers. The following are some of the many providers with their cloud-based services: the *Elastic Compute Cloud* is from **Amazon, IBM** offers *Cloudburst,* **EMC** has *Decho,* and **Microsoft** provides *Azure.*

Confidentiality and Security   Communication technology is great, but it is challenging to keep our information confidential and secure.[20] Businesses are working to stop information theft by employees and hackers who have managed to steal information leading to identity theft at **Yahoo, Home Depot,** and others.

The Downside of Technology   One of the downsides of electronic communications is that it is dehumanized and depersonalized, which is less effective at developing relationships.[21] Our brains actually respond differently to in-person interactions vs. virtual.[22] Face-to-face communications can make us healthier, happier, and smarter.[23] With text and e-mails, you can't see the person and therefore miss nonverbal social cues and body language. When you push the "send" or "like button" you miss seeing people smile and laugh.

Another issue related to the business of getting work done is that technology is inappropriately used on the job. Some 83 percent of employees admitted using work computers for personal use.[24] In a survey, 23 percent of recent graduates said they wouldn't take a job if they couldn't make personal phone calls.[25] Would you? On the other side, employees are expected to be using mobile devices to check for messages during nonbusiness hours, contributing to workaholic tendencies as professional and personal lives blur.[26] Are you addicted to your smartphone?

/// **In the opening case,** Ford is a large MNC with a complex organizational structure with communications flowing in all directions both with and without the use of digital technology. Janet wants to make new friends at work, and will likely use social media. ///

Learning Outcome 4-2

List and explain the four steps in the communication process.

THE COMMUNICATION PROCESS, BARRIERS, AND DIFFERENCES

Now that we have a foundation in organizational structure and communication flow organizationwide, for the rest of the chapter, let's focus more on interpersonal communications, which are often between two people face-to-face.[27] In this section, we begin with an explanation of the communication process, followed by barriers to communications. Next we discuss differences in communications between genders, and we end with difference by culture.

The Communication Process

WORK APPLICATION 4-8

Which message transmission channels do you use most often at work?

The **communication process** consists of *a sender who encodes a message and transmits it through a channel to a receiver who decodes it and may give feedback.* Exhibit 4.3 illustrates the communication process. Below is a brief explanation of each step in the communication process;[28] you will learn the details of each step in separate sections of this chapter.

In step 1, the sender encodes the message and selects the transmission channel. The *sender* of the message is the person who initiates the communication. **Encoding** is *the sender's process of putting the message into a form that the receiver will understand.* The message is *the physical form of the encoded information.* The **message** is transmitted through a channel. The three primary *communication channels* you can use are oral, nonverbal, and written. See Exhibit 4.4 for the various transmission channel options.[29] When selecting a channel, you need to remember that people do have different preferences.[30] For example, many younger people like to text, whereas older people do not. You also need to select proper words to convey what you actually mean.[31]

In step 2, the sender transmits the message through a channel. As the sender, after you encode the message and select the channel, you transmit the message through the channel to one or more receivers.[32]

In step 3, the receiver decodes the message and decides whether feedback is needed. The person receiving the message decodes it. **Decoding** is *the receiver's process of translating the message into a meaningful form.* We all decode words so that the message makes sense to us. The receiver decides if feedback, a response, or a new message is needed.

Step 4 is feedback: a response or a new message may be transmitted. After decoding the message, the receiver may give feedback to the sender. Note that the roles of sender and receiver can change during a communication exchange.

EXHIBIT 4.3 | The Communication Process

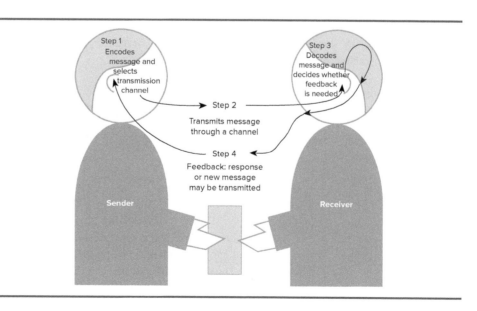

EXHIBIT 4.4 | Message Transmission Channels

Oral Communication	Nonverbal Communication	Written Communication
Face-to-face conversations	Setting	Memos
Presentations	Body language	Letters
Meetings	Facial expressions	Reports
Telephone conversations	Vocal quality	E-mails, instant messages, texts
Voice-mail messages	Gestures	Faxes
	Posture	Bulletin boards
	Posters (pictures)	Posters (words)
		Newsletters
Personal or Digital	**Personal or Digital**	**Personal or Digital**
Face-to-face is personal communications; presentations can use digital PowerPoint; meetings can be in person or via webcam teleconferencing; and telephone calls and messages use digital technology.	Nonverbal communications can be seen in person and digitally via webcam teleconferencing.	Most of these channels can be a more personal hard copy or digital copy. Memos are commonly used for internal communications and sent digitally or e-mailed, whereas letters are commonly on company letterhead and mailed.

APPLICATION SITUATIONS / / /

Channel Selection   AS 4-2

Select the most appropriate channel for each message.

A. Face-to-face   D. Presentation   G. Report

B. Telephone   E. Memo   H. Poster

C. Meeting   F. Letter

_____ 6. An employee came in late for work again today. This is not acceptable behavior and needs to stop.

_____ 7. The supervisor is getting together with a few employees to discuss a new procedure that will be going into effect in a week.

_____ 8. Shelly, the supervisor, is expecting needed material for production this afternoon. She wants to know whether it will arrive on time to make the product.

_____ 9. Employees have been leaving the lights on when no one is in the break room. As the manager concerned for saving electricity, you want employees to shut off the lights when they leave.

_____ 10. The boss asked for the sales data for the quarter.

Here is an example of the communication process: (1) A professor (sender) prepares for a class and encodes a message by preparing a lecture; (2) the professor transmits the message orally through a lecture during class; (3) the students (receivers) decode the lecture (message) by listening and/or taking notes in a meaningful way; and (4) students usually have the option of asking questions (feedback) during or after class.

Communication Skills
Refer to CS Question 4.

WORK APPLICATION 4-9

Give at least two different barriers to communication you have experienced at work. Explain the situation and how the barrier could have been overcome.

Communication Barriers

When we communicate, there are barriers that can lead to miscommunications. The top of Exhibit 4.5 lists 11 common barriers that interfere with effective communication. The bottom of Exhibit 4.5 lists the barriers, their descriptions, and ways to overcome the communication barriers to help prevent communication breakdowns. Emotions are important barriers,[33] so we will discuss this topic in more detail in the last section of this chapter.

EXHIBIT 4.5 | Communication Barriers

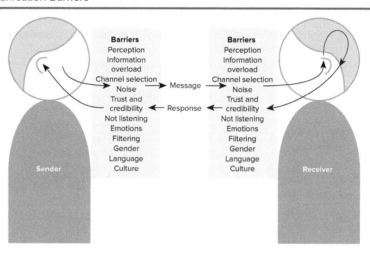

Barrier	Description	Overcoming the Barrier
a. Perception	Receivers use their perceptions to decode messages. *Semantics* and *jargon* can be communication barriers.	Consider how the receiver will perceive the message and select appropriate words and terminology.
b. Information overload	People have a limit on the amount of information they can understand at any given time.	Send messages in a quantity that the receiver can understand.
c. Channel selection	Some channels are more appropriate for certain messages than others.	Give careful thought to selecting the most effective channel for the situation.
d. Noise	Noise is anything that interferes with message transmission.	Stop the noise or distraction, or move to a quiet location.
e. Trust and credibility	People who lack credibility and fail to create a climate of trust and openness aren't believed.	Be open and honest with people, and get the facts straight before you communicate.
f. Not listening	People don't always pay attention and listen to the message or understand it.	Question receivers and have them paraphrase the message back to you.
g. Emotions	When people are emotional, it is difficult to be objective and to listen.	Remain calm and be careful not to make others emotional by your behavior.
h. Filtering	Filtering is altering or distorting information (lying) to project a more favorable image.	Be honest and treat errors as a learning experience rather than as an opportunity to blame and criticize others.
i. Gender	Gender difference can lead to miscommunications.	Be empathetic with the other gender.
j. Language	Speaking different languages makes communication very difficult.	Try to use a translator or nonverbal methods to get the message across.
k. Culture	Having different cultures can lead to miscommunications.	Get to know the other person's culture.

Communication Barriers   AS 4-3

Using Exhibit 4.5, identify the communication barriers indicated by the statements below using the letters a through k.

_____ 11. "I said I'd do the task in a little while. It's only been 15 minutes. I'll get to it in a little while."

_____ 12. "Come on. You don't know what you're talking about. You don't really expect me to believe that, do you?"

_____ 13. "She doesn't understand you. Let me explain it to her in Spanish for you."

_____ 14. "I'm sorry, I was thinking about last night. What did you say?"

_____ 15. "When you go overseas, don't use the thumbs up sign because it is considered an insult there."

_____ 16. "Why are you angry? It's no big deal. You are missing my point."

_____ 17. "Don't you know you are wasting your time sending him a text message because he will not respond?"

_____ 18. "The employee is saying, 'Yes, I got it,' to the boss, but is thinking, 'That's a lot to remember; I'm not sure I got it all.'"

_____ 19. "The employee is telling the boss that the project is on schedule, but is thinking 'I'm behind but I will catch up and the boss will never know.'"

_____ 20. "What did you say? Please shut that thing off! Now."

Gender Conversation Differences

Gender biases influence communications and cause communication barriers. Research has shown that, generally, men and women behave differently and that they converse for different reasons.[34] Men tend to talk to emphasize status. Women tend to talk to create connections and develop relationships.[35] Women spend more time talking about their feelings and personal lives, including their families, than do men.

As a result of gender diversity, men tend to complain that women talk about their problems, and women criticize men for not listening. When men hear a problem, they tend to want to provide a solution. However, at times when women mention their feelings, it tends to be to promote closeness; they generally are not looking for advice. So men may want to just listen and give reflecting responses, rather than focusing on solving problems. Men may also talk more about their feelings and personal lives to improve human relations. You'll learn how to listen and reflect later in the chapter.

Women tend to want more personal face-to-face communications to develop close relationships. When Angela Ahrendts took the Senior Vice President of Retail and Online Stores job at Apple, rather than send an e-mail to introduce herself, she personally visited more than 100 stores to talk to employees and customers.[36]

Cross-Cultural Communication Differences

In the global economy, when conducting international business, you should be aware that cultural differences can cause barriers to communication.[37] Let's discuss some of the barriers.

Cultural Context   The process of encoding and decoding is based on an individual's culture; therefore, the message meaning is different for people of diverse cultures. The greater the

Communication Skills
Refer to CS Question 5.

WORK APPLICATION 4-10

Describe a gender communication difference you have observed at work.

EXHIBIT 4.6 |
High-Context to
Low-Context Cultures

High-Context

▲

Chinese

Korean

Vietnamese

Arab

Greek

Spanish

Italian

English

North American

Scandinavian

Swiss

▼

German

Low-Context

Source: Based on the work
of E.T. Hall, from R.E. Dulck,
J.S. Fielden, and J.S. Hill,
"International Communication:
An Executive Primer," Business
Horizons, January–February
1991, p. 21.

Communication Skills
Refer to CS Question 6.

EXHIBIT 4.7 | High-Context versus Low-Context Cultures: Communication Importance

Context	High-Context Culture	Low-Context Culture
Focus on nonverbal communications and subtle cues	X	
Focus on actual spoken and written word		X
Importance of credibility and trust	X	
The need to develop relationships	X	
Importance of position, age, and seniority	X	
Use of precisely written legal contracts		X
Use of direct, get-down-to-business conversation		X
Managers telling employees (giving orders) what to do		X

difference in culture between the sender and receiver, the greater are the chances of encountering communication barriers. People around the globe see, interpret, and evaluate behavior differently. As a result, they act on behavior differently

Understanding high- and low-context culture differences can help you communicate better. A person's behavioral actions varies by culture.[38] See Exhibit 4.6 for a list of high- and low-context cultures. See Exhibit 4.7 for a list of some of the differences between high-context and low-context cultures in terms of communication.

Social Conventions   The directness of how business is conducted varies. North Americans tend to favor getting down to business quickly and concisely. If you use this approach with Arab or Japanese people, however, you may lose the business because they prefer a more indirect, informal chat to begin business meetings. What constitutes punctuality varies greatly around the world. North American and Japanese people want you to be on time, while being late for a meeting with an Arab or Latin American person is not viewed as negative. So you need to follow social conventions,[39] face-to-face and when using social media.[40]

Language, Etiquette, and Politeness   Even when you are speaking English to people outside North America, words mean different things, and the same thing may be called by different names (e.g., *lift* rather than *elevator, petrol* rather than *gasoline*). What is considered rude in one country may not be rude in another. So be careful not to accidentally offend people; be pleasant, patient, and professional.[41]

Nonverbal Communication   As Exhibit 4.7 shows, nonverbals are important, and more so in some cultures than others. Especially seeing a face helps us detect and understand who they are, what they feel, and if they are trustworthy.[42] Make sure your body language, tone of voice, and word choice project a positive, calm, honest demeanor.[43] What you say is important, but how you say it (happy or angry) is just as important, and a pause helps send messages.[44] Also, silence with a look of approval or disappointment can often send a powerful message better than words.

Be sure to look for nonverbal communications and realize that when using communication technology, including social media such as Facebook, you usually lose important facial messages.[45] Also, gestures do not translate well across cultures because they involve symbolism that is not shared. One gesture can mean different things in different cultures.

Overcoming Global Barriers   This section is not meant to teach you how to overcome all the possible barriers to global communication. The objective is to make you realize the importance of learning the cultures of other countries if you plan to do business with them successfully. Most major multinational companies train their employees to be sensitive to specific cultural differences when doing business with people from other cultures.

To help overcome global barriers to communications, you can follow these guidelines:

- Believe there are differences until similarity is proved. We need to ignore our natural tendency to think that people are like us until we are sure they really are.

- Delay judgment of a person's behavior until you are sure you are being culturally sensitive. You may think a particular behavioral statement or action is inappropriate or insulting to you, but that may not be the intended meaning; the behavior may be appropriate in the other person's culture.

WORK APPLICATION 4-11

Describe a cross-cultural barrier to communication you have experienced. Explain the situation and how the barrier could have been overcome.

- When in doubt, ask. If you are not sure what is appropriate, ask someone who knows. Then, for example, you will know to expect a gift exchange.

- Follow the other person's lead, and watch his or her behavior. For example, if a person bows, bow back. If you do or don't do something and the other person's nonverbal communication indicates discomfort, be quick to apologize and to do it or avoid the behavior.

/// **In the opening case,** Janet is concerned about making friends, which is based on her interpersonal communication skills. ///

Keep in mind the overview of the steps in the communication process and the potential barriers as we discuss the details of sending, receiving, and responding to messages in the rest of this chapter.

SENDING MESSAGES

How you communicate makes a difference in outcomes.[46] Have you ever heard a manager say, "This isn't what I asked for"? When this happens, it is usually the manager's fault for not doing a good job of sending the message. In this section, you will learn how to plan, send, and check to ensure the message has been transmitted successfully.

Planning the Message

Learning Outcome 4-3

List the five steps in the message-sending process.

Recall that before we send a message we should carefully encode it and select the channel—this is planning how to send the message. Encode to keep it simple.[47] Your messages shouldn't just be easy to understand, they should be impossible to misunderstand. Plan before sending a message.[48] You should plan *What* to send (set an objective, end result of the message), *Who* to send it to, *How* (channel), *When,* and *Where* you will transmit the message.

Skill-Building Exercise 4-1 develops this skill.

Sending the Message Face-to-Face

Face-to-face, and the phone, are more personal and often a faster and better way to send a message needing multiple responses than e-mailing or texting.[49] It is helpful to follow the steps in the *message-sending process.* Below is a discussion of the five steps.

Step 1: Develop rapport. Put the receiver at ease with small talk related to the message. It helps prepare the person to receive the message and to form relationships.

Step 2: State the communication objective. It is helpful for the receiver to know the end result of the communication before getting to all the details.

WORK APPLICATION 4-12

Recall a present or past boss. How well did the boss send messages? Which steps in the message-sending process were followed, and which were not commonly followed?

Step 3: Transmit the message. To influence, tell the people what you want them to do, give instructions, and so forth with deadlines for completing tasks. If the goal is to inform, tell them the information.

Step 4: Check understanding. To simply ask "Do you have any questions?" does not check understanding. After transmitting the message, ask questions and for paraphrasing to check to see if the message has been understood. **Paraphrasing** is *the process of having the receiver restate the message in his or her own words.*

MODEL 4.1 | The
Message-Sending Process

| Step 1: Develop rapport | → | Step 2: State the communication objective | → | Step 3: Transmit the message | → | Step 4: Check understanding | → | Step 5: Get a commitment and follow up |

Step 5: Get a commitment and follow up. Make sure the other person can do the task and have it done by the deadline. Follow up as needed to ensure that the task is completed by the deadline. Model 4.1 lists the five steps in the message-sending process.

Learning Outcome 4-4

Describe how to get feedback.

Checking Understanding: Feedback

The best way to ensure mutual understanding is to get feedback from the receiver. **Feedback** is *the process of verifying messages.* Questioning, paraphrasing, and allowing comments and suggestions are all forms of feedback. Feedback facilitates job performance.[50]

The Common Approach to Getting Feedback on Messages and Why It Doesn't Work The most common approach to getting feedback is to send the entire message, followed by asking, "Do you have any questions?" Feedback usually does not follow because people have a tendency not to ask questions. Regardless of the reason, the result is the same: Employees don't ask questions; generally, students don't either.

After sending messages and asking if there are questions, we often proceed to make another common error. We assume that no questions means communication is complete and that there is mutual understanding of the message. In reality, the message is often misunderstood. When a message does not result in communication, the most common cause is the sender's lack of getting feedback to ensure mutual understanding. The proper use of questioning and paraphrasing can help ensure that our messages are communicated successfully.

How to Get Feedback on Messages Below are four guidelines we should use when getting feedback on messages:

Be Open to Feedback First of all, you must be open to feedback and must ask for it.[51] When someone asks a question, you need to be responsive and patiently answer questions and explain things.

Be Aware of Nonverbal Communication You must be sure that your nonverbals encourage feedback. If you say you encourage questions but when people ask questions, you act impatient or look at them as though they are stupid, people will learn not to ask you questions.

You must also be aware of the receivers' nonverbal communications. If you are explaining a task to Larry, and Larry has a puzzled look on his face, he is probably confused but may not be willing to say so. In such a case, you should stop and clarify things before going on.

Communication Skills
Refer to CS Question 7.

WORK APPLICATION 4-13

Describe how a boss in either your present or your past used feedback. How could his or her feedback skills be improved?

Ask Questions Direct questions dealing with the information you have given will indicate whether the receivers have been listening and if they understand enough to give a direct reply. If the response is not accurate, repeating, giving more examples, or elaborating the message is needed.

Use Paraphrasing The most accurate indicator of understanding is paraphrasing. However, the way you ask others to paraphrase will affect their attitude. For example, if you say, "Jose, tell me what I just said so that I can be sure you will not make a mistake

WORK APPLICATION 4-14

Do you use paraphrasing now? Will you use it more, less, or with the same frequency in the future? Why?

as usual," the result will probably be defensive behavior. Here are two proper requests for paraphrasing:

- "Now tell me what you are going to do so we will be sure that we are in agreement."
- "Please tell me what you are going to do so that I can be sure that I explained myself clearly."

RECEIVING MESSAGES

How we listen affects our relationships,[52] and good leadership is about listening.[53] You may have heard that you learn more by listening than talking,[54] and that you should listen more and talk less.[55] Employers rate communications and especially listening skills as a critical criteria in job candidates.[56] So let's begin this section by completing Self-Assessment Exercise 4-1 to determine how good of a listener you are.

/ / / Self-Assessment Exercise 4-1 / / /

Your Listening Skills

Select the response that best describes the frequency of your actual behavior. Place the letter A, U, F, O, or S on the line before each of the 15 statements.

Almost always (A)   Usually (U)   Frequently (F)   Occasionally (O)   Seldom (S)

_____ 1. I like to listen to people talk. I encourage them to talk by showing interest, by smiling and nodding, and so forth.

_____ 2. I pay closer attention to speakers who are more interesting or similar to me.

_____ 3. I evaluate speakers' words and nonverbal communication ability as they talk.

_____ 4. I avoid distractions; if it's noisy, I suggest moving to a quieter spot.

_____ 5. When people interrupt me to talk, I put what I was doing out of sight and mind and give them my complete attention.

_____ 6. When people are talking, I allow them time to finish. I do not interrupt, anticipate what they are going to say, or jump to conclusions.

_____ 7. I tune out people whose views do not agree with mine.

_____ 8. While the other person is talking or the professor is lecturing, my mind wanders to personal topics.

_____ 9. While the other person is talking, I pay close attention to the nonverbal communication to help me fully understand what the sender is trying to get across.

_____ 10. I tune out and pretend I understand when the topic is difficult.

_____ 11. When the other person is talking, I think about what I am going to say in reply.

_____ 12. When I feel there is something missing or contradictory, I ask direct questions to get the person to explain the idea more fully.

_____ 13. When I don't understand something, I let the sender know.

_____ 14. When listening to other people, I try to put myself in their position and see things from their perspective.

_____ 15. During conversations, I repeat back to the sender what has been said in my own words (paraphrase) to be sure I understand correctly what has been said.

If you were to have people to whom you talk regularly answer these questions about you, would they have the same responses that you selected? Have friends fill out the questions for you and compare answers.

To determine your score, give yourself 5 points for each A, 4 for each U, 3 for each F, 2 for each O, and 1 for each S for statements 1, 4, 5, 6, 9, 12, 13, 14, and 15. Place the scores on the line next to your response letter. For items 2, 3, 7, 8, 10, and 11, the score reverses: Give yourself 5 points for each S, 4 for each O, 3 for each F, 2 for each U, and 1 for each A. Place these scores on the line next to your response letter. Now add your total number of points. Your score should be between 15 and 75. Place your score here and place an X on the continuum below at the point that represents your score. Generally, the higher your score, the better your listening skills.

Poor listener   15 ---------- 25 ---------- 35 ---------- 45 ---------- 55 ---------- 65 ---------- 75   Good listener

Learning Outcome 4-5

List the three steps in the message-receiving process.

If someone asked us, Are you a good listener?, most likely we would say yes. What was your score on the self-assessment? For how long can you pay attention and listen effectively at school and work? Next time you begin reading a textbook, time how long you can go before you "have" to stop and do something else. By using the message-receiving process and listening tips in this section, you can become a better listener.

The Message-Receiving Process

The message-receiving process has three parts. First we have to listen to the message, next we should analyze what was said as we decode the message, and then we should check understanding through paraphrasing and watching nonverbal behavior to ensure the message was received accurately.

To improve your listening skills, focus your attention on listening for a week by concentrating on both what other people say and their nonverbal communication. Talk only when necessary so that you can listen to what others are saying. The 13 listening tips below are presented in the sequence of the message-receiving process.

Listening Tips

Listening

1. *Pay attention.* When people interrupt you to talk, stop what you are doing and give them your complete attention.[57] Quickly relax and clear your mind so that you are receptive to them.

2. *Avoid distractions.* Shut off your digital machines and other distractions. Keep your eye on the speaker.

3. *Stay tuned in.* Do not let your mind wander. If it does, gently bring it back. It is also very helpful to repeat in your mind what the speaker is saying. Do not think about what you are going to say in reply; just listen.

4. *Do not assume and interrupt.* Listen to the entire message without interrupting the speaker other than to clarify the message.

5. *Watch for nonverbal cues.* Watch as you listen to be sure that the speaker's eyes, body, and face are sending the same message as the verbal message. If something seems out of place, clarify by asking questions.

6. *Ask questions.* When you feel there is something missing or contradictory, or you just do not understand, ask direct questions to get the person to explain the idea more fully.

7. *Take notes.* Part of listening is writing down important things so you can remember them later. This is especially true when listening to instructions.

8. *Convey meaning.* The way to let the speaker know you are listening to the message is to use verbal clues such as "you feel ...," "uh huh," "I see," and "I understand." You should also use eye contact, appropriate facial expressions, nodding of the head, and sitting on the edge of the chair, leaning slightly forward to indicate you are interested and listening.

Communication Skills
Refer to CS Question 8.

Skill-Building Exercise 4-2
develops this skill.

Analyzing

9. *Think.* Listen actively by organizing, summarizing, reviewing, interpreting, and critiquing often. Again, repeat in your mind what the speaker is saying.

10. *Evaluate after listening.* You should listen to the entire message and then come to your conclusions.

11. *Evaluate facts presented.* Base your conclusion on the facts presented rather than on opinions, stereotypes, and generalities.

WORK APPLICATION **4-15**

Refer to Self-Assessment
Exercise 4-1 and the 13 tips
to improve your listening
skills. What is your weakest
listening skill? How will you
improve your listening
ability?

Checking Understanding

12. *Paraphrase.* Begin speaking by paraphrasing the message back to the sender to convey that you have listened and understood. Now you are ready to offer your ideas, advice, solution, or decision in response to the sender of the message.

13. *Watch for nonverbal cues.* If the person does not seem to understand what you are talking about, clarify the message before finishing the conversation.

See Model 4.2 for a review of the message-sending process with the 13 listening tips.

MODEL 4.2 | The Message-Receiving Process

1. Listening	→	2. Analyzing	→	3. Checking understanding
1. Pay attention 2. Avoid distractions 3. Stay tuned in 4. Do not assume and interrupt 5. Watch for nonverbal cues 6. Ask questions 7. Take notes 8. Convey meaning		9. Think 10. Evaluate after listening 11. Evaluate facts presented		12. Paraphrase 13. Watch for nonverbal cues

---

APPLICATION SITUATIONS / / /

Listening   AS 4-4

Identify each statement by its number (1 to 13) from the 13 listening tips in Model 4.2.

_____ 21. "I can do it. But how long will it take me to get the task done?"

_____ 22. "That's all I need to know. I don't need any more details."

_____ 23. "Are you finished? I'm not sure we can implement this suggestion."

_____ 24. "Uh huh. I get it. That is a great idea."

_____ 25. "Do you have any data to support that your suggestion will solve the problem?"

_____ 26. "Hold on; I just got a text. What did you say again?"

_____ 27. "I'll write down the instructions so I don't forget them later when I do the assignment."

_____ 28. "I missed the beginning of what you said. Please start over again."

_____ 29. "You look confused. Let me explain it a bit differently."

_____ 30. "Let me see if I got this straight. You want me to. . . ."

RESPONDING TO MESSAGES

Learning Outcome 4-6

Define five response styles.

The fourth and last step in the communication process is responding to the message. Not all messages require a response, but most face-to-face messages do. In this section, we present five response styles to choose from.

Response Styles

Before learning about response styles, complete Self-Assessment Exercise 4-2 to determine your preferred response style.

/ / / **Self-Assessment Exercise 4-2** / / /

Your Preferred Response Style

Select the response you would actually make as the supervisor in the five situations that follow:

_____ 1. I cannot work with Paul. That guy drives me crazy. He is always complaining about me and everyone else, including you, boss. Why does he have to be my job partner? We cannot work together. You have to assign someone else to be my partner.

   a. I'm sure there are things that you do that bother Paul. You'll have to work things out with him.

   b. What has he said about me?

   c. Can you give me some examples of the specific things that he does that bother you?

   d. I'll talk to Paul. I'm sure we can improve or change the situation.

   e. So Paul is really getting to you.

_____ 2. We cannot make the deadline on the Procter Project without more help. We've been having some problems. A major problem is that Betty and Phil are recent college grads, and you know they don't know anything. I end up doing all the work for them. Without another experienced person, my team will not get the job done on time.

   a. Tell me more about these problems you are having.

   b. Did you see the game last night?

   c. You are really concerned about this project, aren't you?

   d. You will have to stop doing the work and train the new people. They will come through for you if you give them a chance.

   e. Don't worry. You're a great project leader. I'm sure you will get the job done.

_____ 3. Congratulations on being promoted to supervisor. I was wondering about what to expect. After all, we go back five years as good friends in this department. It will seem strange to have you as my boss.

   a. Things will work out fine, you'll see.

   b. I take it that you don't like to see things change. Is that what you mean?

   c. Just do a good job and there will not be any problems between us.

   d. Is Chris feeling any better?

   e. Tell me how you think things will change.

_____ 4. I wish you would do something about Gloria. Because of her short, tight clothes, the men are always finding some excuse to come by here. She loves it; you can tell by the way she is always flirting with all the guys. Gloria could turn this place into a soap opera if you don't do something.

   a. So you think this situation is indecent, is that it?

   b. I cannot tell Gloria how to dress. Why don't you turn your desk so you don't have to watch.

   c. Don't let it bother you. I'm sure it's innocent and that nothing is really going on. You know how these younger kids are these days.

   d. What do you think I should do?

   e. Are you feeling well today?

_____ 5. I cannot take it anymore. I've been running around like a fool waiting on all these customers and all they do is yell at me and complain.

   a. Are you going to the party tonight?

   b. What is the most irritating thing the customers are doing?

(continued)

   c. With Erin being out today, it's been crazy. But tomorrow she should be back and things should be back to normal. Hang in there; you can handle it.

   d. The customers are really getting to you today, hey?

   e. I told you during the job interview that this is how it is. You have to learn to ignore the comments.

To determine your preferred response style, in the following table circle the letter you selected in situations 1 to 5. The column headings indicate the style you selected.

	Advising	Diverting	Probing	Reassuring	Reflecting
1	A	B	C	D	E
2	D	B	A	E	C
3	C	D	E	A	B
4	B	E	D	C	A
5	E	A	B	C	D
	___	___	___	___	___
Total	___	___	___	___	___

Add up the number of circled responses per column. The total for all columns should equal 5. The column with the highest number represents your preferred response style. The more evenly distributed the numbers are among the styles, the more flexible you are at responding.

EXHIBIT 4.8 | Response Styles

Style	Definition	Appropriate Use
Advising	Providing evaluation, personal opinion, direction, or instructions.	Give advice when directly asked for it.
Diverting	Switching the message; changing the subject.	Use to avoid needless arguments.
Probing	Asking for more information.	Ensure understanding by getting more information.
Reassuring	Giving supportive statements.	Give to provide confidence.
Reflecting	Paraphrasing the message back to the sender.	Use to convey understanding and acceptance.

Communication Skills
Refer to CS Question 9.

WORK APPLICATION 4-16

Give situations in which any two of the five response styles would be appropriate. Give the sender's message and your response. Identify its style.

How you respond to the message directly affects communication.[58] See Exhibit 4.8 for a list of the five response styles, their definitions, and when it is appropriate to use each style.

Don't be too quick to give advice; you are not listening.[59] Psychologist Carl Rogers stated that reflecting responses should be used in the beginning stages of most communications because they lead to developing good human relations—as people want to be listened to and know that they are valued. However, there is no one best response style. The response should be appropriate for the situation. Probing does help clarify the message,[60] but more importantly, everyone you meet knows more about something than you do, so probe to get their knowledge.[61] Also, be aware that your nonverbals also give responses.[62]

/// **In the opening case,** Janet's interpersonal skills of sending, receiving, and responding to messages will affect her personal satisfaction in making friends, as well as her job satisfaction and performance. ///

Identifying Response Styles   AS 4-5

Below are two situations with 10 responses. Identify each as:

A. Advising   C. Probing   E. Reflecting

B. Diverting   D. Reassuring

LYNN: Michael, do you have a minute to talk?

MICHAEL: Sure, what's up?

LYNN: Can you do something about all the swearing the men use around the plant? It carries through these thin walls into my work area. It's disgusting. I'm surprised you haven't done anything.

MICHAEL:

_____ 31. Just ignore it and it will not bother you.

_____ 32. Are you behind in your work today?

_____ 33. What specific swears are the ones that bother you?

_____ 34. So you find this swearing offensive?

_____ 35. I didn't know anyone was swearing. I'll look into it and everything will be fine.

JIM: Mary, I have a complaint.

MARY: Sit down and tell me about it.

JIM: Being the AD [athletic director], you know that I use the weight room after the football team. Well, my track team has to return the plates to the racks, put the dumbbells back, and so forth. I don't get paid to pick up after the football team. After all, they have the use of the room longer than we do. I've complained to Ted [the football coach], but all he says is that's the way he finds it, or that he'll try to get the team to do a better job. But nothing happens.

MARY:

_____ 36. So you don't think it's unfair to pick up after the football team.

_____ 37. For how long have you been picking up after the football team?

_____ 38. I want you to go and work it out with Ted.

_____ 39. Thanks for telling me about it; I'll talk to Ted to see what's going on.

_____ 40. I almost forget to tell you, congratulations on beating Ohio State.

In the above two situations, which response is the most appropriate?

SITUATIONAL COMMUNICATION

Learning Outcome 4-7

List the four situational supervisory styles and the four variables to consider in selecting the appropriate communication style.

There are four situational communications styles, outlined below, and each style is based primarily on four behaviors. These behaviors can be characterized as a combination of two dimensions: task and relationship. In *task behavior*, you focus on getting the job done primarily through directing the receiver in what to do and how to do it. In *relationship behavior*, you elicit others' input, and you listen and respond with supportive behavior. Task and relationship behavior can be described as high or low, depending on the amount of emphasis placed on each of the two dimensions during communication. The most appropriate communication style to use in a specific situation varies based on communication control[63] of task and relationship behaviors, as discussed below.

Situational Communication Styles

- *Autocratic communication style (S-A)* demonstrates high task–low relationship (HT-LR) behavior, initiating a closed presentation. The other party has little, if any, information and is generally low in capability. You initiate and control the communication with minimal, if any, response. You make a presentation letting the other parties know they are expected to comply with your message.

- *Consultative communication style (S-C)* demonstrates high task–high relationship (HT-HR) behavior, using a closed presentation for the task with an open elicitation for the relationship. The other party has moderate information and capability. You initiate the communication by letting the other party know that you want him or her to buy into your influence. You are closed to having your message accepted (task) but open to the person's feelings (relationship).

- *Participative communication style (S-P)* demonstrates low task–high relationship (LT-HR) behavior, responding with open elicitation, some initiation, and little presentation. The other party is high in information and capability. You respond by eliciting others' input on how to do things or convey personal support and make decisions together.

- *Laissez-faire communication style (S-L)* demonstrates low task–low relationship (LT-LR) behavior. The other party is outstanding in information and capability. You respond to the other party with the information, structure, and so forth that the sender wants.

Situational Variables

When selecting the appropriate communication style, you should consider four variables: time, information, acceptance, and capability. Answering the questions related to each variable below can help you select the appropriate style for the situation.

- **Time:** Do I have enough time to communicate? When there is no time, the other three variables are not considered; the autocratic style is appropriate. When time is available, any of the other styles may be appropriate, depending on the other variables.

- **Information:** Do I have the necessary information to communicate my message, make a decision, or take action? The more information you have, the less need there is to communicate with others (autocratic), and laissez-faire style is more appropriate.

- **Acceptance:** Will the other party accept my message without any input? If the receiver will like or willingly accept your message, be autocratic; if they will reject it, be more consultative or participative.

- **Capability:** Capability has two parts: (1) Ability–does the other party have the experience or knowledge to participate in two-way communication? Will the receiver put the organization's goals ahead of personal needs or goals? and (2) Motivation–does the other party want to participate?

Skill-Building Exercise 4-3 develops this skill with the use of Model 4.3 that puts the variable and communication styles together to select the most appropriate communication style for the situation.

The more capable the other party is, the higher the level or involvement they can have. Capability levels can change from one task to another. For example, a professor may have outstanding capability in classroom teaching but be low in capability for advising students. So a supervisor would use a different communication style for each of the two tasks.

/// **In the opening case,** Janet's ability to use the best communication style for the situation will affect her personal and job satisfaction and performance. ///

DEALING WITH EMOTIONS AND CRITICISM

Communicating with people brings out emotions, and our feelings affect our behavior, human relations, happiness, and performance in our personal and professional lives.[64] Emotions overpower rational thought,[65] and others' behavior influences our emotions and how we handle emotions.[66] Thus, understanding emotions and how to manage your and others' emotions is important to personal and career success.[67] Recall from Chapter 2 that adjustment (or emotional stability) is part of our personality and the importance of emotional intelligence.

Emotions, Emotional Labor, and Global Differences

Here we discuss these three related topics, which are the foundation for our next topic, dealing with emotional people.

Understanding Feelings   Emotions are often just called feelings, and we express them when we communicate.[68] There are six universal emotions: happiness, surprise, fear, sadness, anger, and disgust.

We Can Control Behavior, Not Feelings   We should realize that feelings are subjective; they tell us people's attitudes and needs. Feelings are usually disguised as factual statements. Most important, feelings are neither right nor wrong, but behavior is, so we should not make judgments and evaluate feelings, only behavior.

We cannot choose our feelings or control them. However, we can control how we express our feelings. You can use self-control over your behavior, such as not letting fear lead us to failure,[69] which is called managing emotions. Also, if someone says something that upsets you, you will feel the emotion and then choose your behavior, such as to say nothing, give the person a dirty look, or yell or throw something. People can't see our feelings, only our behavior that expresses those feelings. So we will feel our emotions, but we should control our behavior.

Nonverbals Convey Feelings   Emotions are more clearly revealed through nonverbal communications than verbally. If people are angry, they don't usually tell us. But we can tell by the look on the person's face, the tone of voice, the pointing of a finger at us, and so on. A person's smile or frown conveys happy or sad feelings. So to truly understand feeling, pay attention to nonverbal emotional behavior as you interact with people.[70]

Emotional Labor   At work, we are expected to control our behavior, not our feelings. **Emotional labor** requires *the expression of feeling through desired behavior.* You are expected to be cheerful with customers, to be pleasant with coworkers, and to avoid expressing feeling through negative behavior at work.[71] /// **In the opening case,** Janet is emotionally excited and dedicated to doing her best. ///

Managers should encourage employees to express their feelings in a positive way. However, they shouldn't allow employees to go around yelling, swearing, bullying, or hitting others. Therefore, dealing with emotions effectively, which you are learning to do, can help prevent negative behavior. Although we may not like some of our coworkers, we should treat them with respectful emotional labor.[72] We should also watch out not to stereotype women as being too emotional at work.[73]

Also, we shouldn't get caught up in others' emotions. You don't want to match their negative behavior. When someone yells at you, it doesn't mean you have to yell back. Returning negative behavior usually only makes the interaction worse and hurts human relations. Stay calm; don't have a hissy fit.

Don't let others control your emotions. Realize that your expressed emotions reinforce themselves. If you smile, you will be happier, and when you act angry, you feel angrier.[74] Do you want to be happy or sad? Think and act that way.

Communication Skills
Refer to CS Question 10.

WORK APPLICATION 4-17

How well do you hide your feelings from others, such as being disappointed or upset, while using emotional labor?

Global Differences   What is acceptable in one culture may not be acceptable in another. Some cultures lack words to express feelings such as anxiety, depression, sadness, and guilt, and they interpret the same emotions differently. Emotional labor expectations vary culturally. In the United States, employees are generally expected to be friendly and to smile at customers. However, in Muslim cultures, smiling is commonly taken as a sign of sexual attraction, so women are discouraged from smiling at men.

There are also cultural differences in the acceptance of crying at work. Wealthier and more democratic countries (Chile, Sweden, and the United States) are more accepting of crying than others (Ghana, Nepal, and Nigeria). Criticism (which we will discuss) is the most common reason for emotional breakdowns at work.[75] Next we discuss how to deal with emotions.

Learning Outcome 4-8

Discuss what should and should not be done to calm an emotional person.

Communication Skills
Refer to CS Question 11.

Dealing with Emotional People

You will have better communications and human relations if you can deal with emotional employees effectively.[76] Let's begin by discussing what not to do and then what to do when dealing with emotional people.

Don't Argue, Return Negative Behavior, or Belittle the Emotional Person   When dealing with an emotional person, don't argue. And don't return the negative behavior.[77] In the early days of **Apple** and **Microsoft**, when **Bill Gates** worked together with **Steve Jobs** to create software for Apple, Steve would sometimes express his anger through rude behavior, but Bill responded by becoming very calm. Think about it: Does arguing or negative behavior really help?

When someone is emotional, *never* make put-down statements such as these:[78] "You shouldn't be angry," "Don't be upset," "Don't be a baby," "Just sit down and be quiet," or "I know how you feel." (No one knows how anyone else feels; recall perceptions in Chapter 2.) Don't try to make the person feel guilty or bad with statements like, "I'm ashamed of you," "I'm disappointed in you," or "You should be ashamed of yourself." These types of statements only make the feelings stronger. While you may get the person to be quiet, effective communication will not take place. And your human relations will suffer.[79]

Be Empathic and Use Reflecting Statements   Recall that strong emotions are a barrier to communications because people can't think and talk logically when they are highly emotional. Being logical with them doesn't work because when we are highly emotional, it doesn't matter what we know or don't know; all that counts is what we feel.[80] Therefore, we have to first deal with the emotion and calm them, and then deal with the content of the issue to resolve any conflicts. To calm emotional people, encourage them to express their feelings in a positive way by being empathic and using reflective responses.[81] However, if emotions are too strong (yours or theirs), it may be wiser to wait until a later time after emotions cool down. Make statements such as, "Let's wait until after lunch (and set a time) to discuss this issue."

Employers are looking for new hires with empathy.[82] Be empathic by attempting to see things from the other person's perception and use empathy.[83] **Empathic listening** is *the ability to understand and relate to another's situation and feelings.* To listen with empathy doesn't mean you have to agree with the person. Just try to put yourself in his or her shoes/place.[84] Do not agree or disagree with the feelings (recall that feelings are not right or wrong, so don't belittle people); simply identify them verbally with reflecting statements.[85]

WORK APPLICATION 4-18

Recall a situation in which a manager had to handle an emotional employee (which can be you). Did the manager follow the guidelines for calming an emotional person?

Reflecting statements *paraphrase feelings back to the person.* Use statements like these: "You were *hurt* when you didn't get the assignment." "You *resent* Bill for not doing his share of the work. Is that what you mean?" "Is that what you're saying?" Using empathic listening allows the person to get out the feelings, thus calming him or her. After you deal with emotions, you can go on to work on content (solving problems). Understanding feelings is often the solution, as sometimes all people want is someone to listen to them and understand what they are going though; they are not seeking advice or solutions.

Getting and Giving Criticism

Learning Outcome 4-9

Describe how to get criticism effectively.

Communication Skills
Refer to CS Question 12.

Criticism is about getting and giving feedback,[86] which can lead to increased performance.[87] Criticism (finding fault with our behavior) and emotions are related topics because criticism tends to bring out feelings, as people tend to get emotional and defend their behavior. So when we deal with criticism, we tend to have to deal with emotions. Here are some tips on getting and giving criticism.

Getting Criticism   It is great to hear praise for the job we are doing, and we need to hear it as a motivator,[88] but the only way we can improve is to openly seek criticism. However, if you ask someone for critical feedback, remember that you are asking to hear things that may surprise, upset, or insult you, or hurt your feelings.[89]

Let's face it, criticism of our behavior from our boss, peers, or employees is painful. We do not really enjoy being criticized, even when it is constructive, and many people handle criticism poorly. Ask your boss the best way to check in on how you're doing, including how often and which channel (instant message, e-mail, phone, or in person) to use for feedback.[90]

Many managers will not tell you how they really view your performance, so if you want to advance, you need to ask them without getting defensively emotional. Even when you think the feedback is wrong, look for ways to improve.[91] During a performance review, if you don't get the rating you want, ask what "specifically" you need to do to get the higher rating during the next review period—and do it.

Do you like being told you did something wrong or your performance was not up to par? How well do you listen to criticism and change your behavior to improve? See Exhibit 4.9 for some dos and don'ts for when you get criticism. Don't take it personally or react emotionally. Focus on the positive side, realizing that the feedback can lead to improved performance.[92] Also, admitting your lack of exceptional performance and working to improve will improve your relationship with your boss.[93]

EXHIBIT 4.9 | Getting Criticism

Don't	Why Not?	If You Do	What to Do/Say Instead
Cry	It is what the boss will remember about the criticism session.	Apologize and ask for another meeting.	"Will you give me some time to think about the criticism and we'll talk later?"
Get upset	The boss will get angry with you and may not trust you.	Apologize for getting angry and ask for another meeting.	Stay calm and use paraphrasing to make sure you understand the criticism, and use reflective statements. If you are too upset to calm down as suggested, ask for a later meeting to discuss it.
Deny it	The boss will doubt your credibility and may not trust you.	Meet again and state that after thinking about it, you would like more details of the behavior and how to improve.	Can you give me some examples of the specific behavior being criticized, and how to improve?
Blame others	The boss will lose respect for you and may not trust you.	Take responsibility for your behavior and apologize if you did something wrong. Reexamine your behavior and what you can learn from the criticism; then meet again.	I'm not sure I see it that way. Please tell me how you perceive my behavior.

Do	Why Do It?	If You Do	What to Do/Say
Seek criticism	It is the way to learn from your mistakes and continuously improve your performance.	You will get higher performance ratings, which can lead to raises and promotions (career success).	Make action plans and improve your performance. Follow-up with your boss to see how you are doing.

Source: Adapted from S. Shellenbarger, "It's Not My Fault! A Better Response to Criticism at Work," *The Wall Street Journal* (June 18, 2014): D1, D4.[78]

WORK APPLICATION 4-19

How would you rate
yourself on your ability to
accept criticism without
getting emotional and
defensive? How could you
improve your ability to
accept criticism?

/// **In the opening case,** Janet is sensitive and hopes not to be criticized too often. How well she performs her job and accepts criticism and improves will affect how often she needs to be criticized. ///

Giving Criticism   An important part of the manager's job is to improve employee performance through constructive criticism. If you are (or want to be) a manager, if you are not willing to criticize, maybe you should ask yourself this question: Do I really want to be a manager? In our personal lives, and if we are not managers at work, we don't have the authority to tell people that they need to change their behavior through criticism. However, if we want to help people improve their behavior on or off the job, we need to give criticism.

Get the Other Person to Ask for Your Feedback   Criticize carefully using behavior that will not make the person emotional or defensive. A good approach is not to just come out with criticism. Ask the person if he or she wants it. For example, if you see a person do a task that is not effective, ask, "Would you like me to show you an easier (faster/better) way to do that?" If the person says yes, he or she is open to your criticism. Keep it short, but clearly and descriptively state the undesired performance and tell the person exactly what needs to be changed to improve. Chapter 5 will provide more details on how to accomplish this task.

Remember that what you think about affects how you feel, and how you feel affects your behavior, human relations, happiness, and performance. Think happy, confident thoughts that you will improve to help you stay calm and in control of your emotional behavior and deal effectively with emotional people. Keep in mind that we will continue to deal with emotions in the next chapter, as people are often emotional when they deal with conflict. Complete Self-Assessment Exercise 4-3 to determine how your personality affects your communications, emotions, and acceptance of criticism.

/// **Self-Assessment Exercise 4-3** ///

Your Personality Traits and Communications, Emotions, and Criticism

Let's tie personality traits from Chapter 2 together with what we've covered in this chapter. We are going to present some general statements about how your personality may affect your behavior, human relations, and performance. For each area, determine how the information relates to you. This will help you better understand your behavioral strengths and weaknesses and the areas you may want to improve.

If you have a high *surgency* personality, you most likely are an extrovert and have no difficulty initiating conversations and communicating with others orally. However, you may be dominating communication and prefer vertical communications following the chain of command with centralized authority. Be a team player. Surgency types are often not good at dealing with emotions. You may need to be more attentive to nonverbal communication and emotions. You may be better at giving than getting feedback, so you may need to work at being receptive to feedback. You may also need to work at giving more praise and less criticism.

If you are high in *agreeableness* personality traits, you are most likely a good listener and communicator, preferring oral horizontal communications as a team player. You are probably connected to the grapevine, so be careful not to spread false rumors. You are probably in tune with emotions and nonverbal communication cues. You may be reluctant to give criticism even though it will help others improve.

Your *adjustment* level affects the emotional tone of your communications. If you tend to get emotional, and it is a barrier to communications, you may want to work to keep your emotional response behavior under control. Watch your nonverbal communication because it tells people how you feel about them and it can hurt your human relations. Try not to be sensitive to criticism and not to become defensive, blame others, and give excuses for your negative behavior and performance. At the same time, don't be too critical of others.

If you are high in *conscientiousness,* you tend to have reliable communications. If you are not conscientious, you may want to work at returning messages quickly. You may be so concerned with your own success that you don't pay attention to emotions and nonverbal communication. Criticism may be painful to you, because you try hard to do a good job. But remember that it can lead to more conscientiousness and greater success.

(continued)

/// **Self-Assessment Exercise 4-3** /// (*continued*)

People who are *open to new experience* often initiate communications, because communicating is often part of the new experience. If you are not open to new experience, you may be reluctant to change organizational structure and flows of communication.

Action plan: Based on your personality, what specific things will you do to improve your communications, emotional labor, and acceptance of criticism?

_____

_____

_____

_____

As we bring this chapter to a close, you should understand how organizations are structured and the *flow of communications* throughout the organization. You should know the *communication process* and *barriers* to communications and how to overcome them. You should be able to effectively send, receive, and respond to *messages*. You should understand how *emotions* affect communications and be able to deal effectively with emotional people. You should be able to effectively give and receive *criticism*.

/// REVIEW ///

The chapter review is organized to help you master the 10 learning outcomes for Chapter 5. First provide your own response to each learning outcome, and then check the summary provided to see how well you understand the material. Next, identify the final statement in each section as either true or false (T/F). Correct each false statement. Answers are given at the end of the chapter.

LO 4-1 Describe how communication flows through organizations.

Formal communication flows through communication networks in vertical and horizontal directions. The grapevine is also a major source of informal communication flowing in all directions.

When an employee goes to talk to the boss, the employee is using vertical upward communication. T F

LO 4-2 List and explain the four steps in the communication process.

The four steps in the communication process are: (1) The sender encodes the message and selects the transmission channel; (2) the sender transmits the message; (3) the receiver decodes the message and decides whether feedback is needed; and (4) feedback, in the form of a response or a new message, may be transmitted.

Low-context cultures rely heavily on nonverbal communication and subtle situational cues during the communication process. T F

LO 4-3 List the five steps in the message-sending process.

The steps in the message-sending process are: (1) develop rapport, (2) state the communication objective, (3) transmit the message, (4) check understanding, and (5) get a commitment and follow up.

A good way to check understanding is to just ask, "Do you have any questions?" T F

LO 4-4 Describe how to get feedback.

To get feedback, one must be open to feedback, be aware of nonverbal communication, ask questions, and paraphrase.

Effective managers take the time to listen to employee complaints and suggestions for change. T F

LO 4-5 List the three steps in the message-receiving process.

The first step is to listen to the message; the second step is to analyze what has been communicated; the third step is to check understanding by paraphrasing what has been said while watching for nonverbal cues.

Asking questions while listening is part of effective listening. T F

LO 4-6 Define five response styles.

(1) Advising responses provide evaluation, opinion, direction, or instructions. (2) Diverting responses switch the message; change the subject. (3) Probing responses ask for more information. (4) Reassuring responses

give supportive statements. (5) Reflecting responses paraphrase the message back to the sender.

Reflecting responses should be used in the beginning stages of most communications. T F

LO 4-7 List the four situational supervisory styles and the four variables to consider in selecting the appropriate communication style.

The autocratic communication style (S-A) demonstrates high task–low relationship (HT–LR) behavior, initiating a closed presentation. The consultative communication style (S-C) demonstrates high task–high relationship (HT–HR) behavior, using a closed presentation for the task with an open elicitation for the relationship. The participative communication style (S-P) demonstrates low task–high relationship (LT–HR) behavior, responding with open elicitation, some initiation, and little presentation. The laissez-faire communication style (S-L) demonstrates low task–low relationship (LT–LR) behavior, responding with the necessary open presentation. The other party is outstanding in information and capability. You respond to the other party with the information, structure, and so forth that the sender wants.

When selecting the appropriate communication style, you should consider four variables: Time–Do I have enough time to use two-way communication? Information–Do I have the necessary information to communicate my message, make a decision, or take action? Acceptance–Will the other party accept my message without any input? Capability (two parts): Ability–Does the other party have the experience or knowledge to participate in two-way communication? Motivation–Does the other party want to participate?

If you don't have time, you use the laissez-faire communication style. T F

LO 4-8 Discuss what should and should not be done to calm an emotional person.

First, don't use behavior that gets people emotional so you don't have to calm them. Don't argue, return negative behavior, or belittle the emotional person because these behaviors tend to make the feelings stronger. Do use empathic listening and reflecting statements because this behavior calms emotions.

When dealing with an emotional person, it is a good idea to determine what the feeling is and if it is right or wrong. T F

LO 4-9 Describe how to get criticism effectively.

First we need to accept the fact that the only way to improve our behavior, human relations, and performance is to accept criticism and change our behavior accordingly. To this end, realizing that criticism is painful, but that without pain there is no gain, openly seek criticism without becoming emotional, defensive, and blameful with excuses for our faulty behavior and performance.

If we don't believe we need to change our behavior, but others do, there is a perception problem and in most cases we should change our behavior. T F

LO 4-10 Define the following 14 key terms.

Select one or more methods: (1) fill in the missing key terms for each definition given below from memory; (2) match the key terms from the end of the review with their definitions below; and/or (3) copy the key terms in order from the key terms at the beginning of the chapter.

_____ refers to the way managers design their firms to achieve the organization's mission and goals.

_____ is the compounded interpersonal communications process across an organization.

_____ is the flow of information both up and down the chain of command.

_____ is the flow of information between colleagues and peers.

The _____ is the informal vehicle through which messages flow throughout the organization.

The _____ consists of a sender who encodes a message and transmits it through a channel to a receiver who decodes it and may give feedback.

_____ is the sender's process of putting the message into a form that the receiver will understand.

The _____ is the physical form of the encoded information.

_____ is the receiver's process of translating the message into a meaningful form.

_____ is the process of having the receiver restate the message in his or her own words.

_____ is the process of verifying messages.

_____ requires the expression of feelings through desired behavior.

_____ is the ability to understand and relate to another's situation and feelings.

_____ paraphrase feelings back to the person.

/ / / KEY TERMS / / /

communication
   process   105
decoding   105
emotional labor   119
empathic listening   120

encoding   105
feedback   111
grapevine   103
horizontal
   communication   102

message   105
organizational
   communication   102
organizational
   structure   101

paraphrasing   110
reflecting
   statements   120
vertical
   communication   102

/ / / COMMUNICATION SKILLS / / /

The following critical thinking questions can be used for class discussion and/or as written assignments to develop communication skills. Be sure to give complete explanations for all questions.

1. Many employees, including managers, complain about organizational communications. What are some of the complaints, and how can communications be improved?

2. E-mail is preferred over oral communication at work, and texting is increasingly used. What are the pros and cons of oral versus e-mail or text communication? Which form of communication do you use more often? Which one do you prefer?

3. Many employees waste time using social media at work. Should organizations ban the use of social media for personal reasons during work hours? If so, how?

4. Which two barriers to communication do you believe are the most common in organizations today? What can firms do to help eliminate these two barriers?

5. Do men and women really converse differently? Do you speak about different things with your male and female friends and coworkers? If so, what do you talk about with men versus women?

6. Which is preferable to you, a high-context culture or a low-context culture?

7. How often do you use paraphrasing and ask others to paraphrase to ensure mutual understanding? How effective are you at paraphrasing and asking others to paraphrase, and how can you improve your paraphrasing skills?

8. Select a few friends and/or coworkers. Do you spend more time talking or listening, or do you spend an equal amount of time talking and listening when you are with them? Write down each person's name and the percentage of time you spend talking and listening; for example, 25 percent talking and 75 percent listening, 50–50, 35–65, and so on. After recording the percentages, ask each person what percentage he or she believes you talk and listen. How accurate was your perception? Should you change the amount of time you spend talking versus listening, and if so, how will you go about changing?

9. Which response style do you believe is most commonly used at work? Should the most commonly used response style be reflecting? Why or why not?

10. How do you rate your ability to read nonverbal communications (e.g., facial expressions, vocal quality, gestures, and posture)? What can you do to improve your ability to understand nonverbal communications?

11. Do you agree that women are more emotional than men? Do they show greater emotional expression, experience emotions more intensely, express both positive and negative feelings (except anger) more often, feel more comfortable expressing feelings, and read nonverbal clues better than men?

12. Do you actively seek criticism? How do you rate your ability to accept criticism? Do you get emotional and defensive? How can you improve your ability to accept criticism? After getting criticized, do you change to improve? What advice would you give others to help them accept criticism and change to improve performance?

CASE   / / /   Oprah Winfrey: Her Ability to Communicate, Connect, and Influence Others

It would appear that Oprah knew quite early in life that she had a genuine gift of the gab. The dictionary defines a "conversationalist" as *a person who enjoys and contributes to good conversation; an interesting person in conversation.* This is Oprah! She had an interest to be on television. After high school, Oprah was awarded a full scholarship to Tennessee State University. However, she withdrew after a year to pursue a career in media. Oprah's first job on television came when at age 20, she became the first black female news anchor in Nashville. Her next opportunity was in Baltimore where she was co-anchor. Less than a year into it, she was fired but soon after landed a job hosting a struggling morning talk show in Chicago appropriately named *AM Chicago*. Within a few months, Ms. Winfrey turned *AM Chicago* from the lowest-rated talk show in Chicago to the highest-rated. She was finally coming into her own as a talk-show host. Three years later the show would be renamed *The Oprah Winfrey Show*.[i]

The Oprah Winfrey Show aired its first episode on September 8, 1986. The show ran for 25 seasons. Oprah had the instinct to know what topics would interest her diverse audience, and like the perfect conversationalist, she knew how to explore a topic using her guests, invited experts, and the audience. Her audience felt like it was their life story being told, and you could see the nodding of heads, the laughter, and the tears. Winfrey's personal and engaging approach to interviewing guests touched a cord in American homes. Oprah tackled stories ranging from infidelity, sexual abuse, child trafficking, and postpartum depression to racism. There were also positive stories of overcoming the odds and "how-to" stories for achieving career success, marital bliss, a good education, and strong friendships. To say that Oprah was and still is the ultimate communicator is an understatement. She uses emotion, passion, criticism, rationale, and energy to tell a story that captivates her audiences like no one can. Viewers and guests found Oprah to be sympathetic, empathetic, and enlightening, qualities that endeared her to millions. Guests often found themselves revealing things they never imagined telling anyone, much less a national TV audience.

Oprah believes in her power to inspire and motivate others. Her message of positivity and self-improvement has captured the interests of millions of Americans from all ages, genders, ethnicities, and socioeconomic backgrounds. She wants her loyal followers to follow their bliss and be the best they can be. Using her own life as an example, Oprah explains that she does not see herself "as a poor, deprived ghetto girl who made good but rather as somebody who from an early age knew she was responsible for herself—and had to make good."

She made a strategic move in 1986 when she formed Harpo ("Oprah" spelled backwards) Productions Inc. She executed the strategy a couple of years later by purchasing a state-of-the-art production studio in Chicago and then taking over ownership and production of *The Oprah Winfrey Show*. The move made her only the third woman in history to own and produce her own show as well as the first African American, male or female, to own her own entertainment production company. The "Oprah Effect," a term coined to describe the power of Oprah's opinions and endorsements to influence public opinion, was well known. Anything she endorses or mentions in a favorable light becomes an instant best seller in its category. Her influence is unparalleled. She also published her own magazine, *The Oprah Magazine*; started a radio channel, Oprah Radio; and most recently collaborated with Discovery Communications to launch a cable channel, the Oprah Winfrey Network.[ii]

Oprah has also been involved in films, television series, and plays. She was nominated for an Academy Award for Best Supporting Actress for her performance in the 1985 drama *The Color Purple*. In 2015, she produced and stared in the film *Selma*. The movie chronicles Martin Luther King Jr.'s march from Selma to Montgomery, Alabama. The film was nominated for Best Picture.

By any objective measure, Oprah is quite possibly the most influential woman in the world. In 2013, she received the Presidential Medal of Freedom awarded by President Barack Obama. That same year, she also received an honorary doctorate degree from Harvard. Oprah was ranked the richest African American of the 20th century. Winfrey has been featured in TIME Magazine's 100 most influential people on an impressive 10 occasions. *Forbes* magazine estimates that Oprah's net worth is about $3 billion and so far, she is the only black woman on the publication's list of the 400 richest people in America.[iii]

Former Chicago Mayor Richard Daley renamed the blocks in front of Harpo Studios "Oprah Winfrey Way." Now 63, Winfrey has a lifestyle that she could only have dreamed of during her traumatic childhood. Her accomplishments as a global media leader and philanthropist have made her one of the most respected and admired public figures today.[iv]

Go to the Internet: To learn more about Oprah Winfrey, visit her website at www.oprah.com.

Support your answers to the following questions with specific information from the case and text.

1. Assess the how well Oprah's communication and interpersonal skills have affected her career as a media mogul.

2. Would you agree with the statement that Oprah's decision to form her own production studio (Harpo) and take over ownership and production of *The Oprah Winfrey Show* was about creating a different organizational structure for herself and the show? Explain.

3. To what extent has digital technology influenced the way Oprah communicates and interacts with her audience?

4. How would you assess Oprah's abilities at encoding her messages when she was holding court with her audience during *The Oprah Winfrey Show*? Use evidence from the case to support your answer.

5. Following up Question 4, what is the evidence from the case that Oprah's guests and audiences effectively decoded her messages and that communication and understanding was achieved?

Cumulative Questions

6. Based on Oprah Winfrey's media persona as revealed in the case, which of the Big Five Dimensions of Traits does she score high on in your opinion (Chapter 2)?

7. Assess Oprah's attitude, self-concept, values, and ethics (Chapter 3).

Case Exercise and Role

Preparation: Assume that you are Oprah Winfrey. On your television talk show, you have decided to tackle a growing problem in our society today—the abuse of prescription drugs. It is a problem that affects every age, gender, socioeconomic, and racial group. So many lives have been lost, and many affected communities are running out of options. You have invited a number of guests, some of them recovering addicts, some still actively using, parents of a dead teenager from an overdose, and a medical expert on opioid addiction.

Remember, not everyone in your audience believes this is a problem; they see addiction as an individual's responsibility to do something about it and no one else. They believe addicts can stop anytime they want to and that it is their choice to keep up with the behavior. It will be helpful for students to Google the topic to have more information/data for their presentation.

Role-Play: Your task is to prepare a 2 to 3 minute opening monologue that is part informative, part compelling, sympathetic, empathetic, and part critical of users. You are to deliver this monologue to the audience before involving your guests and experts to share their stories. Break up the class into groups. Each group is to prepare their monologue and appoint a representative to do the oral presentation to the class. Be sure to follow the steps in Model 5.1, The Message-Sending Process. After the presentations, the class should discuss and critique the effectiveness of each presenter.

OBJECTIVE CASE   / / /   **Communication?**

In the following dialogue, Chris is the manager and Sandy is the employee.

CHRIS: I need you to get a metal plate ready for the Stern job.

SANDY: OK.

CHRIS: I need a ¾-inch plate. I want a ½-inch hole a little off center. No, you'd better make it ⅝. In the left corner I need about a ⅜-inch hole. And on the right top portion, about ⅞ of an inch from the left side, drill a ¼-inch hole. You got it?

SANDY: I think so.

CHRIS: Good, I'll be back later.

Later.

CHRIS: Do you have the plate ready?

SANDY: It's right here.

CHRIS: This isn't what I asked for. I said a ½-inch hole a little off center; this is too much off center. Do it again so it will fit.

SANDY: You're the boss. I'll do it again.

Answer the following questions. Then in the space between questions, state why you selected that answer.

_____   1. Chris and Sandy communicated.

   a. true   *b.* false

_____   2. Chris's primary goal of communication was to:

   a. influence   *b.* inform   *a.* express feelings

_____   3. Chris was the:

   a. sender/decoder   *c.* sender/encoder
   b. receiver/decoder   *d.* receiver/decoder

_____   4. Sandy was the:

   a. sender/decoder   *c.* sender/encoder
   b. receiver/decoder   *d.* receiver/encoder

_____   5. The message transmission medium was:

   a. oral   *c.* nonverbal
   b. written   *d.* combined

_____   6. Chris followed guidelines to getting feedback on messages by

   a. being open to feedback   *c.* asking questions
   b. being aware of nonverbal   *d.* paraphrasing communication
       communication   *e.* none of these

_____   7. Which step(s) did Chris follow in the message-sending process? (You may select more than one answer.)

   a. step 1   *d.* step 3
   b. step 2   *e.* step 5
   c. step 3

_____   8. Sandy was an active listener.

   a. true   *b.* false

_____   9. Sandy's response style was primarily:

   a. advising   *d.* reassuring
   b. diverting   *e.* reflecting
   c. probing

_____   10. Chris used the _____ supervisory style.

   a. autocratic   *c.* participative
   b. consultative   *d.* laissez-faire

_____   11. In Chris's situation, how would you have given the instructions to Sandy?

(*Note:* Students may role-play giving instructions.)

/ / / SKILL-BUILDING EXERCISE 4-1 / / /

Giving Instructions

Experience: In-Class Small Group Exercise

You will plan, give, and receive instructions for the completion of a drawing of three objects.

Objective: To develop your ability to give and receive messages (communication skills).

AACSB Competencies: Communication abilities, analytical thinking, and application of knowledge.

Preparation: No preparation is necessary except reading the chapter. The instructor will provide the original drawings.

Procedure 1 (3–7 minutes)

Read all of procedure 1 twice. The task is for the manager to give an employee instructions for completing a drawing of three objects. The objects must be drawn to scale and look like photocopies of the originals. You will have 15 minutes to complete the task.

The exercise has four separate parts, or steps.

1. The manager plans.
2. The manager gives the instructions.
3. The employee does the drawing.
4. The results are evaluated.

Rules: The rules are numbered to correlate with the four parts above.

1. *Planning.* While planning, the manager may write out instructions for the employee but may not do any drawing of any kind.
2. *Instructions.* While giving instructions, the manager may not show the original drawing to the employee. (The instructor will give it to you.) The instructions may be given orally, and/or in writing, but no nonverbal hand gestures are allowed. The employee may take notes while the instructions are being given but cannot do any drawing with or without a pen. The manager must give the instructions for all three objects before drawing begins.
3. *Drawing.* Once the employee begins the drawing, the manager should watch but no longer communicate in any way.
4. *Evaluation.* When the employee is finished or the time is up, the manager shows the employee the original drawing. Discuss how you did. Turn to the integration section and answer the questions. The manager writes down the answers.

Procedure 2 (2–5 minutes)

Half of the class members act as the manager first and give instructions. Managers move their seats to one of the four walls (spread out). They should be facing the center of the room with their backs close to the wall.

Employees sit in the middle of the room until called on by a manager. When called on, they bring a seat to the manager. They sit facing the manager so that they will not be able to see any manager's drawing.

Procedure 3 (15–20 minutes)

The instructor gives each manager a copy of the drawing. Be careful not to let any employees see it. The manager plans the instructions. When managers are ready, they call an employee and give the instructions. It may be helpful to use the message-sending process. Be sure to follow the rules. The employee should do the drawing on the page titled "Employee Drawing." If using written instructions, use nonbook paper. You have 15 minutes to complete the drawing, and possibly 5 minutes for integration (evaluation). When you finish the drawing, turn to the evaluation questions in the integration section below.

Procedure 4 (15–20 minutes)

The employees are now the managers and sit in the seats facing the center of the room. New employees go to the center of the room until called on.

Follow procedure 3, with the instructor giving a different drawing. Do not work with the same person; change partners.

Evaluating Questions: You may select more than one answer.

_____ 1. The goal of communication was to:

     a. influence   *b.* inform   *c.* express feelings

_____ 2. Feedback was:

     a. immediate   *c.* performance-oriented

     b. specific and accurate   *d.* positive

_____ 3. The manager transmitted the message:

     a. orally   *c.* nonverbally

     b. in writing   *d.* using a combined method

_____ 4. The manager spent _____ time planning.

     a. too much   *b.* too little   *c.* the right amount of

The next six questions relate to the message-sending process:

_____ 5. The manager developed rapport (step 1).

     a. true   *b.* false

_____ 6. The manager stated the communication objective (step 2).

     a. true   *b.* false

_____ 7. The manager transmitted the message _____ (step 3).

     a. effectively   *b.* ineffectively

_____ 8. The manager checked understanding by using _____ (step 4).

     a. direct questions   *c.* both direct questions and paraphrasing

     b. paraphrasing   *d.* neither direct questions nor paraphrasing

Integration

_____ 9. The amount of checking was:

     a. too frequent   *b.* too infrequent   *c.* about right

_____ 10. The manager got a commitment and followed up (step 5).

     a. true   *b.* false

_____ 11. The manager and/or employee got emotional.

     a. true   *b.* false

_____ 12. The primary response style used by the manager was:

     a. advising   *c.* probing   *e.* reflecting

     b. diverting   *d.* reassuring

_____ 13. The primary response style used by the employee was:

     a. advising   *c.* probing   *e.* reflecting

     b. diverting   *d.* reassuring

_____ **14.** The manager used the _____ supervisory style.

     a. autocratic   *c* participative

     b. consultative   *d.* laissez-faire

_____ **15.** The appropriate style was:

     a. autocratic   *c* participative

     b. consultative   *d.* laissez-faire

_____ **16.** Were the objects drawn to approximate scale? If not, why not?

_____ **17.** Did you follow the rules? If not, why not?

_____ **18.** If you could do this exercise over again, what would you do differently?

Conclusion: The instructor leads a class discussion and/or makes concluding remarks.

Application (2–4 minutes):   What did I learn from this experience? How will I use this knowledge in the future?

Sharing: Volunteers give their answers to the application section.

/ / / SKILL-BUILDING EXERCISE 4-2 / / /

Listening Skills

Experience: In-Class Small Group Exercise

Objective: To experience and/or observe and assess listening skills.

AACSB Competencies: Communication abilities and application of knowledge.

Preparation: Recall a time when you did something really good that you shared with a friend. It should take around 5 minutes to describe. Write a brief description._____

Procedure 1 (2–3 minutes)

Select an option and set up for the role play.

Options: A. One person tells his or her good news to one other person as the class observes.

   B. Break into groups of 6 to 8. One person tells his or her good news to one other person as the other group members observe.

Procedure 2 (5–7 minutes)

Tell the other person your good news as though it just happened.

Procedure 3 (8–12 minutes)

Assess the listening skills below by giving specific examples of how the person did or did not do a good job of listening. Was the person an empathic listener? Explain.

   Assess the listener on the 13 listening tips: Turn to the tips on pages 113–114 and assess the person on each of the 13 tips, with examples of what was done well and what could be improved. Which response styles did the listener use (advising, diverting, probing, reassuring, or reflecting)?

Conclusion: The instructor leads a class discussion and/or makes concluding remarks.

Application: (2–4 minutes):   What did I learn from this experience? How will I use this knowledge in the future?

Sharing: Volunteers give their answers to the application section.

/ / / SKILL-BUILDING EXERCISE 4-3 / / /

Situational Communication

Experience: Individuals can share answers and/or work in groups to select the most appropriate communication style for the 12 situations. Or entire class can share answers in class or online.

Objective: To develop your ability to communicate using the appropriate style for the situation.

AACSB Competencies: Analytic skills communication abilities and application of knowledge.

Preparation: You should have completed the 12 situations in Self-Assessment Exercise 4-4. In the self-assessment, you were selecting the alternative that you would choose in the situation. In this part of the skill-building exercise, you are trying to select the most appropriate alternative that will result in the most effective communication. Thus, you may be selecting different answers.

Exercise: You will work at selecting the appropriate style for the 12 situations in Self-Assessment Exercise 4-4. On the time, information, acceptance, and capability lines, place the letters S-A, S-C, S-P, or S-L, whichever is appropriate for the situation. Based on your diagnoses, select the one style you would use. Place the letters S-A, S-C, S-P, or S-L on the style line. On the four S lines write the letters S-A, S-C, S-P, or S-L to identify each style being used.

Begin this exercise by determining your preferred communication style in Self-Assessment Exercise 4-4.

/ / / BMV–4-4 Self-Assessment Exercise 4-4 / / /

Determining Your Preferred Communication Style

To determine your preferred communication style, select the *one* alternative that most closely describes what you would do in each of the 12 situations below. Do not be concerned with trying to pick the correct answer; select the alternative that best describes what *you* would actually do. Circle the letter *a, b, c,* or *d.* Ignore the _____ time _____ information _____ acceptance _____ capability/ _____ style and S _____ lines. They will be explained later.

_____ 1. Wendy, a knowledgeable person from another department, comes to you, the engineering supervisor, and requests that you design a special product to her specifications. You would: _____ time _____ information _____ acceptance _____ capability/ _____ style

    a. Control the conversation and tell Wendy what you will do for her. S _____

    b. Ask Wendy to describe the product. Once you understand it, you would present your ideas. Let her realize that you are concerned and want to help with your ideas. S _____

    c. Respond to Wendy's request by conveying understanding and support. Help clarify what is to be done by you. Offer ideas, but do it her way. S _____

    d. Find out what you need to know. Let Wendy know you will do it her way. S _____

_____ 2. Your department has designed a product that is to be fabricated by Saul's department. Saul has been with the company longer than you have; he knows his department. Saul comes to you to change the product design. You decide to: _____ time _____ information _____ acceptance _____ capability/ _____ style

    a. Listen to the change and why it would be beneficial. If you believe Saul's way is better, change it; if not, explain why the original design is superior. If necessary, insist that it be done your way. S _____

    b. Tell Saul to fabricate it any way he wants to. S _____

    c. You are busy; tell Saul to do it your way. You don't have time to listen and argue with him. S _____

    d. Be supportive; make changes together as a team. S _____

_____ 3. Upper management has a decision to make. The managers call you to a meeting and tell you they need some information to solve a problem they describe to you. You: _____ time _____ information _____ acceptance _____ capability/ _____ style

    a. Respond in a manner that conveys personal support and offer alternative ways to solve the problem. S _____

    b. Respond to their questions. S _____

    c. Explain how to solve the problem. S _____

    d. Show your concern by explaining how to solve the problem and why your solution is an effective one. S _____

_____ 4. You have a routine work order. The work order is to be placed verbally and completed in three days. Sue, the receiver, is very experienced and willing to be of service to you. You decide to: _____ time _____ information _____ acceptance _____ capability/ _____ style

    a. Explain your needs, but let Sue make the order decision. S _____

    b. Tell Sue what you want and why you need it. S _____

    c. Decide together what to order. S _____

    d. Simply give Sue the order. S _____

_____ 5. Work orders from the staff department normally take three days; however, you have an emergency and need the order today. Your colleague, Jim, the department supervisor, is knowledgeable and somewhat cooperative. You decide to: _____ time _____ information _____ acceptance _____ capability/ _____ style

    a. Tell Jim that you need the work order by three o'clock and will return at that time to pick it up. S _____

    b. Explain the situation and how the organization will benefit by expediting the order. Volunteer to help in any way you can. S _____

    c. Explain the situation and ask Jim when the order will be ready. S _____

    d. Explain the situation and together come to a solution to your problem. S _____

(*continued*)

/// BMV–4-4 Self-Assessment Exercise 4-4 /// (continued)

_____ 6. Danielle, a peer with a record of high performance, has recently had a drop in productivity. Her problem is affecting your performance. You know Danielle has a family problem. You: _____ time _____ information _____ acceptance _____ capability/ _____ style

    a. Discuss the problem; help Danielle realize the problem is affecting her work and yours. Supportively discuss ways to improve the situation. S _____

    b. Tell the boss about it and let him decide what to do about it. S _____

    c. Tell Danielle to get back on the job. S _____

    d. Discuss the problem and tell Danielle how to solve the work situation; be supportive. S _____

_____ 7. You are a knowledgeable supervisor. You buy supplies from Peter regularly. He is an excellent salesperson and very knowledgeable about your situation. You are placing your weekly order. You decide to: _____ time _____ information _____ acceptance _____ capability/ _____ style

    a. Explain what you want and why. Develop a supportive relationship. S _____

    b. Explain what you want and ask Peter to recommend products. S _____

    c. Give Peter the order. S _____

    d. Explain your situation and allow Peter to make the order. S _____

_____ 8. Jean, a knowledgeable person from another department, has asked you to perform a routine staff function to her specifications. You decide to: _____ time _____ information _____ acceptance _____ capability/ _____ style

    a. Perform the task to her specifications without questioning her. S _____

    b. Tell her that you will do it the usual way. S _____

    c. Explain what you will do and why. S _____

    d. Show your willingness to help; offer alternative ways to do it. S _____

_____ 9. Tom, a salesperson, has requested an order for your department's services with a short delivery date. As usual, Tom claims it is a take-it-or-leave-it offer. He wants your decision now, or within a few minutes, because he is in the customer's office. Your action is to: _____ time _____ information _____ acceptance _____ capability/ _____ style

    a. Convince Tom to work together to come up with a later date. S _____

    b. Give Tom a yes or no answer. S _____

    c. Explain your situation and let Tom decide if you should take the order. S _____

    d. Offer an alternative delivery date. Work on your relationship; show your support. S _____

_____ 10. As a time-and-motion expert, you have been called in regard to a complaint about the standard time it takes to perform a job. As you analyze the entire job, you realize one element of the complaint should take longer, but other elements should take less time. The end result is a shorter total standard time for the job. You decide to: _____ time _____ information _____ acceptance _____ capability/ _____ style

    a. Tell the operator and supervisor that the total time must be decreased and why. S _____

    b. Agree with the operator and increase the standard time. S _____

    c. Explain your findings. Deal with the operator's or supervisor's concerns, but ensure compliance with your new standard. S _____

    d. Together with the operator, develop a standard time. S _____

_____ 11. You approve budget allocations for projects. Marie, who is very competent in developing budgets, has come to you. You: _____ time _____ information _____ acceptance _____ capability/ _____ style

    a. Review the budget, make revisions, and explain them in a supportive way. Deal with concerns, but insist on your changes. S _____

    b. Review the proposal and suggest areas where changes may be needed. Make changes together, if needed. S _____

    c. Review the proposed budget, make revisions, and explain them. S _____

    d. Answer any questions or concerns Marie has and approve the budget as is. S _____

(continued)

/// BMV–4-4 Self-Assessment Exercise 4-4 /// (continued)

_____ 12. You are a sales manager. A customer has offered you a contract for your product with a short delivery date. The offer is open for two days. The contract would be profitable for you and the organization. The cooperation of the production department is essential to meet the deadline. Tim, the production manager, and you do not get along very well because of your repeated requests for quick delivery. Your action is to: _____ time _____ information _____ acceptance _____ capability/ _____ style

    a. Contact Tim and try to work together to complete the contract. S _____

    b. Accept the contract and convince Tim in a supportive way to meet the obligation. S _____

    c. Contact Tim and explain the situation. Ask him if you and he should accept the contract, but let him decide. S _____

    d. Accept the contract. Contact Tim and tell him to meet the obligation. If he resists, tell him you will go to his boss. S _____

To determine your preferred communication style, in the table below, circle the letter corresponding to the alternative you chose in situations 1 to 12. The column headings indicate the style you selected.

	Autocratic	Consultative	Participative	Laissez-faire
1.	a	b	c	d
2.	c	a	d	b
3.	c	d	a	b
4.	d	b	c	a
5.	a	b	d	c
6.	c	d	a	b
7.	c	a	b	d
8.	b	c	d	a
9.	b	d	a	c
10.	a	c	d	b
11.	c	a	b	d
12.	d	b	a	c
Total	_____	_____	_____	_____

Add the number of circled items per column. Adding the numbers in the Total row should equal 12. The column with the highest number represents your preferred communication style. There is no one best style in all situations. The more evenly distributed the numbers are between the four styles, the more flexible your communication style is. A total of 0 or 1 in any column may indicate a reluctance to use that style. You could have problems in situations calling for the use of that style.

Selecting the Appropriate Communication Style

Successful people understand different styles of communication and select communication styles based on the situation. There are three steps to follow when selecting the appropriate communication style in a given situation. Read through the bulleted items below, then follow the example for the first problem to better understand the remaining steps in this exercise.

- *Step 1: Diagnose the situation.* Answer the questions for each of the four situation variables. In Self-Assessment Exercise 4-4 you were asked to select one situation (S-A, S-C, S-P, or S-L). You were told to ignore the time information acceptance capability/style and S lines. Now you will complete this part in the In-Class Skill-Building Exercise 4-3 by placing the style letters (S-A, S-C, S-P, S-L) on the lines provided for each of the 12 situations.

- *Step 2: Select the appropriate style for the situation.* After analyzing the four variables, select the appropriate style for the situation. In some situations, where variables support conflicting styles, select the style of the most important variable for the situation. For example, capability may be outstanding (C-4), but you have all the information needed (S-A). If the information is more important, use the autocratic style even though the capability is outstanding. When doing In-Class Skill-Building Exercise 4-3, place the letters (S-A, S-C, S-P, S-L) for the appropriate styles on the style lines.

- *Step 3: Implement the appropriate communication style.* During In-Class Skill-Building Exercise 4-3, you will identify one of the four communication styles for each alternative action; place S-A, S-C, S-P, or S-L on the S lines. Select the alternative *a, b, c,* or *d* that represents the appropriate communication for each of the 12 situations.

The table below summarizes the material from the chapter on pages 117–118 and in this section. Use it to determine the appropriate communication style in situation 1 below and during In-Class Skill-Building Exercise 4-3. During In-Class Skill-Building Exercise 4-3, you will identify each communication style and select the alternative (*a, b, c,* or *d*) that represents the appropriate style.

Determining the Appropriate Communication Style for Situation 1

Step 1: Diagnose the situation. Answer the four variable questions from the model, and place the letters on the four variable lines below.

1. Wendy, a knowledgeable person from another department, comes to you, the engineering supervisor, and requests that you design a special product to her specifications. You would: time _____ information _____ acceptance _____ capability/ _____ style

    a. Control the conversation and tell Wendy what you will do for her. S _____

    b. Ask Wendy to describe the product. Once you understand it, you would present your ideas. Let her realize that you are concerned and want to help with your ideas. S _____

    c. Respond to Wendy's request by conveying understanding and support. Help clarify what is to be done by you. Offer ideas, but do it her way. S _____

    d. Find out what you need to know. Let Wendy know you will do it her way. S _____

Step 2: Select the appropriate style for the situation. Review the four variables. If they are all consistent, select one style. If they are conflicting, select the most important variable as the style to use. Place its letters (S-A, S-C, S-P, or S-L) on the style line.

Step 3: Select the appropriate action. Review the four alternative actions. Identify the communication style for each, placing its letters on the S _____ line, then check the appropriate match alternative.

MODEL 4.3 | Situational Communications

Step 1: Diagnose the Situation.

Variable	Use of Communication Style
Time	No S-A (do not consider the other three variables) Yes S-A, S-C, S-P, or S-L (consider other three variables)
Information	All S-A, some S-C, little S-P or S-L
Acceptance	Accept S-A, reluctance S-C, reject S-P or S-L
Capability	Low S-A, moderate S-C, high S-P, outstanding S-L

Step 2: Select the Appropriate Style for the Situation.

Autocratic (S-A)	Consultative (S-C)	Participative (S-P)	Laissez-Faire (S-L)
High task–low relationship behavior	High task–high relationship behavior	Low task–high relationship behavior	Low task–low relationship behavior
You take charge. You want things done your way.	You want things done your way, but you are willing to discuss things.	You are seeking others' input on how to do things, or supporting them.	You are willing to do things the other person's way; help as needed.

Step 3: Implement the Appropriate Communication Style.

Let's see how you did.

1. *Time* is available; it can be either S-C, S-P, or S-L. *Information:* You have little information, so you need to use a participative or laissez-faire style to find out what Wendy wants done: S-P or S-L. *Acceptance:* If you try to do it your way rather than Wendy's way, she will most likely reject it. You need to use a participative or laissez-faire style: S-P or S-L. *Capability:* Wendy is knowledgeable and is highly capable: S-P.

2. Reviewing the four variables, you see that there is a mixture of S-P and S-L. Since you are an engineer, it is appropriate to participate with Wendy to give her what she needs. Therefore, the choice is S-P.

3. *Alternative a* is S-A; this is the autocratic style, high task–low relationship. *Alternative b* is S-C; this is the consultative style, high task–high relationship. *Alternative c* is S-P; this is the participative style, low task–high relationship. *Alternative d* is S-L; this is laissez-faire, low task–low relationship behavior.

If you selected *c* as your action, you chose the most appropriate action for the situation. This was a 3-point answer. If you selected *d* as your answer, this is also a good alternative; it scores 2 points. If you selected *b,* you get 1 point for overdirecting. If you selected *a,* you get zero points; this is too much directing and will most likely hurt communication.

The better you match your communication style to the situation, the more effective you will be at communicating.

Procedure 1 (3–8 minutes)

The instructor reviews the Situational Communications Model and explains how to apply it to determine the appropriate style for situation 1.

Procedure 2 (6–8 minutes)

Turn to situation 2. Using the model, select the appropriate style. If you have time, identify each alternative style (3–4 minutes). The instructor goes over the recommended answers (3–4 minutes).

Procedure 3 (20–50 minutes)

A. Break into groups of two or three. As a team, apply the model to situations 3 through 7 (15–20 minutes). The instructor will go over the appropriate answers when all teams are done or the time is up (4–6 minutes).

B (Optional) Break into new groups of two or three and do situations 8 through 12 (15–20 minutes). The instructor will go over the appropriate answers (4–6 minutes).

Conclusion: The instructor leads a class discussion and/or makes concluding remarks.

Application (2–4 minutes): What did I learn from this experience? How will I use this knowledge in the future?

Sharing: Volunteers give their answers to the application section.

/ / / SKILL-BUILDING EXERCISE 4-4 / / /

Developing New Habits

Experience: Individual may share habits in groups or entire class, in-class or online.

AACSB Competencies: Analytic and application of knowledge.

Objective: To develop and share new habits.

Preparation: Select one or more topics from this chapter that will help you improve your human relations. Develop a new habit following the guideline from Chapter 1, section Habits and Skill-Building Exercise 1-4, on how to develop your cure, routine, and reward-change.

Procedure (5–30 minutes)

Follow the procedures from Skill Builder 1-4.

1. T.
2. F. High-context cultures rely heavily on nonverbal communication and subtle situational cues during the communication process.
3. F. Asking direct questions and paraphrasing are two techniques used to check understanding.
4. T.
5. T.
6. T.
7. F. With no time, you use the autocratic communication style.
8. F. Feelings are neither right or wrong, and identifying a feeling as wrong is a form of belittling a person, which should be avoided. Again, we can't control our feelings, only how we express our feelings as behavior.
9. T.

/ / / NOTES / / /

1. G. Colvin, "Humans Are Underrated," *Fortune* (August 1, 2015): 100–113.
2. L. Tomkins and E. Ulus, "Is Narcissism Undermining Critical Reflection in Our Business Schools?" *Academy of Management Learning & Education* 14(4) (2015): 595–606.
3. R.D. Costigan and K.E. Brink, "Another Perspective on MBA Program Alignment: An Investigation of Learning Goals," *Academy of Management Learning & Education* 14(2) (2015): 260–276.
4. L. Wiseman, "Five Not-to-Be-Missed Books," Fortune.com, accessed April 21, 2017.
5. K.E. Brink and R.D. Costigan, "Oral Communication Skills: Are the Priorities of Workplace and AACSB-Accredited Business Programs Aligned?" *Academy of Management Learning & Education* 14(2) (2015): 205–221.
6. AACSB www.aacsb.org, accessed April 21, 2017.
7. M. Voronov and K. Weber, "The Heart of Institutions: Emotional Compentence and Institutional Actorhood," *Academy of Management Review* 41(3) (2016): 456–478.
8. B.R. Spisak, M.J. O'Brien, N. Nicholson, and M. Van Vugt, "Niche Construction and the Evolution of Leadership," *Academy of Management Review* 40(2) (2015): 291–306.
9. F.P. Morgeson, T.R. Mitchell, and D. Liu, "Event System Theory: An Event-Oriented Approach to the Organizational Sciences," *Academy of Management Review* 40(4) (2015): 515–537.
10. F.P. Morgeson, T.R. Mitchell, and D. Liu, "Event System Theory: An Event-Oriented Approach to the Organizational Sciences," *Academy of Management Review* 40(4) (2015): 515–537.
11. F.P. Morgeson, T.R. Mitchell, and D. Liu, "Event System Theory: An Event-Oriented Approach to the Organizational Sciences," *Academy of Management Review* 40(4) (2015): 515–537.
12. R.D. Costigan and K.E. Brink, "Another Perspective on MBA Program Alignment: An Investigation of Learning Goals," *Academy of Management Learning & Education* 14(2) (2015): 260–276.
13. R. McCammon, "A Little Talk Therapy," *Entrepreneur* (November 2014): 28–29.
14. M.M Butts, W.J. Becker, and W.R. Boswell, "Hot Buttons and Time Sinks: The Effects of Electronic Communication During Nonwork Time on Emotions and Work-Nonwork Conflicts," *Academy of Management Journal* 58(3) (2015): 763–788.
15. G. Colvin, "Humans Are Underrated," *Fortune* (August 1, 2015): 100–113.
16. A. Handley, "Before You Hit Send..." *Entrepreneur* (January 2015): 28.
17. S. Dembling, "Should I Stay or Should I Go?" *Entrepreneur* (August 2014): 28.
18. L. Hochwald, "The Personal Touch," *Entrepreneur* (December 2014): 96.

19. S. McGregor, "Margin Advice," *Fortune* (November 17, 2014): 133.

20. T.L. Stanko and C.M. Beckman, "Watching You Watching Me: Boundary Control and Capturing Attention in the Context of Ubiquitous Technology Use," *Academy of Management Journal* 58(3) (2015): 712-738.

21. L. Hochwald, "The Personal Touch," *Entrepreneur* (December 2014): 96.

22. S. Dembling, "Should I Stay or Should I Go?" *Entrepreneur* (August 2014): 28.

23. L. Hochwald, "The Personal Touch," *Entrepreneur* (December 2014): 96.

24. T.L. Stanko and C.M. Beckman, "Watching You Watching Me: Boundary Control and Capturing Attention in the Context of Ubiquitous Technology Use," *Academy of Management Journal* 58(3) (2015): 712-738.

25. L. Weber, "No Personal Calls on the Job? No Thanks," *Wall Street Journal* (May 9, 2012): B10.

26. T.L. Stanko and C.M. Beckman, "Watching You Watching Me: Boundary Control and Capturing Attention in the Context of Ubiquitous Technology Use," *Academy of Management Journal* 58(3) (2015): 712-738.

27. L. Hochwald, "The Personal Touch," *Entrepreneur* (December 2014): 96.

28. L.R. Weingart, K.J. Behfar, C. Bendersky, G. Todorova, and K.A. Hehn, "The Directness and Oppositional Intensity of Conflict Expression," *Academy of Management Review* 40(2) (2015): 235-262.

29. J.P. Cornelissen, R. Durand, P.C. Fiss, J.C. Lammers, and E. Vaara, "Putting Communication Front and Center in Institutional Theory and Analysis," *Academy of Management Review* 40(1) (2015): 10-27.

30. R. McCammon, "A Little Talk Therapy," *Entrepreneur* (November 2014): 28-29.

31. S. Pinker, "When Being Too Smart Ruins Writing," *The Wall Street Journal* (September 27-28, 2014): C3.

32. J.P. Cornelissen, R. Durand, P.C. Fiss, J.C. Lammers, and E. Vaara, "Putting Communication Front and Center in Institutional Theory and Analysis," *Academy of Management Review* 40(1) (2015): 10-27.

33. M. Voronov and K. Weber, "The Heart of Institutions: Emotional Compentence and Institutional Actorhood," *Academy of Management Review* 41(3) (2016): 456-478.

34. J. Gray, *Men Are from Mars, Women Are from Venus* (New York: HarperCollins, 1992).

35. D. Tannen, *You Just Don't Understand: Women and Men in Conversation* (New York: Ballantine, 1991); and *Talking from 9 to 5* (New York: Morrow, 1995).

36. J. Reingold, "Angela Ahrendts," *Fortune* (September 15, 2015): 101-108.

37. G. Colvin, "Humans Are Underrated," *Fortune* (August 1, 2015): 100-113.

38. Staff, "Crying at Work," *Entrepreneur* (October 2014): 18.

39. J.P. Cornelissen, R. Durand, P.C. Fiss, J.C. Lammers, and E. Vaara, "Putting Communication Front and Center in Institutional Theory and Analysis," Academy of Management Review 40(1) (2015): 10-27.

40. L. Hochwald, "The Personal Touch," *Entrepreneur* (December 2014): 96

41. C. Hann, "Keep a Level Head," *Entrepreneur* (January 2016): 23.

42. S. Dembling, "Should I Stay or Should I Go?" *Entrepreneur* (August 2014): 28.

43. C. Hann, "Keep a Level Head," *Entrepreneur* (January 2016): 23.

44. R. McCammon, "A Little Talk Therapy," *Entrepreneur* (November 2014): 28-29.

45. M.M Butts, W.J. Becker, and W.R. Boswell, "Hot Buttons and Time Sinks: The Effects of Electronic Communication During Nonwork Time on Emotions and Work-Nonwork Conflicts," *Academy of Management Journal* 58(3) (2015): 763-788.

46. V. Harnish, "Five Not-to-Be-Missed Books," Fortune.com, accessed April 26, 2017.

47. F.M. Bell, "Best Advice," *Fortune* (November 17, 2014): 138.

48. S. Shellenbarger, "Raise a Glass, Give a Speech, Without a Stumble," *The Wall Street Journal* (December 23, 2015): D1.

49. L. Hochwald, "The Personal Touch," *Entrepreneur* (December 2014): 96.

50. S. Shellenbarger, "Find Out What Your Boss Really Thinks About You," *The Wall Street Journal* (June 29, 2016): D1, D2.

51. S.H. Harrison and E.D. Rouse, "An Inductive Study of Feedback Interactions Over the Course of Creative Projects," *Academy of Management Journal* 58(2) (2015): 375-404.

52. Video, Dynamic Catholic.com, viewed March 23, 2017.

53. J. Lauder, "Most Powerful Women Advice!" *Fortune* (November 17, 2014): 149.

54. R.B. Pollock, "Advice," *Fortune* (November 17, 2014): 130.

55. J. Steinberg, "Advice to My 20-Year-Old Self," *Fortune* (October 1, 2015): 116.

56. K.E. Brink and R.D. Costigan, "Oral Communication Skills: Are the Priorities of Workplace and AACSB-Accredited Business Programs Aligned?" *Academy of Management Learning & Education* 14(2) (2015): 205–221.

57. Video, Dynamic Catholic.com, viewed March 23, 2017.

58. Bernstein, "You Can Do IT! Be a Motivator" *The Wall Street Journal* (June 16, 2016): D1, D3.

59. R. McCammon, "The Worst of Times," *Entrepreneur* (February 2016): 15–16.

60. B. Murphy, "4 Habits of Exceptional Bosses," *INC.* (June 2016): 12.

61. W. Beasley, "Listen Up," *Fortune* (December 15, 2015): 7.

62. G. Colvin, "Employers Are Looking for New Hires With Something Extra: Empathy," *Fortune* (September 4, 2014): 55.

63. T.L. Stanko and C.M. Beckman, "Watching You Watching Me: Boundary Control and Capturing Attention in the Context of Ubiquitous Technology Use," *Academy of Management Journal* 58(3) (2015): 712–738.

64. M. Voronov and K. Weber, "The Heart of Institutions: Emotional Compentence and Institutional Actorhood," *Academy of Management Review* 41(3) (2016): 456–478.

65. Staff, "Boost Your Limbic Brain," *AARP The Magazine*: 40, accessed online www.aarp.com April 30, 2017.

66. C.C. Manz, "Takeing the Self-Leadership High Road: Smooth Surface or Potholes Ahead?" *Academy of Management Perspectives* 29(1) (2015): 132–151.

67. A. Chen, "More Rational Resolutions," *The Wall Street Journal* (December 31, 2013): D1, D3.

68. R. McCammon, "Don't Pop Your Top," *Entrepreneur* (May 2016): 15–16.

69. A.C. Cosper, "Meet Fear's Antidote: Hope," *Entrepreneur* (January 2016): 10.

70. R. McCammon, "A Little Talk Therapy," *Entrepreneur* (November 2014): 28–29.

71. M. Voronov and K. Weber, "The Heart of Institutions: Emotional Compentence and Institutional Actorhood," *Academy of Management Review* 41(3) (2016): 456–478.

72. M. Voronov and K. Weber, "The Heart of Institutions: Emotional Compentence and Institutional Actorhood," *Academy of Management Review* 41(3) (2016): 456–478.

73. L.M. Little, V.S. Major, A.S. Hinojosa, D.L. Nelson, "Professional Image Maintenance: How Women Navigate Pregnancy in the Workplace," *Academy of Management Journal* 58(1) (2015): 8–37.

74. R. McCammon, "Don't Pop Your Top," *Entrepreneur* (May 2016): 15–16.

75. Staff, "Crying at Work," *Entrepreneur* (October 2014): 16.

76. R. McCammon, "Don't Pop Your Top," *Entrepreneur* (May 2016): 15–16.

77. D. Worowitz, "When Customer Service Goes Wrong," *Costco Connection* (October 2014): 15.

78. S. Shellenbarger, "Relax Don't You Tell Me to Relax!" *The Wall Street Journal* (August 17, 2016): D1, D2.

79. S. Shellenbarger, "Relax Don't You Tell Me to Relax!" *The Wall Street Journal* (August 17, 2016): D1, D2.

80. M. Voronov and K. Weber, "The Heart of Institutions: Emotional Compentence and Institutional Actorhood," *Academy of Management Review* 41(3) (2016): 456–478.

81. G. Colvin, "Humans Are Underrated," *Fortune* (August 1, 2015): 100–113.

82. G. Colvin, "Employers Are Looking for New Hires With Something Extra: Empathy," *Fortune* (September 4, 2014): 55.

83. B. Murphy, "4 Habits of Exceptional Bosses," *INC.* (June 2016): 12.

84. H. Ersek, "Margin Advice," *Fortune* (November 17, 2014): 132.

85. S. Shellenbarger, "Relax Don't You Tell Me to Relax!" *The Wall Street Journal* (August 17, 2016): D1, D2.

86. R. Feintzeig, "When Nice Is a Four-Letter Word," *The Wall Street Journal* (December 31, 2015): D1, D3.

87. S.H. Harrison and E.D. Rouse, "An Inductive Study of Feedback Interactions Over the Course of Creative Projects," *Academy of Management Journal* 58(2) (2015): 375–404.

88. R. McCammon, "Words of Encouragement," *Entrepreneur* (October 2015): 26.

89. S. Shellenbarger, "Find Out What Your Boss Really Thinks About You," *The Wall Street Journal* (June 29, 2016): D1, D2.

90. S. Shellenbarger, "Find Out What Your Boss Really Thinks About You," *The Wall Street Journal* (June 29, 2016): D1, D2.

91. S. Shellenbarger, "Find Out What Your Boss Really Thinks About You," *The Wall Street Journal* (June 29, 2016): D1, D2.

92. S. Shellenbarger, "Find Out What Your Boss Really Thinks About You," *The Wall Street Journal* (June 29, 2016): D1, D2.

93. P. Lencioni, "Innovation Won't Get You Very Far," *INC.* (December 2014 / January 2015): 102.

  i. http://www.oprah.com/pressroom/oprah-winfreys-official-biography, accessed May 17, 2017

 ii. http://madamenoire.com/345185/60-year-oprah-effect-still-going-strong-oprah-winfrey-changed-face-media/ accessed May 17, 2017

iii. Oprah Winfrey's Greatest Accomplishments, by Banji Ganchrow - https://longevity.media/oprah-winfreys-greatest-accomplishments, accessed May 17, 2017

 iv. http://www.oprah.com/pressroom/oprah-winfreys-official-biography, accessed May 17, 2017

Dealing with Conflict

© PhotoAlto/Eric Audras/Getty Images

LEARNING OUTCOMES

After completing this chapter, you should be able to:

LO 5-1   Describe the three ego states of transactional analysis.

LO 5-2   Explain the three types of transactions.

LO 5-3   Identify the differences between passive, aggressive, and assertive behavior.

LO 5-4   List the four steps of assertive behavior.

LO 5-5   State when and how to use five conflict management styles.

LO 5-6   List the steps of initiating, responding to, and mediating conflict resolutions.

LO 5-7   Define the following 14 key terms (in order of appearance in the chapter):

transactional analysis (TA)	compromising conflict style
ego states	collaborating conflict style
types of transactions	initiating conflict resolution steps
assertiveness	XYZ model
conflict	responding to conflict resolution steps
forcing conflict style	mediating conflict resolution steps
avoiding conflict style	
accommodating conflict style	

OPENING CASE WORK SCENARIO

/ / / Larry and Helen work together doing the same job at Harvey's, a department store in Springfield. They share a special calculator because it is expensive and it is used for only part of their job. The calculator is generally kept in one person's possession until the other person requests it. Recently, the amount of time each needs to use the calculator has increased.

When Larry wants the calculator, he says, "I need the calculator now" (in a bold, intimidating voice), and Helen gives it to him, even when she is using it. When Helen needs the calculator, she says, "I don't like to bother you, but I need the calculator." If Larry is using it, he tells Helen that he will give it to her when he is finished with it, and

Helen says, "OK." Helen doesn't think this arrangement is fair and is getting upset with Larry. But she hasn't said anything to Larry yet. Larry comes over to Helen's desk, and this conversation takes place:

LARRY: I need the calculator right now.

HELEN: I'm sick and tired of you pushing me around. Go back to your desk, and I'll bring it to you when I'm good and ready.

LARRY: What's wrong with you? You've never acted like this before.

HELEN: Just take the calculator and go back to your desk and leave me alone.

LARRY: *(Says nothing; just takes the calculator and leaves.)*

HELEN: *(Watches Larry walk back to his desk with the calculator, feels a bit guilty, and thinks to herself:)* Why do I let little annoyances build up until I explode and end up yelling at people? It's rather childish behavior to let people walk all over me, then to reverse and be tough and rude. I wish I could stand up for my rights in a positive way without hurting my relations. / / /

HOW INTERPERSONAL DYNAMICS AFFECT BEHAVIOR, HUMAN RELATIONS, HAPPINESS, AND PERFORMANCE

The three topics of this chapter—transactional analysis, assertiveness, and conflict management—all involve interpersonal dynamics through communication. All three deal with your *emotions* and those of others in an effective way to enhance behavior, human relations, happiness, and performance as we continue to develop your interpersonal skills,[1] or soft skills that employers value.[2]

Transactional analysis is a method for determining how people interact.[3] When we interact, behavior can be passive, aggressive, or assertive.[4] During human relations, transactions can go poorly, people can be aggressive, and it is common for people to disagree and be in *conflict*.[5] Putting these topics together, you should realize that during human relations (transactional analysis), the behavior used (passive, aggressive, or assertive) affects performance and potential conflict.

Dealing with your emotions and transacting with people on the appropriate level, assertively standing up for your rights, and resolving your conflicts without hurting human relations will improve your effectiveness in organizations and in your personal life because "the ability to get along with others" is the key to success.[6] That's what this chapter is about.

TRANSACTIONAL ANALYSIS

Before we begin, complete Self-Assessment Exercise 5-1 to determine your preferred transactional analysis (TA) style.

Communication Skills
Refer to CS Question 1.

Transactional analysis (TA) *is a method of understanding behavior in interpersonal dynamics.* In fact, there is an International Transactional Analysis Association (itaaworld.org) that publishes the *Transactional Analysis Journal.* Eric Berne applied TA to business in his bestselling book, *Games People Play.*[7]

In this section you will learn about your preferred TA style (called *ego state* in TA jargon), the types of human relations transactions you have, and your attitude toward yourself and others (called *life positions*). You will also learn about giving positive and negative feedback (called *stroking*) during human relations.

/ / / Self-Assessment Exercise 5-1 / / /

Your Preferred Transactional Analysis Style

Turn to Skill-Building Exercise 5-1, Transactional Analysis, on page 168. Ignore the directions, steps 1 to 4. Go directly to the 10 situations. Put yourself in the responder's position (1–Sue, 2–Saul, . . . 10–Mike), and place a check mark after the letter (*not* on the line) of the one response that best describes what you would say in each situation. Be honest; don't try to pick the response you think is correct. After selecting your 10 responses, circle the letter of your response for each situation in the following table.

(continued)

/ / / **Self-Assessment Exercise 5-1** / / / (*continued*)

Situation	Critical Parent	Sympathetic Parent	Natural Child	Adapted Child	Adult
1.	a	b	d	c	e
2.	d	c	e	a	b
3.	b	d	a	c	e
4.	c	e	b	d	a
5.	e	b	d	a	c
6.	a	b	e	d	c
7.	e	a	b	c	d
8.	b	c	e	d	a
9.	a	c	d	b	e
10.	a	e	d	c	b
Total					

Scoring: Add the number of letters circled in each column. The number in each column should be between 0 and 10, and the total of all columns should equal 10. The column with your highest total is your preferred TA style. If it's not adult, or even if it is, you may want to improve your TA behavior.

Learning Outcome 5-1

Describe the three ego states of transactional analysis.

Learning Outcome 5-2

Explain the three types of transactions.

Communication Skills
Refer to CS Question 2.

Ego States and Types of Transactions

Ego States   According to Berne, we all have three major ego states that affect our behavior or the way we transact through communication. The three **ego states** are the *parent, child,* and *adult:* (1) *parent:* the critical parent is evaluative while the sympathetic parent is supportive; (2) *child:* the natural child is curious while the adapted child is rebellious; and (3) *adult:* the adult is a thinking, unemotional state of ego. We change ego states throughout the day; even during a single discussion, a series of transactions can take place between different ego states. See Exhibit 5.1 for a more detailed description of the ego states.

Generally, the most effective behavior, human relations, and performance come from the adult ego state.[8] When interacting with others, you should be aware of their ego state because it will help you understand why they are behaving the way they are and help you determine which ego state you should use during the interaction.

EXHIBIT 5.1 | Transactional Analysis Ego States

TA Ego State	Description
Parent	
1. Critical parent	Controls the conversation using advising responses (Chapter 4) that are judgmental, opinionated, demanding, disapproving, or disciplining, telling others what to do.
2. Sympathetic parent	Uses reassuring responses (Chapter 4) that are protecting, permitting, consoling, caring, or nurturing, to be supportive.
Child	
1. Natural child	Uses probing responses (Chapter 4) that show curiosity, fun, fantasy, or impulsiveness.
2. Adapted child	Responds with confrontational advising responses (Chapter 4) that express rebelliousness, pouting, anger, fear, anxiety, inadequacy, or procrastination.
Adult	Behaves in a thinking, rational, calculating, factual, unemotional manner with cool and calm behavior. Avoids getting caught up in others' emotions.

EXHIBIT 5.2 | Types of Transactions

WORK APPLICATION 5-1

Give an example of a complementary transaction you experienced. Be sure to identify the ego states involved.

Transaction	Example	Common Result
Complementary	An employee makes a mistake and, wanting some sympathy, apologizes to the boss. *Employee:* "I just dropped the thing when I was almost done. Now I have to do it all over again." *Supervisor:* "It happens to all of us; don't worry about it."	Generally, complementary transactions result in more effective communication with fewer hurt feelings and arguments. Exceptions are if an employee uses an adapted child or critical parent ego state and the supervisor does too. These complementary transactions can lead to problem transactions.
Crossed	Let's return to our first example. *Employee:* "I just dropped the thing when I was almost done. Now I have to do it all over again." *Supervisor:* "You are so clumsy."	Generally, crossed transactions result in surprise, disappointment, and hurt feelings for the sender of the message. The unexpected response often gets the person emotional, which can result in his or her changing to the adapted child ego state, which causes the communication to deteriorate further, often into an argument. Crossed transactions can be helpful when the negative parent or child ego response is crossed with an adult response. This crossover may result in the preferred adult-to-adult conversation.
Ulterior	A person came up to a consultant and complained about his boss in the adult ego state. When the consultant gave advice, the participant twice had quick responses as to why the advice would not work (child rather than adult behavior). The consultant realized that what the participant actually wanted was sympathetic understanding for his situation, not advice. The consultant stopped making suggestions and used reflecting responses (Chapter 4) from the sympathetic parent ego state.	Sometimes people don't know what they want or how to ask for it in a direct way, so they use ulterior transactions. When possible, it is best to avoid ulterior transactions because they tend to waste time. Avoid making people search for your hidden meaning. Plan your message (Chapter 4) before you send it. When receiving messages, look for ulterior transactions and turn them into complementary transactions as illustrated in the ulterior example.

WORK APPLICATION 5-2

Give an example of a crossed transaction you experienced. Be sure to identify the ego states involved.

WORK APPLICATION 5-3

Give an example of an ulterior transaction you experienced. Be sure to identify the ego states involved.

Types of Transactions   Within ego states there are three different **types of transactions:** *complementary, crossed, and ulterior:* (1) *complementary:* the sender of the message gets the intended response from the receiver; (2) *crossed:* the sender does not get the expected response; and (3) *ulterior:* the person appears to be in one ego state, but his or her behavior comes from a different ego state. See Exhibit 5.2 for examples and common results of each transaction.

APPLICATION SITUATIONS / / /

Transactional Analysis   AS 5-1

Identify each transaction as being:

A. Complementary   B. Crossed   C. Ulterior

(continued)

_____ 1. John: So Karen, will you serve on my recycling committee? Karen: Yes, I'm concerned about the environment (thinking—I want to date you, you're attractive).

_____ 2. Sandy: Rob, will you help me do this project? Rob: You have done several of them. Do it on your own; then I will check it for you.

_____ 3. Latoya: Shawn, please take out the trash for me. Shawn: Are you kidding me? That's not my job, I'm not doing it!

_____ 4. Hank: You're lying. Brenda: No, I'm not! You're a liar.

_____ 5. Holly: Pete, please help me move this desk over there? Pete: OK. Let's do it now.

Life Positions and Stroking

Life Positions   As stated in Chapter 3, attitudes affect your behavior and human relations. Within the TA analysis framework, you have attitudes toward yourself and toward others.[9] Positive attitudes are described as "OK," and negative attitudes are described as "not OK." The four life positions are illustrated in Exhibit 5.3. It is your emotional state.[10]

The most desirable life position is shown in the upper right-hand box: "I'm OK—You're OK." With a positive attitude toward yourself and others, you have a greater chance for having adult-to-adult ego state communication. You can change your attitudes (Chapter 3), and you should if they are not positive.

Communication Skills
Refer to CS Question 3.

Stroking   Stroking is any behavior that implies recognition of another's presence. Strokes can be positive and make people feel good about themselves, or they can be negative and hurt people in some way. Giving praise (positive strokes) is a powerful motivation technique that is easy to use and costs nothing.

Through work and effort, you can control your adult-to-adult level transactions in most situations. Skill-Building Exercise 5-1 can help you. Remember that what you think about affects how you feel, and how you feel affects your behavior, human relations, happiness, and performance. So think "I'm OK—You're OK" thoughts to help you communicate from the adult ego state, and give lots of strokes.

Skill-Building Exercise 5-1
develops this skill.

/// **In the opening case,** Larry was behaving out of the critical parent ego state. He showed disapproval of Helen by asking, "What's wrong with you? You never acted like this before." Helen responded to Larry's request for the calculator from the adapted child ego state. Helen was rebellious and showed her anger. They had a crossed transaction because Larry opened in his usual manner but was surprised when Helen did not respond in her typical manner. Larry was in the "I'm OK—You're not OK" life position, while Helen was in the "I'm not OK—You're not OK" life position. Both used negative strokes. ///

WORK APPLICATION 5-4

Identify your present or past boss's life position and use of stroking.

EXHIBIT 5.3 | Life Positions

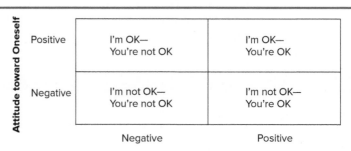

Learning Outcome 5-3

Identify the differences between passive, aggressive, and assertive behavior.

ASSERTIVENESS

Begin this section by completing Self-Assessment Exercise 5-2 to determine your use of the assertiveness style.

In this section, you will learn to express feelings, ask for favors, give and receive compliments, request behavior changes, and refuse unreasonable requests. You can ask for what you want in a direct, straightforward, deliberate, and honest way that conveys self-confidence without being obnoxious or abusive.[11]

Assertiveness is *the process of expressing thoughts and feelings while asking for what one wants in an appropriate way.* You need to present your message without falling into stereotypical "too pushy" (aggressive) or "not tough enough" (nonassertive–passive) traps; women must be especially aware of this.[12]

Assertiveness Is Becoming More Global   For example, employees in Thailand are becoming more assertive, and the Japanese now include more strategies of assertiveness. In China, workers are assertively asking for raises and better working conditions, and getting them.

Passive Behavior

Passive or nonassertive behavior comes primarily through the obedient child or supportive parent ego state. Passive behavior is an avoidance of behavior or an accommodation of the other party's wishes without standing up for one's own rights. Passive people tend to deny the importance of things. They rationalize things—"It doesn't matter to me."

When people know someone is passive, they tend to take advantage of the person. They make unreasonable requests, knowing the person cannot say no, and refuse to meet the

---

/ / / Self-Assessment Exercise 5-2 / / /

Your Use of the Assertiveness Style

Turn to Skill-Building Exercise 5-2, Assertiveness, on page 171. Ignore the directions. Go directly to the 10 situations. Put yourself in the situation, and place a check mark after the letter (*not* on the line) of the one response that best describes what you would say or do in each situation. Be honest; don't try to pick the response you think is correct. After selecting your 10 responses, circle the letter of your response for each situation in the table below.

Situation	Passive		Assertive	Aggressive	
1.	*b*	*d*	*c*	*a*	*e*
2.	*d*	*e*	*c*	*a*	*b*
3.	*c*	*e*	*a*	*b*	*d*
4.	*b*	*d*	*c*	*a*	*e*
5.	*a*	*e*	*b*	*c*	*d*
6.	*a*	*d*	*b*	*c*	*e*
7.	*b*	*d*	*a*	*c*	*e*
8.	*b*	*c*	*d*	*a*	*e*
9.	*a*	*c*	*d*	*b*	*e*
10.	*b*	*c*	*a*	*d*	*e*
Total					

Scoring: Add the number of letters circled in each column. The number in each column should be between 0 and 10, and the total of all three columns should equal 10. The column with your highest total is your preferred style. Regardless of the result, you may want to improve your assertiveness behavior.

Communication Skills
Refer to CS Question 4.

passive person's rare mild request. When the passive person does speak, others tend not to listen and tend to interrupt, especially women.[13]

Passivity is often based on fear: fear of rejection, retaliation, hurting others, being hurt, getting into trouble, and so on. If you tend to be passive, determine what really is important, and stand up for your rights in an assertive way.

Aggressive Behavior

As you read, you will realize that aggressive behavior is not the same as assertive; aggression is "abusive mistreatment of others" and not appropriate behavior.[14]

Aggressive behavior comes primarily through the adapted child and the critical parent ego states, often through anger.[15] Aggressive people are demanding, tough, rude, and pushy. They are very competitive, hate to lose to the point of cheating, and tend to violate the rights of others to get what they want.

When faced with aggressive behavior, the other party often retaliates with aggressive behavior (fights back) or withdraws and gives in (takes flight). People often avoid contact with the aggressive person or prepare themselves for a fight when transacting. Abusive employees and supervisors decrease work performance.[16]

Violence is clearly aggressive behavior at the extreme level. Because anger and workplace violence are so important, we will discuss these issues separately in the next major section.

Unfortunately, women are stereotyped as being passive.[17] When they use the same aggressive behavior as men, they are often criticized and told to be less aggressive, whereas the identical behavior is often considered acceptable by men.[18]

If you are continually aggressive, work at becoming more sensitive to the needs of others. Learn to replace aggressive behavior with assertive behavior.

Passive–Aggressive Behavior

Passive–aggressive behavior is displayed in three major ways:

1. The person uses both types of behavior sporadically. The person may be passive one day or moment and aggressive the next.

2. The person uses passive behavior during the situation, then shortly after uses aggressive behavior. An employee may agree to do something, then leave and slam the door or yell at the next person he or she sees or sabotage the task.

3. The person uses passive behavior but inside is building up hostility. After the repeated behavior happens often enough, the passive person becomes aggressive.[19] Too often the person who was attacked really doesn't understand the full situation and blames everything on the exploder, rather than examining his or her self-behavior and changing it.

Communication Skills
Refer to CS Question 5.

The person who becomes aggressive often feels guilty. The end result is usually hurt human relations and no change in the situation. For example, during a meeting, Carlos interrupted Latoya three times when she was speaking. Latoya said nothing each time, but was building up hostility. The fourth time Carlos interrupted Latoya, she attacked him by yelling at him for being so inconsiderate of her. He simply said, "What's wrong with you?" It would have been better for Latoya to assertively tell Carlos not to interrupt her the first time he did it. Be quick to address passive-aggressive behavior during meetings.[20]

If you use passive–aggressive behavior, try to learn to be assertive on a consistent basis and you will be easier to work with. You will also get the results you want more often.

WORK APPLICATION 5-5

Recall an example of when you used or observed passive–aggressive behavior. How did it affect human relations?

Assertive Behavior

Assertive behavior comes through the adult ego state, with an "I'm OK–You're OK" life position. As stated earlier, the assertive person expresses feelings and thoughts and asks for things without aggressive behavior. The person stands up for his or her rights without violating the rights of others. Organizations, such as **Bridgewater Associates**, value assertive behavior and encourage and train employees to be honest in giving feedback.[21]

People who use assertive behavior are not threatened by others, and they do not let others control their behavior. They stay calm[22] in the adult ego state. Assertive people project a positive image (Chapter 3) of being confident, friendly, and honest.[23] Using assertive behavior wins the respect of others.[24] Use it on a consistent basis.

Being Assertive   Being assertive can create a win-win situation. Assertive behavior is different from aggressive behavior, and the terms are not interchangeable. To better understand the differences between passive, aggressive, and assertive behavior, see Exhibit 5.4. The phrases can be thought of as dos and don'ts. Do make assertive phrases and don't make passive and aggressive phrases. But remember, there are times when passive and aggressive behavior are appropriate. You will learn when later in this chapter.

Below is an example that puts it all together. When a person who is talking is interrupted, which is more frequently women,[25] he or she can behave in one of three ways:

1. Passively. The person can say and do nothing.

2. Aggressively. The person can say, "I'm talking; mind your manners and wait your turn" in a loud voice, while pointing to the interrupter.

3. Assertively. The person can say, "Excuse me; I haven't finished making my point," with a smile and in a friendly but firm voice using eye contact.[26]

Men need to be more aware of their stereotyping of women as passive, stop judging their same behavior as men as being aggressive, and stop interrupting them. And men need assertive women to make them aware of the situation to stop gender biases.[27] We will further explain how to be assertive in the next section, which deals with conflict management.

Communication Skills
Refer to CS Question 6.

EXHIBIT 5.4 | Passive, Assertive, and Aggressive Phrases

Passive Phrases

Passive speakers use self-limiting, qualifying expressions without stating their position or needs.
- I don't know/care (when I do).
- It doesn't matter (when it does).
- Either one/way is fine with me (when I have a preference).
- I'm sorry (when I don't mean it).
- It's just my opinion . . .
- I don't want to bother you, but . . .
- It's not really important, but . . .

Assertive Phrases

Assertive speakers state their position or needs without violating the rights of others.
- I don't understand . . .
- I need/want/prefer . . .
- I would like . . .
- No, I won't be able to . . .
- I'd prefer that you don't tell me these jokes anymore.
- My opinion is . . .
- I need some of your time to . . .
- I thought that you would like to know . . .

Aggressive Phrases

Aggressive speakers state their position or needs while violating the rights of others using "you-messages" and absolutes.
- You don't need/want . . .
- Your opinion is wrong.
- You don't know what you're talking about.
- You're doing it wrong.
- That won't work!
- You have to . . .
- You need to know . . .

MODEL 5.1 |

Assertiveness Steps

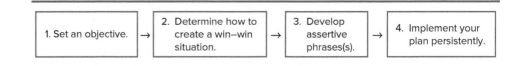

| 1. Set an objective. | → | 2. Determine how to create a win–win situation. | → | 3. Develop assertive phrases(s). | → | 4. Implement your plan persistently. |

WORK APPLICATION 5-6

Recall an actual conflict you faced. Identify passive, aggressive, and assertive responses to the situation.

Learning Outcome 5-4

List the four steps of assertive behavior.

Skill-Building Exercise 5-2 develops this skill.

/// **In the opening case,** before the conversation took place, Helen used passive behavior, while Larry used aggressive behavior. During the confrontation Helen used aggressive behavior, but when Larry responded with aggressive behavior, she returned to passive behavior, giving him the calculator. In other words, Helen used passive–aggressive–passive behavior with Larry. ///

Assertiveness Steps Below are the four assertive steps that Helen, in the opening case, could have used. These steps are summarized in Model 5.1.

Step 1: Set an objective. Specify what you want to accomplish. Helen's objective could have been "to tell Larry that I will give him the calculator after I'm finished with it."

Step 2: Determine how to create a win-win situation. Assess the situation in terms of meeting your needs and the other person's needs. Larry's needs are already being met by Helen's giving him the calculator any time he wants it. At present, there is a win-lose situation. Helen needs to be assertive to meet her own needs to get her work done. Equitably sharing the use of the calculator will create a win-win situation. The present system of giving it to each other when done may work fine if Helen finishes using it before giving it to Larry.

Step 3: Develop assertive phrase(s): Before confronting Larry, Helen could have developed a statement such as, "I'm using it now, and I'll give it to you as soon as I'm finished with it."

Step 4: Implement your plan persistently. Helen could have used the above statement. If Larry continued to use aggressive behavior to get the calculator, Helen could persistently repeat the phrase until it sinks in, until Larry leaves without the calculator. It is not necessary, but Helen could explain why she feels the situation is not fair and repeat that she will give the calculator to Larry when she is done with it.

APPLICATION SITUATIONS / / /

Assertiveness AS 5-2

Identify each response to a supervisor's request for an employee to make a personal purchase for him on company time:

A. Passive   B. Aggressive   C. Assertive

_____ 6. "I've never done that before. Is that part of my job description?"

_____ 7. "I'll do it right now (thinking, 'What I'm doing is much more important.')"

_____ 8. "You don't really expect me to do that for you, do you? Forget it, and don't ask me again."

_____ 9. "Your asking me to shred the documents is against company policy. I will not do it."

_____ 10. "After being interrupted for the fourth time during a conversation, Charlene doesn't say anything."

Remember that what you think about affects how you feel, and how you feel affects your behavior, human relations, happiness, and performance. Don't let people take advantage of you, but you can't afford to blow your top. Don't fight jerkiness with jerkiness. Think about being assertive, not passive; be aware of your feelings of anger; and keep your aggressive behavior under control to help you have effective human relations.[28]

ANGER AND VIOLENCE IN THE WORKPLACE

Now that we know the difference between passive, aggressive, and assertive behavior, let's focus on aggressive behavior with anger that can lead to incivility, bullying, and violence, and how to prevent it. The key to preventing workplace violence is to recognize and handle suspicious behavior before it becomes violent.

Causes of Anger and Violence

You have most likely heard of road rage. In business we have *desk rage* and *customer rage,* which can take the form of yelling, verbal abuse, and physical violence. Anger leads to incivility and violence. Frustration, stress, fear, ostracism, and bullying can bring out anger. People who are angry are disappointed, or who have been hurt/bullied in some way, may become aggressive and seek revenge, sometimes through violence.[29] The behavior of one person affects those of others, so anger can spread.[30] Also, complaining about the boss and company (*venting*) is bad for you because it only makes you angrier.[31]

Dealing with Anger

Anger can be tough to deal with, so here are some ideas to help.

Your Anger and Emotional Behavior Control   Recall our discussion of emotions in Chapter 4. It is natural to get angry sometimes. Although we cannot control the feeling of anger, we can control our behavior. Letting anger build up often leads to passive–aggressive behavior. Here are some tips for effectively getting rid of your anger:

- Remember that what you think about affects how you feel, and how you feel affects your behavior, human relations, happiness, and performance. So don't think about and dwell on your angry feelings—don't vent.[32] Let it go because you only get more upset. Buddha said, "You will not be punished *for* your anger; you will be punished *by* your anger." Be assertive, not passive, to help keep from using passive-aggressive behavior.

- Develop a positive attitude about how you deal with anger. Use the techniques from Chapter 3 for changing your attitudes and building a positive self-concept. Review Skill-Building Exercise 3-2. Develop positive affirmations, such as "I stay calm when in traffic" (not "I must stop getting mad in traffic"); "I get along well with Joe" (not "I must stop letting Joe make me angry").

- Use rational thinking. For example, when dealing with customers, tell yourself their anger is to be expected; it's part of your job to stay calm.

- Look for positives. In many bad situations, there is some good.

- Use an anger journal. A first step to emotional control of anger is self-awareness. Try to understand why you get angry and how to deal with it more productively, then write it down and continuously improve. This method is an effective way to let out the anger and change your angry behavior.

Anger of Others and Emotional Behavior Control   Below are some tips to help you deal with the anger of others through your emotional control and to prevent violence.

- Think and be like **Bill Gates**. When people get angry, Bill responds by becoming very calm. Here is a positive affirmation: "I'm good at staying calm when people get emotional."[33]

- Remember to be empathic and use reflecting statements (Chapter 4) to calm the person.[34] Apologize even if you didn't do anything wrong. You can say, "I'm sorry this happened. How can we make it right?"

- Our tips in Chapter 4 for dealing with emotional employees apply here. Again, never make any type of put-down statement; it can make the person angrier.
- Don't respond to anger and threats with the same behavior.
- Don't threaten or give orders or ultimatums. This approach can increase anger and push the person to violence.
- Watch your nonverbal communication; show concern and avoid appearing aggressive. Talking loud and with frustration, anger, or annoyance in your tone of voice will convey aggression. Don't move rapidly, point at the person, get too close (stay 2 to 5 feet apart), or touch the person.
- Get away from the person. If necessary, call in a third party (security) to deal with the person; then leave.

Preventing Violence

Signs of Potential Violence   Workplace violence is rarely spontaneous; it's more commonly passive–aggressive behavior in rising steps, related to an unresolved conflict. Employees do give warning signs that violence is possible, so it can be prevented if you look for these signs and take action to defuse the anger before it becomes violent.

- Take verbal threats and bullying seriously. Most violent people do make a threat of some kind before they act.
- Watch nonverbal communication. Gestures or other body language that convey anger can indicate a threat of violence. Talk to the person to find out what's going on.
- Watch for stalking, harassment, and bullying. It usually starts small but can lead to violence. Put a stop to it.
- Watch for damage to property. People who damage property can become violent to coworkers.
- Watch for indications of alcohol and drug use. Get them out of the workplace and get them professional help if it's a recurring problem.
- Include the isolated and ostracized employee.[35] It is common for violent people to be employees who don't fit in, especially if they are bullied by coworkers. Reach out to such employees and help them fit in, or get them to a place where they do.

Communication Skills
Refer to CS Question 7.

- Look for the presence of weapons or objects that might be used as weapons. You may try talking to the person if you feel safe, but get security personnel involved.

WORK APPLICATION 5-7

Recall a situation in which someone was angry with you, preferably your boss. What was the cause of the anger? Did the person display any signs of potential violence? If so, what were they? How well did the person deal with his or her anger? Give the specific tips the person did and did not follow.

Individual Prevention of Violence   One thing you should realize is that the police department will not help you prevent personal or workplace violence. Police get involved only after violence takes place.

- Never be alone with a potentially violent person or stand between the person and the exit.
- Know when to get away from the person.
- Be aware of the organization's policy for calling in security help.
- Report any troubling incidents, such as bullying, to security staff.

/// **In the opening case,** Helen got angry and used passive–aggressive behavior. If the issue is not resolved, Helen could end up being violent, such as throwing the calculator at Larry, or Larry could get angry and physically take the calculator away from Helen, which could be a violent struggle. ///

CONFLICT MANAGEMENT STYLES

Some people think that a conflict exists only in serious issues with anger. However, in human relations, a **conflict** exists whenever *two or more parties are in disagreement*. Do you agree with everything people do and say in your human relations? If not, you are in conflict,

WORK APPLICATION 5-8

Recall a situation in which you were angry with someone. What was the cause of your anger? Did you display any signs of potential violence? If so, what were they? How well did you deal with your anger? Give the specific tips you did and did not follow.

most likely every day. Your ability to manage conflict is critical to your success.[36] In this section, we discuss reasons for conflict as well as the five conflict management styles you can use when you are in conflict.

Reasons for and Types of Conflict

The Psychological Contract   We all rely on unwritten, implicit expectations by each other, called the *psychological contract.*[37] Often we are not aware of our expectations until they have not been met. Communication problems or conflicts arise for three primary reasons: (1) we fail to make our expectations known to other parties, (2) we fail to find out the expectations of other parties, and (3) we assume that the other parties have the same expectations that we have.

In any relationship, to avoid conflict, share information and assertively discuss expectations early, before the conflict escalates. Unfortunately, avoiding conflict is easier said than done.

Idea and Personal Conflict   There are different types of conflict, such as task, process, and relationships, negative and positive.[38] Let's combine them into conflicts of ideas and personal. *Conflict of ideas* are positive because they can lead to improvements, such as solving problems,[39] changing how you do tasks and the process of making products, and innovating new products.[40] **Christopher Koelsch, CEO** of the **Los Angeles Opera,** says, "Don't fear conflict."[41]

WORK APPLICATION 5-9

Describe a conflict you observed in an organization, preferably an organization with which you are or were associated. Explain the conflict by the people involved and the reasons for the conflict.

Conversely, *personal conflict* tends to be negative because it can hurt relationships and performance.[42] The focus of this course is developing good relationships so that you don't have personal conflicts. However, when you do, and we all do, you will learn how to resolve personal conflicts in the next section. But in this section, we discuss five conflict styles.

/// **In the opening case,** Larry expected Helen to give him the calculator when he wanted it, which he made explicit to Helen. Larry failed to find out Helen's expectations (probably did not care), and he may have assumed that she did not mind giving him the calculator whenever he wanted it. Helen's expectation was that Larry would share the calculator, and she found out his expectations were not the same as hers. However, she did not assertively tell Larry this early. Thus, they are in conflict and need to talk about their expectations. Also, there are times when the other party (Larry) is emotional and/or not being reasonable, making conflict more common and more difficult to resolve. Helen is going to need to be assertive with Larry. ///

Before learning the five conflict management styles, complete Self-Assessment Exercise 5-3 to determine your preferred style.

Communication Skills
Refer to CS Question 8.

/ / / **Self-Assessment Exercise 5-3** / / /

Determining Your Preferred Conflict Management Style

Below are four situations. Rank all five alternative actions from 1, the first approach you would use (most desirable), to 5, the last approach you would use (least desirable). Don't try to pick a best answer. Select the alternative that best describes what you would actually do in the situation based on your past experiences.

1.   You are the general manager of a manufacturing plant. The purchasing department has found a source of material at a lower cost than the one being used. However, the production manager says the current material is superior, and he doesn't want to change. The quality control manager says that both will pass inspection with similar results. You would:

_____ *a.* Do nothing; let the purchasing and production managers work it out between themselves.

_____ *b.* Suggest having the purchasing manager find an alternative material that is cheaper but acceptable to the production manager.

_____ *c.* Have the purchasing and production managers compromise.

(continued)

/ / / **Self-Assessment Exercise 5-3** / / / (continued)

      _____ *d.* Decide who is right and make the other comply.

      _____ *e.* Get the purchasing and production managers together and work out an agreement acceptable to both parties.

2. You are a professor at a college. You have started a consulting organization and have the title of director of consulting services, which the dean has approved. You run the organization through the business department, using other faculty and yourself to consult. It has been going well. Randy, the director of continuing education, says that your consulting services should come under his department and not be a separate department. You would:

      _____ *a.* Suggest that some services be under continuing education, but that others, like your consulting service, remain with you in the business department.

      _____ *b.* Do what you can to stop the move. Go to the dean and request that the consulting services stay under your direction in the business department, as originally approved by the dean.

      _____ *c.* Do nothing. The dean will surely see through this "power grab" and turn Randy down.

      _____ *d.* Go and talk to Randy. Try to come up with an agreement you are both satisfied with.

      _____ *e.* Go along with Randy's request. It's not worth fighting about; you can still consult.

3. You are a branch manager for a bank. One of your colleagues cut you off twice during a managers' meeting that just ended. You would:

      _____ *a.* Do nothing; it's no big deal.

      _____ *b.* Discuss it in a friendly manner, but try to get the colleague to stop this behavior.

      _____ *c.* Don't do or say anything because it might hurt your relations, even if you're a little upset about it.

      _____ *d.* Forcefully tell the colleague that you put up with being cut off, but you will not tolerate it in the future.

      _____ *e.* Tell the colleague that you will listen without interrupting if he or she does the same for you.

4. You are the human resources/personnel manager. You have decided to have visitors sign in and wear guest passes. However, only about half of the employees sign their guests in before taking them to their offices to do business. You would:

      _____ *a.* Go talk to the general manager about why employees are not signing in visitors.

      _____ *b.* Try to find a method that will please most employees.

      _____ *c.* Go to the general manager and request that she require employees to follow your procedures. If the general manager says to do it, employees will comply.

      _____ *d.* Do not require visitors to sign in; require them only to wear guest passes.

      _____ *e.* Let employees do things the way they want to.

To determine your preferred conflict management style, place your numbers 1 to 5 on the lines below.

Situation 1	**Situation 2**
_____ *a.* Avoiding	_____ *a.* Compromising
_____ *b.* Accommodating	_____ *b.* Forcing
_____ *c.* Compromising	_____ *c.* Avoiding
_____ *d.* Forcing	_____ *d.* Collaborating
_____ *e.* Collaborating	_____ *e.* Accommodating
Situation 3	**Situation 4**
_____ *a.* Avoiding	_____ *a.* Collaborating
_____ *b.* Collaborating	_____ *b.* Accommodating
_____ *c.* Accommodating	_____ *c.* Forcing
_____ *d.* Forcing	_____ *d.* Compromising
_____ *e.* Compromising	_____ *e.* Avoiding

(continued)

Now place your ranking numbers 1 to 5 that correspond to the styles from the four situations in order; then add the four numbers.

Situation 1	Situation 2	Situation 3	Situation 4		
_____ *a.*	_____ *b.*	_____ *d.*	_____ *c.*	= _____	total, Forcing style
_____ *b.*	_____ *c.*	_____ *a.*	_____ *e.*	= _____	total, Avoiding style
_____ *c.*	_____ *e.*	_____ *c.*	_____ *b.*	= _____	total, Accommodating style
_____ *d.*	_____ *a.*	_____ *e.*	_____ *d.*	= _____	total, Compromising style
_____ *e.*	_____ *d.*	_____ *b.*	_____ *a.*	= _____	total, Collaborating style

The total with the lowest score is your preferred conflict management style. There is no one best conflict style in all situations. The more even the totals are, the more flexible you are at changing conflict management styles. Very high and very low totals indicate less flexibility.

It is also helpful to identify others' preferred styles so that you can plan how to resolve conflicts with them.

See Exhibit 5.5 for an overview of the five styles integrated with TA and assertiveness. Be sure to review this exhibit as you read about each style to understand its behavior.

Learning Outcome 5-5

State when and how to use five conflict management styles.

Forcing Conflict Style

The **forcing conflict style** user attempts to *resolve the conflict by using aggressive behavior.* The forcing approach attempts to satisfy one's own needs at the expense of others, if necessary. Forcers use authority, threat, and intimidation powers.

Advantages and Disadvantages of the Forcing Conflict Style   Better organizational decisions will be made (assuming the forcer is correct), rather than less effective, compromised decisions. The disadvantage is that overuse of this style leads to poor relationships, hostility, and resentment toward its user.

EXHIBIT 5.5 | Conflict Management Styles

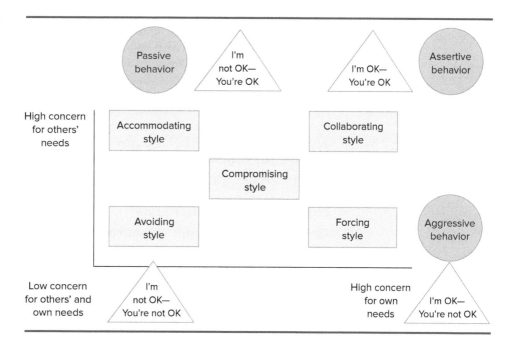

Appropriate Use of the Forcing Conflict Style   Use it when: (1) the conflict is about personal differences between others; (2) maintaining close, supportive relationships is not critical; and (3) conflict resolution is urgent.

Avoiding Conflict Style

Communication Skills
Refer to CS Question 9.

The **avoiding conflict style** user attempts to *passively ignore the conflict rather than resolve it.* Its user wants to avoid or postpone confrontation. Avoiders refuse to take a stance, physically leaving it, or escaping the conflict by mentally leaving.

Advantages and Disadvantages of the Avoiding Conflict Style   Avoiding may maintain relationships that would be hurt through conflict resolution. The disadvantage of this style is the fact that conflicts do not get resolved. An overuse of this style leads to conflict within the individual. People tend to walk all over the avoider. Avoiding problems usually does not make them go away; the problems usually get worse—so be assertive.

Appropriate Use of the Avoiding Conflict Style   Use it when: (1) one's stake in the issue is not high, (2) confrontation will damage a critical working relationship, and (3) a time constraint necessitates avoidance.

Accommodating Conflict Style

The **accommodating conflict style** user attempts to *resolve the conflict by passively giving in to the other party.* It attempts to satisfy the other party while neglecting one's own needs.

Advantages and Disadvantages of the Accommodating Conflict Style   Relationships are developed and maintained by accommodating. The disadvantage is that giving in to the other party may be counterproductive when you have a better solution. An overuse of this style leads to people's taking advantage of the accommodator, and the relationship the accommodator tries to maintain is often lost.

Appropriate Use of the Accommodating Conflict Style   Use it when: (1) maintaining the relationship outweighs all other considerations; (2) the changes agreed to are not important to you, but are to the other party; and (3) the time to resolve the conflict is limited. This is often the only style one can use with an autocratic boss.[43]

Accomodating is an important part of family and friendship—it's about giving to help others. Think about how many things your parents/partners/family members/friends/co-workers do or did for you that they really would rather not do. How often do you do things for them that you don't really want to do to help them—or spending time with them? True happiness comes more from giving than taking from others.

The Difference between Avoiding and Accommodating   With the avoiding style, you can simply say or do nothing. However, with the accommodating style, you have to do or say something you don't really want to. For example, if your boss says something you disagree with, you can avoid by saying nothing. However, if your boss asks you to take a letter to the mailroom, and you don't want to but do it anyway, you have accommodated the boss.

Compromising Conflict Style

The **compromising conflict style** user attempts to *resolve the conflict through assertive give-and-take concessions.* This approach attempts to meet one's need for harmonious relationships by finding common interest. It is used in negotiations.

Advantages and Disadvantages of the Compromising Conflict Style   Using compromising conflict style, the conflict may be resolved quickly and relationships are maintained. The disadvantage is that the compromise often leads to counterproductive results (suboptimum decisions). An overuse of this style leads to people's playing games, such as asking for twice as much as they need in order to get what they want. It is commonly used during management and labor collective bargaining.

Appropriate Use of the Compromising Conflict Style   Use it when: (1) the issues are complex and critical, and there is no simple and clear solution; (2) all parties have a strong interest in different solutions; and (3) time is short.

Collaborating Conflict Style

The **collaborating conflict style** user assertively attempts to *resolve the conflict with the best solution agreeable to all parties.* It is also called the *problem-solving style.* The focus is on finding the best solution to the problem that is satisfactory to all parties. This is the only style that creates a true win–win situation.

Advantages and Disadvantages of the Collaborating Conflict Style   Collaborating tends to lead to the best solution to the conflict using assertive behavior. One great disadvantage is that the time and effort it takes to resolve the conflict is usually greater and longer than with the other styles.

Appropriate Use of the Collaborating Conflict Style   The collaborating style is appropriate when: (1) maintaining relationships is important, (2) time is available, and (3) it is a peer conflict. The collaborating conflict style is generally considered the best style because it confronts the conflict assertively, rather than passively ignoring it or aggressively fighting.

The Difference between Compromising and Collaborating   Here's an example. With the compromising style, when you and a coworker are delivering furniture, you take turns listening to the radio station you like; thus, each of you wins and loses some. With collaborating, you would agree on a station you both like to listen to—you both win. Unfortunately, collaboration is not always possible.

The Most Appropriate Conflict Style Is Based on the Situation   There is no one best style for resolving all conflicts. Your preferred style tends to meet your needs. Some people enjoy forcing, others prefer to avoid conflict, and so forth. Success lies in one's ability to use the appropriate style to meet the situation. Of the five styles, the most difficult to implement successfully (and probably the most underutilized when appropriate) is the collaborative style. Therefore, the collaborative style is the only one that will be given detailed coverage in the next section of this chapter. In Chapter 9 you will learn how to use the compromising style when negotiating.

/// **In the opening case,** Larry consistently used the forcing conflict resolution style, while Helen began by using the accommodating style, changed to the forcing style, and returned to the accommodating style. To create a true win–win situation for all parties, Helen could have used the collaborating conflict management style. ///

WORK APPLICATION 5-10

Give an example of a conflict situation you face or have faced. Identify and explain the appropriate conflict management style to use.

APPLICATION SITUATIONS / / /

Selecting Conflict Management Styles   AS 5-3

Identify the most appropriate conflict management style as:

A. Forcing   C. Compromising   E. Collaborating

B. Avoiding   D. Accommodating

_____ 11. Your committee has been meeting for some time now, but at today's meeting you have to finalize the total budget for each department.

(continued)

_____ 12. You and a coworker are assigned to complete a project. You disagree on the process to use to complete the project.

_____ 13. You're over budget. It's slow today, so you asked a part-time employee to go home early. He tells you he doesn't want to go because he needs the money.

_____ 14. You are taking a class that uses small groups as part of your grade. Under normal class conditions, what is the most appropriate style?

_____ 15. You have joined a committee so that you can meet people. Your interest in its function itself is low. While serving on the committee, you make a recommendation that is opposed by another member. You realize that you have the better idea. The other party is using a forcing style.

_____ 16. You are the supervisor of a production department. An important order is behind schedule. Two of your employees are in conflict, as usual, over who is doing more work than the other.

_____ 17. You are on a committee that has to select a new production machine. The six alternatives will all do the job. It's the brand, price, and service that people disagree on.

_____ 18. You are a sales manager. One of your competent salespersons is trying to close a big sale. The two of you are discussing the next sales call she will make. You disagree on strategy.

_____ 19. You are on your way to an important meeting. You're late. As you turn a corner, you see one of your employees goofing off instead of working.

_____ 20. You have a department crisis. Your boss calls you and tells you, in a stern voice, "Get up here right away."

RESOLVING CONFLICTS WITH THE COLLABORATING CONFLICT STYLE

Learning Outcome 5-6

List the steps of initiating, responding to, and mediating conflict resolutions.

Recall the importance of getting along with people[44] and that conflict of ideas can bring improvements, but personal conflicts can have negative effects on relationships if not successfully resolved. Thus, your ability to resolve conflicts is an important skill in your personal and professional lives.[45] Some organizations encourage and teach employees to confront others, through a culture of candor.[46]

The manner in which conflict is expressed influences reactions and how the conflict process unfolds successfully or not.[47] Therefore, the objective of this section is to develop your ability to assertively confront (or be confronted by) people in a manner that resolves the conflict without damaging interpersonal relationships. We examine the roles of initiator, responder, and mediator in conflict resolution.

Initiating Conflict Resolution

An initiator is a person who confronts another person (or other people) about a conflict. Your attitude will have a major effect on the outcome of the confrontation.[48] If you go into a confrontation expecting to argue and fight, you probably will.

To resolve conflicts, you should develop a plan of action. When you initiate a conflict resolution using the collaborating style, follow the **initiating conflict resolution steps:** *(1) plan to maintain ownership of the problem using the XYZ model; (2) implement your plan persistently; and (3) make an agreement for change.* (See Model 5.2.) The **XYZ model** *describes a problem in terms of behavior, consequences, and feelings.*

Step 1: Plan to Maintain Ownership of the Problem Using the XYZ Model   Part of the reason we are not successful at resolving conflict is that we wait too long before confronting the other party, and we are in an emotional state without planning (passive–aggressive behavior). We end up saying things we don't mean because we haven't given thought to what it is we want to say and accomplish through confrontation.

You should realize that when you are upset and frustrated, the problem is yours, not the other party's. For example, you don't smoke and someone visits you who does smoke. The smoke bothers you, not the smoker. It's your problem. Open the confrontation with a request for the respondent to help you solve your problem. This approach reduces defensiveness and establishes an atmosphere of problem solving.

There are four things we should not do during the opening XYZ statement: (1) Don't *judge* the person's behavior; "You shouldn't smoke; it's bad for you." (2) Don't give *advice* (this is done in steps 2 and 3). (3) Don't make *threats;* "If you do smoke again I will report you to the boss." (4) Don't try to determine who is to *blame.* Both parties are usually partly to blame. Fixing blame only gets us defensive, which is counterproductive to conflict resolution.

Keep the opening statement short. The longer the statement, the longer it will take to resolve the conflict. People get defensive when kept waiting for their turn to talk. Use the XYZ model. When you do X (behavior), Y (consequences) happens, and I feel Z (feelings). When you smoke in my room (their behavior), I have trouble breathing and become nauseated (consequence to you), and I feel uncomfortable and irritated (your feeling). You can vary the sequence and start with a feeling or consequence to fit the situation.

Timing is also important. If the other party is busy, set an appointment to discuss the conflict. In addition, don't confront a person on several unrelated issues at once, or when they are highly emotional.

Step 2: Implement Your Plan Persistently   After making your short, planned XYZ statement, let the other party respond. If they acknowledges the problem and say they will change, you may have succeeded. Often people do not realize there is a conflict and when approached properly, they are willing to change. However, if the other party does not understand or avoids acknowledgment of the problem, persist. You cannot resolve a conflict if the other party will not even acknowledge its existence. Repeat your planned statement, and/or explain it in different terms, until you get an acknowledgment or realize that the situation is hopeless. But don't give up too easily, and be sure to listen to the other party and watch for nonverbal clues.

When the other party acknowledges the problem but is not responsive to resolving it, appeal to common goals. Make the other party realize the benefits to him or her, your relationship, and the department and organization as well.

Step 3: Make an Agreement for Change   Try to agree on a specific action you both will take to resolve the conflict. Remember that you are collaborating, not forcing. If possible, get a commitment statement describing the change.

Below is an example of conflict resolution:

PAM: Hi, Bill! Got a few minutes to talk?

BILL: Sure, what's up?

PAM: Something's been bothering me lately, and I wanted you to know about it. When you come to class without doing your homework [*behavior*], I get irritated [*feeling*], and our group has to wait for you to read the material or make a decision without your input [*consequences*].

BILL: Hey, I'm busy!

PAM: Do you think the rest of the group isn't?

BILL: No.

PAM: Are grades important to you?

BILL: Yeah. If I don't get good grades, I can't play on the football team.

PAM: You get a grade for doing your homework, and we all get the same group grade. Your input helps us all get a better grade.

Skill-Building Exercise 5-3 develops this skill.

WORK APPLICATION 5-11

Use the XYZ model to describe a conflict problem you face or have faced.

BILL: You're right; sometimes I forget about that. Well, sometimes I don't do it because I don't understand the assignment.

PAM: I'll tell you what; when you don't understand it, call me, or come over, and I'll explain it. You know my number and address.

BILL: I'd appreciate that.

PAM: So you agree to do your homework before class, and I agree to help you when you need it.

BILL: OK, I'll do it from now on.

Skill-Building Exercise 5-4 develops this skill.

Responding to Conflict Resolution

You are the responder when someone confronts you. Most initiators do not follow the model above. Therefore, as the responder, you must take responsibility for successful conflict resolution by following the conflict resolution model. The **responding to conflict resolution steps** are as follows: *(1) listen to and paraphrase the problem using the XYZ model; (2) agree with some aspect of the complaint; (3) ask for, and/or give, alternative solutions; and (4) make an agreement for change.* (See Model 5.2.)

Apologize and Change Your Behavior   When confronted, it is important to restore relationships that may have been hurt by the conflict, and apologizing really helps. You will be surprised at how your human relations can improve simply by telling people you are sorry for your behavior that bothers them. During step 2 it is helpful to apologize. Even if you don't believe you did anything wrong, it is helpful to at least say something like, "I'm sorry I offended you," or "I'm sorry you are upset." But apologizing isn't enough; you need to change your behavior that offends others to improve your human relations.[49]

Mediating Conflict Resolution

Frequently, conflicting employees cannot resolve their dispute. In these cases, the manager or an outside mediator should mediate to help them resolve their differences. Be a mediator, not a judge. Make employees realize it's their problem, not yours, and that they are responsible for solving it. Get the employees to resolve the conflict, if possible. Remain impartial, unless one party is violating company policies. Don't belittle the parties in conflict. Don't make comments like, "I'm disappointed in you two; you're acting like babies."

When bringing conflicting parties together, follow the mediating conflict model. The **mediating conflict resolution steps** are as follows: *(1) have each party state his or her complaint using the XYZ model; (2) agree on the problem(s); (3) develop alternative solutions; and (4) make an agreement for change, and follow up.* The steps for initiating, responding to, and mediating conflict resolution are summarized in Model 5.2.

Remember that what you think about affects how you feel, and how you feel affects your behavior, human relations, happiness, and performance. Think about the specific behavior that is causing the conflict and how to resolve the issue.

MODEL 5.2 | Conflict Resolution

Initiating Conflict Resolution Steps	Responding to Conflict Resolution	Mediating Conflict Resolution
1. Plan to maintain ownership of the problem using the XYZ model.	1. Listen to and paraphrase the problem using the XYZ model.	1. Have each party state his or her complaint using the XYZ model.
2. Implement your plan persistently.	2. Agree with some aspect of the complaint.	2. Agree on the problem(s).
3. Make an agreement for change.	3. Ask for, and/or give, alternative solutions.	3. Develop alternative solutions.
	4. Make an agreement for change.	4. Make an agreement for change, and follow up.

/// In the discussion of assertiveness, there was an example of how Helen could have been assertive with Larry in the opening case. In addition to being assertive with Larry, Helen could have used the collaborating conflict style to resolve the calculator problem. Helen could have suggested to Larry that the two of them go to the boss and ask for another calculator so that they could each have their own. A second calculator could create a win-win situation for all parties. Obtaining a second calculator is a good conflict resolution. However, the department or organization may not have the money in the budget to buy a new calculator, or the idle time may actually be cheaper. If this is the case, Helen can be assertive and keep the calculator until she is finished—this is a win-win situation; or she and Larry could work out some other collaborative agreement, such as each having the calculator during specific hours. If Larry is not willing to collaborate, their boss will have to mediate the conflict resolution. ///

WORK APPLICATION 5-12

Describe an actual situation in which the initiating, responding, and/or mediating conflict resolution model would be appropriate.

PUTTING IT ALL TOGETHER

To see the relationship between TA, assertiveness, and conflict management, see Exhibit 5.6. Notice that the first two columns come from conflict management, the third from assertiveness, and the fourth and fifth from TA. The last column relates to the goal of human relations. The last column shows the order of priority of which interpersonal behavior to

EXHIBIT 5.6 | Interpersonal Dynamics Styles

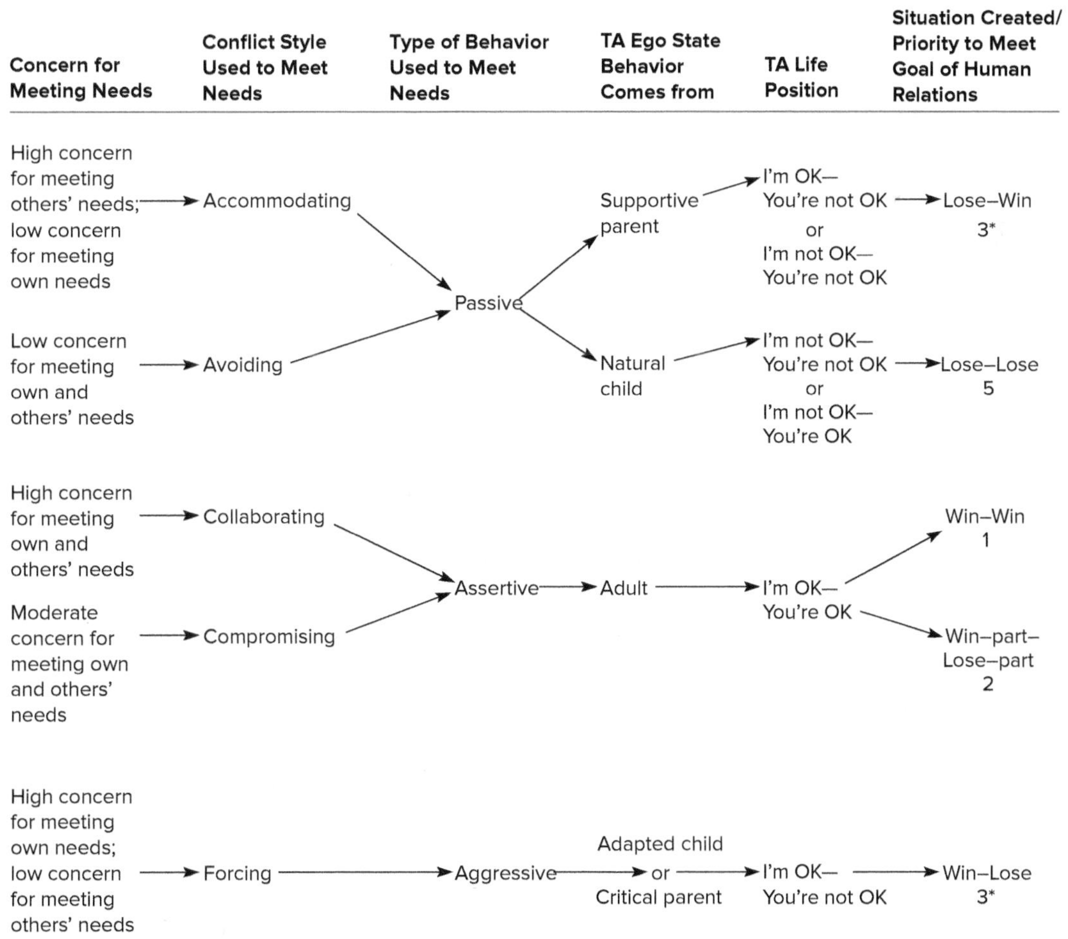

*The win–lose and lose–win situations are equal in priority to the group or organization because both an individual and the group or organization lose. The individual's loss is more important to the loser than to the group.

use to meet the goal of human relations. However, remember that this is general advice. As stated in the chapter, at times other behavior is appropriate. In the majority of your human relations, you should strive to have a high concern for meeting your needs while meeting the needs of others. You should use an assertive, adult, collaborating style to create a win–win situation for all parties.

In reviewing Exhibit 5.6, you should see that the behavior of people using the passive, accommodating, or avoiding conflict styles is the opposite of the behavior of people who use the aggressive or forcing conflict styles. Assertive people use the collaborating and compromising conflict styles, and their behavior is between the other two extremes.

You should also understand that people using the passive, accommodating, and avoiding conflict styles tend to have human relations that are the opposite of people using the aggressive and forcing conflict styles. The passive person tends to shy away from making friends and being actively involved, while the aggressive person tries to take over and is offensive to the group. Assertive people use the collaborating style and tend to be friendly and outgoing as they work to create win–win situations for all parties. Generally, people who are passive don't get their needs met; they get walked over by the aggressive people. Aggressive people are disliked because they violate the rights of others. Assertive people tend to have the best human relations. What is your style, and how can you improve your human relations?

By following the guidelines in this chapter, you can develop assertive collaborating skills.

Let's discuss how your personality affects your ego state, assertiveness, and preferred conflict style in Self-Assessment Exercise 5-4.

/ / / Self-Assessment Exercise 5-4 / / /

Your Personality and Interpersonal Dynamics

People with the same personality type (Chapter 2) tend to get along better and have less conflict than those with different personality types. So be careful during human relations with people different from you.

If you have a high *surgency* personality, watch your use of the critical parent ego state and be sure to give lots of positive strokes to help human relations. You may be in the "I'm OK" life position, but make sure that you treat others as "You're OK." As a surgency, you also need to be careful not to use aggressive behavior to get what you want. You most likely have no problem confronting others when in conflict. However, be careful not to use the forcing style with others.

If you have a high *agreeableness* personality, you tend to get along well with others. But be careful not to use the sympathetic parent ego state, and watch the appropriate use of the child ego state. Don't let others take advantage of you so that you put them in the "You're not OK" life position, and so that you can stay in the "I'm OK" position. Be careful not to be passive and not to use the avoiding and accommodating conflict styles to get out of confronting others; you need to satisfy your needs too.

How well you deal with your emotions, especially anger, is what *adjustment* is about. If you are not high on adjustment personality traits, you will tend to use the parent or child ego states. You may be in the "I'm not OK" position, and others will be in the "You're not OK" position. Based on your adjust-

ment personality, you can be passive (let people take advantage of you) or aggressive (try to take advantage of others), and poor adjustment can lead to violence. Low adjustment people are usually poor at dealing with conflict, because they tend to avoid and accommodate or to use force in conflict situations. Try not to be low in adjustment and get too emotional. Use the tips on dealing with emotions, especially anger.

There is a relationship between adjustment and *openness to experience*. If you are not well adjusted, you are probably not open to experience. If you are low on openness, you may not handle conflicts well since their resolution often requires change. So try to be open to new experiences.

If you are a high *conscientious* personality, you can still transact from the parent or child ego state. You may be in the "I'm OK" life position, but be sure not to put others in the "You're not OK" position. Watch your use of aggressive behavior to achieve your objectives. You may be good at conflict resolution, but be careful to meet others' needs too.

Action plan: Based on your personality, what specific things will you do to improve your TA, assertiveness, and conflict management skills?

_____

_____

_____

_____

As we bring this chapter to a close, you should understand *transactional analysis* ego states, types of transactions, life positions, and stroking, and use behavior from the adult ego state during human relations. You should know the difference between passive, aggressive, and *assertive* behavior and be able to avoid being passive and aggressive and use assertive behavior. You should be able to deal with your anger, the anger of others, and help prevent workplace violence. You should know the reasons for *conflict and* how to use five conflict management styles, and you should be able to successfully initiate a conflict resolution.

Putting these topics together briefly, you should realize that during your human relations (transactional analysis), the behavior you use (passive, aggressive, or assertive) affects whether or not you are in conflict and affects your performance.

/ / / R E V I E W / / /

The chapter review is organized to help you master the seven learning outcomes for Chapter 5. First provide your own response to each learning outcome, and then check the summary provided to see how well you understand the material. Next, identify the final statement in each section as either true or false (T/F). Correct each false statement. Answers are given at the end of the chapter.

LO 5-1   Describe the three ego states of transactional analysis.

The three ego states of transactional analysis are: (1) *parent*: the critical parent is evaluative, while the sympathetic parent is supportive; (2) *child:* the natural child is curious, while the adapted child is rebellious; and (3) *adult:* the adult is a thinking, unemotional state of ego.

Transactional analysis was first developed for the field of psychology and later applied to business. T F

LO 5-2   Explain the three types of transactions.

The three types of transactions are: (1) *complementary:* the sender of the message gets the intended response from the receiver; (2) *crossed:* the sender does not get the expected response; and (3) *ulterior:* the person appears to be in one ego state, but his or her behavior comes from a different ego state.

Complementary transactions always come from the same ego state. T F

LO 5-3   Identify the differences between passive, aggressive, and assertive behavior.

Passive behavior is nonassertive. The passive person gives in to the other party without standing up for his or her rights.

Aggressive behavior includes the use of force to get one's own way, often at the expense of violating others' rights.

Assertive behavior involves standing up for one's rights without violating the rights of others.

Passive–aggressive behavior occurs when a person says nothing when irritated, lets anger build up, and then blows up. T F

LO 5-4   List the four steps of assertive behavior.

The four steps of assertive behavior are: (1) set an objective; (2) determine how to create a win–win situation; (3) develop an assertive phrase; and (4) implement your plan persistently.

Assertive behavior should be used to get what you want, while the other party loses. T F

LO 5-5   State when and how to use five conflict management styles.

The five conflict management styles are: (1) *forcing,* when the user attempts to resolve the conflict by using aggressive behavior; it should be used when the conflict is one involving personal differences; (2) *avoiding,* when the user attempts to passively ignore the conflict rather than resolve it; it should be used when one's stake in the issue is not high; (3) *accommodating,* when the user attempts to resolve the conflict by passively giving in to the other party; it should be used when maintaining relations outweighs all other considerations; (4) *compromising,* when the user attempts to resolve the conflict through assertive give-and-take concessions; it should be used when the issues are complex and critical, and when there is no simple and clear solution; and (5) *collaborating,* when the user assertively attempts to jointly resolve the conflict with the best solution agreeable to all parties; it should be used for peer conflicts.

When an employee doesn't do what the supervisor requests, the forcing conflict style is appropriate. T F

LO 5-6   List the steps of initiating, responding to, and mediating conflict resolutions.

The initiating conflict resolution steps are: (1) plan to maintain ownership of the problem using the XYZ model; (2) implement your plan persistently; and (3) make an agreement for change. The responding to conflict resolution steps are: (1) listen to and paraphrase the problem using the XYZ model; (2) agree with some aspect of the complaint; (3) ask for, and/or give, alternative solutions; and (4) make an agreement for change. The mediating conflict resolution steps are: (1) have each party state his or her complaint using the XYZ model; (2) agree on the problem(s); (3) develop alternative solutions; and (4) make an agreement for change, and follow up.

Initiating, responding to, and mediating a conflict all take the same level of skill. T F

LO 5-7 Define the following 14 key terms.

Select one or more methods: (1) fill in the missing key terms for each definition given below from memory; (2) match the key terms from the end of the review with their definitions below; and/or (3) copy the key terms in order from the key terms at the beginning of the chapter.

_____ is a method of understanding behavior in interpersonal dynamics.

_____ are the parent, child, and adult.

_____ are complementary, crossed, and ulterior.

_____ is the process of expressing thoughts and feelings while asking for what one wants in an appropriate way.

_____ exists whenever two or more parties are in disagreement.

The _____ user attempts to resolve the conflict by using aggressive behavior.

The _____ user attempts to passively ignore the conflict rather than resolve it.

The _____ user attempts to resolve the conflict by passively giving in to the other party.

The _____ user attempts to resolve the conflict through assertive give-and-take concessions.

The _____ user assertively attempts to resolve the conflict with the best solution agreeable to all parties.

The _____ are these: step (1) plan to maintain ownership of the problem using the XYZ model; step (2) implement your plan persistently; and step (3) make an agreement for change.

The _____ describes a problem in terms of behavior, consequences, and feelings.

The _____ are as follows: step (1) listen to and paraphrase the problem using the XYZ model; step (2) agree with some aspect of the complaint; step (3) ask for, and/or give, alternative solutions; and step (4) make an agreement for change.

The _____ are these: step (1) have each party state his or her complaint using the XYZ model; step (2) agree on the problem(s); step (3) develop alternative solutions; and step (4) make an agreement for change, and follow up.

/ / / KEY TERMS / / /

accommodating conflict
    style   156
assertiveness   147
avoiding conflict style   156
collaborating conflict
    style   157

compromising conflict
    style   156
conflict   152
ego states   144
forcing conflict
    style   155

initiating conflict resolution
    steps   158
mediating conflict
    resolution steps   160
responding to conflict
    resolution steps   160

transactional
    analysis   143
types of
    transactions   145
XYZ model   158

The following critical thinking questions can be used for class discussion and/or as written assignments to develop communication skills. Be sure to give complete explanations for all questions.

1. Some people say that because transactional analysis was developed in the 1960s, it is outdated. Do you agree, or do you believe that TA can help us understand behavior and improve human relations?

2. Some people intentionally use ulterior transactions to get what they want without others knowing it. Are ulterior transactions ethical?

3. Some people have negative attitudes and use negative strokes that hurt others. Is giving negative strokes unethical behavior?

4. Select a person you know who is consistently passive. Do people take advantage of this person, such as getting them to do more work? Do you? Is it ethical to take advantage of passive people?

5. Select a person you know who is consistently aggressive. Do people let this person get his or her way? Do you? What is the best way to deal with an aggressive person? What is the best way to deal with a passive-aggressive person?

6. Select a person you know who is consistently assertive. Do people tend to respect this person, and does this person have effective human relations? Do you have effective human relations? What will you do to improve your assertiveness?

7. Recall an occasion of violence at school or work. Describe the situation. Were there signs that violence was coming? What can you do to help prevent violence?

8. Which conflict management style do you use most often? Why do you tend to use this conflict style? How can you become more collaborative?

9. How do you feel about the use of the forcing conflict style? Do you use it often? Is using the forcing style ethical?

CASE   / / /   **Trying Times for Uber's Co-founder Travis Kalanick**

In less than a decade, many people (especially in urban areas) have come to know of Uber but not its cofounder and CEO, Travis Kalanick. However, recently, Mr. Kalanick has become one of the most talked-about people in Silicon Valley and the media. He has been described as ruthless, pugnacious, "emotionally unintelligent," unethical, an evil genius, or a loose cannon.[i]

In May 2010, Travis Kalanick and his friend Garrett Camp co-founded Ubercab, as they called it then. It all started when Camp went from frustration to determination in his attempt to hail a private luxury car with a smartphone app after being unable to catch cabs in San Francisco. Mr. Camp and Mr. Kalanick selected the name to emphasize the convenience of calling a car on demand from an app. In October 2010, the company shortened its name to Uber after receiving a cease-and-desist letter from San Francisco officials for marketing itself as a taxi company without the proper licenses and permits. Uber is emblematic of the "sharing economy." Think of Airbnb, DogVacay, or RelayRides. The sharing economy is an emerging, highly flexible economic network that allows people to share resources—such as cars, homes, services, and skills—with one another, often at significantly lower cost than traditional retail establishments.

In his quest to leapfrog everyone else in this emerging sector, Mr. Kalanick has knowingly ignored regulatory standards and business norms, backing down only when he is near the edge of the cliff. An example of this is when Kalanick thought he could ignore Apple's privacy guidelines by directing his employees to help camouflage the ride-hailing app from Apple's engineers so that Apple would not find out that Uber had been secretly identifying and tagging iPhones even after its app had been deleted and the devices erased. He only apologized and stopped the action when Apple's fraud detection technology discovered Uber's unlawful act. This led to a tense and uncomfortable face-to-face meeting between Kalanick and Apple's CEO Tim Cook. Tim Cook effectively threatened to remove Uber's app from Apple's App Store. Some have speculated that if Tim Cook had followed through with his threat, Uber would lose access to millions of iPhone customers—essentially destroying the ride-hailing company's business.[ii] Mr. Kalanick has ignored or fought against transportation and safety regulations, stood up against entrenched competitors, and capitalized on legal loopholes and gray areas to gain a business advantage.

This unflattering description of Mr. Kalanick only tells half the story. Travis Kalanick is also a creative, hardworking, driven, and super-smart CEO who has transformed Uber into the most powerful startup in history, with a valuation of $70 billion in less than a decade. Comparatively, Uber has outpaced the likes of tech giants such as Google and Facebook when they were at a similar point in their evolution. Uber has a workforce of more than 9,000 employees and

1.5 million drivers. In terms of job creation, more people earn a paycheck—or part of one—from Uber than from any other private employer in the world except corporate chains such as Wal-Mart and McDonald's. Today, Uber operates in more than 450 cities across 73 countries. In any given month, 40 million people will take an Uber ride, and its drivers will collectively cover 1.2 billion miles.[iii]

Uber's value proposition is simple—push a button, get a ride. It is about speed, efficiency, convenience, and better value. The algorithm that delivers on this promise comprises an elaborate and complex computer code system. Miguel Helft of *Forbes* describes the sequence of events that takes place once a customer opens an Uber app: His or her location gets beamed to Uber's servers, and dispatching software begins searching for pricing algorithms and scouring the map for nearby vehicles. Once a driver accepts a ride, the routing software directs the car to a location, updating ETAs based on GPS readings every four seconds. That near-continuous tracking goes on during the ride, and often before it is over, the driver is predispatched to the next trip. Then there is billing, processing, ratings, and the company's analytics to evaluate the quality of the ride. This algorithm is the backbone of Kalanick's vision and strategy to exploit opportunities in transportation globally.[iv] [v]

As pointed out in the opening, it has not been the best of times for Uber and Kalanick lately. A former employee went public with allegations of sexual harassment and a condoning work culture. Kalanick was recorded berating an Uber driver over its fare structure. Uber's critics mounted a grassroots campaign with the hashtag #deleteUber. Poor judgment with some business deals and increasing concern that Mr. Kalanick's reckless behavior and pattern of risk-taking could bring down the business empire he is creating. His mindset of "win at any cost" is a trait that some believe has now plunged Uber into its most sustained set of crises since its founding in 2009. To say that Mr. Kalanick's leadership is at a precarious point is an understatement. Even his strongest supporters and institutional investors such as Goldman Sachs are putting pressure on him to change. On April 25, 2017, CNBC reported that these scandals may have knocked $10 billion off Uber's value.[vi]

Mr. Kalanick has publicly apologized for some of his behavior, and acknowledged that he needs management help. On June 6, 2017, Uber announced that it fired more than 20 employees as a result of the investigation.[vii] On June 13, 2017, Kalanick took an indefinite leave of absence from Uber.[viii] On June 20, 2017, after multiple shareholders reportedly demanded his resignation, Kalanick resigned as CEO.[ix] Only time will tell how Uber will perform without its founding CEO.

Go to the Internet: To learn more about Uber and Travis Kalanick, visit the company's website at www.uber.com.

Support your answers to the following questions with specific information from the case and text or with information from the web or another source.

1. Explain why some have described Travis Kalanick as "emotionally unintelligent." Cite some examples to support your answer.

2. The three ego states that affect our behavior and the way we transact with others are: parent, child, and adult. In the incident described in the case between Kalanick and Apple CEO Tim Cook, who in your opinion displayed the parent or adult role and who displayed the child role? Explain your answer.

3. Which of the implied behaviors (passive, aggressive, or assertive) has Travis Kalanick been known to employ in his interactions and transactions with others?

4. The text describes four Conflict Resolution Styles: accommodating, avoiding, forcing, and collaborating. Which style is Mr. Kalanick more likely to exercise given his personality and ambition?

Cumulative Case Question

5. Chapter 2 discusses the Big Five Model of Personality and categorizes leadership traits into five dimensions: surgency, agreeableness, adjustment, conscientiousness, and openness to experience. Based on your knowledge of Travis Kalanick, which of these dimensions is he strong or weak in as a leader?

6. Chapter 3 discusses attitudes, self-concept, values, and ethics. More specifically, a manager's attitudes, values, and ethics can affect employees' job behavior and performance. How will you relate these concepts to Travis Kalanick and his leadership at Uber?

Case Exercise and Role Play

Preparation: In March 2017, Mr. Kalanick is seen in the backseat of an Uber car with two women. When they reach their destination, he begins talking with the driver, Fawzi Kamel. During the exchange, Mr. Kamel complains about what he says is Uber's history of lowering earnings for drivers, and Mr. Kalanick says Mr. Kamel should "take responsibility" for his own problems. The conversation quickly gets out of hand with Mr. Kalanick using obscenities and generally being dismissive of Mr. Kamel's complaints. Unbeknown to Mr. Kalanick, the driver taped the exchange and released the video to the media. It creates a media firestorm, and Mr. Kalanick goes on an apology tour to calm the waters.

Assume you are Mr. Kalanick and prepare a 2 to 3 minute alternative response to the driver's concerns that Mr. Kalanick should have given rather than the tone he took.

Role-Play: Matched pairs of Travis Kalanick and Mr. Kamel role-play the exchange. The role-play may be done in small groups or two students may role-play before the entire class. The first exchange should present the original scenario as published in the video and the second exchange should take an alternative approach of how the situation should have been handled. This should be followed by a question and answer period.

OBJECTIVE CASE   / / /   Bill and Saul's Conflict

The following conversation takes place over the telephone between Bill, the salesperson, and Saul, the production manager.

BILL: Listen, Saul, I just got an order for 1,000 units and promised delivery in two days. You'll get them out on time, won't you?

SAUL: Bill, you know the normal delivery time is five days.

BILL: I know, but I had to say two days to get the order, so fill it.

SAUL: We don't have the capability to do it. You should have checked with me before taking the order. The best I can do is four days.

BILL: What are you—my mother, or the production manager?

SAUL: I cannot have 1,000 units ready in two days. We have other orders that need to be filled before yours. Four days is the best I can do on short notice.

BILL: Come on, Saul, you cannot do this to me, I want to keep this account. It can mean a lot of business.

SAUL: I know, Bill; you've told me this on three other orders you had.

BILL: But this is a big one. Don't you care about sales?

SAUL: Yes, I do, but I cannot produce the product as fast as you sales reps are selling it lately.

BILL: If I don't meet my sales quota, are you going to take the blame?

SAUL: Bill, we are going in circles here. I'm sorry, but I cannot fulfill your request. The order will be ready in four days.

BILL: I was hoping you would be reasonable. But you've forced me to go to Mr. Carlson. You know he'll be telling you to fill my order. Why don't you just do it and save time and aggravation?

SAUL: I'll wait to hear from Mr. Carlson. In the meantime, have a good day, Bill.

Answer the following questions. Then in the space between the questions, state why you selected that answer.

_____ 1. Bill was transacting from the _____ ego state.

   a. critical parent   *b.* sympathetic parent   *c.* adult

   d. natural child   *e.* adapted child

_____ 2. Saul was transacting from the _____ ego state.

   a. critical parent   *b.* sympathetic parent   *c.* adult   *d.* natural child   *e.* adapted child

_____ 3. The telephone discussion was a(n) _____ transaction.

   a. complementary   *b.* crossed   *c.* ulterior

_____ 4. Bill's life position seems to be:

   a. I'm OK– You're not OK   *b.* I'm OK–You're OK

   c. I'm not OK–You're not OK   *d.* I'm not OK–You're OK

_____   5. Bill's behavior was:

      a. passive   *b.* aggressive   *c.* assertive

_____   6. Saul's behavior was:

      a. passive   *b.* aggressive   *c.* assertive

_____   7. Bill and Saul have an _____ conflict.

      a. individual   *b.* interpersonal

      c. individual/group   *d.* intragroup

_____   8. Their source of conflict is:

      a. personal differences   *b.* information

      c. objectives   *d.* environment

_____   9. Bill used the _____ conflict style.

      a. forcing   *b.* avoiding   *c.* accommodating

      d. compromising   *e.* collaborating

_____   10. Saul used the _____ the conflict style.

      a. forcing   *b.* avoiding   *c.* accommodating

      d. compromising   *e.* collaborating

      11. What would you have done if you were Bill?

      12. Assume you are Mr. Carlson, the boss. How will you respond when Bill calls?

Note: The conversation between Bill and Saul and/or their meeting with Mr. Carlson can be role-played in class.

/ / / SKILL-BUILDING EXERCISE 6-1 / / /

Transactional Analysis

Experience: Individual may share answers in groups or entire class, in class or online.

AACSB Competencies: Analytic skills, communication abilities, interpersonal relations, and application of knowledge.

Objective: To improve your ability to use transactional analysis.

Preparation: You should complete the 10 situations below.

For each situation:

1. Identify the sender's communication ego state as:

   CP–Critical Parent

   SP–Sympathetic Parent

   NC–Natural Child

   AC–Adapted Child

   A–Adult

2. Place the letters CP, SP, NC, AC, or A on the S _____ to the left of each numbered situation.

3. Identify each of the five alternative receiver's ego states as in instruction 1 above. Place the letters CP, SP, NC, AC, or A on the R _____.

4. Select the best alternative to achieve effective communication and human relations. Circle the letter *a, b, c, d,* or *e.*

S _____ 1. Ted delegates a task, saying, "It's not much fun, but someone has to do it. Will you please do it for me?" Sue, the delegatee, says:

    a. "A good boss wouldn't make me do it."   R _____

    b. "I'm always willing to help you out, Ted."   R _____

    c. "I'm not cleaning that up."   R _____

    d. "You're not being serious, are you?"   R _____

    e. "I'll get right on it."   R _____

S _____ 2. Helen, a customer, brought a dress to the cleaners, and later she picked it up, paid, and went home. At home she opened the package and found that the dress was not clean. Helen returned to the cleaners and said, "What's wrong with this place? Don't you know how to clean a dress?" The cleaning person, Saul, responds:

    a. "It's not my fault. I didn't clean it personally."   R _____

    b. "I'm sorry this happened. We'll do it again right now."   R _____

    c. "I can understand your disappointment. Were you planning on wearing it   R _____ today? What can I do to make this up to you?"

    d. "These are stains caused by your carelessness, not ours."   R _____

    e. "Gee whiz, this is the first time this has happened."   R _____

S _____ 3. In an office, Bill drops a tray of papers on the floor. Mary, the manager, comes over and says, "This happens once in a while to all of us. Let me help you pick them up." Bill responds:

    a. "Guess I slipped, ha ha ha."   R _____

    b. "This wouldn't have happened if people didn't stack the papers so high."   R _____

    c. "It's not my fault; I'm not picking up the papers."   R _____

    d. "Thanks for helping me pick them up, Mary."   R _____

    e. "It will not take long to pick them up."   R _____

S _____ 4. Karl and Kelly were talking about the merit raise given in their branch of the bank. Karl says: "I heard you did not get a merit raise." Kelly responds:

    a. "It's true; how much did you get?"   R _____

    b. "I really don't need a raise anyway."   R _____

    c. "The branch manager is unfair."   R _____

    d. "The branch manager didn't give me a raise because he is   R _____ prejudiced. The men got bigger raises than the women."

    e. "It's nice of you to show your concern. Is there anything I can do to   R _____ help you out?"

S _____ 5. Beckie, the store manager, says to an employee: "Ed, there is no gum on the counter; please restock it." Ed responds:

    a. "Why do I always get stuck doing it?"   R _____

    b. "I'd be glad to do it. I know how important it is to keep the shelves stocked   R _____ for our customers."

    c. "I'll do it just as soon as I finish this row."   R _____

    d. "I'll do it if I can have a free pack."   R _____

    e. "Why don't we buy bigger boxes so I don't have to do it so often?"   R _____

S _____ 6. Carol, the manager, asked Tim, an employee, to file some forms. A while later Carol returned and asked Tim why he hadn't filed the forms. Tim said: "Oh, no! I forgot about it." Carol responds:

    a. "I've told you before; write things down so you don't forget to do them."   R _____

    b. "It's OK. I know you're busy and will do it when you can."   R _____

    c. "Please do it now."   R _____

    d. "What's wrong with you?"   R _____

    e. "You daydreaming or what?"   R _____

S _____ 7. Joan just finished making a budget presentation to the controller, Wayne. He says: "This budget is padded." Joan responds:

    a. "I'm sorry you feel that way. What is a fair budget amount?"   R _____

    b. (*laughing*) "I don't pad any more than the others."   R _____

    c. "You don't know what you're talking about. It's not padded."   R _____

    d. "What items do you believe are padded?"   R _____

    e. "You can't expect me to run my department without some padding for emer- R _____
gencies, can you?"

S _____ 8. Jill, a computer repair technician, says to the customer: "What did you do to this computer to make it malfunction like this?" The customer responds:

    a. "Can you fix it?"   R _____

    b. "I take good care of this machine. You'd better fix it fast."   R _____

    c. "I'm sorry to upset you. Are you having a rough day?"   R _____

    d. "I'm going to tell your boss what you just said."   R _____

    e. "I threw it down the stairs, ha ha."   R _____

S _____ 9. Pete is waiting for his friend, Will, whom he hasn't seen for some time. When Will arrives, Pete says, "It's good to see you," and gives Will a hug, spinning him around. Will responds:

    a. "Don't hug me on the street; people can see us."   R _____

    b. "I'm not late; you got here early."   R _____

    c. "Sorry I'm late. Is there anything I can do to make it up to you? Just name it."   R _____

    d. "Let's go party, party, party."   R _____

    e. "Sorry I'm late; I got held up in traffic."   R _____

S _____ 10. Sally gives her secretary, Mike, a note saying: "Please type this when you get a chance." About an hour later, Sally returns from a meeting and asks: "Mike, is the letter I gave you done yet?" Mike responds:

    a. "If you wanted it done by 11, why didn't you say so?"   R _____

    b. "I'm working on it now. It will be done in about 10 minutes."   R _____

    c. "You said to do it when I got a chance. I've been too busy doing more   R _____
important things."

    d. "Sure thing, boss lady, I'll get right on it."   R _____

    e. "I'm sorry, I didn't realize how important it was. Can I type it right now   R _____
and get it to you in about 15 minutes?"

Procedure 1 (5–50 minutes)

Select one option:

1. The instructor goes over the recommended answers to the 10 situations.

2. The instructor asks students for their answers to the situations, followed by giving the recommended answers.

3. Break into groups of two or three and together follow the three-step approach for two to three situations at a time, followed by the instructor's going over the recommended answers. Discuss the possible consequences of each alternative response in the situation. Would it help or hurt human relations and performance? How?

Conclusion: The instructor leads a class discussion and/or makes concluding remarks.

Application: What have I learned from this experience? How will I use this knowledge in the future?

Sharing: Volunteers give their answers to the application section.

/ / / SKILL-BUILDING EXERCISE 5-2 / / /

Assertiveness

Experience: Individual may share answers in groups or entire class, in class or online.

AACSB Competencies: Analytic skills and communication abilities, interpersonal relations, and application of knowledge.

Objective: To improve your ability to be assertive.

Preparation: You should complete the 10 situations below.

In this exercise there are 10 situations with 5 alternative statements or actions. Identify each as assertive (A), aggressive (G), or passive (P). Place the letter A, G, or P on the line before each of the five alternatives. Circle the letter (*a* to *e*) of the response that is the most appropriate in the situation.

1. In class, you are in small groups discussing this exercise; however, two of the members are talking about personal matters instead. You are interested in this exercise.

    _____ *a.* "Don't you want to learn anything in this class?"

    _____ *b.* Forget the exercise, join the conversation.

    _____ *c.* "This is a valuable exercise. I'd really appreciate your input."

    _____ *d.* "This exercise is boring, isn't it?"

    _____ *e.* "Stop discussing personal matters, or leave the class!"

2. You and your roommate do not smoke. Smoke really bothers you. However, your roommate has friends over who smoke in your room regularly.

    _____ *a.* Throw them out of your room.

    _____ *b.* Purposely cough, repeatedly saying, "I cannot breathe."

    _____ *c.* Ask your roommate to have his guests refrain from smoking, or meet at a different place.

    _____ *d.* Complain to your favorite professor.

    _____ *e.* Do and say nothing.

3. Your boss has repeatedly asked you to go get coffee for the members of the department. It is not part of your job responsibility.

    _____ *a.* "It is not part of my job. Why don't we set up a rotating schedule so that everyone has a turn?"

    _____ *b.* "Go get it yourself."

    _____ *c.* Continue to get the coffee.

    _____ *d.* File a complaint with the personnel department or the union.

    _____ *e.* "Why don't we skip coffee today?"

4. You are riding in a car with a friend. You are nervous because your friend is speeding, changing lanes frequently, and passing in no-passing zones.

    _____ *a.* "Are you trying to kill me?"

    _____ *b.* "What did you think of Professor Lussier's class today?"

    _____ *c.* "Please slow down and stay in one lane."

    _____ *d.* Try not to look where you are going.

    _____ *e.* "Stop driving like this or let me out right here."

5. You are in a department meeting to decide on the new budget. However, some of the members are going off on tangents and wasting time. Your boss hasn't said anything about it.

_____ a. Don't say anything. After all, it's your boss's meeting.

_____ b. "So far we agree on XYZ, and we still need to decide on ABC. Does anyone have any ideas on these line items?"

_____ c. "Let's stop wasting time and stay on the subject."

_____ d. "Let's just vote so we can get out of here."

_____ e. "Excuse me, I have to go to the bathroom."

6. One of your coworkers repeatedly tries to get you to do her work with all kinds of excuses.

_____ a. Do the work.

_____ b. "I have no intention of doing your work, so please stop asking me to do it."

_____ c. "Buzz off. Do it yourself, freeloader."

_____ d. "I'd like to do it for you, but I'm tied up right now."

_____ e. "Get away from me and don't bother me again."

7. You bought a watch. It doesn't work, so you return to the store with the receipt. The salesclerk says you cannot exchange it.

_____ a. Insist on the exchange. Talk to the person's boss and his or her boss if necessary.

_____ b. Leave with the watch.

_____ c. Drop the watch on the counter and pick up a new watch and walk out.

_____ d. Come back when a different salesclerk is there.

_____ e. Create a scene, yell, and get other customers on your side. Disrupt business until you get the new watch.

8. You are about to leave work and go to see your child perform in a play. Your boss comes to you and asks you to stay late to do a report she needs in the morning.

_____ a. "Sorry, I'm on my way to see a play."

_____ b. "I'd be happy to stay and do it."

_____ c. "Are you sure I cannot do it tomorrow?"

_____ d. "I'm on my way to see a play. Can I take it home and do it later tonight?"

_____ e. "Why should I get stuck here? Why don't you do it yourself?"

9. You believe that cheating is wrong. Your roommate just asked you if he could copy the homework you spent hours preparing.

_____ a. "Here you go."

_____ b. "I don't help cheaters."

_____ c. "OK, if you don't copy it word for word."

_____ d. "I'd like to help you. You're my friend, but in good conscience I cannot let you copy my homework."

_____ e. "You go out and have a good time, then you expect me to be a fool and get you off the hook? No way."

10. Some people you know stop by your dorm room. One of them pulls out some drugs, takes some, and passes them along. You don't take drugs.

_____ a. "You can get me into trouble. Please put them away or leave."

_____ b. Grab them and get rid of them.

_____ c. Take some drugs because you don't want to look bad.

_____ d. Pass them along without taking any.

_____ e. "Get out of here with that stuff."

Procedure (5–50 minutes)

Select one option:

1. The instructor goes over the recommended answers to the 10 situations.

2. The instructor asks students for their answers to the situations, followed by giving the recommended answers.

3. Break into groups of two or three and together follow the three-step approach for two or three situations at a time, followed by the instructor's going over the recommended answers. Discuss the possible consequences of each alternative response in the situation. Would it help or hurt human relations and performance? How?

Conclusion: The instructor leads a class discussion and/or makes concluding remarks.

Application: What have I learned from this experience? How will I use this knowledge in the future?

Sharing: Volunteers give their answers to the application section.

/ / / SKILL-BUILDING EXERCISE 5-3 / / /

Using the XYZ Conflict Model

Experience: Individual may share answers in groups or with entire class, in class or online.

AACSB Competencies: Analytic skills, communication abilities, interpersonal relations, and application of knowledge.

Objective: To improve your ability to initiate conflict resolution with positive statements

Preparation: You should complete the five situations below.

Below are five conflict situations. Write the XYZ statement you would use to resolve the conflict. Remember the goal of resolving the conflict while maintaining human relations.

1. A coworker has asked you to go out after work for the second time. The first time you gave an excuse for not being able to go, but you really don't want to go out with this person. What would you say?

   X _____

   Y _____

   Z _____

2. A coworker keeps coming to your work area to socialize. You have been talking as long as the person wants to. But it is affecting getting your work done, and you have had to stay late. What would you say?

   X _____

   Y _____

   Z _____

3. A coworker has been taking it easy and not doing his share of the work on your two-person assignment. You have had to do more than your share, and you don't want it to continue. What would you say?

   X _____

   Y _____

   Z _____

4. A coworker has continued to interrupt another coworker friend of yours as she speaks. It is upsetting you, and you have decided to talk to the interrupter privately about it. What would you say?

   X _____

   Y _____

   Z _____

5. A coworker is playing music loud for the third time. You don't like the music, and it affects your ability to concentrate. You haven't said anything, but you plan to now. What would you say?

X _____

Y _____

Z _____

Procedure (5–30 minutes)

Select one option:

1. The instructor goes over possible answers to the five situations.

2. The instructor asks students for their XYZ statements to the situations, followed by giving possible answers.

3. Break into groups of two or three, and together come up with an XYZ statement, followed by the instructor's going over the recommended answers. Discuss the possible consequences of each alternative response in the situation. Would it help or hurt human relations and performance? How?

Conclusion: The instructor leads a class discussion and/or makes concluding remarks.

Application: What have I learned from this experience? How will I use this knowledge in the future?

Sharing: Volunteers give their answers to the application section.

/// SKILL-BUILDING EXERCISE 5-4 ///

Initiating Conflict Resolution

Experience: Small group in-class exercise.

You will initiate, respond to, and observe a conflict role-play, and then evaluate the effectiveness of its resolution.

AACSB Competencies: Analytic skills, communication abilities, interpersonal relations, and application of knowledge.

Objective: To experience and develop skills in resolving a conflict.

Preparation: You should complete the information and written plan in preparation for this exercise.

During class you will be given the opportunity to role-play a conflict you face, or have faced, to develop your conflict skills. Fill in the information below, and also record your answers on a separate sheet of paper.

Other party (or parties) (You may use fictitious names) _____
     Define the situation:

1. List pertinent information about the other party (e.g., relationship with you, knowledge of the situation, age, background).

2. State what you wish to accomplish (objective) as a result of the conflict confrontation or discussion.

3. Identify the other party's possible reaction to your confrontation (resistance to change: intensity, source, focus).

4. How will you overcome this resistance to change?

5. Using the three steps in initiating conflict resolution, on a separate sheet of paper write out your plan to initiate the conflict resolution. Bring your written plan to class.

BMV 5-1

Procedure 1 (2–3 minutes)

Break into as many groups of three as possible. If there are any people not in a triad, make one or two groups of two. Each member selects the number 1, 2, or 3. Number 1 will be the first to initiate a conflict role-play, then 2, followed by 3.

Procedure 2 (8–15 minutes)

1. Initiator number 1 gives his or her information from the preparation to number 2 (the responder) to read. Once number 2 understands, role-play (see number 2 below). Number 3 is the observer.

2. Role-play the conflict resolution. Number 3, the observer, writes his or her observations on the feedback sheet (see below).

3. Integration: When the role-play is over, the observer leads a discussion on the effectiveness of the conflict resolution. All three should discuss the effectiveness. Number 3 is not a lecturer. Do not go on until told to do so.

Procedure 3 (8-15 minutes)

Follow procedure 2; this time number 2 is the initiator, number 3 is the responder, and number 1 is the observer.

Procedure 4 (8-15 minutes)

Follow procedure 2; this time number 3 is the initiator, number 1 is the responder, and number 2 is the observer.

Conclusion: The instructor leads a class discussion and/or makes concluding remarks.

Application (2-4 minutes):   What did I learn from this experience? How will I use this knowledge in the future?

BMV 6-2

Mediating Conflict Resolution may be shown.

Sharing: Volunteers give their answers to the application section.

Feedback for _____

Try to have positive improvement comments for each step in initiating conflict resolution. Remember to be descriptive and specific, and for all improvements have an alternative positive behavior (APB) (i.e., if you would have said /done . . . , it would have improved the conflict resolution by . . .).

Step 1: Did the initiator *maintain ownership* of the problem?

Did he or she have and implement a well-thought-out *XYZ plan*?

Step 2: Did he or she *persist* until the confrontee acknowledged the problem?

Step 3: Did the initiator get the confrontee to *agree to a change* or solution?

/ / / S K I L L - B U I L D I N G   E X E R C I S E   5 - 5   / / /

Developing New Habits

Experience: Individual may share habits in groups or entire class, in class or online.

AACSB Competencies: Analytic and application of knowledge.

Objective: To develop and share new habits.

Preparation: Select one or more topics from this chapter that will help you improve your human relations. Develop a new habit following the guideline from Chapter 1, section Habits and Skill-Building Exercise 1-4, on how to develop your cure, routine, and reward-change.

Procedure (5-30 minutes)

Follow the procedures from Skill Builder 1-4.

1. T.

2. F. Complementary transactions can come from *any* ego state, such as parent to child.

3. T.

4. F. Assertive behavior is used to create a win-win situation, not a win-lose situation as stated.

5. T.

6. F. It is more difficult to mediate a conflict.

1. W.L. Bedwell, S.M. Fiore, and E. Salas, "Developing the Future Workforce," *Academy of Management Learning & Education* 13(2) (2014): 171-186.

2. GE, "Identifying the Leadership Skills That Matter Most," *INC.* (December 2014 / January 2015): 78.

3. Transactional Analysis Journal http://journals.sagepub.com/home/tax, accessed May 2, 2017.

4. D.L. Ferris, H. Lian, D.J. Brown, and R. Morrison, "Ostracism, Self-Esteem and Job Performance" When Do We Self-Verify and When Do We Self-Enhance?" *Academy of Management Journal* 58(1) (2015): 279-297.

5. P. Lencioni, "Innovation Won't Get You Very Far," *INC.* (December 2014 / January 2015): 102.

6. W.L. Bedwell, S.M. Fiore, and E. Salas, "Developing the Future Workforce," *Academy of Management Learning & Education* 13(2) (2014): 171-186.

7. Eric Berne, *Games People Play* (New York: Grove Press, 1964); International Transactional Analysis Association Web site, http://itaaworld.org, retrieved on May 3, 2017.

8. International Transactional Analysis Association Web site, http://itaaworld.org, retrieved on May 3, 2017.

9. T. Harris, *I'm OK–You're OK.* (New York: HarperCollins, 1967; Quill edition, 2004).

10. R. McCammon, "Don't Pop Your Top," *Entrepreneur* (May 2016): 15-16.

11. M.J. Williams, "The Price Assertive Women Pay–and How to Minimize It," *The Wall Street Journal* (May 31, 2016): R3.

12. R.E. Silverman, "Managers: Watch Your Language," *The Wall Street Journal* (September 30, 2015): R9.

13. M.J. Williams, "The Price Assertive Women Pay–and How to Minimize It," *The Wall Street Journal* (May 31, 2016): R3.

14. R. McCammon, "The Anger Games," *Entrepreneur* (November 2013): 32-33.

15. R. McCammon, "Don't Pop Your Top," *Entrepreneur* (May 2016): 15-16.

16. A.C. Peng, J.M. Schaubroeck, and L. Li, "Social Exchange Implications of Own and Coworkers' Experiences of Supervisor Abuse," *Academy of Management Journal* 57(5) (2014): 1385-1405.

17. R.E. Silverman, "Managers: Watch Your Language," *The Wall Street Journal* (September 30, 2015): R9.

18. M.J. Williams, "The Price Assertive Women Pay–and How to Minimize It," *The Wall Street Journal* (May 31, 2016): R3.

19. E. Bernstein, "Venting Isn't Good for Us," *The Wall Street Journal* (August 11, 2015): D1, D4.

20. E. Bernstein, "Venting Isn't Good for Us," *The Wall Street Journal* (August 11, 2015): D1, D4.

21. R. Feintzeig, "When Nice Is a Four-Letter Word," *The Wall Street Journal* (December 31, 2015): D1, D3.

22. S. Shellenbarger, "Find Out What Your Boss Really Thinks About You," *The Wall Street Journal* (June 29, 2016): D1, D2.

23. R. McCammon, "How to Own the Room," *BusinessWeek* accessed online March 24, 2017.

24. M.J. Williams, "The Price Assertive Women Pay—and How to Minimize It," *The Wall Street Journal* (May 31, 2016): R3.

25. M.J. Williams, "The Price Assertive Women Pay—and How to Minimize It," *The Wall Street Journal* (May 31, 2016): R3.

26. M.J. Williams, "The Price Assertive Women Pay—and How to Minimize It," *The Wall Street Journal* (May 31, 2016): R3.

27. R.E. Silverman, "Managers: Watch Your Language," *The Wall Street Journal* (September 30, 2015): R9.

28. R. McCammon, "Don't Pop Your Top," *Entrepreneur* (May 2016): 15-16.

29. D.L. Ferris, H. Lian, D.J. Brown, and R. Morrison, "Ostracism, Self-Esteem and Job Performance: When Do We Self-Verify and When Do We Self-Enhance?" *Academy of Management Journal* 58(1) (2015): 279-297.

30. D.H. Wo, M.L. Ambrose, and M. Schminke, "What Drives Trickle-Down Effects? A Test of Multiple Mediation Processes," *Academy of Management Journal* 58(6) (2015): 1484-1868.

31. E. Bernstein, "Venting Isn't Good for Us," *The Wall Street Journal* (August 11, 2015): D1, D4.

32. E. Bernstein, "Venting Isn't Good for Us," *The Wall Street Journal* (August 11, 2015): D1, D4.

33. W. Isaascon, "Steve Jobs: The Biography—His Rivalry with Bill Gates," *Fortune* (November 7, 2011): 97-112.

34. G. Colvin, "Employers Are Looking for New Hires With Something Extra: Empathy," *Fortune* (September 4, 2014): 55.

35. D.L. Ferris, H. Lian, D.J. Brown, and R. Morrison, "Ostracism, Self-Esteem and Job Performance: When Do We Self-Verify and When Do We Self-Enhance?" *Academy of Management Journal* 58(1) (2015): 279-297.

36. P. Lencioni, "Innovation Won't Get You Very Far," *INC.* (December 2014 / January 2015): 102.

37. D.H. Wo, M.L. Ambrose, and M. Schminke, "What Drives Trickle-Down Effects? A Test of Multiple Mediation Processes," *Academy of Management Journal* 58(6) (2015): 1484-1868.

38. L.R. Weingart, K.J. Behfar, C. Bendersky, G. Todorova, and K.A. Hehn, "The Directness and Oppositional Intensity of Conflict Expression," *Academy of Management Review* 40(2) (2015): 235-262.

39. G. O'Brian, "Fixing the First Impression," *Entrepreneur* accessed online May 5, 2017.

40. P. Lencioni, "Innovation Won't Get You Very Far," *INC.* (December 2014 / January 2015): 102.

41. C. Kilesch, "CEO 101," *Fortune* (November 17, 2014): 150.

42. L.R. Weingart, K.J. Behfar, C. Bendersky, G. Todorova, and K.A. Hehn, "The Directness and Oppositional Intensity of Conflict Expression," *Academy of Management Review* 40(2) (2015): 235-262.

43. T. Gutner, "Why You May Be Deferential to Peers—But Not Your Boss," *Wall Street Journal* (April 28, 2014): R6.

44. W.L. Bedwell, S.M. Fiore, and E. Salas, "Developing the Future Workforce," *Academy of Management Learning & Education* 13(2) (2014): 171-186.

45. R.D. Costigan and K.E. Brink, "Another Perspective on MBA Program Alignment: An Investigation of Learning Goals," *Academy of Management Learning & Education* 14(2) (2015): 260-276.

46. R. Feintzeig, "When Nice Is a Four-Letter Word," *The Wall Street Journal* (December 31, 2015): D1, D3.

47. L.R. Weingart, K.J. Behfar, C. Bendersky, G. Todorova, and K.A. Hehn, "The Directness and Oppositional Intensity of Conflict Expression," *Academy of Management Review* 40(2) (2015): 235-262.

48. L.R. Weingart, K.J. Behfar, C. Bendersky, G. Todorova, and K.A. Hehn, "The Directness and Oppositional Intensity of Conflict Expression," *Academy of Management Review* 40(2) (2015): 235-262.

49. R. McCammon, "How to Own the Room," *BusinessWeek* accessed online May 4, 2017

 i. M. Helft, "How Travis Kalanick Is Building The Ultimate Transportation Machine," *Forbes* (Dec. 14, 2016).

 ii. M. Isaac, "Uber's C.E.O. Plays With Fire," *New York Times* (April 23, 2017).

 iii. M. Helft, "How Travis Kalanick Is Building The Ultimate Transportation Machine," *Forbes* (Dec. 14, 2016).

 iv. M. Helft, "How Travis Kalanick Is Building The Ultimate Transportation Machine," *Forbes* (Dec. 14, 2016).

 v. M. Isaac, "Uber's C.E.O. Plays With Fire," *New York Times* (April 23, 2017).

 vi. http://www.cnbc.com/2017/04/25/uber-stock-price-drops-amid-sexism-investigation-greyballing-and-apple-run-in-the-information.html. Accessed May 18, 2017

vii. Solon, O. (June 7, 2016). "Uber fires more than 20 employees after sexual harassment investigation". *The Guardian.* ISSN 0261–3077; Marinova, P. (June 6, 2017). "Uber Fires More Than 20 Employees After Harassment Investigation: Report". Fortune Magazine.

viii. Wong, J.C. (June 13, 2017). "Embattled Uber CEO Travis Kalanick takes indefinite leave of absence". *The Guardian.* Bensinger, G. (June 13, 2017). "Uber CEO Travis Kalanick to take a leave of absence". MarketWatch.

ix. Isaac, M. (June 21, 2017). "Uber Founder Travis Kalanick Resigns as C.E.O.". *The New York Times.* Segall, L. and Mullen, J. (June 21, 2017). "Uber CEO Travis Kalanick resigns after months of crisis". CNN.

Leadership Skills: Influencing Others

Leading and Trust

©bowdenimages/Getty Images

After completing this chapter, you should be able to:

LO 6-1   Explain what leadership is and how it affects behavior, human relations, and performance.

LO 6-2   Describe leadership trait theory.

LO 6-3   List and describe three behavioral leadership theories.

LO 6-4   List and describe three contingency leadership theories.

LO 6-5   Explain four situational supervisory styles.

LO 6-6   Briefly describe the five dimensions of trust.

LO 6-7   Define the following 14 key terms (in order of appearance in the chapter):

leadership
leadership trait theory
behavioral leadership theories
Leadership Grid
contingency leadership theories
contingency leadership theory

leadership continuum
normative leadership theory
situational leadership
autocratic style (S-A)
consultative style (S-C)
participative style (S-P)
laissez-faire style (S-L)
trust

OPENING CASE WORK SCENARIO

/// Mike Templeton is a branch manager at the Northwest Bank. Mike has authority over subordinates to make decisions regarding hiring and firing, raises, and promotions. Mike gets along well with his subordinates. The branch atmosphere is friendly. His boss has asked for a special report about the loans the branch has made so far this year. Mike could have done the report himself, but he thought it would be better to delegate the task to one of the three loan officers. After thinking about the qualifications of the three loan officers, Mike selected Jean. He called her into his office to talk about the assignment.

MIKE: Hi, Jean, I've called you in here to tell you that I've selected you to do a year-to-date loan report for the branch. It's not mandatory; I can assign the report to someone else. Are you interested?

JEAN: I don't know; I've never done a report before.

MIKE: I realize that, but I'm sure you can handle it. I selected you because of my faith in your ability.

JEAN: Will you help me?

MIKE: Sure. There is more than one way to do the report. I can give you the details on what must be included in the report, but you can use any format you want, as long as I approve it. We can discuss the report now; then as you work on it, you can come to me for input. I'm confident you'll do a great job. Do you want the assignment?

JEAN: OK, I'll do it.

Together, Mike and Jean discuss how she will do the report.

What leadership style would you use to get the report done? This chapter explains 10 leadership theories. Each will be applied to the loan report. ///

In Part 1 (Chapters 1 to 3) we focused on developing intrapersonal skills, and in Part 2 (Chapters 5 to 6) we built on those skills to develop interpersonal skills. We are now in Part 3, so we turn to developing leadership skills, which are clearly based on intrapersonal and interpersonal skills. These three skills form a natural, overlapping developmental sequence. Again, organizations are recruiting employees with interpersonal skills, including leadership.[1]

HOW LEADERSHIP AFFECTS BEHAVIOR, HUMAN RELATIONS, HAPPINESS, AND PERFORMANCE

Learning Outcome 6-1

Explain what leadership is and how it affects behavior, human relations, and performance.

Leadership is *the process of influencing employees to work toward the achievement of objectives.* The essence of leadership in organizations is influencing and facilitating individual and collective efforts to accomplish objectives. A managers' leadership behavior affects employees' behavior, human relations, and their happiness, as well as job performance.[2] Clearly, leadership affects company success.[3] Therefore, organizations recruit for and spend millions of dollars to develop employee leadership skills. **General Electric (GE)** is known for its great leadership programs.[4]

Leadership in Your Personal Life Do you ever ask anyone to do something for you—a favor?[5] If you think about it, every day you use your leadership skill when you try to persuade others to do what you want them to do.[6] Are you happier when you get your way? Leadership skills are important in your personal life as well as your career,[7] or if you want to be a manager or not. Also, don't you try to influence your boss?

But effective leadership is not about manipulating people to get what you want. Once people realize you are trying to manipulate them for your own personal gain at their expense, you lose your ability to influence them. In this chapter, you can develop your leadership skills to attain the goal of human relations—create win-win situations in which you give people what they want, and you get what you want in return—or balancing self-interest and others' interest.[8]

Participative Leadership The trend today is away from the old-school autocratic leadership to participative leadership. It is called *shared leadership* because the leader shares influence and joint decision making through participation in implementing the management functions.[9] Shared leadership entails the serial emergence of both official and unofficial leaders as part of a simultaneous, ongoing, mutual influence process. Hence, all leadership is shared leadership, as it is simply a matter of degree of participation in a given situation.[10] Another trend is the use of self-managing teams that have no organizationally assigned leaders, as leaders emerge informally.[11] Therefore, leadership skills will affect your career success.[12]

Leadership and Management Are Not the Same People tend to use the terms *manager* and *leader* interchangeably. However, that usage is not correct. Management and leadership are related but different concepts. Leadership is one of the five management functions (planning, organizing, staffing, leading, and controlling), and leadership is critical to management success. Someone can be a manager without being a true leader. There are managers—you may know of some—who are not leaders because they do not have the ability to influence others. There are also good leaders who are not managers. The informal leader, an employee group member who takes charge, voices issues, and initiates change, is a case in point. You may have worked in a situation where one of your peers had more influence in the department than the manager.[13]

Our definition of leadership does not suggest that influencing employees is the task of the manager alone; employees do influence other employees. Anyone can be a leader within any group or department, and everyone in a team is expected to be a leader. Thus, regardless of your position, you are expected to share leadership.

WORK APPLICATION 6-1

Give detailed reasons why leadership skills are important to a specific organization, and to you personally and professionally.

Theory and Application   Leadership is a topic of great interest to researchers and practitioners alike,[14] as bridging the gap is a key issue to both.[15] But some people like leadership theories and want to know about them and the history of leadership, while others just want the practical, "how to lead" material. In this chapter, we provide both. In the first three major sections we provide the history of leadership theory based on the three schools of leadership: trait, behavioral, and contingency. In the fourth section, based on the theories, we provide situational supervision that explains how to select the most appropriate leadership style for a given situation. So you can put your focus on one or the other, or both.

For more than 50 years researchers have been trying to answer these questions: "What does it take to be an effective leader?" and "What is the most effective leadership style?" There is no universal agreement about the answers to these questions. We will now turn to a chronological review of how researchers have tried to answer these questions. After studying the major leadership theories, you can select the one you like best, combine some, or develop your own.

LEADERSHIP TRAIT THEORY

Learning Outcome 6-2

Describe leadership trait theory.

In the early 1900s, an organized approach to studying leadership began. The early studies were based on the assumption that leaders are born, not made. Researchers wanted to identify a set of characteristics, or traits, that distinguished leaders from followers or effective from ineffective leaders.[16] **Leadership trait theory** assumes that *there are distinctive physical and psychological characteristics accounting for leadership effectiveness*. In fact, personality traits do affect leadership style.[17] Researchers analyzed traits, or qualities, such as appearance, aggressiveness, self-reliance, persuasiveness, and dominance in an effort to identify a set of traits that all successful leaders possess.[18] The list of traits was to be used as a prerequisite for the promotion of candidates to leadership positions. Only candidates possessing all the identified traits were to be given leadership positions.

Inconclusive Findings: In 70 years, more than 300 trait studies were conducted. However, no one has come up with a universal list of traits that all successful leaders possess.[19] In all cases, there were exceptions. Indeed, if leaders were simply born and not made (in other words, if leadership skills could not be developed), there would be no need for courses in management and human relations.

The Ghiselli Study

Probably the most widely publicized trait theory study was conducted by **Edwin Ghiselli**.[20] His study concluded that there are traits important to effective leadership, though not all are necessary for success. Ghiselli identified the following six traits, in order of importance, as being significant traits for effective leadership: (1) *supervisory ability* (you will develop these skills in this course); (2) *need for occupational achievement;* (3) *intelligence;* (4) *decisiveness;* (5) *self-assurance;* and (6) *initiative.*

/// **In the opening case,** Mike appears to have supervisory ability. He is getting the job done through Jean, using the supervisory process. Based on the case, one cannot determine whether Mike has the other five traits. ///

WORK APPLICATION 6-2

What are your views on leadership trait theory? Recall a manager you have now or have had in the past. Which of Ghiselli's six traits does or did the person have? Which traits does or did the person lack?

Current Studies

Even though it is generally agreed that there is no universal set of leadership traits or qualities, people continue to study and write about the importance of leadership traits.[21] Why? Because leadership style is shaped according to a leader's traits[22] and behavior.[23] The Big Five personality does have a preferred leadership profile, with high surgency and conscientiousness being positively related to successful leadership and high agreeableness and low adjustment being negatively related to leadership success.[24] In a survey, 782 top executives were asked, "What are the most important traits for success as a supervisor?"[25] Before the results are revealed, complete Self-Assessment Exercise 6-1 to determine whether you have the qualities necessary to be a successful leader.

/ / / Self-Assessment Exercise 6-1 / / /

Your Leadership Traits

Select the response that best describes the frequency of your actual behavior. Place the number 1 to 5 on the line before each statement.

Almost always	Usually	Frequently	Occasionally	Seldom
5	4	3	2	1

_____ 1. I am trustworthy. If I say I will do something by a set time, I do it.

_____ 2. I am loyal. I do not do or say things that hurt my friends, relatives, coworkers, boss, or others.

_____ 3. I can take criticism. If people tell me negative things about myself, I give them serious thought and change when appropriate.

_____ 4. I am honest. I do not lie, steal, cheat, or the like.

_____ 5. I am fair. I treat people equally. I don't take advantage of others.

_____ 6. I want to be successful. I do things to the best of my ability.

_____ 7. I am a self-starter. I get things done without having to be told to do them.

_____ 8. I am a problem solver. If things aren't going the way I want them to, I take corrective action to meet my objectives. I don't give up easily.

_____ 9. I am self-reliant. I don't need the help of others.

_____ 10. I am hardworking. I enjoy working and getting the job done.

_____ 11. I enjoy working with people. I prefer to work with others rather than work alone.

_____ 12. I can motivate others. I can get people to do things they may not really want to do.

_____ 13. I am respected. People enjoy working with me.

_____ 14. I am cooperative. I strive to help the team do well, rather than to be the star.

_____ 15. I am a leader. I enjoy teaching, coaching, and instructing people.

To determine your score, transfer the numbers 1 to 5 that represent your responses below. The column headings represent the trait or quality listed in each statement. Total each column; then add those numbers to determine the grand total.

Integrity	Industriousness	Ability to Get Along with People	
_____ 1.	_____ 6.	_____ 11.	
_____ 2.	_____ 7.	_____ 12.	
_____ 3.	_____ 8.	_____ 13.	
_____ 4.	_____ 9.	_____ 14.	
_____ 5.	_____ 10.	_____ 15.	
_____ Total	_____ Total	_____ Total	_____ Grand Total

Your total for each column will range from 5 to 25, and your grand total will range from 15 to 75. In general, the higher your score, the better your chances of being a successful manager. If you are interested in being (or are) a manager, you can work on improving your integrity, industriousness, and ability to get along with others. As a start, review the list of traits. In which were you strongest? Weakest? Set objectives and develop plans to improve.

Answers to the survey revealed integrity, industriousness, and the ability to get along with people (human relations skills) as the three most important traits for success. Whatever your score of traits was, remember that traits are important to leadership,[26] but there is no universal list of traits, and you don't need every trait to be a successful leader.

BEHAVIORAL LEADERSHIP THEORIES

Learning Outcome 6-3

List and describe four behavioral leadership theories.

By the late 1940s, most of the leadership research had switched from trait theory to a focus on the leader's behavior. In the continuing quest to find the one best leadership style in all situations, thousands of studies have been conducted in an attempt to identify the differences in the behavior of effective leaders versus ineffective leaders.[27] **Behavioral leadership theories** assume that *there are distinctive styles that effective leaders use consistently; that is, that good leadership is rooted in behavior.*

In this section you will learn about two-dimensional leadership styles, the Leadership Grid, and transformational, charismatic, transaction, servant, stewardship, authentic, and LMX leadership theories.

Two-Dimensional Leadership Styles

Structuring and Consideration Styles   In 1945, **Ohio State University** began a study to determine effective leadership styles. In their attempt to measure leadership styles, the researchers developed an instrument known as the Leader Behavior Description Questionnaire (LBDQ). Respondents to the questionnaire perceived their leaders' behavior toward them on two distinct dimensions[28]:

- *Initiating structure.* The extent to which the leader takes charge to plan, organize, direct, and control as the employee performs the task.

- *Consideration.* The extent to which the leader communicates to develop trust, friendship, support, and respect.

Job-Centered and Employee-Centered Styles   At approximately the same time the Ohio State studies began, the **University of Michigan**'s Survey Research Center began leadership studies. Researchers at Michigan identified the same two dimensions, or styles, of leadership behavior. However, they called the two styles by different names[29]:

- *Job-centered.* This is the same *as initiating structure.*

- *Employee-centered. This is the same as consideration.*

Leadership Styles   Different combinations of the two dimensions of leadership result in four leadership styles, illustrated in Exhibit 6.1.

/// **In the opening case,** Mike is using the high-consideration (employee-centered) and low-structure (job-centered) style, box 3, because he is telling Jean what needs to be in the report, but how she does the report is up to her. Mike also offers supportive statements. ///

The Leadership Grid

Robert Blake and **Jane Mouton** developed the **Managerial Grid**. It became the **Leadership Grid**, with **Anne Adams McCanse** replacing Mouton.[30]

EXHIBIT 6.1 | Two-Dimensional Leadership Models

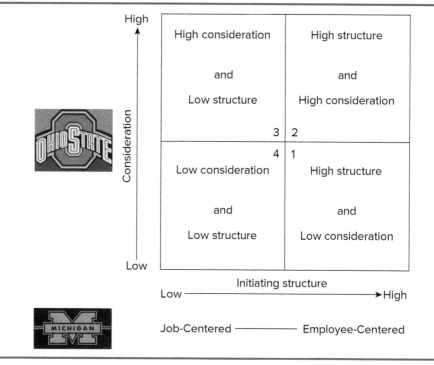

OSU image: ©aceshot1/Shutterstock; UM image: ©Steve Pepple/Shutterstock

---

APPLICATION SITUATIONS / / /

Two-Dimensional Leadership Styles   AS 6-1

Using Exhibit 6.1, identify the behavior by its quadrant:

A. 1   B. 2   C. 3   D. 4

_____ 1. "Get back to work now. The break is over."

_____ 2. "This is a complex task, and you're new. I'll work with you until you get the hang of it. Here is a demonstration of the task . . ."

_____ 3. "I know you can complete the report. You're just not too sure of yourself because you never did one before. Try it on your own, and if you have a problem I will help you."

_____ 4. "Jose, I want you to clean the work area. It's your turn; you haven't done it for quite awhile."

_____ 5. "I will let you select the new computer without my input."

The Leadership Grid is based on the two leadership dimensions called *concern for production* and *concern for people*. The **Leadership Grid** is *Blake and Mouton's model identifying the ideal leadership style as having a high concern for both production and people.* The model, shown in Exhibit 6.2, identifies five major styles:

The impoverished manager (1,1). This leader has low concern for both production and people. The leader does the minimum required.

The sweatshop manager (9,1). This leader has a high concern for production and a low concern for people. The leader uses position power to coerce employees to do the work.

EXHIBIT 6.2 | The Leadership Grid

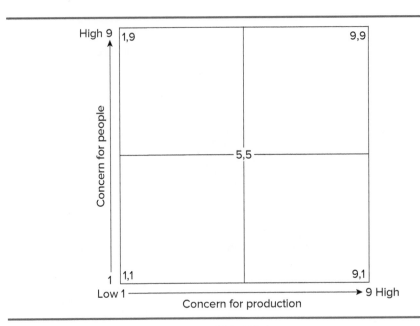

Source: Adapted from Robert R. Blake and Anne Adams McCanse, *Leadership Dilemmas—Grid Solutions*, Houston: Gulf Publishing Company, 29. Copyright 1991, by Scientific Methods, Inc.

The country club manager (1,9). This leader has a high concern for people and a low concern for production. The leader strives to maintain good relations.

The organized-person manager (5,5). This leader has balanced, medium concern for both production and people.

The team manager (9,9). This leader has a high concern for both production and people. This leader strives for maximum performance and employee satisfaction.

Leadership Grid training identifies a person's preferred leadership style as 1 of 81 combinations of concern for production and people. Then trainees are taught to always use the one ideal leadership style—the team manager (9,9).

/// **In the opening case,** Mike has a high concern for getting the report done and a high concern for Jean. If you had to select one of the five major styles, you would probably choose the 9,9 team manager. However, Mike is giving more support to Jean than direction for doing the report. Mike is actually using closer to a 9,7 leadership style. ///

Communication Skills
Refer to CS Question 3.

WORK APPLICATION 6-3

What are your views on the Leadership Grid? Recall a manager you have now or have had. Which of the five styles does or did the manager use?

APPLICATION SITUATIONS / / /

The Leadership Grid   AS 6-2

Match the five situations with the leader's probable style. (Refer to Exhibit 6.2.)

A. 1,1 (impoverished)   C. 9,1 (sweatshop)   E. 9,9 (team manager)

B. 1,9 (country club)   D. 5,5 (organized person)

_____ 6. The department is one of the lowest producers, and it has a low level of morale.

_____ 7. The department has very high morale; the members enjoy their work. But productivity in the department among the lowest in the company.

_____ 8. The department has adequate morale, with average productivity levels.

_____ 9. The department is one of the top performers, and employees have high morale.

_____ 10. The department has one of the lowest levels of morale, but it is the top performer.

Transformational, Charismatic, Transactional, Servant, Stewardship, Authentic, and LMX Leadership

Although scholars gave up trying to find the one best leadership style, today researchers continue to further develop behavioral theories.[31]

Transformational Leadership   Transformational leadership, a contemporary view of leadership, is a behavioral theory because it focuses on the behavior of successful leaders.[32] Transformational leadership is about change, innovation, and entrepreneurship.[33] Clearly, **Steve Jobs** was a transformational leader.

Charismatic Leadership   Transformational leaders also can be charismatic leaders.[34] Although charisma is not needed to lead, it can help.[35] Charismatic leaders have the ability to engage employees by energizing them to meet challenging objectives[36] and inspiring them to greatness.[37] **Martin Luther King Jr.** and **Mother Teresa** are considered to have been charismatic. **Steve Jobs** was charismatic, and he was even called a Pied Piper as employees followed his lead.

Transactional Leadership   Transformational leadership has been contrasted with transactional leadership.[38] The transaction is based on the behavioral strategy[39] of "you do this work for me and I'll give this reward to you."

Servants and Stewardship   *Stewardship theory* states that leaders should be *servants* of the employees and organization.[40] Stewards focus least on satisfying their own personal needs to fulfill followers' needs, as they live the values such as honesty, altruism, and courage and treat employees well.[41]

Authentic Leadership   Authentic leadership is about being yourself.[42] Use self-leadership or influencing yourself,[43] because if we try to copy someone else we are not being our true self, and it is usually unsuccessful. **Integrate CEO Jeremy Boom** says, "Learn from others, read autobiographies of your favorite leaders, pick up skills along the way...but never lose your authentic voice, opinions and, ultimately, how you make decisions."[44]

Leader-Member Exchange (LMX)   Positive manager-subordinate relationships are invaluable to organizations,[45] as employees want to have inclusive leaders who they feel they can relate to and see as a person.[46] **New York Times bestselling author Lewis Howes** says, "The more you focus on genuine connections with people, and look for ways to help them...the more likable and personable you become."[47] LMX is about developing positive dyadic relationships with each person,[48] everyone should feel included—or there shouldn't be an in-group and out-group.[49] Your most important job as a leader is to develop relationships with others.[50]

CONTINGENCY LEADERSHIP THEORIES

Learning Outcome 6-4

List and describe four contingency leadership theories.

Both the trait and behavioral leadership theories were attempts to find the one best leadership style in all situations. In the late 1960s, it became apparent that there is no one best leadership style in all situations. **Contingency leadership theories** assume that *the appropriate leadership style varies from situation to situation.* Contingency, also called situational leadership, is based on the two-dimensional behaviors. The major difference is selecting the appropriate leadership style based on the person and the situational factors.[51] Changes in a dynamic environment may require changes in leadership styles,[52] and the frequency of checking on employees varies based on the situation.[53] **Meg Whitman, CEO of IBM,** says that she is a big believer in situational leadership.[54]

In this section, we discuss some of the most popular contingency leadership theories, including contingency leadership theory, leadership continuum, normative leadership theory, and situational leadership.

Contingency Leadership Theory

In 1951, **Fred E. Fiedler** began to develop the first situational leadership theory. He called the theory "Contingency Theory of Leader Effectiveness."[55] Fiedler believed that one's leadership style is a reflection of one's personality (trait theory–oriented) and is basically constant. Leaders do not change styles. **Contingency leadership theory** developed by Fiedler, is *used to determine whether a person's leadership style is task- or relationship-oriented and if the situation matches the leader's style.* If there is no match, Fiedler recommends that the leader change the situation, rather than the leadership style.

Leadership Style   The first major factor is to determine whether one's leadership style is task- or relationship-oriented. To do so, the leader fills in the Least Preferred Coworker (LPC) scales. This is followed by determining the favorableness of the leader's situation.

Situational Favorableness   Situational favorableness refers to the degree to which a situation enables the leader to exert influence over the followers. The more favorable the situation, the more power the leader has. The three variables, in order of importance, are:

1. *Leader-member relations.* Is the relationship good or poor? The better the relations, the more favorable the situation.

2. *Task structure.* Is the task structured or unstructured? Do employees perform routine, unambiguous, standard tasks? The more structured the jobs are, the more favorable the situation.

3. *Position power.* Is position power strong or weak? The more power, the more favorable the situation.

Determining the Appropriate Leadership Style   To determine whether task or relationship leadership is appropriate, the user answers the three questions pertaining to situational favorableness, using the Fiedler contingency theory model. See Exhibit 6.3 for an adapted model. The user starts with question 1 and follows the decision tree to determine the situation (1 to 8) and appropriate leadership style (task or relationship).

One of the criticisms of Fiedler's model comes from those who believe that the leader should change his or her style rather than the situation. The other contingency writers in this chapter take this position.

/// **In the opening case,** Mike has good relations with Jean, the task is unstructured, and Mike's position power is strong. This is situation 3, in which the appropriate leadership style is task (Exhibit 6.3). However, Mike is using a relationship style. Fiedler would suggest that Mike change the situation to meet his preferred relationship style. ///

Leadership Continuum

Robert Tannenbaum and **Warren Schmidt** state that leadership behavior is on a continuum from boss-centered to employee-centered leadership. Their model focuses on who makes the decisions. They identify seven major styles the leader can choose from. Exhibit 6.4 is an adaptation of their model, which lists the seven styles.[56] The **leadership continuum,** developed by Tannenbaum and Schmidt, *identifies seven leadership styles based on the use of boss-centered versus employee-centered leadership.*

Communication Skills
Refer to CS Question 4.

WORK APPLICATION 6-4

What are your views on contingency leadership theory? Do you agree with Fiedler's recommendation to change the situation rather than the leader's style?

EXHIBIT 6.3 | Fiedler's Contingency Leadership Theory Model

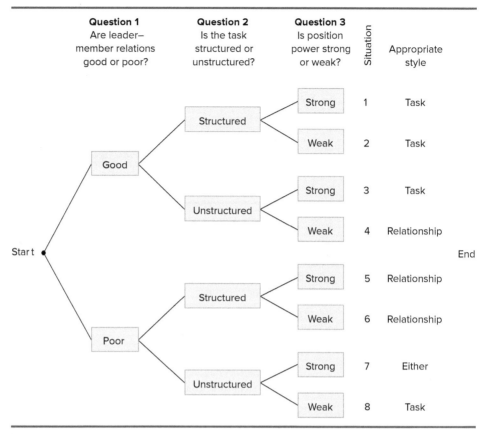

	Question 1 Are leader–member relations good or poor?	Question 2 Is the task structured or unstructured?	Question 3 Is position power strong or weak?	Situation	Appropriate style
	Good	Structured	Strong	1	Task
			Weak	2	Task
		Unstructured	Strong	3	Task
			Weak	4	Relationship
	Poor	Structured	Strong	5	Relationship
			Weak	6	Relationship
		Unstructured	Strong	7	Either
			Weak	8	Task

Start ● ... End

Source: F. Fiedler, A Theory of Leadership Effectiveness Copyright © 1967, by McGraw-Hill.

APPLICATION SITUATIONS / / /

Contingency Leadership Theory   AS 6-3

Using Exhibit 6.3, match the situation with its corresponding appropriate leadership style. Select two answers for each situation.

A. 1   C. 3   E. 5   G. 7

B. 2   D. 4   F. 6   H. 8

a. Task-oriented   b. Relationship-oriented

_____ 11. Fernando is from the corporate planning staff. He helps the other departments plan. Fernando is viewed as being a dreamer; he doesn't understand the departments. People tend to be rude in their dealings with him.

_____ 12. Jennie is the supervisor of processing canceled checks for the bank. She is well liked by the workers. Jennie's boss enjoys hiring and evaluating her employees' performance.

_____ 13. Henry is the principal of a high school and assigns teachers to classes and various other duties. He hires teachers and decides on tenure appointments. The school atmosphere is tense.

_____ 14. Sam is the chairperson of the quality improvement committee. She is highly regarded by its volunteer members from a variety of departments. They are charged with recommending ways to increase organizational performance.

_____ 15. Carleen is the supervisor of the assembly of mass-produced containers. She has the power to reward and punish and is viewed as a very tough supervisor.

EXHIBIT 6.4 | The Leadership Continuum

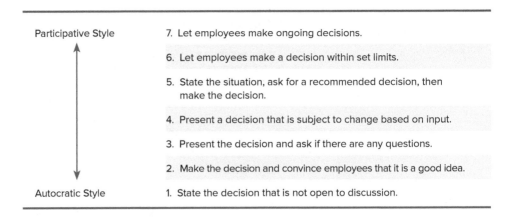

Participative Style

7. Let employees make ongoing decisions.

6. Let employees make a decision within set limits.

5. State the situation, ask for a recommended decision, then make the decision.

4. Present a decision that is subject to change based on input.

3. Present the decision and ask if there are any questions.

2. Make the decision and convince employees that it is a good idea.

Autocratic Style

1. State the decision that is not open to discussion.

Skill-Building Exercise 6-2 develops this skill.

Before selecting one of the seven leadership styles, the user must consider the following three factors, or variables:

The manager. What is the leader's preferred style, based on experience and confidence in the subordinates?

The subordinates. What is the subordinates' preferred style for the leader?

The situation. What are the environmental considerations, such as the organization's size, structure, goals, and technology?

As you read about the situational variables, you will realize that they are descriptive; the model does not state which style to use in a situation. The leadership styles discussed in the "Situational Supervision" tell the leader which style to use in a given situation.

/// In the opening case, Mike began the discussion using style 4, in which the leader presents a tentative decision subject to change. Jean did not have to do the report. Mike would have given it to another employee if she did not want to do it. Mike also used style 5, leader presents problem—the need for the report and what must be included in

---

APPLICATION SITUATIONS / / /

Leadership Continuum AS 6-4

Using Exhibit 6.4, identify the statements by their leadership style:

A. 1   C. 3   E. 5   G. 7
B. 2   D. 4   F. 6

_____ 16. "Thanks for agreeing to be on this committee. I'd like your ideas on how to improve performance in the department. But I have the final say on any changes we implement."

_____ 17. "Shawn, I selected you to chair the committee, but you don't have to if you prefer not to."

_____ 18. "Tanya, pick up in lane 4 right away."

_____ 19. "Until the end of the month, this is the way it will be done. Does anyone have any questions about the procedure?"

_____ 20. "Your committee has come up with three good ideas. Please select one and implement it soon."

the report—and told Jean he would allow her to select the form, subject to his final approval. ///

Normative Leadership Theory

Victor Vroom and **Philip Yetton** attempted to bridge the gap between leadership theory and managerial practice. To do so, they developed a model that tells the manager which leadership style to use in a given situation. **Normative leadership theory,** developed by Vroom and Yetton, is *a decision-tree model that enables the user to select from five leadership styles the one that is appropriate for the situation.*

Leadership Styles   In 2000 Victor Vroom published a revised version of this normative leadership model with the title *Leadership and the Decision Making Process.*[57] Vroom identified five leadership styles based on the level of participation in the decision by the followers. Here is Vroom's latest version of the five leadership styles:

1. *Decide.* Leader makes decision alone.
2. *Consult individually.* Talk to employees individually to get information and suggestions; then leader makes decision.
3. *Consult group.* Talk to group of employees to get information and suggestions; then leader makes decision.
4. *Facilitate.* Have group meeting for employee participation with leader in making decision.
5. *Delegate.* Group makes the decision.

Although the normative leadership model is primarily a leadership model, it is also used to determine the level of participation in decision making. There are actually two different models and a series of seven questions to answer, making it quite complex. Therefore, we will not present the model. Refer to endnote 36 for a copy of the model and details on how to use the model.

/// In the opening case, Mike used the consult individually style. Mike told Jean that she could select the style subject to his approval. Mike makes the final decision based on Jean's input. ///

Situational Leadership

Situational leadership, developed by Paul Hersey and Kenneth Blanchard, is *a model for selecting from four leadership styles the one that matches the employees' maturity level in a given situation.* For the most part, situational leadership[58] takes the two-dimensional leadership styles and the four quadrants (see Exhibit 6.1), and develops four leadership styles, which **Hersey** and **Blanchard** call *telling* (lower-right quadrant—high task, low relationship); *selling* (upper-right quadrant—high task, high relationship); *participating* (upper-left quadrant—high relationship, low task); and *delegating* (lower-left quadrant—low relationship, low task).

Hersey and Blanchard went beyond the behavioral theory by developing a model that tells the leader which style to use in a given situation. To determine the leadership style, one determines the followers' maturity level. If it is low, the leader uses a telling style; if it is moderate to low, the leader uses a selling style; if it is moderate to high, the leader uses the participating style; and if it is high, the leader uses a delegating style.

/// In the opening case, Mike used the participating style with Jean. Since Mike had a higher concern for Jean than for the task, he gave Jean more support than directions. Mike gave her the specifics of what had to be included, but he let her decide on the format, subject to his approval. ///

See Exhibit 6.5 for a review of the major theories of leadership.

EXHIBIT 6.5 | Leadership Theories

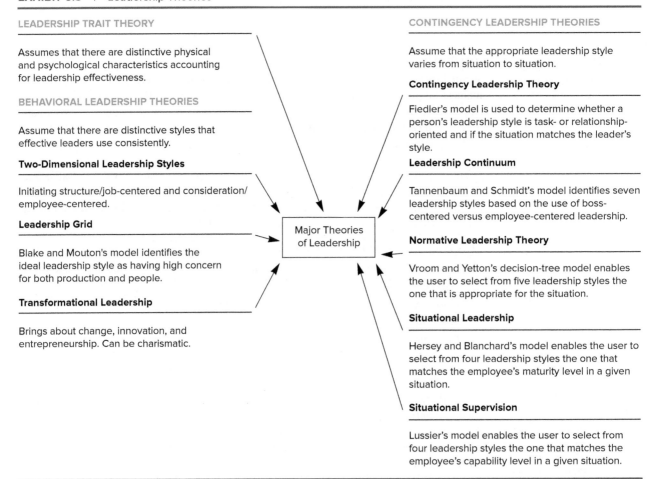

LEADERSHIP TRAIT THEORY

Assumes that there are distinctive physical and psychological characteristics accounting for leadership effectiveness.

BEHAVIORAL LEADERSHIP THEORIES

Assume that there are distinctive styles that effective leaders use consistently.

Two-Dimensional Leadership Styles

Initiating structure/job-centered and consideration/employee-centered.

Leadership Grid

Blake and Mouton's model identifies the ideal leadership style as having high concern for both production and people.

Transformational Leadership

Brings about change, innovation, and entrepreneurship. Can be charismatic.

Major Theories of Leadership

CONTINGENCY LEADERSHIP THEORIES

Assume that the appropriate leadership style varies from situation to situation.

Contingency Leadership Theory

Fiedler's model is used to determine whether a person's leadership style is task- or relationship-oriented and if the situation matches the leader's style.

Leadership Continuum

Tannenbaum and Schmidt's model identifies seven leadership styles based on the use of boss-centered versus employee-centered leadership.

Normative Leadership Theory

Vroom and Yetton's decision-tree model enables the user to select from five leadership styles the one that is appropriate for the situation.

Situational Leadership

Hersey and Blanchard's model enables the user to select from four leadership styles the one that matches the employee's maturity level in a given situation.

Situational Supervision

Lussier's model enables the user to select from four leadership styles the one that matches the employee's capability level in a given situation.

SITUATIONAL SUPERVISION

Now that we have explained the various leadership theories, we present the practical "how to lead" with the appropriate style for the situation model based on situational variables.[59] Recall that we can all be leaders (supervisors) of others (employees) even if we are not managers. Although the terms *supervisor* and *employee* are used, anyone can use the model in their personal and professional lives. Our goal is to learn to select the most appropriate style for the situation. Let's begin with Self-Assessment Exercise 6-2, which identifies your preferred supervisory style.

/ / / Self-Assessment Exercise 6-2 / / /

Determining Your Preferred Supervisory Style

This exercise is designed to determine your preferred supervisory style. Below are 12 situations. Select the one alternative that most closely describes what you would do in each situation. Don't be concerned with trying to pick the right answer; select the alternative you would really use. Circle the letter *a*, *b*, *c*, or *d*. Ignore the C and S lines, which will be explained later in this chapter and used in class in Skill-Building Exercise 7-1.

(continued)

C _____   1. Your rookie crew members seem to be developing well. Their need for direction and close supervision is diminishing. You would:

    a. Stop directing and overseeing performance unless there is a problem. S _____

    b. Spend time getting to know them personally, but make sure they maintain performance levels. S _____

    c. Make sure things keep going well; continue to direct and oversee closely. S _____

    d. Begin to discuss new tasks of interest to them. S _____

C _____   2. You assigned Joe a task, specifying exactly how you wanted it done. Joe deliberately ignored your directions and did it his way. The job will not meet the customer's standards. This is not the first problem you've had with Joe. You decide to:

    a. Listen to Joe's side, but be sure the job gets done right away. S _____

    b. Tell Joe to do it again the right way and closely supervise the job. S _____

    c. Tell him the customer will not accept the job and let Joe handle it his way. S _____

    d. Discuss the problem and what can be done about it. S _____

C _____   3. Your employees work well together. The department is a real team. It's the top performer in the organization. Because of traffic problems, the president OK'd staggered hours for departments. As a result, you can change your department's hours. Several of your workers have suggested changing. The action you take is to:

    a. Allow the group to decide the hours. S _____

    b. Decide on new hours, explain why you chose them, and invite questions. S _____

    c. Conduct a meeting to get the group members' ideas. Select new hours together, with your approval. S _____

    d. Send around a memo stating the hours you want. S _____

C _____   4. You hired Bill, a new employee. He is not performing at the level expected after one month's training. Bill is trying, but he seems to be a slow learner. You decide to:

    a. Clearly explain what needs to be done and oversee his work. Discuss why the procedures are important; support and encourage him. S _____

    b. Tell Bill that his training is over and it's time to pull his own weight. S _____

    c. Review task procedures and supervise his work closely. S _____

    d. Inform Bill that although his training is over, he can feel free to come to you if he has any problems. S _____

C _____   5. Helen has had an excellent performance record for the past five years. Recently you have noticed a drop in the quality and quantity of her work. She has a family problem. You would:

    a. Tell her to get back on track and closely supervise her. S _____

    b. Discuss the problem with Helen. Help her realize her personal problem is affecting her work. Discuss ways to improve the situation. Be supportive and encourage her. S _____

    c. Tell Helen you're aware of her productivity slip and that you're sure she'll work it out soon. S _____

    d. Discuss the problem and solution with Helen and supervise her closely. S _____

C _____   6. Your organization does not allow smoking in certain areas. You just walked by a restricted area and saw Joan smoking. She has been with the organization for 10 years and is a very productive worker. Joan has never been caught smoking before. The action you take is to:

    a. Ask her to put it out, then leave. S _____

    b. Discuss why she is smoking and what she intends to do about it. S _____

    c. Encourage Joan not to smoke in this area again, and check up on her in the future. S _____

    d. Tell her to put it out, watch her do it, and tell her you will check on her in the future. S _____

(*continued*)

/ / / Self-Assessment Exercise 6-2 / / / (continued)

C _____ 7. Your department usually works well together with little direction. Recently a conflict between Sue and Tom has caused problems. As a result, you:

    a. Call Sue and Tom together and make them realize how this conflict is affecting the department. Discuss how to resolve it and how you will check to make sure the problem is solved. S _____

    b. Let the group resolve the conflict. S _____

    c. Have Sue and Tom sit down and discuss their conflict and how to resolve it. Support their efforts to implement a solution. S _____

    d. Tell Sue and Tom how to resolve their conflict and closely supervise them. S _____

C _____ 8. Jim usually does his share of the work with some encouragement and direction. However, he has migraine headaches occasionally and doesn't pull his weight when they occur. The others resent doing Jim's work. You decide to:

    a. Discuss his problem and help him come up with ideas for maintaining his work; be supportive. S _____

    b. Tell Jim to do his share of the work and closely watch his output. S _____

    c. Inform Jim that he is creating a hardship for the others and should resolve the problem by himself. S _____

    d. Be supportive, but set minimum performance levels and ensure compliance. S _____

C _____ 9. Bob, your most experienced and productive worker, came to you with a detailed idea that could increase your department's productivity at a very low cost. He can do his present job plus this new assignment. You think it's an excellent idea and you:

    a. Set some goals together. Encourage and support his efforts. S _____

    b. Set up goals for Bob. Be sure he agrees with them and sees you as being supportive of his efforts. S _____

    c. Tell Bob to keep you informed and to come to you if he needs any help. S _____

    d. Have Bob check in with you frequently so that you can direct and supervise his activities. S _____

C _____ 10. Your boss asked you for a special report. Fran, a very capable worker who usually needs no direction or support, has all the necessary skills to do the job. However, Fran is reluctant because she has never done a report. You:

    a. Tell Fran she has to do it. Give her direction and supervise her closely. S _____

    b. Describe the project to Fran and let her do it her own way. S _____

    c. Describe the benefits to Fran. Get her ideas on how to do it and check her progress. S _____

    d. Discuss possible ways of doing the job. Be supportive; encourage Fran. S _____

C _____ 11. Jean is the top producer in your department. However, her monthly reports are constantly late and contain errors. You are puzzled because she does everything else with no direction or support. You decide to:

    a. Go over past reports, explaining exactly what is expected of her. Schedule a meeting so that you can review the next report with her. S _____

    b. Discuss the problem with Jean and ask her what can be done about it; be supportive. S _____

    c. Explain the importance of the report. Ask her what the problem is. Tell her that you expect the next report to be on time and free of errors. S _____

    d. Remind Jean to get the next report in on time and without errors. S _____

C _____ 12. Your workers are very effective and like to participate in decision making. A consultant was hired to develop a new method for your department using the latest technology in the field. You:

    a. Explain the consultant's method and let the group decide how to implement it. S _____

    b. Teach them the new method and closely supervise them. S _____

    c. Explain the new method and why it is important. Teach them the method and make sure the procedure is followed. Answer questions. S _____

    d. Explain the new method and get the group's input on ways to improve and implement it. S _____

(continued)

/// Self-Assessment Exercise 6-2 /// (continued)

To determine your supervisory style:

1. In the table below, circle the letter you selected for each situation. The column headings represent the supervisory style you selected.

Situation	S-A	S-C	S-P	S-L	
1.	c	b	d	a	S-A Autocratic
2.	b	a	d	c	S-C Consultative
3.	d	b	c	a	S-P Participative
4.	c	a	d	b	S-L Laissez-faire
5.	a	d	b	c	
6.	d	c	b	a	
7.	d	a	c	b	
8.	b	d	a	c	
9.	d	b	a	c	
10.	a	c	d	b	
11.	a	c	b	d	
12.	b	c	d	a	
Total					

2. Add the number of circled items per column. The highest number is your preferred supervisory style. Is this the style you tend to use most often?

The more evenly distributed the numbers are, the more flexible your style is. A score of 1 or 0 in any column may indicate a reluctance to use the style.

Note that there is no "right" leadership style. This part of the exercise is designed to enable you to better understand the style you tend to use or prefer to use.

Defining the Situation

Having determined a preferred supervisory style, it is time to learn about the four supervisory styles and when to use each. As mentioned, no one best supervisory style exists for all situations. Instead, the effective supervisor adapts his or her style to meet the capabilities of the individual or group. Based on Ohio State two-dimensional leadership styles, supervisor-employee interactions fall into two distinct categories: directive and supportive. When we use the term *supervisor,* we are referring to *you,* and employees can be others if you are not in an official supervisory role.

- *Directive behavior.* You focus on directing and controlling behavior to ensure that the task gets done. Tell employees what the task is and when, where, and how to do it, and oversees performance.

- *Supportive behavior.* You focus on encouraging and motivating behavior. Explains things and listens to employee views, helping employees make their own decisions.

In other words, when a supervisor interacts with employees, the focus can be on directing (getting the task done), supporting (developing relationships), or both.

These definitions lead us to the question, What style should I use and why? The answer is, It depends on the situation. And the situation is determined by the capability of the employee(s). There are two distinct aspects of capability:

- *Ability.* Do the employees have the experience, education, skills, and so on to do the task without direction?

- *Motivation.* Do the employees want to do the task? Will they perform the task without encouragement and support?

Employee capability can be located on a continuum from low to outstanding, which you will determine by selecting the one capability level that best describes the employee's ability and motivation for the specific task. These levels are as follows:

- *Low (C-1).* The employees can't do the task without detailed directions and close supervision. Employees in this category may have the ability to do the task, but they lack the motivation to perform without close supervision.

- *Moderate (C-2).* The employees have moderate ability and need specific direction and support to get the job done properly. The employees may be highly motivated but still need direction, support, and encouragement.

- *High (C-3).* The employees are high in ability but may lack the confidence to do the job. What they need most is support and encouragement to motivate them to get the task done.

- *Outstanding (C-4).* The employees are capable of doing the task without direction or support.

It is important to realize that capability may vary depending on the specific task. For example, a bank teller may be a C-4 for routine transactions, but a C-1 for opening new or special accounts. Employees tend to start working with a C-1 capability, needing close direction. As their ability to do the job increases, supervisors can begin to be supportive and stop supervising closely. A supervisor must gradually develop employees from C-1 to C-3 or C-4 levels over time.

Using the Appropriate Supervisory Style

Learning Outcome 6-5

Explain four situational supervisory styles.

Each of the supervisory styles, discussed in greater detail below, also involves varying degrees of supportive and directive behavior. In some situations, you need to be in control of people being autocratic,[60] whereas in other situations you need to empower others[61] using a laissez-faire leadership style.

The four supervisory styles—autocratic, consultative, participative, and laissez-faire—are summarized in Model 6.1 in relation to the different levels of employee capability.

The **autocratic style (S-A)** *involves high-directive–low-supportive behavior (HD–LS) and is appropriate when interacting with low-capability employees (C-1).* You give very detailed instructions, describing exactly what the task is and when, where, and how to perform it. Closely oversees performance. The supportive style is largely absent. You make decisions without input from the employees.

The **consultative style (S-C)** *involves high-directive–high-supportive behavior (HD–HS) and is appropriate when interacting with moderate-capability employees (C-2).* You give specific instructions, overseeing performance. At the same time, you would support the employees by explaining why the task should be performed as requested and answering their questions. Work on relationships. When making decisions, you may consult employees, but you have the final say.

The **participative style (S-P)** *is characterized by low-directive–high-supportive behavior (LD–HS) and is appropriate when interacting with employees with high capability (C-3).* You give

MODEL 6.1 | Situational Supervision Model

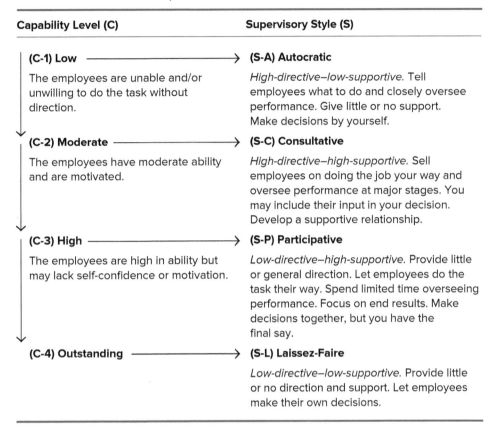

Capability Level (C)	Supervisory Style (S)
(C-1) Low →	**(S-A) Autocratic**
The employees are unable and/or unwilling to do the task without direction.	*High-directive–low-supportive.* Tell employees what to do and closely oversee performance. Give little or no support. Make decisions by yourself.
(C-2) Moderate →	**(S-C) Consultative**
The employees have moderate ability and are motivated.	*High-directive–high-supportive.* Sell employees on doing the job your way and oversee performance at major stages. You may include their input in your decision. Develop a supportive relationship.
(C-3) High →	**(S-P) Participative**
The employees are high in ability but may lack self-confidence or motivation.	*Low-directive–high-supportive.* Provide little or general direction. Let employees do the task their way. Spend limited time overseeing performance. Focus on end results. Make decisions together, but you have the final say.
(C-4) Outstanding →	**(S-L) Laissez-Faire**
	Low-directive–low-supportive. Provide little or no direction and support. Let employees make their own decisions.

general directions and spend limited time overseeing performance, letting employees do the task their way and focusing on the end result. You support the employees by encouraging them and building up their self-confidence. If a task needs to be done, you should not tell them how to do it, but ask them how they will accomplish it. You should make decisions together with employees or allow employees to make the decision subject to your limitations and approval.

The **laissez-faire style (S-L)** *entails low-directive–low-supportive behavior (LD-LS) and is appropriate when interacting with outstanding employees (C-4).* You merely inform employees about what needs to be done. You answer their questions but provide little, if any, direction. These employees are highly motivated and need little, if any, support. You allow these employees to make their own decisions subject to limitations, although approval will not be necessary.

Applying the Situational Supervision Model

The situation below comes from Self-Assessment Exercise 6-2. Now the information in Model 6.1 will be applied to this situation.

To begin, identify the employee capability level described. The levels are listed in the left-hand column of the exhibit. Indicate the capability level (1 through 4) on the line marked "C" to the left of the situation. Next, determine the style that each response (*a, b, c,* or *d*) represents. Indicate that style (A, C, P, or L) on the line marked "S" at the end of each response. Finally, identify the most appropriate response by placing a check mark (✓) next to it.

C _____ 1. Your rookie crew members seem to be developing well. Their need for direction and close supervision is diminishing. You would:

    a. Stop directing and overseeing performance, unless there is a problem.
    S _____

    b. Spend time getting to know them personally, but make sure they maintain performance levels. S _____

    c. Make sure things keep going well; continue to direct and oversee closely.
    S _____

    d. Begin to discuss new tasks of interest to them. S _____

Let's see how well you did.

1. The capability was C-1, but they have now developed to the C-2 level. If you put the number 2 on the C line, you were correct.

2. Alternative *a* is S-<u>L</u>, the laissez-faire style. There is no direction or support. Alternative *b* is S-<u>C</u>, the consultative style. There is both direction and support. Alternative *c* is S-<u>A</u>, the autocratic style. There is direction but no support. Alternative *d* is S-<u>P</u>, the participative style. There is low direction and high support (in discussing employee interests).

3. If you placed a check mark next to *b* as the appropriate response, you were correct. However, in the business world, there is seldom only one way to handle a problem successfully. Therefore, in this exercise, you receive points based on how successful your behavior would be in each situation. In this situation, *b* is the most successful alternative because it involves developing the employees gradually; it's a three-point answer. Alternative *c* is the next best alternative, followed by *d*. It is better to keep things the way they are now than try to rush employee development, which would probably cause problems. So *c* is a two-point answer, and *d* is a one-point answer. Alternative *a* is the least effective because you are going from one extreme of supervision to the other. This is a zero-point answer because the odds are great that this style will cause problems that will affect supervisory success.

    The better you match your supervisory style to employees' capabilities, the greater the chances of being successful. Don't forget that you don't have to be a supervisor to use the model when you influence others as a leader.

    In completing Skill-Building Exercise 6-1, Situational Supervision, you will apply the model to the remaining situations and be given feedback on your success at applying the model as you develop your situational supervision skills. Remember that what you think about is how you feel, and what you feel is how you behave. Now that you know how to be a situational supervisor, think and act like a leader and others will follow you whether or not you are a manager.

PUTTING THE LEADERSHIP THEORIES TOGETHER

This chapter has presented nine different leadership theories. Exhibit 6.6 puts the nine leadership theories together, converting them into four leadership style categories. A review of this exhibit should lead to a better understanding of the similarities and differences between these leadership theories.

DIVERSITY AND GLOBAL LEADERSHIP

Although leadership is important globally,[62] most leadership theories were developed in the United States, so they do have an American bias. Theories assume employee responsibility, rather than employee rights; self-gratification, rather than employee commitment to duty or altruistic motivation; democratic values, rather than autocratic values; rationality, rather than spirituality, religion, or superstition. Thus, the theories may not be as effective in cultures based on different assumptions.[63] We need to abandon the one-size-fits-all assumption.[64] However, charisma tends to be idealized across cultures.[65]

Skill-Building Exercise 6-1 develops this skill.

WORK APPLICATION 6-7

What are your views on situational supervision? Recall a manager you have now or have had. Which of the four styles does or did the manager use? Would you use the model on the job?

WORK APPLICATION 6-8

Which of the four supervisory styles would you like your boss to use with you? Why would you prefer this particular style?

WORK APPLICATION 6-9

Which leadership theory or model do you prefer? Why?

WORK APPLICATION 6-10

Describe the type of leader you want to be.

Communication Skills
Refer to CS Question 5.

EXHIBIT 6.6 | Leadership Styles

Leadership Trait Theory[1]

Behavioral Leadership Theories

	Leadership Style Categories			
	Autocratic	**Democratic**		**Laissez-Faire**
Two-dimensional leadership styles, Ohio State and Michigan U	High structure/job-centered Low consideration/employee-centered	High structure/job-centered High consideration/employee-centered	High consideration/employee-centered Low structure/job-centered	Low consideration/employee-centered Low structure/job-centered
Leadership Grid	High concern for production; low concern for people (9,1 sweatshop manager)	High concern for both production and people (9,9 team manager)	High concern for people; low concern for production (1,9 country club manager)	Low to moderate concern for both people and production (1,1 impoverished and 5,5 organized managers)
Transformational, Sevant, Stewardship, Authentic, LMX leadership theory	Charismatic, Transactional	No actual behavior style		

Contingency Leadership Theories

Contingency Leadership Theory	Task Orientation		Relationship Orientation	
Leadership continuum	1. Make decision and announce it	2. Sell decision 3. Present ideas and invite questions	4. Present tentative decision subject to change 5. Present problem, get suggestions, and make decision	6. Define limits and ask group to make decision 7. Permit subordinates to function within limits defined by leader
Normative leadership theory	Make decision alone using available information (Decide)	Meet individually or as a group with subordinates, explain the situation, get information and ideas on how to solve the problem, make final decision alone (Consult individual and group)	Have group meeting for employee participation with leader in decision making (Facilitate)	Meet with subordinates as a group, explain the situation, and allow the group to make decision (Delegate)
Situational leadership	High task, low relationship (Telling)	High task, high relationship (Selling)	High relationship, low task (Participating)	Low relationship, low task (Delegating)
Situational supervision	High directive, low support (Autocratic)	High directive, high support (Consultative)	High support, low directive (Participative)	Low support, low directive (Laissez-faire)

[1]Based on traits of leader; no actual style

Within Europe there are diverse management models, which raise a range of management education issues. European managers deal more with cultural than technical issues in the context of diverse value systems and religious backgrounds. Management is organized more as a language than as a set of techniques. Thus, leaders in different MNCs need autonomy to lead differently.[66]

American, European, and Japanese executives realize that they must manage and lead their business units in other countries differently than they do at home. Toyota and Honda run their plants in the United States somewhat differently from those in Japan. Similarly,

IBM's management style in Japan differs from its style in the United States. Thus, an understanding of multicultural leadership is important.[67]

Here are a few examples of differences in leadership styles based on national culture. Korean leaders are expected to be paternalistic toward employees. Arab leaders are viewed as weak if they show kindness or generosity without being asked to do so. Japanese leaders are expected to be humble and speak infrequently. Scandinavian and Dutch leaders embarrass, rather than motivate, employees with public, individual praise. Autocratic leadership styles tend to be appropriate in high-context cultures, such as those in Arab, Far Eastern, and Latin American countries, whereas participative leadership styles tend to be appropriate in low-context cultures, such as those in the United States, Norway, Finland, Denmark, and Sweden. Thus, different cultures make cross-business-unit collaboration in MNCs difficult.[68]

Leadership is also different in e-organizations, which are often global companies. According to executives who have worked in e-org and traditional organizations, e-org leaders focus more on speed in decision making, flexibility, and a vision of the future. Online leadership, managing people from all over the world in virtual and boundaryless organizations, calls for much less face-to-face communication and more written communication to get the job done. You may lead or be part of a virtual team, working interdependently with shared purpose across space, time, and organization boundaries, using technology to communicate and collaborate.[69]

Although cultural differences will continue to affect leadership, the instant communication, individualism, and material acquisition of global products in our society today threaten traditional family, religious, and social structures, as the trend toward the development of a more global blended culture continues. But don't look for a one-size-fits-all solution or leadership style.[70]

Communication Skills
Refer to CS Question 6.

TRUST

Effective leadership is based on trust.[71] As leaders, we must be trusted by others to influence them.[72] Managers who are not trusted by employees don't have their respect.[73] Employees who trust their supervisors have better job performance,[74] whereas abusive supervisors aren't trusted and negatively affect performance.[75] Unfortunately, the public's trust in business leaders in most countries is low because of unethical behavior.[76] As you probably already realize, being trustworthy is important in your personal and professional life. So before reading about trust, complete Self-Assessment Exercise 6-3, Your Trustworthiness.

/ / / **Self-Assessment Exercise 6-3** / / /

Your Trustworthiness

For each statement, select the frequency with which you use, or would use, the behavior at work. Be honest; that's part of trustworthiness.

Almost always				Almost never
1	2	3	4	5

_____ 1. I tell the truth; I tell it like it is.

_____ 2. When I make a commitment to do something, I do it.

_____ 3. I strive to be fair by creating a win–win situation for all parties.

_____ 4. I do the task to the best of my ability.

_____ 5. I volunteer to help others when I can, and I seek help when I need it.

_____ 6. I am humble; I don't brag about my accomplishments.

(continued)

_____   7. When I make a mistake, I admit it rather than try to cover it up or downplay it.

_____   8. I don't overcommit to the point of breaking commitments.

_____   9. I practice what I preach; I don't say one thing and do another.

_____   10. I treat coworkers—both friends and others—fairly.

_____   11. I stand by, protect, and save face for coworkers.

_____   12. When someone tells me something in confidence, I don't tell anyone else.

_____   13. I say only positive things, or nothing, about coworkers; I don't gossip.

_____   14. I am viewed by coworkers as being collaborative rather than competitive.

_____   15. I let coworkers know the real me—what I stand for and what I value. I share my feelings.

_____   16. When coworkers tell me something private about themselves, I offer acceptance and support and share something about myself.

_____   17. I deal effectively with diverse opinions, people, and types of conflict.

Place the numbers (1 to 5) you recorded for the situations on the lines below. Total each by column; then add the totals of the five columns and place the grand total on the continuum (17–85) below the totals.

Integrity	Competence	Consistency	Loyalty	Openness
____ 1.	____ 4.	____ 8.	____ 11.	____ 15.
____ 2.	____ 5.	____ 9.	____ 12.	____ 16.
____ 3.	____ 6.	____ 10.	____ 13.	____ 17.
	____ 7.		____ 14.	
____	____	____	____	____ Totals

Trustworthy 17 --- 20 --- 30 --- 40 --- 50 --- 60 --- 70 --- 80 --- 85 Untrustworthy

The lower your score, the more trustworthy you are. Note your strongest (lowest-score column) and weakest (highest-score column) dimensions of developing trust. You will learn how to develop trust in all five dimensions in the following section.

Are you trustworthy? In this section, we discuss types of trust and how to develop trust.

Types of Trust

Trust is *the positive expectation that another will not take advantage of you.* See Exhibit 6.7 for a list of trust levels and dimensions.

- **Deterrence-based trust.** Most new human relations begin with deterrence-based trust because we lack experience dealing with the other person. It is the most fragile since one violation or inconsistency can destroy the human relations. The relationship is based on fear of reprisal if the trust is violated. So we try to avoid being untrustworthy; we are on our best behavior when we first meet people.

- **Knowledge-based trust.** Knowledge-based trust is the most common organizational trust. Trust is based on experience dealing with the other person. The better you know people, the better you can predict their behavior—and trust them.

- **Identification-based trust.** Identification-based trust occurs when there is an emotional connection—friend rather than just coworker. It is the highest level of trust. People look out for each other's best interests and act for the other.

WORK APPLICATION 6-11

Give an example of each of the three levels of trust you have experienced on the job.

EXHIBIT 6.7 | Three Levels and Five Dimensions of Trust

Learning Outcome 6-6

Briefly describe the five dimensions of trust.

Developing Trust

Now let's discuss how to develop trust[77] so that you can achieve the identification-based level of trust. As shown in Exhibit 6.7, there are five dimensions of trust. Note that integrity is in the center, holding the other four dimensions together, because without integrity, trust breaks apart.

The five columns in Self-Assessment Exercise 6-3, Your Trustworthiness, are the five dimensions of trust. Although they are all important, you may want to pay particular attention to your weaker areas.

Integrity   People who have *integrity* are honest and sincere, and people want to work in a culture of integrity.[78]

Tips to develop your integrity include:

- *Be honest.* Trust is based on honesty. Don't lie, steal, or cheat; be sincere and tell it like it is and people will trust you.
- *Be fair.* According to **Gene Lee (CEO of Darden Restaurants)**, integrity and fairness are the important core values to business. Perceived unfairness causes distrust and a desire for revenge, restitution, and retaliation.[79]

Communication Skills
Refer to CS Questions 7 and 8.

Competence   People need to believe that you have the skills and abilities to carry out your commitments.

Tips to develop your competence include:

- *Be conscientious.* Do the job to the best of your ability.
- *Admit your mistakes and apologize.* Others will think, "I can trust you."

Consistency   *Consistent* people use the same behavior in similar situations; they are predictable.

Tips to develop your consistency include:

- *Keep your commitments.* To trust you, people must believe that you are dependable. If you say you will do something, follow through.
- *Practice what you preach.* Actions speak louder than words.

Loyalty   People who are *loyal* look out for others' interests (they don't take advantage of others). Betrayal triggers intense emotional reactions, as you may have experienced.[80] It hurts, so don't do it.

Tips to develop your loyalty include:

- *Maintain confidences.* When someone tells you something in confidence—a secret—that person is being vulnerable in trusting you, so don't tell others. One time could be your last.
- *Don't gossip negatively about individuals.* If people hear you gossip about others, they may assume you do the same behind their backs. Your gossip can cause someone to

EXHIBIT 6.8 | The Johari Window

	Known to Self	Unknown to Self
Known to Others	Open	Blind
Unknown to Others	Hidden	Unknown

Source: J. Luft, *Of Human Interaction* Copyright © 1969, by Mayfield Publishing Company, imprint of McGraw-Hill Education. ISBN 9780874841985

lose the trust of others,[81] so don't do it. Follow this rule: If you don't have anything nice to say, don't say anything.

Openness   People who are *open* accept new ideas and change. They give the full truth. Tips to develop your openness include:

- *Self-disclosure and the Johari Window.* Self-disclosure enhances human relations and is what takes the level of trust to the identification level. As shown in Exhibit 6.8, the Johari Window has four regions representing the intersection of two axes: (1) the degree to which information about you (values, attitudes, beliefs) is known to or understood by you, and (2) the degree to which information about you is known by others.

  Based on our understanding of self, we select those aspects of self that are appropriate to share with others; we *open* the *hidden* self areas of the window. As we self-disclose, we also find out things about ourselves that others know, such as irritating things we do; we open the *blind* area. The *unknown* area cannot be open until we experience a new situation, such as getting laid off, because we don't know how we will behave until it happens. Thus, to develop trust and improve human relations, we gradually share self-disclosure to *open* the *hidden* and *blind* areas of the Johari Window.

- *Risk self-disclosure.* Developing trust through self-disclosure does include the risk of vulnerability—being hurt, disappointed, and taken advantage of.[82] Although people often fear the risk of self-disclosure, the rewards of improved human relations and personal friendship are worth the risk. If you follow the guidelines above, you can minimize your risk.

Skill-Building Exercise 6-3 develops this skill.

WORK APPLICATION 6-12

What are your strongest and weakest dimensions of trust at work? How will you improve your trustworthiness? What tips will you implement?

WORK APPLICATION 6-13

How often do you apologize? Should you apologize more often, and especially to the people closest to you, when you break their trust?

Repairing Trust

Trust is earned and builds over time. Years of trust can be hurt or destroyed with one bad act of distrust. For example, if you get caught in a lie, miss a deadline or do a poor job, or are disloyal, you may hurt your relationship. Your relationship may never be the same again, or it could end. Be sure to always be trustworthy to avoid having to repair trust.

After trust is broken, we obviously need to follow all of the tips to building trust. However, to truly repair trust, the starting point is to admit mistakes and give a sincere apology. People apologize more often to strangers than to their romantic partners and family members. When we do something that breaks trust, the other person is likely to be emotional, so we do need to stay calm and calm the other person, and apologizing helps. Even if you don't believe you did anything wrong, you can apologize for breaking trust with the other person. For example, you can say in a sincere voice, "I'm sorry I upset you with my (state the specific behavior, i.e., comment), I will try not to do it again." It takes only a minute to give a sincere apology, and apologizing can help develop, maintain, and repair trust that is critical to effective human relations. But to be trusted, you need to change the behavior that resulted in mistrust.

Complete Self-Assessment Exercise 6-4 to determine how your personality affects your leadership style and ability to develop trust.

Your Personality and Leadership and Trust

Recall that your personality is based on traits. So your personality does affect your leadership behavior and your use of contingency leadership styles. What was your preferred situational leadership style? Are you flexible? Can you change styles to meet the situation?

If you have a high *surgency* personality, you most likely have a higher task-oriented leadership style than people-oriented, so you may want to work on the people side. Watch your use of autocratic leadership behavior. Use participation (participative and laissez-faire styles) when appropriate. You may be competent and consistent, but because getting the job done is more important to you than developing human relations, you may need to work on integrity, loyalty, and openness to develop greater *trust.*

If you have a high *agreeableness* personality, you most likely have a high people-oriented leadership style, but you need to make sure the job gets done. You may be reluctant to use the autocratic leadership style when it is appropriate. You are most likely high on openness and are loyal on *trust* dimensions and you may have integrity, but you may need to work on competence and consistency, because getting the job done is less important to you than developing human relations.

How well you deal with your emotions is what *adjustment* is about. If you are not high on adjustment personality traits, you may tend to be reluctant to be a leader. Low adjustment personalities are usually not open to disclosure, so you may have trouble being *trusted* for competence, consistency, and integrity.

If you are a high *conscientious* personality, you may push others to be conscientious too. Are you more task- or people-oriented? That orientation will affect your leadership style more than your conscientiousness. Conscientiousness tends to lead to competence and consistency *trust* dimensions. However, you may need to work on integrity, loyalty, and openness, based on your task or people orientation.

If you have a high *openness to experience,* you may use participative leadership styles to bring about change. You will use openness to develop *trust,* but you may need to work on other dimensions of trust.

Action plan: Based on your personality, what specific things will you do to improve your leadership style and develop trust?

_____

_____

_____

_____

_____

As we bring this chapter to a close, you should realize that you can be a leader even if you are not a manager. You should know that leadership traits are important but that there is no universal list of traits that determine leadership success. You should understand the two-dimensional leadership styles of task and relationship behavior, and that they have different terms based on the behavioral theory; and you should be able to define contemporary behavioral theories. You should also be able to describe four contingency leadership theories. Importantly, you should be able to select the most appropriate leadership style for the situation using the situational supervision model. In addition, there is diversity in global leadership. Leadership is based on trust, so you should understand the types of trust and be able to develop and repair trust. Remember that what you think is how you feel, and how you feel is how you behave. Think, feel, and act like a leader whom people can trust.

/ / / R E V I E W / / /

The chapter review is organized to help you master the 7 learning outcomes for Chapter 6. First provide your own response to each learning outcome, and then check the summary provided to see how well you understand the material. Next, identify the final statement in each section as either true or false (T/F). Correct each false statement. Answers are given at the end of the chapter.

LO 6-1 Explain what leadership is and how it affects behavior, human relations, and performance.

Leadership is the process of influencing employees to work toward the achievement of objectives. A leader using one style will behave differently than another leader using a different style. The leader's style also affects the type of human relations between the leader and followers. Leaders can affect followers' performance, but not always.

The terms *leadership* and *management* mean the same thing. T F

LO 6-2   Describe leadership trait theory.

Leadership trait theory assumes that distinct physical and psychological characteristics account for effective leadership. According to Ghiselli, the major leadership trait needed for success is supervisory ability. However, there is no universally accepted set of effective leadership traits.

Leadership trait theory is outdated and no longer studied. T F

LO 6-3   List and describe three behavioral leadership theories.

Behavioral leadership theories assume that there are distinctive styles that effective leaders use consistently. The three theories are: (1) two-dimensional leadership styles—initiating structure and consideration styles (Ohio State) and job-centered and employee-centered styles (University of Michigan); (2) the Leadership Grid—Blake and Mouton's model identifying the ideal leadership style as having a high concern for both production and people; and (3) transformational leadership—leaders bring about change, innovation, and entrepreneurship.

Charismatic leadership is a behavioral leadership theory. T F

LO 6-4   List and describe four contingency leadership theories.

Contingency leadership theories assume that the appropriate leadership style varies from situation to situation. The four theories are: (1) contingency leadership theory—Fiedler's model used to determine whether leadership style is task- or relationship-oriented, and whether the situation matches the style; (2) leadership continuum—Tannenbaum and Schmidt's identified boss-centered and employee-centered leadership at the extremes; (3) normative leadership theory—Vroom and Yetton's decision-tree model that enables the user to select from five leadership styles the one that is appropriate for the situation; and (4) situational leadership—Hersey and Blanchard's model for selecting from four leadership styles the one that fits the employees' maturity level in a given situation.

Contingency leadership theory is the only one that recommends changing the situation, rather than your leadership style. T F

LO 6-5   Explain four situational supervisory styles.

The four situational supervisory styles are: (1) autocratic–high-directive-low-support; (2) consultative–high-directive–high-support; (3) participative–low-directive-high-support; and (4) laissez-faire–low-directive-low-support.

When the employee's capability level is high (C-3), the consultative leadership style is appropriate. T F

LO 6-6   Briefly describe the five dimensions of trust.

The five dimensions of trust are: (1) integrity—being honest, truthful, and sincere; (2) competence—having technical and interpersonal knowledge, ability, and skill; (3) consistency—using the same behavior in similar situations; (4) loyalty—looking out for the interests of others; and (5) openness—accepting new ideas and change.

The Johari Window is a measure of openness. T F

LO 6-7   Define the following 14 key terms.

Select one or more methods: (1) Fill in the missing key terms for each definition given below from memory; (2) match the key terms from the end of the review with their definitions below; and/or (3) copy the key terms in order from the key terms at the beginning of the chapter.

_____ is the process of influencing employees to work toward the achievement of objectives.

_____ assumes that there are distinctive physical and psychological characteristics accounting for leadership effectiveness.

_____ assume that there are distinctive styles that effective leaders use consistently.

The _____ is Blake and Mouton's model identifying the ideal leadership style as having a high concern for both production and people.

_____ assume that the appropriate leadership style varies from situation to situation.

_____ is Fiedler's model, which is used to determine if a person's leadership style is task- or relationship-oriented, and if the situation matches the leader's style.

The _____ is Tannenbaum and Schmidt's model, which identifies seven leadership styles based on the use of boss-centered versus employee-centered leadership.

_____ is Vroom and Yetton's decision-tree model, which enables the user to select from five leadership styles the one that is appropriate for the situation.

_____ is Hersey and Blanchard's model for selecting from four leadership styles the one that matches the employees' maturity level in a given situation.

The four situational supervision styles are _____, which involves high-directive–low supportive behavior and is appropriate when interacting with low-capability employees; _____, which involves high-directive–high-supportive behavior and is appropriate when interacting with moderate-capability employees; _____, which is characterized by low-directive–high-supportive behavior and is appropriate when interacting with employees with high capability; and _____, which entails low-directive-low-supportive behavior and is appropriate when interacting with outstanding employees.

_____ is the positive expectation that another will not take advantage of you.

/ / / KEY TERMS / / /

autocratic style   196
behavioral leadership
   theories   184
consultative style   196
contingency leadership
   theories   187

contingency leadership
   theory   188
laissez-faire style   197
leadership   181
leadership
   continuum   188

Leadership Grid   184
leadership trait
   theory   182
normative leadership
   theory   191
participative style   196

situational
   leadership   191
trust   201

/ / / COMMUNICATION SKILLS / / /

The following critical thinking questions can be used for class discussion and/or as written assignments to develop communication skills. Be sure to give complete explanations for all questions.

1. There are many traits that are said to be important to leadership success. Which three traits do you believe are the most important? List in order of priority.

2. The two-dimensional leadership styles developed at Ohio State University and the University of Michigan back in the 1940s still serve as the bases for the current contingency leadership theories. Are the task and relationship dimensions outdated?

3. The Leadership Grid states that the one best style to use in all situations is the 9,9 team manager style, with a high concern for both people and production. Do you agree with this statement?

4. Fiedler's contingency leadership theory states that managers can't change their leadership style; they are either task- or relationship-oriented. Do you agree with this statement?

5. Which of the five contingency leadership theories (Exhibit 7.5) do you prefer?

6. Give some examples of global cultural diversity that you have experienced.

7. Do you agree that integrity is at the center of trust, holding the other four dimensions together? Can competence, consistency, loyalty, and/or openness lead to trusting relationships if there is no integrity?

8. Based on your life and work experience, what percentage of people would you say really have integrity (that is, are honest—don't lie, steal, or cheat—and sincere)? Give some examples of how certain people damaged your trust in them.

CASE   / / /   Tony Hsieh and Zappos.com

Tony Hsieh is a CEO who subscribes to a leadership style that is more people-centered than job-centered; more participative than autocratic; more transformational than transactional; and definitely more relationship than task-oriented. Tony Hsieh is a serial entrepreneur who has started and sold several successful business ventures. He was a millionaire at just 24 years old. His net worth is valued at close to $1 billion.

So what makes Tony Hsieh such a great leader? Tony Hsieh is a young, dynamic, creative, risk-taking CEO. After graduating from Harvard, Hsieh worked for Oracle Corporation. Less than a year into his employment at Oracle, Hsieh found himself very unhappy with the corporate environment and quit to co-found LinkExchange, an advertising network that allowed members to advertise their sites using banner ads. The site grew, and within 90 days had more than 20,000 participating web pages and had its banner ads displayed over 10 million times. By 1998, the site had more than 400,000 members and 5 million ads rotated daily. Despite such phenomenal growth, Tony felt something had changed. Tony enjoyed working at LinkExchange in the beginning because he would hire his friends or friends of friends, and everyone got along. However, the company ran into a problem when they started hiring people they did not know. Hsieh says that, while competent people with the right skill set were hired, they were not a good culture fit. By the time LinkExchange grew to around 100 employees, the culture was lost. Hsieh says that it was difficult to get out of bed in the morning to go work at his own company. Looking to get out, he sold the company to Microsoft in 1998 for $265 million.

Soon after selling LinkExchange, Nick Swinmurn approached Hsieh with the idea of selling shoes online. Nick's company, already in operations, was called Zappos. At the time, the idea was relatively new and unique. People were used to buying their shoes at a brick and mortar store where they had the opportunity to try the shoes before buying. Naturally, skeptics, including Tony himself, wondered if this new retail model had legs. After Tony joined Zappos and assumed the role of CEO, he brought a leadership style or approach that has helped the company achieve great success. Today, the company has revenues in excess of $1 billion annually, and in 2009, Amazon acquired Zappos for around $1 billion. Zappos' success has attracted the interest of scholars and business analysts trying to understand the Zappos phenomenon. According to Zach Bulygo, a blogger for KISSmetrics, "it's not what it sells that makes Zappos successful. It's how it sells (that is, what it does for its employees and customers) that makes Zappos what it is today."[i] Tony wants Zappos to be known and remembered as the best customer service and customer experience company. He believes he can only do this if he has a company culture that values its employees and empowers them to serve customers well. Tony likes to help employees grow both personally and professionally. He wants his company and employees to seek to change the world. But, he is also in business to still make money too.[ii]*Fortune* magazine listed Zappos as one of the Best Companies to Work For.[iii]

Tony had learned from LinkExchange that he wanted to build a different kind of company, one that had a better corporate culture. He brought this knowledge and experience to Zappos. At Zappos, Hsieh wanted to be a more creative and passionate leader. He believed having the right culture was the key to success. As he puts it, "Our number one priority is company culture. Our whole belief is that if you get the culture right, most of the other stuff like delivering great customer service or building a long-term enduring brand will just happen naturally on its own." He developed the following 10 Key Core Values and prominently displays them on the company web-site.[iv]

1. Deliver Wow Through Customer Service.
2. Embrace and Drive Change.
3. Create Fun and a Little Weirdness.
4. Be Adventurous, Creative, and Open Minded.
5. Pursue Growth and Learning.
6. Build Open and Honest Relationship with Communication.
7. Build a Positive Team & Family Spirit.
8. Do More with Less.
9. Be Passionate and Determined.
10. Be Humble.[v]

Mr. Hsieh wrote a popular book *Delivering Happiness* that focuses on company culture as the #1 priority. Tony learned (from reading management books) that two key strategies needed to be employed. The first strategy was a strong corporate culture and the second was a purpose beyond money. [vi]The core component of Hsieh's culture is the concept of happiness. He likes to ask employees how happy they are.

One of his most unique examples for creating and maintaining a happy culture at Zappos is their unique training program. New employees are offered $2,000 during their training program. New employees can take the money if they want to leave the company because they feel they are not well-suited to working within the Zappos culture. New employees are also offered this option for a short time after training to make sure they like the company and their job. Tony wants his employees to feel their own values match the values of his company. He wants them to be able to go home and say they believe in the culture of Zappos and are ready to be an active participant.[vii]

The acquisition by Amazon was not your typical transaction where the founder and team got rich, left the company, and went off to explore new opportunities. Today, nearly four years after the acquisition, Zappos still operates independently from Amazon. The takeover acquisition agreement allowed Tony Hsieh to stay on and continue leading the brand. A quick look at the Zappos website and you may might think it is a competitor of Amazon.

You can watch a video of Tony Hsieh and his ideas about Zappos at https://www.youtube.com/watch?v=JjzrbDfeV9M.

Go to the Internet: To learn more about Zappos.com, visit the company website at http://about.zappos.com, where you can read about customer service, which is not just a department in his organization but is actually the whole organization.

Support your answers to the following questions with specific information from the case and text or with information you get from the web or another source.

1. What traits does Tony Hsieh exhibit that would indicate he is an effective leader?

2. How would you rate Hsieh's leadership using the Leadership Grid?

3. What factors might lead you to believe that Hsieh is a transformational and charismatic leader?

4. Which leadership challenges might occur if Zappos goes international?

Cumulative Questions

5. How is personality (Chapter 2) best associated with which leadership theory?

6. What is the role of communication (Chapter 4) in leadership?

Case Exercise and Role-Play

Preparation: The instructor assigns a student to be Tony Hsieh and another to be a reporter from a television business news station such as CNBC. Assume that the two of you are meeting at a national shoe industry conference in Las Vegas. Prepare for the interview, at which you will be asking Tony about his leadership style. Write down a list of the specific leadership theories in the book, and ask Tony if he believes that theory would work at Zappos.

Role-Play: Matched pairs of Tony Hsieh and the reporter will role-play. The role-play may be done in small groups, or two people may role-play before the entire class.

After the interview, the group or class discusses and critiques the leadership theories from the textbook and how they are used by Tony at Zappos. Identify any leadership theories that Tony used that are not found in the textbook. Also, identify questions and leadership theories not discussed that would have been useful to learn about.

OBJECTIVE CASE   / / /   The Cleanup Job

Brenda is the head meat cutter in the Big K Supermarket. Brenda hires and has fired meat cutters; she also determines raises. Although it has never been said, she speculates that the all-male meat-cutting crew isn't friendly toward her because they resent having a female boss. They are all highly skilled.

Once a month the meat and frozen foods cases are supposed to be cleaned by a meat cutter; they are all equally capable of doing it. It is not any one person's job, and no one likes to do it. It's that time of the month again, and Brenda has to select someone to clean up. She just happens to see Rif first, so she approaches him.

BRENDA: Rif, I want you to clean the cases this month.

RIF: Why me? I just did it two months ago. Give someone else a turn.

BRENDA: I didn't ask you to tell me when you did it last. I asked you to do it.

RIF: I know, but I'm a meat cutter, not a janitor. Why can't the janitor do it? Or something more fair?

BRENDA: Do I have to take action against you for not following an order?

RIF: OK, I'll do it.

Answer the following questions. Then in the space between questions, state why you selected that answer.

_____ 1. The basic leadership style Brenda used with Rif was:

    a. autocratic   *b.* democratic   *c.* laissez-faire

_____ 2. With Rif, Brenda used the _____ quadrant leadership style in Exhibit 7.1.

    a. 1   *c.* 3

    b. 2   *d.* 4

_____ 3. With Rif, Brenda should have used the _____ quadrant leadership style in Exhibit 7.1.

    a. 1   *c.* 3

    b. 2   *d.* 4

_____ 4. The Leadership Grid style Brenda used with Rif was _____ (see Exhibit 7.2).

    a. 1,1   *c.* 1,9   *e.* 9,9

    b. 9,1   *d.* 5,5

_____ 5. According to Leadership Grid theory, Brenda used the appropriate leadership style.

    a. true   *b.* false

_____ 6. According to Fiedler's contingency theory model (see Exhibit 7.3), Brenda is in a _____ situation, and _____ -oriented behavior is appropriate.

    a. task   *b.* relationship

_____ 7. Brenda used the _____ leadership continuum style (see Exhibit 7.4).

    a. 1   *c.* 3   *e.* 5   *g.* 7

    b. 2   *d.* 4   *f.* 6

_____ 8. The appropriate normative leadership style to resolve the monthly cleanup job is:

    a. decide   *c.* consult group   *e.* delegate

    b. consult individually   *d.* facilitate

_____ 9. The situational supervision style Brenda used with Rif was _____ (see Model 7.1).

    a. autocratic   *c.* participative

    b. consultative   *d.* laissez-faire

_____ 10. The situational supervision style Brenda should use to resolve the monthly cleanup job is _____ (see Model 7.1).

    a. autocratic   *c.* participative

    b. consultative   *d.* laissez-faire

_____ 11. In Brenda's situation, how would you get the cases cleaned each month?

(*Note:* Different leadership styles can be role-played by Brenda in class.)

Situational Supervision

Experience: Individual may share answers in groups or entire class, in class or online.

AACSB Competencies: Reflective and analytic thinking and application of knowledge.

Objectives: To learn to use the situational supervision model. To develop your ability to supervise employees using the appropriate situational supervisory style for their capability level.

BMV 6-1

Preparation: In groups of two, you will apply the Situational Supervision Model in Model 6.1 to situations 2 through 12 in Self-Assessment Exercise 6-2. After you have finished, your instructor will give you the recommended answers, enabling you to determine your level of success at selecting the appropriate style.

For each situation, use the left-hand column in Model 6.1 to identify the employee capability level the situation describes. Write the level (1 through 4) on the line marked "C" to the left of each situation in Self-Assessment Exercise 6-2. Now identify the supervisory style that each response (*a* through *d*) represents. (These are listed in the right-hand column of the exhibit.) Indicate the style (A, C, P, or L) on the line marked "S" at the end of each response (*a* through *d*). Finally, indicate the management style you think is best for each situation by placing a check mark (✓) next to the appropriate response (*a, b, c,* or *d*).

Procedure 1 (3–8 minutes)

The instructor reviews the Situational Supervision Model, Model 6.1, and explains how to use the model for situation 1.

Procedure 2 (29–43 minutes)

1. Turn to situation 2 in Self-Assessment Exercise 6-2, page 192, and to Model 6.1, page 197, Situational Supervision Model. (You may tear the exhibit out of your book.) Apply the model to the situation to select what you believe is the best course of action (3–4 minutes). The instructor will go over the answers and scoring (3–4 minutes).

2. Divide into teams of two; you may have one group of three if there is an odd number in the class. Apply the model as a team to situations 3 through 6. Team members may select different answers if they don't agree (8–12 minutes). Do not do situations 7 through 12 until you are told to do so. Your instructor will go over the answers and scoring for situations 3 through 6 (2–4 minutes).

3. As a team, select your answers to situations 7 through 12 (11–15 minutes). Your instructor will go over the answers and scoring for situations 7 through 12 (2–4 minutes).

Caution: There is no proven relationship between how a person performs on a pencil-and-paper test and how he or she actually performs on the job. People have a tendency to choose the answer they think is correct, rather than what they would actually do. The objective of this exercise is to help you better understand your supervisory style and how to improve it.

Conclusion: The instructor leads a class discussion and/or makes concluding remarks.

Application (2–4 minutes):   What have I learned from this experience? How will I use this knowledge in the future?

Sharing: Volunteers give their answers to the application section.

A Leadership Style Role-Play

Experience: Group In-Class Exercise

AACSB Competencies: Analytic thinking and application of knowledge

Objectives: To experience leadership in action. To identify the leadership style, and how using the appropriate versus inappropriate leadership style affects the organization.

Preparation: All necessary material is below; no preparation is necessary.

Procedure 1 (5-10 minutes)

Break into groups and select the style (autocratic, consultative, participative, or laissez-faire) your group would use to make the following decision:

You are an office manager with four subordinates who all do typing on outdated computers. You will be receiving a new computer to replace one of the outdated ones. (Everyone knows about it because several salespeople have been in the office.) You must decide who gets the new computer. Below is some information about each subordinate.

- Pat—He or she has been with the organization for 20 years, is 50 years old, and presently has a two-year-old computer.
- Chris—He or she has been with the organization for 10 years, is 31 years old, and presently has a one-year-old computer.
- Fran—He or she has been with the organization for five years, is 40 years old, and presently has a three-year-old computer.
- Sandy—He or she has been with the organization for two years, is 23 years old, and presently has a five-year-old computer.

Possible Leadership Styles

Instructor selects one option:

Option A: Continuum of Leadership Behavior Styles 1 through 7. See Exhibit 6.4 for definitions of these seven styles.

Option B: Situational Supervisory Styles

S-A Autocratic	*a.* Make the decision alone; then tell each subordinate individually your decision and how and why you made it.
	b. Make the decision alone; then have a group meeting to announce the decision and how and why you made it. No discussion is allowed.
S-C Consultative	*a.* Before deciding, talk to the subordinates individually to find out if they want the word processor, and why they think they should get it. Then make the decision and announce it to the group or to each person individually.
	b. Before deciding, have a group meeting to listen to why all the subordinates want it, and why they think they should get it. Have no discussion among subordinates. Then make the decision and announce it to the group or to each person individually.
S-P Participative	*a.* Tentatively decide to whom you want to give it. Then hold a meeting to tell the group your plans, followed with a discussion that can lead to you changing your mind. After the open discussion, you make the decision and announce it, explaining the rationale for selection.
	b. Call a group meeting and explain the problem. Lead an open discussion about who should get the word processor. After the discussion, make your decision and explain the rationale for it.
S-L Laissez-faire	*a.* Call a meeting and explain the situation. Tell the group that they have X amount of time (5-7 minutes for the exercise) to make the decision. You do not become a group member; you may or may not stay for the decision. However, if you do stay, you cannot participate.

Procedure 2 (5-10 minutes)

1. Four volunteers from different groups go to the front of the class. Take out a sheet of 8½-by-11-inch paper and write the name of the person you are role-playing (in big, dark letters), fold it in half, and place it in view of the manager and class. While the managers are planning, turn to the end of this exercise and read your role and the roles of your colleagues. Try to put yourself in the person's position, and do and say what he or she actually would during the role-play. No one but the typist should read this additional subordinate role information.

2. The instructor will tell each group which leadership style their manager will role-play; it may or may not be the one selected.

3. The group selects a manager to do the actual role-play of making the decision; the group plans "who, what, when, where, how." The manager will perform the role-play. No one should read the additional subordinate role information.

Procedure 3 (1–10 minutes)

One manager goes to the front of the class and conducts the leadership role-play.

Procedure 4 (1–5 minutes)

The class members (other than the group being represented) vote for the style (1 to 7 or Tell *a. b.*; Sell *a. b.*; Participate *a. b.*; Delegate *a.*) they think the manager portrayed. Then the manager reveals the style. If several class members didn't vote for the style portrayed, a discussion can take place.

Procedures 3 and 4 continued (25–40 minutes)

Repeat procedures 3 and 4 until all managers have their turn or the time runs out.

Procedure 5 (2–3 minutes)

The class members individually determine the style they would use when making the decision. The class votes for the style the class would use in this situation. The instructor gives his or her recommendation and/or the author's.

Conclusion: The instructor leads a class discussion and/or makes concluding remarks.

Application (2–4 minutes):   What did I learn from this experience? How will I apply this knowledge in the future?

Sharing: Volunteers give their answers to the application section.

Subordinate Roles

Additional information (for subordinates' role-playing only):

Pat	You are happy with the way things are now. You do not want the new computer. Be firm and assertive in your stance.
Chris	You are bored with your present job. You really want the new computer. Being second in seniority, you plan to be aggressive in trying to get it. You are afraid that the others will complain because you got the last new computer. So you have a good idea: You will take the new one, and Sandy can have your old one.
Fran	You are interested in having the new computer. You spend more time each day typing than any of the other employees. Therefore, you believe you should get the new computer.
Sandy	You want the new computer. You believe you should get it because you are by far the fastest typist, and you have the oldest computer. You do not want a hand-me-down computer.

/ / / SKILL-BUILDING EXERCISE 6-3 / / /

Self-Disclosure and Trust (Johari Window)

Experience: Group In-Class Exercise

AACSB Competencies: Communication abilities, interpersonal relations, and application of knowledge.

Objectives: To develop trust by self-disclosing to open your Johari Window.

Preparation: You will self-disclose by asking and answering questions to develop trust.

Rules:

1. Take turns asking questions.
2. You may refuse to answer a question as long as you did not ask it (or plan to).
3. You don't have to ask the questions in order.
4. You can add your own questions to ask anytime during the exercise.

Procedure 1 (7–15 minutes)

Break into groups of two or three. Take a minute to read the questions. Check questions you want to ask, and add your own questions. Follow the rules above.

1. What is your name and major?

2. Why did you select your major?

3. What career plans do you have?

4. How do you feel about doing this exercise?

5. What do you do in your spare time?

6. What is your Big Five Personality profile, or what do you think my profile is?

7. In Self-Assessment Exercise 6-3 what was your trustworthiness score and what were your strongest and weakest dimensions, or what do you think my score was, and which are my strongest and weakest dimensions?

8. What was your first impression of me?

9. How do you and/or others view me?

10. _____

11. _____

12. _____

Procedure 2 (5–15 minutes)

Review the tips for developing trust. How well did I follow the tips, or did I not follow any of the tips?

   Answer the following questions in the same group. Then you may ask the questions from the list above and/or your own questions to further self-disclose.

1. Have I/you taken any risk during this self-disclosure?

2. What level of trust have we developed (deterrence-, knowledge-, identification-based)?

3. Did I/you not follow any of the tips for developing trust?

4. With regard to the Johari Window, have I/you simply focused on opening the unknown to others (hidden), or have I/you opened the unknown to self (blind)?

5. Have I/you learned anything unknown to self?

Conclusion: The instructor may lead a class discussion and/or make concluding remarks.

Application (2–4 minutes):   What did I learn from this experience? How will I apply this knowledge in the future?

Sharing: Volunteers give their answers to the application section.

///   SKILL-BUILDING EXERCISE 6-4   ///

Developing New Habits

Experience: Individual may share habits in groups or entire class, in class or online.

AACSB Competencies: Analytic and application of knowledge.

Objectives: To develop and share new habits.

Preparation: Select one or more topics from this chapter that will help you improve your human relations. Develop a new habit following the guideline from Chapter 1, section Habits and Skill-Building Exercise 1-4, on how to develop your cure, routine, and reward-change.

Procedure (5–30 minutes)

Follow the procedures from Skill Builder 1-4.

1. F. Leadership and management are not the same thing.
2. F. As stated in the text, although there is no universal list of leadership traits, leadership trait theory is still being studied today.
3. T.
4. T.
5. F. In Model 6.1, with C-3 employees the participative leadership style is appropriate.
6. T.

1. GE, "Identifying the Leadership Skills That Matter Most," *INC.* (December 2014 / January 2015): 78.
2. J.P. Doh and N.R. Quigley, "Responsible Leadership and Stakeholder Management: Influence Pathways and Organizational Outcomes," *Academy of Management Perspectives* 28(3) (2014): 255–274.
3. B.R. Spisak, M.J. O'Brien, N. Nicholson, M. Van Vugt, "Niche Construction and the Evolution of Leadership," *Academy of Management Review* 40(2) (2015): 291–306.
4. GE, "Identifying the Leadership Skills That Matter Most," *INC.* (December 2014 / January 2015): 78.
5. R. McCammon, "Do Me A Solid?" *Entrepreneur* (March 2016): 15-16.
6. E. Bernstein, "If You Want to Persuade People, Try Altercasting," *The Wall Street Journal* (September 5, 2016): D1, D2.
7. J.P. Doh and N.R. Quigley, "Responsible Leadership and Stakeholder Management: Influence Pathways and Organizational Outcomes," *Academy of Management Perspectives* 28(3) (2014): 255–274.
8. B.R. Spisak, M.J. O'Brien, N. Nicholson, M. Van Vugt, "Niche Construction and the Evolution of Leadership," *Academy of Management Review* 40(2) (2015): 291–306.
9. C.K. Lam, X. Huang, and S.C.H. Chan, "The Treshold Effect of Participative Leadership and the Role of Leader Information Sharing," *Academy of Management Journal* 58(3) (2015): 836–855.
10. C.L. Pearce, C.L. Wassenaar, and C.C. Manz, "Is Shared Leadership the Key to Responsible Leadership?" *Academy of Management Perspectives* 28(3) (2014): 275–288.
11. K. Lanaj and J.R. Hollenbeck, "Leadership Over-Emergence in Self-Managing Teams: The Role of Gender and Countervailing Biases," *Academy of Management Journal* 58(5) (2015): 1476-1494.
12. The discussion of personal and participative leadership was added based on the suggestion of reviewer, added May 12, 2017.
13. C.L. Pearce, C.L. Wassenaar, and C.C. Manz, "Is Shared Leadership the Key to Responsible Leadership?" *Academy of Management Perspectives* 28(3) (2014): 275–288.
14. D. Collinson and D. Tourish, "Teaching Leadership Critically: New Directions for Leadership Pedagogy," *Academy of Management Learning & Education* 14(4) (2015): 576–594.
15. R.L. Dipboye, "Bridging the Gap in Organizational Behavior," *Academy of Management Learning & Education* 13(3) (2014): 487–491.
16. D. Collinson and D. Tourish, "Teaching Leadership Critically: New Directions for Leadership Pedagogy," *Academy of Management Learning & Education* 14(4) (2015): 576–594.
17. 17 S.M. Martin, S. Cote, and T. Woodruff, "Ecoes of Our Upbringing: How Growing Up Wealth or Poor Relates to Narcissism, Leader Behavior, and Leader Effectiveness," *Academy of Management Journal* 59(6) (2016): 2157-2177.
18. T.A. Judge and C.P. Zapata, "The Person-Situation Debate Revisited: Effect of Situation Strength and Train Activation on the Validity of the Big Five Personality Traits in Predicting Job Performance," *Academy of Management Journal* 58(4) (2015): 1149-179.

19. T.A. Judge and C.P. Zapata, "The Person-Situation Debate Revisited: Effect of Situation Strength and Train Activation on the Validity of the Big Five Personality Traits in Predicting Job Performance," *Academy of Management Journal* 58(4) (2015): 1149-1179.

20. E. Ghiselli, *Exploration in Management Talent* (Santa Monica, CA: Goodyear, 1971).

21. A. and J. Bornstein, "What Makes a Great Leader?" *Entrepreneur* (March 2016): 36-44.

22. V. Bamiaizi, S. Jones, S. Mitchelore, and K, Nikolopoulos, "The Role of Competencies in Shaping the Leadership Style of Female Entrepreneurs: The Case of North West of England, Yorkshire, and North Wales," *Journal of Small Business Management* 53(3) (2015): 627-644.

23. F.K. Matta, B.A. Scott, J. Koopman, and D.E. Conlon, "Does Seeing Eye to Eye Affect Work Engagement and Organizational Citizenship Behavior? A Role Theory Perspective on LMX Agreements," *Academy of Management Journal* 58(6) (2015): 1686-1708.

24. T.A. Judge and C.P. Zapata, "The Person-Situation Debate Revisited: Effect of Situation Strength and Train Activation on the Validity of the Big Five Personality Traits in Predicting Job Performance," *Academy of Management Journal* 58(4) (2015): 1149-1179.

25. Staff, "What Are the Most Important Traits for Success as a Supervisor," *The Wall Street Journal* (November 14, 1980): 33.

26. GE, "Identifying the Leadership Skills That Matter Most," *INC.* (December 2014 / January 2015): 78.

27. B.R. Spisak, M.J. O'Brien, N. Nicholson, M. Van Vugt, "Niche Construction and the Evolution of Leadership," *Academy of Management Review* 40(2) (2015): 291-306.

28. R. Likert, *New Patterns of Management* (New York: McGraw-Hill, 1961).

29. R.M. Stogdill and A.E. Coons (Eds.), *Leader Behavior: The Description and Measurement* (Columbus: Ohio State University Bureau of Business Research, 1957).

30. R. Blake and J. Mouton, *The Managerial Grid* (Houston: Gulf, 1964); R. Blake and J. Mouton, *The New Managerial Grid* (Houston: Gulf, 1978); R. Blake and J. Mouton, *The Managerial Grid III: Key to Leadership Excellence*(Houston: Gulf, 1985); R. Blake and A.A. McCanse, *Leadership Dilemmas—Grid Solutions* (Houston: Gulf, 1991).

31. B.R. Spisak, M.J. O'Brien, N. Nicholson, M. Van Vugt, "Niche Construction and the Evolution of Leadership," *Academy of Management Review* 40(2) (2015): 291-306 .

32. M.R. Barrick, G.R. Thurgood, T.A. Smith, and S.H. Courtright, "Collective Organizational Engagement: Linking Motivational Antecedents, Strategic Implementation, and Firm Performance," *Academy of Management Journal* 58(1) (2015): 111-135.

33. C.L. Pearce, C.L. Wassenaar, and C.C. Manz, "Is Shared Leadership the Key to Responsible Leadership?" *Academy of Management Perspectives* 28(3) (2014): 275-288.

34. M.A. LePine, Y. Zhang, E.R. Crawford, and B.L Rich, "Turning Their Pain to Gain: Charismatic Leader Influence on Follower Stress Appraisal and Job Performance," *Academy of Management Journal* 59(3) (2016): 1036-1059.

35. D.L. Gamache, G. McNamara, M.J. Mannor, R.E. Johnson, "Motivated to Acquire? The Impact of CEO Regulatory Focus on Firm Acquisitions," *Academy of Management Journal* 58(4) (2015): 1261-1282.

36. P. Jacquart and J. Antonakis, "When Does Charisma Matter for Top-Level Leaders? Effect of Attributional Ambiguity," *Academy of Management Journal* 58(4) (2015): 1051-1074.

37. D. Collinson and D. Tourish, "Teaching Leadership Critically: New Directions for Leadership Pedagogy," *Academy of Management Learning & Education* 14(4) (2015): 576-594.

38. C.L. Pearce, C.L. Wassenaar, and C.C. Manz, "Is Shared Leadership the Key to Responsible Leadership?" *Academy of Management Perspectives* 28(3) (2014): 275-288.

39. H.R. Greven, "Microfoundations of Management: Behavioral Strategies and Levels of Rationality in Organizational Action," *Academy of Management Perspectives 27*(2) (2013): 103-119.

40. B.M. Galvin, D. Lange, and B.E. Ashforth, "Narcissistic Organizational Identification: Seeing Oneself as Central to the Orgnization's Identity," *Academy of Management Review* 40(2) (2015): 163-181.

41. R.C. Liden, S.J. Wayne, C. Liao, J.D. Meuser, "Servant Leadership and Serving Culture: Influence on Individual and Unit Performance," *Academy of Management Journal* 57(5) (2014): 1434-1452.

42. I. Berkovich, "Between Person and Person: Dialogical Pedagogy in Authentic Leadership Development," *Academy of Management Learning & Education* 13(2) (2014): 245-264.

43. C.C. Manz, "Taking the Self-Leadership High Road: Smooth Surface or Potholes Ahead?" *Academy of Management Perspectives* 29(1) (2015): 132–151.

44. J. Bloom, "Authenticity," *Entrepreneur* (March 2016): 39.

45. S.J. Creary, B.B. Caza, and L.M. Roberts, "Out of the Box? How Managing a Subordinate's Multiple Identities Affects the Quality of a Manager-Subordinate Relationship," *Academy of Management Review* 40(4) (2015): 538–562.

46. GE, "Identifying the Leadership Skills That Matter Most," *INC.* (December 2014 / January 2015): 78.

47. GE, "Identifying the Leadership Skills That Matter Most," *INC.* (December 2014 / January 2015): 78.

48. F.K. Matta, B.A. Scott, J. Koopman, and D.E. Conlon, "Does Seeing Eye to Eye Affect Work Engagement and Organizational Citizenship Behavior? A Role Theory Perspective on LMX Agreements," *Academy of Management Journal* 58(6) (2015): 1686–1708.

49. D. Collinson and D. Tourish, "Teaching Leadership Critically: New Directions for Leadership Pedagogy," *Academy of Management Learning & Education* 14(4) (2015): 576–594.

50. V. Harnish, "5 Crucial Performance Metrics," *Fortune* (August 1, 2016): 322.

51. T.A. Judge and C.P. Zapata, "The Person-Situation Debate Revisited: Effect of Situation Strength and Train Activation on the Validity of the Big Five Personality Traits in Predicting Job Performance," *Academy of Management Journal* 58(4) (2015): 1149–1179.

52. Y. Zhang, D.A. Waldman, U.L. Han, and X.B. Li, "Paradoxical Leaders Behaviors in People Management: Antecedents and Consequences," *Academy of Management Journal* 58(2) (2015): 538–566.

53. T.L. Stanko and C.M. Beckman, "Watching You Watching Me: Boundary Control and Capturing Attention in the Context of Ubiquitous Technology Use," *Academy of Management Journal* 58(3) (2015): 712–738.

54. M. Whitman, "Most Powerful Women," *Fortune* (November 17, 2014): 149.

55. F. Fiedler, *A Theory of Leadership Effectiveness* (New York: McGraw-Hill, 1967).

56. R. Tannenbaum and W. Schmidt, "How to Choose a Leadership Pattern," *Harvard Business Review* (May–June 1973): 166.

57. V. Vroom and P. Yetton, *Leadership and Decision Making* (Pittsburgh: University of Pittsburgh Press, 1973); V. Vroom, "Leadership and the Decision Making Process," *Organizational Dynamics* 28 (Spring 2000): 82–94.

58. P. Hersey, K. Blanchard, and D. Johnson, *Management of Organizational Behavior,* 10th ed. (Upper Saddle River, NJ: Prentice Hall, 2013).

59. T.A. Judge and C.P. Zapata, "The Person-Situation Debate Revisited: Effect of Situation Strength and Train Activation on the Validity of the Big Five Personality Traits in Predicting Job Performance," *Academy of Management Journal* 58(4) (2015): 1149–1179.

60. T.L. Stanko and C.M. Beckman, "Watching You Watching Me: Boundary Control and Capturing Attention in the Context of Ubiquitous Technology Use," *Academy of Management Journal* 58(3) (2015): 712–738.

61. Y. Zhang, D.A. Waldman, U.L. Han, and X.B. Li, "Paradoxical Leaders Behaviors in People Management: Antecedents and Consequences," *Academy of Management Journal* 58(2) (2015): 538–566.

62. G. Colvin, "Ignore These Leadership Lessons at Your Peril," *Fortune* (October 28, 2013): 85.

63. Editors, "Cross-Cultural Management Learning and Education—Exploring Multiple Aims, Approaches, and Impacts, *Academy of Management Learning & Education* 12(3) (2013): 323–329.

64. Editors, "Cross-Cultural Management Learning and Education—Exploring Multiple Aims, Approaches, and Impacts," *Academy of Management Learning & Education* 12(3) (2013): 323–329.

65. P. Jacquart and J. Antonakis, "When Does Charisma Matter for Top-Level Leaders? Effect of Attributional Ambiguity," *Academy of Management Journal* 58(4) (2015): 1051–1074.

66. J.A. Martin and K.M. Eisenhardt, "Rewiring: Cross-Business-Unit Collaborations in Multi-Business Organizations," *Academy of Management Journal* 53(2) (2010): 265–301.

67. Reviewer, suggestion of reviewer added May 15, 2017.

68. M. Mazmanian, "Avoiding the Trap of Constant Connectivity: When Congruent Frames Allow for Heterogeneous Practices," *Academy of Management Journal* 56(5) (2013): 1125–1250.

69. Editors, "Cross-Cultural Management Learning and Education—Exploring Multiple Aims, Approaches, and Impacts," *Academy of Management Learning & Education* 12(3) (2013): 323–329.

70. Editors, "Cross-Cultural Management Learning and Education—Exploring Multiple Aims, Approaches, and Impacts," *Academy of Management Learning & Education* 12(3) (2013): 323–329.

71. A.C. Peng, J.M. Schaubroeck, and L. Li, "Social Exchange Implications of Own and Coworkers' Experiences of Supervisor Abuse," *Academy of Management Journal* 57(5) (2014): 1385–1405.

72. Y. Liu, G.R. Ferris, J. Xu, B.A. Weitz, and P.L. Perrewe, "When Ingratiation Backfires: The Role of Political Skill in the Ingratiation-Internship Performance Relationship," *Academy of Management Learning & Education 13*(3) (2014): 569–586.

73. E.G.R. Barends and R.B. Briner, "Teaching Evidence-Based Practice: Lessons from the Pioneers," *Academy of Management Learning & Education 13*(3) (2014): 476–483.

74. M.D. Baer, R.K.D. Kahlon, J.A. Colquitt, J.B. Rodell, R. Outlaw, and D.M. Long, "Uneasy Lies the Head that Bears the Trust: The Effects of Feeling Trusted on Emotional Exhaustion," *Academy of Management Journal* 58(6) (2015): 1637–1657.

75. C.M. Barnes, L. Lucianetti, D.P. Bhave, and M.S. Christian, "You Wouldn't Like Me When I'm Sleepy: Leaders' Sleep, Daily Abusive Supervision, and Work Unit Engagement," *Academy of Management Journal* 58(5) (2015): 1419-1437.

76. C.L. Pearce, C.L. Wassenaar, and C.C. Manz, "Is Shared Leadership the Key to Responsible Leadership?" *Academy of Management Perspectives* 28(3) (2014): 275–288.

77. D. Eng, "Does Joy Help You Sell?" *Fortune* (January 1, 2016): 30.

78. W.L. Bedwell, S.M. Fiore, and E. Salas, "Developing the Future Workforce," *Academy of Management Learning & Education* 13(2) (2014): 171–186.

79. A.C. Peng, J.M. Schaubroeck, and L. Li, "Social Exchange Implications of Own and Coworkers' Experiences of Supervisor Abuse," *Academy of Management Journal* 57(5) (2014): 1385–1405.

80. M.D. Baer, R.K.D. Kahlon, J.A. Colquitt, J.B. Rodell, R. Outlaw, and D.M. Long, "Uneasy Lies the Head that Bears the Trust: The Effects of Feeling Trusted on Emotional Exhaustion," *Academy of Management Journal* 58(6) (2015): 1637–1657.

81. G. O'Brian, "Fixing the First Impression," *Entrepreneur* accessed online May 5, 2017.

82. W.L. Bedwell, S.M. Fiore, and E. Salas, "Developing the Future Workforce," *Academy of Management Learning & Education* 13(2) (2014): 171–186.

  i. https://blog.kissmetrics.com/zappos-art-of-culture/ accessed May 26, 2017.

 ii. http://www.deliveringhappiness.com/about-us/about-2/ accessed May 26, 2017.

iii. http://www.inc.com/magazine/20090501/the-zappos-way-of-managing.html accessed May 26, 2017.

 iv. http://about.zappos.com/our-unique-culture/zappos-core-values accessed May 26, 2017.

  v. http://money.cnn.com/2009/01/21/news/companies/obrien_zappos10.fortune/index.htm?utm_source=feedburner&utm_medium=feed&utm_campaign=Feed%3A+rss%2Fmoney_latest+(Latest+News) accessed May 26, 2017.

 vi. http://bluesky.chicagotribune.com/originals/chi-zappos-ceo-tony-hsieh-company-culture-bsi,0,0.story accessed May 26, 2017.

vii. http://www.greatplacetowork.com/storage/documents/Publications_Documents/Zappos_-_How_Zappos_Creates_Happy_Customers_and_Employees.pdf accessed May 26, 2017.

Motivating Performance

©Jacobs Stock Photography/Getty Images

LEARNING OUTCOMES

After completing this chapter, you should be able to:

LO 7-1 Explain the motivation process and the three factors affecting performance.

LO 7-2 Describe four content motivation theories.

LO 7-3 Describe two process motivation theories.

LO 7-4 State how reinforcement is used to increase performance.

LO 7-5 List the four steps in the model for giving praise.

LO 7-6 List the criteria for setting objectives.

LO 7-7 Identify the four parts of the model for writing objectives.

LO 7-8 State ways to enrich, design, and simplify jobs.

LO 7-9 Explain possible limitations of using motivation theories outside North America.

LO 7-10 Define the following 16 key terms (in order of appearance in the chapter):

motivation	equity theory
performance formula	reinforcement theory
content motivation	giving praise
theories	objectives
needs hierarchy	management by objectives
two-factor theory	(MBO)
manifest needs theory	job enrichment
process motivation	job design
theories	job simplification
expectancy theory	

OPENING CASE WORK SCENARIO

/ / / Latoia Henderson was recently promoted to a management position at The Gap headquarters. She is enthusiastic about her work. Generally, things are going well, but Latoia is having a problem with Hank. Hank is often late for work, and even though he can do a good job, he does not regularly perform to expectations. Latoia had a talk with Hank to find out what the problem was. Hank said the money and benefits were great, and the people in the department were nice, but the job was boring. He complained that he didn't have any say about how to do his job and that Latoia was always checking up on him. Hank believes he is treated fairly because of the union, which gives him job protection. But because everyone is paid the same, working hard is a waste of time. If you were in Latoia's position, how would you motivate Hank? This chapter examines specific motivation theories and techniques that can be used to motivate not only Hank but employees in all organizations, as well as to motivate yourself. / / /

THE IMPORTANCE OF MOTIVATION

Learning Outcome 7-1

Explain the motivation process and the three factors affecting performance.

In this section, we discuss what motivation is, why it is important, and how motivation affects behavior, human relations, happiness, and performance.

What Is Motivation?

Motivation is *the internal process leading to behavior to satisfy needs.* Have you ever wondered why people do the things they do? The primary reason people do what they do is to meet their needs or wants—or to bring happiness. So motivating is about answering people's often unasked question, "What's in it for me?" by helping them meet their needs and wants, while achieving organizational objectives.[1] Effective leaders are good motivators,[2] as they influence others,[3] as they satisfy their own needs and the followers' needs to benefit the organization,[4] which is the goal of human relations. The process people go through to meet their needs is

Need → Motive → Behavior → Satisfaction or Dissatisfaction.

WORK APPLICATION 7-1

Give an example of how you have gone through the motivation process. Identify the need, motive, behavior, and satisfaction or dissatisfaction.

For example, you are thirsty (need) and have a drive (motive) to get a drink (behavior) that quenches (satisfaction) your thirst. However, if you could not get a drink, or a drink of what you really wanted, you would be dissatisfied. Motivation is satisfaction-based. Satisfaction is usually short-lived. Getting that drink satisfied you, but soon you will need another drink.

Managers often view motivation as an employee's willingness to put forth effort and commitment to achieve organizational objectives, which is called *employee engagement*[5] and *organizational citizenship behavior (OCB).*[6] Employee engagement is one of the top three challenges of businesses today, but only 32 percent of U.S. workers say they are motivationally engaged in their jobs.[7] /// **In the opening case,** Latoia is concerned because Hank is not motivated to work hard. ///

How Motivation Affects Behavior, Human Relations, Happiness, and Performance

Recall the Pygmalion effect (Chapter 3) as how managers treat employees affects their behavior, happiness, and performance,[8] either positively or negatively. People who are happy with their jobs are generally motivated to work harder and have high levels of performance.[9] Conversely, those who don't have job satisfaction can be demotivated.[10] An unengaged worker costs an organization approximately $3,400 for every $10,000 in annual salary.[11] With the trend of team structures, one of the key drivers of effective team performance is the motivation of team members.[12] Happiness, which affects motivation, comes from relationships, so effective Leader-member exchange (LMX) leaders (Chapter 6) have higher levels of performance.[13]

The Performance Formula   However, performance is not based simply on motivation. The level of performance attained is determined by three interdependent factors: ability (IQ, skills), motivation (willingness to work hard), and resources (things needed to do the task). This relationship can be stated as a **performance formula:** *Performance = Ability × Motivation × Resources.*

For performance levels to be high, all three factors must be high. If any one factor is low or missing, the performance level will be adversely affected. For example, Mary Lou, a very intelligent student, has the books, but because she does not care about grades, she does not study (low motivation) and does not get an A.

When performance is not at the standard level or above, you must determine which performance factor needs to be improved, and improve it. /// **In the opening case,** Hank has the ability and resources, but he lacks motivation.

Communication Skills
Refer to CS Question 1.

APPLICATION SITUATIONS / / /

The Performance Formula   AS 7-1

Identify the factor contributing to low performance in the five situations below.

A. Ability   B. Motivation   C. Resources

_____ 1. I spend more time practicing shooting baskets than my teammates Jamal and Tyron. I don't understand why they constantly score more points than me.

_____ 2. I could get all As if I wanted to. But I'd rather relax and have a good time in college.

_____ 3. The government would be more efficient if it cut down on waste.

_____ 4. Sherry went on a sales call, but when she pulled out her laptop to show a demonstration of the products, it wouldn't work. So she didn't get any sales.

_____ 5. You don't do as much work as the rest of us because you're lazy.

Hank finds the job boring and is not performing to expectations. To increase Hank's performance, Latoia needs to motivate him to perform to her expectations. As each motivation theory and technique is presented, you will learn how Latoia can apply it to motivate Hank or others. ///

Theory and Application   Based on learning styles (Chapter 2), some people like motivation theories and want to know them, while others just want the practical "how to motivate" material. In this chapter, we provide both. In the first three major sections we provide the theories based on the three schools of motivation: content, process, and reinforcement, but we do include advice on how to motivate with each theory. The section on reinforcement theory is also practical because it tells you how to get people to do what you want them to do. Then, based on the theories, we provide motivation techniques that can be used to motivate others and yourself. So you can put your focus on one or the other, or both.

Your Motivation   When you are motivated, do you have different behavior, happiness, human relations, and a higher level of performance than when you are not motivated? Let's be honest. Do you like to have things your way (meet your needs and wants), rather than help others satisfy their needs? At some level, we all try to influence (motivate) people to help us get what we want. For most of us it's a daily habit. Thus, your ability to motivate yourself and others is critical to your personal and career success, and the goal of this chapter is to increase your ability to do both. Success is a choice, so do you want to improve your ability to motivate yourself and others? As you read the motivation theories and techniques, keep in mind that you can be a leader and influence others to help you meet your needs and wants, while helping them meet their needs and wants—the goal of human relations.

CONTENT MOTIVATION THEORIES

Learning Outcome 7-2

Describe four content motivation theories.

To influence others, we need to understand their needs[14] so that we can add value to the relationship.[15] Thus, to increase performance, we must know our own needs and others' needs, and satisfy them.[16] This is the goal of human relations.

The **content motivation theories** focus on *identifying people's needs in order to understand what motivates them.* In this section, you will learn four content motivation theories: (1) needs hierarchy, (2) ERG theory, (3) two-factor theory, and (4) manifest needs theory. You will also learn how organizations use these theories to motivate employees.

Needs Hierarchy

The **needs hierarchy** is *Maslow's theory of motivation, which is based on five needs.* In the 1940s, **Abraham Maslow** developed one of the most popular and widely known motivation theories based on three major assumptions:[17]

1. People's needs are arranged in order of importance (hierarchy), going from basic needs (physiological) to more complex needs (self-actualization).

2. People will not be motivated to satisfy a higher-level need unless the lower-level need has been at least minimally satisfied.

3. There are five classifications of needs. Listed below are these five classes of needs in order of importance to the individual.

   • *Physiological needs.* These are your primary or basic needs. They include air, food, shelter, sex, and relief or avoidance of pain. These needs include adequate salary, breaks, and working conditions.

   • *Safety needs.* These needs include safe working conditions, salary increases to meet inflation, job security, and fringe benefits that protect the physiological needs.

   • *Social needs.* These needs include the opportunity to interact with others, be accepted, and have friends.

   • *Esteem needs.* Your ego, status, self-respect, recognition for accomplishments, and a feeling of self-confidence and prestige. These needs include titles, the satisfaction of completing the job itself, merit pay raises, recognition, challenging tasks, and the chance for advancement. Recall the importance of a positive self-concept (Chapter 3).

   • *Self-actualization.* You develop your full potential by seeking growth, achievement, and advancement. These needs include the development of one's skills; the chance to be creative; achievement and promotions; and the ability to have complete control over one's job.

Communication Skills
Refer to CS Question 2.

Sources: A. Maslow, "A Theory of Human Motivation," *Psychological Review* Vol 50, 1943, 370–396; A. Maslow, *Motivation and Personality*, New York: Harper & Row, 1954.

See Exhibit 7.1 for an illustration of Maslow's five needs.

EXHIBIT 7.1 | Needs Hierarchy and ERG Theory

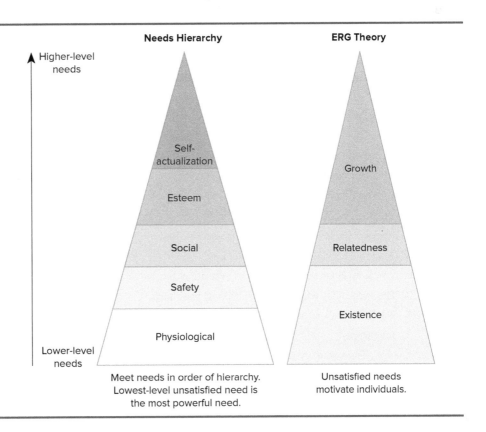

ERG Theory

As Exhibit 7.1 illustrates, **Clayton Alderfer** reorganizes Maslow's needs hierarchy into three levels of needs: existence (physiological and safety needs), relatedness (social), and growth (esteem and self-actualization). Today's companies focus on fulfilling higher-level needs. /// In the opening case, Hank's performance was poor, but he can be motivated to meet Latoia's expectations if his performance results in satisfying his needs. ///

Motivating with Needs Hierarchy and ERG Theory   The major recommendation is to meet employees' lower-level needs so that they will not dominate the employees' motivational process. To use ERG theory, answer six questions: (1) What need does the individual have? (2) What needs have been satisfied? (3) Which unsatisfied need is the lowest in the hierarchy? (4) Have some higher-order needs been frustrated? If so, how? (5) Has the person refocused on a lower-level need? (6) How can the unsatisfied needs be satisfied?

/// In the opening case, Latoia observed Hank and took the time to talk to him to determine his needs. Hank's needs for existence and relatedness have been met. However, his need for growth has been frustrated. To motivate Hank, Latoia must meet his need for growth. In this chapter, you will learn ways to satisfy growth needs. ///

Two-Factor Theory

The **two-factor theory** is *Herzberg's classification of needs as hygienes and motivators.* Before learning Herzberg's theory, complete Self-Assessment Exercise 7-1 to learn what motivates you.

In the 1950s, **Frederick Herzberg** and associates' research findings disagreed with the traditional view that satisfaction and dissatisfaction were at opposite ends of a continuum.[18]

/// / **Self-Assessment Exercise 7-1** / / /

Your Motivators and Hygienes

Below are 12 job factors that contribute to job satisfaction. Rate each according to how important it is to you. Place the number 1 to 5 on the line before each factor.

Very important		Somewhat important		Not important
5	4	3	2	1

_____ 1. An interesting job I enjoy doing.

_____ 2. A good boss who treats everyone the same, regardless of circumstances.

_____ 3. Recognition and appreciation for the work I do.

_____ 4. The opportunity for advancement.

_____ 5. A job that is routine, without much change from day to day.

_____ 6. A prestigious job title regardless of pay.

_____ 7. Job responsibility that gives me the freedom to do the job my way.

_____ 8. Good working conditions (nice office).

_____ 9. A focus on following company rules, regulations, procedures, and policies.

_____ 10. The opportunity to grow through learning new things.

_____ 11. A job I can do well and succeed at.

_____ 12. Job security.

To determine if hygienes or motivators are important to you, on the lines below place the numbers (1 to 5) that represent your answers for the statements.

(continued)

Hygienes Score	Motivators Score
2. _____	1. _____
5. _____	3. _____
6. _____	4. _____
8. _____	7. _____
9. _____	10. _____
12. _____	11. _____
Total _____	Total _____

Add each column. Did you select hygienes or motivators as being more important to you? Now we'll find out their significance.

Herzberg classifies two needs that he calls *factors*. Herzberg combines lower-level needs into one classification he calls *hygienes*; and he combines higher-level needs into one classification he calls *motivators*. Hygienes are also called *extrinsic factors* because attempts to motivate come from outside the job itself. Motivators are called *intrinsic factors* because motivation comes from the job itself. See Exhibit 7.2 for an illustration of Herzberg's theory.

Herzberg contends that providing hygiene factors keeps people from being dissatisfied, but it does not motivate people. For example, if people are dissatisfied with their pay and they get a raise, they will no longer be dissatisfied. They may even be satisfied for a short period of time. However, before long they get accustomed to the new standard of living and will no longer be satisfied. The vicious cycle goes on. If you got a pay raise, would you be motivated and be more productive?

WORK APPLICATION 7-2

In Self-Assessment Exercise 7-1, did you select motivators or hygienes as being important to you? Explain.

To motivate, Herzberg says that you must first ensure that hygiene factors are adequate. Once employees are satisfied with their environment, they can be motivated through their jobs.

Review Self-Assessment Exercise 7-1. Do not expect external rewards for everything you are asked to do. To be satisfied, you must seek and attain internal rewards.

Using Two-Factor Theory to Motivate Employees   /// **In the opening case,** Hank said he was not dissatisfied with hygiene factors. He lacked job satisfaction. If Latoia is going to motivate him, she will have to focus on intrinsic motivation, not hygiene. Hank says the job is boring. Will a pay raise or better working conditions make the job more interesting and challenging? Motivation and happiness come from doing what you like and enjoy doing; it helps you meet higher-order needs. Herzberg has developed a method for increasing motivation, which he calls *job enrichment*. In a later section of this chapter, you will learn about job enrichment and how Latoia could use it to motivate Hank. ///

EXHIBIT 7.2 | Two-Factor Theory

Hygiene Factors (Needs) (physiological, safety, social/existence, and relatedness needs)	Motivator Factors (Needs) (esteem, self-actualization, and growth needs)
Extrinsic Factors	**Intrinsic Factors**
Dissatisfaction ◄─────────► No Dissatisfaction	No Job Satisfaction ◄─────────► Job Satisfaction
• Pay • Status • Job security • Fringe benefits • Policies and administrative practices	• Meaningful and challenging work • Recognition for accomplishments • Feeling of achievement • Increased responsibility • Opportunity for growth • Opportunity for advancement

EXHIBIT 7.3 | Classification of Needs by Four Theories of Motivation

Maslow's Needs Hierarchy Theory	Alderfer's ERG Theory	Herzberg's Two-Factor Theory	McClelland's Manifest Needs Theory
Self-actualization	Growth	Motivators	Achievement Power
Esteem			
Social	Relatedness	Hygienes	Affiliation
Safety	Existence		
Physiological			

Manifest Needs Theory

Communication Skills
Refer to CS Question 3.

Skill-Building Exercise 7-1
develops this skill.

The **manifest needs theory** of motivation is primarily *McClelland's classification of needs as achievement, power, and affiliation.* It is a personality-based approach to motivation. **David McClelland** does not have a classification for lower-level needs. His affiliation needs are the same as social and relatedness needs, and power and achievement are related to esteem and self-actualization and growth.[19] See Exhibit 7.3 for a comparison of the need classifications of the four theories of motivation.

Unlike Maslow, he believes that needs are based on personality and are developed as people interact with the environment. All people possess the need for achievement, power, and affiliation, but to varying degrees. One of these three needs tends to be dominant in each one of us and motivate our behavior. Before getting into the details of each need, complete Self-Assessment Exercise 7-2 to determine your dominant or primary need.

/// Self-Assessment Exercise 7-2 ///

Your Manifest Needs

Identify each of the following 15 statements according to how accurately it describes you. Place the number 1 to 5 on the line before each statement.

Like me		Somewhat like me		Not like me
5	4	3	2	1

_____ 1. I enjoy working hard.

_____ 2. I enjoy competition and winning.

_____ 3. I want/have lots of friends.

_____ 4. I enjoy a difficult challenge.

_____ 5. I enjoy leading and being in charge.

_____ 6. I want to be liked by others.

_____ 7. I want to know how I am progressing as I complete tasks.

_____ 8. I confront people who do things I disagree with.

_____ 9. I enjoy frequent parties.

_____ 10. I enjoy setting and achieving realistic goals.

_____ 11. I enjoy influencing other people to get my way.

_____ 12. I enjoy belonging to lots of groups or organizations.

_____ 13. I enjoy the satisfaction of completing a difficult task.

_____ 14. In a leaderless situation I tend to take charge.

_____ 15. I enjoy working with others more than working alone.

(continued)

/ / / **Self-Assessment Exercise 7-2** / / / (*continued*)

To determine your primary need, on the lines below, place the numbers (1 to 5) that represent your scores for the statements.

Achievement	Power	Affiliation
1. _____	2. _____	3. _____
4. _____	5. _____	6. _____
7. _____	8. _____	9. _____
10. _____	11. _____	12. _____
13. _____	14. _____	15. _____
Total _____	Total _____	Total _____

Add the numbers in each column. Each column total should be between 5 and 25. The column with the highest score is your dominant or primary need.

The Need for Achievement (n-Ach)

People with a high *n*-Ach tend to be characterized as: wanting to take personal responsibility for solving problems; goal-oriented (they set moderate, realistic, attainable goals); seeking challenge, excellence, and individuality; taking calculated, moderate risks; desiring concrete feedback on their performance; willing to work hard. Need for achievement is correlated with performance. Managers tend to have a high, but not a dominant, *n*-Ach.

Motivating Employees with a High* n-*Ach   Give them nonroutine, challenging tasks in which there are clear, attainable objectives. Give them fast and frequent feedback on their performance. Continually give them increased responsibility for doing new things.

The Need for Power (n-Pow)

People with a high need for power tend to be characterized as: wanting to control the situation; wanting influence or control over others; enjoying competition in which they can win (they do not like to lose); willing to confront others. People with high *n*-Pow tend to have a low need for affiliation. Managers tend to have a dominant need for power.

Motivating Employees with a High* n-*Pow   Let them plan and control their jobs as much as possible. Try to include them in decision making, especially when they are affected by the decision. They tend to perform best as leaders or alone rather than as team members.

People are motivated to gain power as leaders because having it meets their needs. /// In the opening case, Hank's primary need seems to be power. Hank wants more say in how to do his job, and he wants Latoia to do less checking up on him. If Latoia empowers Hank by giving him more job-related responsibility, it may satisfy Hank's needs, resulting in higher performance. ///

The Need for Affiliation (n-Aff)

People with a high *n*-Aff tend to be characterized as: seeking close relationships with others; wanting to be liked by others; enjoying lots of social activities; seeking to belong (they join groups and organizations). They tend to have a low *n*-Pow. They also tend to avoid supervision because they like to be one of the group rather than its leader.

Motivating High* n-*Aff Employees   Be sure to let them work as part of a team. They derive satisfaction from the people they work with rather than the task itself. Give them lots of praise and recognition. Delegate responsibility for orienting and training new employees to them. They make great mentors.

WORK APPLICATION 7-3

Explain how your personal *n*-Ach, *n*-Pow, and *n*-Aff affect your motivation, behavior, and performance. How can you use manifest needs theory to motivate employees?

EXHIBIT 7.4 | How Organizations Meet Employee Needs

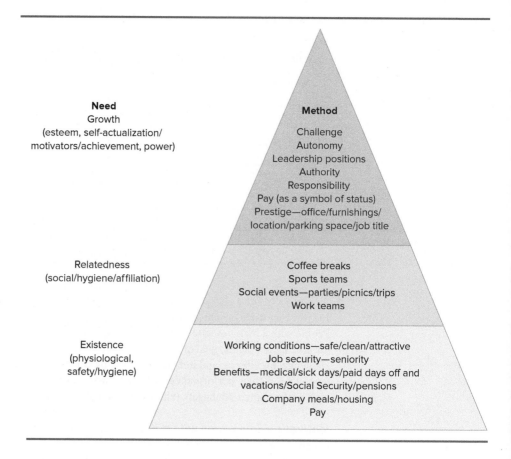

Need
Growth
(esteem, self-actualization/
motivators/achievement, power)

Method
Challenge
Autonomy
Leadership positions
Authority
Responsibility
Pay (as a symbol of status)
Prestige—office/furnishings/
location/parking space/job title

Relatedness
(social/hygiene/affiliation)

Coffee breaks
Sports teams
Social events—parties/picnics/trips
Work teams

Existence
(physiological,
safety/hygiene)

Working conditions—safe/clean/attractive
Job security—seniority
Benefits—medical/sick days/paid days off and
vacations/Social Security/pensions
Company meals/housing
Pay

How Organizations Meet Employee Needs

See Exhibit 7.4 for a list of methods used by organizations to meet employee needs. Note that pay is important and can meet both higher- and lower-level needs. Many companies are meeting relatedness needs by creating a fun place to work,[20] such as **Acuity** insurance, **Facebook**, and **Google**.

PROCESS MOTIVATION THEORIES

Learning Outcome 7-3

Describe two process motivation theories.

Content motivation theories attempt to understand what motivates people, whereas **process motivation theories** *attempt to understand how and why people are motivated.* Their focus is more on behavior than needs. Why do people select certain goals to work toward? Why do people select particular behavior to meet their needs? How do people evaluate need satisfaction? Expectancy and equity theories attempt to answer these questions.

Expectancy Theory

The **expectancy theory,** which is *Vroom's formula, states that Motivation = Expectancy × Valence.* Motivation depends on how much people want something and how likely they are to get it.[21] Expectancy and valence are two important variables in **Victor Vroom**'s formula that must be met for motivation to take place.

Expectancy   Expectancy refers to the person's perception of his or her ability (probability) to accomplish an objective.[22] Generally, the higher one's expectancy, the better the chance for motivation. When employees do not believe that they can accomplish objectives, they will not be motivated to try.

Also important is the perception of the relationship between performance and the outcome or reward. Generally, the higher one's expectancy of the outcome or reward, the better the chance for motivation. This is called *instrumentality*. If employees are certain to get a reward or to be successful, they probably will be motivated. When not sure, employees may not be motivated.

Valence   Valence refers to the value a person places on the outcome or reward. Generally, the higher the value (importance) of the outcome or reward, the better the chance of motivation.

Motivating with Expectancy Theory   The following conditions should be implemented to motivate employees:

1. Clearly define objectives and the performance needed to achieve them.

2. Tie performance to rewards. High performance should be rewarded. When one employee works harder to produce more than other employees and is not rewarded, he or she may slow down productivity.

3. Be sure rewards are of value to the employee. You need to realize that what motivates you may not motivate someone else. You should treat others as individuals.

4. Make sure your employees believe you will do as what you say you will do. You need people's trust (Chapter 6) to motivate them.

/// **In the opening case,** Hank says that because of the union, everyone is paid the same, so working hard is a waste of time. In the expectancy formula, since expectancy is low, there is no motivation. Latoia may find some other need to help him meet. If Latoia can find a need with expectancy and valence, Hank will be motivated to perform to expectations, creating a win–win situation for all parties. ///

WORK APPLICATION 7-4

Give an example of how expectancy theory has affected your motivation. How can you use expectancy theory to motivate employees?

Equity Theory

The **equity theory** is *primarily Adams's motivation theory, which is based on the comparison of perceived inputs and outputs.* **J. Stacy Adams** popularized equity theory with his contention that people seek social equity in the rewards they receive (output) for their performance (input).[23]

According to equity theory, people compare their inputs (effort, experience, seniority, status, intelligence, and so forth) and outputs (praise, recognition, pay promotions, increased status, supervisor's approval, and the like) with those of relevant others. A relevant other could be a coworker or a group of employees from the same or from different organizations or even from a hypothetical situation. Notice that our definition mentions *perceived,* not *actual,* inputs and outputs. Equity may actually exist. However, if employees believe there is inequity, they will change their behavior to create equity, such as doing less work, changing the situation (like getting a raise), or getting another job.

Studies have demonstrated the importance of fairness.[24] It is important to treat people ethically and fairly,[25] because it is difficult to influence people when they don't trust you.[26] Abusive supervisors use unfair treatment and tend to demotivate employees and hurt performance.[27]

Pay equity does affect performance, but most employees tend to inflate their own efforts or performance when comparing themselves with others. They also overestimate what others earn.[28]

Motivating with Equity Theory   Using equity theory in practice can be difficult because you don't know: (1) who the employee's reference group is and (2) what his or her view of inputs and outcomes is. However, it does offer some useful general recommendations:

• Equity is difficult for managers because they are expected to treat employees uniformly and consistently, while considering individual needs and sometimes making exceptions that can be viewed as unfair by others.[29]

- You need to treat people fairly. But be aware that equity is based on perception of being treated fairly, which may not be correct. You may perceive that you are treating another person fairly, but they may not.

WORK APPLICATION 7-5

Give an example of how equity theory has affected your motivation. How can you use equity theory to motivate employees?

- Realize that what people know or don't know isn't important. All that really counts is what they feel. The perception of large inequity gets people emotional. So you have to deal effectively with emotions (follow the guidelines from Chapter 4).

- Rewards should be equitable. High performance should be rewarded, but employees must understand the inputs needed to attain certain outputs.

/// **In the opening case,** Hank said that he was equitably treated because of the union. Therefore, Latoia does not need to be concerned about equity theory with Hank. However, it could be an issue with another employee. ///

Communication Skills
Refer to CS Question 4.

Learning Outcome 7-4

State how reinforcement is used to increase performance.

REINFORCEMENT THEORY

As you have seen, content motivation theories focus on meeting people's needs to motivate them, and process motivation theories focus on how and why people are motivated; reinforcement theory focuses on getting people to do what you want them to do. **Reinforcement theory** is *primarily Skinner's motivation theory: Behavior can be controlled through the use of positive or negative consequences.* It is also called *behavior modification* and *operant conditioning.*

B. F. Skinner contends that people's behavior is learned through experiences of positive and negative consequences. He believes that rewarded behavior tends to be repeated, while unrewarded behavior tends not to be repeated. The three components of Skinner's framework are:[30]

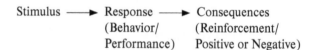

Stimulus ⟶ Response ⟶ Consequences
(Behavior/   (Reinforcement/
Performance)   Positive or Negative)

An employee learns what is, and is not, desired behavior as a result of the consequences for specific behavior. **Kimberly Clark**'s focus is on rewarding good performance and punishing poor performance.[31]

Reinforcement is not about meeting needs, it's about getting people to do what we want them to do by answering their often unasked question, "What's in it for me?" In essence you are saying, "If you do this behavior [stimulus calling for response behavior] I will give you this reward or this punishment if you don't [consequence—types of reinforcement] and this is how often I will give you the reward or punishment [schedules of reinforcement]."

Skinner states that supervisors can control and shape employees' behavior while at the same time making them feel free. The two important concepts used to control behavior are the types of reinforcement and the schedule of reinforcement.

Types of Reinforcement

The four types of reinforcement are as follows:

Positive Reinforcement   A method of encouraging continued behavior is to offer attractive consequences (rewards) for desirable performance.[32] For example, an employee is on time for a meeting and is rewarded by the supervisor's thanking him or her. The praise is used to reinforce punctuality. Other reinforcers are pay, promotions, time off, and increased status. Positive reinforcement is the best motivator for increasing productivity. Recall that developing habits is based on rewards.[33]

Avoidance Reinforcement   Avoidance is also called *negative reinforcement.* The employee avoids the negative consequence. For example, an employee is punctual for a meeting to avoid negative reinforcement, such as a reprimand. Rules are designed to get employees to avoid certain behavior. Notice that with avoidance there is no actual punishment; it's the threat of the punishment that controls behavior.

Extinction   Extinction attempts to reduce or eliminate undesirable behavior by withholding reinforcement when the behavior occurs. For example, an employee who is late for the meeting is not rewarded with praise. Or a pay raise is withheld until the employee performs to set standards.

Punishment   Punishment is used to provide an undesirable consequence for undesirable behavior. For example, an employee who is late for a meeting is reprimanded. Other methods of punishment include harassing, taking away privileges, probation, fining, and demoting. Using punishment may reduce the undesirable behavior, but it may cause other undesirable behavior, such as poor morale, lower productivity, and acts of theft or sabotage. Punishment is the most controversial method and the least effective at motivating employees.

Schedules of Reinforcement

The second reinforcement consideration in controlling behavior is when to reinforce performance. Recall the importance of timely feedback (Chapter 4). The frequency and magnitude of the reinforcement may be as important as the reinforcement itself. The two major classifications are continuous and intermittent:

Continuous Reinforcement   With a continuous method, each desired and undesired behavior is reinforced. Examples of this method would be a machine with an automatic counter that lets the employee know exactly how many units have been produced, or a supervisor who punishes employees for breaking rules every time.

Intermittent Reinforcement   With intermittent reinforcement, the reward is given based on the passage of time or output. When the reward is based on the passage of time, it is called an *interval schedule*. When it is based on output, it is called a *ratio schedule*. When electing to use intermittent reinforcement, there are four alternatives:

1. *Fixed interval schedule* (giving a salary paycheck every week, breaks and meals at the same time every day).
2. *Variable interval schedule* (giving praise only now and then, a surprise inspection, a pop quiz).
3. *Fixed ratio schedule* (giving a piece rate or bonus after producing a standard rate).
4. *Variable ratio schedule* (giving praise for excellent work, a lottery for employees who have not been absent for a set time).

Ratios are generally better motivators than intervals. The variable ratio tends to be the most powerful schedule for sustaining behavior.

Motivating with Reinforcement   Generally, positive reinforcement is the best motivator. Continuous reinforcement is better at sustaining desired behavior; however, it is not always possible or practical. Following are some general guidelines:

- Make sure employees know exactly what is expected of them. Set clear objectives.[34]
- Select appropriate rewards. A reward to one person could be considered a punishment by another.[35]
- Select the appropriate reinforcement type and schedule.
- Do not reward mediocre or poor performance.[36]

- Look for the positive and give praise, rather than focusing on the negative and criticizing.[37] Make people feel good about themselves (Pygmalion effect).

- Never go a day without giving praise.

- Do things *for* people, instead of *to* them, and you will see human relations and productivity increases. Treat employees well.

/// **In the opening case,** Hank has been coming to work late and performing below expectations. Latoia can try giving Hank positive, encouraging statements to do a good job. But Latoia should try some other positive reinforcement such as job enrichment. If positive reinforcement doesn't change Hank's behavior, Latoia can use avoidance reinforcement. Based on her authority, she could tell Hank that the next time he is late or performs below a specific level, he will receive a specific punishment, such as having part of his pay withheld. If Hank does not avoid this behavior, Latoia must follow up and give the punishment. /// As a manager, try the positive first. Positive reinforcement is a true motivator because it creates a win–win situation by meeting both the employee's and the manager's or organization's needs. From the employees' perspective, avoidance and punishment create a lose–win situation. The organization or manager wins by forcing them to do something they really don't want to do.

Communication Skills
Refer to CS Question 5.

APPLICATION SITUATIONS / / /

Motivation Theories   AS 7-2

Identify each supervisor's statement of how to motivate employees by the theory underlying the statement.

A. Expectancy   C. Needs hierarchy   E. Two-factor

B. Equity   D. Manifest needs   F. Reinforcement

_____ 6. "I know what is of value to my employees, and I offer rewards that will motivate them."

_____ 7. "We offer good working conditions and compensation, so I'm working at developing more teamwork."

_____ 8. "When an employee does something well, I thank him or her for a job well done."

_____ 9. "I used to try to improve working conditions to motivate employees. But I stopped and now focus on giving employees more responsibility so they can grow and develop new skills."

_____ 10. "I set clear objectives that are attainable. And I offer rewards that employees like when they achieve their objectives."

_____ 11. "I now realize that I tend to be an autocratic supervisor because it helps meet my needs. I will work at giving some of my employees more autonomy."

_____ 12. "I motivate employees by making their jobs interesting."

_____ 13. "I make sure I treat everyone fairly."

_____ 14. "I know Hector is a real people person, so I give him jobs in which he works with other employees."

_____ 15. "Betty would give me a dirty look because she knew it bothered me. So I decided to ignore it and she stopped."

WORK APPLICATION 7-6

What reinforcement type(s) and schedule(s) does/did your present/past supervisor use to motivate you? Explain each. How can you use reinforcement to motivate employees?

MOTIVATION TECHNIQUES

The previous sections discussed the major motivation theories. Now we examine specific on-the-job techniques to motivate employees: incentives and recognition—giving praise, MBO, job enrichment, and job design.

Incentives and Recognition

Incentive and Recognition Programs   As discussed with reinforcement theory, people do respond to incentives, and we can nearly always get them to do what we want them to do as long as we find the right levers (combination of types and schedules of reinforcement) to motivate the desired behavior. People respond to incentives, even though not necessarily in the expected way. If people don't do what we expect or want, you can certainly find some hidden incentives that explain why.[38]

Pay practices are an important incentive in attracting and retaining employees. Because managers know financial incentives do motivate employees to higher levels of performance, many organizations have formal incentive programs, such as pay-for-performance, bonuses, profit sharing, and stock options. Along with pay, companies provide good benefits, or perks to motive employees.[39]

Many organizations also have recognition programs, which tend to offer nonfinancial (not cash) rewards, such as banquets and employee of the year/month/week awards. Recognition programs can also include things like luncheons, plaques, gift certificates, mugs, t-shirts, and so on. Incentive and recognition programs are generally two separate programs. One great method of recognition that we all can use and that is not part of a formal program is giving praise—our next topic.

Learning Outcome 7-5

List the four steps in the model for giving praise.

Giving Praise   Recognition is a motivator,[40] as employees want full appreciation for work done. When was the last time your boss gave you a thank-you or some praise for a job well done? When was the last time your boss complained about your work? When was the last time you praised someone? What is the ratio of praise to criticism?

Giving praise develops a positive self-concept and leads to better performance through the Pygmalion effect. Praise is a motivator (not a hygiene) because it meets employees' needs for esteem/self-actualization, growth, and achievement. Praise is a complement that encourages desired behavior,[41] and it works better than criticism.[42] It is probably the most powerful, least expensive, simplest, and yet most underused motivational technique.

Ken Blanchard and **Spencer Johnson** popularized giving praise through their best-selling book, ***The One-Minute Manager***.[43] They developed a technique that involves giving one minute of praise. Model 7.1 is an adaptation. The steps in **giving praise** are as follows: *(1) tell the person exactly what was done correctly; (2) tell the person why the behavior is important; (3) stop for a moment of silence; and (4) encourage repeat performance.* Blanchard calls it one-minute praise because it should not take more than one minute to give the praise. It is not necessary for the employee to say anything. The four steps are illustrated below.

Step 1: Tell the person exactly what was done correctly. When giving praise, look the person in the eye to show sincerity. It is important to be very specific and descriptive. General statements like "You're a good worker" are not as effective.

SUPERVISOR: Julio, I just overheard you deal with that customer's complaint. You did an excellent job of keeping your cool; you were polite. That person came in angry and left happy.

MODEL 7.1 | Model for Giving Praise

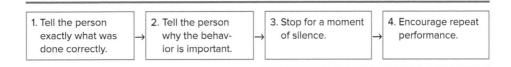

| 1. Tell the person exactly what was done correctly. | → | 2. Tell the person why the behavior is important. | → | 3. Stop for a moment of silence. | → | 4. Encourage repeat performance. |

Step 2: Tell the person why the behavior is important. Briefly state how the organization and/or person benefits from the action. It is also helpful to tell the employee how you feel about the behavior. Be specific and descriptive.

SUPERVISOR: Without customers we don't have a business. One customer bad-mouthing us can cause hundreds of dollars in lost sales. It really made me proud to see you handle that tough situation the way you did.

Step 3: Stop for a moment of silence. This is a tough one. The rationale for the silence is to give the person the chance to feel the impact of the praise. It's like "the pause that refreshes."

SUPERVISOR: (*Silently counts to five.*)

Step 4: Encourage repeat performance. This is the reinforcement that motivates the person to keep up performance. Blanchard recommends touching the person because it has a powerful impact. However, he recommends it only if both parties feel comfortable. Others say not to touch because it could lead to a sexual harassment charge.

SUPERVISOR: Thanks, Julio; keep up the good work (*while touching him on the shoulder or shaking hands*).

As you can see, giving praise is easy, and it doesn't cost a penny. Several managers trained to give praise say it works wonders. It's a much better motivator than giving a raise or other monetary reward. One manager stated that an employee was taking his time stacking cans on a display. He gave the employee praise for stacking the cans so straight. The employee was so pleased with the praise that the display went up with about a 100 percent increase in productivity. Notice that the manager looked for the positive and used positive reinforcement, rather than punishment. The manager could have made a comment such as, "Quit goofing off and get the display up faster." That statement would not have motivated the employee to increase productivity. All it would have done was hurt human relations, and it could have ended in an argument. Notice that in the above example the cans were straight. The employee was not praised for the slow work pace. However, if the praise had not worked, the manager should have used another reinforcement method.

/// **In the opening case,** Latoia should give him praise for coming in on time and increasing his performance to encourage him to continue this behavior. /// Praise is a reinforcement that is very effective when used with a variable interval schedule.

Thank-You Videos and Notes   In today's global business world, you may never see people you work with face-to-face, but you can video conference or Skype them. Praise can also be given as a written thank-you note (50 to 70 words is all it takes), especially when you can't give praise in person. You can follow the giving praise model steps 1 to 2 and 4, skipping the obvious silence. It can be an e-mail, but even today some people consider the handwritten thank-you note more personal and powerful. **Doug Conant,** CEO of **Campbell Soup,** sent out more than 30,000 handwritten notes to the company's 20,000 employees because he finds it to be a powerful way to motivate them through recognition.

Communication Skills
Refer to CS Question 6.

Skill-Building Exercise 7-2 develops this skill.

Objectives and MBO—Goal Setting Theory

Learning Outcome 7-6

List the criteria for setting objectives.

Goal setting is a great motivator. In fact, goal setting theory was rated number 1 in importance among 73 management theories.[44]

The **objectives** *state what is to be accomplished within a given period of time.* Objectives are end results; they do not state how the objective will be accomplished.[45] How to achieve the objective is the plan. In this section, you will learn the five criteria objectives should meet, how to write objectives, and how to use management by objectives (MBO).

Criteria for Setting Objectives   To motivate people to high levels of performance, objectives should be:

- *Difficult but achievable.* To have high levels of performance, you need to set high standards. **Sam Walton** (founder of **Walmart**) said, "High expectations are the key to everything." Individuals perform better when assigned difficult objectives, as opposed to being assigned easy ones, or having no goals, or simply being told to "do your best." **GE** employees develop "stretch goals."[46] However, if people do not believe that the objectives are achievable (expectancy theory), they will not be motivated to work for their accomplishment. Worse, when objectives are too difficult and incentives are high enough, many people will use unethical and illegal means to achieve the objectives, for example, **Wells Fargo**.

- *Observable and measurable.* You can't manage what you don't measure, so measure what matters.[47] If people are to achieve objectives, they must be able to observe and measure their progress regularly. Individuals perform better when their performance is measured and evaluated. Leaders need to be evaluated based on actual measures of results.[48] **Johnson & Johnson** gives bonuses based on revenue, profits, and other metrics including diversity.[49]

- *Specific, with a target date.* To be motivated, employees must know exactly what is expected of them[50] and when they are expected to have the task completed—a deadline. Deadlines help motivate us,[51] but tight deadlines can be stressful.[52] Some objectives do not require or lend themselves to target dates. For example, the objectives in the skill-building exercises do not list a target date.

- *Participatively set when possible.* With the increase use of teams,[53] people need to work together to set collective goals.[54] Managers should use the appropriate level of participation for the employees' capabilities ("Situational Supervision," Chapter 6).

- *Accepted.* For objectives to be met, employees must accept them by taking responsibility to achieve them.[55] Without acceptance, even meeting the above four criteria can lead to failure. Using participation helps get employees to accept objectives.

Some people use the *SMART goals* approach when setting objectives making sure they are Specific, Measurable, Achievable, Realistic, and Time-based.

APPLICATION SITUATIONS / / /

Objectives   AS 7-3

For each objective, state which criterion is *not* met.

A. Difficult but achievable   B. Observable and measurable   C. Specific, with a target date

_____ 16. To improve the company's reputation by December 31, 2020.

_____ 17. To write objectives within two weeks.

_____ 18. To pass this course this semester.

_____ 19. To increase production of iPads during the fiscal year 2020.

_____ 20. To increase GE total revenue by 40 percent during 2020.

Learning Outcome 7-7

Identify the four parts of the model for writing objectives.

Writing Objectives   Objectives should be written. To help write objectives that meet the five criteria above, use Max E. Douglas's model, shown in Model 7.2.

Management by Objectives (MBO)   **Management by objectives (MBO)** is *the process in which managers and their employees jointly set objectives for the employees, periodically evaluate the performance, and reward according to the results.* MBO was started by **Peter Drucker**.

Skill-Building Exercise 7-3
develops this skill.

MODEL 7.2 | Model for Writing Objectives

Objectives Model
To + Action verb + Specific, measurable, and singular result + Target date
Example Objectives for a Student:
To + receive + a B as my final grade in human relations + in December/May 20____.
To increase my cumulative grade point average to 3.0 by May 20____.
Example Objectives for a Manager:
To produce 1,000 units per day.
To keep absences to three or fewer per month.
To decrease accidents by 5 percent during 20____.

Example Objectives for an Organization:	
Apple	To build a driverless car by 2019.[56]
Telsa	To sell 500,000 vehicles by 2020.[57]
Unilever	To double the company size by 2020.[58]
AB InBev	To halve $100 billion in annual revenue by 2020.[59]

The three steps of an MBO program are as follows:

Step 1. Set Individual Objectives and Plans.   Each subordinate jointly sets objectives with the manager. The objectives are the heart of the MBO program and should meet the five criteria discussed earlier.

Step 2. Give Feedback and Evaluate Performance.   Employees must know how they are progressing toward their objectives. Thus, the manager and employee must meet frequently to review the latter's progress.

Step 3. Reward According to Performance.   Employees' performance should be measured against their objectives. Employees who meet their objectives should be rewarded through recognition, praise, pay raises, promotions, and so on. Those that don't meet personalized goals are not rewarded, or even punished.[60]

An MBO program is a motivator (not a hygiene) because it meets employees' needs for esteem/self-actualization, growth, and power/achievement. An MBO program empowers employees to increase responsibility with an opportunity for creating meaningful, challenging work to help them grow and accomplish what *they* and the manager want to accomplish.

In a union situation, such as the opening case, using an MBO program may not be possible without union consent and input.

Communication Skills
Refer to CS Question 8.

Job Enrichment and Design

Learning Outcome 7-8

State ways to enrich, design, and simplify jobs.

Work designs are a key way to motivate better job performance.[61] **Job enrichment** is *the process of building motivators into the job itself by making it more interesting and challenging.*
Here are some simple ways managers can enrich jobs:

- *Delegate more variety and responsibility.* Give employees challenging assignments that help them grow and develop new skills.

- *Form natural work groups.* The work group can also perform its own identifiable work with increased responsibility.[62]

- *Make employees responsible for their own identifiable work.* Let employees make the entire product rather than one part of it.

WORK APPLICATION 7-7

Describe how to enrich a present or past job of yours.

• *Give employees more autonomy.* Allow employees to plan, schedule, organize, and control their own jobs. Making employees responsible for checking their own work eliminates the need for checkers.

Job design is *the employee's system for transforming inputs into outputs.* The more effective and efficient the method, the more productive the employee.

A common approach to job design is work simplification. The idea behind work simplification is to work smarter, not harder. **Job simplification** is *the process of eliminating, combining, and/or changing the work sequence to increase performance.* To motivate employees, have them break the job down into steps and see if they can:

WORK APPLICATION 7-8

Describe how to simplify a present or past job of yours. Does an elimination, combination, or change in sequence help simplify the job?

• *Eliminate.* Does the task have to be done at all? If not, don't waste time doing it.

• *Combine.* Doing more than one thing at a time often saves time.

• *Change sequence.* Often a change in the order of doing things results in a lower total time.

WORK APPLICATION 7-9

Which motivation theory is the best? Explain why.

When used appropriately, work simplification can be effective at motivating employees. However, the danger lies in making a job too simple and boring rather than making it more interesting and challenging, as with job enrichment.

According to Herzberg, job enrichment and job design are motivators (not hygienes) because they meet employees' needs for esteem, self-actualization, growth, power, and achievement. Thus, job design and job enrichment are processes used to motivate employees.

/// **In the opening case,** in a union situation, job enrichment and/or job design may not be possible without union consent and input. Assuming Latoia can use these techniques, she and Hank could work together to transform Hank's present boring job into a challenging and interesting one. This is the most appropriate motivation technique to use with Hank because it directly addresses the boring job. If Hank finds his job interesting, he will most likely come to work on time and perform to expectation. ///

WORK APPLICATION 7-10

What is your motivation theory? What are the major methods, techniques, and so on you plan to use on the job as a manager to increase motivation and performance?

PUTTING THE MOTIVATION THEORIES TOGETHER

In this section, we put the theories together and discuss how to be self-motivated. Start by reviewing the major motivation theories in Exhibit 7.5. For a review of the four steps in the motivation process, see Exhibit 7.6.

Communication Skills
Refer to CS Question 9.

Self-Motivation

Intrapersonal Skills   Self-motivation is based on your intrapersonal skills (Chapters 1–3). Recall that you become what you think about, or what you think is what you get.[63] To be self-motivated, you need to have a positive attitude about yourself (self-concept) and your job. A starting place to self-motivation is knowing what you want (Content Motivation Theories) so that you can better understand what motivates you (Process Motivation Theories). When you know your own motivations, you make better decisions.[64] So you need to take responsibility for your self-motivation and happiness.

Career Success   Successful careers are usually based on two factors: knowing what you like to do and doing what you are good at. **GM CEO Mary Barra** says, "If you are doing something you are passionate about, you are just naturally going to succeed."[65] **Berkshire Hathaway CEO Warren Buffett** says, follow your passions and you will get noticed if you really go for it.[66] **Foot Locker CEO Ken Hicks** says, "Try your hardest."[67] It takes self-motivation to succeed, and organizations are recruiting self-starters.[68]

EXHIBIT 7.5 | Motivation Theories

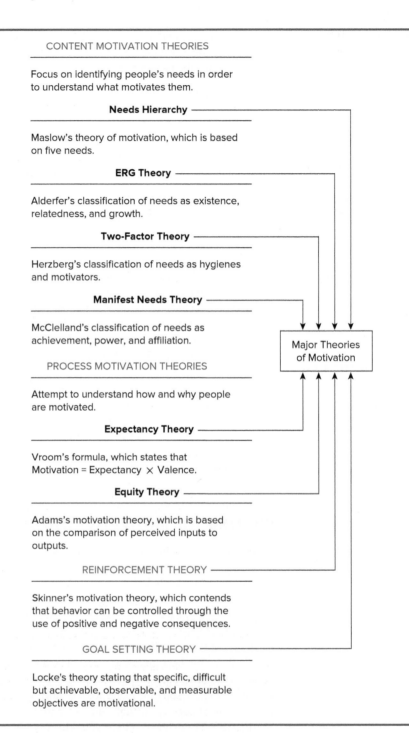

CONTENT MOTIVATION THEORIES

Focus on identifying people's needs in order to understand what motivates them.

Needs Hierarchy

Maslow's theory of motivation, which is based on five needs.

ERG Theory

Alderfer's classification of needs as existence, relatedness, and growth.

Two-Factor Theory

Herzberg's classification of needs as hygienes and motivators.

Manifest Needs Theory

McClelland's classification of needs as achievement, power, and affiliation.

PROCESS MOTIVATION THEORIES

Attempt to understand how and why people are motivated.

Expectancy Theory

Vroom's formula, which states that Motivation = Expectancy × Valence.

Equity Theory

Adams's motivation theory, which is based on the comparison of perceived inputs to outputs.

REINFORCEMENT THEORY

Skinner's motivation theory, which contends that behavior can be controlled through the use of positive and negative consequences.

GOAL SETTING THEORY

Locke's theory stating that specific, difficult but achievable, observable, and measurable objectives are motivational.

Major Theories of Motivation

The Self-Motivation Model

As stated, a starting place to self-motivation is knowing what you want. But that's not enough. You need to set objectives to get what you want and then develop plans to accomplish the objectives. Below is a four-step model to follow to motivate yourself, followed by some other advice if you are not motivated and feel bored or trapped on the job.

Set Objectives   What do you want? To be motivated, develop objectives using Model 7.2 to be sure to meet the criteria with high expectations for yourself. Intelligence is overrated; the drive to win and persistence are better predictors of success.[69]

EXHIBIT 7.6 | The Motivation Process

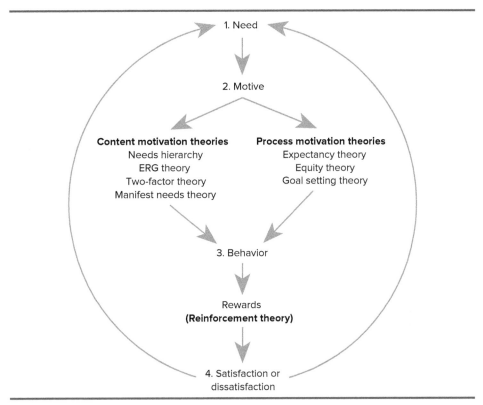

Notice that the motivation process is circular, or ongoing, because meeting needs is a never-ending process.

Develop Plans—Willpower Alone Fails   Why do so many people make New Year's resolutions and fail to keep them? It's because willpower, or self-discipline, alone without a plan doesn't work. Be specific. What exactly are you going to do step-by-step to accomplish your objective? You may need to develop new habits, as happiness is about behavior change.[70] Do you need to improve your skills and qualifications, such as getting a college degree and passing a certification exam, to meet your objective?

Measure Results   Get feedback to know how you are progressing toward your objective. Compare your actual performance to your objective. For longer-term objectives, check regularly, not only at the end. How are you progressing? Are you there yet?

Reinforce Results   Be sure to use *reinforcement theory* on yourself. If you are missing the objective, consider punishing yourself; for example, if your weight is up, eat less next time. If you are on track, reward yourself in some way (have a special dessert). Recall that developing new habits includes rewards.

Remember, what you think about is how you feel and what you feel is how you behave. So develop a self-motivation objective and then plan, measure, and reinforce and think about it, and visualize yourself accomplishing the objective. Model 7.3 reviews the steps of self-motivation.

MODEL 7.3 | Self-Motivation Model

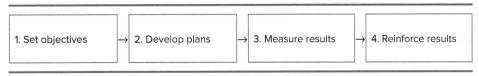

Communication Skills
Refer to CS Question 10.

WORK APPLICATION 7-11

Using Model 7.3, set an objective and develop a plan to achieve it to motivate yourself.

Learning Outcome 7-9

Explain possible limitations of using motivation theories outside North America.

Bored or Feeling Trapped on the Job?   If you are in these situations, you can keep things the same, or you can take responsibility and change it with two major alternatives. One, you can look for another job (within or leaving the firm) following the four steps of the self-motivation model, which may require developing new skills, more education, or getting some type of certification. Two, you can think about how your job can be enriched or change the design. With ideas in mind, talk to your boss about implementing ways to improve your job satisfaction.

DO MOTIVATION THEORIES APPLY GLOBALLY?

As discussed, managers need to adequately motivate employees, and the trend is toward increased globalization and technological advances; therefore, you have to know how to motivate people who speak different languages and who have different cultural contexts.[71] The motivation theories you have learned were developed in North America and may present cultural limitations in the global village.

Cross-Cultural Differences in Motivation

Let's discuss how the specific motivation theories differ across cultures.

Hierarchy of Needs, ERG, and Two-Factor Theory   Cultural differences suggest that the order of hierarchy may vary across cultures. In risk-averse countries such as Japan, Greece, and Mexico, security needs would be at the top of the needs hierarchy. In countries such as Denmark, Sweden, Norway, the Netherlands, and Finland, which prefer quality of life (relationships) over quantity of life (possessions), social needs would be at the top. As related to two-factor theory, the intrinsic motivation of higher-level needs can be more relevant to wealthy societies than to poor societies.

Manifest Needs Theory   Cultures also differ in the extent to which they value need for achievement. The concern for high performance is common in high quantity-of-life countries, including the United States, Canada, and Great Britain; it is almost absent in high quality-of-life countries, including Chile and Portugal.

One major cultural difference is in the focus on individualistic versus group approaches to business. Individualistic societies (the United States, Canada, Great Britain, Australia) tend to value self-accomplishment. Collective societies (Japan, Mexico, Singapore, Pakistan) tend to value group accomplishment and loyalty. Individual versus group incentives tend to vary by country.

Equity Theory   Equity theory as it relates to fairness tends to be a value upheld in most cultures. However, equity can call for higher producers to be paid more. This tends to be more of a motivator in individualistic countries than it is in collective countries, where people tend to prefer equality and all are paid the same regardless of output. On the other hand, U.S. unions, including teachers, also tend to prefer equal pay to merit pay.

Expectancy Theory   Expectancy theory holds up fairly well cross-culturally because it is flexible. It allows for the possibility that there may be differences in expectations and valences across cultures. For example, societal acceptance may be of higher value than individual recognition in collective societies. So managers in different countries can offer rewards that are of value to their employees.

Reinforcement Theory   Reinforcement theory also holds up well cross-culturally. People everywhere tend to use behavior that is reinforced. We all can be told or can figure out what behavior is rewarded and use the behavior to our benefit. Management everywhere tends to set up rules and penalties for breaking them. However, how well the punishment fits the offense can vary. In the United States it is much easier to fire employees than it is in Europe.

Goal Setting   Motivational goal setting relies on a need for achievement and high levels of performance, and it is based on quantity-of-life issues. Thus, the United States sets challenging objectives and achieves them. However, goal setting is less motivational to cultures in which achievement is not important and quality of life is important, such as Portugal and Chile.

Complete Self-Assessment Exercise 7-3 to determine how your personality affects your motivation.

/ / / **Self-Assessment Exercise 7-3** / / /

Your Personality and Motivation

If you have a high *surgency* personality, you most likely have a high need for power. You are probably realistic in your expectations, tend to know what you want and set reasonable objectives, and work to achieve your objectives. You may be concerned about being treated equitably but not too concerned if others are. You may like positive reinforcement for yourself, but you have no problem using punishment to get what you want. You like praise but may not give much praise to others. You tend to like jobs in which you are in control of what you do and how you do it.

If you have a high *agreeableness* personality, you most likely have a high need for affiliation. Your expectations are most likely related more to relationships than to setting task objectives and working to achieve them. You may be concerned about your being treated equitably, and you tend to help others get equal treatment. You may like positive reinforcement for yourself, but you may need to be careful not to use extinction (do nothing and the problem will solve itself) if you are not being treated fairly—be assertive. You need acceptance and like praise, and you tend to give both to others. You tend to like jobs in which you work with others.

If you have a high *conscientiousness* personality, you most likely have a high need for achievement. You are most likely realistic in your expectations, tend to know what you want and set reasonable objectives, and work to achieve your objectives. You may be concerned about being treated equitably but are not too concerned if others are. You like positive reinforcement of your accomplishments and tend to avoid punishment. You like praise but may not give much praise to others. You tend

to like jobs in which you can measure your accomplishments and succeed.

The *adjustment* personality dimension is not a need in the manifest needs motivation theory. However, it clearly affects behavior in a positive or negative way. If you are low in adjustment, you most likely have unrealistic expectations, don't really know what you want, and don't set goals and work to achieve them. You are probably being treated fairly, but you perceive that you are not being treated equitably. You probably get more punishment than rewards. You may not like your job, but changing jobs may not make you happy or more adjusted. A new job will not change your personality; you need to change.

The *openness to experience* personality dimension is not a need in the manifest needs motivation theory. However, it clearly affects behavior in a positive or negative way. If you are open to experience, you are more of a risk taker and tend to set more challenging, realistic objectives than people who are closed to new experiences.

Action plan: Based on your personality, what specific things will you do to improve how you motivate yourself and others?

_____

_____

_____

_____

As we bring this chapter to a close, we discussed the motivation process and the importance of motivation and how it affects behavior, human relations, and performance. You should know four content motivation theories (needs hierarchy, ERG, two-factor, and manifest needs) and how organizations meet employee needs, and two process motivation theories (expectancy and equity) and how to motivate others and yourself through these six theories. We also covered reinforcement theory and how to motivate using types (positive, avoidance, extinction, and punishment) and schedules (continuous and intermittent) of reinforcement. You learned about incentive and recognition programs, job enrichment and job design, how the motivation theories fit together, and cross-cultural differences in motivation. More important, you should have the skill to give recognition or praise, to write objectives meeting four criteria, and how to motivate yourself using these three 4-step models.

The chapter review is organized to help you master the 10 learning outcomes for Chapter 7. First provide your own response to each learning outcome, and then check the summary provided to see how well you understand the material. Next, identify the final statement in each section as either true or false (T/F). Correct each false statement. Answers are given at the end of the chapter.

LO 7-1   Explain the motivation process and the three factors affecting performance.

The motivation process steps are: need → motive → behavior → satisfaction or dissatisfaction. The three factors affecting performance are Ability × Motivation × Resources.

Motivation is the most important factor in the performance formula. T F

LO 7-2   Describe four content motivation theories.

Content motivation theories focus on identifying people's needs in order to understand what motivates them. *Needs hierarchy* is Maslow's theory of motivation based on five categories of needs. Alderfer's *ERG theory* classifies existence, relatedness, and growth needs. The *two-factor theory* is Herzberg's classification of needs as hygienes and motivators. The *manifest needs theory* of motivation is primarily McClelland's classification of needs as achievement, power, and affiliation.

Motivating factors are primarily extrinsic factors. T F

LO 7-3   Describe two process motivation theories.

Process motivation theories attempt to explain how and why people are motivated. *Expectancy theory* is Vroom's formula, which states that Motivation = Expectancy × Valence. *Equity theory* is primarily Adams's motivation theory, which is based on the comparison of perceived inputs to outputs.

Valence refers to one's need for perceived inputs to match outputs. T F

LO 7-4   State how reinforcement is used to increase performance.

Reinforcement theory is primarily Skinner's motivation theory, which contends that behavior can be controlled through the use of positive or negative consequences. Through the use of four types of reinforcement—positive, avoidance, extinction, and punishment—and two schedules of reinforcement—continuous and intermittent—employees can learn which behavior is and is not appropriate. Appropriate behavior that is productive is encouraged, while nonproductive behavior is discouraged.

The two variables of intermittent reinforcement are passage of time (fixed or variable interval) and output (fixed or variable ratio), resulting in four alternative schedules. T F

LO 7-5   List the four steps in the model for giving praise.

The four steps for giving praise are: (1) tell the person exactly what was done correctly; (2) tell the person why the behavior is important; (3) stop for a moment of silence; and (4) encourage repeat performance.

Praise works best when it is not used very often. T F

LO 7-6   List the criteria for setting objectives.

In setting objectives, they should be: difficult but achievable; observable and measurable; specific, with a target date; participatively set when possible; and accepted.

Letting employees set their own objectives generally leads to their acceptance and achievement. T F

LO 7-7   Identify the four parts of the model for writing objectives.

The formula for writing objectives is as follows: To + Action verb + Specific, measurable, and singular behavior + Target date.

"To make a profit this year" is a well-written objective. T F

LO 7-8   State ways to enrich, design, and simplify jobs.

Job enrichment is the process of building motivators into the job itself by making it more interesting and challenging. *Job design* is the employee's system for transforming inputs into outputs. *Job simplification* is the process of eliminating, combining, and/or changing the work sequence to increase performance.

The objective of all three methods is the same—to make the job more interesting and challenging and to motivate employees to higher levels of performance. T F

LO 7-9   Explain possible limitations of using motivation theories outside North America.

People of different cultures have different needs and values. What works well in one country may not be effective in a different one.

Hierarchy of needs, ERG, two-factor, and manifest needs theories don't tend to work well across cultures, but equity, expectancy, reinforcement, and goal setting theories do. T F

LO 7-10   Define the following 16 key terms.

Select one or more methods: (1) fill in the missing key terms for each definition given below from memory; (2) match the key terms from the end of the review with their definitions below; and/or (3) copy the key terms in order from the key terms at the beginning of the chapter.

_____ is the internal process leading to behavior to satisfy needs.

The _____ is: Performance = Ability × Motivation × Resources.

_____ focus on identifying people's needs in order to understand what motivates them.

_____ is Maslow's theory of motivation, which is based on five needs.

_____ is Herzberg's classification of needs as hygienes and motivators.

The _____ of motivation is primarily McClelland's classification of needs as achievement, power, and affiliation.

_____ attempt to understand how and why people are motivated.

_____ is Vroom's formula, which states that Motivation = Expectancy × Valence.

_____ is primarily Adams's motivation theory, which is based on the comparison of perceived inputs and outputs.

_____ is primarily Skinner's motivation theory: Behavior can be controlled through the use of positive or negative consequences.

The steps in _____ are as follows: (1) tell the person exactly what was done correctly; (2) tell the person why the behavior is important; (3) stop for a moment of silence; and (4) encourage repeat performance.

_____ state what is to be accomplished within a given period of time.

_____ is the process by which managers and their employees jointly set objectives for the employees, periodically evaluate the performance, and reward according to results.

_____ is the process of building motivators into the job itself by making it more interesting and challenging.

_____ is the employee's system for transforming inputs into outputs.

_____ is the process of eliminating, combining, and/or changing the work sequence to increase performance.

/ / / KEY TERMS / / /

content motivation
  theories   220
equity theory   227
expectancy theory   226
giving praise   231

job design   235
job enrichment   234
job simplification   235
management by objectives
  (MBO)   233

manifest needs
  theory   224
motivation   219
needs hierarchy   220
objectives   232

performance formula   219
process motivation
  theories   226
reinforcement theory   228
two-factor theory   222

/ / / COMMUNICATION SKILLS / / /

The following critical thinking questions can be used for class discussion and/or as written assignments to develop communication skills. Be sure to give complete explanations for all questions.

1. Some people have stated that the performance formula is oversimplified. Do you agree? Can it really be used to increase performance?

2. Give examples of how all five of your needs in Maslow's hierarchy of needs have been or are being met.

3. Herzberg says that pay is a hygiene factor, whereas others say it is a motivator. What do you say?

4. Which do you believe are more useful in motivating employees: content or process motivation theories?

5. Some people say that reinforcement theory is a means of manipulating employees to do what the company wants them to do. Do you agree? Is the use of reinforcement theory ethical?

6. Does giving praise really motivate employees, or do they view it as a means of getting them to do more work?

7. Some managers say that what gets measured gets done. Do you agree? What does this have to do with setting objectives?

8. What are the advantages and disadvantages of an MBO program?

9. Which of the motivational theories do you prefer? Why?

10. Will you actually use Model 7.3 to motivate yourself?

CASE   / / /   Kevin Plank: Founder, CEO, and Chair of Under Armour

It is often said that necessity is the mother of invention. In 1995 Kevin Plank, then special team's captain of University of Maryland football had an idea born of a problem every athlete could relate to but could do nothing about; that is, until Kevin Plank decided to do something about it. Tired of repeatedly changing the cotton T-shirt under his jersey as it became wet and heavy during practice or a game, Kevin set out to design a different type of shirt that would remain drier and lighter, a shirt that worked with your body to regulate temperature and enhance performance. Working from his grandmother's townhouse in Washington, D.C., Kevin produced and sold his revolutionary new product out of the trunk of his car. He named his company Under Armour (UA) and built it into a leading developer, marketer, and distributor of performance apparel, footwear, and accessories. The brand's innovative products are sold worldwide today.

Under Armour's mission is to make all athletes better through passion, design, and the relentless pursuit of innovation. Since 1996, Mr. Plank has served as UA's Chief Executive Officer and Chairman of the Board of Directors. Not bad for someone who came in as a walk-on for his university's football team and went on to become a special team's captain. More than two decades later, UA is a multi-billion-dollar global brand. UA still sells those shirts it started with, but it has expanded into many corners of the athletic/casual wear market, from compression shorts to sports bras, innovative mouth guards, and basketball shoes.

In a 2003 *Inc* article, titled "How I Did It," Kevin Plank provides a glimpse into his early motivations to pursue a career in entrepreneurship. Unlike many college football players, Plank never considered football his only option. He always wanted to be in business. Even though Nike was a giant in the sports apparel industry, Plank never thought he could not make it. He relays a childhood story that led him to believe in his entrepreneurial instincts. Plank describes himself as a "hustler," not in the literal sense but as an aggressive entrepreneur. When he was 14 or 15, he and his brother (Scott) returned from Guatemala with a bunch of knitted bracelets such as those you will see at Grateful Dead concerts. Scott presented a business proposition to Kevin and his other brother, Colin. "Listen, there's a Dead show coming to town. We'll go down and sell these bracelets and make a lot of money."

They took him on his offer. After just three hours of running around selling the bracelets, the brothers got back together to discuss their progress. According to Kevin, his brother Colin said, "I sold the first two. Then I started feeling guilty about how much money I was charging, so I gave the rest away." His brother Scott said, "I made about 70 bucks." Kevin then said, "I have about 580 bucks in my pocket. And I need more bracelets." Right there Kevin knew he was good at business. It seems self-motivation has been a big part of Mr. Plank's success. He has always been motivated to achieve whatever he sets his mind to achieve.

Not everyone believed Kevin Plank could translate his ideas into a real-life business. Plank recalls one of his strength coaches telling him to "stop worrying about all this other [business] crap and just commit yourself to playing football." However, Plank said he knew he could never stop. He envisioned himself running his own business and making important decisions long before he actually launched Under Armour. As he put it, "I remember thinking how much fun it would be just to sit at a desk and think, all right, how are we going to make a buck?"[i] His confidence in himself paid off. Today as CEO and Chairman of the Board at UA, Mr. Plank tries to model his work ethic and motivations for his employees. He understands the importance of motivation as a key factor in influencing follower behaviors. Plank abides by what he calls the "four pillars of greatness": "Build a great product." "Tell a great story." "Service the business." "Build a great team." He employed time-tested concepts such as positive reinforcement, management by objectives, and job enrichment to fulfill these promises.

In its recent financial reporting, UA announced financial results for the first quarter ended March 31, 2017. Plank characterized the results as in line with expectations and indication that the company was off to a solid start in 2017.

Despite this positive outlook, many analysts believe that UA is showing some competitive weakness. During the past year, the company's stock has gone from a 52-week high of $44.86 to a low of $18.40 and currently (as of 05/16/17) trading at $19.52. At the end of 2016, Kevin Plank acknowledged that numerous challenges and disruptions in the North American retail sector had tempered the company's fourth quarter results. He projected the company's 2017 full-year revenues to increase 11 to 12 percent to nearly $5.4 billion. Everyone is looking to Mr. Plank to lead the company out of what has been a difficult and challenging period. His leadership of UA is under scrutiny, and many are watching to see how he comes out.

In every public presentation that Mr. Plank makes, he emphasizes three things: "Passion," "Vision," and "People," as his set of principles for success in the way he leads UA. On people, Plank says he wants to have the best type of people "—team, team, team. I can't underscore that need [enough]."[ii] The relationship between Mr. Plank and his employees is based on friendship and respect for each other. He has encouraged a very informal culture at UA but also very results-oriented. At UA, the prevailing mantra is "get-it-done." If you need to get something done, any obstacles that are in the way, you find a way to get it done. There is an expectation that you are going to figure it out somehow. There is support for employee creativity and risk-taking. At UA, employees—the majority of whom are around 30 years old—are called "teammates."

Go to the Internet: To learn more about Kevin Plank and Under Armour, visit the company's website at www.underarmour.com. You can also watch a 20-minute talk he gave about entrepreneurship at the University of Maryland at www.youtube.com/watch?v=C8zI1mcmEkM.

Support your answers to the following questions with specific information from the case and text or with information you get from the web or another source.

1. According to Herzberg's two-factor theory of motivation, was Plank's motivation to create a new category of performance apparel driven by extrinsic (hygiene) factors or intrinsic (motivator) factors?

2. According to McClelland's manifest theory of motivation, people are motivated by the needs for achievement, power, and affiliation. Which of these needs would you attribute to Plank? If you were to rank them in order of significance to Plank, which will be first, second, and third?

3. What's the evidence in the case that job enrichment is a key part of the way work is done at Under Armour?

4. Watch Kevin Plank give the keynote speech at the 2010 Cupid's Cup for the Robert H. Smith School of Business at the University of Maryland (https://www.youtube.com/watch?v=C8zI1mcmEkM). From the video, what are some of his motivational team themes that he lists?

Cumulative Questions

5. Chapter 6 distinguished between transformational, charismatic, and transactional leadership theories; which one of these best describes Kevin Plank?

6. Based on the discussion in Chapter 5 on passive, aggressive, and assertive behavior, what type of behavior do you think Kevin Plank has shown in the case narrative on him?

7. The Big Five Model of Personality (Chapter 2) categorizes traits into the dimensions of surgency, agreeableness, adjustment, conscientiousness, and open to experience. Which of these dimensions can you attribute to Kevin Plank?

Case Exercise and Role-Play

Preparation: Under Armour went from $17,000 in revenue in 1996 to $110,000 in 1997 to $400,000 to $1.3 million to $5 million to $20 million, $50 million and up, and this last quarter to more than a $5 billion in sales. It is one of those only-in-America stories that went from one employee to more than 2,700 today. According to the case, one of Kevin Plank's "four pillars of greatness" is to tell a great story.

In-Class Groups: According to the discussion on giving praise in the text, giving recognition to employees motivates them. Divide the class into groups of four or five students. Each group should select a leader to play the role of Kevin Plank and the rest of the group members are employees. Given how far the company has come, Plank wants to give a rousing motivational speech to his employees. He has a vision for the company to become number one in its industry in five years—its 20th anniversary.

Role-Play: Using the different motivational theories presented in the chapter, each group should craft a three-minute speech that will be presented to the class by the group's leader. As Plank puts it, "tell a great story." The instructor or the class as a whole will decide who made the most compelling speech.

OBJECTIVE CASE   / / /   Friedman's Motivation Technique

The following conversation took place between Art Friedman and Bob Lussier. In 1970, Art Friedman implemented a new business technique. At that time the business was called Friedman's Appliances. It employed 15 workers in Oakland, California. Friedman's is an actual business that uses the technique you will read about.

BOB: What is the reason for your success in business?

ART: My business technique.

BOB: What is it? How did you implement it?

ART: I called my 15 employees together and told them, "From now on I want you to feel as though the company is ours, not mine. We are all bosses. From now on you decide what you're worth and tell the accountant to put it in your pay envelope. You decide which days and hours you work and when to take time off. We will have an open petty cash system that will allow anyone to go into the box and borrow money when they need it."

BOB: You're kidding, right?

ART: No, it's true. I really do these things.

BOB: Did anyone ask for a raise?

ART: Yes, several people did. Charlie asked for and received a $100-a-week raise.

BOB: Did he and the others increase their productivity to earn their raises?

ART: Yes, they all did.

BOB: How could you run an appliance store with employees coming and going as they pleased?

ART: The employees made up schedules that were satisfactory to everyone. We had no problems of under- or overstaffing.

BOB: Did anyone steal from the petty cash box?

ART: No.

BOB: Would this technique work in any business?

ART: It did work, it still works, and it will always work for me!

In 1976, Art Friedman changed his business to Friedman's Microwave Ovens. He developed a franchise operation to use his motivation technique of making everyone a boss.

Today, the business is called Friedman's Appliances, and for more information visit its website (friedmansappliance.com).

Answer the following questions. Then in the space between questions, state why you selected that answer.

_____   1. Art's business technique increased performance.

        a. true   *b.* false

_____   2. Art focused on the _____ factor in the performance formula.

        a. ability   *b.* motivation   *c.* resources

_____   3. Art's employees seem to be on the _____ needs level.

        a. physiological   *c.* social   *e.* self-actualization

        b. safety   *d.* esteem

_____   4. Art's technique has less emphasis on meeting _____ needs.

        a. achievement   *b.* power   *c.* affiliation

_____ 5. Frederick Herzberg would say Art is using:

    a. hygienes   *b.* motivators

_____ 6. Victor Vroom would say that Art uses expectancy motivation theory.

    a. true   *b.* false

_____ 7. J. Stacy Adams would say Art:

    a. has equitable rewards   *b.* underrewards   *c.* overrewards

_____ 8. Art uses _____ reinforcement.

    a. positive   *c.* extinction

    b. avoidance   *d.* punishment

_____ 9. Art's technique is most closely associated with:

    a. giving praise   *c.* job enrichment

    b. MBO   *d.* job design

_____ 10. Art's technique focuses most on:

    a. delegating variety   *c.* making work identifiable

    b. forming natural work groups   *d.* giving autonomy

11. Do you know of any organizations that use any of Art's or other unusual techniques? If yes, what is the organization's name? What does it do?

12. Could Art's technique work in all organizations? Explain your answer.

13. In a position of authority, would you use Art's technique? Explain your answer.

What Do You Want from a Job?

Experience: Individual may share answers in groups or entire class, in class or online

AACSB Competencies: Reflective thinking and application of knowledge.

Objectives: To help you better understand how job factors affect motivation. To help you realize that people are motivated by different factors. What motivates you may turn off someone else.

Preparation: You should have completed Self-Assessment Exercise 7-1.

Experience: You will discuss the importance of job factors.

Procedure 1 (8-20 minutes)

Break into groups of five or six, and discuss job factors selected by group members in Self-Assessment Exercise 7-1. Come to a consensus on the three factors that are most important to the group. They can be either motivators or hygienes. If the group mentions other job factors not listed, such as pay, you may add them.

Procedure 2 (3-6 minutes)

A representative from each group goes to the board and writes his or her group's three most important job factors.

Conclusion: The instructor leads a class discussion and/or makes concluding remarks.

Application (2-4 minutes):   What did I learn from this experience? How will I use this knowledge in the future?

Sharing: Volunteers give their answers to the application section.

/ / / SKILL-BUILDING EXERCISE 7-2 / / /

Giving Praise

Experience: Group in-class exercise, may be used in personal and professional life to develop this skill.

AACSB Competencies: Communication abilities and application of knowledge.

Objective: To develop your skill at giving praise.

BMV 7-1

Preparation:

Think of a job situation in which you did something well, deserving of praise and recognition. You may have saved the company some money, you may have turned a dissatisfied customer into a happy one, and so on. If you have never worked or done something well, interview someone who has. Put yourself in a supervisory position and write out the praise you would give to an employee for doing what you did.

Briefly describe the situation:

Step 1. Tell the employee exactly what was done correctly.

Step 2. Tell the employee why the behavior is important.

Step 3. Stop for a moment of silence. (Count to five silently.)

Step 4. Encourage repeat performance.

Procedure (12-17 minutes)

Break into groups of five or six. One at a time, give the praise.

1. Explain the situation.
2. Select a group member to receive the praise.
3. Give the praise. (Talk; don't read it off the paper.) Try to select the position you would use if you were actually giving the praise on the job (for example, both standing, both sitting).
4. Integration. The group gives the giver of praise feedback on how he or she did:

   • Step 1. Was the praise very specific and descriptive? Did the giver look the employee in the eye?
   • Step 2. Was the importance of the behavior clearly stated?

- Step 3. Did the giver stop for a moment of silence?
- Step 4. Did the giver encourage repeat performance? Did the giver of praise touch the receiver [optional]?
- Did the praise take less than one minute? Was the praise sincere?

Conclusion: The instructor leads a class discussion and/or makes concluding remarks.

Application (2-4 minutes):   What did I learn from this experience? How will I use this knowledge in the future?

Sharing: Volunteers give their answers to the application section.

/ / / SKILL-BUILDING EXERCISE 7-3 / / /

Setting Objectives

Experience: Individual may share answers in groups or entire class, in class or online.

AACSB Competencies: Analytic skills and application of knowledge.

Objective: To gain skill at setting objectives.

Preparation: Written nine objectives in preparation for this exercise.

In Chapter 1, you were asked to write five course objectives. Rewrite the five objectives, or new ones, using the Douglas model below:

To + Action verb + Specific, measurable, and singular result + Target date

1.
2.
3.
4.
5.

Also write two personal objectives and two career objectives using Douglas's model:

Personal

1.
2.

Career

1.
2.

Procedure (2-12 minutes)

Break into groups of five or six people and share your objectives. One person states one objective and the others give input to be sure it meets the criteria of effective objectives. A second person states one objective, followed by feedback. Continue until all group members have stated all their objectives or the time runs out.

Conclusion: The instructor may lead a discussion and/or make concluding remarks.

Application (2-4 minutes):   What did I learn from this experience? How will I use this knowledge in the future?

Sharing: Volunteers give their answers to the application section.

Developing New Habits

Experience: Individual may share habits in groups or entire class, in class or online.

AACSB Competencies: Analytic and application of knowledge.

Objective: To develop and share new habits.

Preparation: Select one or more topics from this chapter that will help you improve your human relations. Develop a new habit following the guideline from Chapter 1, section Habits and Skill-Building Exercise 1-4, on how to develop your cure, routine, and reward-change.

Procedure (5-30 minutes)

Follow the procedures from Skill Builder 1-4.

1. F. They are all important because if any of the factors are missing, performance will be lower.
2. F. Motivating factors are primarily "intrinsic" factors.
3. F. Valence refers to the value a person places on the outcome or reward in expectancy theory, not equity theory.
4. T.
5. F. We should praise good behavior often.
6. T.
7. F. Because it is not specific, it is not a well-written objective. How much profit? Also, stating the month and year, rather than simply "this year," would provide a better target date.
8. T.
9. T.

1. B.M. Galvin, D. Lange, and B.E. Ashforth, "Narcissistic Organizational Identification: Seeing Oneself as Central to the Orgnization's Identity," *Academy of Management Review* 40(2) (2015): 163-181.
2. P. Wahba, "She Thanks You for Not Smoking," *Fortune* (September 15, 2015): 125-130.
3. R. Fehr, K.C. Yam, and C. Dang, "Moralized Leadership: The Construction and Consequences of Ethical Leader Perceptions," *Academy of Management Review* 40(2) (2015): 182-209.
4. R.C. Liden, S.J. Wayne, C. Liao, and J.D. Meuser, "Servant Leadership and Serving Culture: Influence on Individual and Unit Performance," *Academy of Management Journal* 57(5) (2014): 1434-1452.
5. M.R. Barrick, G.R. Thurgood, T.A. Smith, and S.H. Courtright, "Collective Organizational Engagement: Linking Motivational Antecedents, Strategic Implementation, and Firm Performance," *Academy of Management Journal* 58(1) (2015): 111-135.
6. N. Li, B.L. Kirkman, and C.O.L.H. Porter, "Toward a Model of Work Team Altruism," *Academy of Management Review* 39(4) (2014): 541-565.
7. R. King, "Companies Want to Know: How Do Workers Feel?" *The Wall Street Journal* (October 14, 2015): R3.

8. A.C. Peng, J.M. Schaubroeck, and L. Li, "Social Exchange Implications of Own and Coworkers' Experiences of Supervisor Abuse," *Academy of Management Journal* 57(5) (2014): 1385–1405.

9. C.K. Lam, X. Huang, and S.C.H. Chan, "The Treshold Effect of Participative Leadership and the Role of Leader Information Sharing," *Academy of Management Journal* 58(3) (2015): 836–855.

10. Reviewer suggestion, added May 24, 2017.

11. K. Rockwood, "Tracking the Mood of Your Employees," *INC.* (January 2016): 106–107.

12. J. Hu and R.C. Liden, "Making a Difference in the Teamwork: Linking Team Prosocial Motivation to Team Processes and Effectiveness," *Academy of Management Journal* 58(3) (2015): 836–855.

13. F.K. Matta, B.A. Scott, J. Koopman, and D.E. Conlon, "Does Seeing Eye to Eye Affect Work Engagement and Organizational Citizenship Behavior? A Role Theory Perspective on LMX Agreements," *Academy of Management Journal* 58(6) (2015): 1686–1708.

14. E. Bernstein, "You Can Do IT! Be a Motivator" *The Wall Street Journal* (June 16, 2016): D1, D3.

15. B. O'Keefe, "Robbins' Rules: How to Give a Presentation," *Fortune* (November 17, 2014): 131.

16. R.C. Liden, S.J. Wayne, C. Liao, and J.D. Meuser, "Servant Leadership and Serving Culture: Influence on Individual and Unit Performance," *Academy of Management Journal* 57(5) (2014): 1434–1452.

17. A. Maslow, "A Theory of Human Motivation," *Psychological Review 50*(1943): 370–396; A. Maslow, *Motivation and Personality* (New York: Harper & Row, 1954).

18. F. Herzberg, "One More Time: How Do You Motivate Employees?"*Harvard Business Review* (January–February 1968): 53–62.

19. D. McClelland, *The Achieving Society* (New York: Van Nostrand Reinhold, 1961); and D. McClelland and D.H. Burnham, "Power Is the Great Motivator," *Harvard Business Review* (March–April 1978): 103.

20. Ad, "Company Spotlight: Acuity," *Fortune* (March 15, 2016): no page number.

21. V. Vroom, *Work and Motivation* (New York: Wiley, 1964).

22. S.J. Creary, B.B. Caza, and L.M. Roberts, "Out of the Box? How Managing a Subordinate's Multiple Identities Affects the Quality of a Manager-Subordinate Relationship," *Academy of Management Review* 40(4) (2015): 538–562.

23. S. Adams, "Toward an Understanding of Inequity," *Journal of Abnormal and Social Psychology 67*(4) (1963): 422–436.

24. B.A. Scott, A.S. Garza, D.E. Conlong and Y.J. Kim, "Why Do Managers Act Fairly in the First Place? A Daily Investigation of Hot and Cold Motives and Discretion," *Academy of Management Journal* 57(6) (2014): 1571–1591.

25. R. Fehr, K.C. Yam, and C. Dang, "Moralized Leadership: The Construction and Consequences of Ethical Leader Perceptions," *Academy of Management Review* 40(2) (2015): 182–209.

26. D.T. Kong, K.T. Dirks, and D.L. Ferrin, "Interpersonal Trust Within Negotiations: Mata-Analytic Evidence, Critical Contingencies, and Directions for Future Research," *Academy of Management Journal* 57(5) (2014): 1235–1255.

27. A.C. Peng, J.M. Schaubroeck, and L. Li, "Social Exchange Implications of Own and Coworkers' Experiences of Supervisor Abuse," *Academy of Management Journal* 57(5) (2014): 1385–1405.

28. News, National Public Radio (NPR), aired November 18, 2015.

29. Y. Zhang, D.A. Waldman, U.L. Han, and X.B. Li, "Paradoxical Leaders Behaviors in People Management: Antecedents and Consequences," *Academy of Management Journal* 58(2) (2015): 538–566.

30. B.F. Skinner, *Beyond Freedom and Dignity* (New York: Knopf, 1971).

31. E.L. Weber, "Nowhere to Hide for Dead Wood Workers," *The Wall Street Journal* (August 22, 2017): A1, A10.

32. S.J. Creary, B.B. Caza, and L.M. Roberts, "Out of the Box? How Managing a Subordinate's Multiple Identities Affects the Quality of a Manager-Subordinate Relationship," *Academy of Management Review* 40(4) (2015): 538–562.

33. M. Rosenwald, "Bound by Habit," *BusinessWeek* (March 19–25, 2012): 106–107.

34. S.F. Collins, "Success Steps," *Costco Connection* (January 2016): 29.

35. D. Elzinga, "Optimizing Happiness," *INC.* (June 2016): 107.

36. E.L. Weber, "Nowhere to Hide for Dead Wood Workers," *The Wall Street Journal* (August 22, 2017): A1, A10.

37. R. McCammon, "Words of Encouragement," *Entrepreneur* (October 2015): 26.

38. R. Pinheiro, "SuperFreakonomics: Global Cooling, Patriotic Prostitutes, and Why Suicide Bombers Should Buy Life Insurance," *Academy of Management Perspectives* 25(2) (2011): 86-87.

39. S. Leibs, "Perks That Work," *INC.* (November 2014): 64-65.

40. S.J. Creary, B.B. Caza, and L.M. Roberts, "Out of the Box? How Managing a Subordinate's Multiple Identities Affects the Quality of a Manager-Subordinate Relationship," *Academy of Management Review* 40(4) (2015): 538-562.

41. E. Bernstein, "If You Want to Persuade People, Try Altercasting," *The Wall Street Journal* (September 5, 2016): D1, D2.

42. R. McCammon, "Words of Encouragement," *Entrepreneur* (October 2015): 26.

43. K. Blanchard and J. Johnson, *The One-Minute Manager* (New York: Morrow, 1982).

44. E.A. Locke, "Guest Editor's Introduction: Goal-Setting Theory and Its Applications to the World of Business," *Academy of Management Executive* 18(4) (2004): 124-125.

45. D. Baden and M. Higgs, "Challenging the Perceived Wisdom of Management Theories and Practice," *Academy of Management Learning & Education* 14(4) (2015): 539-555.

46. C. Duhigg, "Smarter Faster Better," *Fortune* (March 15, 2016): 28.

47. V. Harnish, "5 Crucial Performance Metrics," *Fortune* (August 1, 2016): 322.

48. A. Murray, "Should Leaders Be Modest," *Fortune* (September 15, 2015): 28.

49. R. Feintzeig, "More Firms Say Targets Are the Key to Diversity," *The Wall Street Journal* (September 30, 2015): R1, R7.

50. R. McCammon, "Words of Encouragement," *Entrepreneur* (October 2015): 26.

51. J. Fried, "In Praise of Deadlines," *INC.* (December 2015 / January 2016): 128.

52. L.M. Maruping, V. Venkatesh, S.M.B. Thatcher, and P.C. Patel, "Folding Under Pressure of Rising to the Occasion?" *Academy of Management Journal* 58(5) (2015): 1313-1333.

53. L. Alexander and D. Van Knippenberg, "Teams in Pursuit of Radical Innovation: A Goal Orientation Perspective," *Academy of Management Review* 39(4) (2014): 423-438.

54. G. Colvin, "Humans Are Underrated," *Fortune* (August 1, 2015): 100-113.

55. S. Shellenbarger, "Leader? No, Be a Follower," *The Wall Street Journal* (September 30, 2015): D1, D3.

56. D. Wakabayashi, "Apple Sets 2019 Goal to Build an Auto," *The Wall Street Journal* (September 22, 2015): A1.

57. D. Hull, "The Bottom Line," *BusinessWeek* (Sept 28 to October 4, 2015): 23.

58. G. Colvin, "Ignore These Leadership Lessons at Your Peril," *Fortune* (October 28, 2013): 85.

59. T. Mickle, "AB InBev Sets Lofty Goal," *The Wall Street Journal* (April 2-3, 2016): B1.

60. E.L. Weber, "Nowhere to Hide for Dead Wood Workers," *The Wall Street Journal* (August 22, 2017): A1, A10.

61. M.R. Barrick, G.R. Thurgood, T.A. Smith, and S.H. Courtright, "Collective Organizational Engagement: Linking Motivational Antecedents, Strategic Implementation, and Firm Performance," *Academy of Management Journal* 58(1) (2015): 111-135.

62. N. Li, B.L. Kirkman, and C.O.L.H. Porter, "Toward a Model of Work Team Altruism," *Academy of Management Review* 39(4) (2014): 541-565.

63. S.F. Collins, "Success Steps," *Costco Connection* (January 2016): 29.

64. L. Daska, "4 Pieces of Advice Most People Ignore (but Great Entrepreneurs Don't)," *INC.* (July/August 2015): 8.

65. M. Barra, "Most Powerful Women Advice!" *Fortune* (November 17, 2014): 149.

66. W. Buffett, "Most Powerful Women Advice!" *Fortune* (November 17, 2014): 149.

67. K. Hicks, "Best Advice," *Fortune* (November 17, 2014): 132.

68. S. Shellenbarger, "Leader? No, Be a Follower," *The Wall Street Journal* (September 30, 2015): D1, D3.

69. G.J. Kilduff, H.A. Eefenbein, and B.M. Staw, "The Psychology of Rivalry: A Relationally Dependent Analysis of Competition," *Academy of Management Journal* 53(5) (2010): 943-969; J.C. Dencker, "Outliers: The Story of Success," *Academy of Management Perspectives* 24(3) (2010): 97-99.

70. N. Pasricha, "The Happiness Equation," *Fortune* (March 15, 2016): 28.

71. O.E. Varela and R.G. Watts, "The Development of the Global Manager: An Empirical Study on the Role of Academic International Sojourns," *Academy of Management Learning & Education* 13(2) (2014): 187–207.

  i. http://cnsmaryland.org/2012/04/11/maryland-under-armour-relationship-beneficial-for-school-and-company/ accessed May 26, 2017.

 ii. http://knowledge.wharton.upenn.edu/article/under-armours-kevin-plank-creating-the-biggest-baddest-brand-on-the-planet/ accessed May 26, 2017.

CHAPTER 8

Ethical Power and Politics

©Dave and Les Jacobs/Blend Images/Alamy Stock Photo

LEARNING OUTCOMES

After completing this chapter, you should be able to:

LO 8-1   State how power, politics, and ethics affect behavior, human relations, and performance.

LO 8-2   Describe seven bases of power.

LO 8-3   List techniques to increase your power bases.

LO 8-4   Describe five influencing tactics.

LO 8-5   Discuss the necessity of organizational politics and three political behaviors.

LO 8-6   Identify techniques to develop effective human relations with superiors, subordinates, peers, and members of other departments.

LO 8-7   List the steps in the handling customer complaints model.

LO 8-8   Define the following 11 key terms (in order of appearance in the chapter):

power	information power
coercive power	expert power
connection power	politics
reward power	reciprocity
legitimate power	open-door policy
referent power	

OPENING CASE WORK SCENARIO

/ / / **Bob and Sally are at the water fountain, talking. They both are employed at Tightens Corporation.**

BOB: I'm sorry the Peterson account was not assigned to you. You deserved it. Roger's claim of being more qualified to handle the job is not true. I'm really surprised that our boss, Ted, believed Roger's claim.

SALLY: I agree. Nobody likes Roger because he always has to get his own way. I can't stand the way Roger puts down coworkers and members of other departments to force them to give him his own way. Roger has pulled the old emergency routine so many times now that purchasing and maintenance ignore his requests. This hurts our department.

BOB: You're right. Roger only thinks of himself; he never considers other people or what's best for the company. I've overheard Ted telling him he has to be a team player if he wants to get ahead.

SALLY: The way he tries to beat everyone out all the time is sickening. He'll do anything to get ahead. But the way he behaves, he will never climb the corporate ladder.

Besides good work, what does it take to get ahead in an organization? In most cases, getting ahead involves gaining power and using ethical political skills with superiors, subordinates, peers, and members of other departments and using proper business etiquette. That's what this chapter is all about. / / /

Learning Outcome 8-1

State how power, politics, and ethics affect behavior, human relations, and performance.

HOW POWER, POLITICS, AND ETHICS AFFECT BEHAVIOR, HUMAN RELATIONS, HAPPINESS, AND PERFORMANCE

Power and organizational politics are often viewed negatively because some people abuse them using unethical behavior,[1] which causes unhappiness, hurts relationships, and decreases performance.[2] For example, /// **In the opening case,** Roger uses unethical power and politics in hopes of getting ahead. But according to his peers, he will not climb the corporate ladder. Bob and Sally don't have effective human relations with Roger because of his unethical political behavior. The purchasing and maintenance department members ignore Roger's requests because of his behavior, while Bob and Sally have good relations with these departments. As a result of Roger's behavior, the performance of the organization as a whole is affected negatively. Ted gave the Peterson account to Roger, which will affect both Roger's and Sally's behavior and human relations. Roger may not perform as well as Sally and may hurt department performance. ///

But power and politics in and of themselves are neither good nor bad; it's how they are used. Whether you have a positive or negative attitude toward power and organizational politics, they are a reality of organizational life that is important to performance.[3] Power and politics are used to influence people to achieve objectives.[4] Organizations have power structures,[5] as a source of power,[6] and colleges prepare students for powerful positions.[7] So, your ability to influence others[8] by gaining power[9] and using politics skills[10] are important in your career success. But, as discussed in Chapter 3, your behavior must be ethical.[11] You should strive to meet the goal of human relations by creating win-win situations for all stakeholders (Chapter 3).

WORK APPLICATION 8-1

Give an example of ethical and unethical politics, preferably from an organization for which you work or have worked. Describe the behavior and the consequences for all parties involved.

Let's admit it—we all have a desire for influence and power,[12] as we try to influence people at work and off the job to get what we want every day, unless you always just go along with doing whatever others want you to do. This comes naturally, and there is nothing wrong with looking out for your self-interest, so long as you are not narcissistic and aim to get your way at the expense of others. Recall that looking out for others, and even putting their needs ahead of your own, is the foundation of good relationships and happiness. They are interpersonal skills.[13]

APPLICATION SITUATIONS / / /

Ethical and Unethical Politics   AS 8-1

Identify the type of politics represented in each statement.

A. Ethical politics   B. Unethical politics

_____ 1. Carlos drops off the daily figures at 10:00 on Mondays because he knows he will run into higher-level managers going to a meeting. On the other days, he delivers them at noon on his way to lunch.

_____ 2. Aisha goes around asking about what is happening in other departments during her work time.

_____ 3. Claire sent a copy of her very positive department's performance record to three high-level managers to whom she does not report even though they didn't ask for a copy.

_____ 4. Troy tells everyone about mistakes his boss and peers make.

_____ 5. Tanya is taking golf lessons so she can join the company league that most of the managers belong to.

Communication Skills
Refer to CS Question 1.

POWER

Some people want and seek power, while others wouldn't take it if you offered it to them. You discovered the reason for this difference in Chapter 7, where you learned about the need for power in **McClelland**'s manifest needs theory. Do you have a need for power? Recall that managers need to use power to achieve organizational goals,[14] but that they must use ethical behavior,[15] as abusive supervisors hurt performance.[16] In this section, we discuss the importance of power in organizations, bases of power and how to increase your power, and influencing tactics. Begin by completing Self-Assessment Exercise 8-1, Your Power Base, to determine your preferred use of power.

/ / / Self-Assessment Exercise 8-1 / / /

Your Power Base

When you want to get something and need others' consent or help, which approach do you use most often? Think of a recent specific situation in which you tried to get something. If you cannot develop your own example, assume you and a coworker both want the same job assignment for the day. How would you get it? Rank all seven approaches below from 1, the first approach you would most commonly use, to 7, the last approach you would most commonly use. Be honest.

_____   I did/would somehow use a form of *coercive power*—pressure, blackmail, force, threat, retaliation, and so forth—to get what I want.

_____   I did/would use the influential *connection power* I have. I'd refer to my friend, or actually have my friend tell the person with authority (such as my boss) to let me get (or do) what I want.

_____   I did/would use *reward power* by offering the coworker something of value to him or her as part of the process or in return for compliance.

_____   I did/would convince the coworker to give me what I want by making a *legitimate* request (such as referring to my seniority over the coworker).

_____   I did/would convince the coworker by using *referent power*—relying on our relationship. Others would comply because they like me or are my friends.

_____   I did/would convince my coworker to give me what I want with *information power.* The facts support the reason why he or she should do what I want. I have information my coworker needs.

_____   I did/would convince my coworker to give me what I want by making him or her realize that I have the skill and knowledge. Since I'm the *expert,* it should be done my way.

Your selection rank (1 to 7) prioritizes your preferred use of power. Each power base is a key term and will be explained in this chapter.

Organizational Power

Within an organization, power should be viewed in a positive sense. "The fundamental concept of social science is power."[17] Leadership and power go hand in hand.[18] For our purposes, **power** is *a person's ability to influence others to do something they would not otherwise do.* The good news is that power skills can be developed,[19] or you can improve your ability to influence others to help you get what you want.[20]

Learning Outcome 8-2

Describe seven bases of power.

Bases of Power and How to Increase Your Power

There are two sources of power: position power and personal power, also called structural and social power.[21] Position power is derived from top-level management and is delegated down the chain of command. Personal power is derived from the person. We all have personal power to varying degrees.

Learning Outcome 8-3

List techniques to increase your power bases.

Below, we will examine seven bases of power and how to increase each. You do not have to take power away from others to increase your power base. Contrary to the Machiavellian cliche, nice people are more likely to rise to power because people give it to others that they genuinely like.

Coercive Power   The use of **coercive power** involves *threats and/or punishment to influence compliance.* Out of fear that noncompliance will lead to negative consequences, people do as requested. Other examples of abusive coercive power include verbal abuse, humiliation, ostracism, and bullying.[22] /// **In the opening case,** when Roger puts down coworkers and members of other departments to force them to give him his own way, he is using coercive power. ///

Coercive power is appropriate to use in maintaining discipline when enforcing rules. When an employee is not willing to do as the manager requests, the manager may use coercive power to gain compliance. However, it is advisable to keep the use of coercive power to a minimum because it hurts human relations and often productivity as well. Narcissists tend to be coercive, resulting in dysfunctional consequences.[23]

Increasing Coercive Power   To have strong coercive position power, you need to have a management job that enables you to gain and maintain the ability to hire, discipline, and fire your employees. However, some people can pressure others to do what they want without management authority.

Communication Skills
Refer to CS Question 2.

Connection Power   **Connection power** is *based on the user's relationship with influential people.* People who have the "right" connections tend to get ahead.[24] It relies on the use of contacts or friends who can influence the person you are dealing with. The right connections can give you the perception of having power, and they can give you actual power. If people know you are friendly with people in power, they are more apt to do as you request—proximity is power.[25] The Objective Case, Politicking, at the end of the chapter illustrates how people use networking connection power to get ahead.

Increasing Connection Power   To increase your connection power, expand your network of contacts with important managers who have power. Join the "in crowd" and the "right" clubs. When you want something, identify the people who can help you attain it, make alliances, and win them over to your side. Have your accomplishments known by the people in power.

Reward Power   **Reward power** is *based on the user's ability to influence others with something of value to them.* You can exchange favors, known as reciprocity,[26] as a reward or give something of value to the other party. Let people know what's in it for them. If you have something attractive to others, use it.

Increasing Reward Power   Get a management position, and gain and maintain control over resources. Have the power to evaluate your employees' performance and determine their raises and promotions. Find out what others value, and try to reward them in that way. Using praise can help increase your power using the giving praise model in Chapter 7. When people feel that they are appreciated rather than being used, you will gain more power.

Legitimate Power   **Legitimate power** is *based on the user's position power,* which is given by the organization. Employees tend to feel that they ought to do what the supervisor says within the scope of the job.[27]

The use of legitimate power is appropriate when asking people to do something that is within the scope of their jobs. Most day-to-day interactions are based on legitimate power, which need to be based on communicating legitimacy effectively to influence thoughts and behavior.[28]

Increasing Legitimate Power   Let people know the power you possess, and work at gaining people's perception that you do have power. Remember, people's perception that you have power gives you power.

Referent Power   **Referent power** is *based on the user's personal power.* A person using referent power relies on personality and the relationship to gain compliance. For example, say, "Will you please do it for me?" not "This is an order." Identification stems primarily from the attractiveness of the person using power and is manifested in personal feelings of liking someone. /// **In the opening case,** since Roger is not well liked in the organization, he has weak referent power. ///

The use of referent power is particularly appropriate for people with weak, or no, position power. Today, managers are sharing power, or empowering employees through participative leadership.[29]

Increasing Referent Power   To gain referent power, develop your relationship with others; stand up for them. Using the guidelines in this book can help you win referent power. To get more power, work at your relationship with the boss. We will discuss this in more detail later in the chapter.

Information Power   **Information power** is *based on the user's information being desired by others.* People with access to information have more power because information is the new source of power.[30]

Increasing Information Power   Have information flow through you. Know what is going on in the organization. Provide service and information to other departments. Serve on committees; it gives you both information and a chance to increase connection power. Attend seminars and other meetings.

Expert Power   **Expert power** is *based on the user's skill and knowledge.* Being an expert makes other people dependent on you. "Knowledge is power." The fewer the people who possess the skill or knowledge, the more power the individual who does possess it has. For example, because there are so few people possessing the ability to become top athletes and executives, they command multimillion-dollar contracts.

Expert power is essential to people who have to work with people from other departments and organizations. They have no direct position power to use, so being seen as an expert gives credibility and power. /// **In the opening case,** Roger, rather than Sally, got the Peterson account because he convinced Ted of his expertise. ///

Increasing Expert Power   Actor **Steve Martin** said, "Be so good they can't ignore you."[31] To become an expert, take all the training and educational programs your organization provides. Stay away from routine tasks, in favor of more complex, hard-to-evaluate tasks. Project a positive image.[32]

Remember to use the appropriate type of power in a given situation. Exhibit 8.1 matches the two sources of power and the seven bases of power with the four situational supervision and communication styles (from Model 7.1). You should also realize that power can shift between team members based on the situation.[33]

EXHIBIT 8.1 | Sources and Bases of Power with Situational Supervision and Communication Styles

Personal power ——————→ ←—————— Position power
Expert   Referent   Reward   Coercive
Information   Legitimate   Connection
Laissez-faire   *Participative*   *Consultative*   *Autocratic*

Using Power   AS 8-2

Identify the appropriate power base to use in each situation.

A. Coercive   C. Reward or legitimate   E. Information or expert

B. Connection   D. Referent

_____ 6. Hank, your worst worker, didn't do what you asked him to do again.

_____ 7. Anita, who needs some direction and encouragement to maintain production, is not working to standard today. Anita claims to be ill, as she does occasionally.

_____ 8. Tony is one of your best workers. He needs little direction, but Tony has slowed down his production level. You know he has a personal problem, but the work needs to get done.

_____ 9. You want a new machine to help you do a better job.

_____10. Latoya, one of your best workers, wants a promotion. She has asked you to help prepare her for when an opening comes.

Learning Outcome 8-4

Describe five influencing tactics.

Influencing Tactics

Your power is your ability to influence others to do something they would not otherwise do to help you meet your objectives, so influencing tactics are an important part of gaining and using power.[34] Persuasion takes careful preparation and proper presentation of arguments and supporting evidence in an appropriate and compelling way; it is not coercive power or manipulation.

To help persuade people you don't supervise, you can use influencing tactics that focus primarily on personal power. Before we discuss each of the five tactics, let's discuss reading people and creating and presenting a win–win situation so you know which influencing tactic may work best in a given situation.

Reading People   Reasons for or an argument presenting your view may sound good to you, but they may seem irrelevant to the other person. If you are going to influence someone, you have to understand the person's values, attitudes, beliefs, and use incentives that will motivate that individual (Chapter 7). **Racecar champion Mario Andretti** has an uncanny knack of being able to work with and read people.[35] Reading people is a key interpersonal skill and has four parts:

1. Put yourself in the place of the person you want to persuade (your boss, coworker). Anticipate how the person sees the world (perception [Chapter 2]) and what his or her expectations are during your persuasion interaction.

2. Get the other person's expectations right. If you don't, you most likely will not influence the person.

3. Incorporate the information about the other person's expectations into your persuasive presentation. In other words, use the influencing tactic that will work best with the person. For example, if you know the person likes to be praised, use ingratiation. If the person likes or expects a rational persuasion with facts and figures, use that tactic. If the person doesn't care much about facts and figures and is more emotional, use an inspirational appeal.

4. Keep the focus on the other person's expectations when trying to persuade. What's in it for them?

Creating and Presenting a Win–Win Situation   When you want someone to do something to help you, it is easy to focus just on yourself and your personal gain.[36] But recall that the key to human relations success is to develop a win–win situation for all relevant parties. Spend time reading the other person, as suggested above, and answer the other person's often unasked question, "What's in it for me?" Remember that most people are concerned about themselves, not about you. What they want to hear is how they will benefit, so, as it says in step 4 above, keep the focus on the other person's expectations.

Ingratiation (Praise)   With the *ingratiation tactic,* you are friendly and give praise to get the person in a good mood before making your request. You learned the importance of, and how to give, praise in Chapter 7. Never go a day without giving praise.

Appropriate Use of Ingratiation   Ingratiation works best as a long-term influencing strategy to improve relationships. The ingratiation must also be sincere to be effective. If you usually don't compliment a person and all of a sudden you compliment him or her and then ask for a favor, the person will think you are trying to manipulate him or her. Thus, you can come across as a suck-up, and this technique can backfire on you.[37]

Using Ingratiation   When using ingratiation, follow these guidelines:

1. Be sensitive to the individual's moods. Start out with some compliments to determine their mood. If it's good, make the request; if not, wait for a more opportune time, if possible.
2. Compliment the person's past related achievements. Use the model for giving praise in Chapter 7.
3. You can also use *altercasting*—you characterize the person as a certain type of person to encourage him or her to behave in a desired manner. "Shak, I know you're a good writer and know the test. Will you please write the report?" People want to rise to the occasion.[38]
4. Ask for a *favor*—Do me a solid? People do like to do favors, when you ask simply and directly. (a) Open with a phrase such as, "I'd like to ask you a favor," "I could really use a favor from you," or "Could you do this favor for me?" (b) then say something like, "Here is what I'm hoping you will do for me," "Can you please?" and (c) just state what you want. Don't offer a reward in your request for a favor—if you do, it's a transaction, not a real favor.[39]
5. Praise and thank the person for their willingness to help you, and acknowledge inconveniences.

Rational Persuasion   The *rational persuasion tactic* includes logical arguments with factual evidence to persuade the person that the behavior will result in meeting the objective. Use facts and figures to build a persuasive case; visuals are also helpful. Remember that how information is presented, such as using **Excel** and **PowerPoint**, affects persuasiveness.

Appropriate Use of Rational Persuasion   Logical arguments generally work well with people whose behavior is more influenced by thinking than by feeling *learning styles* (Chapter 2) . It works well when you share the same objective and create a true win–win situation.

Using Rational Persuasion   When you develop rational persuasion, follow these guidelines:

1. Explain the reason your objective needs to be met. To get a commitment to meet your objective, you want people to know why it needs to be met and why it is important.
2. Explain how the other person, department, and/or organization will benefit by meeting your objective; again, create a win–win situation.

3. Provide evidence that your objective can be met. Remember the importance of expectancy motivation theory (Chapter 7). Offer a detailed, step-by-step plan.

4. Explain how potential problems and concerns will be handled. Know the potential problems and concerns, and deal with them in the rational persuasion. If others bring up problems that you have not anticipated when reading the person, which is likely, be sure to address them. Do not ignore people's concerns or make simple statements like "That will not happen" or "We don't have to worry about that." Get the person's input on how to resolve any possible problems as they come up. This will help gain commitment.

5. If there are competing plans to meet the objective, explain why your proposal is better than the competing ones. Again, do your homework. You need to be well versed about the competition. To simply say "My idea is better than theirs" won't cut it. Be sure to state how your plan is superior to the others and to identify the weaknesses and problems within the other plans.

Inspirational Appeal   The *inspirational appeal tactic* attempts to arouse people's enthusiasm. You appeal to the other person's values, ideals, and aspirations or increase his or her self-confidence by displaying feelings that appeal to the person's emotions and enthusiasm.

Appropriate Use of Inspirational Appeals   Inspirational appeals generally work well with people whose *learning style* is more influenced by feelings than by logical thinking *learning styles* (Chapter 2).   Great sports coaches, such as **Vince Lombardi**, are well respected for their inspirational appeals to get the team to win the game. Have you heard the saying from **Notre Dame**, "Win one for the **Gipper**"?

Using Inspirational Appeals   When you develop an inspirational appeal, it is helpful to phrase your own ideas as if they came from the other person. Follow these guidelines:

1. When you use inspirational appeals, you need to develop emotions and enthusiasm. When dealing with multiple individuals, different inspirational appeals may be made to meet individual values.

2. Link the appeal to the person's self-concept. Appeal to his or her self-image as a professional or a member of a team, department, or organization.

3. Link the request to a clear, appealing vision. Create a vision of how things will be when your objective is achieved.

4. Be positive and optimistic. Make your confidence and optimism that the objective can be met contagious. For example, talk about when, not if, the objective will be accomplished.

5. Use nonverbal communication to bring emotions to the verbal message. Raise and lower your voice tone, and pause to intensify key points. Maintain eye contact. Using facial expressions, body movement, and gestures can effectively reinforce verbal messages with emotions.

Personal Appeal   With the *personal appeal tactic,* you request the person to meet your objective based on loyalty and friendship. Present your request as a favor to you: "Please do it for me," not "This is an order."

Appropriate Use of Personal Appeals   Personal appeals are especially important when you have weak power. Thus, personal appeals are more commonly used with peers and outsiders. It is also important to have a good relationship with the person. If you ask a personal favor of a person who doesn't like you, the request may end in resistance.

Using Personal Appeals   When using personal appeals, follow these guidelines:

1. Review how to ask for a favor in the "Ingratiation Tactic" section. But be sure not to be viewed as manipulative and hurt the relationship.

2. Appeal to your friendship. When you have a relationship, a friendship appeal is usually not needed, and it will generally not work with people you don't know.

3. Tell the person that you are counting on him or her. This helps the person realize the importance to you and your friendship.

Legitimization   With the *legitimization tactic,* you rely on organizational authority that a reasonable request is being made and that the person should meet your objective.[40] Yes, legitimization is closely tied to legitimate power, but the tactic is used when you don't have position power, such as with people at higher levels in the organization.

Communication Skills
Refer to CS Question 3.

Appropriate Use of Legitimization   Legitimization is an appropriate tactic to use when you have legitimate authority or the right to make a particular type of request.

Using Legitimization   When using legitimization, follow these guidelines:

SB

Skill-Building Exercises 8-2 and 8-3 develops this skill.

1. Refer to organizational policies, procedures, rules, and other documentation. Explain how the request is verified within the organization structure.

2. Refer to written documents. If the person doesn't believe your reference to documents, show the policy manual or the like that makes your request legitimate.

WORK APPLICATION 8-4

Give an example of when you or someone else in an organization for which you work or have worked used one of the five influencing tactics to achieve an objective. Be sure to state the tactic used.

3. Refer to precedent. If some other person has made the same request, refer to it for equity in support of your request.

You should realize that the five influencing tactics can be used together to help you influence others. For example, praise usually needs to be backed up with another tactic. When one tactic does not work, you may need to change to another. Remember that people do like to do favors, and many people have a hard time saying no when asked directly for a favor.[41]

APPLICATION SITUATIONS / / /

Influencing Tactics   AS 8-3

Select the most appropriate individual tactic for each situation.

A. Rational persuasion   C. Legitimization   E. Personal appeal
B. Inspirational appeal   D. Ingratiation

_____ 11. You have a large order that should be shipped out at the end of the day. Two of your five crew members did not come in to work today. It will be tough for the small crew to meet the deadline.

_____12. Although the crew members in situation 11 have agreed to push to meet the deadline, you would like to give them some help. You have an employee whose job is to perform routine maintenance and cleaning. He is not one of your five crew workers. However, you realize that he could be of help filling in for the two missing workers. You decide to talk to this nonunion employee about working with the crew for two hours today.

_____13. The nonunion employee in situation 12 is resisting helping the other workers. Without directly saying it, you read him as thinking, "What's in it for me?"

_____14. You believe you deserve a pay raise, so you decide to talk to your boss about it.

_____15. Apple is known to be very secretive. You are in sales and want some information about a new product that has not been produced yet, nor publicly stated internally or externally. You know a person in the production department who has been working on the new product, so you decide to contact her.

ORGANIZATIONAL POLITICS

In this section, you will learn the nature of politics and how to develop political skills[42] ethically for a successful career.[43] Begin by determining your use of political behavior by completing Self-Assessment Exercise 8-2.

/ / / **Self-Assessment Exercise 8-2** / / /

Your Political Behavior

Select the response that best describes your actual or planned use of the following behavior on the job. Place the number 1 to 5 on the line before each statement.

(5) Usually   (4) Frequently   (3) Occasionally   (2) Seldom   (1) Rarely

_____ 1. I get along with everyone, even those recognized as difficult. I avoid or delay giving my opinion on controversial issues.

_____ 2. I try to make people feel important and compliment them.

_____ 3. I compromise when working with others and avoid telling people they are wrong; instead, I suggest alternatives that may be more effective.

_____ 4. I try to get to know the managers and what is going on in as many of the other departments as possible.

_____ 5. I take on the same interests as those in power (watch or play sports, join the same clubs, and the like).

_____ 6. I purposely seek contacts and network with higher-level managers so they will know who I am by name and face.

_____ 7. I seek recognition and visibility for my accomplishments.

_____ 8. I form alliances with others to increase my ability to get what I want.

_____ 9. I do favors for others and use their favors in return.

_____10. I say I will do things when I am not sure I can deliver; if I cannot meet the obligation, I explain why it was out of my control.

To determine your political behavior, add the 10 numbers you selected as your answers. The number will range from 10 to 50. The higher your score, the more political behavior you use. Place your score here _____ and mark the point that represents your score on the continuum below.

Nonpolitical   10 ---- 20 ---- 30 ---- 40 ---- 50   Political

These 10 statements are generally considered ethical behavior.

Learning Outcome 8-5

Discuss the necessity of organizational politics and three political behaviors.

The Nature of Organizational Politics

Millennials (born 1980–2000) often don't understand the importance of organizational politics. However, politics is critical to your career success, as it is part of EI.[44] In our economy, money is the medium of exchange; in an organization, politics is the medium of exchange. Managers cannot meet their objectives without the help of other people and departments over which they have no authority or position power. So you need to work with the system. **Politics** is *the process of gaining and using power.* As you can see from the definition, power and politics go hand in hand as they are both used to influence others to help you get what you want.[45]

The amount and importance of politics varies from organization to organization. However, larger organizations tend to be more political, and the higher the level of management, the more important politics becomes.[46] But try to avoid and prevent unethical politics that is dysfunctional.[47]

Political Behavior

Political behavior is used to develop relationships that are necessary to get the job done.[48] Three primary political behaviors commonly used in organizations are networking, reciprocity, and coalition building. As you will learn below, these three behaviors are interrelated.

Networking   Networking is the process of developing relationship alliances with key people for the purpose of politicking. Your network of people helps you get your job done. Navigating networks of people in organizations has been shown to help win promotions.[49] Networking is such an important topic that we discuss it in detail in the next chapter.

WORK APPLICATION 8-5

Give an example of reciprocity, preferably from an organization for which you work or have worked. Explain the trade-off.

Reciprocity   Politics is about reciprocal exchanges.[50] **Reciprocity** involves *creating obligations and debts, developing alliances, and using them to accomplish objectives.* Have you ever heard the expression "You owe me one"? When others do something for you, you incur an obligation that they may expect to be repaid. When you do something for others, you create a debt that you may be able to collect at a later date when you need a favor. Politics creates mutual reciprocity obligations.[51] As **Zig Ziglar** said, if you help others get what they want, they will help you get what you want.[52]

Coalition Building   A coalition is a network of alliances that helps you achieve a specific objective. Reciprocity is primarily used to achieve ongoing objectives, whereas coalitions are developed for achieving a specific objective. Many organizational decisions that are supposed to be made during a meeting or vote are actually decided through coalition building. For example, let's say that the selection of the department chair at your college is by election at a department meeting.

Professor Smith would like to replace the current chair. Rather than just put her name on the ballot for the department election at the next meeting, she goes around to several people in the department telling them she wants to be chair. Members of her coalition may also get votes for Smith. She gets a majority of the department members saying they will vote for her, so Smith puts her name on the ballot. So going into the meeting, the coalition has really already made the decision to elect Smith.

Putting the Political Behaviors Together   So to put the three political behaviors together, political success is about developing networks of alliances and coalitions in reciprocal exchanges. When the exchanges create a win–win situation for all members of the alliance and the organization, the goal of human relations is met. And it pays to be polite.[53]

Developing Political Skills

Communication Skills
Refer to CS Question 4.

Human relations skills are also political skills in organizations, as political skills are part of EI.[54] Following the human relations guidelines throughout this book can help you develop political skills. More specifically, review the 10 statements in Self-Assessment Exercise 8-2 and consciously increase your use of these behaviors. Successfully implementing these behaviors results in increased political skills. However, if you don't agree with a political behavior, don't use it. You may not need to use all the political behaviors to be successful. Learn what it takes in the organization where you work. It is important to know who can help you. Use number 10, saying you will do something when you are not sure you can, sparingly and don't use the word *promise*. You don't want to be viewed as a person who doesn't keep his or her word. Developing trust is very important, and being honest builds trust[55] (Chapter 6).

WORK APPLICATION 8-6

Of the 10 political behaviors in Self-Assessment Exercise 8-2, which two need the most effort on your part? Which two need the least? Explain your answer.

Business Etiquette   Although not a specific political behavior, part of political skills includes business etiquette—often referred to as manners, or the code of behavior expected in work situations. You have most likely also heard about the need to be politically correct in what you say and do. Using behavior that is considered inappropriate can result in not getting a job offer, it can hurt your relationships, and poor business etiquette can limit your career success. Because business etiquette is important to your career success, we will give you tips on proper business etiquette in Appendix A.

VERTICAL POLITICS

Vertical politics are relations with superiors and subordinates. They are the most important persons with whom to develop effective relations.[56] To be successful, honor relationships and commitments.[57]

Relations with Your Boss

Your relationship with your boss will affect your job satisfaction and can mean the difference between success or failure on the job. Needless to say, you should develop a good working relationship with your boss. Doing so is also called *managing* your boss and *leader-member exchange (LMX) theory*[58] (Chapter 6).

Don't try to change your boss. Analyze your boss's style and preferences, and if necessary, change your style to match his or hers.[59] For example, if your boss is very businesslike and you are informal and talkative, be businesslike when you are with your boss. If your boss likes you and your work to be early, not just on time, be early. Remember, people generally like people who behave like themselves, and being liked can lead to career advancement.

Knowing your boss can lead to better human relations between the two of you. It is helpful to know your boss's primary responsibility, what your boss regards as good performance, how your performance will be evaluated, and what your boss expects of you. So get feedback from your boss to make sure you are on the same page. As discussed in Chapter 6, your boss must trust you.[60] It's your job to help your boss be successful and to offset his or her weaknesses.

Common Expectations of Bosses   Your boss will expect loyalty, cooperation, initiative, information, and openness to criticism.

Loyalty   Recall that loyalty is an important part of trust. You need to be loyal and have a proper attitude. You should not talk negatively about your boss behind his or her back; gossip gets back to the boss. When it does, it can seriously hurt your relationship. Your boss may never forget it or forgive you for doing it. The benefits, if any, don't outweigh the cost of not being loyal.

Also, venting negatively about your boss is actually bad for you, as it just makes you angrier and unhappier. Remember that what you put on the Internet stays on it, so you could damage your reputation and career.[61] Some employees have been fired for social media venting. Focus on the positives about your job and be happy.

Going over Your Boss's Head   Also, be careful about going over his or her head (to your boss's boss) because you may be viewed as a betrayer of loyalty and as unethical. Going to complain about your boss can create more problems for you than solutions. Before you do, think, "What are the chances that my boss's boss will take my side against my boss?" It is especially doubtful if you don't have a good relationship with the higher-level manager and your boss does. Going over the boss's head is an issue in the first case at the end of this chapter.

Cooperation   Your boss expects you to cooperate with him or her and with everyone else you must work with; be a team player.[62] If you cannot get along with others, you can be an embarrassment to your boss. And bosses don't like to be embarrassed. /// **In the opening case,** Roger is not cooperative; his boss Ted has told him that if he wants to get ahead, he will have to be a team player. ///

Initiative   Your boss will expect you to know your responsibility and authority and to act without having to be told to do so. If you do only what your boss tells you to do, you haven't done enough—overdeliver. If you really want to advance, don't meet your boss's expectations, exceed them. Volunteer for assignments.[63]

Information   Your boss expects you to keep him or her informed about what your objectives are and how you are progressing. You should not cover up mistakes. Bosses don't like to be surprised.

Openness to Criticism   We all make mistakes. When your boss criticizes you, try not to become defensive and argumentative. Go back to Chapter 4 and review the guidelines for accepting criticism.

Regaining Your Boss's Trust   If you have done something that makes your boss look bad or in some way hurt your relationship, such as breaking any of the above expectations, you need to earn back his or her trust to reestablish your good working relationship. Your boss can give you poor evaluations and make your life miserable. So *admit shortcomings, apologize,* and state how you will improve. To regain trust, follow the guidelines in Chapter 6.

Communication Skills
Refer to CS Question 5.

WORK APPLICATION 8-7

Of the five common expectations of bosses, which is your strongest area? Your weakest area? Explain your answers.

Relations with Subordinates

The manager must consider the work to be accomplished as ultimately more important than the needs and desires of those doing the work, including the manager's own needs.[64] Managers get so busy getting the job done that they forget about the needs of the employees doing the work, and some even become abusive.[65] Think about the best and worst boss you ever had. Chances are the difference was in the relationship you had. As a manager, you must take the time to develop effective LMX relations[66] (Chapter 6) based on trust.[67]

Developing Manager–Employee Relations   In developing manager–employee relations, you should follow the guidelines to human relations throughout this book. You should strive for harmonious relations where questions and differences of opinion are encouraged and settled in a peaceful manner.[68] You can have good working human relations without being well-liked personally or popular. Don't forget to give more praise than criticism.[69]

WORK APPLICATION 8-8

Assume you are hired for or promoted to a management position. Will you develop a relationship with your employees based on friendship? Describe the relationship you plan to develop.

Friendship   The relationship between manager and employee cannot be one of real friendship. The nature of supervision excludes true friendship because the manager must evaluate the employee's performance; true friends don't evaluate or judge each other in any formal way. The manager must also give employees directions; friends don't order each other around. Some experts also don't advise being **Facebook** (or other social media) friends with subordinates. Will your friend try to take advantage of your friendship to get special favors?

Not being true friends to employees does not mean that you should not be friendly. As in most cases, there are exceptions to the rule. Some managers are friends with employees and are still effective managers.

WORK APPLICATION 8-9

Does/did your present/past boss use the open-door policy? Explain.

Communication Skills
Refer to CS Question 6.

The Open-Door Policy   The **open-door policy** is *the practice of being available to employees.* For effective human relations, you must be available to employees to give them the help they need, when they need it. If employees view you as too busy or not willing to help them, poor human relations and low morale can result. Managers are also using an *open e-mail policy.*

Use your power wisely. Remember, your success as a manager depends on your subordinates and teamwork.[70] If you want employees to meet your expectations, create a win–win situation. Help your subordinates meet their needs while attaining the high performance that will make you a success. When you ask subordinates to do something, answer their unasked question, "What's in it for me?"

HORIZONTAL POLITICS

Horizontal politics are your relations with your peers and with members of other departments and organizations. Let's discuss how to develop effective horizontal politics. Realize that when you give anyone praise or thanks for helping you, it influences them to continue to help you with favors. So give lots of praise to everyone.[71]

Relations with Peers

To be successful, you must cooperate with, compete with, and sometimes even criticize your peers.

Cooperating with Peers   Your success as an employee is linked to other employees in the organization. If you are cooperative and help them, they should have a positive attitude toward you and be willing to help you meet your objectives through reciprocity.[72]

Competing with Peers   Your boss will compare you with your peers when evaluating your performance, giving raises, and granting promotions. Like a great athlete, you must learn to be a team player and do your share of the work and help your peers be successful. But at the same time, you have to look good as well, without being a selfish,[73] bragging ball hog.

WORK APPLICATION 8-10

Give an example, preferably from an organization for which you work or have worked, of a situation in which you had good human relations with your peers. Describe how you cooperated with, competed with, and/or criticized your peers.

Criticizing Peers   If your peers do something they shouldn't, you owe it to them to try to correct the situation or prevent it from recurring. Sometimes peers are not aware of the situation. Chapter 5 provides details on how to approach peers, and others, to resolve conflicts, and Chapter 4 offers suggestions for giving criticism, including asking if they want feedback that can help them.

Be ethical. Do not cover for a peer in trouble—you will most likely only make things worse for everyone involved including yourself. And don't expect or ask others to cover for you.

/// **In the opening case,** Roger violates peer relations. He always has to get his own way. Roger is uncooperative and too competitive; he criticizes coworkers and members of other departments to force them to give him his own way. ///

Learning Outcome 8-6

Identify techniques to develop effective human relations with superiors, subordinates, peers, and members of other departments.

Relations with Members of Other Departments

You will most likely need the help of other departments and organizations to succeed. You will need the human resources department to hire new employees, accounting to approve budgets, purchasing to get materials and supplies, and so forth.

Some of these departments have procedures you should follow. Develop good human relations through being cooperative and following the guidelines set by the organization. It is also advisable to develop good relations with people in other organizations, including giving them praise for a job well done.[74]

/// **In the opening case,** Roger's pulling "the old emergency routine" so many times has resulted in purchasing and maintenance ignoring him. This is an embarrassment for Ted and the department, and it is hurting performance. ///

WORK APPLICATION 8-11

Give an example, preferably from an organization you work(ed) for, of a situation in which you had good human relations with members of other departments. Describe how your relations affected your performance, the other departments, and the organization as a whole.

Putting It All Together   See Exhibit 8.2 for an illustration that puts the concepts of power, politics, and ethics together. You need to develop and honor your relationships and commitments.[75] Starting in the center, with the goal of human relations, you create a win-win situation through horizontal politics with your peers and people in other departments and through vertical politics with your superiors and subordinates. You also use appropriate power with your politics.

EXHIBIT 8.2 | Human Relations Guide to Ethical Decision Making

If you are proud to tell all relevant parties your decision, it is probably ethical.

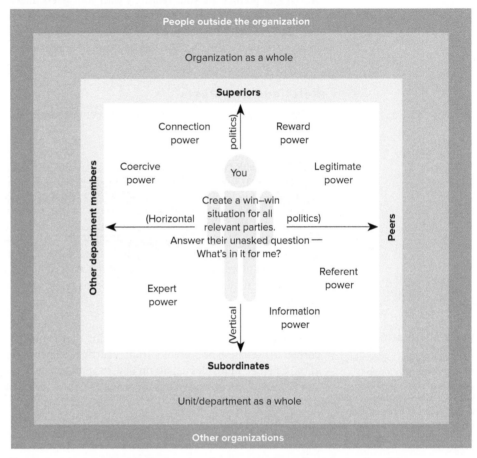

If you are embarrassed to tell all relevant parties your decision or if you keep rationalizing, the decision is probably unethical.

APPLICATION SITUATIONS / / /

Relations with Others   AS 8-4

Identify the other party being mentioned in each statement.

A. Subordinate   B. Superior   C. Peers   D. Other departments

_____ 16. "Let me introduce you to Ted Danson, he is the CEO and owner of the company."

_____ 17. "The other workers are getting together for a discussion of unionization. Will you join us?"

_____ 18. "I'm a first-line supervisor, and I report to a middle manager named Taylor."

_____ 19. "I'm in production, but the guys in sales are always trying to rush me to ship the product."

_____ 20. "Tyron is reluctant to accept the task I delegated to him."

CUSTOMER SATISFACTION AND COMPLAINTS

All organizations provide a good or service or a combination of the two to customers (also called clients, patients, and guests). Therefore, customer service is critical to business success because without customers, you don't have a business. Everyone in the organization should be focusing on customer satisfaction. Although the same human relations skills apply to both employees and customers, dealing with customers is different from dealing with employees. In this section, we provide basic information on customer service and how to deal with customer complaints.

Customer Satisfaction

The goal of sales is to provide customer satisfaction so that customers will buy your product now and become repeat customers. Customer satisfaction is based on perception (Chapter 2) of the sales and service of the transaction, and perceptions are often more heavily based on emotions than logic—or on how people feel about the experience or situation. So we want to make the experience as pleasant as possible. Satisfied and dissatisfied customers will tell others about their experience, which will result in more or fewer future sales.

Customer Needs and Solving Problems—Listening   To provide customer satisfaction, you have to understand what the customers want from your product. The only way to do this is to listen carefully and ask probing questions to find out. Follow the listening tips from Chapter 4.

Attitudes Lead to Behavior   The underlying behavior that makes or breaks the customer experience is attitude (Chapter 3). What we think about customers is how we feel, and what we feel is how we behave toward customers. Do you enjoy working with customers? If you don't, jobs dealing directly with customers may not be a good career choice.

Proper Customer Etiquette   You want to develop a welcoming attitude, or service with a smile, not a frown; convey that you care about the customers and want to meet their needs and solve their problems; make buyers feel good about the sales and service experience as you build effective human relations; and invite customers back for repeat business.

Improper Customer Etiquette   Here we list three major things not to do, followed by what to do to avoid these problems.

Don't Ignore Customers   Do you like walking into a business without being acknowledged when you want service? When customers arrive, greet them immediately by at least looking at them (eye contact is best) and saying, "I will be with you shortly," and do help them as soon as you can.

Don't Conduct Personal Business While Waiting on Customers   Do you like to be kept waiting for a service while you can hear the employee talking to a coworker or on a cell phone about personal things, or seeing the employee reading something? Proper etiquette is to give the customer your full undivided attention without distractions.

Don't Use Rude Behavior and Get the Customer Defensive—Do Apologize   Even if the customer is being rude to you, don't return the behavior. If you apologize, again even if you didn't do anything wrong, such as by saying "I'm sorry you are not satisfied with the product," it goes a long way to calming an emotional customer. Stay calm and control your

Learning Outcome 8-7

List the steps in the handling customer complaints model.

WORK APPLICATION 8-12

Give a job example of when a coworker behaved with improper customer etiquette; and/or give an example of when you were treated poorly as a customer.

MODEL 8.1 | Handling Customer Complaints

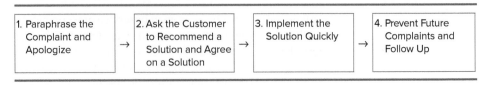

| 1. Paraphrase the Complaint and Apologize | → | 2. Ask the Customer to Recommend a Solution and Agree on a Solution | → | 3. Implement the Solution Quickly | → | 4. Prevent Future Complaints and Follow Up |

behavior; don't raise your voice and verbally abuse customers. Watch your nonverbal communication; don't let your anger show through actions.

Dealing with Customer Complaints

Although organizations try hard to satisfy customers, there will be some customers who are dissatisfied for a variety of reasons; mistakes do happen, products don't always meet expectations, some customers make unreasonable requests, and some people have highly disagreeable personalities and like to have something to complain about. If you have to deal with a dissatisfied customer, follow the guidelines. Model 8.1 shows ways to handle customer complaints that will help turn a dissatisfied customer into a satisfied customer.

Step 1: Paraphrase the Complaint and Apologize   Realize that you will have to deal with dissatisfied customers and there is a good chance that they will be emotional. Stay calm and deal with emotions (Chapter 5) to calm the customers. Focus on the goal of satisfying them by solving the problem without arguing, because arguing makes them dissatisfied and you lose. Don't get them defensive by blaming them or telling them that they are wrong, and remember the importance of apologizing to calm emotions and retain good human relations.

You can't resolve a complaint unless you clearly understand what the complaint is, so you have to listen carefully (Chapter 5). Repeating the complaint in your own words helps calm the emotional person because he or she realizes that you are listening, and it ensures that you do know what the person is complaining about. When you paraphrase the complaint and apologize, use statements like, "I understand that the problem is . . . , and I'm sorry it happened" or "I agree that . . . shouldn't have happened, and I apologize for the inconvenience it has caused you."

Step 2: Ask the Customer to Recommend a Solution and Agree on a Solution   If it is routine, like a simple return, ask if the customer would like cash or a store credit, for example. When it is not routine, make statements like, "How would you like us to handle this situation?" or "What can I do to fix this problem?" Often customers have simple solutions that are easy and inexpensive. Letting customers come up with the solution to their problem really turns them around to be satisfied customers.

But asking for a solution doesn't mean you have to do what the customer recommends when it is unreasonable. Realize the customer may be asking for more than he or she expects, hoping to get a good deal (this is negotiation, and you will learn to negotiate in the next chapter). Again, avoid arguing but be firm and calmly repeat the facts that don't justify the customer's solution. Be willing to say no to unreasonable solutions, and state what you are willing to do to resolve the problem. Some customers are not worth keeping anyway.

Step 3: Implement the Solution Quickly   The faster the complaint is solved, the happier the customer and the greater the chance of not losing him or her. Let's face it, if your cable is not working and you can't watch TV or go online, do you want a discount coupon, or do you want to have it fixed quickly?

Communication Skills
Refer to CS Question 7.

Step 4: Prevent Future Complaints and Follow Up   Take action to make sure the problem doesn't happened again; for example, stop making the same error or stop selling a faulty product. To follow up, you can call or send an e-mail simply asking whether the solution is working. Both prevention and follow-up help satisfy customers and lead to customer retention.

DO POWER AND POLITICS APPLY GLOBALLY?

If you said no, you are correct. Based on cultural values and history, *power* is perceived and exercised differently around the globe. A method of understanding global differences is called *power distance*. Power distance centers on the extent to which employees feel comfortable interacting across hierarchical levels. In high power distance, employees believe management should have the power and make the decisions, whereas in low power distance, employees want power and want to be involved with management in decision making.

In high power-distance cultures (for example, in Mexico, Venezuela, the Philippines, Yugoslavia, and France), using strong power and politics is acceptable because leaders are expected to behave differently from people in low ranks, and differences in rank are more apparent. In low power-distance cultures (for example, in the United States, Ireland, Australia, New Zealand, Denmark, Israel, and the Netherlands), using strong power and politics is not acceptable because power is expected to be shared with employees through empowerment. In low power-distance cultures, people are less comfortable with differences in power and there is less emphasis on social class distinction and hierarchical rank. Thus, when U.S. companies try to empower their business units in high power-distance cultures, they need to integrate and change the culture within the business unit slowly to be effective.

There still exists a tremendous gap in accepted ethical behavior between the East and West. Like business ethics, proper business *etiquette* in one culture may not be appropriate in another. For example, pointing with the index finger is considered rude in most Asian and Middle Eastern countries. Be aware of possible differences in etiquette, such as gift giving, dining, and drinking alcoholic beverages, as well as when and where to discuss business. When in doubt about whether something is proper etiquette, ask, and if you do offend someone, apologize, stating your ignorance. Also, follow the behavior of the culture, such as bowing back. Other differences in business etiquette have been presented in discussions on global differences in other chapters.

Complete Self-Assessment Exercise 8-3 to determine how your personality affects your use of power and politics.

/ / / **Self-Assessment Exercise 8-3** / / /

Your Personality and Power and Politics

If you have a high *surgency* personality, you most likely have a high need for power. Watch your use of coercive power and the use of the autocratic leadership style with subordinates. The way to get power is through politics, so you may be inclined to use political behavior; just make sure you use ethical politics to get what you want. Although you may not be too concerned with what others think of you, watch your use of proper etiquette so that you don't offend others. Being liked does help you gain power. You also need the help of peers and members of other departments, so create win–win situations for all parties. Don't expect your boss to agree with all your ideas. Remember that your relationship with your boss is critical to your advancement. If you want to advance, do what your boss wants, the way the boss wants it done, no matter how much you disagree.

(continued)

If you have a high *agreeableness* personality, you most likely have a high need for affiliation, and you most likely have a low need for power. However, you may be political to gain relationships. Being concerned about what others think of you, you may be good at etiquette and have good relations with your boss, peers, and others. Watch out for others using power to take advantage of you; be assertive.

If you have a high *conscientious* personality, you most likely have a high need for achievement. You may not care for politics, but you most likely try to gain power to achieve your specific objectives. You most likely use good, rational persuasion; however, you may not be good at reading people and may need to develop this skill to help you get what you want. To maintain a good relationship with your boss, you may need to make sure what you want to accomplish is what your boss wants you to accomplish. Watch the tendency to seek individual objectives unrelated to those of your peers and others if you want to advance.

How high your *adjustment* is affects how you use power and politics. People low on adjustment (and some can fake it) generally don't use power and politics ethically; they seek to get what they want and to take advantage of others. If you are not high on adjustment personality traits, you may want to stop being self-centered and work on creating win–win situations. You will be surprised at how much more you can get when you give.

There is a lot of truth in the adage, "The more you give, the more you receive." Have you ever noticed that the givers are usually happier than the takers? Have you ever done something for someone figuring there is nothing in it for you, only to find out that you got more than you expected?

Your *openness to experience* will have a direct affect on how much power you have. To maintain expert power, you have to keep up with the latest developments in your field. Be the first to get the latest training; volunteer for assignments. Read the appropriate journals to keep up in your field. Go to trade or professional meetings, and network with others outside your organization to stay current. Be a part of the learning organization's quest for continual improvement; try to bring new developments into your department or organization.

Action plan: Based on your personality, what specific things will you do to improve your power, ethical political skills (vertical and horizontal), and etiquette?

_____

_____

_____

_____

As we bring this chapter to a close, be aware that what you think is how you feel, and what you feel is how you behave. So if your attitude toward power, politics, and etiquette is positive, you should be better at these skills, which will help you be more successful. You should understand two sources of power and seven power bases (Exhibit 8.1) and how to increase your power, and be able to better read people and influence them to help you through five influencing tactics. You should realize that power and politics are related, as politics is the process of gaining and using power.

You should be able to use three political behaviors (networking, reciprocity, and coalition building) to get others to help you meet your objectives. You should also be effective in vertical politics (with your boss and subordinates) and horizontal politics (with peers and other departments).

When using power and politics, your behavior should be ethical, using proper business etiquette. Also important is your ability to use proper etiquette in person and digitally, and to satisfy customers and handle dissatisfied customers using Model 8.1. Last, you should realize that how power and politics are used effectively does vary by culture, and that business etiquette varies as well.

The chapter review is organized to help you master the eight learning outcomes for Chapter 8. First provide your own response to each learning outcome, and then check the summary provided to see how well you understand the material. Next, identify the final statement in each section as either true or false (T/F). Correct each false statement. Answers are given at the end of the chapter.

LO 8-1 State how power, politics, and ethics affect behavior, human relations, and performance.

The use of power and politics is needed in organizations to perform successfully to meet goals. People who use abusive power and politics tend to use unethical behavior and hurt human relations and performance. In the long run, people using ethical power and political behavior with integrity have more positive human relations and outperform people who use unethical behavior.

Power is the ability to influence others to do something they would not otherwise do, and politics is the process of gaining and using power. T F

LO 8-2 Describe seven bases of power.

The seven bases of power are: (1) *coercive power,* which is based on threats and/or punishment to influence compliance; (2) *connection power,* which is based on relationships with influential people; (3) *reward power,* which is based on the ability to influence others with something of value to them; (4) *legitimate power,* which is based on position power; (5) *referent power,* which is based on personal power; (6) *information power,* which is based on information desired by others; and (7) *expert power,* which is based on skill and knowledge.

The bases of position power include coercive, connection, reward, and legitimate; referent, information, and expert power are bases of human relations power. T F

LO 8-3 List techniques to increase your power bases.

Techniques to increase your power bases include: (1) To have *coercive power,* you need to gain and maintain the ability to hire, discipline, and fire employees. (2) To increase your *connection power,* you need to expand your network of contacts with important managers who have power and to get in with the "in crowd." (3) *Reward power* can be gained by evaluating employees' performance and determining their raises and promotions. Using praise can help increase your power. (4) *Legitimate power* can be increased by letting people know the power you do possess, and by working at gaining people's perception that you do have power. (5) To gain *referent power,* you need to develop your relationships with others. Show a sincere interest in others. (6) To increase *information power,* have information

flow through you. Know what is going on in the organization. Provide services and information to other departments. Serve on committees; it gives you both information and a chance to increase connection power. (7) To increase your *expert power,* take all the training and educational programs your organization provides. Stay away from routine tasks, in favor of more complex, hard-to-evaluate tasks.

People don't actually have to use power to influence others. T F

LO 8-4 Describe five influencing tactics.

Five influencing tactics include: (1) ingratiation, giving praise; (2) rational persuasion, giving logical arguments with factual evidence; (3) inspirational appeal, arousing people's enthusiasm; (4) personal appeal, focusing on loyalty and friendship; and (5) legitimization, using organizational authority.

Rational persuasion is the most effective influencing tactic. T F

LO 8-5 Discuss the necessity of organizational politics and three political behaviors.

In our economy, money is the medium of exchange; in an organization, politics is the medium of exchange. Political behavior is used to develop relationships that are necessary to get your job done. Three political behaviors that people use include: (1) networking, the process of developing relationship alliances with key people for the purpose of politicking; (2) reciprocity, which involves creating obligations and debts, developing alliances, and using them to accomplish objectives; and (3) coalition building, which involves creating a network of alliances to help you achieve a specific objective.

Power and politics are interrelated, as they are often used together. T F

LO 8-6 Identify techniques to develop effective human relations with superiors, subordinates, peers, and members of other departments.

To develop effective human relations with superiors, meet the common expectations of your boss: be loyal, be cooperative, use initiative, keep your boss informed, and be open to criticism. With subordinates, be friendly, but remember that you cannot be real friends with employees. Use an open-door policy. With peers, be cooperative while competing with them and help them to do an effective job. In your relations with other departments, be cooperative, and follow the requirements they set.

Your relations with your boss and peers are called vertical politics, and your relations with subordinates and other departments are called horizontal politics. T F

LO 8-7 List the steps in the handling customer complaints model.

The steps include: (1) paraphrase the complaint and apologize; (2) ask the customer to recommend a solution and agree on a solution; (3) implement the solution quickly; and (4) prevent future complaints and follow up.

It is important to know who to blame for the customer complaint. T F

LO 8-8 Define the following 11 key terms.

Select one or more methods: (1) fill in the missing key terms for each definition given below from memory; (2) match the key terms from the end of the review with their definitions below; and/or (3) copy the key terms in order from the key terms at the beginning of the chapter.

_____ is a person's ability to influence others to do something they would not otherwise do.

The seven bases of power are:

_____, based on threats and/or punishment to influence compliance.

_____, based on the user's relationship with influential people.

_____, based on the user's ability to influence others with something of value to them.

_____, based on the user's position power.

_____, based on the user's personal power.

_____, based on the user's information being desired by others.

_____, based on the user's skill and knowledge.

_____, the process of gaining and using power, is an important part of meeting organizational objectives.

_____ involves creating obligations and debts, developing alliances, and using them to accomplish objectives.

A(n) _____ is the practice of being available to employees.

_____

///   KEY TERMS   ///

coercive power   255
connection power   255
expert power   256

information power   256
legitimate power   255
open-door policy   264

politics   261
power   254
reciprocity   262

referent power   256
reward power   256

///   COMMUNICATION SKILLS   ///

The following critical thinking questions can be used for class discussion and/or as written assignments to develop communication skills. Be sure to give complete explanations for all questions.

1. Some people say that power and politics can't be used ethically. Do you agree?

2. Do you agree with the saying, "It's not what you know, it's who you know that is important"? Is it ethical to use connection power to get jobs and other things?

3. When someone tries to influence you, which influencing tactic works best and why? Why doesn't this same tactic work best for everyone?

4. How would you assess your political skill at using networking, reciprocity, and coalition building to help you get what you want? What can you do to improve?

5. Describe your relationship with your current or past boss. Did you meet the five common expectations of bosses? How can you improve your relationship with your current and/or future boss?

6. Describe your relationship with your current peers and members from other departments. How do you cooperate with them, compete with them, and criticize them? How can you improve your relationship with your current peers and members of other departments?

CASE / / / **Latoya Jefferson Use of Power and Politics**

Latoya Jefferson is a tenured professor of business at a small teaching college in the Midwest. The Department of Business (DB) has nine faculty members; it is one of 10 departments in the School of Arts and Sciences (SAS). The business department chair is Beth Sweeny, who is in her first year as chair. Six faculty members, including Latoya, have been in the department for longer than Beth. She likes to have policies so that faculty members have guides for their behavior. On the collegewide level, there is no policy about the job of graduate assistants. Beth asked the dean of the SAS what the policy was. The dean stated that there is no policy, and he had spoken to the vice president for academic affairs. The vice president and the dean suggested letting the individual departments develop their own policy regarding what graduate assistants can and cannot do. So Beth put "use of graduate assistants" on the department meeting agenda.

During the DB meeting, Beth asked for members' views on what graduate assistants should and should not be allowed to do. Beth was hoping that the department would come to a consensus on a policy. Latoya Jefferson was the only faculty member who was using graduate assistants to grade exams. All but one of the other faculty members spoke out against the use of having graduate assistants grade exams. Other faculty members believed it was the job of the professor to grade the exams. Latoya made a few statements in hopes of not having to correct her own exams. She stated that her exams were objective; thus, because there was a correct answer for each item on the exams, it was not necessary for her to personally correct the exams. She also pointed out that across the campus, and across the country, other faculty members were using

graduate assistants to teach entire courses and to correct subjective papers and exams. Latoya stated that she did not think it would be fair to tell her that she could not use graduate assistants to grade objective exams when others could do so. She also stated that the department did not need to have a policy, and she requested that the department not set a policy. But Beth stated that she wanted a policy. She held a single minority view during the meeting. However, after the meeting, one other member of the department, Ted Brown, who had said nothing during the meeting, told Latoya that he agreed that it was not fair to deny her the use of a graduate assistant.

There was no department consensus, as Beth hoped there would be. Beth said that she would draft a department policy, which would be discussed at a future DB meeting. The next day, Latoya sent a memo to department members asking if it was ethical and legal to deny her the use of the same resources as others across the campus. She also stated that if the department set a policy stating that she could no longer use graduate assistants to correct objective exams, she would appeal the policy decision to the dean, the vice president, and the president.

Go to the Internet: This case actually did happen. However, the names have been changed for confidentiality. Thus, you cannot go to the college Web site where the case really happened. Therefore, go to your own college Web site and get information that you did not know about your college.

Support your answer to the following questions with specific information from the case and text, or with other information you get from the web or other sources.

1. What source of power does Beth have, and what type of power is she using during the meeting?

2. (*a*) What source of power does Latoya have, and what type of power is she using during the meeting? (*b*) Is the memo a wise political move for Latoya? What may be gained/lost by sending it?

3. What would you do if you were Beth? (*a*) Would you talk to the dean, letting him know that Latoya said she would appeal the policy decision? (*b*) Which political behavior would that discussion represent? (*c*) Would you draft a policy directly stating that graduate assistants cannot be used to grade objective exams? (*d*) Would your answer to (*c*) be influenced by your answer to (*a*)?

4. If you were Latoya, (*a*) knowing you had no verbal supporters during the meeting, would you have continued to defend your position or agreed to stop using a graduate assistant? (*b*) What do you think of Latoya's sending the memo? (*c*) As a tenured full professor, Latoya is secure in her job. Would your answer change if you had not received tenure or promotion to the top rank?

5. If you were Latoya and Beth drafted a policy and department members agreed with it, what would you do? (*a*) Would you appeal the decision to the dean? (*b*) Again, would your answer change if you had not received tenure or promotion to the top rank?

6. If you were the dean of the SAS, knowing that the vice president does not want to set a collegewide policy, and Latoya appealed to you, what would you do? Would you develop a schoolwide policy for the SAS?

7. At what level (collegewide, by schools, or by departments within each school) should a graduate assistant policy be set?

8. (*a*) Should Ted Brown have spoken up in defense of Latoya during the meeting? (*b*) If you were Ted, would you have taken Latoya's side against the seven other members? (*c*) Would your answer change if you were or were not friends with Latoya, and if you were or were not a tenured full professor?

Cumulative Questions

9. What is the role of perception (Chapter 2) and attitudes and values (Chapter 3) in this case?

10. What type of communications (Chapter 5) were used in this case? What was the major barrier to communications?

11. Which conflict management style (Chapter 6) did Beth and Latoya use in setting the policy? Which conflict management style would you have used if you were in Latoya's situation?

12. Which situational supervisory business style (Chapter 7) was Beth using to set the policy?

13. Which motivation theory (Chapter 8) was Latoya using to defend her position to use graduate assistants?

CASE   / / /   Exercise and Role-Play

Preparation: Read the case and think about whether you agree or disagree with using graduate assistants to correct objective exams. If you do this exercise, we recommend that you complete it before discussing the questions and answers to the case.

In-Class Meeting: A person who strongly agrees with Latoya Jefferson's position volunteers to play this role (can be male or female) during a DB meeting. A second person who also agrees with the use of graduate assistants correcting exams plays the role of Ted Brown (can be female). However, recall that Ted cannot say anything during the meeting to support Latoya. One person who strongly disagrees with Beth Sweeny—who doesn't want graduate assistants to correct exams, and who also feels strongly that there should be a policy stating what graduate assistants can and cannot do—volunteers to play the role of the department chair who runs the DB meeting. Six others who are neutral or disagree with graduate assistants grading exams play the roles of other department members.

The 10 role-players sit in a circle in the center of the room, with the other class members sitting around the outside of the circle. Observers just quietly watch and listen to the meeting discussion.

Role-Play: *(about 15 minutes)* Beth opens the meeting by simply stating that the agenda item is to set a graduate assistants policy stating what they can and cannot do, and that he or she hopes the department can come to a consensus on a policy. Beth states her (or his) position on why graduate students should not be allowed to correct exams, and then asks for other views. Latoya and the others, except Ted, jump in anytime with their opinions.

Discussion: After the role-play is over, or when time runs out, the person playing the role of Latoya expresses to the class how it felt to have everyone against him (or her). Other department members state how they felt about the discussion, followed by observers' statements as time permits. A discussion of the case questions and answers may follow.

OBJECTIVE CASE / / / Politicking

Karen Whitmore is going to be promoted in two months. She will be replaced by one of her subordinates, Jim Green or Lisa Fesco. Both Jim and Lisa know they are competing for the promotion. Their years of experience and quality and quantity of work are about the same. Below is some of the political behavior each used to help get the promotion.

Lisa has been going to night classes and company training programs in management to prepare herself for the promotion. Lisa is very upbeat; she goes out of her way to be nice to people and compliment them. She gets along well with everyone. Knowing that Karen was an officer in a local businesswomen's networking organization, Lisa joined the club six months ago and now serves on a committee. At work Lisa talks regularly to Karen about the women's organization. Lisa makes an effort to know what is going on in the organization. One thing Karen doesn't like about

Lisa is the fact that when she points out Lisa's errors, Lisa always has an answer for everything.

Jim is good at sports and has been playing golf and tennis with upper-level managers for over a year now. In the department, especially with Karen, Jim refers to conversations with managers all the time. When Jim does something for someone, he expects that person to do a favor in return. Jim really wants this promotion, but he fears that with more women being promoted to management positions, Lisa will get the job just because she is a woman. To increase his chances of getting the job, Jim stayed late and made a few changes—errors—in the report Lisa was working on. Jim sees nothing wrong with making the changes to get ahead. When Lisa passed in the report, without checking prior work, Karen found the errors. The one thing Karen doesn't like about Jim is the fact that, on occasion, she has to tell him what to do before he acts.

Answer the following questions. Then in the space between the questions, state why you selected that answer.

_____ 1. We know that Karen has _____ power.

   a. position   *b.* personal

_____ 2. To be promoted, Lisa is stressing _____ power. Refer to the opening statement about Lisa.

   a. coercive   *c.* reward   *e.* referent   *g.* expert
   b. connection   *d.* legitimate   *f.* information

_____ 3. To be promoted, Jim is stressing _____ power. Refer to the opening statement about Jim.

   a. coercive   *c.* reward   *e.* referent   *g.* expert
   b. connection   *d.* legitimate   *f.* information

_____ 4. _____ appears to use reciprocity the most.

   a. Lisa   *b.* Jim

_____ 5. Lisa _____ conducted unethical political behavior.

   a. has   *b.* has not

_____ 6. Jim _____ conducted unethical political behavior.

   a. has   *b.* has not

_____ 7. Jim has committed _____ behavior in changing the report.

   a. Type I   *b.* Type II

_____ 8. Jim's changing the report did *not* affect:

   a. supervisors   *c.* peers   *e.* other departments
   b. subordinates   *d.* Karen's department   *f.* the organization

_____ 9. Lisa does not meet Karen's expectation of:

   a. loyalty   *c.* initiative   *e.* openness to criticism
   b. cooperation   *d.* information

_____ 10. Jim does not meet Karen's expectation of:

    a. loyalty   *c.* initiative   *e.* openness to criticism

    b. cooperation   *d.* information

_____ 11. In Lisa's situation, she suspects Jim made the changes in the report, but she has no proof. What would you do?

_____ 12. In Karen's situation, she suspects Jim made the changes in the report, but she has no proof. What would you do?

Note: Meetings between Lisa and Jim, Karen and Jim, or all three may be role-played in class.

/ / / SKILL-BUILDING EXERCISE 8-1 / / /

Who Has the Power?

Experience: Groups in-class exercise discuss power within the group.

Note: This exercise is designed for permanent groups that have worked together at least twice.

AACSB Competencies: Reflective thinking and application of knowledge.

Objective: To better understand power and how people gain power.

Preparation: You should have read and understood the text chapter.

Procedure 1 (5–10 minutes)
Permanent teams get together and decide which member has the most power at this time (greatest ability to influence group members' behavior). Power can change with time. Before discussion, all members select the member they believe has the most power. You may select yourself. Write the most powerful person's name here: _____. After everyone has made their selection, each member should state who was selected and explain why. Record the names of those selected below.

Procedure 2 (7–12 minutes)
Come to an agreement on the one person with the most power. Write the group's choice here: _____.

Was there a struggle for power?

Why is this person the most powerful in the group? To help you answer this question, as a group, answer the following questions about your most powerful person:

1. Which of the 10 human relations guidelines (discussed in Chapter 1) does he or she follow: (1) be optimistic, (2) be positive, (3) be genuinely interested in other people, (4) smile and develop a sense of humor, (5) call people by name, (6) listen to people, (7) help others, (8) think before you act, (9) apologize, and (10) create win–win situations?

2. How does this person project a positive image? What type of image does his or her appearance project? What non-verbal communication does this person project that sends a positive image? What behavior does this person use that gains him or her power?

3. What is the primary source of this person's power (position, personal)?

4. What is the primary base for this person's power in the group (coercive, connection, reward, legitimate, referent, information, expert)?

5. Which political behaviors does this person use (gets along with everyone, makes people feel important and compliments them, compromises and avoids telling people they are wrong)?

6. Does this person use ethical or unethical politics?

7. Does this person cooperate with, compete with, or criticize group members?

Overall, why is this person the most powerful? (Agree and write the reason below.) Share the feeling you experienced doing this exercise. How did you feel about not being, or being, selected as the most powerful group member? Who wanted power and who didn't? Is it wrong or bad to want and seek power?

Optional:

1. A spokesperson from each group tells the class which member was selected as the most powerful, and the overall reason why the person is considered to be the most powerful.

2. A spokesperson from each group does not tell the class which member was selected as the most powerful, but does state the overall reason why the person is considered to be the most powerful.

Conclusion: The instructor leads a class discussion and/or makes concluding remarks.

Application (2-4 minutes):   What did I learn from this exercise? How will I use this knowledge in the future?

Sharing: Volunteers give their answers to the application section.

/ / / SKILL-BUILDING EXERCISES 8-2 AND 8-3 / / /

Influencing Tactics

Experience: Individual or group may share answers in groups or entire class, in class or online.

AACSB Compentencies: Analytic skills and application of knowledge.

Objective: To develop your persuasion skills by using influencing tactics.

Preparation: You should understand the five influencing tactics and complete the preparation below. You will discuss which influencing tactics are most appropriate for the preparation situations. You may also be given the opportunity to role-play how you would handle the one situation you selected; you will also play the role of the person to be influenced and the observer.

Below are three situations. For each situation, select the most appropriate influencing tactic(s) to use. Write the tactics on the lines following the situations. At this time, don't write out how you would behave (what you would say and do).

1. You are doing a college internship, which is going well. You would like to become a full-time employee a few weeks after you graduate.

Which influencing tactic(s) would you use?

_____

Who would you try to influence? How would you do so (behavior)?

_____

_____

2. You have been working for six months. As you are approaching the elevator, you see a powerful person, one who could potentially help you advance in your career, waiting for the elevator. You have never met her, but you do know that her

committee has recently completed a new five-year strategic plan for the company and that she plays tennis and is active in the same religious organization as you. Although you have only a couple of minutes, you decide to try to develop a connection.

Which influencing tactic(s) would you use?

_____

How would you strike up a conversation? What topic(s) would you raise?

_____

_____

3. You are the manager of the production department. Some of the sales staff has been scheduling delivery dates for your product that your department can't meet. Customers are blaming you for late delivery. This situation is not good for the company, so you decide to talk to the sales staff manager about it over lunch.

Which influencing tactic(s) would you use?

_____

How would you handle the situation (behavior)?

_____

_____

Select one situation that seems real to you, that is, one you can imagine yourself in. Or write in a real-life situation that you can quickly explain to a small group. Now, briefly write out the behavior (what you would do and say) that you would use in the situation to influence the person to do what you want.

Situation # _____ or my situation:

_____

_____

Influencing tactic(s) to use:

_____

Behavior:

_____

_____

_____

_____

_____

SB 8-2

Procedure 1 (10–20 minutes)

Break up into groups of three, with one or two groups of two if needed. Try not to have in the group two members that selected the same situation; use people who selected their own situation. First, try to agree quickly on which influencing tactics are most appropriate in each situation. Select a spokesperson to give group answers to the class. In preparation for role playing, have each person state the behavior to handle the situation selected. The others give feedback to improve how to handle the situation—by avoiding, changing, and/or adding to the behavior (for example, "I would not say _____; I'd say _____; I'd add _____ to what you have now").

Procedure 2 (5-10 minutes)
SB 8-3
One situation at a time, each group spokesperson tells the class which influencing styles it would use, followed by brief remarks from the instructor. The instructor may also ask people who selected their own situation to tell the class the situation.

Preparation (1-2 minutes)
During the three role-plays, you will be the influencer, influencee, and observer. In preparation, determine who will be the first to role-play the selected situation, who will play the role of the person being influenced, and who will be the observer. Do the same for each of the other two role-plays, giving each person a chance to play all three roles.

Role-play 1 (7-15 minutes)
The influencer role-plays influencing the influencee while the observer takes notes on what was done well and how the influencing could be improved. After the role-play, both the influencee and observer give the influencer feedback for future improvement. Do not start the next role-play until told to do so.

Role-play 2 (7-15 minutes)
The second influencer role-plays influencing the influencee while the observer takes notes on what was done well and how the influencing could be improved. After the role-play, both the influencee and observer give the influencer feedback for future improvement. Do not start the next role-play until told to do so.

Role-play 3 (7-15 minutes)
The third influencer role-plays influencing the influencee while the observer takes notes on what was done well and how the influencing could be improved. After the role-play, both the influencee and observer give the influencer feedback for future improvement.

Conclusion: The instructor may lead a class discussion and/or make concluding remarks.

Application (2-4 minutes):   What did I learn from this exercise? How will I use this knowledge in the future?

Sharing: Volunteers give their answers to the application section.

/ / / SKILL-BUILDING EXERCISE 8-4 / / /

Developing New Habits

Experience: Individual may share habits in groups or entire class, in class or online.

AACSB Competencies: Analytic and application of knowledge.

Objective: To develop and share new habits.

Preparation: Select one or more topics from this chapter that will help you improve your human relations. Develop a new habit following the guideline from Chapter 1, section Habits and Skill-Building Exercise 1-4, on how to develop your cure, routine, and reward-change.

Procedure (5-30 minutes)
Follow the procedures from Skill Builder 1-4.

1. T.
2. F. "Human relations" is not a source of power—personal power is the power source.
3. T.
4. F. There is no most effective influencing tactic; it depends on the situation.
5. T.
6. F. Relations with bosses and subordinates are called vertical politics; relations with peers and others are called horizontal politics.
7. F. Placing blame only makes people defensive, so it should be avoided.

/ / / NOTES / / /

1. L. Tomkins and E. Ulus, "Is Narcissism Undermining Critical Reflection in Our Business Schools?" *Academy of Management Learning & Education* 14, no. 4 (2015): 595–606.
2. A.C. Peng, J.M. Schaubroeck, and L. Li, "Social Exchange Implications of Own and Coworkers' Experiences of Supervisor Abuse," *Academy of Management Journal* 57(5) (2014): 1385–1405.
3. D. Collinson and D. Tourish, "Teaching Leadership Critically: New Directions for Leadership Pedagogy," *Academy of Management Learning & Education* 14(4) (2015): 576–594.
4. I. Sutherland, J.R. Gosling, and J. Jelinek, "Aesthetics of Power: Why Teaching About Power Is Easier Than Learning for Power, and What Business Schools Could Do About It," *Academy of Management Learning & Education* 14, no. 4 (2015): 607–624.
5. Q.N. Huy, K.G. Corley, and M.S. Kraatz, "From Support to Mutiny: Shifting Legitmacy Judgments and Emotional Reactions Impacting the Implementation of Radical Change," *Academy of Management Journal* 57, no. 6 (2014): 1650–1680.
6. J.D. Westphal and G. Shani, "Psyched-Up to Suck-Up: Self-Regulated Cognition, Interpersonal Influence, and Recommendations for Board Appointments in the Corporate Elite," *Academy of Management Journal* 59, no. 2 (2016): 479–509.
7. I. Sutherland, J.R. Gosling, and J. Jelinek, "Aesthetics of Power: Why Teaching About Power Is Easier Than Learning for Power, and What Business Schools Could Do About It," *Academy of Management Learning & Education* 14, no. 4 (2015): 607–624.
8. R.D. Costigan and K.E. Brink, "Another Perspective on MBA Program Alignment: An Investigation of Learning Goals," *Academy of Management Learning & Education* 14(2) (2015): 260–276.
9. L.M. Little, V.S. Major, A.S. Hinojosa, D.L. Nelson, "Professional Image Maintenance: How Women Navigate Pregnancy in the Workplace," *Academy of Management Journal* 58(1) (2015): 8–37.
10. Y. Liu, G.R. Ferris, J. Xu, B.A. Weitz, and P.L. Perrewe, "When Ingratiation Backfires: The Role of Political Skill in the Ingratiation-Internship Performance Relationship," *Academy of Management Learning & Education* 13(3) (2014): 569–586.
11. D. Baden, "Look on the Bright Side: A Comparison of Positive and Negative Role Models in Business Ethics Education," *Academy of Management Learning & Education* 13(2) (2014): 154–170.
12. A.A. Cannella, C.D. Jones, and M.C. Withers, "Family-Versus Lone-Founder-Controlled Public Corporations: Social Identity Theory and Boards of Directors," *Academy of Management Journal* 58, no. 2 (2015): 436–459.
13. J.D. Westphal and G. Shani, "Psyched-Up to Suck-Up: Self-Regulated Cognition, Interpersonal Influence, and Recommendations for Board Appointments in the Corporate Elite," *Academy of Management Journal* 59, no. 2 (2016): 479–509.

14. Statement added at the suggestion of a reviewer, May 30, 2017.

15. I. Sutherland, J.R. Gosling, and J. Jelinek, "Aesthetics of Power: Why Teaching About Power Is Easier Than Learning for Power, and What Business Schools Could Do About It," *Academy of Management Learning & Education* 14, no. 4 (2015): 607-624.

16. A.C. Peng, J.M. Schaubroeck, and L. Li, "Social Exchange Implications of Own and Coworkers' Experiences of Supervisor Abuse," *Academy of Management Journal* 57(5) (2014): 1385-1405.

17. D. Ma, M. Rhee, and D. Yang, "Power Sources Mismatch and the Effectiveness of Interorganizational Relations: The Case of Venture Capital Syndication," *Academy of Management Journal* 56(3) (2013): 711-734.

18. D. Collinson and D. Tourish, "Teaching Leadership Critically: New Directions for Leadership Pedagogy," *Academy of Management Learning & Education* 14(4) (2015): 576-594.

19. R.D. Costigan and K.E. Brink, "Another Perspective on MBA Program Alignment: An Investigation of Learning Goals," *Academy of Management Learning & Education* 14(2) (2015): 260-276.

20. I. Sutherland, J.R. Gosling, and J. Jelinek, "Aesthetics of Power: Why Teaching About Power Is Easier Than Learning for Power, and What Business Schools Could Do About It," *Academy of Management Learning & Education* 14, no. 4 (2015): 607-624.

21. J.D. Westphal and G. Shani, "Psyched-Up to Suck-Up: Self-Regulated Cognition, Interpersonal Influence, and Recommendations for Board Appointments in the Corporate Elite," *Academy of Management Journal* 59, no. 2 (2016): 479-509.

22. A.C. Peng, J.M. Schaubroeck, and L. Li, "Social Exchange Implications of Own and Coworkers' Experiences of Supervisor Abuse," *Academy of Management Journal* 57(5) (2014): 1385-1405.

23. D. Collinson and D. Tourish, "Teaching Leadership Critically: New Directions for Leadership Pedagogy," *Academy of Management Learning & Education* 14(4) (2015): 576-594.

24. M. Kilduff, D. Crossland, W. Tsai, and M.T. Bowers, "Magnification and Correction of the Acolyte Effect: Initial Benefits and Ex Post Settling Up in NFL Coaching Careers," *Academy of Management Journal* 59(1) (2016): 352-375.

25. T. Robbins,"On Keys to Success," *INC.* (June 2015): 12.

26. S.J. Creary, B.B. Caza, and L.M. Roberts, "Out of the Box? How Managing a Subordinate's Multiple Identities Affects the Quality of a Manager-Subordinate Relationship," *Academy of Management Review* 40(4) (2015): 538-562.

27. D.J. Harmon, S.E. Green, and G.T. Goodnight, "A Model of Rhetorical Legitimation: The Structure of Communication and Cognition Underlying Institutional Maintenance and Change," *Academy of Management Review* 40(1) (2015): 76-95.

28. R.L. Hoefer and S.E. Green, "A Rhetorical Model of Institutional Decision Making: The Role of Rhetoric in the Formation and Change of Legitimacy Judgments," *Academy of Management Review* 41(1) (2015): 130-150.

29. C.K. Lam, X. Huang, and S.C.H. Chan, "The Threshold Effect of Participative Leadership and the Role of Leader Information Sharing," *Academy of Management Journal* 58(3) (2015): 836-855.

30. J. Naisbitt, "On Power," *Forbes* (November 23, 2015): 160.

31. M. Andeessen, "Steve Martin Quote taken from" *Fortune* (November 17, 2014): 126.

32. L.M. Little, V.S. Major, A.S. Hinojosa, D.L. Nelson, "Professional Image Maintenance: How Women Navigate Pregnancy in the Workplace," *Academy of Management Journal* 58(1) (2015): 8-37.

33. Aime et al., "The Riddle of Heterarchy."

34. Y. Liu, G.R. Ferris, J. Xu, B.A. Weitz, and P.L. Perrewe, "When Ingratiation Backfires: The Role of Political Skill in the Ingratiation-Internship Performance Relationship," *Academy of Management Learning & Education* 13(3) (2014): 569-586.

35. A. Lawrence, "A Racing Champ's High-Octane Encore," *Fortune* (June 15, 2015): 67-71.

36. B.M. Galvin, D. Lange, and B.E. Ashforth, "Narcissistic Organizational Identification: Seeing Oneself as Central to the Organization's Identity," *Academy of Management Review* 40(2) (2015): 163-181.

37. J.D. Westphal and G. Shani, "Psyched-Up to Suck-Up: Self-Regulated Cognition, Interpersonal Influence, and Recommendations for Board Appointments in the Corporate Elite," *Academy of Management Journal* 59, no. 2 (2016): 479-509.

38. E. Bernstein, "If You Want to Persuade People, Try Altercasting," *The Wall Street Journal* (September 5, 2016): D1, D2.

39. R. McCammon, "Do Me A Solid?" *Entrepreneur* (March 2016): 15-16.

40. D.J. Harmon, S.E. Green, G.T. Goodnight, "A Model of Rhetorical Legitimation: The Structure of Communication and Cognition Underlying Institutional Maintenance and Change," *Academy of Management Review* 40(1) (2015): 76-95.

41. R. McCammon, "Do Me A Solid?" *Entrepreneur* (March 2016): 15-16.

42. Y. Liu, G.R. Ferris, J. Xu, B.A. Weitz, and P.L. Perrewe, "When Ingratiation Backfires: The Role of Political Skill in the Ingratiation-Internship Performance Relationship," *Academy of Management Learning & Education* 13(3) (2014): 569-586.

43. D. Baden, "Look on the Bright Side: A Comparison of Positive and Negative Role Models in Business Ethics Education," *Academy of Management Learning & Education* 13(2) (2014): 154-170.

44. E. Grialva and P.D. Harms, "Narcissism: An Integrative Synthesis and Dominance Complementary Model," *Academy of Management Perspectives* 28(2) (2014): 106-127.

45. Y. Liu, G.R. Ferris, J. Xu, B.A. Weitz, and P.L. Perrewe, "When Ingratiation Backfires: The Role of Political Skill in the Ingratiation-Internship Performance Relationship," *Academy of Management Learning & Education* 13(3) (2014): 569-586.

46. J. Pfeffer, "Don't Dismiss Office Politics—Teach It," *Wall Street Journal* (October 24, 2011): R6.

47. P. Lencioni, "Being Smart Is Overrated," *INC.* (October 2014): 128.

48. S.J. Creary, B.B. Caza, and L.M. Roberts, "Out of the Box? How Managing a Subordinate's Multiple Identities Affects the Quality of a Manager-Subordinate Relationship," *Academy of Management Review* 40(4) (2015): 538-562.

49. J. Pfeffer, "Don't Dismiss Office Politics—Teach It," *Wall Street Journal* (October 24, 2011): R6.

50. G. Di Stenfano, A.A. King, and G. Verona, "Sanctioning in the Wild: Rational Calculus and Retributive Instincts in Gourmet Cuisine," *Academy of Management Journal* 58(3) (2015): 906-931.

51. S.J. Creary, B.B. Caza, and L.M. Roberts, "Out of the Box? How Managing a Subordinate's Multiple Identities Affects the Quality of a Manager-Subordinate Relationship," *Academy of Management Review* 40(4) (2015): 538-562.

52. Zig Ziglar website www.Ziglar.com accessed June 1, 2017.

53. J. Pfeffer, "Don't Dismiss Office Politics—Teach It," *Wall Street Journal* (October 24, 2011): R6.

54. E. Grialva and P.D. Harms, "Narcissism: An Integrative Synthesis and Dominance Complementary Model," *Academy of Management Perspectives* 28(2) (2014): 106-127.

55. M.D. Baer, R.K.D. Kahlon, J.A. Colquitt, J.B. Rodell, R. Outlaw, and D.M. Long, "Uneasy Lies the Head that Bears the Trust: The Effects of Feeling Trusted on Emotional Exhaustion," *Academy of Management Journal* 58(6) (2015): 1637-1657.

56. S.J. Creary, B.B. Caza, and L.M. Roberts, "Out of the Box? How Managing a Subordinate's Multiple Identities Affects the Quality of a Manager-Subordinate Relationship," *Academy of Management Review* 40(4) (2015): 538-562.

57. G. O'Brian, "Fixing the First Impression," *Entrepreneur* accessed online May 31, 2017.

58. S.J. Creary, B.B. Caza, and L.M. Roberts, "Out of the Box? How Managing a Subordinate's Multiple Identities Affects the Quality of a Manager-Subordinate Relationship," *Academy of Management Review* 40(4) (2015): 538-562.

59. R. McCammon, "How to Own the Room," *BusinessWeek* accessed online March 24, 2017.

60. M.D. Baer, R.K.D. Kahlon, J.A. Colquitt, J.B. Rodell, R. Outlaw, and D.M. Long, "Uneasy Lies the Head that Bears the Trust: The Effects of Feeling Trusted on Emotional Exhaustion," *Academy of Management Journal* 58(6) (2015): 1637-1657.

61. E. Bernstein, "Venting Isn't Good for Us," *The Wall Street Journal* (August 11, 2015): D1, D4.

62. N. Li, B.L. Kirkman, and C.O.L.H. Porter, "Toward a Model of Work Team Altruism," *Academy of Management Review* 39(4) (2014): 541-565.

63. N. Li, B.L. Kirkman, and C.O.L.H. Porter, "Toward a Model of Work Team Altruism," *Academy of Management Review* 39(4) (2014): 541-565.

64. B.M. Galvin, D. Lange, and B.E. Ashforth, "Narcissistic Organizational Identification: Seeing Oneself as Central to the Organization's Identity," *Academy of Management Review* 40(2) (2015): 163-181.

65. A.C. Peng, J.M. Schaubroeck, and L. Li, "Social Exchange Implications of Own and Coworkers' Experiences of Supervisor Abuse," *Academy of Management Journal* 57(5) (2014): 1385-1405.

66. S.J. Creary, B.B. Caza, and L.M. Roberts, "Out of the Box? How Managing a Subordinate's Multiple Identities Affects the Quality of a Manager-Subordinate Relationship," *Academy of Management Review* 40(4) (2015): 538-562.

67. M.D. Baer, R.K.D. Kahlon, J.A. Colquitt, J.B. Rodell, R. Outlaw, and D.M. Long, "Uneasy Lies the Head that Bears the Trust: The Effects of Feeling Trusted on Emotional Exhaustion," *Academy of Management Journal* 58(6) (2015): 1637-1657.

68. G. O'Brian, "Fixing the First Impression," *Entrepreneur* accessed online May 31, 2017.

69. R. McCammon, "Do Me A Solid?" *Entrepreneur* (March 2016): 15-16.

70. N. Li, B.L. Kirkman, and C.O.L.H. Porter, "Toward a Model of Work Team Altruism," *Academy of Management Review* 39(4) (2014): 541-565.

71. R. McCammon, "Do Me A Solid?" *Entrepreneur* (March 2016): 15-16.

72. G. Di Stenfano, A.A. King, and G. Verona, "Sanctioning in the Wild: Rational Calculus and Retributive Instincts in Gourmet Cuisine," *Academy of Management Journal* 58(3) (2015): 906-931.

73. N. Li, B.L. Kirkman, and C.O.L.H. Porter, "Toward a Model of Work Team Altruism, *Academy of Management Review* 39(4) (2014): 541-565.

74. R. McCammon, "Do Me A Solid?" *Entrepreneur* (March 2016): 15-16.

75. G. O'Brian, "Fixing the First Impression," *Entrepreneur* accessed online May 31, 2017.

Networking and Negotiating

©Design Pics/Don Hammond

LEARNING OUTCOMES

After completing this chapter, you should be able to:

LO 9-1 List and explain the steps in the networking process.

LO 9-2 Describe what a one-minute self-sell is and what it contains.

LO 9-3 Briefly describe how to conduct a networking interview.

LO 9-4 List and explain the steps in the negotiating process.

LO 9-5 Briefly describe how to plan for negotiations.

LO 9-6 Briefly describe how to bargain.

LO 9-7 Explain the influencing process.

LO 9-8 Define the following 11 key terms (in order of appearance in the chapter):

networking	coalition
networks	negotiating
networking process	negotiating process
one-minute self-sell	negotiating planning
networking interview	bargaining
process	influencing process

OPENING CASE WORK SCENARIO

/ / / Toyota started as a family business, and the Toyoda family still has power over the company. Hiroshi Okuda was the first nonfamily member in over 30 years to head Toyota as president. Toyota had become lethargic and overly bureaucratic and had lost market share in Japan to both Mitsubishi and Honda. Hiroshi was not the typical Japanese president, that is, one who would make changes slowly and with consensus.

President Hiroshi Okuda moved quickly and powerfully to change Toyota, going against Japanese cultural traditions to embrace a more global (primarily American) perspective of managing. Even though lifetime employment is common in Japan, Hiroshi replaced almost one-third of the highest-ranking executives. He changed the long-standing Japanese promotion system based on seniority by adding performance as a factor. Some outstanding performers moved up several management levels at one time—a practice unheard of in the history of Toyota.

Hiroshi Okuda turned Toyota around; in a few short years, the company better understood the Japanese customer, and market share and sales were growing. However, it has been speculated that although Hiroshi did a great job, at the same time he offended Toyoda family members. Thus, he was promoted to board chair to keep him out of day-to-day management and then replaced. Today the company is run by family member Akio Toyoda.[1] It was under his leadership that Toyota ran into quality problems. For more information about Toyota and to update the information provided, visit Toyota's Web site at www .toyota.com. / / /

HOW NETWORKING AND NEGOTIATING AFFECT BEHAVIOR, HUMAN RELATIONS, HAPPINESS, AND PERFORMANCE

WORK APPLICATION 9-1

Explain how networking and/or negotiating have affected behavior, human relations, and performance where you work or have worked.

As discussed in prior chapters, much of our happiness comes from our relationships.[2] Establishing and maintaining effective interpersonal relationships with people inside and outside organizations is important to the firm and your career success.[3] Networking and negotiating are interpersonal skills.[4] So, whether you are starting or advancing in your career, your career success will be based on relationships.[5] Thus, your ability to network and negotiate will affect how you behave, your human relations, happiness, and your performance.

Networking and negotiating are influencing tactics, but they are not about unethical narcissistic manipulation of people.[6] We all have something unique to offer others, and the more you focus on genuine connections with others, and look for ways to help them—rather than just focus on what they can do for you—the more likeable and successful you become.[7] In this chapter, you will learn how to network and negotiate to influence people to help you achieve your objectives.

NETWORKING

Recall that networking is a form of political behavior (Chapter 8). Before we get into the details of networking, complete Self-Assessment Exercise 9-1 to determine your networking skill.

/ / / Self-Assessment Exercise 9-1 / / /

Your Networking Skill

Identify each of the 16 statements according to how accurately they describe your behavior. Place the number (1 to 5) on the line before each statement.

Describes me				Does not describe me
5	4	3	2	1

_____ 1. When I take on a task (a new project, a career move, a major purchase), I seek help from people I know and from new contacts.

_____ 2. I view networking as a way to create win–win situations.

_____ 3. I like to meet new people; I can easily strike up a conversation with people I don't know.

_____ 4. I can quickly state two or three of my most important accomplishments.

_____ 5. When I contact businesspeople who can help me (such as with career information), I have goals for the communication.

_____ 6. When I contact businesspeople who can help me, I have a planned, short opening statement.

_____ 7. When I contact businesspeople who can help me, I praise their accomplishments.

_____ 8. When I contact people who can help me, I have a set of questions to ask.

_____ 9. I know contact information for at least 100 people who can potentially help me.

_____ 10. I have a file or database with contact information of people who can help me in my career, and I keep it updated and continue to add new names.

_____ 11. During communications with people who can help me, I ask them for names of others I can contact for more information.

_____ 12. When seeking help from others, I ask how I might help them.

_____ 13. When people help me, I thank them at the time, and for big favors, I write a follow-up thank-you note.

(continued)

_____ 14. I keep in touch with people who have helped or can potentially help me in my career at least once a year, and I update them on my career progress.

_____ 15. I have regular communications with people in my industry who work for different organizations, such as members of trade or professional organizations.

_____ 16. I attend trade, professional, and career meetings to maintain relationships and to make new contacts.

Add up your score and place it here _____. Then on the continuum below, mark the point that represents your score.

Effective networking   80 ---- 70 ---- 60 ---- 50 ---- 40 ---- 30 ---- 20 ---- 10   Ineffective networking

If you are a full-time student, you may not score high on networking effectiveness, but that's OK. You can develop networking skills by following the steps and guidelines in this chapter.

Networking is *the ongoing process of building interconnected relationships for the purpose of politicking and socializing.* Networking is about building professional relationships and friendships using ethical behavior.[8] **Networks** are *clusters of people joined by a variety of links,* as illustrated in Exhibit 9.1. Your primary connections give you access to their networks, which are secondary connections for you.

Networking is about marketing yourself; *you* are responsible for your career and the exposure of your talents and skills. Whenever you start something—working on a new project, planning a career move, buying a car or a house—use networking.

The Why and Reality of Networking

Let's begin by stating some of the objectives of networking, followed by stating its importance, and ending with the networking process steps.

EXHIBIT 9.1 | Networks

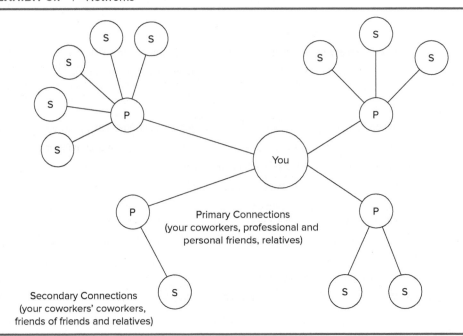

Networking Objectives   Here are some of the many reasons to develop your networking skills:

- *To get a job or a better position.* Many jobs being filled today are not posted, and many that are posted are unofficially filled before they are posted. Without networking, you will never know about these job opportunities.[9]

- *To perform better at your current job.* Don't reinvent the wheel; find someone who has "been there and done that" for help. Some jobs, such as sales, require networking to acquire new business.

- *To advance within an organization.* Network to get to know the power players, to gain support and recognition from higher-level managers, and to find a mentor to help you advance.[10]

- *To stay current in your field.* Network through trade and professional organization meetings with people outside your organization to understand the latest developments in your field.

- *To maintain mobility.* If you think that once you have a job, you don't have to network or stay current in your field, you may be in for a big surprise. People today use networking to get better jobs.[11]

- *To develop relationships.* We all want to have both professional and personal friends.[12] Networking is especially important if you take a job in a new location.

Communication Skills
Refer to CS Question 1.

WORK APPLICATION 9-2

Explain how you have used or will use networking to help your career.

Communication Skills
Refer to CS Question 2.

Learning Outcome 9-1

List and explain the steps in the networking process.

It's Not What You Know, It's Who You Know That's Important   To a large extent, this statement is true, but there are exceptions. Its also been said that its not who you know, but who knows you. Here is a general job-related illustration. Sending out resumes and posting them on the web in areas such as www.ideed.com are not how most people are getting jobs today. Of the many ways to secure a job, networking is by far the most successful way to discover employment opportunities. According to the **U.S. Department of Labor**, two-thirds of all jobs are located through word of mouth, informal referrals, relatives, friends, and acquaintances. Networking results in more job opportunities than all the other job search methods combined.[13]

If you get a job through networking, is that fair? Being fair is really not the issue—reality is. You have two choices: complain about how unfair networking is, or develop your networking skills.

Professional networking sounds easy and we tend to think it should come naturally. However, the reality is that networking is a learned skill that just about everyone struggles with at some time or another.

The Networking Process   The next five subsections provide a how-to network process that will enhance your career development.[14] The networking process is summarized in Model 9.1. The **networking process** includes these tasks: *(1) perform a self-assessment and set objectives, (2) create a one-minute self-sell, (3) develop a network, (4) conduct networking interviews, and (5) maintain the network.*

Although the same networking process applies to broad career development, as discussed under networking objectives, we'll focus more on the job search for an internship or part-time or full-time jobs.

MODEL 9.1 | The Networking Process

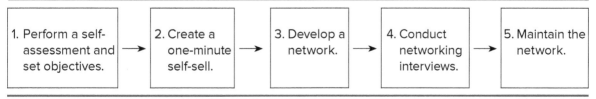

1. Perform a self-assessment and set objectives. → 2. Create a one-minute self-sell. → 3. Develop a network. → 4. Conduct networking interviews. → 5. Maintain the network.

Source: A. Gumbus and R. N. Lussier, "Career Development: Enhancing Your Networking Skills," *Clinical Leadership & Management Review,* vol. 17, no. 1, 2003, 16–20.

Perform a Self-Assessment and Set Objectives

The task of self-assessment can help clarify your skills, competencies, and knowledge. Self-assessment can also give you insight into your transferable skills and the criteria that are important to you in a new job. **Appendix A** has a Career Planning Skill-Building Exercise A-2 that includes a self-assessment. You can go to Appendix A and do so now.

Communication Skills
Refer to CS Question 3.

Accomplishments and Job Interviews   After completing a self-assessment, you are ready to translate your talents into accomplishments. The results you achieved in your jobs and/or college are the best evidence of your skills. Accomplishments are what set you apart and provide evidence of your skills and abilities. You must articulate what you have accomplished in your past in a way that is clear, concise, and compelling. Write down your accomplishments (at least two or three), and include them in your resume, and be sure to discuss them during job interviews.

If you are asked a broad general question, such as, "Tell me about yourself," you can use the accomplishment statements in your resume as your answer.

WORK APPLICATION 9-3

Write a networking objective.

Set Networking Objectives   Next, you need to clearly state your goal, for example, to get a mentor; to determine the expertise, skills, and requirements needed for . . .; to get feedback on my resume and job and/or career preparation for a career move into . . .; to attain a job as . . .; and so on.

Create Your One-Minute Self-Sell

Learning Outcome 9-2

Describe what a one-minute self-sell is and what it contains.

You have most likely seen the TV show *Shark Tank* and know the importance of the elevator pitch. Well, the one-minute self-sell is your networking self-pitch.

Based on your goal, your next step is to create a one-minute self-sell to help you accomplish your goal. The **one-minute self-sell** is *an opening statement used in networking that quickly summarizes your history and career plan and asks a question.* To take 60 seconds or less, your message must be concise, but it also needs to be clear and compelling. It stimulates conversation by asking your network for help in the area of support, coaching, contacts, knowledge of the industry, and the like.[15]

History   Start with a summary of the highlights of your career to date. Include your most recent career and/or school history and a description of the type of work or internship performed and/or the courses you have taken. Be sure to include the industry and type of organization.

Plans   Next, state the target career you are seeking, the industry you prefer, and a specific function or role. You can also mention names of organizations you are targeting as well as letting the acquaintance know why you are looking for work.

Question   Last, ask a question to encourage two-way communication. The question will vary depending on the contact person and your goal or the reason you are using the one-minute self-sell. Following are some sample questions:

- In what areas might there be opportunities for a person with my experience?
- In what other fields can I use these skills or this degree?
- In what other positions in your organization could my skills be used?
- How does my targeted future career sound to you? Is it a match with my education and skills?
- Do you know of any job openings in my field?

Communication Skills
Refer to CS Question 4.

WORK APPLICATION 9-4

Write a one-minute self-sell to achieve your networking objective from Work Application 9.3.

Write and Practice Your One-Minute Self-Sell—Example   Here's a sample self-sell: *"Hello, my name is Will Smith. I am a senior at Springfield College, graduating in May with a major in marketing, and I have completed an internship in the marketing department at the Big Y supermarket. I'm seeking a job in sales in the food industry. Can you give me some ideas on the types of sales positions available in the food industry?"*

Practice delivering your self-sell with family and friends, and get feedback to improve it. Skill-Building Exercise 9-1, Networking Skills, will give you the opportunity to develop and practice a one-minute self-sell.

Develop Your Network

Here is sequential approach to developing your network.

Primary Contacts   Begin with people you know—your primary contacts. Everyone can create a network list of about 200 people consisting of professional and personal contacts. Address books (paper, Facebook, and e-mail) and phone lists are written network listings. A simple way to start is to set up a separate e-mail or **LinkedIn** account. Professional contacts include colleagues (past and present), trade and professional organizations, alumni associations, vendors, suppliers, managers, and mentors. On a personal level, your network includes family, neighbors, friends, religious groups, and personal service providers (doctor, insurance agent, hairstylist, politician).

Secondary Contacts   Ask your primary contacts for secondary contacts with whom you can network. Continually update and add to your list with referrals from others. Your network can get you closer to the decision makers in a hiring position.

Using Your Self-Sell   When meeting your primary and secondary contacts, introduce yourself with your one-minute sell. When you are introduced to people, call them by name two or three times during the conversation. If you think they can help you, don't stop with casual conversation; make an appointment at a later time for a phone conversation, personal meeting, coffee, or lunch. Get their business cards to add to your network list, and give them your card and/or resume when appropriate.

Expanded Contacts   Next, expand your list to include people you don't know. Where should you go? Anywhere people gather. Get more involved with professional associations and attend their meetings and conferences;[16] many have special student memberships and some even have college chapters. Other places to go to network with people you don't know include the Chamber of Commerce; college alumni clubs and reunions; civic organizations (**Rotary, Lions, Knights of Columbus, Kiwanis, Elks, Moose**); trade shows and career fairs; charity, community, and religious groups (your local church); and social clubs (exercise, boating, golf, tennis). E-groups and chat rooms are available for all types of interests.

Starting Conversations   As stated, you can use your self-sell as a conversation starter with anyone. Here are some additional ways to start a conversation.

In any setting

- Any questions about the seasons or weather—Is it hot enough for you?
- A question about traffic—Did you get stuck in traffic getting here?
- How is your day going?
- Where are you from?
- What do you do?

At a networking event   Any of the questions above and

- Ask or comment about the information on the person's name badge
- What brought you here today?
- How long have you been doing what you do—and/or with XYX organization?
- What do you enjoy most about what you do—and/or your organization?

- How did you get involved in ... (networking event, career, company, association)?
- What trends or challenges do you see in your company and/or industry?
- How do you stay current in your field?
- Is there anyone you can suggest I speak to to learn more about your company/field? (ask secondary contacts)

At a conference   Any of the questions above and

- Are you presenting?
- What session are you planning to attend?
- What do you think of the keynote speaker and/or session presenter?
- What sessions have you attended?
- What do you hope to gain from this conference
- Is there anyone you can introduce me to, or suggest I speak to to learn more about your company/field? (ask secondary contacts)

Job Search Networking Form   Computer software is available to help you. See Exhibit 9.2 for an example Networking Form. Of course, you can customize your system to suit your needs.

Conduct Networking Interviews

Set up a networking interview to meet your objective. It may take many interviews to meet a goal, such as the goal of getting a job. An informational interview is a phone call or, preferably, a face-to-face meeting that you initiate to meet objectives, such as to gain information from a contact with hands-on experience in your field of interest. You are the interviewer, so you need to be prepared with specific questions to ask the contact regarding your targeted career or industry. Be sure to dress appropriately and be polite. You will learn about proper job interviewing etiquette in Appendix A.

Ask for a 15- to 20-Minute Meeting   Ask for a 15- to 20-minute meeting and many people will talk to you because they are flattered, and most people do like doing favors,[17] like meeting with you. Such a meeting can be most helpful when you have accessed someone within an

EXHIBIT 9.2 | Job Search Network Form

Primary Contact: Bill Smith, fraternity brother
Secondary Contact: John Smith
Smith Brothers Corporation
225 Westwood Street
Anytown, WI 59025
643-986-1182
john_smith@smith.com
Contacts with Person:
6/2/18 Bill called his dad from our fraternity house and I spoke with John and set up an appointment to meet him at his office on 6/5.
6/5/18 Talked for 20 minutes about Smith Brothers and career opportunities. No openings.
6/6/18 Mailed thank-you note for meeting and career info and advice, with copy of business card and resume.
6/18/18 Sent e-mail telling Smith I met with Peter Clark.
Secondary Contacts Received [Make separate page for each.]
Peter Clark, The Ranch Golf Club
Tom Broadhurst, Lobow Mercedes Dealer
Carol Shine, Consultant

Learning Outcome 9-3

Briefly describe how to conduct a networking interview.

organization you'd like to join or have a contact in an industry you are targeting. Be sure not to linger beyond the time you have been offered, unless you are invited to stay. Leave a business card and resume so the person can contact you in case something comes up. If you are a full-time student or between jobs, you can have professional business cards made up for a relatively low cost. Some college career centers will help you develop business cards and have them printed.

The **networking interview process** includes these steps: *(1) establish rapport—praise and read the person, (2) deliver the one-minute self-sell, (3) ask prepared questions, (4) get additional contacts for your network, (5) ask your contacts how you might help them, and (6) follow up with a thank-you note and status report.* Let's discuss each step.

Establish Rapport—Praise and Read the Person   Provide a brief introduction (your name and title—which can be "student at . . . college"), and thank the contact for his or her time. Give the person a copy of your business card and resume. Clearly state the purpose of the meeting. Do some research, and impress the person by stating an accomplishment, such as "I enjoyed your presentation at the CLMA meeting on . . ." As we discussed in Chapter 8, you should read the person and try to match his or her style.

Deliver Your One-Minute Self-Sell   Even if the person has already heard it, say it again. This enables you to quickly summarize your background and career direction and start your questions.

Ask Prepared Questions   Ask questions. Your questions should vary depending on your objective, the contact, and how the person may be able to help you with your job search. Sample questions include:

- What do you think of my qualifications for this field?
- With your knowledge of the industry, what career opportunities do you see in the future?
- What advice do you have for me as I begin/advance in my career?
- If you were exploring this field, with whom would you talk?

During the interview, if the interviewee mentions anything that could hinder your search, ask how such obstacles could be overcome.

Get Additional Contacts for Your Network   The last question above is an example of how to ask for additional contacts. Always ask for names of others you should speak with. Most people can give you three names, so if you are offered only one, ask for others. Add the new contact to your network list. Note that this is done in the job search network form in Exhibit 9.2. When contacting new people, be sure to refer to your primary network person's name as an introduction.

Ask Your Contacts How You Might Help Them   Offer a copy of a recent journal article, or any additional information that came up in your conversation. Remember, it's all about building relationships and reciprocity.[18] CEO of Pixel Mobb Christopher Perilli say to be generous and help others grow as individuals.[19] Do favors for others.

Follow up with a Thank-You Note and Status Report   Keeping them posted on your job search progress as well as sending a thank-you note (or e-mail) after the meeting also solidifies the relationship. By sending a thank-you note (or e-mail) with another business card and/or resume and following up with your progress, you are continuing the networking relationship and maintaining a contact for the future. Notice that this is noted in the job search network form in Exhibit 9.2.

It is always helpful to create a log of calls, meetings, and contacts to maintain your network as it expands. See Model 9.2 for a review of the networking interview steps.

MODEL 9.2 | Networking Interview Process

```
┌──────────────────┐     ┌──────────────────┐     ┌──────────────────┐
│ Step 1: Establish │     │ Step 2: Deliver  │     │ Step 3: Ask      │
│ rapport—praise    │ ──▶ │ your one-minute  │ ──▶ │ prepared         │
│ and read the      │     │ self-sell.       │     │ questions.       │
│ person.           │     │                  │     │                  │
└──────────────────┘     └──────────────────┘     └──────────────────┘

┌──────────────────┐     ┌──────────────────┐     ┌──────────────────┐
│ Step 4: Get       │     │ Step 5: Ask      │     │ Step 6: Follow up │
│ additional        │ ──▶ │ your contacts    │ ──▶ │ with a thank-you │
│ contacts for      │     │ how you might    │     │ note and status  │
│ your network.     │     │ help them.       │     │ report.          │
└──────────────────┘     └──────────────────┘     └──────────────────┘
```

Maintain Your Network

Keep your network informed of your career progress. If an individual was helpful in finding your new job, be sure to let that person know the outcome. It is also a good idea to notify everyone in your network that you are in a new position and to provide contact information. Networking doesn't stop once you've made a career change. Make a personal commitment to continue networking to be in charge of your career development. Continue to update, correct, and add to your network list. Always thank others for their time.

As you have been helped, you should help others (reciprocity). Besides, you will be amazed at how helping others comes back to you. Try to contact everyone on your network list at least once a year.

Coalitions

Like networking, building coalitions is an influencing tactic of political behavior. It helps to have alliances—people who will help you. Recall our discussion of coalitions in Chapter 8, and how to influence others. A **coalition** is *a short-term network used to meet an objective.* Try to get powerful people on your side, and they can help you get other people in your coalition either directly (they can ask others) or indirectly (you can use their name as connection power to get others to join you).

/// **In the opening case,** Hiroshi Okuda was good at networking within Toyota and with its family owners. If he hadn't been a good networker, he never would have been the first nonfamily member in more than 30 years to head the company. It was through networking that Hiroshi climbed the corporate ladder. A coalition of family members who were against Okuda got him promoted to board chair to remove him from day-to-day management to allow family member Akio Toyoda to take over as CEO. ///

Digital Networking

College-age students and recent college grads grew up networking through social media. Today's employees of all ages are communicating more online through social media networks, and their personal and professional lives are colliding.[20] **Facebook** is generally considered more appropriate for your personal networking and **LinkedIn** more for your professional networking, and some people suggest keeping them separate.[21]

There are nearly 2 billion Facebook social networking users,[22] so you may already have a Facebook account. But do you have a LinkedIn account? As already stated, you can conduct your networking online, but don't neglect in-person communications. A person you interview in-person will know you better and be more likely to help you than a person you've never met.

WORK APPLICATION 9-5

Give a job example of how a coalition was used to achieve an objective.

Networking Do's and Don'ts   AS 9-1

State if you should or should not do each item.
A. Do   B. Don't

_____ 1. Network to know the latest developments in your field.

_____ 2. Network to get help with your current job.

_____ 3. View networking as being unfair.

_____ 4. To keep networking flexible, stay away from having specific goals.

_____ 5. Focus on your weakness during the networking self-assessment.

_____ 6. Develop a self-sell with your history, plans, and question.

_____ 7. During the networking interview, be sure to ask directly for what you want, especially if you are asking for a job.

_____ 8. Ask for a 30-minute networking interview.

_____ 9. Begin the networking interview with your one-minute self-sell.

_____ 10. Be sure to ask for additional contacts during the networking interview; try for three.

_____ 11. When a networking interview is helpful, send a thank-you note and status report.

_____ 12. Contact the people in your network at least once a month.

_____ 13. Start networking with secondary contacts.

Skill-Building Exercise 9-1 develops this skill.

WORK APPLICATION 9-6

What are your strongest and weakest areas of networking? How will you improve your networking skills? Include two or three of the most important tips you learned that you will use.

Clearly, digital social networks have advantages and disadvantages. Some companies encourage their employees to use social networking on the job while others don't. Some firms claim that personal sharing of information skills can be used to improve workplace collaboration and productivity, whereas others point to studies stating that social networking at work hampers business productivity. The big question that is hard to answer is, "Is it business? Or is it personal?" Many firms have developed digital social networking corporate policies.

So how does this relate to you as a student and worker? A study found that the more time young people spend on Facebook, the more likely they are to have weaker study habits and lower grades, as about 25 percent of students check Facebook more than 10 times a day.[23] As a worker, you need to follow the company policy on using digital networking while on the job and focus on doing business, not on personal socializing with friends at work.

NEGOTIATING

Like power and politics, negotiating sometimes has a negative connotation because some people do lie and take advantage of others. Like networking, negotiating is about developing relationships and using the stakeholders' approach to ethics by making sure all parties get a good deal.[24] You may never have to negotiate official company contracts, but as you search for a job, you may be able to negotiate your pay and benefits, as well as salary raises.[25]

Negotiating is *a process in which two or more parties have something the other wants and attempt to come to an exchange agreement.* Negotiation is also called *bargaining.* You may not realize it, but every time you try to meet an objective—to get your way or what you want with the help of others—you are negotiating. So like it or not, you have to negotiate to get what you want. Negotiating is an interpersonal skill[26] that is important to career success.[27] When you negotiate, use your power, influencing tactics, and political

/ / / **Self-Assessment Exercise 9-2** / / /

Your Negotiating Skill

Identify each of the 16 statements according to how accurately they describe your behavior. Place the number (1 to 5) on the line before each statement.

Describes me   Does not describe me

5	4	3	2	1

_____ 1. Before I negotiate, if possible, I find out about the person I will negotiate with to determine what she or he wants and would be willing to give up.

_____ 2. Before I negotiate, I set objectives.

_____ 3. When planning my negotiating presentation, I focus on how the other party will benefit.

_____ 4. Before I negotiate, I have a target price I want to pay, a lowest price I will pay, and an opening offer.

_____ 5. Before I negotiate, I think through options and trade-offs in case I don't get my target price.

_____ 6. Before I negotiate, I think of the questions and objections the other party might have, and I prepare answers.

_____ 7. At the beginning of negotiations, I develop rapport and read the person.

_____ 8. I let the other party make the first offer.

_____ 9. I listen to what the other parties are saying and focus on helping them get what they want, rather than focusing on what I want.

_____ 10. I don't give in too quickly to others' offers.

_____ 11. When I compromise and give up something, I ask for something in return.

_____ 12. If the other party tries to postpone the negotiation, I try to create urgency and tell the other party what he or she might lose.

_____ 13. If I want to postpone the negotiation, I don't let the other party pressure me into making a decision.

_____ 14. When I make a deal, I don't second-guess my decision.

_____ 15. If I can't make an agreement, I ask for advice to help me with future negotiations.

_____ 16. During the entire business negotiating process, I'm trying to develop a relationship, not just a one-time deal.

Add up your score and place it here: ____. Then on the continuum below, mark the point that represents your score.

Effective negotiating   80 ---- 70 ---- 60 ---- 50 ---- 40 ---- 30 ---- 20 ---- 10   Ineffective negotiating

If you did not score high on negotiating effectiveness, that's OK. You can develop negotiating skills by following the steps and guidelines in this chapter.

Communication Skills
Refer to CS Question 5.

behavior (Chapter 8) to help you meet your objectives. If you want to improve your negotiation skills, read on.

In this section, we discuss negotiating and the negotiating process. Before we begin, complete Self-Assessment Exercise 9-2 to determine the behavior you use during negotiating.

The Negotiating Process

Learning Outcome 9-4

List and explain the steps in the negotiating process.

The **negotiating process** has three, and possibly four, steps: *(1) planning, (2) bargaining, (3) possibly a postponement, and (4) an agreement or no agreement.* These steps, which are summarized in Model 9.3, are discussed in separate subsections. Like other models in this

MODEL 9.3 | The Negotiating Process

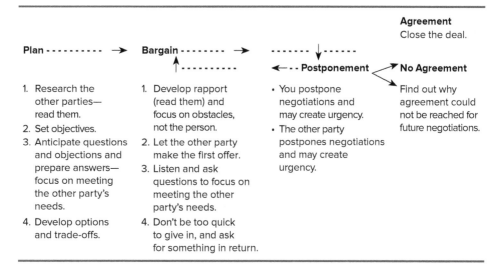

book, Model 9.3 is meant to give you step-by-step guidelines to follow. However, in applying it to multiple types of negotiations, you may have to make slight adjustments.

Negotiating Planning

Learning Outcome 9-5

Briefly describe how to plan for negotiations.

Success or failure in negotiating is often based on preparation. Be clear about what it is you are negotiating over.[28] **Negotiating planning** includes *researching the other parties, setting objectives, anticipating questions and objections and preparing answers, and developing options and trade-offs.* It is helpful to write out your plan; Exhibit 9.3 is a sample negotiating plan sheet, with a professional job offer compensation. You can use the headings and write in your own plan.

EXHIBIT 9.3 | Sample Negotiating Plan

Negotiating Situation

Job offer from the X Company

1. Research the other parties—read them.

What is the cost of living in the job area? What is the going pay for this job in other organizations? What does this company pay others in this job? What is the job market like? Are there lots of others with my qualifications seeking this job (expert power)? What is the negotiation style of the person who will make me the offer? What can I expect to be offered for compensation?

2. Set objectives.

Based on my research, what is the lowest compensation I will accept? What is my target compensation? What is my opening "asking" compensation, if I make the first offer? What is my best alternative to a negotiated agreement [BATNA]? If I don't get my minimum limit, I'll continue to work part-time/keep my current job/get a job with a temporary agency.

3. Anticipate questions and objections and prepare answers.

I may be asked why I should be paid my target compensation or told that it is too high. If so, I'll say that the competitors pay . . . and your company pays . . . and I have this to offer to earn my compensation. I'll say that I have other possible jobs or that I really need . . . to make it worth moving.

4. Develop options and trade-offs.

If I can't get the pay I want, I'll ask for more days off, more in my retirement account, a nice office, an assistant, or the like.

Source: A. Coombes, "The Biggest Mistakes Executives Make When Negotiating a Retirement Package," The Wall Street Journal, June 13, 2016, R1, R2.

Step 1: Research the Other Parties—Read Them   Researching the other party doesn't mean only the person; it includes the person's situation. For example, if you are buying or selling something, find out about competing brands, quality, prices, and so on. For a job, know the average salary in the area.

Know the key power players. When negotiating with one person, find out to whom that person reports and who really makes the decision. Try to meet with the decision maker to negotiate. Try to read the other party; follow the guidelines from Chapter 8 before you even meet to negotiate. Get into their heads.[29] Try to find out what the other parties want and what they will and will not be willing to give up *before* you meet to negotiate.[30]

Find out their personality traits and negotiation style through networking with people who have negotiated with the person you will negotiate with. Match their negotiation style. Do they like to get right down to business or socialize; do they want facts and figures or emotional appeal?[31] If possible, establish a personal relationship before the negotiation. If you have worked with the other party, such as your boss or a potential customer, recall what worked and did not work in the past.

Step 2: Set Objectives   Based on your research, what can you expect? You have to identify the bottom line—one thing you must come away with.[32]

- Set a specific *limit* objective, and be willing to walk away (not come to an agreement) unless you get it. The limit can be considered an upper (most you will pay) or lower (least you will sell for) limit. You need to be willing to walk away from a bad deal.[33]

- Set a *target* objective of what you really want.

- Set an *opening* objective offer that is higher than you expect; you might get it.

- Plan your *Best Alternative to a Negotiated Agreement (BATNA)*— the most advantageous alternative course of action a party can take if negotiations fail and an agreement cannot be reached. Know in advance what you will do if you don't get your limit objective. A BATNA helps you walk away from a bad deal. See Exhibit 9.3 for job BATNAs.

Communication Skills
Refer to CS Question 6.

Remember that the other party is probably also setting three objectives with a BATNA. So don't view the opening offer as final. Also, if you are told there are not exceptions—there usually are, so ask to be an exception.[34] Most successful negotiations result in all parties reaching an agreement that is between their limit and target objectives. This creates a good deal for all, a win-win situation.[35]

As you know, most people don't come right out and identify their objective range and BATNA. These objectives and alternatives come out through negotiations. We'll discuss objectives again later in this section (see "Agreement or No Agreement").

Step 3: Anticipate Questions and Objections and Prepare Answers   You need to be prepared to answer the unasked question—"What's in it for me?" Don't focus on what you want, but on how your deal will benefit the other party (common interest). What will they think is a good deal for them?[36] Talk in "you" and "we," not "I," terms, unless you are telling others what you will do for them.

WORK APPLICATION 9-7

Write negotiating objectives that include limit, target, and opening objectives and a BATNA.

There is a good chance that you will be given objections—reasons why the negotiations will not result in an agreement or a sale. Unfortunately, not everyone will come out and directly tell you their real objections. Thus, you need to listen and ask questions to find out what is preventing an agreement or what the other party wants from you.[37]

You need to fully understand your product or deal and project positive self-esteem that shows enthusiasm and confidence. If the other party does not trust you and believes the deal is not a good one, you will not reach an agreement.[38]

Step 4: Develop Options and Trade-Offs   If you have multiple sellers or job offers, you are in a stronger power position to get your target price. It is common practice to quote other offers and to ask if the other party can beat them. Let other parties know what they have to lose.

You have to plan for alternatives. If you're giving something, you ought to get something.[39] If you have to give up something, or cannot get exactly what you want, be prepared to ask for something in *return*. When an airline was having financial difficulty, it asked employees to take a pay cut. Rather than simply accept a cut, the union asked for a trade-off and got company stock. If the other party asks for a lower price, ask for a concession, such as a larger-volume sale or a longer delivery time. If you can't get the salary you are asking for, ask for more vacation days, paying more of your health benefit, or retirement match.

Bargaining

Learning Outcome 9-6

Briefly describe how to bargain.

After you have planned, you are ready to bargain. Face-to-face negotiations are generally preferred because you can see (read) the other person's nonverbal behavior (Chapter 4) and better understand objections.[40] However, telephone and digital written negotiations work too. **Bargaining** includes: *(1) developing rapport and focusing on obstacles, not on the person, (2) letting the other party make the first offer, (3) listening and asking questions to focus on meeting the other party's needs, (4) not being too quick to give in, and (5) asking for something in return.* As we go through the bargaining steps, you will realize that you have already planned for each step of bargaining.

Step 1: Develop Rapport (Read the Person) and Focus on Obstacles, Not on the Person   Smile and call other parties by name as you greet them. Open with some small talk. Start developing trust and a buy-in relationship. How much time you should wait until you get down to business depends on the other party's style. Some people like to get right down to business, while others want to get to know you before discussing business.[41] Read their style and try to match it.

Focusing on the obstacle, not on the person, means never attacking the other's personality or putting someone down with negative statements, such as, "You are being unfair to ask for such a price cut." Don't make demands or threats.[42] If you do so, the other party will become defensive, you may end up arguing, and it will be harder to reach an agreement.

Step 2: Let the Other Party Make the First Offer   Without setting objectives in preparation for bargaining, how do you know if an offer is any good? With objectives in mind, you have the advantage because if the other party offers you more than your opening and target objective, you can close the agreement. Let's assume you are expecting to be paid $45,000 a year (your target objective), your minimum limit is $40,000, and your opening offer to the employer is $47,000. If the employer offers you $50,000, are you going to say "That's too high; give me $45,000"? However, letting the other person make the first offer is general advice, and there may be times when you would want to make the first offer high to get the other party thinking they got a deal by bringing your price down.

Use the opening offer as a starting point. Remember that the other party probably is starting with an opening offer that can be negotiated up. So start the negotiations from this offer to get to your target objective when you need to. If you are offered $41,000, which is below your limit, you can work the compensation up toward your target. Often, the key to a large raise or beginning salary is bargaining; you must be willing to ask for it and not back down too easily (bargaining step 4), so be persistent.[43]

If the other party seems to be waiting for you to make the first offer, get the other party to make the first offer with questions like these: "What is the salary range?" "What do you expect to pay for such a fine product?"

Try to avoid negotiating simply on price. When others pressure you to make the first offer with a comment like, "Give us your best price, and we'll tell you whether we'll take it," try asking them a question such as, "What do you expect to pay?" or "What is a reasonable price?" When this does not work, say something like, "Our usual [or list] price is . . . However, if you make me a proposal, I'll see what I can do for you."

If things go well during steps 1 and 2 and you get or exceed your opening offer or target objective, you may skip steps 3 and 4 and go to closing the agreement. If you are not ready to agree, proceed to the next step.

Communication Skills
Refer to CS Question 7.

Step 3: Listen and Ask Questions to Focus on Meeting the Other Party's Needs   Listen with empathy during bargaining, especially when you are in conflict. This is your opportunity to give your prepared answers to the objections while focusing on the other party's needs.

Create opportunities for the other party to disclose reservations and objections. When you speak, you give out information, but when you ask questions and listen, you receive information that will help you overcome the other party's objections. Ask questions like these: "Is the price out of the ballpark?" "Is it fast enough for you?" "Is any feature you wanted missing?" If the objection is something you cannot meet, at least you find out and don't waste time chasing a deal that will not happen.

Steps 4 and 5: Don't Be Too Quick to Give In, and Ask for Something in Return   Those who ask for more get more. If you've planned, you have developed options (at least a BATNA) and you have trade-offs ready. After bargaining, you won't have to say, "I should have asked for. . . ." Don't simply give up whatever it takes to get the agreement. If your competitive advantage is service and you quickly give in during negotiation for a lower price, you blow all the value in a minute. You want to satisfy the other party without giving up too much during the negotiation. Remember not to go below your limit objective; if that limit is realistic, be prepared to walk away and you can calmly threaten to walk away. Having other planned options can help give you bargaining power. If you do walk away, you may be called back, and if not, you may be able to come back for the same deal.

Avoid Desperation and Being Intimidated   If others know you are desperate, or just weak, and will accept a low agreement, they will likely take advantage of you. Have you ever seen someone's sign on a product saying, "Must sell, need cash bad"? What type of price do you think such a person gets? You also need to avoid being intimidated by comments such as, in a loud voice, "Are you kidding me? That's too much." Many people will quickly drop the price, but don't be intimidated by such tactics.

Communication Skills
Refer to CS Question 8.

Make the First Concession   When you are involved with a complex deal, with trade-offs, be willing to be the first to make a concession. Concessions tend to be reciprocated and to lead to agreements. The other party tends to feel obligated, and then you can come back with a counter trade-off that is larger than the one you gave up.

Postponement

When there doesn't seem to be any progress, it may be wise to postpone the negotiations.

When the Other Party Is Postponing, You May Create Urgency   The other party says, "I'll get back to you." Let other parties know what they have to lose. When you are not getting what you want, you may try to create urgency, for example, by saying, "This is on sale and it ends today," "It's our last one," or "They are going fast and it may not be here when you come back." But to create long-term relations, you need to be sure you are giving the other party a good deal. Honesty is the best policy. Establishing a relationship of trust is the necessary first step in closing a deal. If you do have other options, you can use them to create urgency. For example, you might say, "I have another job offer pending; when will you let me know if you want to offer me the job?"

If urgency does not apply or does not work, and the other party says, "I'll think about it," say, "That's a good idea." Then at least review the major features the other party liked about your proposed deal and ask if your offer meets their needs. The other party may decide to come to an agreement. If not, and they don't tell you when they will get back to you, ask, "When can I expect to hear if I got the job?" Try to pin the other party down for a specific time, and tell the person that if you don't hear anything by then, you will call. If you are really interested, follow up with a letter (mail, e-mail, or fax) of thanks for their time and again highlight your features they liked. If you forgot to include any features during the negotiation, add them in the letter.

One thing to remember when the other party resists making the agreement is that the hard sell often will not work. Take off the pressure. For example, you might say to a boss, "Why don't we think about it and discuss it some more later?"

You also need to learn to read between the lines, watching for nonverbal communications, especially when working with people from different cultures. Some people will not come right out and tell you "no deal."

When You Want to Postpone, the Other Party May Create Urgency   If you are not satisfied with the deal, or want to shop around, tell the other party you want to think about it. You may also need to check with your boss, or someone else, which simply may be for advice, before you can finalize the deal. If the other party is creating urgency, be sure it really is urgent. In any case, you may get the same deal at a later date; don't be pressured into making a deal you are not satisfied with or may regret later. If you do want to postpone, give the other party a specific time that you will get back to them, and then do so—whether it is with more prepared negotiations or to simply say you cannot make an agreement.

Agreement or No Agreement

Agreement   You may sometimes get your opening offer, or better, if the other party offers more before you open with an offer. If your target and the other party's target are the same, you could both get that target and have a great deal. So when you get your opening offer and both parties get their target objective, there is no real bargaining compromise.

However, it is common for targets to be in opposition. The *bargaining range* is the range between your limit and the other party's limit, which falls between each party's target and limit. Within that range, there is a good deal for both parties. See Exhibit 9.4 for an illustration of the bargaining range; we continue the job example from page 301, using its objectives. Note that the negotiated pay will most likely be between $43,000 and $45,000. In reality, most people don't tell the other parties their objectives and settle between those objectives; it just happens through bargaining.

Once the agreement has been made, restate it and/or put it in writing when appropriate.[44] It is common to follow up an agreement with a letter of thanks and a restatement of the agreement to ensure the other parties have not changed their minds as to what they agreed to.

After the deal is made, stop selling it. Change the subject to a personal one and/or leave, depending on the other person's preferred negotiation style. If the other person wants to work on the relationship, stick around; if not, leave.

EXHIBIT 9.4 | The Bargaining Range

Your Objective Range					Other Party's Objective Range
Your BATNA					Other party's BATNA
		Bargaining Range			
Your opening offer	Your target	Other party's limit [upper]	Your limit [lower]	Other party's target	Other party's opening offer
($47,000)	($45,000)	($45,000)	($43,000)	($44,000)	($41,000)

Avoid the so-called *winner's curse.* Be happy that you got a good deal. Don't start second-guessing your decision. Don't ask yourself, "Could I have bought (or sold) it for less (or more) than I did?" After you make the deal, it's usually too late to change anything, so why worry about it? By planning (researching the negotiation and setting effective objectives), you can reduce your chances of experiencing the winner's curse and be more confident that you did get a good deal.

No Agreement   Rejection, refusal, and failure happen to us all, even the superstars. The difference between the also-rans and the superstars lies in how they respond to the failure. The successful people keep trying and learn from their mistakes and continue to work hard; failures usually don't persevere. Remember that success is the ability to go from failure to failure without losing your enthusiasm, and happiness is nothing more than a poor memory for the bad things (failures) that happen to us.

If you cannot come to an agreement, analyze the situation and try to determine where you went wrong so you can improve in the future. You may also ask the other party for advice. For instance, you could say, "I realize I did not get the job, but thanks for your time. Can you offer me any ideas for improving my resume or my interview skills? Do you have any other ideas to help me get a job in this field?"

/// **In the opening case,** former Toyota chair Hiroshi Okuda was viewed as a tough negotiator who used his power to get what he wanted. He had to negotiate to become president and to take the position of chair. Toyota is also known to be a tough company to negotiate with. It negotiates with hundreds of suppliers to provide top quality at low prices. At the same time, Toyota uses its network and develops long-term relationships with its suppliers. It is agreed that Hiroshi Okuda was a successful businessperson. /// However, you don't have to try to be like him or anyone else. You need to be the authentic you, and to be the best that you can be. Skill Building Exercise 9-2 gives you the opportunity to develop your negotiating skills.

Skill-Building Exercise 9-2 develops this skill.

WORK APPLICATION 9-8

What are your strongest and weakest areas of negotiating? How will you improve your negotiating skills? Include two or three of the most important tips you learned that you will use.

APPLICATION SITUATIONS / / /

Negotiating Do's and Don'ts   AS 9-2

State if you should or should not do each item.
A. Do   B. Don't

_____ 14. If you can't come to an agreement, ask for suggestions that can help you in future negotiations.

_____ 15. Strive to develop rapport.

_____ 16. Make sure you get the best deal.

_____ 17. Research the other parties before you meet with them.

_____ 18. Set one objective.

_____ 19. Keep your focus on helping the other person meet his or her objective.

_____ 20. Get down to business quickly.

_____ 21. Make the first offer.

_____ 22. Present a take-it-or-leave-it offer.

_____ 23. Spend most of your negotiating time telling the other parties how great a deal they are getting.

_____ 24. Don't be too quick to give in, and ask for something in return.

_____ 25. Try to postpone bargaining.

DO NETWORKING AND NEGOTIATING APPLY GLOBALLY?

The Internet makes networking even easier. You can communicate with people from all over the world through **LinkedIn, Facebook, Twitter,** and e-mail and by joining online lists, chat rooms, blogs, and web boards. As an alternative to traveling around the world, you can negotiate online too. So get online and do some cyber-schmoozing.

Yes there are cultural differences in networking, and you need to appreciate and embrace the host culture. Networking is part of politicking and socializing, which we discussed in the last chapter, so we'll keep it brief here. The need to *network* to develop relationships to get business does vary culturally. We'll discuss networking within the context of negotiating. Be aware that your normal behavior may seem rude and callous to others, so try not to offend others.[45] Here we present some general guidelines.

With increased globalization, there is an increase in cross-cultural *negotiating*. There is strong support for the existence of negotiating style differences among national cultures. For example, the Israelis like to argue, so a heated emotional negotiation is often common behavior, but that is not the case for the Japanese. The amount of time you need to spend researching the other party and the type of information you will need will vary based on the culture, but in general, you need to spend more time when you don't know the customs, practices, and expectations of a particular culture.

There are many implications for negotiating globally. Throughout this section, we refer to classic studies comparing cultural differences regarding the following issues:[46]

- *Time to reach an agreement and deadlines.* The French like conflict and tend to take a long time in negotiating agreements, and they are not too concerned about being liked by the other parties. The Chinese like to drag out negotiations. Americans are different in that they are known globally to be impatient and eager for quick agreement, and they want to be liked. So good negotiators often drag out the negotiations with Americans and make relationships conditional on the final settlement.

- *The focus on task versus relationship.* In Japan and many South American countries, without a relationship there will be no task accomplishment of an agreement, or the task will be to develop the relationship. Like the Japanese, the Chinese tie close networking relationships and negotiating together in conducting business, and gift giving is expected.

- *The use of power and influencing tactics* (plus concessions with reciprocity). The power base to use also varies, based on the power distance of the culture. Influencing tactics (Chapter 8) used during negotiating also vary across cultures. To counter arguments or obstacles to closing the deal, Americans tend to use the rational persuasion tactic, using logical arguments with facts and figures. Arabs tend to use the inspirational tactic, using emotional appeal with feelings. Russians tend to assert their ideas with power, more than with influencing tactics. Concessions are made and reciprocated by both Americans and Arabs, but not often by Russians, because they view concessions as a sign of weakness.

- *Communications—both verbal and nonverbal.* In some cultures (the United States, Germany, England, Switzerland) negotiators use direct verbal messages, whereas in other cultures (Japan, China, Egypt, France, and Saudi Arabia) they rely more on nonverbal communications, so you have to read between the lines.

- *Where the negotiations should take place and the use of alcohol.* These are important considerations. You should know the proper place and when (time of day can vary) to talk business. For example, the CEO of Saber Enterprises says that when Japanese executives come to the United States and when American executives go to Japan, it is almost expected that you will go out to dinner and have several drinks and some sake while talking business. But you certainly don't want to offer and order a drink with a Mormon client.

- *Name, rank or title, dress, greetings, and rituals.* Note that these issues also apply to same-culture negotiations. During your research or, when with the other party, find out how the person prefers to be addressed (is it Christine/Chris, Ms. Smith, President Smith?). Also find out what he or she will wear (a suit, a casual outfit). Note that special or sacred articles may be worn. Know if there are certain greetings (such as bowing) or rituals (such as praying before eating) that you may be expected to participate in.

THE INFLUENCING PROCESS

Learning Outcome 9-7

Explain the influencing process.

Recall that Part 3 of this book is titled Leadership Skills: Influencing Others. In Chapters 6 through Chapter 8 and in this chapter, we have covered many factors that can help you influence others to get what you want by developing trust and motivating others with power, influencing tactics, politics, networking, and negotiating. We have focused on getting what we want by being ethical and giving others what they want; thus, we meet the goal of human relations by creating a win-win situation for all parties. Here, we put all the influencing concepts together and create the influencing process.

Review of Influencing Key Terms   Let's begin by reviewing definitions. *Leadership* is the process of influencing employees to work toward the achievement of objectives. So leadership is about getting people to do what the organization wants. *Motivation* is the internal process leading to behavior to satisfy needs. *Power* is a person's ability to influence others to do something they would not otherwise do. *Politics* is the process of getting and using power. *Networking* is the ongoing process of building interconnected relationships for the purpose of politicking and socializing. *Negotiating* is a process in which two or more parties have something the other wants and attempt to come to an exchange agreement. *Trust* is the positive expectation that another will not take advantage of you.

The Influencing Process   The **influencing process** *begins with an objective; ethical leadership, power, politics, etiquette, networking, and negotiating are used to motivate others to help reach the objective; and through trust and creating a win-win situation for all parties, the objective is met.* See Exhibit 9.5 for an illustration of this influencing process, which shows the interrelationships among our influencing key terms.

EXHIBIT 9.5 | The Influencing Process

Motivation	Behavior	Human Relations	Performance
You begin with a need or something you want, so you set an objective. You need to motivate others to get them to help you meet the objective.	You use power, politics, and networking to motivate others to help you meet the objective. When others have something you want and you have something they want, you negotiate so you both can meet your objectives.	Effective human relations are based on good intrapersonal and interpersonal skills (Chapters 1 to 5) and on using ethical behavior to develop trust.	Using good human relations based on trust leads to a win–win situation for all parties, which results in meeting the objective.

Communication Skills
Refer to CS Question 10.

We can view leadership skills from the personal level within and outside organizations as they relate to your behavior, human relations, and performance. You begin with a need or something you want, so you set an objective. (Referring to "setting an objective" rather than to "getting what you want" is using politically correct language; after all, we don't want to appear selfish or to offend anyone.) Often, you need other people to help you get what you want, so you have to motivate them to help you. You use power, politics, and networking behavior to get others to help you meet your objective, and you, in turn, do favors for others in your network. So there is mutual influence. When others have something you want and you have something they want, you negotiate so you both meet your objectives—creating a win–win situation. But to get people to help you, you need to develop trust by using ethical behavior to get what you want.

Let's discuss how your personality affects your networking and negotiating style in Self-Assessment Exercise 9-3.

/ / / Self-Assessment Exercise 9-3 / / /

Your Personality and Networking and Negotiating

You should realize that personality can be used more accurately to predict networking behavior than negotiating style. This is why in bargaining, you should focus on obstacles, not on the person. When you research the other party, you do so to find out negotiating style, not personality. Thus, in this exercise, when we discuss negotiating and how it may affect your behavior, the generalities noted may not be accurate in all cases. But keep in mind that there are always exceptions to the generalities presented regarding personality and behavior.

If you have a high *surgency* personality, you most likely have a high need for power and try to network with people who can help you. Remember, however, that even people who you don't think can help you might be the key to something you want down the road, so network with people of all levels. Often the secretary to an important person can get the key person to help you. Watch your use of coercive power during negotiations. Remember that being the first to make a concession usually results in the other person's reciprocating. At that point you can come back with a counter trade-off that is larger than the one you gave up.

If you have a high *agreeableness* personality, you most likely have a high need for affiliation and you enjoy networking at all levels to gain relationships. Watch out for others who might use power during negotiating to take advantage of you. Be assertive, don't give in too easily, and ask for something in return.

If you have a high *conscientious* personality, you most likely have a high need for achievement and don't care too much about having a large network. But you enjoy reciprocity with friends. You may need to work on developing your networking skills, such as making small talk and meeting new people. You probably develop good

rational reasons to get what you want in negotiations, but remember to read the other parties and focus on giving them what they want so that you get what you want.

How high your *adjustment* is affects how you network and negotiate. People low on adjustment generally don't use networking and negotiating ethically; they seek to get what they want and to take advantage of others through distributive bargaining. If you are not high on adjustment personality traits, you may want to stop being self-centered and work on creating win–win situations. You will be surprised at how much more you can receive in your network when you learn to give in return. There is truth in the adage, "The more you give, the more you receive." Have you ever done something for someone figuring there was nothing in it for you, only to find out that you got more than you expected?

Your *openness to experience* will have a direct effect on your networking skills. People who are open to new experiences are generally outgoing and enjoy meeting new people. Introverts tend not to enjoy meeting new people and thus are not good at networking, so they may need to work harder at it than others. Openness often leads to compromise and integrative bargaining, which is needed in negotiating successfully.

Action plan: Based on your personality, what specific things will you do to improve your networking and negotiating skills?

_____

_____

_____

_____

As we bring this chapter to a close, you should understand the importance of networking and negotiating and be able to network using Model 9.1, the networking process, including interviewing with Model 9.2. You should also be able to negotiate using Model 9.3, the negotiating process.

Where We've Been and Where We Are Going   To sum up Parts 2 and 3, Chapters 5 through Chapter 9, interpersonal and leadership skills are all about how you interact with people and your relationships in your personal and professional lives. It's *not* about what you know or technical skills; it's about how you behave (what you say and do) in teams and organizations, which is the topic of Part 4, Leadership Skills: Team and Organizational Behavior, Human Relations, and Performance.

/ / / R E V I E W / / /

The chapter review is organized to help you master the eight learning outcomes for Chapter 9. First provide your own response to each learning outcome, and then check the summary provided to see how well you understand the material. Next, identify the final statement in each section as either true or false (T/F). Correct each false statement. Answers are given at the end of the chapter.

LO 9-1   List and explain the steps in the networking process.
The first step in the networking process is to perform a self-assessment to determine your accomplishments and to set objectives. Second, create a one-minute self-sell that quickly summarizes your history and career plan and asks a question. Next, develop a written network list. Fourth, conduct networking interviews to meet your objective. Finally, maintain your network for meeting future objectives.

People in the workforce use networking primarily to get a job. T F

LO 9-2   Describe what a one-minute self-sell is and what it contains.
The one-minute self-sell is an opening statement used in networking to begin developing a relationship with another person. It briefly summarizes one's career/educational history, states one's career plans, and asks a question.

A good one-minute self-sell question to ask is, "Can you give me a job?" T F

LO 9-3   Briefly describe how to conduct a networking interview.
The steps for conducting a networking interview are as follows: (1) establish rapport—praise and read the person; (2) deliver the one-minute self-sell; (3) ask prepared questions; (4) get additional contacts for your network; (5) ask your contacts how you might help them; and (6) follow up with a thank-you note and status report.

When establishing rapport, it is a good idea to praise the person and to "read" the person. T F

LO 9-4   List and explain the steps in the negotiating process.
The negotiating process has three, and possibly four, steps: (1) planning, (2) bargaining, (3) possibly a postponement, and (4) an agreement or no agreement.

The best negotiating strategy is to give all parties a good deal.

LO 9-5   Briefly describe how to plan for negotiations.
Negotiating planning includes: (1) researching the other parties, (2) setting objectives, (3) anticipating questions and objections and preparing answers, and (4) developing options and trade-offs.

Planning for the negotiation should include three objectives: a limit, a target, and an opening objective. T F

LO 9-6   Briefly describe how to bargain.
Steps for bargaining include: (1) develop rapport and focus on obstacles, not the person; (2) let the other party make the first offer; (3) listen and ask questions to focus on meeting the other party's needs; (4) don't be too quick to give in; and (5) ask for something in return.

If you don't get your limit objective, you should not come to an agreement. T F

LO 9-7   Explain the influencing process.
The influencing process begins with an objective. To achieve it, ethical leadership, power, politics, networking, and negotiating are used to motivate others to help reach the objective. Through trust and creating a win-win situation for all parties, the objective is met.

If people actually followed the influencing process—were ethical and tried to meet the goal of human relations—performance in organizations would increase. T F

LO 9-8 Define the following 13 key terms.

Select one or more methods: (1) Fill in the missing key terms for each definition given below from memory; (2) match the key terms from the end of the review with their definitions below; and/or (3) copy the key terms in order from the key terms at the beginning of the chapter.

_____ is the ongoing process of building interconnected relationships for the purpose of politicking and socializing.

_____ are clusters of people joined by a variety of links.

The _____ includes these tasks: perform a self-assessment and set objectives, create a one-minute self-sell, develop a network, conduct networking interviews, and maintain the network.

The is an opening statement used in networking that quickly summarizes your history and career plan and asks a question.

The _____ includes these steps: establish rapport—praise and read the person; deliver your one-minute self-sell; ask prepared questions; get additional contacts for your network; ask your contacts how you might help them; and follow up with a thank-you note and status report.

A(n) _____ is a short-term network used to meet an objective.

_____ is a process in which two or more parties have something the other wants and attempt to come to an exchange agreement.

The _____ has three, and possibly four, steps: (1) planning, (2) bargaining, (3) possibly a postponement, and (4) an agreement or no agreement.

_____ includes researching the other parties, setting objectives, anticipating questions and objections and preparing answers, and developing options and trade-offs.

_____ includes developing rapport and focusing on obstacles, not on the person; letting the other party make the first offer; listening and asking questions to focus on meeting the other party's needs; and not being too quick to give in, and asking for something in return.

The _____ begins with an objective. Ethical leadership, power, politics, networking, and negotiating are used to motivate others to help reach the objective. Through trust and creating a win–win situation for all parties, the objective is met.

/ / / KEY TERMS / / /

bargaining 297	negotiating 293	networking 286	networking process 287
coalition 292	negotiating planning 295	networking interview	networks 286
influencing process 302	negotiating process 294	process 291	one-minute self-sell 288

The following critical thinking questions can be used for class discussion and/or as written assignments to develop communication skills. Be sure to give complete explanations for all questions.

1. This chapter lists six networking objectives (see page 291). For which of these reasons (or for what other reasons) do you have to network?

2. You have heard the expression, "It's not what you know, it's who you know, that's important." Do you agree? If it is true, is it fair?

3. The first step of the networking process is to perform a self-assessment. What are your three most important accomplishments?

4. If you didn't write out a one-minute self-sell for Work Application 9-4, do so now.

5. College students are poor at negotiating. Do you agree with this statement?

6. The next time you negotiate, will you actually set three—limit, target, and opening—objectives? Why or why not?

7. In bargaining, does it really matter who makes the first offer?

8. Think of a past, present, or future negotiation situation. Describe the situation and state what you can ask for in return if you don't get your target.

9. Can the influencing process really be conducted ethically and in a way that meets the goal of human relations, or is it just manipulation?

CASE / / / Carol Frohlinger: President of Negotiating Women, Inc.

Most people fail to recognize the importance of networking and negotiating to their career success. People who are good at networking tend to form better human relations with key individuals who can help them in advancing their professional careers. People who are good at negotiating have a better chance of getting what they truly desire. One's ability to negotiate affects his or her compensation in the workplace.

Negotiating Women, Inc. is a consulting company that focuses on women exclusively by providing negotiation and leadership training for them. The mission statement for Negotiating Women, Inc is twofold: first, to provide women with the resources—conceptual frameworks as well as practical skill sets—to succeed in the workplace, and second, to help organizations create cultures that value and can profit from the diverse talents women bring.[i] Its areas of expertise include negotiating, leadership, conflict resolution, gender analysis, alliances/coalitions, and sales management. The company specializes in live negotiation training, online e-learning courses, and consulting services designed to help women at every stage of their careers claim their value and create conditions for success.

Carol Frohlinger is the president of Negotiating Women, Inc. She is a lawyer, negotiation expert, cofounder of Negotiating Women, Inc., and coauthor of *Her Place at the Table: A Woman's Guide to Negotiating Five Key Challenges to Leadership Success*. She recently coauthored *Nice Girls Just Don't Get It: 99 Ways to Win the Respect You Deserve, the Success You've Earned, and the Life You Want*.

Ms. Frohlinger has consulted for organizations such as **Microsoft, JPMorgan Chase**, the **Healthcare Business Women's Association, Pricewaterhouse Coopers, The Principal Financial Group,** the **New York State Bar Association**, and the **National Association of Women Lawyers.** She has been invited by media outlets including **CBS MoneyWatch, NPR, Martha Stewart Living Radio, Newsday, Cosmopolitan Magazine, Women's Health,** and **The New York Times** to share her expertise on how to attract, retain, and promote talented women.[ii]

At Networking Women Inc., workshops are conducted in which participants learned to make their value visible and to avoid sabotaging themselves. In a recent interview, Ms. Frohlinger echoed the view of many when she said that the playing field in the workforce is still not equal, so women are impacted unintentionally in a disproportionately negative way. She said women are left out of the informal networks where information is shared about new positions and openings on the next managerial level. More often than not, women do not have access to hiring managers or other influential individuals who could put out a feeler for them.

This is where networking makes a big difference; unfortunately, in some industries, women are left out of these networks. According to Ms. Frohlinger, it is not intentional, but it is just the way things are. She points out that companies may say they promote solely on performance, "but you are naïve if you think that your promote-ability is based only on your work." Having a strong relationship with the right people is just as important, she reminds women.[iii]

On its Web site, Negotiating Women, Inc. has posted 15 questions about women, leadership, and negotiation that Negotiating Women, Inc. can address through their workshops. Among them are the following:[iv]

- I have a really exciting plan to change the ways our group does its work. How do I negotiate to make the changes?

- I was just offered a great opportunity to lead a highly visible project at work. I am so excited that I am ready to take it. But I am worried that I won't be able to take on this extra work and do my current job. What should I do?

- My boss just offered me a new job that doesn't interest me very much, but I know that if I say no, that will be the last promotion to come my way. What should I do?

- My boss always supports me and consistently gives me great opportunities. I feel I am underpaid relative to my colleagues, but I hesitate to bring it up because I am afraid he will see me as ungrateful. What should I do?

- I have a hard time negotiating for myself when it comes to salary. I know I bring value to my company; I have the reviews and promotions to show it. But every time I start to negotiate about money, I lose my conviction and accept what is offered. What should I do?

- I have just been appointed to a new leadership role over others in the group. I am concerned that people will not accept me in the role. How can I change their perceptions?

- I am having trouble pulling the team together. There are some people who are trying to make it difficult for me to succeed. What can I do?

- At my annual performance review in a year when my bottom line has been outstanding, my boss surprised me. He didn't discuss my outstanding year but instead focused on my style, telling me that I am too aggressive and that I need to change my style. What should I do?

Carol Frohlinger's theories on women in leadership positions have received support from other highly respected women like **Sheryl Sandberg, COO of Facebook**. Sheryl is a leading technologist who has worked for **Yahoo** and Facebook. Her book, ***Lean In: Women and the Will to Work,*** encourages women to pursue their ambitions, and it focuses on how women can be more successful in the business world.[v]

Go to the Internet: To learn more about Carol Frohlinger, visit Negotiating Women, Inc.'s Web site at www.negotiating women.com. You can also visit http://4020vision.com to learn more about women in their 40s helping women in their 20s.

Support your answers to the following questions with specific information from the case and text or with information you get from the Web or another source.

1. Why has Negotiating Women, Inc. focused its attention on women?

2. The text discusses some of the many reasons to develop your networking skills (such as to get a job or a better position, to perform better at your current job, or to advance within your organization). In what ways does Negotiating Women, Inc. address some of these needs?

3. The case listed examples of questions that can be addressed by Negotiating Women Inc. Select any two questions on the list and indicate whether they can be addressed using networking, negotiating, or both.

4. Experts in the field of negotiation generally agree that setting goals too low "is likely to become a self-fulfilling prophecy," especially for women. Therefore, the advice is for women to develop a backbone, something that takes preparation to accomplish. How can networking help someone in this situation?

5. A good negotiation tactic is to not make unilateral concessions during negotiations. Instead, experts advise that you should figure out the other side's hidden agenda, devise an alternative if you cannot reach an agreement, and plan to deflect moves that put you on the defensive. The textbook describes the negotiating process as consisting of four steps: *planning, bargaining, possibly a postponement, and an agreement or no agreement.* In which step does this scenario belong?

Cumulative Questions

6. In Chapter 3 we discussed job satisfaction and its determinants—*the work itself, pay, growth and upward mobility, supervision, coworkers, and attitudes toward work.* Which of these determinants can be greatly enhanced through negotiating?

7. In Appendix A the "Career Management" section defines career planning as the process of setting career objectives and determining how to accomplish them. How can networking help with one's career planning?

Case Exercise and Role-Play

Preparation: Have students read the section on creating your one-minute self-sell in the text. Assume you are attending a Negotiating Women, Inc. workshop and your task is to develop and present your one-minute self-sell.

In-Class Groups: Divide the class into groups of four or five students. Each group member should develop his or her one-minute self-sell and present it to group members for feedback. The group should then select the member with the best one-minute self-sell. This individual will represent the group in front of the rest of the class.

Role-Play: Each person selected from a group will then present his or her one-minute self-sell to the rest of the class. The class will vote on who had the best presentation.

OBJECTIVE CASE   / / /   John Stanton: Amway

Charley Roys wanted to get more consulting jobs, so he went to a Rotary International meeting to make more contacts that could lead to consulting jobs. During the meeting he was talking to different people and giving out his business card.

One guy, John Stanton, said to Charley, "Hi, my name is John Stanton, and I have an interesting part-time business. I'm looking for people to share this business opportunity with. Would you be interested in making an additional $50,000 a year part-time?" Charley said yes, and he tried to get some ideas of what the business was all about, but all John would say was, "Let's meet for a half hour or so and I will tell you about it." So they agreed to meet the next day at Charley's house.

Charley asked John what the business name was, and John said, "Let me explain the opportunity first." John started drawing layers of people, stating how much Charley would earn from each layer of people selling products for him. All Charley would have to do is sign people up like John was doing and the money would come in. The figures were showing that Charley could make $50,000 a year from a part-time business.

Before John finished, Charley asked, "Is this Amway?" John said, "Yes, it is." Charley said, "I've seen this type of presentation before, and I'm not interested in being an Amway distributor." John said, Amway is an $8.8 billion global direct sales company. It offers one of the world's leading models for entrepreneurs looking to own their own business, which includes a multilevel marketing compensation plan. Its purpose is to help people live better lives. Amway offers hundreds of unique, high-quality nutrition, beauty, and home products and helps million of people around the world reach their full potential.[vi]

Charley told him that he did not want to sell products. John replied, "That's not where the money is. You don't have to actually sell the Amway products yourself. You just sign people up and get them to sell the products."

Charley asked John why he did not tell him it was Amway when he asked him at the Rotary Club meeting. John said, "Many people have the wrong impression of Amway, and you really have to have time to see the presentation."

Charley said that he knew that there were some Amway distributors who were really making a lot of money, but that it was not the type of business he would be successful in. Amway was not for him. Before John left, he asked Charley if he knew of anyone who would be interested in making a lot of money part-time. But Charley said no, so John left.

To learn more about Amway, visit its Web site at www .amway.com.

Answer the following questions. Then in the space between questions, state why you selected that answer.

_____ 1. This case is mainly about:

   a. networking   *b.* negotiating

_____ 2. Was John successful at networking at the Rotary Club meeting?

   a. yes   *b.* no

_____ 3. To sell Amway products, salespeople need to start with _____ connections.

   a. primary   *b.* secondary

_____ 4. John's networking objective was to:

   a. get a job or a better one   *d.* stay current in his field

   b. perform better at his current job   *e.* maintain mobility

   c. advance within Amway   *f.* develop relationships

_____ 5. Did John have a good one-minute self-sell?

   a. yes   *b.* no

_____ 6. Which part of the networking interview did John clearly try to do?

   a. develop rapport   *d.* get additional contacts

   b. deliver one-minute self-sell   *e.* offer help

   c. ask questions   *f.* follow up

_____ 7. Are coalitions needed for John to be successful at Amway?

   a. yes   *b.* no

_____ 8. Did John and Charley bargain?

   a. yes   *b.* no

_____ 9. Amway's business is based mainly on _____ bargaining.

   a. distributive   *b.* integrative

_____ 10. Does Amway, and other similar businesses, try to give all parties a good deal?

   a. yes   *b.* no

_____ 11. Why wasn't John successful in using the influencing process with Charley?

_____ 12. Was it unethical for John not to tell Charley the business was Amway at the Rotary Club meeting?

/ / / S K I L L - B U I L D I N G E X E R C I S E 9 - 1 / / /

Networking Skills

Experience: Group in-class exercise.

AACSB Competencies: Reflective thinking, communication and application of knowledge.

Objective: To develop networking skills by implementing the steps in the networking process.

   You will deliver your one-minute self-sell from the preparation and get feedback for improvement. You will also share your network list and interview questions and get feedback for improvement.

Preparation: Complete the following steps:

1. Perform a self-assessment and set objectives. List two or three of your accomplishments. Clearly state your goal, which can be to learn more about career opportunities in your major; to get an internship; to get a part-time, summer, or full-time job; and so on.

2. Create your one-minute self-sell. Write it out. See page 293 for an example.

History:

Plan:

Question:

3. Develop your network. List at least five people to be included in your network, preferably people who can help you achieve your objective.

4. Conduct networking interviews. To help meet your objective, select one person to interview by phone if it is difficult to meet in person for a 20-minute interview. List the person and write questions to ask during the interview. This person can be someone in your college career center or a professor in your major.

In-Class Exercise

Procedure 1 (7–10 minutes)

A. Break into groups of two. Show each other your written one-minute self-sell. Are the history, plan, and question clear (do you understand it?), concise (does it take 60 seconds or less to say?), and compelling (does it generate interest in helping?)? Offer suggestions for improvement.

B. After the self-sell is perfected, each person states (no reading) the one-minute self-sell. Was it stated clearly, concisely, and with confidence? Offer improvements. State it a second and third time, or until told to go on to the next procedure.

Procedure 2 (7–10 minutes)

Break into groups of three with people you did not work with during procedure 1. Follow steps A and B above in your triad. Repeating your self-sell should improve your delivery and confidence.

Procedure 3 (10-20 minutes)
Break into groups of four with people you did not work with during procedures 1 and 2, if possible. Share your answers to preparation steps 3 (your network list) and 4 (your interview questions). Offer each other improvements to the list and the questions.

Application (outside class):   Expand your written network list to at least 25 names. Conduct the networking interview using the questions developed through this exercise.

Conclusion: The instructor leads a class discussion and/or makes concluding remarks. Written network lists and/or interview questions and answers may be passed in.

Sharing: Volunteers may share what they have learned about networking.

Source: This exercise was developed by Andra Gumbus, professor, College of Business, Sacred Heart University. © Andra Gumbus, 2002. It is used with Dr. Gumbus's permission.

/ / / SKILL-BUILDING EXERCISE 9-2 / / /

Car Dealer Negotiation
Experience: Group in-class exercise.

AACSB Competencies: Reflective thinking, communication and application of knowledge.

Objective: To develop negotiation skills.

You will be the buyer or seller of a used car.

Preparation: You should have read and should understand the negotiation process.

Procedure 1 (1-2 minutes)
Break into groups of two and sit facing each other so that you cannot read each other's confidential sheet. Each group should be as far away from other groups as possible so that they cannot overhear each other's conversations. If there is an odd number of students in the class, one student will be an observer or work with the instructor. Select who will be the buyer and who will be the seller of the used car.

Procedure 2 (1-2 minutes)
The instructor goes to each group and gives the buyer and seller their confidential sheets.

Procedure 3 (5-6 minutes)
Buyers and sellers read their confidential sheets and in the space below write some plans (what your basic approach will be, what you will say) for the lunch meeting.

Procedure 4 (3-7 minutes)
Negotiate the sale of the car. Try not to overhear your classmates' conversations. You do not have to buy or sell the car. After you make the sale or agree not to sell, read the confidential sheet of your partner in this exercise and discuss the experience.

Integration (3-7 minutes)
Answer the following questions:

1. Which of the seven bases of power (Chapter 8) did you use during the negotiations? Did both parties believe that they got a good deal?

2. Which of the influencing tactics (Chapter 8) did you use during the negotiations?

3. During your planning, did you: (1) research the other party, (2) set an objective (limit, target, open—price to pay or accept), (3) anticipate questions and objections and prepare answers, and (4) develop options and trade-offs?

4. During the negotiations, did you: (1) develop a rapport and focus on obstacles, not on the person, (2) let the other party make the first offer, (3) listen and ask questions to focus on meeting the other party's needs, (4) avoid being too quick to give in, and (5) ask for something in return?

5. Did you reach an agreement on the price of the car? If you were the seller, did you get your target price? Or did you get more or less than your target?

6. When you are negotiating, is it a good practice to open high, that is, to ask for more than you expect to receive?

7. When you are negotiating, is it better to be the one to give or to receive the initial offer?

8. When you are negotiating, is it better to appear to be dealing with strong or weak power? In other words, should you try to portray that you have other options and don't really need to make a deal with this person? Or should you appear to be in need of a deal?

9. Can having the power to intimidate others be helpful in negotiations?

Conclusion: The instructor leads a class discussion or simply gives the answers to the integration questions and makes concluding remarks.

Application: What did I learn from this experience? How will I use this knowledge in the future?

Sharing: Volunteers give their answers to the application section.

Source: The car dealer negotiation confidential information is from Arch G. Woodside, Tulane University. The car dealer game is part of a paper, "Bargaining Behavior in Personal Selling and Buying Exchanges," that was presented at the 1980 Eighth Annual Conference of the Association for Business Simulation and Experiential Learning (ABSEL). It is used with Dr. Woodside's permission.

Developing New Habits

Experience: Individual may share habits in groups or entire class, in class or online.

AACSB Competencies: Analytic and application of knowledge.

Objective: To develop and share new habits.

Preparation: Select one or more topics from this chapter that will help you improve your human relations. Develop a new habit following the guideline from Chapter 1, section Habits and Skill-Building Exercise 1-4, on how to develop your cure, routine, and reward-change.

Procedure (5–30 minutes)
Follow the procedures from Skill Builder 1-4.

1. F. Most people in the workforce have jobs, so they network primarily for other reasons. Networking is not all about getting a job: it's about developing relationships to help you meet your personal and professional goals.

2. F. In a one-minute self-sell, you should not directly ask for a job.

3. T.

4. T.

5. T.

6. T.

7. T.

1. Toyota website, http://www.toyota.com, retrieved on August 5, 2014.

2. Staff "Optimum Happiness," *INC.* (June, 2016): 107.

3. R.D. Costigan and K.E. Brink, "Another Perspective on MBA Program Alignment: An Investigation of Learning Goals," *Academy of Management Learning & Education* 14(2) (2015): 260–276.

4. W.L. Bedwell, S.M. Fiore, and E. Salas, "Developing the Future Workforce," *Academy of Management Learning & Education* 13(2) (2014): 171–186.

5. R.D. Costigan and K.E. Brink, "Another Perspective on MBA Program Alignment: An Investigation of Learning Goals," *Academy of Management Learning & Education* 14(2) (2015): 260–276.

6. B.M. Galvin, D. Lange, and B.E. Ashforth, "Narcissistic Organizational Identification: Seeing Oneself as Central to the Orgnization's Identity," *Academy of Management Review* 40(2) (2015): 163–181.

7. L. Howes, "Personableness," *Entrepreneurship* (March 2016): 40.

8. A. Shipilov, R. Gulati, M. Kilduff, S. Li, and W. Tsai, "Relational Pluralism Within and Between Organizations," *Academy of Management Journal* 57(2) (2014): 449–459.

9. A. Gumbus and R.N. Lussier, "Career Development: Enhancing Your Networking Skills," *Clinical Leadership & Management Review* 17(1) (2003): 16–20.

10. I. Sutherland, J.R. Gosling, and J. Jelinek, "Aesthetics of Power: Why Teaching About Power Is Easier Than Learning for Power, and What Business Schools Could Do About It," *Academy of Management Learning & Education* 14, no. 4 (2015): 607-624.

11. A. Gumbus and R.N. Lussier, "Career Development: Enhancing Your Networking Skills," *Clinical Leadership & Management Review 17*(1) (2003): 16-20.

12. Staff "Optimum Happiness," *INC.* (June, 2016): 107.

13. A. Gumbus and R.N. Lussier, "Career Development: Enhancing Your Networking Skills," *Clinical Leadership & Management Review 17*(1) (2003): 16-20.

14. A. Gumbus and R.N. Lussier, "Career Development: Enhancing Your Networking Skills," *Clinical Leadership & Management Review 17*(1) (2003): 16-20.

15. A. Gumbus and R.N. Lussier, "Career Development: Enhancing Your Networking Skills," *Clinical Leadership & Management Review 17*(1) (2003): 16-20.

16. C. Mariani, "How to Network as if You Aren't Nervous at All," *Inc.* (November 2013): 60.

17. R. McCammon, "Do Me A Solid?" *Entrepreneur* (March 2016): 15-16.

18. A.C. Peng, J.M. Schaubroeck, and L. Li, "Social Exchange Implications of Own and Coworkers' Experiences of Supervisor Abuse," *Academy of Management Journal* 57(5) (2014): 1385-1405.

19. C. Perilli, "#17 Generosity," *Entrepreneur* (March 2016): 42.

20. A.O. Malaterre, N.P. Rothbard, and J.M. Berg, "When Worlds Collide in Cyberspace: How Boundary Work in Online Social Networks Impact Professional Relationships," *Academy of Management Review 38*(4) (2013): 645-669.

21. A.O. Malaterre, N.P. Rothbard, and J.M. Berg, "When Worlds Collide in Cyberspace: How Boundary Work in Online Social Networks Impact Professional Relationships," *Academy of Management Review 38*(4) (2013): 645-669.

22. Staff, The Fast Tech 25: *Forbes* (June 13, 2017): 48.

23. J. Zaslow, "The Greatest Generation (of Networkers)." *The Wall Street Journal* (November 4, 2009): D1, D3.

24. A. Coombes, "The Biggest Mistakes Executives Make When Negotiating a Retirement Package," *The Wall Street Journal* (June 13, 2016): R1, R2.

25. C. Hann, "Fair Pay," *Entrepreneur* (May 2016): 23.

26. W.L. Bedwell, S.M. Fiore, and E. Salas, "Developing the Future Workforce," *Academy of Management Learning & Education* 13(2) (2014): 171-186.

27. R.D. Costigan and K.E. Brink, "Another Perspective on MBA Program Alignment: An Investigation of Learning Goals," *Academy of Management Learning & Education* 14(2) (2015): 260-276.

28. A. Coombes, "The Biggest Mistakes Executives Make When Negotiating a Retirement Package," *The Wall Street Journal* (June 13, 2016): R1, R2.

29. C. Hann, "Fair Pay," *Entrepreneur* (May 2016): 23.

30. A. Coombes, "The Biggest Mistakes Executives Make When Negotiating a Retirement Package," *The Wall Street Journal* (June 13, 2016): R1, R2.

31. G. O'Brien, "Points of Difference," *Entrepreneur* (January 2016): 20.

32. A. Coombes, "The Biggest Mistakes Executives Make When Negotiating a Retirement Package," *The Wall Street Journal* (June 13, 2016): R1, R2.

33. Evans, "Be a Temp Forever."

34. A. Coombes, "The Biggest Mistakes Executives Make When Negotiating a Retirement Package," *The Wall Street Journal* (June 13, 2016): R1, R2.

35. Silverman, "Stay Calm, and Don't Have a Hissy Fit."

36. A. Coombes, "The Biggest Mistakes Executives Make When Negotiating a Retirement Package," *The Wall Street Journal* (June 13, 2016): R1, R2.

37. G. O'Brien, "Points of Difference," *Entrepreneur* (January 2016): 20.

38. E. Bernstein, "Don't Apologize So Fast," *Wall Street Journal* (July 15, 2014): D1, D4.

39. G. O'Brien, "Points of Difference," *Entrepreneur* (January 2016): 20.

40. G. Colvin, "Humans Are Underrated," *Fortune* (August 1, 2015): 100–113.

41. G. O'Brien, "Points of Difference," *Entrepreneur* (January 2016): 20.

42. A. Coombes, "The Biggest Mistakes Executives Make When Negotiating a Retirement Package," *The Wall Street Journal* (June 13, 2016): R1, R2.

43. N. Kagan, "#18 Persistence," *Entrepreneur* (March 2016): 42.

44. C. Hann, "Fair Pay," *Entrepreneur* (May 2016): 23.

45. G. O'Brien, "Points of Difference," *Entrepreneur* (January 2016): 20.

46. *N.J. Adler, International Dimensions of Organizational Behavior 5th ed. (Cincinnati: South-Western, 2008).*

i. http://www.negotiatingwomen.com/ accessed June 6, 2017.

ii. http://www.negotiatingwomen.com/about-us/carol-frohlinger/ accessed June 6, 2017.

iii. http://4020vision.com/index.php/2011/08/negotiating-women-inc-co-founder-carol-frohlinger-on-hidden-bias-in-the-workplace/ accessed June 6, 2017.

iv. http://www.negotiatingwomen.com/ accessed June 6, 2017.

v. Sandberg, Sheryl, *Lean In: Women and the Will to Work*, New York: Alfred A. Knopf, 2013.

vi. Away.com, accessed June 6, 2017.

Team Dynamics, Creativity and Problem Solving, and Decision Making

©Patrick Ryan/Getty Images

LEARNING OUTCOMES

After completing this chapter, you should be able to:

LO 10-1 Explain the six components of team dynamics and how they affect team performance.

LO 10-2 Describe the five stages of a team's development.

LO 10-3 Explain the four situational supervisory styles to use with a group, based on its stage of development.

LO 10-4 Explain how to plan for and conduct effective meetings.

LO 10-5 Identify six problem members and explain how to handle them so they do not have a negative effect on your meetings.

LO 10-6 List the five steps in the decision-making model.

LO 10-7 Describe five techniques for generating creative alternatives.

LO 10-8 Define the following 16 key terms (in order of appearance in the chapter):

teamwork	self-interest roles
team performance model	problem
team dynamics	problem solving
norms	decision making
group cohesiveness	creativity
status	stages in the creative
roles	process
task roles	brainstorming
maintenance roles	

OPENING CASE WORK SCENARIO

/ / / Bonnie Sue Swinaski is a machine operator for the Western Pacific Manufacturing Company. In the past, she has recommended ways to increase performance, which management used. As a result, management appointed Bonnie Sue to lead an ad hoc committee charged with recommending ways to increase performance in her work area. Her group has six members, all from her department, who volunteered to serve on the committee. The committee has been meeting biweekly now for three weeks for one- to two-hour sessions. The members have grown quite close over the weeks, and participation has been fairly equal.

Bonnie Sue, however, has not been very pleased with the group's performance. Only three weeks remain before the group's report is to be presented to management. She has been thinking about some of the problems and wondering how to handle them. At first, the members came to the meetings enthusiastic and came up with crazy ideas.

But over time, they lost some of the enthusiasm, even though they were developing better ideas for improving the performance of the department. During meetings, members have been suggesting the need for work to be done outside the meeting, but no one seems to do it. Three of the members cause different kinds of problems in the group. Kirt is destructive—he is constantly putting down other people's ideas, and others have followed his lead. Kirt always thinks his way is better, and he never gives an inch, even when he knows he is wrong. Kirt ends up fighting with members over whose idea is better. Shelby is very pleasant—she tries to keep peace in the group. The problem with Shelby is that she is consistently getting the group off the topic at hand. Carlos is the opposite of Shelby—he puts the group back on the topic. He doesn't believe in wasting any time, but he's a motor mouth. Carlos dominates the airtime at meetings.

What are the issues? If you were in Bonnie Sue's situation, how would you turn the group into a top performer ? / / /

HOW TEAMS, CREATIVITY AND PROBLEM SOLVING, AND DECISION MAKING AFFECT BEHAVIOR, HUMAN RELATIONS, AND PERFORMANCE

We use the term *team* to refer to groups and teams. **Teamwork** involves *working together to achieve something beyond the capabilities of individuals working alone.* The common organizational structure (Chapter 4) today is based on teams.[1] So, developing teamwork skills is an important part of interpersonal skills.[2] Recall that much of our happiness comes from relationships, and working in teams is about getting the job done through relationships.[3] People behave differently in teams. Teams with good working relationships perform at high levels.[4]

Team work is a popular tactic for fostering creativity that leads to innovative changes in products and processes.[5] Groups with members that share ideas and work together develop creative innovations.[6]

Organizations and groups encounter problems,[7] and there is a need for better decision making.[8] Groups can solve problems far better than individuals can.[9] Clearly the decisions you make affect your behavior, happiness, relationships, and performance. Thus, critical thinking to solve problems and make decisions is an important skill in your personal and professional lives.[10] Team skills can be developed, and that is what this chapter is all about.

TEAMS

The type of team, its structure, and its process[11] and dynamics will affect organizational performance.[12] In this section, you will learn about the different types of groups, the team performance model, and team structure.

Types of Teams

There are *formal groups,* which are sanctioned by the organization (i.e., departments), and *informal groups,* which develop spontaneously when members get together voluntarily because of similar interests. Two of the major types of formal groups are functional and task.

Functional Teams **Functional teams** are formal, ongoing teams that consist of managers and their employees. Each work unit or department makes up a functional group. There are also *cross-functional* groups with members from different groups, which can be ongoing or temporary.[13] Some functional groups are called *self-directed* groups or *self-managed* teams because team leadership is shared.[14] Organizations also develop a hybrid form of *networks of teams* called *multi-team systems* that have interdependencies in their pursuit of shared goals.[15]

Task Teams **Task teams** work together on a specific activity. Being a member of a task group is in addition to your job in a functional group, so you can have two bosses. Task groups are often called committees. There are two common types of task groups or committees.

The *ad hoc committee,* or *task force,* is a formal, temporary team that disbands when its purpose is accomplished. For example, a task force can be created to select a new computer. The *standing committee* is a formal, ongoing team that often has rotating members. For example, labor and management commonly have standing committees that work together to negotiate the ongoing collective bargaining agreements that result in a new contract.

Virtual Teams—Working Digitally In the global economy, people from around the world work in teams digitally. *Virtual teams* conduct almost their entire group work by electronic digital communications, rather than face-to-face. Recall that you learned about digital communications and networking in Chapters 4, 8, and 9. This information also applies to virtual teams,

Communication Skills
Refer to CS Question 1.

as well as developing trust (Chapter 6). An additional digital tool commonly used is group-ware. *Groupware* allows team members of any size to edit a document at the same time, or in sequence.

Before we get into the details of the components of the team performance model, complete Self-Assessment Exercise 10-1 to determine your use of team behavior.

/ / / Self-Assessment Exercise 10-1 / / /

Your Team Behavior

For each statement, identify how accurately it describes your behavior. Place the number (1 to 5) on the line before each statement.

Describes me				Does not describe me
5	4	3	2	1

_____ 1. I influence the team members to do a good job of meeting organizational objectives.

_____ 2. I try to include the ideas and perspectives of all team members.

_____ 3. I offer creative ways to solve problems that help my team get the job done well.

_____ 4. I offer input in the decisions my team makes.

_____ 5. When there are team conflicts, I help members resolve the differences.

_____ 6. I make sure the team develops clear objectives.

_____ 7. When completing a task, I consider how many members are needed to accomplish the task and include the best team members for the task.

_____ 8. I use behavior that will help meet the organization's or team's objectives, and I encourage others to develop and enforce positive norms.

_____ 9. I try to include every member of the team so that they all feel like full, active members of the team. I don't exclude others in any way.

_____ 10. I'm comfortable with my place on the team; I can be a star or just one of the team's members. I try to help others be comfortable with their status.

_____ 11. I do and say things that directly help the team get the job done.

_____ 12. I do and say things that directly help the team develop and maintain good human relations.

_____ 13. I don't do and say things that benefit me at the expense of the team.

_____ 14. When I join a team that is just starting, such as a new committee, I help the team clarify and set objectives.

_____ 15. If members are dissatisfied with the team, I try to help resolve the issues so that everyone is satisfied with the team.

_____ 16. If a team member has a drop in commitment to the team, such as having personal problems or a bad day, I try to help that person get through the situation and keep his or her commitment to the team.

_____ 17. When the team is doing a good job, I don't interfere with the team members' getting along or the team's performance.

Add your score and place the total here:_____. Then on the continuum below, mark the point that represents your score.

Effective team behavior	85 ----- 75 ----- 65 ----- 55 ------ 45 ----- 35 ----- 25 ----- 17	Ineffective team behavior

You don't need to do all these things for the team to be effective as long as someone else on the team does them. An important part of team skills is knowing the behavior that is needed to have a successful team and providing the needed behavior to help the team continue to develop.

Questions 1 to 5 refer to team structure, 6 to 13 to team dynamics, and 14 to 17 to team development. As you read about each of the three components, you may want to turn back and review your answers.

EXHIBIT 10.1 | The Team Performance Model

| Team Performance | (f)* | Team Structure | + | Team Dynamics | + | Team Development Stage |

*(f) = is a function of.

The Team Performance Model

The **team performance model** states that *a team's performance is based on its structure, dynamics, and stage of development.* The performance model can be stated as a formula. *Team performance* is a function of team structure + team dynamics + team development stage. The three components of the model are shown in Exhibit 10.1. You should realize that to have high levels of performance the team must have an effective structure for working together as a team, have good dynamic human relations, and develop its ability to work as a team. Teams face the systems effect: if any one of the components is weak, performance suffers. In this chapter, we discuss each component in sequence in separate sections, starting with team structure.

Communication Skills
Refer to CS Question 2.

Team Structure

As shown in Exhibit 10.2, there are four team structure components that, along with team dynamics and development, affect team performance. We spend the least amount of time with team structure here because we already discussed some of the components of structure in other chapters, and we will discuss others in detail later in this chapter. *Conflict,* which we discussed in Chapter 5, and effectively resolving conflicts without hurting human relations, is important to performance.[16]

Leadership, covered in Chapter 6, is important to team performance.[17] Therefore, in this chapter we expand the coverage to leading teams as a situational supervisor, based on team development stages. We also cover how to run a meeting using leadership skills.

Composition refers to the diversity of team members. Team mix, or diversity, involves more than gender and race, which we will discuss in Chapter 12. Important to team performance are the knowledge, abilities, and skills of the team members that should complement each other so that the team can achieve better results than its individuals.

Creative problem solving and decision making also affect team performance. Teams encounter problems and need to make decisions in getting the job done. How decisions are made, autocratic or participative (Chapter 6), and the decisions themselves also affect performance.[18] Problem solving and decision making and creativity are discussed in separate sections later in this chapter.

Learning Outcome 10-1

Explain the six components of team dynamics and how they affect team performance.

EXHIBIT 10.2 | Team Structure Components

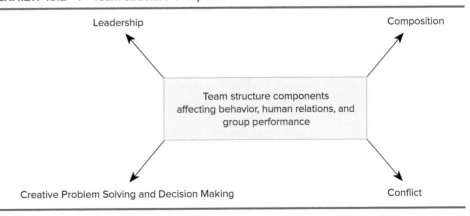

Leadership

Composition

Team structure components
affecting behavior, human relations, and
group performance

Creative Problem Solving and Decision Making

Conflict

Source: L.R. Weingart, K.J. Behfar, C. Bendersky, G. Todorova, and K.A. Hehn, "The Directness and Oppositional Intensity of Conflict Expression," Academy of Management Review, vol. 40, no. 2, 2015, 235–262.

/// **In the opening case,** Bonnie Sue is leading a formal task team called an ad hoc committee. Her team structure includes her as the leader. The group composition is six people from her department. There is some conflict and problems within the team, which is charged with coming up with creative ideas to improve performance. ///

TEAM DYNAMICS

Team dynamics refers to *the patterns of interactions that emerge as groups develop.* These interactions are also called *group process*[19] and group dynamics.[20] It's not about the work done, but rather about how effective the human relations are, because they affect performance.[21] In this section, we discuss the six components of group dynamics: objectives, team size, team norms, group cohesiveness, status within the team, and group roles. As you read the implications for leaders, *recall that you don't have to be a manager to be a leader*—rise to the occasion to help the group dynamics.

Objectives

WORK APPLICATION 10-1

For Work Applications 10-1 through 10-8, recall a specific group to which you belong or have belonged. If you will be doing Skill-Building Exercise 10-1, do not use your class group for this specific group now.

Does the group agree on, and are members committed to, clear objectives? Explain your answer.

To be effective, teams must agree on clear objectives and be committed to achieving them, and networks of teams share goals.[22] The leader should allow the group to have input in setting objectives, based on its capability to participate, which you will learn to do later in this chapter.

Implications for Leaders   Get the group to set specific, measurable objectives with a target date following the guidelines in the setting objectives model (Chapter 7).

Team Size

What is the ideal team size? The number varies, depending on the team's purpose. If the group is too small, it tends to be too cautious and there may not be enough members to share the work. Smaller groups allow more participation and often better performance,[23] and 5 to 9 members is commonly recommended.[24] Groups of 20 or more tend to be too large to reach consensus on decisions, and they tend to form subgroups. But larger groups tend to generate more alternatives and higher-quality ideas because they benefit from diverse participation.

WORK APPLICATION 10-2

How large is the group? Is the size appropriate? Explain.

Implications for Leaders   Usually leaders have no say in the size of their functional groups. However, the appropriate leadership style may vary with team size. Leaders who chair a committee may be able to select the team size. In doing so, be sure to get the right people on the committee, while trying to keep the group size appropriate for the task.[25]

Team Norms

Functional groups generally have standing plans (policies and rules) to help provide the necessary guidelines for behavior. However, groups tend to form their own unwritten rules about how things are done.[26] **Norms** are *the group's shared expectations of its members' behavior.* Professional norms determine develop indicating what should, ought to, or must be done.[27]

How Norms Develop and Teams Enforce Them   Members, influenced by leaders, determine what is acceptable and unacceptable behavior, such as how to talk and dress. Violations of norms is usually sanctioned to encourage cooperation.[28] If a team member does not follow the norm, the other members may try to enforce compliance—*peer pressure.*[29] The common ways teams enforce norms include ridicule, ostracism, sabotage, and physical abuse. You most likely have experienced peer pressure at school, socially, and at work.

Implications for Leaders   Team norms can be positive, helping the team meet its objective(s), or they can be negative, hindering the group. Be aware of the group's norms, and work toward maintaining and developing positive norms while trying to eliminate negative norms. Confront groups with negative norms and try to work out agreeable solutions to have positive norms.

Group Cohesiveness

WORK APPLICATION 10-3

List at least three of the team's norms. Identify them as positive or negative. How does the team enforce these norms?

The extent to which a group will abide by and enforce its norms depends on its degree of cohesiveness. **Group cohesiveness** is *the attractiveness and closeness group members have for one another and for the group.* The more cohesive the group, the more its members stick together as a team. The more desirable group membership is, the more willing the members are to behave according to the team's norms. For example, if some team members drink too much and/or take drugs, the team may develop a norm of taking drugs. This peer pressure often wins out.[30] To be accepted by the team, members will behave in ways they really don't agree with.

How Cohesiveness Affects Team Performance   Many research studies have compared cohesive and noncohesive teams and concluded that cohesive teams tend to have a higher level of success at achieving their objectives, with greater job satisfaction. Unfortunately, sometime the objectives and norms are personal negative that hold back team and organizational performance.

Implications for Leaders   Strive to develop cohesive groups that accept positive norms. The use of participation helps the group develop cohesiveness while it builds agreement and commitment toward its objective(s) (goal orientation). While some intragroup competition may be helpful, focus primarily on intergroup competition—think like sports. The **NBA** national basketball champion **Warriors** are highly cohesive.

Status within the Team

WORK APPLICATION 10-4

Is the group cohesive? How does the level of cohesiveness affect the group's performance? Explain your answers.

As team members interact, they develop respect for one another on numerous dimensions. The more respect, prestige, influence, and power a group member has, the higher his or her status within the team.[31] **Status** is *the perceived ranking of one member relative to other members of the group.*

The Development of Status and How It Affects Team Performance   Managers usually have higher status,[32] and their level of status does affect their behavior and decisions.[33] But status is based on several factors: a member's job title, wage or salary, seniority, knowledge or expertise, interpersonal skills, appearance, education, race, age, sex, and so on. High-status members have more influence on the development of the group's norms.[34] Lower-level members tend to copy high-status members' behavior.

Status congruence is the acceptance and satisfaction members receive from their group status. Members who are not satisfied with their status may feel excluded from the team, and they may not be active team participants. They may physically or mentally escape from the team and not perform to their full potential. Or they may cause team conflict as they fight for a higher status level.

Implications for Leaders   To be an effective leader, you need to have high status within the group because your status affect your ability to influence others and your performance.[35] Maintain good human relations with the group, particularly with the high-status informal leaders, to be sure they endorse positive norms and objectives. In addition, be aware of conflicts that may be the result of lack of status congruence. Use the conflict management model (Chapter 5) to be sure conflicts are resolved.

Group Roles

WORK APPLICATION 10-5

List each team member in order by status in the team, including yourself. What are some of the characteristics that lead to high or low status on the team?

Team members have their own roles and responsibilities, as roles determine how you can contribute to the team and its performance.[36] **Roles** are *shared expectations of how group members will fulfill the requirements of their position.* When interacting with the team, you learn the team's expectations—its norms. People often have multiple roles within the same position. For example, a professor may have the roles of teacher, researcher, consultant, adviser, and committee member.

Classifying Group Roles and How They Affect Team Performance   Chapter 6 stated that when leaders interact with employees, they can use directive behavior, supportive behavior, or both. These same two dimensions can also be performed by group members as they interact. When used to relate to group interactions, they are commonly called *task roles* and *maintenance roles.* A third category, called *self-interest roles,* is often added.[37] Below we will discuss each type of role in more detail.

The group's **task roles** are *the things group members do and say that directly aid in the accomplishment of its objective(s).* Task roles focus on getting the job done (and influencing others to help). Task roles can be subclassified as: objective clarifiers, planners, organizers, leaders, and controllers. Clearly, task roles need to be fulfilled for the team to perform its functions.

The group's **maintenance roles** are *the things group members do and say to develop and sustain group dynamics.* Maintenance roles focus on people working effectively together (and influencing others to work as team members). Maintenance roles can be subclassified as: involvers and encouragers of others, consensus seekers, gatekeepers of norms, compromisers, and harmonizers who keep the peace through conflict resolution. As discussed, a group will perform only to the level of how well team members work together effectively to achieve its objectives.[38]

In contrast to these two types of roles that help team performance, **self-interest roles** are *the things group members do and say to meet their own needs or objectives at the expense of the team.* Self-interest seekers are often narcissistic,[39] giving the impression that they are concerned about others and the organization, when in reality such behavior is a cover to get what they want. They may use unethical politics (Chapter 8) and the forcing conflict style (Chapter 5) to push others to get what they want.[40] Self-interest roles can be subclassified as: aggressors, blockers, recognition seekers, and withdrawers.

Communication Skills
Refer to CS Question 6.

Implications for Leaders   To be effective, a team must have members who play task roles and maintenance roles, while minimizing self-interest roles. When in a group, you should be aware of the roles its members play. If the members are not playing the task and/or maintenance role required at a given time, you should play the role. The next section discusses group development and the manager's use of task and maintenance roles as the group develops.

/// **In the opening case,** the objective is fairly clear, group size is adequate, and cohesiveness, status, and roles are not major problems. Kirt has been discrediting others' ideas, and others have followed his lead. A negative norm has developed that needs to be addressed by Bonnie Sue as the leader to ensure success of the group. Bonnie Sue can begin the next meeting by stating that the norm has developed and explain how it is destructive to the group. She can interrupt when Kirt and others put down ideas by reminding the group to be positive. The group can also discuss whether there are other negative norms that should be stopped. In addition, they can discuss the development of positive norms that can help the group do a better job. In terms of group roles, Carlos is playing a task role for the group. Shelby is playing a maintenance role for the group. Kirt is playing a self-interest role. How to handle Kirt, Shelby, and Carlos as problem individuals will be discussed later in this chapter. ///

WORK APPLICATION 10-6

Using your list from Work Application 10-5, identify the major roles played by each group member, including yourself.

In summary, effective groups should have clear objectives with agreement and commitment to those objectives by its members, appropriate group size to achieve its objectives, positive norms, cohesiveness, status congruence, and members who play task and maintenance roles while minimizing self-interest roles. Developing effective group dynamics that meet the needs of the individuals and the group or organization creates a win–win situation for all parties. See Exhibit 10.3 for a review of the six components of team dynamics.

EXHIBIT 10.3 | Team Dynamics Components

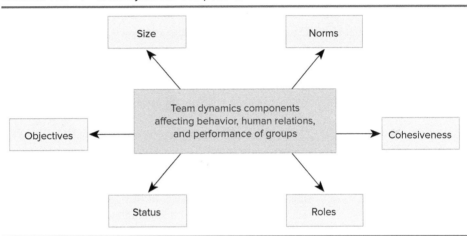

APPLICATION SITUATIONS / / /

Group Dynamics   AS 10-1

Match each statement with the group dynamics issue it represents.

A. Objectives   C. Norms   E. Status

B. Size   D. Cohesiveness   F. Roles

_____ 1. "We really need another employee, but there is no work space available for one."

_____ 2. "I wish management would make up its mind. One month we have a policy, and the next month we change to another."

_____ 3. "When you need advice, go see Jose; he knows the ropes around here better than anyone."

_____ 4. "Henry, you're late for the meeting. Everyone else was on time, so we started without you."

_____ 5. "I'm a member of the union because we would not be getting the pay we do. Collective bargaining really works."

TEAM DEVELOPMENT STAGES AND LEADERSHIP

When you bring a group of people together to work as a team, they need to develop effective team dynamics to develop through the states of team development.[41] As discussed in Chapter 6, leadership is important to team and organizational success,[42] and it is important

Roles   AS 10-2

Match each statement with the role it fulfills.

A. Task   B. Maintenance   C. Self-interest

_____ 6. "I like that idea better than mine. Let's implement your idea instead of mine."

_____ 7. "Wait, we have not heard a good idea yet."

_____ 8. "Could you explain to us all how to do the assignment again?"

_____ 9. "That idea will never work here. My idea is much better, so let's do it my way."

_____ 10. "What does this have to do with the decision we have to make? Let's get back on our objective for this meeting."

Learning Outcome 10-2

Describe the five stages of a team's development.

to share leadership.[43] Thus, everyone should contribute to the team process[44] by supporting team members.[45] Managing and working with people is an important skill.[46] So whether you are a manager, informal leader, or a follower, you can help the team progress through the stages of team development. In this section, we discuss the stages that teams go through, followed by a model for understanding which situational supervision style (Chapter 6) to use based on the stage of development.

Stages of Team Development

Below we will describe each of the group development stages (GDSs) that task groups may go through. However, not all groups progress through all the stages, or they get stuck in one stage and never reach the group's full potential. So it's your job to help the team develop.[47]

Communication Skills
Refer to CS Question 7.

Stage 1: Orientation   This *forming* stage is characterized by low development level (D1), high commitment, and low competence. When people first form a group, they tend to come to the group with a moderate to high commitment to the group. However, because they have not worked together, they do not have the competence to achieve the task. Members tend to have anxiety over how they will fit in, what will be required of them, and what the group will be like.

Stage 2: Dissatisfaction   This *storming* stage is characterized by moderate development level (D2), lower commitment, and some competence. As members work together for some time, they tend to become dissatisfied with the group. Members start to question: Why am I a member? Is the group going to accomplish anything? Why don't other group members do what is expected? and so forth. However, the group does develop some competence to perform the task.

Stage 3: Resolution   This *norming* stage is characterized by high development level (D3), variable commitment, and high competence. As members develop competence, they often become more satisfied with the group and committed to it. Relationships develop that satisfy group members' affiliation needs. They learn to work together as they develop a group structure with acceptable norms and cohesiveness.

Stage 4: Production   This *performing* stage is characterized by outstanding development level (D4), high commitment, and high competence. This high commitment enhances productivity and performance, as does the high competence skill level. The group works as a

EXHIBIT 10.4 | Team Development Stages 1 through 4

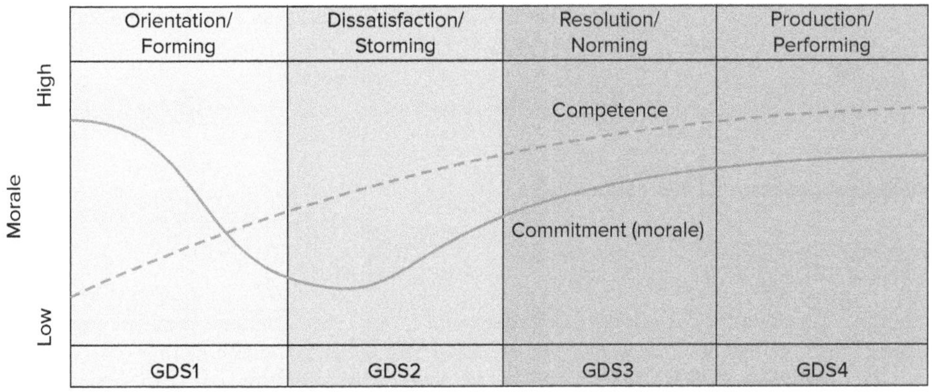

Note: If a team is at stage 5, it terminates and has no competence and commitment. There is no development.

Source: G. Yukl, "Effective Leadership Behavior: What We Know and What Questions Need More Attention," Academy of Management Perspectives, vol. 26, no. 4, 2012, 66–85.

team and there is a high level of satisfaction of members' affiliation needs. The group maintains a positive group structure and dynamics.

Stage 5: Termination   In functional groups, the *adjourning* stage is not reached unless there is some drastic reorganization; however, it does occur in task groups. During this stage, members experience feelings about leaving the group.

The two key variables identified through each stage of group development are work on the task[48] (*competence*) and the socioemotional tone or morale (*commitment*). The two variables do not progress in the same manner. Competence tends to continue to increase through each of the first four stages, while commitment tends to start high in stage 1, drop in stage 2, and then rise through stages 3 and 4. This pattern is illustrated in Exhibit 10.4.

/// **In the opening case,** Bonnie Sue's committee is in stage 2–dissatisfaction. The group has had a decrease in commitment and an increase in competence. The group needs to resolve the dissatisfaction to progress to stages 3 and 4 of development. Being an ad hoc committee, the group will go through stage 5–termination–in three weeks. The next part of this section discusses how Bonnie Sue can help the group develop to stages 3 and 4 as a situational supervisor. ///

WORK APPLICATION 10-7

Identify the group's stage of development and the leader's situational supervisory style. Does the leader use the appropriate style?

WORK APPLICATION 10-8

What can be done to improve the group's dynamics? Explain.

APPLICATION SITUATIONS / / /

Group Development Stages   AS 10-3

Identify the group's development stage as:

A. GDS1   B. GDS2   C. GDS3   D. GDS4   E. GDS5

_____ 11. The task team members are trying to get to know one another.

_____ 12. The group sets a new all time high number of units produced.

_____ 13. At the team meeting, several members are complaining.

_____ 14. The group isn't meeting all members' initial expectations, but they accept the situation and are working well as a team.

_____ 15. The ad hoc committee has presented to management its task force recommendations on which new machine to buy.

Team Development and Situational Supervision

Before we discuss leading teams as a situational supervisor, complete Self-Assessment Exercise 10-2.

/ / / **Self-Assessment Exercise 10-2** / / /

Determining Your Preferred Group Leadership Style

In the 12 situations below, select the response (a, b, c, or d) that represents what you would actually do as the group's leader. Ignore the D and S lines; they will be used as part of Skill-Building Exercise 10-2.

1. Your group works well together; members are cohesive, with positive norms. They maintain a fairly consistent level of production that is above the organizational average, as long as you continue to provide maintenance behavior. You have a new assignment for them. To accomplish it, you would: D _____
   a. Explain what needs to be done and tell them how to do it. Oversee them while they perform the task. S _____
   b. Tell the group how pleased you are with their past performance. Explain the new assignment, but let them decide how to accomplish it. Be available if they need help. S _____
   c. Tell the group what needs to be done. Encourage them to give input on how to do the job. Oversee task performance. S _____
   d. Explain to the group what needs to be done. S _____

2. You have been promoted to a new supervisory position. The group appears to have little talent to do the job, but members do seem to care about the quality of the work they do. The last supervisor was terminated because of the department's low productivity level. To increase productivity, you would: D _____
   a. Let the group know you are aware of its low production level, but let them decide how to improve it. S _____
   b. Spend most of your time overseeing group members as they perform their jobs. Train them as needed. S _____
   c. Explain to the group that you would like to work together to improve productivity. Work together as a team. S _____
   d. Tell the group some ways productivity can be improved. With their ideas, develop methods, and make sure they are implemented. S _____

3. Your department continues to be one of the top performers in the organization. It works well as a team. In the past, you generally let members take care of the work on their own. You decide to: D _____
   a. Go around encouraging group members on a regular basis. S _____
   b. Define members' roles, and spend more time overseeing performance. S _____
   c. Continue things the way they are; let them alone. S _____
   d. Hold a meeting. Recommend ways to improve and get members' ideas as well. After agreeing on changes, oversee the group to make sure it implements the new ideas and does improve. S _____

4. You have spent much of the past year training your employees. However, they do not need as much of your time to oversee production as they used to. Several group members no longer get along as well as they did in the past. You've played referee lately. You: D _____
   a. Have a group meeting to discuss ways to increase performance. Let the group decide what changes to make. Be supportive. S _____
   b. Continue things the way they are now. Supervise them closely and be the referee when needed. S _____
   c. Let the members alone to work things out for themselves. S
   d. Continue to supervise closely as needed, but spend more time playing maintenance roles; develop a team spirit. S _____

5. Your department has been doing such a great job that it has grown in numbers. You are surprised at how fast the new members were integrated. The team continues to come up with ways to improve performance on its own. As a result of the growth, your department will be moving to a new, larger location. You decide to: D _____
   a. Design the new layout and present it to the group to see if they can improve it. S _____
   b. In essence, become a group member and allow the group to design the new layout. S _____
   c. Design the new layout and put a copy on the bulletin board so employees know where to report for work after the move. S _____
   d. Hold a meeting to get employee ideas on the layout of the new location. After the meeting, think about it and finalize the layout. S _____

(continued)

/ / / Self-Assessment Exercise 10-2 / / / (continued)

6. You are appointed to head a task group. Because of the death of a relative, you had to miss the first meeting. At the second meeting, the group seems to have developed objectives and some ground rules. Members have volunteered for assignments that have to be accomplished. You: D _____
   a. Take over as a strong leader. Change some ground rules and assignments. S _____
   b. Review what has been done so far, and keep things as is. However, take charge and provide clear direction from now on. S _____
   c. Take over the leadership but allow the group to make the decisions. Be supportive and encourage them. S _____
   d. Seeing that the group is doing so well, leave and do not attend any more meetings. S _____

7. Your group was working at, or just below, standard. However, there has been a conflict within the group. As a result, production is behind schedule. You: D _____
   a. Tell the group how to resolve the conflict. Then closely supervise to make sure your plan is followed and production increases. S _____
   b. Let the group work it out. S _____
   c. Hold a meeting to work as a team to come up with a solution. Encourage the group to work together. S _____
   d. Hold a meeting to present a way to resolve the conflict. Sell the members on its merits, include their input, and follow up. S _____

8. The organization has allowed flextime. Two of your employees have asked if they could change work hours. You are concerned because all busy work hours need adequate coverage. The department is very cohesive, with positive norms. You decide to: D _____
   a. Tell them things are going well; keep things as they are now. S _____
   b. Hold a department meeting to get everyone's input; then reschedule members' hours. S _____
   c. Hold a department meeting to get everyone's input; then reschedule members' hours on a trial basis. Tell the group that if there is any drop in productivity, you will go back to the old schedule. S _____
   d. Tell them to hold a department meeting. If the department agrees to have at least three people on the job during the busy hours, they can make changes, giving you a copy of the new schedule. S _____

9. You have arrived 10 minutes late for a department meeting. Your employees are discussing the latest assignment. This surprises you because, in the past, you had to provide clear direction and employees rarely would say anything. You: D _____
   a. Take control immediately and provide your usual direction. S _____
   b. Say nothing and just sit back. S _____
   c. Encourage the group to continue, but also provide direction. S _____
   d. Thank the group for starting without you, and encourage them to continue. Support their efforts. S _____

10. Your department is consistently very productive. However, occasionally, the members fool around and someone has an accident. There has never been a serious injury. You hear a noise and go to see what it was. From a distance you can see Sue sitting on the floor, laughing, with a ball made from company material in her hand. You: D _____
    a. Say and do nothing. After all, she's OK, and the department is very productive; you don't want to make waves. S _____
    b. Call the group together and ask for suggestions on how to keep accidents from recurring. Tell them you will be checking up on them to make sure the fooling around does not continue. S _____
    c. Call the group together and discuss the situation. Encourage them to be more careful in the future. S _____
    d. Tell the group that from now on, you will be checking up on them regularly. Bring Sue to your office and discipline her. S _____

11. You are at the first meeting of an ad hoc committee you are leading. Most of the members are second- and third-level managers from marketing and financial areas; you are a supervisor from production. You decide to start by: D _____
    a. Working on developing relationships. Get everyone to feel as though they know each other before you talk about business. S _____
    b. Going over the group's purpose and the authority it has. Provide clear directives. S _____
    c. Asking the group to define its purpose. Because most of the members are higher-level managers, let them provide the leadership. S _____
    d. Providing both direction and encouragement. Give directives and thank people for their cooperation. S _____

12. Your department has done a great job in the past. It is now getting a new computer, somewhat different from the old one. You have been trained to operate the computer, and you are expected to train your employees to operate it. To train them, you: D _____
    a. Give the group instructions. Work with them individually, providing direction and encouragement. S _____
    b. Get the group together to decide how they want to be instructed. Be very supportive of their efforts to learn. S _____

(continued)

/ / / Self-Assessment Exercise 10-2 / / / (continued)

c. Tell them it's a simple system. Give them a copy of the manual and have them study it on their own. S _____

d. Give the group instructions. Then go around and supervise their work closely, giving additional instructions as needed. S _____

To determine your preferred group leadership style, in the table below, circle the letter you selected in situations 1 through 12. The column headings indicate the style you selected.

	Autocratic (S-A)	Consultative (S-C)	Participative (S-P)	Laissez-faire (S-L)
1.	*a*	*c*	*b*	*d*
2.	*b*	*d*	*c*	*a*
3.	*b*	*d*	*a*	*c*
4.	*b*	*d*	*a*	*c*
5.	*c*	*a*	*d*	*b*
6.	*a*	*b*	*c*	*d*
7.	*a*	*d*	*c*	*b*
8.	*a*	*c*	*b*	*d*
9.	*a*	*c*	*d*	*b*
10.	*d*	*b*	*a*	*c*
11.	*b*	*d*	*a*	*c*
12.	*d*	*a*	*b*	*c*
Total				

Add the number of circled items per column. The total for all four columns should equal 12. The column with the highest number represents your preferred group leadership style. There is no one best style in all situations.

The more evenly distributed the numbers are among the four styles, the more flexible you are at leading groups. A total of 0 or 1 in any column may indicate a reluctance to use that style. You could have problems in situations calling for that style.

Is your preferred group leadership style the same as your preferred situational supervision style (Chapter 6) and situational communication style (Chapter 4)?

Learning Outcome 10-3

Explain the four situational supervisory styles to use with a group, based on its stage of development.

Situational supervision can be applied to the stages of group development. Chapter 6 presented the situational supervision model. In that chapter, the focus was on supervising individual employees. Below you will find changes that place the focus on applying the model to group development. Recall the need for contingency leadership. With each stage of group development, a different supervisory style is needed to help the group perform effectively at that stage and to develop to the next level.

When people interact with their groups, they can perform task roles, maintenance roles, or both. Here you will learn which role(s) the leader should play during the different stages of group development. As you read the stages and styles, recall that *you don't have to be a manager to be a leader*—rise to the occasion to help the group develop.

Orientation (D1 Low) = Autocratic Style   The group development stage 1, orientation–low development *D1* (high commitment/low competence), uses the *autocratic supervisory style* (high task–low maintenance), S-A. When task groups first come together, leaders need to help the group clarify its objectives to provide the direction to be sure the group gets off to a good start. Because the members are committed to joining the group, leaders need to help the group develop its competence with task behavior.

Dissatisfaction (D2 Moderate) = Consultative Style   The group development stage 2, dissatisfaction–moderate development *D2* (lower commitment/some competence), uses the *consultative* *supervisory style* (high task–high maintenance), S-C. Even though groups know their objectives and their roles are clear, members become dissatisfied for a variety of reasons, such as not getting along with one or more members or not being happy with the amount of influence (status) they have in the group. When morale drops, leaders need to focus on maintenance roles to encourage members to resolve issues. At the same time, continue to play the task role necessary to help the group develop its level of competence.

Resolution (D3 High) = Participative Style   The group development stage 3, resolution–high development *D3* (variable commitment/high competence), uses the *participative supervisory style* (low task–high maintenance), S-P. There is little need to provide task leadership; the members know how to do the job. When commitment varies, it is usually due to some problem in the group's dynamics, such as a conflict,[49] self-interest roles, or a loss of interest, so focus on the maintenance behavior to get the group through the issue(s) it faces. If leaders continues to provide task directives that are not needed, the group can become dissatisfied and regress or plateau at this level.

Production (D4 Outstanding) = Laissez-faire Style   The group development stage 4, production–outstanding development *D4* (high commitment/high competence), uses the *laissez-faire supervisory style* (low task–low maintenance), S-L. Groups that develop to this stage have members who play the appropriate task and maintenance roles; leaders do not need to play either role unless there is a problem because members share leadership.[50]

As a leader, you should determine your group's current level of development and strive to bring it to the next stage of development. /// **In the opening case,** Bonnie Sue's committee is in stage 2–dissatisfaction. Bonnie Sue needs to play both task and maintenance roles to help the group progress to stages 3 and 4. Focusing on solving the negative norm of putting each other's ideas down works on both task and maintenance levels. Bonnie Sue also needs to provide stronger leadership in the areas of completing meeting assignments and making Kirt, Shelby, and Carlos more productive. You will learn how in the next section. ///

The four stages of group development, along with their appropriate situational supervisory styles, are summarized in Model 10.1.

MODEL 10.1 | Group Situational Supervision

Group Development Stage (D)	Supervisory Styles/Roles (S)
D1 Low Development ⟶ *High commitment—low competence*	**S-A Autocratic** *High task—low maintenance*
Members come to the group committed, but they cannot perform with competence.	Provide direction so that the group has clear objectives and members know their roles. Make the decisions for the group.
D2 Moderate Development ⟶ *Low commitment—some competence*	**S-C Consultative** *High task—high maintenance*
Members have become dissatisfied with the group. They have started to develop competence but are frustrated with results.	Continue to direct the group so it develops task ability. Provide maintenance to regain commitment as the group structure takes place. Include members' input in decisions.
D3 High Development ⟶ *Variable commitment—high competence*	**S-P Participative** *Low task—high maintenance*
Commitment changes over time while production remains relatively constant.	Provide little direction. Focus on developing an effective group structure. Have the group participate in decision making.
D4 Outstanding Development ⟶ *High commitment—high competence*	**S-L Laissez-faire** *Low task—low maintenance*
Commitment remains constantly high and so does production.	Members provide their own task and maintenance roles. The supervisor is a group member. Allow the group to make its own decisions.

LEADERSHIP SKILLS IN MEETINGS

With the trend toward teams, there are more meetings in the workplace. Thus, you need meeting leadership skills for career success to run meetings and/or to be a productive member in meetings. The meeting skills presented here apply to both face-to-face and the increasing use of audio conference and videoconference meetings.

Let's take a few seconds for a humorous break. How do you define a committee? A committee is a group that takes minutes and waste hours. Top level managers spend as much as one-third of their day in meetings, and many people dislike meetings because they believe they are often an unproductive waste of time.[51] But it doesn't have to be. If you develop the skills in this section you can plan, run, and help lead meetings, and deal with problem members effectively. The success or failure of meetings rests primarily with the leader, but again we can all be leaders, so if the person in charge is not running the meeting effectively, you may be able to help improve the meetings.

Learning Outcome 10-4

Explain how to plan for and conduct effective meetings.

Planning Meetings

There are at least five areas in which meeting planning is needed, as discussed here.

Objectives   A great mistake made by those who call meetings is that they often have no clear idea and purpose for the meeting. Before calling a meeting, you should clearly define its purpose and objective.[52] The objective tells you where you are going, and the plan tells you how you are going to get there.

Participants and Assignments   Before calling the meeting, the leader should decide who is qualified to attend the meeting. Does the full group or department need to attend? Should some nongroup specialist be invited to provide input? Participants should know in advance what is expected of them at the meeting and how they can contribute. If any preparation is expected (reading material, doing some research, preparing a report, and the like), they should have adequate advance notice.

Agenda   The leader should identify the activities that will take place during the meeting to achieve the objective of the meeting. Place agenda items in order of priority. Then if the group does not have time to cover every item, the least important items carry forward. At too many meetings, a leader puts all the so-called quick items first. The group gets bogged down and either rushes through the important items or puts them off until later.

Date, Time, and Place   Clearly specify the beginning and ending time and stick to it. Be sure to select an adequate place for the meeting and plan for the physical comfort of the group.

Leadership   The leader should determine the group's level of development and plan to provide the appropriate task and/or maintenance behavior using the situational supervisor model. Some groups rotate the role of the group moderator or leader for each meeting, with groups that are capable of doing so, to develop meeting skills.

The Written Plan   After leaders have planned the above five items, they should put them in writing and make copies to be distributed, typically e-mailed, to each member who will attend the meeting. Exhibit 10.5 provides the recommended contents, in sequence, of a meeting plan.

Conducting Meetings

Below, you will learn about the group's first meeting, the three parts of each meeting, and leadership, group structure and dynamics, and emotions. If you want to be technically correct when you run meetings, you can follow the well-known Robert's Rules of Order. You can find a summary at http://www.robertsrules.org or at the official Web site at http://robertsrules.org.

EXHIBIT 10.5 | Written Meeting Plan

Time: Date, day, place, beginning and ending times.

Objectives: A statement of the purpose and/or objective of the meeting.

Participants and Assignments: List each participant's name and assignment, if any. If all members have the same assignment, make one assignment statement.

Agenda: List each item to be covered in priority order with its approximate time limit.

The First Meeting and Ground Rules   At the first meeting, the group is in the orientation stage. The leader should use the high task role; however, the members should be given the opportunity to spend some time getting to know one another. Introductions set the stage for subsequent interactions. If members find that their social needs will not be met, dissatisfaction may occur quickly. A simple technique is to start with introductions, then move on to the group's purpose, objectives, and members' roles and ground rules to help meet the objecitves.

As the formal leader, you should set some ground rules, such as shut off or vibrate smartphones and other devises that distract the user and others.[53] For long meetings, have a break that enables members to interact informally and check their screens.

A norm of starting meetings late is common. So a very important ground rule to consider is that meetings will start and end on time. No one's time will be idly wasted waiting for someone to show up late, and latecomers will not be caught up. No one will be late for their next activity; members can walk out if the meeting doesn't end on time. This rule may sound harsh, but many people feel frustrated, disrespected, or insulted by waiting for others, and they do want to get to their next activity on time.[54]

We presented two examples of possible ground rules. However, it is also a good idea to ask the team members for other suggestions for ground rules.

The Three Parts of Each Meeting   Begin the meetings on time; waiting for late members penalizes the members who are on time and develops a norm for coming late. Each meeting should cover the following:

1. *Objectives.* Begin by reviewing progress to date, the group's objectives, and the purpose or objective for the specific meeting. If minutes are recorded, they are usually approved at the beginning of the next meeting. For most meetings, it is recommended that a secretary be appointed to take minutes.

2. *Agenda.* Cover the agenda items. Try to keep to the approximate times, but be flexible. If the discussion is constructive and members need more time, give it to them; however, if the discussion is more of a distractive argument, move ahead.

3. *Summarize and review assignments.* End the meeting on time. The leader should summarize what took place during the meeting. Were the meeting's objectives achieved? Review all of the assignments given during the meeting.[55] Get a commitment to the task that each member should perform for the next or a specific future meeting. The secretary and/or leader should record all assignments. If there is no accountability and follow-up on assignments, members may not complete them.

Leadership, Group Structure and Dynamics, and Emotions   As stated in the previous section, leadership needs to change with the group's level of development. The leader must be sure to provide the appropriate task and/or maintenance behavior when it is needed. The leader and members are responsible for helping the team develop an effective group structure and dynamics as it performs the task (we have already discussed how to do so in this chapter). Members may get emotional during meetings, so use your skills at dealing with emotions from Chapter 4.

Communication Skills
Refer to CS Question 8.

WORK APPLICATION 10-9

Recall a specific meeting you attended. Did the group leader plan for the meeting by stating meeting objectives, identifying participants and their assignments, making an agenda, and stating the date, time, and place of the meeting? Did the leader provide a written meeting plan to the members prior to the meeting? Explain your answers and state what you would do differently if you were the leader.

Learning Outcome 10-5

Identify six problem members and explain how to handle them so they do not have a negative effect on your meetings.

Handling Problem Team Members

Certain personality types tend to emerge in team meetings that can cause the group to be less efficient than possible. As the leader and/or member, you will have to handle difficult people who don't conform with effective meeting rules and norms. Next we will discuss how to handle six problem types to make the member and the group more effective.

The Silent Member   For a team to be fully effective, all group members should participate. If members are silent, the team does not get the benefit of their input.

Encourage the silent member to participate, without being obvious or overbearing. The simple rotation method, in which all members take turns giving their input, helps. To build up the silent members' confidence, call on them with questions they can easily answer.

If you are a silent type, speaking up is hard, but participate more often. Don't be intimidated and quiet because you think others are smarter than you—they most likely are not and may have the same thoughts as you. Go to the meeting prepared with notes, knowing what you want to say. Know when to stand up for your views and be assertive (Chapter 5).

The Talker   Talkers have something to say about everything. They like to dominate the discussion. However, if they do dominate, the other members do not get to participate and may get bored.

Slow down talkers, don't shut them up, and don't let them dominate the group. The simple rotation method is effective with talkers, as they have to wait for their turn. When not using a rotation method, gently interrupt the talker and present your own ideas or call on other members to present their ideas.

If you tend to be a talker, realize that as an extravert you tend to "think out loud" by speaking, whereas introverts prefer to collect their thoughts before speaking and can be overwhelmed in a group, especially a group of extraverts. Slow down and give others a chance to talk and do things for themselves.

The Wanderer   Wanderers distract the team from the agenda items and often like to complain and criticize as they ramble off topic.

Keep the group on track. If the wanderer socializes, cut off the conversation. Be kind, thank the member for the contribution, and then throw a question out to the group to get it back on track. Griping without resolving anything tends to reduce morale and commitment to task accomplishment. If the wanderer complains, make statements like, "We may be underpaid, but we have no control over our pay. Complaining will not get us a raise; let's get back to the issue at hand."

If you tend to be a wanderer, try to be aware of your behavior and stay on the subject at hand.

The Bored Member   Your team may have one or more members who are not interested in the task. The bored person may be preoccupied with other issues and not pay attention or participate in the group meeting. The bored member may be a know-it-all, who feels superior and wonders why the group is spending so much time on the obvious.

Keep members motivated. Assign the bored member a task such as recording ideas on the board or recording the minutes. Call on bored members; bring them into the group. If you allow them to sit back, things may get worse and others may decide not to participate either. Negative feelings can easily be carried to other team members.

If you tend to be bored, try to find ways to help motivate yourself (Chapter 7). Work at becoming more patient and in control of behavior that can have negative effects on other members.

The Arguer   Like the talker, the arguer likes to be the center of attention. Arguers enjoy arguing for the sake of arguing, rather than helping the group.

Resolve conflict, but not in an argumentative way; stay calm. Do not get into an argument with arguers; that is exactly what they want to happen. If an argument starts, bring others into the discussion. If it is personal, cut it off. Personal attacks only hurt the group. Keep the discussion moving on target. Try to minimize arguers' opportunities for confrontation.

If you tend to be an arguer, strive to convey your views in an assertive debate format, not as an aggressive argument (Chapter 5). Listen to others' views and be willing to change if they have better ideas.

The Social Loafer   This *social loafer* problem member doesn't want to take individual responsibility and do a fair share of the work. They are also called *free riders* in groups.[56]

Communication Skills
Refer to CS Question 9.

SB

Skill-Building Exercise 10-1
develops this skill.

WORK APPLICATION 10-10

Identify group problem members at a meeting you attended. Was the leader effective in handling them? What would you have done to make them more productive members? Explain in detail.

Following all the previously mentioned meeting guidelines helps, especially giving clear individual assignments. Don't let the group develop norms that allow social loafing, and use peer pressure to get them to do their work. Confront social loafers assertively using the conflict resolution model in Chapter 5. When necessary, threaten to go to the boss. If these methods do not work, go to the supervisor (professor or boss) and explain the situation stating the specific behavior that is lacking and that you and the group have tried to resolve the problem, but the social loafer refuses to perform to standards.

Conclusion   Whenever you work in a team, do not embarrass, intimidate, or argue with any members, no matter how much they provoke you. If you do, the result will make martyrs of them and a bully of you to the team. If you have serious problem members who do not respond to the above techniques, confront them individually outside the team meeting. Get them to agree to work in a cooperative way.

/// In the opening case, Bonnie Sue's meetings lacked specific assignments. She needs to use more directive leadership and assign tasks to specific members to complete outside the meetings. Recall that the problem members in Bonnie Sue's group were Carlos, a talker; Shelby, a wanderer; and Kirt, an arguer. Bonnie Sue needs to use her leadership skills to slow down Carlos, keep Shelby on topic, keep Kirt from fighting with others, and resolve conflicts quickly. ///

APPLICATION SITUATIONS / / /

Problem Team Members   AS10-4

Identify the problem member as:

A. Silent member   C. Wanderer   E. Arguer

B. Talker   D. Bored member   F. Social loafer

_____ 16. Hank is always first or second to give his ideas. He is always elaborating on ideas.

_____ 17. Jamal is sitting back quietly today for the first time. The other members are doing all the discussing and volunteering for assignments.

_____ 18. As the group is discussing a problem, Tom asks the group if anyone heard about the vice president and the sales clerk.

_____ 19. Eunice is usually last to give her ideas. When asked to explain her position, Eunice often changes her answers to agree with the group.

_____ 20. Kareem enjoys challenging members' ideas. He likes to have the group do things his way. When a group member does not agree with Kareem, he makes wisecracks about the member's past mistakes.

PROBLEM SOLVING AND DECISION MAKING

Recall that problem solving and decision making are an important part of group structure as teams need to solve specific problems.[57] Teams face problems and must make decisions,[58] and better decisions lead to better performance.[59] Decision making skills are important,[60] as the decisions you make will affect your behavior, relationships, happiness, and performance. In this section, we discuss the relationship between problem solving and decision making, decision-making styles, and the decision-making model that can improve your individual and team skills.

The Relationship between Problem Solving and Decision Making

In short, decisions are made to solve problems and take advantage of opportunities. When we discuss problems, we also include opportunities, and when we discuss decision making, we are also including problem solving because they go hand-in-hand.

A **problem** exists *whenever there is a difference between what is actually happening and what the individual or group wants to be happening.* If your objective is to produce 500 units per day, but only 475 units are produced, you have a problem. We typically try to reduce the discrepancy between the actual performance and the objective. Thus, **problem solving** is *the process of taking corrective action in order to meet objectives.* **Decision making** is *the process of selecting an alternative course of action that will solve a problem.* Decisions must be made when you are faced with a problem or opportunity. When making decisions, remember the goal of human relations is to create a win–win situation for stakeholders.

/// **In the opening case,** Bonnie Sue has a problem because her team is not performing to her expectations. She needs to make some decisions about how to get the team to pull together, using the group structure and dynamics, and lead as a situational supervisor to develop the team, as discussed throughout this chapter. ///

WORK APPLICATION 10-11

Give an example of a problem you face now.

Decision-Making Styles

There are various decision-making styles, and your personality affects how you make decisions. Decisions can be classified by information used and decision speed,[61] including reflexive, consistent, and reflective decision making styles. To determine your decision-making style, answer the questions in Self-Assessment Exercise 10-3.

/// Self-Assessment Exercise 10-3 ///

Decision-Making Styles

Select the answer (1 to 3) that best describes how you make decisions.

A. Overall I'm _____ to act.

   1. quick   2. moderate   3. slow

B. I spend _____ amount of time making important decisions as/than I do making less important decisions.

   1. about the same   2. a greater   3. a much greater

C. When making decisions, I _____ go with my first thought.

   1. usually   2. occasionally   3. rarely

D. When making decisions, I'm _____ concerned about making errors.

   1. rarely   2. occasionally   3. often

E. When making decisions, I _____ recheck my work.

   1. rarely   2. occasionally   3. usually

F. When making decisions, I gather _____ information.

   1. little   2. some   3. lots of

(continued)

G. When making decisions, I consider _____ alternative actions.

   1. few   2. some   3. lots of

H. When making a decision, I usually make it _____ before the deadline.

   1. long   2. somewhat   3. just

I. After making a decision, I _____ look for other alternatives, wishing I had waited.

   1. rarely   2. occasionally   3. usually

J. I _____ regret having made a decision.

   1. rarely   2. occasionally   3. often

To determine your style, add the numbers that represent your answers to the 10 questions. The total will be between 10 and 30. Place an X on the continuum at the point that represents your score.

         Reflexive   Consistent   Reflective

10 - 16 - 23 - 30

A score of 10 to 16 indicates a reflexive style; 17 to 23 indicates a consistent style; and 24 to 30 indicates a reflective style. You have determined your preferred personal decision-making style. Groups also have a preferred decision-making style, based on how their members make decisions. Changing the *I* to *we*, you could answer the 10 questions to refer to a group rather than to yourself.

Reflexive Style   A reflexive decision maker likes to make quick decisions ("to shoot from the hip"), without taking the time to get all the information that may be needed and without considering all alternatives. On the positive side, reflexive decision makers are decisive; they do not procrastinate. They can act fast if the decision wasn't right.[62] On the negative side, making quick decisions can lead to waste and duplication when a decision is not the best possible alternative.

If you use a reflexive style, you may want to slow down and spend more time gathering information and analyzing alternatives. Following the steps in the decision-making model, our next topic, can help you develop your skills.

Reflective Style   A reflective decision maker likes to take plenty of time to make decisions, taking into account considerable information and an analysis of several alternatives, or because they are procrastinators avoiding making decisions. On the positive side, the reflective type does not make decisions that are rushed. On the negative side, they may procrastinate and waste valuable time and other resources and lose out on opportunities. Waiting only makes a bad decision worse,[63] and a correct decision is wrong when it is taken too late.[64] The reflective decision maker may be viewed as wishy-washy and indecisive.

If you use a reflective style, you may want to speed up your decision making. As **Andrew Jackson** once said, "Take time to deliberate; but when the time for action arrives, stop thinking and go on."

Learning Outcome 10-6

List the five steps in the decision-making model.

Consistent Style   A consistent decision maker makes decisions without rushing or wasting time. Consistent decision makers know when they have enough information and alternatives to make a sound decision. They have the most consistent record of good decisions. **Steve Jobs** was known for being a great problem solver, and especially for taking advantage of opportunities to introduce new iProducts. Consistent decision makers tend to follow the decision-making steps below.

The Decision-Making Model

You likely agree that decisions should be made logically and rationally. However, recall that emotions tend to overrule rational thinking.[65] Decision making can be more rational when following a critical thinking[66] evidence-based process,[67] which we call the decision-making model. Of course we have to use some intuitive judgment, which is called *bounded rationality*.[68] The five steps are shown in Model 10.2 and discussed here.

Communication Skills
Refer to CS Question 10.

When to Use the Decision-Making Model   The key to effective decision making is knowing when to make quick decisions (without the model) vs. considered ones (using the model).[69] It is not necessary to follow all five steps in the model when making unimportant recurring decisions when the outcome of the decision is known, called certainty. Risk taking is fundamental to decision making. Use the model when making important nonrecurring decisions when the outcome is risky or uncertain.[70]

Following the steps in the model will not guarantee success. However, following the model increases the probability of successful decision making. You most likely followed the steps in the model when selecting a college without consciously knowing it. Consciously use the model for important decisions, and you will improve your ability to make decisions. Let's examine each step here, as it is shown in Model 10.2.

Step 1: Define the Problem   If you misdiagnose the problem, you will not solve it, so slow down. In analyzing a problem, first distinguish the *symptoms* from the *cause* of the problem. To do so, list the observable and describable occurrences (symptoms) that indicate a problem exists. For example, Wayne, an employee with five years' tenure, has been an excellent producer on the job. However, in the past month, Wayne has been out sick and tardy more times than in the past two years. What is the problem? If you say absenteeism or tardiness, you are confusing symptoms and causes. They are symptoms of the problem. If the supervisor simply disciplines Wayne, he or she may decrease the tardiness and absenteeism, but the problem will not be solved. It would be wiser for the supervisor to talk to the employee and find out the reason (cause) for the changed behavior. The real problem may be a personal problem at home or on the job.

MODEL 10.2 | Decision-Making Model

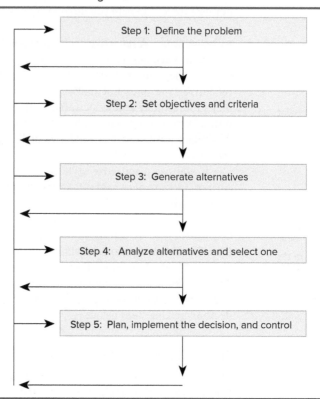

Step 2: Set Objectives and Criteria   After the problem has been defined, you set an objective (end result of the decision) to solve the problem.[71] Refer to Chapter 7 for the setting objectives model.

Next, you identify the criteria the decision must meet to achieve the objective. It is helpful to specify *must* and *want* criteria. Must criteria have to be met, while want criteria are desirable but not necessary. For example: Objective: "To hire a store manager by June 30, 2020." The must criteria are a college degree and a minimum of five years' experience as a store manager. The want criterion is that the hiree should be a minority group member. The organization wants to hire a minority but will not hire one who does not meet the must criteria.

Continuing the example with Wayne: The objective is to improve Wayne's attendance record. The criterion is the organizations stated policy, which was his prior good record of attendance.

Step 3: Generate Alternatives   You need to generate possible methods, or alternatives, for solving the problem through decision making. When making nonroutine decisions, new, creative solutions are often needed. In the next section, we discuss creativity, which is commonly used as part of this step in the decision-making model.

When gathering the information needed to generate alternatives, you can neither expect nor afford complete information. However, you must get enough information to enable you to make good decisions—the consistent decision style—and it should be evidence-based.[72] It is often helpful to ask others for advice on possible solutions to your problem. When generating alternatives, it is important not to evaluate them at the same time (evaluation is in step 4)—just list anything reasonable that can possibly solve the problem.

Continuing the example with Wayne: Some alternatives are giving Wayne a warning, punishing him in some way, or talking to him to determine the reason for the change in his behavior.

Step 4: Analyze Alternatives and Select One   Here you must evaluate each alternative in terms of the objectives and criteria. Think forward and try to predict the outcome of each alternative. One method you can use to analyze alternatives is *cost–benefit* analysis. Each alternative has its positive and its negative aspects, or its costs and benefits. Costs are more than monetary. They may include a sacrifice of time, money, and so forth. Cost–benefit analysis has become popular where the benefits are often difficult to determine in quantified dollars. The benefits of a college degree are more than just a paycheck.

Another approach to improving the quality of decisions is the devil's advocate approach. The *devil's advocate technique* requires the individual to explain and defend his or her position before the group. The group critically asks the presenter questions. They try to shoot holes in the alternative solution to determine any possible problems in its implementation. After a period of time, the group reaches a refined solution.

Continuing the example with Wayne: The alternative selected is to have a talk with him to try to determine why his attendance has changed.

Communication Skills
Refer to CS Questions 11 and 12.

Skill-Building Exercise 10-2
develops this skill.

Step 5: Plan, Implement the Decision, and Control   Step 5 has three separate parts, as the title states. After making the decision, you should develop a *plan* of action with a schedule for its implementation.[73] Lack of planning is a common reason why decisions, including New Year's resolutions, are not *implemented*. Decision making is a waste of time if you don't actually implement the alternative. As with all plans, *controls* should be developed while planning.[74] Checkpoints with feedback should be established to determine whether the decision is solving the problem. If not, corrective action may be needed. You should not be locked into an irrational *escalation of commitment* to a decision that is not solving the problem.[75] When you make a poor decision, you should admit the mistake and change the decision by going back to previous steps in the decision-making model.

WORK APPLICATION 10-12

Solve the problem you gave in Work Application 10-11, following the five steps in the decision-making model. Write it out clearly, labeling each step.

Communication Skills
Refer to CS Question 13.

Communication Skills
Refer to CS Question 14.

Concluding the example with Wayne: The supervisor plans what he or she will say to him during the meeting, conducts the meeting, and follows up to be sure that the problem is solved.

Model 10.2 lists the five steps in the decision-making model. Notice that the steps do not go simply from start to end. At any step, you may have to return to a previous step to make changes. For example, if you are in the fifth step and control and implementation are not solving the problem as planned, you may have to backtrack to take corrective action by generating and selecting a new alternative or by changing the objective. If the problem was not defined accurately, you may have to go back to the beginning.

CREATIVITY AND GROUP PROBLEM SOLVING AND DECISION MAKING

Creativity and innovation go together, but they are different.[76] **Creativity** means *the ability to develop unique alternatives to solve problems.* Innovation is the organizational implementation of the creative ideas. Innovation is important to organizational success, and many companies are working to enhance creativity and innovation.[77] In this section, we'll focus on creativity that can take place during the third step of the decision-making model.

The Creative Process

Creativity is about coming up with ways to improve products and processes by rethinking a problem and creating opportunities.[78] Following the stages in the creative process can help improve your creativity. The four **stages in the creative process** are: *(1) preparation, (2) possible solutions, (3) incubation, and (4) evaluation.* These steps are also listed in Model 10.3.

1. *Preparation.* You must become familiar with the specific problem,[79] so concentrate without multitasking.[80] This is done during steps 1 and 2 of the decision-making model. Get others' opinions, feelings, and ideas as well as the facts. When solving a problem, look for new angles, use imagination and invention, and don't set boundaries—think outside the box!

2. *Possible solutions.* Generate as many possible creative solutions as you can think of, without making any judgments.[81] The brainstorming rules (discussed next) will provide details.

3. *Incubation.* After generating alternatives, take a break. It doesn't have to be long, but take time before working on the problem again—now you can check your screens. During the incubation stage, you may have an insight into the problem's solution. Have you ever worked hard on a problem and become discouraged, but when you had given up or taken a break, the solution came to you?

4. *Evaluation.* Before implementing a solution, you should evaluate the alternative to make sure the idea is practical; use evidence-based management.[82] Evaluation through feedback often leads to more creativity.

WORK APPLICATION 10-13

Give an example of how you solved a problem using the stages in the creative process, or used the creative process to solve an existing problem.

MODEL 10.3 | Stages in the Creative Process

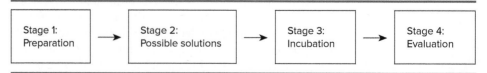

| Stage 1: Preparation | → | Stage 2: Possible solutions | → | Stage 3: Incubation | → | Stage 4: Evaluation |

Source: J. Raffiee and J. Feng, "Should I Quit My Day Job? A Hybrid Path to Entrepreneurship," *Academy of Management Journal,* vol. 57, no. 4, 2014, 936–963.

How people respond to creative ideas affects behavior. For a list of responses that kill creativity, see Exhibit 10.6. Avoid these responses and discourage others from using them as well.

Learning Outcome 10-7

Describe five techniques for generating creative alternatives.

Using Groups to Generate Creative Alternatives

In step 3 of the decision-making process, organizations today are using group input to generate creative alternatives.[83] Exhibit 10.7 lists the five techniques that are described here.

Brainstorming   **Brainstorming** is *the process of suggesting many alternatives, without evaluation, to solve a problem.* When brainstorming, the group is presented with a problem or opportunity and asked to come up with creative solutions.[84] Brainstorming is commonly used for creating new products, naming products, and developing advertising slogans. Here are four interrelated brainstorming rules:

EXHIBIT 10.6 | Responses That Kill Creativity

- It isn't in the budget.
- We're doing fine now, so why change?
- It costs too much.
- We don't have the time.
- That will make other products obsolete.
- We're too small/big for it.
- We've never done it before.
- Has anyone else ever tried it?
- It won't work in our company/industry.

- That's not our problem or responsibility.
- We're not ready for that.
- We tried that before and it doesn't work.
- You're years ahead of your time.
- It can't be done.
- You can't teach an old dog new tricks.
- Let's form a committee.
- It's too radical a change.
- Don't be ridiculous; let's get back to reality.

EXHIBIT 10.7 | Techniques for Generating Creative Alternatives

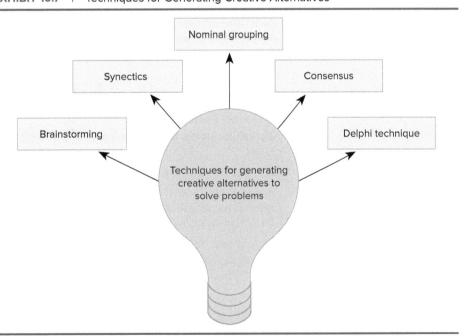

Source: A. Joshi and A.P. Knight, "Who Defers to Whom and Why Dual Pathways Linking Demographic Differences and Dyadic Deference to Team Effectiveness," *Academy of Management Journal*, vol. 58, no. 1, 2015, 59–84.

- *Quantity.* Team members should generate as many ideas as possible. More ideas increase the chances of finding an excellent solution. Generating alternatives is step 3 of the decision-making model.

- *No criticism.* Team members should not criticize or evaluate ideas in any way during the solution-generation phase of brainstorming.[85] Evaluation is done in step 4 of decision making—analyze alternatives and select one.

- *Freewheel.* You can't think outside the box when you are in it. You have to see things from new angles or perspectives. Team members should express any idea that comes to mind, no matter how strange, crazy, or weird—thus, the need to avoid criticism that will hinder members' creativity and to avoid responses that kill creativity (see Exhibit 10.6).

- *Extend.* Team members should try to build on the ideas of others and even take them in new directions.[86] Extending helps build quantity and freewheeling, but watch out for criticism.

- *Brainwriting* is a variation of brainstorming. To eliminate the influence of team peer pressure and other members' suggestions, participants write their ideas down. Then ideas are recorded, and members try to improve and combine ideas. It is especially relevant for use with virtual teams meeting online.

Synectics   Creativity is about coming up with novel ideas.[87] *Synectics* is the process of generating novel alternatives through role-playing and fantasizing. At first, to expand the group's thinking process, the leader does not state the exact nature of the situation. For example, when **Nolan Bushnell** wanted to develop a new concept in family dining, he began by discussing general leisure activities. Bushnell then moved toward leisure activities having to do with eating out. The idea that came out of this synectics process was a restaurant–electronic game complex where families could play games and purchase pizza and hamburgers. The restaurant–electronic game complex is called **Pizza Time Theatre** and its mascot is **Chuck E. Cheese**, which is also used as the restaurant's name.

Nominal Grouping   It is appropriate to use nominal grouping to ensure that status difference among members doesn't influence the process and decision; some members tend to agree with the boss or informal leader and ignore ideas from low status members. *Nominal grouping* is the process of generating and evaluating alternatives through a structured voting method. This process usually involves six steps:

1. Each member individually generates ideas in writing (brainwriting).

2. In a round-robin fashion, members give ideas. Someone records all ideas where everyone can see them.

3. Alternatives are clarified through a guided discussion and any additional ideas are recorded.

4. Each member rates the ideas and votes; the voting eliminates alternatives.

5. An initial vote discussion takes place for clarification, not persuasion. During this time, it is recommended that members present the logic behind the reasons they gave for the various alternatives.

6. The final vote is taken to select the alternative solution presented to the leader. Management may or may not implement the decision.

Consensus   A *consensus* is a cooperative attempt to develop a solution acceptable to all, rather than a forced decision on some members. The major benefit of consensus is that since the solution is the group's, members generally are more committed to implementing it. The process is to have a discussion trying to get everyone to agree on the decision to solve the problem or take advantage of the opportunity.

Communication Skills
Refer to CS Question 15.

WORK APPLICATION 10-14

Give example situations in which it would be appropriate for a manager to use each of the five techniques for generating creative alternatives (brainstorming, synectics, nominal grouping, consensus mapping, and the Delphi technique).

Delphi Technique   The Delphi technique is considered a variation of nominal grouping, without face-to-face interaction at any point, and it also includes consensus. The *Delphi technique* polls a group through a series of anonymous questionnaires. The opinions of each round of questionnaires are analyzed and resubmitted to the group in the next round of questionnaires. This process may continue for five or more rounds before a consensus emerges. The technique is used for technological forecasts, such as what the next online breakthrough will be.

APPLICATION SITUATIONS / / /

Using Groups to Generate Alternatives   AS10-5

In the five situations below, identify the most appropriate group technique to use to generate alternative solutions.

A. Brainstorming   C. Nominal grouping   E. Delphi technique

B. Synectics   D. Consensus

_____ 21. You want to develop some new and different toys. You are meeting with employees and children together.

_____ 22. Your department is suffering from morale problems.

_____ 23. You must decide on new furniture for the office.

_____ 24. You want to reduce waste in the department.

_____ 25. You want to project future trends of the business.

Skill-Building Exercise 10-3 develops this skill.

Communication Skills
Refer to CS Question 16.

Advantages and Disadvantages of Group Decision Making

Groups can solve problems far better than any individuals can.[88] But they don't always. The challenge in decision making is to maximize the advantages while minimizing the disadvantages and attaining synergy. *Synergy* occurs when the group's solution to a problem or opportunity is superior to all individuals'. Skill Building Exercise 10-3 gives you the opportunity to see if your group can reach synergy. See Exhibit 10.8 for the advantages and disadvantages of using group decision making.

EXHIBIT 10.8 | Advantages and Disadvantages of Group Decision Making

Advantages	Disadvantages
• **Better decisions**—with synergy, including avoiding errors with the help of the devil's advocate technique	• **Time**—it takes a long time to make group decisions
• **More alternatives**—more people provide diverse ideas	• **Domination**—powerful individuals or a coalition may actually make the decision
• **Acceptance and commitment**—people tend to accept and be more committed to implement a decision they help make	• **Conformity of groupthink**—members may go along with the suggested decision without questioning when they disagree with it to avoid conflict and keep social solidarity
• **Morale**—participants have more job satisfaction	• **Responsibility and social loafing**—no one individual is accountable for the decision, so people don't take it as seriously and some don't do their fair share of the work

Skill-Building Exercise 10-4
develops this skill.

When to Use Groups in Decision Making   Use groups when making important nonrecurring decisions when the outcome is risky or uncertain, using the decision-making model. The question today isn't so much about *should* we use groups to make decisions, but what level of participation should we use?[89] Skill Building Exercise 10-4 at the end of the chapter develops this skill.

DOES TEAMWORK AND DECISION MAKING APPLY GLOBALLY?

Globalization may require you to interact effectively with people from many different cultural backgrounds:[90] as an employee with coworkers in teams, and as a student in college working on a project.[91]

At major global multinational corporations (MNCs), teamwork has been important for many years.[92] However, the level of teamwork does vary, and operating in an *individualistic versus a collectivist culture* does affect teamwork. In general, in collectivist cultures of Asian countries such as Japan, teamwork is considered very important and leadership and decision making are participative; the group composition is not very diversified, with shared norms and cohesiveness; and there is less conflict than within the United States and many European countries that are more individualistic. Unlike in the United States and many European countries, there are fewer status differences, as Asians don't want to stand out as being the stars—they just want to be part of the team. New technologies, especially the Internet, have made virtual teams more common and at the same time have increased the speed and quality of global communications and decisions.

The global economy requires decisions to be made that affect operations worldwide, but at the same time, country and cultural differences call for local decisions. People from different cultures don't necessarily make decisions the same way or at the same rate of speed. In countries that are not time-sensitive, such as Egypt, decisions are more reflective. In time-sensitive countries, such as the United States, decisions are more reflexive. Countries using participative decision making take longer than do countries that use autocratic decision making.

Communication Skills
Refer to CS Question 17.

The level of participation in team decision making does vary by culture. In *high power-distance cultures* (for example, Mexico, Venezuela, the Philippines, and Yugoslavia), where more autocratic decisions are made, participation is not as acceptable. In *low power-distance cultures* (the United States, Japan, Ireland, Australia, New Zealand, Denmark, Israel, and the Netherlands), there is greater use of participation in decision making.

English is considered the global language of business. When people work in a foreign language setting the tendency to be a free rider increases, but it is moderated based on the conscientiousness personality trait.[93] Let's complete Self-Assessment Exercise 10-4 to better understand how your personality affects your team behavior.

/ / / **Self-Assessment Exercise 10-4** / / /

Personality Traits and Teams and Decision Making

Read the two statements below:

I enjoy being part of a team and working with others more than working alone.

Strongly agree   7   6   5   4   3   2   1   Strongly disagree

I enjoy achieving team goals more than individual accomplishments.

Strongly agree   7   6   5   4   3   2   1   Strongly disagree

The stronger you agree with these two statements, the higher the probability that you will be a good team player. (However, not agreeing strongly does not mean that you are not a good team player.) Below is some information on how the Big Five personality dimensions and their related motive needs can affect your teamwork.

If you have a high *surgency* personality, you probably have a high need for power. Whether you are the team leader or not, you have to be careful not to dominate the group. Seek

(continued)

/ / / Self-Assessment Exercise 10-4 / / / *(continued)*

others' input, and know when to lead and when to follow. Even when you have great ideas, be sensitive to others so they don't feel that you are bullying them, and stay calm as you influence them. Be aware of your motives to make sure you benefit the team. You have the potential to make a positive contribution to the team with your influencing leadership skills. If you have a low need for power, try to be assertive so that others don't take advantage of you, and speak up when you have good ideas.

With a high need for power, you may make quick, reflexive decisions. Your preferred leadership style may tend to be autocratic or consultative. You may need to allow more participation in decision making to be more effective. Participation will also slow down your decision making.

If you are high in *agreeableness* personality traits, with a high need for affiliation, you will tend to be a good team player. However, don't let the fear of hurting relationships get in your way of influencing the team when you have good ideas. Don't be too quick to give in to others. It doesn't help the performance of the team when you have a better idea that is not implemented. You have the potential to be a valuable asset to the team as you contribute your skills of working well with others and making them feel important. If you have a low need for affiliation, be careful to be sensitive to others.

If you are high in *conscientiousness,* with a high need for achievement, you have to watch your natural tendency to be more of an individualist than a team player. It's good to have your own goals, but if the team and organization fail, so do you. Remember that there is usually more than one good way to do anything; your way is not always the best. Don't be too much of a perfectionist because you can cause problems with team members. Being conscientious, you have the potential to help the team do a good job and reach its full potential. If you have a low need for achievement,

push yourself to be a valuable contributor to the group; pull your own weight.

With a high need for achievement, you may know what you want and may make quick, reflexive decisions. You may change leadership styles to help get what you want. Being conscientious, you may tend to follow the steps in the decision-making model more than the other personality types.

Being high on *adjustment,* in control of your emotions, helps the team. If you have a tendency to get emotional, make an effort to stay calm and help the team.

People low in adjustment tend to make quick, reflexive decisions and tend to push to get what they want using an autocratic style. Try not to make decisions when you are highly emotional, and wait until you can think and act rationally.

If you are *open to new experiences,* you will try new things that may help the team improve. When you have ideas that can help the team improve, share them with the team; use your influencing skills. If you are reluctant to change, strive to be more open-minded and to try new things.

People who are open to new experiences are usually more creative than those who are not. If you are reluctant to try new things, make an effort to continually look for ways to improve and be more creative.

Action Plan: Based on your personality, what specific things will you do to improve your team and decision-making skills? Should you follow the steps in the decision-making model more often?

_____

_____

_____

_____

Communication Skills
Refer to CS Question 18.

PUTTING IT ALL TOGETHER

Organizations use groups to meet performance objectives. As the people in a team interact, they develop group dynamics. The group structure is a major determinant of the group's stage of development. The more effective the group structure and dynamics, the higher the stage of development, and the higher the stage of development, the greater the level of performance of the group. The group's performance, in turn, affects its behavior and human relations. See Exhibit 10.9 for an illustration of how the factors discussed in this chapter influence teams.

As we bring this chapter to a close, you should understand the importance of the team performance model and be effective at helping the group with its structure, dynamics, and development level as you work together and during meetings as a manager, informal leader, or follower. You should be able to lead the team based on its level of development using the group situational supervision model; use the decision-making model to improve your skill at solving problems and making decisions; use the creative process model to improve your creativity; and use the team situational supervision model to select the appropriate level of participation when making decisions (this last skill is developed in Skill Building Exercise 10-4).

EXHIBIT 10.9 | Team Performance Model Components

Team Performance (f)*	Team Structure	Team Dynamics	Team Development Stage, Leadership Style, and Decision Making
High ↔ Low	• Leadership • Composition • Problem solving and decision making • Conflict	• Objectives • Size • Norms • Cohesiveness • Status • Roles	1. Orientation; autocratic; leader makes decisions 2. Dissatisfaction; consultative; leader consults team for input on decisions 3. Resolution; participative; leader makes decisions with team 4. Production; laissez-faire; team makes decisions 5. Termination; none; none

*(f) = is a function of.

/ / / R E V I E W / / /

The chapter review is organized to help you master the eight learning outcomes for Chapter 11. First provide your own response to each learning outcome, and then check the summary provided to see how well you understand the material. Next, identify the final statement in each section as either true or false (T/F). Correct each false statement. Answers are given at the end of the chapter.

LO 10-1 Explain the six components of team dynamics and how they affect team performance.

Team dynamics refers to the patterns of interactions that emerge as groups develop. The six components of team dynamics are: (1) *Objectives*–without clear objectives, groups will not be effective. (2) *Group size*–if the group is too large or small, it will not be effective. (3) *Group norms*–the group's shared expectations concerning members' behavior; with norms that do not support high-level performance the group will not be effective. (4) *Group cohesiveness*–the attractiveness and closeness of the group members; generally, noncohesive groups are not as effective as cohesive groups. (5) *Status within the group*–a member's rank within the group; when members are not satisfied with their status they tend to hold back group performance. (6) *Group roles*–shared expectations of how group members will fulfill the requirements of their position; when members do not understand or do not play their roles as expected, the group's performance suffers.

The best size for teams is five members. T F

LO 10-2 Describe the five stages of a team's development.

There are five stages of team development. In stage 1, *orientation* (low development level D1), members have a high commitment but low competence to perform the task. In stage 2, *dissatisfaction* (moderate development level D2), members have a lower commitment but have developed some competence. In stage 3, *resolution* (high development level D3), members' commitment varies and the competence is high. In stage 4, *production* (outstanding development level D4), members have a high commitment and high competence. In stage 5, *termination,* the group no longer exists.

Functional groups and standing committees don't usually go through a termination stage of development. T F

LO 10-3 Explain the four situational supervisory styles to use with a group, based on its stage of development.

In stage 1, *orientation* (low development level D1), the supervisor should use the autocratic style, S-A, which is high task–low maintenance. In stage 2, *dissatisfaction* (moderate development level D2), the supervisor should use the consultative style, S-C, which is high task–high maintenance. In stage 3, *resolution (*high development level D3), the supervisor should use the participative style, S-P, which is low task–high maintenance. In stage 4, *production* (outstanding development level D4), the supervisor should use the laissez-faire style, S-L, which is low task–low maintenance.

At group stage 4, the leader lets the group make its own decisions. T F

LO 10-4 Explain how to plan for and conduct effective meetings.

Areas in which meeting planning is needed include: (1) setting objectives; (2) determining who will participate, and their assignments; (3) developing an agenda; (4) setting a time and place for the meeting; and (5) determining the appropriate leadership style. In conducting the meeting, the leader should go over objectives, cover agenda items, and summarize and review assignments.

The way the manager runs the meeting should be based on the group's level of development. T F

LO 10-5 Identify six problem members and explain how to handle them so they do not have a negative effect on your meetings.

Problem group members include: (1) The silent member—bring this member into the discussion without pushing him or her; the rotation method is helpful. (2) The talker—slow down this member and gently interrupt and call on other members for their input; the rotation method is helpful. (3) The wanderer—keep him or her on the subject and gently remind the group of its objective, asking a question that will get the group back on track. (4) The bored member—keep this member interested and involved by asking for his or her input; assign tasks that will hold his or her attention. (5) The arguer—don't argue with this type of group member and keep the discussion moving; call on other members to diffuse arguments. (6) The social loafer—give him or her specific assignments, use peer pressure and conflict resolution, threaten to go to the boss, and do so if necessary.

Managers should embarrass, intimidate, or argue with members who provoke them during meetings. T F

LO 10-6 List the five steps in the decision-making model.

The steps in the decision-making model are: (1) define the problem; (2) set objectives and criteria; (3) generate alternatives; (4) analyze alternatives and select one; and (5) plan, implement the decision, and control.

The decision-making model should be used when making unimportant recurring decisions. T F

LO 10-7 Describe five techniques for generating creative alternatives.

Five techniques for generating creative alternatives include: (1) *brainstorming,* the process of suggesting as many alternatives as possible, without evaluation, to solve a problem; (2) *synectics,* the process of generating novel alternatives through role-playing and fantasizing; (3) *nominal grouping,* the process of generating and evaluating alternatives using a structured voting method; (4) *consensus mapping,* the process of developing a group consensus to solve a problem; and (5) the *Delphi technique,* which involves using a series of anonymous questionnaires to refine a solution.

The one thing these five techniques have in common is that they all involve a small group of people who get together to come up with creative ideas. T F

LO 10-8 Define the following 16 key terms.

Select one or more methods: (1) fill in the missing key terms for each definition given below from memory; (2) match the key terms from the end of the review with their definitions below; and/or (3) copy the key terms in order from the key terms at the beginning of the chapter.

_____ involves working together to achieve something beyond the capabilities of individuals working alone.

_____ states that a team's performance is based on its structure, dynamics, and stage of development.

_____ refers to the patterns of interactions that emerge as groups develop.

_____ are the group's shared expectations of its members' behavior.

_____ is the attractiveness and closeness group members have for one another and for the group.

_____ is the perceived ranking of one member relative to other members of the group.

_____ are the things group members do and say that directly aid in the accomplishment of the group's objective(s).

_____ are the things group members do and say to develop and sustain group dynamics.

A(n) _____ exists whenever there is a difference between what is actually happening and what the individual or group wants to be happening.

_____ is the process of taking corrective action in order to meet objectives.

_____ is the process of selecting an alternative course of action that will solve a problem.

_____ is the ability to develop unique alternatives to solve problems.

The _____ are (1) preparation, (2) possible solutions, (3) incubation, and (4) evaluation.

_____ is the process of suggesting many alternatives, without evaluation, to solve a problem.

_____ are shared expectations of how group members will fulfill the requirements of their position.

_____ are the things group members do and say to meet their own needs or objectives at the expense of the team.

/ / / KEY TERMS / / /

brainstorming   341
creativity   340
decision making   336
group cohesiveness   323

maintenance roles   324
norms   322
problem   336
problem solving   336

roles   324
self-interest roles   324
stages in the creative
   process 340
status   323

task roles   324
team dynamics   322
team performance
   model   321
teamwork   319

/ / / COMMUNICATION SKILLS / / /

The following critical thinking questions can be used for class discussion and/or as written assignments to develop communication skills. Be sure to give complete explanations for all questions.

1. Many of the TV reality shows have an element of teamwork. However, they often have members of the teams doing negative things to each other to get ahead. Do you believe that these negative examples of poor teamwork influence people's behavior in real-life groups? Can you think of any TV shows that give *positive* examples of good teamwork?

2. It has been said that the team performance model is too simplistic; group performance is much more complex. Do you agree with this statement? How can the model be used?

3. What is the difference between a rule and a norm? Do norms help or hurt groups? Is it ethical to make group members comply with group norms? Can groups stop having norms?

4. It has been said that success breeds cohesiveness, which in turn leads to more success. What does this

mean? How is it supposed to work? Do you agree with the statement?

5. Select a work or sports team to which you belong/have belonged. Which team member (not the manager or coach) had the highest level of status? Identify the factors that contributed to that person's high status.

6. The younger generations have been called the "me generation" because they care only about themselves. Do you agree with this statement? How does putting oneself as number one affect group performance? Which group role is illustrated through the "me generation" statement?

7. Team development stages state that most people coming to a new group are enthusiastic, but that with time they lose some of their morale. What types of things happen in most groups to cause this decline in morale? Be sure to focus on the components of team structure and team dynamics.

8. Many people complain about meetings. Recall a meeting that you have attended. Do you have any complaints about it? State whether or not the meeting had

each of the four parts of a written meeting plan (Exhibit 10.5) and whether the meeting included (1) reviewing objectives, (2) covering agenda items, and (3) summarizing and reviewing assignments. How could the meeting have been improved?

9. Identity the types of problem team members you have encountered. Did the team leader effectively handle these problem members? How could the leader have done a better job of managing these members?

10. What is the role of intuition in decision making? Should managers use more objective or subjective intuition techniques when making decisions?

11. Is following the steps in the decision-making model really all that important? Which steps of the model do you tend to follow? Which steps do you tend to not use? Will you use the model in your personal and/or professional life?

12. Should managers be ethical in their decision making? If so, how should ethics be used in decision making?

13. Are creativity and innovation really that important to all types of businesses?

14. Is it important to evaluate a creative idea before it becomes an innovation?

15. Have you used any of the five techniques for generating creative alternatives? If yes, which ones?

16. Which of the potential advantages and disadvantages of group problem solving and decision making do you think arise most frequently?

17. With virtual team members from all over the world, how does the global economy affect team performance?

18. How do your personality traits affect your teamwork and decision-making style and your interest and ability to participate in group decision making?

CASE / / / Mark Zuckerberg, Founder and CEO of Facebook

In 2010 Time Magazine name Mark Zuckergerg its Person of the Year. He was being recognized for launching what is today seen as a paradigm shift in the way people socialized and share information. Zuckerberg, along with three close friends, created Facebook 2004, a company focused on building products that enable people to connect and share through mobile devices, personal computers, and other surfaces. The company's products include Facebook, Instagram, Messenger, WhatsApp, and Oculus. Mark Zuckerberg was a pioneer in what is today known as the social media space of the tech economy. Some of his competitors in this space include Twitter and Snapchat. Facebook describes itself as an online social media and social networking service company. Its mission is to give people the power to share and make the world more open and connected. People are using Facebook to stay connected with friends and family, to discover what is going on in the world, and to share and express what matters to them.[i]

In terms of his attitude, emotional stability, sense of self, social skills, and empathy, Zuckerberg is different from the typical billionaire CEO. He lives a very different lifestyle from what most people might think of someone with such power and wealth. Facebook is known for its highly effective team dynamics, creativity, and problem solving, ingredients that have contributed to its incredible success. At Facebook, for example, there are no offices. Zuckerberg does not have one of those plush executive suites typical of corporate CEOs. His desk is near the middle of the office, within arm's length of his most senior employees. He is a hands-on leader. Zuckerberg's coworkers are adamant in their declarations of affection for him. He is described as someone with a high emotional intelligence or quotient (EI or EQ). He values personal relationships over the trappings of wealth. He is someone who is truly comfortable with himself and the values he lives by.

Zuckerberg is not motivated by material things; rather, his desire is to give back and improve the lives of others. In September 2010, Zuckerberg announced that he would put up $100 million of his personal Facebook equity to help the Newark school system. Also, as part of a campaign organized by Bill Gates and Warren Buffett, Mark Zuckerberg pledged to give away at least half of his wealth over the course of his lifetime.

Facebook has been able to recruit and hire some of the best minds in the industry. As one analyst notes, everyone at Facebook was a star in his or her previous employment and yet gave it up to be part of Zuckerberg's dream team. In March 2008, Zuckerberg hired Sheryl Sandberg, a veteran of Google and who prior to Google was the chief of staff for former Treasury Secretary Lawrence Summers. She joined Facebook as the company's chief operating officer (COO). Former Google employees soon followed. This did not stop with Google; other companies such as eBay, Genentech, and Mozilla also saw an exodus of their star employees to Facebook. Chris Cox, Facebook's Chief Product Officer, was completing a master's in artificial intelligence at Stanford when Zuckerberg personally convinced him to join Facebook. "You don't get a lot of shy, retiring types at Facebook," said one writer. These are intelligent, experienced, productive, and highly sought after talents, "power nerds" to say the least. They are a highly effective team whose creativity and performance is matched only by that of their leader, Mark Zuckerberg.

Facebook's team dynamics and creativity are captured by its open, relaxed informal corporate culture. A fitting description of Facebook's team spirit is what one author calls a "militant engineering culture," where employees share an all-consuming work identity similar to the biblical version of an "apostolic sense of devotion to a great cause." Facebook employees are described as true believers who will not stop until every man, woman, and child on earth is staring into a blue-bannered window with a Facebook logo.[ii] Debate is the hallmark of staff meetings at Facebook and employees describe what an intense listener Zuckerberg is during these dynamic debates. It is said that he is often one of the last persons to leave the office. He leads his team by example.

Leadership is also about problem solving and decision-making, areas in which Zuckerberg has also displayed a high level of competency. In 2006, Zuckerberg had to make a key decision. He turned down an offer of $1 billion from Yahoo to buy the company. For a 22-year-old to walk away from such an offer was truly remarkable and indicative of how much he believed in himself and his vision for Facebook. In 2011, Zuckerberg had a major threat to deal with. Google launched its version of Facebook called Google Plus. Google Plus was acknowledgment that Google was finally taking note of Facebook and confronting the company head-on. Zuckerberg saw it as an existential threat. It was during this time that the Facebook faithful heard an oratorical command performance from Zuckerberg that he was not known for. He gathered the troops and issued his now famous phrase, "*Carthago delenda est,*" Latin for "Carthage must be destroyed!" an oratorical phrase that was in popular use in ancient Rome during the latter years of the Punic Wars against Carthage. Cato the Elder used this phrase in every speech to the Roman Senate. During the speech, it is reported that Zuckerberg's tone went from paternal lecture to martial exhortation, the drama mounting with every mention of the threat Google represented. The speech ended to a roar of cheering and applause. Everyone walked out of the room ready to do whatever it took to defeat Google Plus. It was a rousing performance from someone whom others had described as having a reclusive and shy personality.[iii]

Facebook is used by more than a billion people around the world to communicate and exchange social information. Advertisers have learned to market products on Facebook by using the incredibly large database Facebook generates to help companies focus on their target markets.[iv] These advertising revenues are how Facebook monetizes its platform. Its total market capitalization is approaching half a trillion dollars and its stock is trading at an all-time high.[v]

Go to the Internet: To learn more about Mark Zuckerberg and Facebook, visit its Web site at www.facebook.com.

Support your answers to the following questions with specific information from the case and text or with information you get from the web or another source.

1. There are four team structure components that along with team dynamics and development, affect team performance. Which of the four components does the case feature with examples?

2. How would you describe Mark Zuckerberg as a team leader?

3. Describe the team dynamics at Facebook.

4. Based on the facts of the case, at which stage would you categorize teamwork at Facebook? Base your answer on the team development stages in the text.

5. Would you describe Zuckerberg as having a reflexive, reflective, or consistent decision-making style?

Cumulative Questions

6. How do Mark Zuckerberg's values, self-concept, and ethics (Chapter 3) affect his life and leadership of Facebook?

7. According to the two-dimensional leadership style studies (Chapter 6), a leader's behavior toward followers can be classified as either initiating structure or consideration or both or neither (Ohio State University Studies). The

Leadership Grid identifies concern for production or people or both or neither with five leadership styles. Which dimension(s) would you associate with Mark Zuckerberg?

Case Exercise and Role-Play

Preparation: Have students read up on the meaning of "going public" for a private company like Facebook. The question before the class is, Should Facebook go public or stay private? The chapter discusses different techniques to use in group decision making—brainstorming, synectics, nominal grouping, consensus mapping, and the Delphi technique.

In-Class Groups: Divide the class into groups of four or five students. Each group selects one of the techniques and a group leader or facilitator. Each team employs the technique it has been assigned to address the question: Should Facebook go public or stay a private company? This is the rehearsal.

Role-Play: Each team takes the stage and plays out its decision-making process using the assigned technique. Which team made the best use of its technique? The instructor or the class as a whole can vote on the outcome.

OBJECTIVE CASE   / / /   Group Performance

Through reorganization, Christen has been assigned three additional departments that produce the same product. Aiden, Sasha, and Rashid are the supervisors of these departments. Christen would like to increase productivity, so she set up a group to analyze the present situation and recommend ways to increase productivity. The group consists of Christen, the three supervisors, an industrial engineer, and an expert on group dynamics from personnel. The group analyzed the present situation in each department as follows:

Group 1: Aiden's department produces at or above standard on a regular basis. It averages between 102 and 104 percent of standard on a monthly basis (standard is 100 percent). Members work well together; they often go to lunch together. Members' productivity levels are all about the same.

Group 2: Sasha's department produces between 95 and 105 percent on a monthly basis. However, it usually produces 100 percent. The members do not seem to interact too often. Part of the reason for the standard production level is two employees who consistently produce at 115 percent of standard. Sasha will be retiring in six months, and they both want to fill her position. There are three members who consistently produce at 80 to 90 percent of standard.

Group 3: Rashid's department achieves between 90 and 92 percent of standard on a monthly basis. Megan is a strong informal leader who oversees the productivity level. She lets members know if they produce too much or too little. John is the only member in the department who reaches production standards. The rest of the department members do not talk to John. At times they intentionally keep his level of production down. All other department members produce at about 90 percent of standard.

Answer the following questions. Then in the space between the questions, state why you selected that answer.

_____ 1. Christen, Aiden, Sasha, and Rashid make up a(n) _____ group.

       a. functional   *b.* task   *c.* informal

_____ 2. To increase productivity, Christen set up a(n) _____ group.

       a. functional   *b.* ad hoc committee   *c.* standing committee

_____ 3. Which group has high agreement and commitment to its own objectives?

       a. 1   *d.* 1 and 2   *g.* 1, 2, and 3

       b. 2   *e.* 1 and 3

       c. 3   *f.* 2 and 3

_____ 4. Which group has objectives (positive norms) in agreement with those of management?

　　　　　 a. 1　　　　　　　　　*d.* 1 and 2　　　　　*g.* 1, 2, and 3

　　　　　 b. 2　　　　　　　　　*e.* 1 and 3

　　　　　 c. 3　　　　　　　　　*f.* 2 and 3

_____ 5. Which group is cohesive?

　　　　　 a. 1　　　　　　　　　*d.* 1 and 2　　　　　*g.* 1, 2, and 3

　　　　　 b. 2　　　　　　　　　*e.* 1 and 3

　　　　　 c. 3　　　　　　　　　*f.* 2 and 3

_____ 6. Which group most clearly plays self-interest roles?

　　　　　 a. 1　　　　　　　　　*b.* 2　　　　　　　　*c.* 3

_____ 7. Megan primarily plays a _____ role for her group.

　　　　　 a. task　　　　　　　　*b.* maintenance　　　　*c.* self-interest

_____ 8. Group 1 appears to be in stage _____ of group development.

　　　　　 a. 1　　　　　　　　　*c.* 3　　　　　　　　*e.* 5

　　　　　 b. 2　　　　　　　　　*d.* 4

_____ 9. Group 2 appears to be in stage _____ of group development.

　　　　　 a. 1　　　　　　　　　*c.* 3　　　　　　　　*e.* 5

　　　　　 b. 2　　　　　　　　　*d.* 4

_____ 10. Group 3 appears to be in stage _____ of group development.

　　　　　 a. 1　　　　　　　　　*c.* 3　　　　　　　　*e.* 5

　　　　　 b. 2　　　　　　　　　*d.* 4

_____ 11. What would you recommend doing to increase productivity in each of the three groups?

/ / /　SKILL-BUILDING EXERCISE 10-1　/ / /

Team Dynamics

Experience: This exercise is designed for class groups that have worked together for some time. (Five or more hours are recommended.) You will discuss your group's structure and develop plans to improve it.

AACSB Competencies: Interpersonal relations and teamwork; in addition, communication, reflective thinking, analytic skills, and application of knowledge are developed.

Objectives: To gain a better understanding of the group structure components and how they affect group performance, and to improve group structure.

Preparation: Answer the following questions as they apply to your class group.

  1. Based on attendance, preparation, and class involvement, identify each group member's level of commitment to the group, including yourself. (Write each member's name on the appropriate line.)

　　 High commitment _____

Medium commitment _____

Low commitment _____

2. Our group size is:

_____ too large _____ too small _____ OK

Explain why.

3. List at least five norms your group has developed. Identify each as positive or negative.

1.

2.

3.

4.

5.

What positive norms could the group develop to help it function?

4. Based on the group's commitment, size, homogeneity, equality of participation, intragroup competition, and success, identify its cohesiveness level as:

_____ high _____ medium _____ low

How does cohesiveness affect performance? What can be done to increase cohesiveness?

5. Identify each group member's status, including your own. (Write each group member's name on the appropriate line.)

High _____

Medium _____

Low _____

Does the group have status congruence? How can the group improve it?

6. Identify the roles members play. Write the name of each group member who plays each role on the appropriate line. You will most likely use each name several times and have more than one name on each role line, but rank them by dominance.

Task roles

Objective clarifier _____

Planner _____

Organizer _____

Leader _____

Controller _____

Maintenance roles

Former _____

Consensus seeker _____

Harmonizer _____

Gatekeeper _____

Encourager _____

Compromiser _____

Self-interest roles (if appropriate)

Aggressor _____

Blocker _____

Recognition seeker _____

Withdrawer _____

Which roles should be played more, and which less, to increase effectiveness? Who should and should not play them?

7. Our group is in stage _____ of group development.

   1. Orientation/Forming

   2. Dissatisfaction/Storming

   3. Resolution/Norming

   4. Production/Performing

   What can be done to increase the group's level of development?

8. Identify problem people, if any, by placing their names on the appropriate line(s).

   Silent member _____

   Talker _____

   Wanderer _____

   Bored member _____

   Arguer _____

   Social loafer _____

   What should be done to help eliminate the problems caused by these people? Specifically, who should do what?

9. Review the answers to questions 1 through 8. In order of priority, what will the group do to improve its group structure? Specify what each group member will do to help the group's structure.

In Class

Procedure 1 (10-20 minutes)

Groups get together to discuss their answers to the nine preparation questions. Be sure to fully explain and discuss your answers. Try to come up with some specific ideas on how to improve your group's process and dynamics.

Conclusion: The instructor leads a class discussion and/or makes concluding remarks.

Application (2-4 minutes):   What did I learn from this experience? How will I use this knowledge in the future?

Sharing: Volunteers give their answers to the application section.

/ / / SKILL-BUILDING EXERCISE 10-2 / / /

Team Situational Supervision

Experience: Individual or in small groups, in class or online. You will discuss your selected supervisory styles for the 12 preparation situations, and you will be given feedback on your accuracy in selecting the appropriate style to meet the situation.

AACSB Competencies: Interpersonal relations and teamwork; in addition, communication, reflective thinking, analytic skills, and application of knowledge are developed.

Objectives: To help you understand the stages of group development, and to use the appropriate situational supervision style.

Preparation: You should have completed Self-Assessment Exercise 10-2.

Procedure 1 (3–10 minutes)

The instructor reviews the group situational supervision Model 10.1 and explains how to apply it to situation 1 in Self-Assessment Exercise 10-2. The instructor states the group's developmental stage, the supervisory style of each of the four alternative actions, and the scoring for each alternative. Follow the three steps below as you try to select the most appropriate alternative action for each of the 12 situations in Self-Assessment Exercise 10-2.

Step 1. For each situation, determine the team's level of development. Place the number 1, 2, 3, or 4 on the D _____ lines.

Step 2. Identify the supervisory style of all four alternatives *a* through *d.* Place the letters A, C, P, or L on the S _____ lines.

Step 3. Select the appropriate supervisory style for the team's level of development. Circle its letter, either *a, b, c,* or *d.*

Procedure 2

Option A (3–5 minutes):   The instructor gives the class the recommended answers to situations 2 through 12, as in procedure 1, without any explanation.

Option B (10–30 minutes):   Break into teams of two or three, and go over the situations chosen by the instructor. The instructor will go over the recommended answers.

Conclusion: The instructor leads a class discussion and/or makes concluding remarks.

Application (2–4 minutes):   What did I learn from this experience? How will I use this knowledge in the future?

Sharing: Volunteers give their answers to the application section.

///   SKILL-BUILDING EXERCISE 10-3   ///

Individual versus Group Decision Making

Experience: In-Class Group Exercise. During class, you will work in a group that will make the same decisions, followed by an analysis of the results.

AACSB Competencies: Teamwork and leadership; in addition, communication and analytic skills are developed.

Objective: To compare individual and group decision making to better understand when and when not to use a group to make decisions.

Preparation: You should have completed Application Situations 10-1 and 19-2, or the first 10 questions in the Objective Case, whichever your instructor assigned.

Procedure 1 (1–2 minutes)

Place your individual answers to Application Situations 10-1 and 10-2 in the "Individual Answer" column below.

Application Situation Question	Individual Answer (A-E)	Group Answer (A-E)	Recommended Answer (A-E)	Score Individual versus Group
1.				
2.				

(continued)

3.		
4.		
5.		
6.		
7.		
8.		
9.		
10.		
Total score		

Procedure 2 (18–22 minutes)

Break into teams of five; make groups of four or six as necessary. As a group, come to an agreement on the answers to Application Situations 10-1 and 10-2. Place the group answers in the "Group Answer" column above. Try to use consensus rather than the voting technique.

Procedure 3 (4–6 minutes)

Scoring: The instructor will give you the recommended answers to Application Situations 10-1 and 10-2; place the answers in column 4. In column 2, place the number of individual answers you got correct (1–10) on the total score line. In column 3, place the number the group answered correctly (1–10) on the total score line. In column 5, place the number representing the gain/loss of individual versus group answers on the total score line. (For example, if you scored 8 correct and the group scored 6, you beat the group by 2—so put +2 on the total score line. If you scored 5 correct and the group scored 8, the group beat you by 3—so put –3 on the total score line. If you tied, put 0.)

Averaging: Calculate the average individual score by adding all the individual scores and dividing by the number of group members. Average.

Gain or Loss: Find the difference between the average score and the group score. If the group's score is higher than the average individual score, you have a gain of _____ points; if the group's score is lower, you have a loss of _____ points.

Determine the highest individual score _____.

Determine the number of individuals who scored higher than the group's score _____.

Integration (4–8 minutes):   As a group, discuss which advantages and/or disadvantages (Exhibit 10.8) your group had while making the decisions in this exercise.

Advantages:

Disadvantages:

Improvements: Overall, were the advantages of using a group greater than the disadvantages of using a group? If your group continues to work together, how could it improve its problem-solving and decision-making abilities? Write out the answer below.

Conclusion: The instructor leads a class discussion and/or makes concluding remarks.

Application (2–4 minutes):   What did I learn from this experience? How will I use this knowledge in the future?

Sharing: Volunteers give their answers to the application section.

/ / / SKILL-BUILDING EXERCISE 10-4 / / /

Using the Situational Decision-Making Model

Experience: Individual or small groups. You will select the problem-solving and decision-making style in the 10 preparation situations.

In this exercise, you will learn how to use the situational decision-making model. Chapter 6 discussed the situational supervision model. Chapter 4 provided a situational communication model to use when communicating. Now you will learn a similar model to use when deciding which supervisory style to use when solving problems and making decisions. Selecting the appropriate situational supervisory style includes two steps: (1) diagnose the situation and (2) select the appropriate style.

AACSB Competencies: Analytic skills and application of knowledge.

Objective: To develop your situational supervisory problem-solving and decision-making skills.

Preparation: Read how to use the following model and complete the 10 situations. Or the instructor may elect to review the model below before you complete the 10 situations.

Step 1: Diagnose the Situation The first step is to diagnose the situational variables, which include time, information, acceptance, and employee capability level. See Model 10.4 for a list of variables. The top half of Model 10.4 summarizes step 1.

MODEL 10.4 | Situational Decision Making

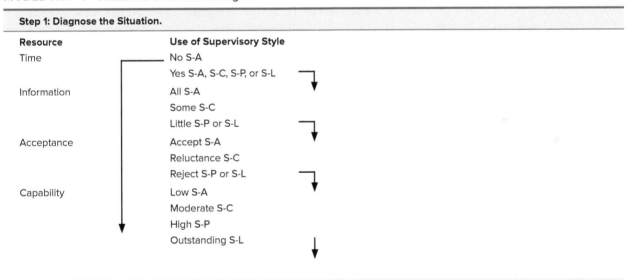

Step 1: Diagnose the Situation.

Resource	Use of Supervisory Style
Time	No S-A
	Yes S-A, S-C, S-P, or S-L
Information	All S-A
	Some S-C
	Little S-P or S-L
Acceptance	Accept S-A
	Reluctance S-C
	Reject S-P or S-L
Capability	Low S-A
	Moderate S-C
	High S-P
	Outstanding S-L

Step 2: Select the Appropriate Style for the Situation.

Autocratic (S-A)

The supervisor makes the decision alone and announces it after the fact. An explanation of the rationale for the decision may be given.

Consultative (S-C)

The supervisor consults individuals or the group for information and then makes the decision. Before implementing the decision, the supervisor explains the rationale for the decision and sells the benefits to the employees. The supervisor may invite questions and have a discussion.

Participative (S-P)

The supervisor may present a tentative decision to the group and ask for its input. The supervisor may change the decision if the input warrants a change. Or the supervisor may present the problem to the group for suggestions. Based on employee participation, the supervisor makes the decision and explains its rationale.

Laissez-Faire (S-L)

The supervisor presents the situation to the group and describes limitations to the decision. The group makes the decision. The supervisor may be a group member.

Time   You must determine if there is enough time to include the group in decision making. If there is not enough time, use the autocratic style and ignore the other three variables–they are irrelevant if there is no time. If time permits, you consider the other three variables and select the style without considering time. Time, however, is a relative term. In one situation, a few minutes may be considered a short time period, while in another, a month or more may be a short period of time.

Information   The more information you have to make the decision, the less need there is to use participation, and vice versa. If you have all the necessary information to make a decision, there is no need to use participation. If you have little information, you need to get it through participation.

Acceptance   If you make the decision alone, will the group implement it willingly? The more the team will like the decision, the less need there is to use participation, and vice versa.

Employee Capability   The leader must decide if the group has the ability and willingness to be involved in problem solving and decision making. The more capable the employees, the higher the level of participation, and vice versa. Realize that a group's capability level can change from situation to situation.

Step 2: Select the Appropriate Supervisory Style for the Situation   After considering the four variables, you select the appropriate style for the situation. In some situations, all variables suggest the same possible style, while other cases indicate conflicting styles. For example, you may have time to use any style and may have all the information necessary (autocratic); employees may be reluctant (consultative or participative); and the capability may be moderate (consultative). In situations where conflicting styles are indicated for different variables, you must determine which variable should be given more weight. In the above example, assume it was determined that acceptance was critical for successful implementation of the decision. Acceptance takes precedence over information. Realizing that employees have a moderate capability, the consultative style would be appropriate. See the bottom half of Model 10.4 for an explanation of how the decision is made using each of the four situational supervisory styles.

Applying the Situational Decision-Making Model

We will apply the model to the following situation as an example:

Ben, a supervisor, can give one of his employees a merit pay raise. He has a week to make the decision. Ben knows how well each employee performed over the past year. The employees really have no option but to accept getting or not getting the pay raise, but they can complain to upper management about the selection. The employees' capability levels vary, but as a group, they have a high capability level under normal circumstances.

Step 1: Diagnose the Situation.

_____ time _____ information _____ acceptance _____ capability

Ben, the supervisor, has plenty of time to use any level of participation. He has all the information needed to make the decision (autocratic). Employees have no choice but to accept the decision (autocratic). And the group's level of capability is normally high (participative).

Step 2: Select the Appropriate Style for the Situation. There are conflicting styles to choose from (autocratic and participative):

_____ yes time _____ S-A information _____ S-A acceptance _____ S-P capability

The variable that should be given precedence is information. The employees are normally capable, but in a situation like this, they may not be capable of putting the department's goals ahead of their own. In other words, even if employees know which employee deserves the raise, they may each fight for it anyway. Such a conflict could cause future problems. Some of the possible ways to make the decision are as follows:

- *Autocratic (S-A).* The supervisor would select the person for the raise without discussing it with any employees. Ben would simply announce the decision and explain the rationale for the selection, after submitting it to the payroll department.

- *Consultative (S-C).* The supervisor would consult the employees as to who should get the raise. Ben would then decide who would get the raise. He would announce the decision and explain the rationale for it. The supervisor may invite questions and discussion.

- *Participative (S-P).* The supervisor could tentatively select an employee to get the raise, but be open to change if an employee or group convinces him that someone else should get the raise. Or Ben could explain the situation to the group and lead a discussion of who should get the raise. After considering their input, Ben would make the decision and explain the rationale for it.

- *Laissez-faire (S-L).* The supervisor would explain the situation and allow the group to decide who gets the raise. Ben may be a group member. Notice that this is the only style that allows the group to make the decision.

Selection   The autocratic style is appropriate for this situation because Ben has all the information needed, acceptance is not an issue, and capability is questionable.

Below are 10 situations calling for a decision. Select the appropriate problem-solving and decision-making style. Be sure to use Model 10.4 above, p. 357, when determining the style to use. On the time, information, acceptance, and capability lines, place S-A, S-C, S-P, or S-L, as indicated by the situation. Based on your diagnoses, select the one style you would use. Note that style on the line preceding the situation.

S-A Autocratic   S-C Consultative   S-P Participative   S-L Laissez-faire

_____   1. You have developed a new work procedure that will increase productivity. Your boss likes the idea and wants you to try it within a few weeks. You view your employees as fairly capable and believe that they will be receptive to the change.

  _____ time _____ information _____ acceptance _____ capability

_____   2. The industry of your product has new competition. Your organization's revenues have been dropping. You have been told to lay off 3 of your 10 employees in two weeks. You have been the supervisor for over one year. Normally, your employees are very capable.

  _____ time _____ information _____ acceptance _____ capability

_____   3. Your department has been facing a problem for several months. Many solutions have been tried, but all have failed. You have finally thought of a solution, but you are not sure of the possible consequences of the change required or of acceptance by the highly capable employees.

  _____ time _____ information _____ acceptance _____ capability

_____   4. Flextime has become popular in your organization. Some departments let each employee start and end work when he or she chooses. However, because of the cooperative effort of your employees, they must all work the same eight hours. You are not sure of the level of interest in changing the hours. Your employees are a very capable group and like to make decisions.

  _____ time _____ information _____ acceptance _____ capability

_____   5. The technology in your industry is changing so fast that the members of your organization cannot keep up. Top management hired a consultant who has made recommendations. You have two weeks to decide what to do. Your employees are normally capable, and they enjoy participating in the decision-making process.

  _____ time _____ information _____ acceptance _____ capability

_____   6. A change has been handed down from top management. How you implement it is your decision. The change takes effect in one month. It will personally affect everyone in your department. Their acceptance is critical to the success of the change. Your employees are usually not too interested in being involved in making decisions.

  _____ time _____ information _____ acceptance _____ capability

_____   7. Your boss called you on the telephone to tell you that someone has requested an order for your department's product with a very short delivery date. She asked you to call her back in 15 minutes with the decision about taking the order. Looking over the work schedule, you realize that it will be very difficult to deliver the order on time. Your employees will have to push hard to make it. They are cooperative, capable, and enjoy being involved in decision making.

  _____ time _____ information _____ acceptance _____ capability

_____   8. Top management has decided to make a change that will affect all your employees. You know the employees will be upset because it will cause them hardship. One or two may even quit. The change goes into effect in 30 days. Your employees are very capable.

_____ time _____ information _____ acceptance _____ capability

_____   9. You believe that productivity in your department could be increased. You have thought of some ways that may work, but you are not sure of them. Your employees are very experienced; almost all of them have been in the department longer than you have.

_____ time _____ information _____ acceptance _____ capability

_____   10. A customer has offered you a contract for your product with a quick delivery date. The offer is open for two days. Meeting the contract deadline would require employees to work nights and weekends for six weeks. You cannot require them to work overtime. Filling this profitable contract could help get you the raise you want and feel you deserve. However, if you take the contract and don't deliver on time, it will hurt your chances of getting a big raise. Your employees are very capable.

_____ time _____ information _____ acceptance _____ capability

In-Class Exercise

Procedure 1 (5–12 minutes)

The instructor reviews Model 10.4 and explains how to use it for selecting the appropriate supervisory style for situation 1 of the exercise preparation.

Procedure 2 (12–20 minutes)

Break into teams of two or three. Apply the model to situations 2 through 5 as a team. You may change your original answers. It may be helpful to tear the model out of the book so you don't have to keep flipping pages. The instructor goes over the recommended answers and scoring for situations 2 through 5. Do not continue on to situation 6 until after the instructor goes over the answers to situations 2 through 5.

In the same teams, select problem-solving and decision-making styles for situations 6 through 10. The instructor will go over the recommended answers and scoring.

Conclusion: The instructor may lead a class discussion and/or make concluding remarks.

Application (2–4 minutes):   What did I learn from this experience? How will I use this knowledge in the future?

Sharing: Volunteers give their answers to the application section.

/ / / SKILL-BUILDING EXERCISE 10-5 / / /

Developing New Habits

Experience: Individual may share habits in groups or entire class, in class or online.

AACSB Competencies: Analytic and application of knowledge.

Objective: To develop and share new habits.

Preparation: Select one or more topics from this chapter that will help you improve your human relations. Develop a new habit following the guideline from Chapter 1, section Habits and Skill-Building Exercise 1–4, on how to develop your cure, routine, and reward-change.

Procedure (5–30 minutes)

Follow the procedures from Skill Builder 1–4.

/ / ANSWERS TO TRUE/FALSE QUESTIONS / /

1. F. There is no one best size for all teams. Size is based on the team's purpose.
2. T.
3. T.
4. T.
5. F. Managers should not embarrass, intimidate, or argue with any team members.
6. F. The decision-making model should be used when making *important nonrecurring* decisions.
7. F. None of these techniques require that a small group of people get together; in fact, they can be used online. With the Delphi technique, members never get together and often don't even know who else is in the group.

/ / / NOTES / / /

1. N. Li, B.L. Kirkman, and C.O.L.H. Porter, "Toward a Model of Work Team Altruism," *Academy of Management Review* 39(4) (2014): 541–565.
2. R.D. Costigan and K.E. Brink, "Another Perspective on MBA Program Alignment: An Investigation of Learning Goals," *Academy of Management Learning & Education* 14(2) (2015): 260–276.
3. R.C. Liden, S.J. Wayne, C. Liao, J.D. Meuser, "Servant Leadership and Serving Culture: Influence on Individual and Unit Performance," *Academy of Management Journal* 57(5) (2014): 1434–1452.
4. T.A. De Vries, F. Walter, G.S. Van Der Vegt, and P.J.M.D. Essens, "Antecedents of Individuals' Interteam Coordination; Broad Functional Experiences as a Mixed Blessing," *Academy of Management Journal* 57(5) (2014): 1334–1359.
5. S.H. Harrison and E.D. Rouse, "Let's Dance! Elastic Coordination in Creative Group Work: A Qualitative Study of Modern Dancers," *Academy of Management Journal* 57(5) (2014): 1256–1283.
6. S.H. Harrison and E.D. Rouse, "An Inductive Study of Feedback Interactions Over the Course of Creative Projects," *Academy of Management Journal* 58(2) (2015): 375–404.
7. M.R. Haas, P. Criscuolo, and G. George, "Which Problems to Solve? Online Knowledge Sharing and Attention Allocation in Organizations," *Academy of Management Journal* 58(3) (2015): 680-711.
8. A. Lim, "Netting the Evidence: A Review of On-Line Evidence-Based Management Resources," *Academy of Management Learning & Education* 13(3) (2014): 495–503.
9. G. Colvin, "Humans Are Underrated," *Fortune* (August 1, 2015): 100–113.
10. K.J. Lovelace, F. Egger, LR. Dyck, "I Do and I Understand: Assessing the Utility of Web-Based Management Simulations," *Academy of Management Learning & Education* 15(1) (2016): 100–121.
11. L.M. Maruping, V. Venkatesh, S.M.B. Thatcher, and P.C. Patel, "Folding Under Pressure of Rising to the Occasion?" *Academy of Management Journal* 58(5) (2015): 1313–1333.
12. R.G. Lord, J.E. Dinh, E.L. Hoffman, "A Quantum Approach to Time and Organizational Change," *Academy of Management Review* 40(2) (2015): 263–290.
13. T.A. De Vries, F. Walter, G.S. Van Der Vegt, and P.J.M.D. Essens, "Antecedents of Individuals' Interteam Coordination; Broad Functional Experiences as a Mixed Blessing," *Academy of Management Journal* 57(5) (2014): 1334–1359.
14. K. Lanaj and J.R. Hollenbeck, "Leadership Over-Emergence in Self-Managing Teams: The Role of Gender and Countervailing Biases," *Academy of Management Journal* 58(5) (2015): 1476–1494.
15. B.M. Firth, J.R. Hollenbeck, J.E. Miles, D.R. Ilgen, and C.M. Barnes, "Same Page, Different Books: Extending Representational Gaps Theory to Enhance Performance in Multiteam Systems," *Academy of Management Journal* 58(3) (2015): 813–835.
16. L.R. Weingart, K.J. Behfar, C. Bendersky, G. Todorova, and K.A. Hehn, "The Directness and Oppositional Intensity of Conflict Expression," *Academy of Management Review* 40(2) (2015): 235–262.

17. B.R. Spisak, M.J. O'Brien, N. Nicholson, M. Van Vugt, "Niche Construction and the Evolution of Leadership," *Academy of Management Review* 40(2) (2015): 291–306.

18. C.Q. Trank, "Reading Evidence-Based Management: The Possibilities of Interpretation," *Academy of Management Learning & Education* 13(3) (2014): 381–395.

19. L.R. Weingart, K.J. Behfar, C. Bendersky, G. Todorova, and K.A. Hehn, "The Directness and Oppositional Intensity of Conflict Expression," *Academy of Management Review* 40(2) (2015): 235–262.

20. R.G. Lord, J.E. Dinh, E.L. Hoffman, "A Quantum Approach to Time and Organizational Change," *Academy of Management Review* 40(2) (2015): 263–290.

21. N. Li, B.L. Kirkman, and C.O.L.H. Porter, "Toward a Model of Work Team Altruism," *Academy of Management Review* 39(4) (2014): 541–565.

22. B.M. Firth, J.R. Hollenbeck, J.E. Miles, D.R. Ilgen, and C.M. Barnes, "Same Page, Different Books: Extending Representational Gaps Theory to Enhance Performance in Multiteam Systems," *Academy of Management Journal* 58(3) (2015): 813–835.

23. R. Karlgaard, "Think Really Small," *Forbes* (April 13, 2015): 32.

24. Staff, "Leader Board," *Forbes* (November 23, 2015): 2015): 32.

25. Staff, "Leader Board," *Forbes* (November 23, 2015): 2015): 32.

26. R.C. Liden, S.J. Wayne, C. Liao, J.D. Meuser, "Servant Leadership and Serving Culture: Influence on Individual and Unit Performance," *Academy of Management Journal* 57(5) (2014): 1434–1452.

27. J.J. Ladge, B.K. Humberd, M.B. Watkins, and B. Harrington, "Updating the Organizational Man: An Examination of Involved Fathering in the Workplace," *Academy of Management Perspectives* 29(1) (2015): 152–171.

28. G. Di Stenfano, A.A. King, and G. Verona, "Sanctioning in the Wild: Rational Calculus and Retributive Instincts in Gourmet Cuisine," *Academy of Management Journal* 58(3) (2015): 906–931.

29. A. Bitektine and P. Haack, "The Macro and the Micro of Legitimacy: Toward a Multilevel Theory of the Legitimacy Process," *Academy of Management Review* 40(1) (2015): 49–75.

30. G. Di Stenfano, A.A. King, and G. Verona, "Sanctioning in the Wild: Rational Calculus and Retributive Instincts in Gourmet Cuisine," *Academy of Management Journal* 58(3) (2015): 906–931.

31. R. Durand and P.A. Kremp, "Classical Deviation: Organizational and Individual Status as Antecedents of Conformity," *Academy of Management Journal* 59(1) (2016): 65–89.

32. S.J. Creary, B.B. Caza, and L.M. Roberts, "Out of the Box? How Managing a Subordinate's Multiple Identities Affects the Quality of a Manager-Subordinate Relationship," *Academy of Management Review* 40(4) (2015): 538–562.

33. R. Durand and P.A. Kremp, "Classical Deviation: Organizational and Individual Status as Antecedents of Conformity," *Academy of Management Journal* 59(1) (2016): 65–89.

34. J.D. Westphal and G. Shani, "Psyched-Up to Suck-Up: Self-Regulated Cognition, Interpersonal Influence, and Recommendations for Board Appointments in the Corporate Elite," *Academy of Management Journal* 59, no. 2 (2016): 479–509.

35. R. Durand and P.A. Kremp, "Classical Deviation: Organizational and Individual Status as Antecedents of Conformity," *Academy of Management Journal* 59(1) (2016): 65–89.

36. T.A. De Vries, F. Walter, G.S. Van Der Vegt, and P.J.M.D. Essens, "Antecedents of Individuals' Interteam Coordination; Broad Functional Experiences as a Mixed Blessing," *Academy of Management Journal* 57(5) (2014): 1334–1359.

37. T.A. De Vries, F. Walter, G.S. Van Der Vegt, and P.J.M.D. Essens, "Antecedents of Individuals' Interteam Coordination; Broad Functional Experiences as a Mixed Blessing," *Academy of Management Journal* 57(5) (2014): 1334–1359.

38. T.A. De Vries, F. Walter, G.S. Van Der Vegt, and P.J.M.D. Essens, "Antecedents of Individuals' Interteam Coordination; Broad Functional Experiences as a Mixed Blessing," *Academy of Management Journal* 57(5) (2014): 1334–1359.

39. B.M. Galvin, D. Lange, and B.E. Ashforth, "Narcissistic Organizational Identification: Seeing Oneself as Central to the Organization's Identity," *Academy of Management Review* 40(2) (2015): 163–181.

40. E. Grialva and P.D. Harms, "Narcissism: An Integrative Synthesis and Dominance Complementary Model," *Academy of Management Perspectives* 28(2) (2014): 106–127.

41. N. Li, B.L. Kirkman, and C.O.L.H. Porter, "Toward a Model of Work Team Altruism," Academy of Management Review 39(4) (2014): 541–565.

42. B.R. Spisak, M.J. O'Brien, N. Nicholson, M. Van Vugt, "Niche Construction and the Evolution of Leadership," *Academy of Management Review* 40(2) (2015): 291–306.

43. M. Javidan, A. Bullough, and R. Dibble, "Mind the Gap: Gender Differences in Global Leadership Self-Efficacies," *Academy of Management Perspectives* 30(1) (2016): 59–73.

44. L.M. Maruping, V. Venkatesh, S.M.B. Thatcher, and P.C. Patel, "Folding Under Pressure of Rising to the Occasion?" *Academy of Management Journal* 58(5) (2015): 1313–1333.

45. G. O'Brien, "Questions and Answers," *Entrepreneur* (September 2015): 36.

46. Editors, "From the Guest Editors: Change the World: Teach Evidence-Based Practice!" *Academy of Management Learning & Education* 13(3) (2014): 305–321.

47. N. Li, B.L. Kirkman, and C.O.L.H. Porter, "Toward a Model of Work Team Altruism," *Academy of Management Review* 39(4) (2014): 541–565.

48. Yukl, "Effective Leadership Behavior."

49. Hogg et al., "Intergroup Leadership in Organizations."

50. N.R. Quigley, "A Longitudinal, Multilevel Study of Leadership Efficacy Development in MBA Teams," *Academy of Management Learning & Education* 12(4) (2013): 579–602.

51. S. Bing, "Productivity Now!" *Fortune* (January 1, 2016): 100.

52. R.S. Schatz, "How to Make Off-Sites Pay Off," *INC.* (December 2014 / January 2015): 82.

53. R.S. Schatz, "How to Make Off-Sites Pay Off," *INC.* (December 2014 / January 2015): 82.

54. S. Shellengarger, "Don't Be Late or You'll Be a Schedule-Wrecker," *The Wall Street Journal* (July 8, 2015): D1, D3.

55. R.S. Schatz, "How to Make Off-Sites Pay Off," *INC.* (December 2014 / January 2015): 82.

56. D. Urbig, S. Terjesen, V. Procher, K. Muehleld, and A. Van Witteloostuijn, "Come on and Take a Free Ride: Contributing to Public Goods in Native and Foreign Language Settings," *Academy of Management Learning & Education* 15(2) (2016): 268–286.

57. M.R. Haas, P. Criscuolo, and G. George, "Which Problems to Solve? Online Knowledge Sharing and Attention Allocation in Organizations," Academy of Management Journal 58(3) (2015): 680–711.

58. E.N. Gamble and R.B. Jelley, "The Case for Competition: Learning About Evidence-Based Management Through Case Competition," *Academy of Management Learning & Education* 13(3) (2014): 433–445.

59. A. Lim, "Netting the Evidence: A Review of On-Line Evidence-Based Management Resources," *Academy of Management Learning & Education* 13(3) (2014): 495–503.

60. B.L. Rau, "Book Review," *Academy of Management Learning & Education* 13(3) (2014): 485–505.

61. D. Kahneman, "Thinking Fast and Slow," *Fortune* (December 1, 2015): 21.

62. S. Boyd, "CEO 101 Advice," *Fortune* (November 17, 2014): 150.

63. S. Boyd, "CEO 101 Advice," *Fortune* (November 17, 2014): 150.

64. L. Iacocca, "Quote," *Forbes* (April 19, 2016): 150.

65. Staff, "Boost Your Limbic Brain," *AARP The Magazine*: 40, accessed online www.aarp.com April 30, 2017.

66. K.J. Lovelace, F. Egger, LR. Dyck, "I Do and I Understand: Assessing the Utility of Web-Based Management Simulations," *Academy of Management Learning & Education* 15(1) (2016): 100–121.

67. R.B. Briner and N.D. Walshe, "From Passively Received Wisdom to Actively Constructed Knowledge: Teaching Systematic Review Skills As a Foundation of Evidence-Based Management," *Academy of Management Learning & Education* 13(3) (2014): 415–432.

68. T. Hahn, L. Preuss, J. Pinkse, and F. Figge, "Cognitive Frames in Corporate Sustainability: Managerial Sensemaking with Paradoxical and Business Case Frames," *Academy of Management Review* 39(4) (2014): 463–487.

69. D. Kahneman, "Thinking Fast and Slow," *Fortune* (December 1, 2015): 21.

70. J. Raffiee and J. Feng, "Should I Quit My Day Job? A Hybrid Path to Entrepreneurship," *Academy of Management Journal* 57(4) (2014): 936–963.

71. T. Hahn, L. Preuss, J. Pinkse, and F. Figge, "Cognitive Frames in Corporate Sustainability: Managerial Sensemaking with Paradoxical and Business Case Frames," *Academy of Management Review* 39(4) (2014): 463–487.

72. E.N. Gamble and R.B. Jelley, "The Case for Competition: Learning About Evidence-Based Management Through Case Competition," *Academy of Management Learning & Education* 13(3) (2014): 433-445.

73. B.L. Rau, "Book Review," *Academy of Management Learning & Education* 13(3) (2014): 485-505.

74. Editors, "Rethinking Governance in Management Research," *Academy of Management Journal* 57(6) (2014): 1535-1543.

75. K.Y. Hsieh, W. Tsai, and M.J. Chen, "If They Can Do It, Why Not US? Competitors as Reference Points for Justifying Escalation of Commitment," *Academy of Management Journal* 58(1) (2015): 38-58.

76. S.H. Harrison and E.D. Rouse, "Let's Dance! Elastic Coordination in Creative Group Work: A Qualitative Study of Modern Dancers," *Academy of Management Journal* 57(5) (2014): 1256-1283.

77. A. Joshi and A.P. Knight, "Who Defers to Whom and Why Dual Pathways Linking Demographic Differences and Dyadic Deference to Team Effectiveness," *Academy of Management Journal* 58(1) (2015): 59-84.

78. J. Raffiee and J. Feng, "Should I Quit My Day Job? A Hybrid Path to Entrepreneurship," *Academy of Management Journal* 57(4) (2014): 936-963.

79. A. Joshi and A.P. Knight, "Who Defers to Whom and Why Dual Pathways Linking Demographic Differences and Dyadic Deference to Team Effectiveness," *Academy of Management Journal* 58(1) (2015): 59-84.

80. C. Webb, "Book Review," *Fortune* (March 15, 2016): 28.

81. S.H. Harrison and E.D. Rouse, "An Inductive Study of Feedback Interactions Over the Course of Creative Projects," *Academy of Management Journal* 58(2) (2015): 375-404.

82. A. Lim, "Netting the Evidence: A Review of On-Line Evidence-Based Management Resources," *Academy of Management Learning & Education* 13(3) (2014): 495-503.

83. A. Joshi and A.P. Knight, "Who Defers to Whom and Why Dual Pathways Linking Demographic Differences and Dyadic Deference to Team Effectiveness," *Academy of Management Journal* 58(1) (2015): 59-84.

84. S.H. Harrison and E.D. Rouse, "Let's Dance! Elastic Coordination in Creative Group Work: A Qualitative Study of Modern Dancers," *Academy of Management Journal* 57(5) (2014): 1256-1283.

85. S.H. Harrison and E.D. Rouse, "An Inductive Study of Feedback Interactions Over the Course of Creative Projects," *Academy of Management Journal* 58(2) (2015): 375-404.

86. S.H. Harrison and E.D. Rouse, "An Inductive Study of Feedback Interactions Over the Course of Creative Projects," *Academy of Management Journal* 58(2) (2015): 375-404.

87. S.H. Harrison and E.D. Rouse, "Let's Dance! Elastic Coordination in Creative Group Work: A Qualitative Study of Modern Dancers," *Academy of Management Journal* 57(5) (2014): 1256-1283.

88. G. Colvin, "Humans Are Underrated," *Fortune* (August 1, 2015): 100-113.

89. C.K. Lam, X. Huang, and S.C.H. Chan, "The Treshold Effect of Participative Leadership and the Role of Leader Information Sharing," *Academy of Management Journal* 58(3) (2015): 836-855. k

90. R.J. Reichard, S.A. Serrano, M. Condren, N. Wilder, M. Dollwet, and W. Wang, "Engaging in Cultural Trigger Events in the Development of Cultural Competence," *Academy of Management Learning & Education* 14(4) (2015): 461-481.

91. D. Urbig, S. Terjesen, V. Procher, K. Muehleld, and A. Van Witteloostuijn, "Come on and Take a Free Ride: Contributing to Public Goods in Native and Foreign Language Settings," *Academy of Management Learning & Education* 15(2) (2016): 268-286.

92. A. Murray, "The Hard Truths of Globalization," *Fortune* (August 1, 2016): 6.

93. D. Urbig, S. Terjesen, V. Procher, K. Muehleld, and A. Van Witteloostuijn, "Come on and Take a Free Ride: Contributing to Public Goods in Native and Foreign Language Settings," *Academy of Management Learning & Education* 15(2) (2016): 268-286.

 i. https://www.facebook.com/pg/facebook/about/?ref=page_internal accessed June 14, 2017.

 ii. http://www.vanityfair.com/news/2016/06/how-mark-zuckerberg-led-facebooks-war-to-crush-google-plus accessed June 14, 2017.

iii. http://www.vanityfair.com/news/2016/06/how-mark-zuckerberg-led-facebooks-war-to-crush-google-plus accessed Jun 14, 2017.

iv. Albergotti, Reed, "Facebook Uses Data to Charm Advertisers Tools Now Allow Advertisers to Target Users Based on Spending Habits in Brick and Mortar Stores," *The Wall Street Journal*, January 30, 2014.

 v. http://data.cnbc.com/quotes/FB/tab/4 accessed June 14, 2017.

Organizational Change and Culture

©Fredrick Kippe/Alamy Stock Photo

LEARNING OUTCOMES

After completing this chapter, you should be able to:

LO 11-1   Describe the four types of change.

LO 11-2   State why people resist change and how to overcome resistance.

LO 11-3   Explain how to use the Lussier change model when making changes.

LO 11-4   Explain the two dimensions of an organization's culture.

LO 11-5   Explain the seven dimensions of an organization's climate.

LO 11-6   Describe five organizational development techniques.

LO 11-7   List the steps in the coaching model.

LO 11-8   Explain the relationship between organizational culture, climate, and development.

LO 11-9   Define the following 16 key terms (in order of appearance in the chapter):

types of change	training
management information	development
systems (MIS)	performance appraisal
automation	standards
resistance to change	coaching model
organizational culture	survey feedback
organizational climate	force field analysis
morale	team building
organizational	
development (OD)	

OPENING CASE WORK SCENARIO

/ / / Ronnie Linkletter now works for the New York City Insurance Company (NYCIC). Ronnie was the manager of the claims department at Rider, a small insurance company in Danbury, Connecticut, until it was bought by NYCIC. Since the purchase of Rider, Ronnie and his peers don't know what to expect. They know there will be many changes, which they don't look forward to. They have been told by the new managers that they are a part of the NYCIC family. "Family" relates to some kind of organizational culture managers keep talking about, which has developed over many years through an ongoing organizational development program. NYCIC has been concerned about its employees' morale. Ronnie feels confused by all these new buzzwords. He wants to know how these changes will affect him. Ronnie knows that at Rider all the managers were white males, and there were very few minorities. But at NYCIC, there are women and minority managers, and more than half of NYCIC employees are minorities.

Is there a way to make changes in organizations so that people don't resist the changes? This is the major topic of Chapter 11. / / /

HOW CHANGE AFFECTS BEHAVIOR, HUMAN RELATIONS, HAPPINESS, AND PERFORMANCE

In the previous chapter, we discussed the importance of creativity and innovation, which of course leads to change[1]—the main topic of this chapter. Companies that don't keep up with the pace of change are not successful and even go bankrupt.[2] Organizational change continues to occur at a high rate,[3] so understanding the process of change is a central theme of business.[4] Clearly, bringing about organizational change requires a change in employee behavior[5] and for them to change the way they work;[6] this in turns often affects their human relations and happiness. Remember that your attitude (Chapter 3) toward change affects your openness to it.[7] If you have a negative attitude toward change, it will affect your behavior, human relations, happiness, and performance, so think positive thoughts about change.[8] Properly implemented, change can increase performance,[9] but attempts to change often fail to meet the intended objectives.[10] This chapter will help you to better understand how to deal with and implement change.

MANAGING CHANGE

WORK APPLICATION 11-1

Give reasons why managing-change skills are important to managers in an organization for which you work or have worked.

Progress is impossible without change,[11] change is faster than ever,[12] and the period between 2015 and 2020 is poised to redefine virtually every facet of how we live and work.[13] Thus, company recruiters seek employees with the skill of adaptability to change.[14] Let's face it, no matter what your age, you have seen changes in organizations that also affect your personal life.

In this section we discuss types of changes and stages in the change process. Our discussion continues in the next section, in which we examine resistance to change and change models. Before we begin, complete Self Assessment Exercise 11-1 to determine your openness to change, which relates to your Big Five personality type (see Chapter 2).

/ / / Self-Assessment Exercise 11-1 / / /

Your Openness to Change

Select the response that best describes what you would do in each situation.

1. In my daily life I:

    _____ *a.* Look for new ways of doing things.
    _____ *b.* Like things the way they are.

2. If my friends were opposed to a change:

    _____ *a.* It would not affect my changing.
    _____ *b.* I would resist the change, too.

3. In my work situation I:

    _____ *a.* Do things differently.
    _____ *b.* Do things the same way.

4. If I had the opportunity to learn to use new computer software to help me in school or at work, I would:

    _____ *a.* Take time to learn to use it on my own.
    _____ *b.* Wait until required to use it.

5. I like to know about a change:

    _____ *a.* Anytime. Short notice is OK with me.
    _____ *b.* Well in advance, to have time to plan for it.

6. When a work change is required, I:

    _____ *a.* Change as quickly as management wants.
    _____ *b.* Want to move slowly to implement change.

(continued)

/ / / **Self-Assessment Exercise 11-1** / / / (*continued*)

7. When leading others, I:

_____ *a.* Use the style appropriate for their capability.
_____ *b.* Use my distinct leadership style.

The more *a* answers you selected, the more open to change you are. The *b* answers show resistance to change. If you tend to be resistant to change and want to have a successful career, you may want to change your attitude and behavior. You can begin by looking for different ways to do things more productively. Look at your routine for getting ready for school or work. Could you make any changes to save time?

Types of Change

Learning Outcome 11-1

Describe the four types of change.

There are different types of change.[15] Organizations are composed of four interactive variables. The four variables, or **types of change**, are *technological change, structural change, task change, and people change.* The proper metaphor for the systems effect for managing change is a balanced mobile in which a change in one variable affects the others. Because of the systems effect, you need to consider the repercussions that a change in one variable will have on the other variables, and plan accordingly.

Communication Skills
Refer to CS Question 1.

Technological Change   With the fast pace of changes in technology, which is moving two to three times faster than management,[16] you need to be flexible and change quickly.[17] The Internet and smartphones have clearly changed the way we live and work.[18] Some of the major areas of technology change are the following:

Machines and Automation   The computer is a sophisticated machine that is also a part of many other machines. **Automation** is *the simplification or reduction of human effort required to do a job.* Computers and other machines have allowed some jobs to be done by robots.[19]

WORK APPLICATION 11-2

Describe the MIS at an organization, preferably one with which you have been associated. If you are not knowledgeable about the organization's MIS, talk with someone who is.

Process   *Process* refers to how the organization transforms inputs (raw materials, parts, data, and so on) into outputs (finished goods and services, information). So *technology* is the essential part of the systems process. The change in the sequence of work in process is a technology change. With the aid of the computer, organizations have changed the way they process information. **Management information systems (MIS)** are *formal systems for collecting, processing, and disseminating the information necessary to aid managers in decision making.* The MIS attempts to centralize and integrate all or most of the organization's information such as production, inventory, and sales information.

WORK APPLICATION 11-3

Describe an automation change in an organization, preferably one with which you have been associated.

Structural Change   It is important to coordinate structure with technology. *Structure* refers to the type of organization principle and departments used, as discussed in Chapter 4. **Google** changes it structure, creating a parent company **Alphabet Inc.** with **Google Inc.** now just one of the business divisions.[20]

Task and People Change   Organizations can't change without changes in people by adopting new behaviors.[21] *Task* refers to the day-to-day things that employees do to perform their jobs. When tasks change with structure and technology, people's skills and performance must change.[22] You need to view learning as a career—lifelong—process to advance, and happiness is about behavior change.[23] A change in team membership and in organizational culture are also considered a people change.

It is people who create, manage, and use technology; therefore, people are the most important resource.[24] What people often resist are the social changes brought about by technological changes. The integration of both people and technology is known as *creating*

EXHIBIT 11.1 | Types of Changes

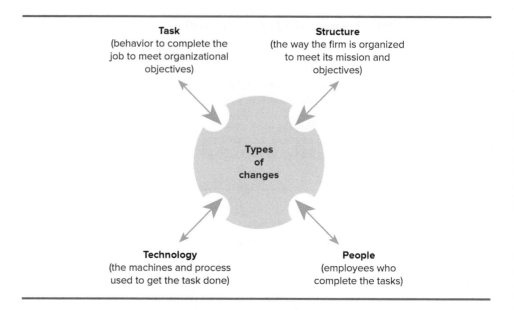

a sociotechnical system. When changing task, structure, or technology, you should never forget the impact of change on people. Changing any of these other variables will not be effective without considering people change.[25]

/// **In the opening case,** Rider Insurance has been bought by NYCIC. The primary change is structural. Rider is no longer a separate entity; it is part of NYCIC. NYCIC will most likely change the structure at Rider to match its present structure. With the change in structure, most likely the tasks, technology, and people will also change./// See Exhibit 11.1 for a review of the types of changes.

Forms of Change

Change also takes one of two broad forms: It is either incremental vs. radical[26] or incremental vs. discontinuous[27] or disruptive.[28]

WORK APPLICATION 11-4

Give one or more examples of a type of change you experienced in an organization. (Identify it as task change, structural change, technological change, or people change.)

APPLICATION SITUATIONS / / /

Types of Changes   AS 11-1

Identify the type of change represented in each statement as:

A. Task change   B. Structural change

C. Technological change   D. People change

_____ 1. "Ajee, because of the increase in the size of our department, we will now split into two departments and you will be the supervisor of the new department."

_____ 2. "Duane is taking Chang's place now that he has retired."

_____ 3. "Shelby, from now on, purchases under $200 will no longer need to be approved by the purchasing manager."

_____ 4. "Casmir, report to the training center to learn proper procedures for running the machine."

_____ 5. "Sergei, from now on, you have to fill in this new form every time you deliver a package."

EXHIBIT 11.2 | Stages in the Change Process

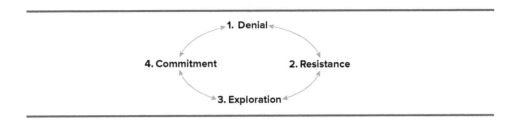

Incremental Change   Incremental change is continual improvement that takes place within the already existing technology cycle. Companies innovate by lowering costs and improving performance of existing products and services. **IBM CEO Virginia Rometty**'s message to employees is that IBM hasn't transformed rapidly enough—she wants employees to think fast and move fast. Incremental changes continue to the point of *technological discontinuity* with advances or unique combinations of existing technologies creating a significant break-through in performance or function.

Discontinuous Change   Discontinuous or disruptive change is a significant breakthrough in technology that leads to design competition and a new technology cycle making the old technology obsolete.[29] Disruptive technology requires the disruptive companies to make radical changes or go out of business.[30] **Western Union** started in 1851 as a telegraph service that was disrupted telephones and long distance calls and the Internet. Today, it's the largest international money transfer MNC.[31] Successful companies discontinue their own success-ful business.[32] **Netflix** disrupted **Blockbuster** in-store DVD rentals with its mail DVDs; then it changed to streaming video content and making it.

Stages in the Change Process

Most people go through four distinct stages in the change process: (1) *Denial:* When peo-ple first hear rumors through the grapevine that change is coming, they deny that it will happen at all, or to them. (2) *Resistance:* Once people get over the initial shock and realize that change is going to be a reality, they resist the change. (3) *Exploration:* When the change begins to be implemented, employees explore the change. (4) *Commitment:* Through exploration, employees determine their level of commitment to making the change a success.

/// **In the opening case,** employees at both Rider and NYCIC will be going through the stages of the change process. How successfully the change process is implemented will affect the behavior, human relations, and performance of the two businesses, which are now one company. ///

Exhibit 11.2 illustrates the stages in the change process. Notice that the stages are in a circular formation because change is an ongoing process, not a linear one, and people can regress, as the arrows show.

RESISTANCE TO CHANGE AND HOW TO OVERCOME IT

Learning Outcome 11-2

State why people resist change and how to overcome resistance.

Why do employees resist change, and how do managers overcome resistance to change? We answer these questions in this section.

Resistance to Change

Why Do People Resist Change?   As stated by **J.C. Penney's chair Michael Ullman**, "only a baby with a wet diaper likes change."[33] We don't want to change our habits and routines.[34] Some people deliberately try to kill good ideas[35] and others to beat the system for their advantage as they attempt to block change efforts.[36]

Communication Skills
Refer to CS Question 2.

People resist change for a variety of reasons, some of which include (1) maintaining the *status quo* (people like things the way they are now, view the change as an inconvenience, or don't agree that a change is needed), (2) *uncertainty* (people tend to fear the unknown and wonder how the change will affect them), (3) *learning anxiety* (the prospect of learning something new itself produces anxiety), and (4) *fear* (people often fear they may lose their jobs, that they will not be successful with learning new ways, or that they may lose control over how they do their jobs).

Before making changes, anticipate how employees will react to or resist the change and how you will overcome it. **Resistance to change** involves the *variables of intensity, source, and focus, which together explain why people are reluctant to change.* **Ken Hultman** identifies these three variables as the major variables of resistance to change.[37]

Intensity   People often have four basic reactions to change: acceptance, tolerance, resistance, and rejection. The resistance intensity can vary from strong to weak or somewhere in between. As a manager of change, you should anticipate the intensity of resistance to change so that you can effectively plan to overcome it.

Sources   There are three major sources of resistance: facts, beliefs, and values. (1) *Facts:* Facts are statements that identify reality. (2) *Beliefs:* Facts can be proved; beliefs cannot. They are subjective. Our beliefs are our opinions that lead us to think and feel that a change is correct or incorrect, good or bad. (3) *Values:* Values are what you believe are worth pursuing or doing. What we value is important to us, whereas beliefs are not very important to us.

People analyze the facts presented from all sources and determine if they believe the change is of value to them. When the facts are clear and logical and people believe the change is of value to them, they tend to have lower resistance to the change.

Focus   There are three major focuses of resistance: self, others, and the work environment. (1) *Self:* It is natural for people to want to know, "What's in it for me? What will I gain or lose?" (Self-interest.) (2) *Others:* After considering what's in it for them, or when they are not affected by the change, people tend to consider how the change will affect their friends, peers (peer pressure), and colleagues. (3) *Work environment:* The work environment includes the job itself and the physical setting and climate. Employees' analysis of the facts about the current versus the changed work environment will affect their resistance to the change.

Exhibit 11.3 is an adapted version of Ken Hultman's resistance matrix, with examples of each area of resistance. For instance, in box 1, "Facts about self," note that one reason

WORK APPLICATION 11-5

Describe a situation in which you were resistant to change. Identify the intensity, source, and focus. Using Exhibit 11.3, which box (by number and statement) describes your resistance?

EXHIBIT 11.3 | Resistance Matrix

Sources of Resistance (facts → beliefs → values)		
1. Facts about self I never did it before. I failed the last time I tried. All my friends are here.	**4. Beliefs about self** I'm too busy to do it. I'll do it, but I'll mess up. I don't think I can accept the change.	**7. Values pertaining to self** I like the job I have now better. I don't want to change; I'm happy. I like working alone.
2. Facts about others He's on probation. She has two children. other people told me it's hard to do.	**5. Beliefs about others** She pretends to be busy to avoid extra work. He's better at it than I am; let him do it. She never understands our side.	**8. Values pertaining to others** Let someone else train her; I'm not interested. What you really think doesn't matter to me. I Don't give a . . . about him.
3. Facts about the work environment Why should I do it? I'm not getting paid extra. I haven't been trained to do it. I make less than anyone else in the department.	**6. Beliefs about the work environment** This is a lousy place to work. The pay here is terrible. It's who you know, not what you khow around here that counts.	**9. Values pertaining to the work environment** Who cares what the goals are? I just do my job. The salary is more important than the benefits. This job gives me the chance to work outside.

Focus of resistance (self → others → work)

Source: Adapted from Ken Hultman's resistance matrix in The Path of Least Resistance, Austin, TX: Learning Concepts, 1979.

Identifying Resistance to Change   AS 11-2

Below are five statements made by employees asked to make a change on the job. Identify the source, focus, and intensity of their resistance using Exhibit 11.3. Place the number of the box (1 to 9) that represents and best describes the major resistance.

_____ 6. One of your employees, Latavia, is busy at work. You tell her to stop what she is doing and begin a new project. Latavia says, "The job I'm working on now is more important."

_____ 7. As the police sergeant you asked Elijah, the patrol officer, to take a rookie cop as his partner. Elijah says, "Do I have to? I broke in the last rookie."

_____ 8. As the tennis coach you asked Tom, the star player, to have Hank as his doubles partner. Tom said, "Come on, Hank is not that good of a player. Zach is better; don't break us up." You disagreed and forced Tom to accept Hank.

_____ 9. As supervisor, you realized that English always uses the accommodating conflict style. You told her to stop giving in to everyone's wishes. English said, "But I like people, and I want them to like me, too."

_____ 10. Tianna went to you, the supervisor, and asked you if she could change the work-order sequence. You said, "No; the procedure is fine the way it is now."

given is "I never did it before." Use the matrix to identify the intensity, source, and focus of resistance. Once you have identified the probable resistance to change, you can work at overcoming it.

Overcoming Resistance to Change

Below are some of the major methods for overcoming resistance to change.

- *Develop a positive climate for change.* Develop and maintain good human relations. Because change and trust are so closely intertwined, the first concern should be to develop ongoing mutual trust.

- *Encourage interest in improvement.* Continually encourage creativity. Constantly look for better ways to do things.

- *Plan.* You need a plan to overcome resistance.[38] Don't consider how you would react. What seems very simple and logical to you may not be to the other person. Try to see things from his or her perspective (Chapter 2). The next eight methods should be part of your plan.

- *Give facts.* Get all the facts and plan how you will present them. Giving half-answers will only make employees more confused and angry, and hiding things and lying is a disaster. Giving the facts as far in advance as possible helps overcome the fear of the unknown.

- *Clearly state why the change is needed and how it will affect employees.* People want and need to know why the change is needed and how it will affect them both positively and negatively. Be open and honest with employees. If employees understand why the change is needed, and it makes sense to them, they will be more willing to change— sensemaking.[39] It is important to create a sense of urgency to kill complacency and get employees to want to change.

- *Create a win-win situation.* People respond to incentives,[40] so be sure to answer, "What's in it for me?" When people can see the benefits to them, and/or what they can lose, they are more willing to change.

EXHIBIT 11.4 |
Overcoming Resistance
to Change

Old		New
R **e** **s** **i** **s** **t** **a** **n** **c** **e**	Develop a positive climate for change. Encourage interest in improvement. Plan. Give facts. Clearly state why the change is needed and how it will affect employees. Create a win–win situation. Involve employees. Provide support. Stay calm. Avoid direct confrontation. Use power and ethical politics.	**C** **h** **a** **n** **g** **e**

Communication Skills
Refer to CS Question 3.

- *Involve employees.* Employees who participate in developing changes are more committed to them than employees who have changes assigned to them.

- *Provide support.* Be a supportive coach,[41] and give as much advance notice and training as possible before the change takes place. Training helps reduce learning anxiety and helps employees realize that they can be successful with the change.

- *Stay calm.* Try not to do or say things that will make people emotional so that you don't create more resistance to change. Follow the guidelines on dealing with emotions in Chapter 4.

- *Avoid direct confrontation.* Trying to persuade people that their facts, beliefs, and values are wrong leads to resistance. Avoid statements that will make people emotional, such as, "You're wrong; you don't know what you're talking about." Deal with conflict following the guidelines in Chapter 5.

- *Use power and ethical politics.* Chapter 8 discussed how to get what you want through the use of power and politics, and it usually involves change. Power and political skills are commonly used to implement changes.[42] Planned radical change fundamentally alters the strategy, culture, and power structure.[43]

See Exhibit 11.4 for a review of the methods for overcoming resistance to change. Remember that the 11 methods for overcoming resistance to change should be a part of your plan for change. Below you will learn about planning for change.

Responding to Resistance

Below are classifications of employee resistance types, resistance statements, and responses you could make to the employee to help overcome resistance to change. The following are presented to acquaint you with some of the possible types of resistance you may face, along with some possible responses you could make:

- *The blocker:* "I don't want to do it that way." Manager: "What are your objections to the change? How would you prefer to do it?"

- *The roller:* "What do you want me to do?" Manager: "I want you to . . ." (Be specific and describe the change in detail; use communication skills. Don't let them give up easily.)

- *The staller:* "I'll do it when I can." Manager: "What is more important?"

- *The reverser:* "That's a good idea." (But she or he never does it.) Manager: "What is it that you like about the change?"

- *The sidestepper:* "Why don't you have XYZ do it?" Manager: "I asked you to do it because . . ."

- *The threatener:* "I'll do it, but the guys upstairs will not like it." Manager: "Let me worry about it. What are *your* objections?"

- *The politician:* "You owe me one; let me slide." Manager: "I do owe you one, but I need the change. I'll pay you back later."

- *The traditionalist:* "That's not the way we do things around here." Manager: "This is a unique situation; it needs to be done."

- *The assaulter:* "You're a . . . (pick a word)." Manager: "I will not tolerate that type of behavior." Or, "This is really upsetting you, isn't it?"

The above supervisory responses will be helpful in most situations, but not all. If employees persist in resisting the change, they may need to be considered problem employees and handled accordingly as discussed in Chapter 10.

Change Models

It is important to know how to implement change. Here are three change models, providing a pro-change orientation.

Lewin's Change Model   In the early 1950s, Kurt Lewin developed a technique, still used today, for changing people's behavior, skills, and attitudes. Lewin viewed the change process as consisting of three steps:

(1) *Unfreezing:* This step usually involves reducing those forces maintaining the status quo. (2) *Moving:* This step shifts the behavior to a new level. This is the change process in which employees learn the new desirable behavior, values, and attitudes. (3) *Refreezing:* The desirable performance becomes the permanent way of doing things. This is the new status quo. Refreezing often takes place through reinforcement and support for the new behavior.

See Exhibit 11.5 for a review of the steps.

Learning Outcome 11-3

Explain how to use the Lussier change model when making changes.

Lussier Change Model

Lewin's model provides a general framework for understanding organizational change. Because the steps of change are broad, the author has developed a more specific model. The Lussier change model consists of five steps:

1. *Define the Change.* Clearly state what the change is. Is it a task, structural, technological, or people change? What are the systems effects on the other variables? Set objectives, following the guidelines in Chapter 8.

2. *Identify Possible Resistance to the Change.* Determine the intensity, source, and focus of possible resistance to the change. Use the resistance matrix in Exhibit 11.3.

3. *Plan the Change.* Plan the change implementation. Use the appropriate supervisory style for the situation. We will discuss planned change in more detail later in this chapter.

4. *Implement the Change.* Follow the 11 guidelines to overcome resistance to change in Exhibit 11.4.

5. *Control the Change.* Remember that people often resist change and may not follow your plan,[44] so you need to follow up to ensure that the change is implemented, reinforced, and maintained. Make sure the objective is met. If not, take corrective action.

EXHIBIT 11.5 | Change Models

Lewin's Change Model	Lussier's Change Model
Step 1: Unfreezing	Step 1: Define the change.
Step 2: Moving	Step 2: Identify possible resistance to the change.
Step 3: Refreezing	Step 3: Plan the change.
	Step 4: Implement the change. Give the facts. Involve employees. Provide support.
	Step 5: Control the change (implementation, reinforcement, maintenance).

Habit Changing Model—Overcoming Your Resistance   Yes, we are discussing habits again. Thus far the focus has been on overcoming others' resistance to change. Now let's focus on overcoming your own resistance to change. Do you really like your daily routine disrupted?[45] Are you bound by your habits of repetition?[46] If you can't change your mind and embrace change, you cannot change anything.[47] The aim is to cultivate a mind-set that embraces change in ourselves and others.[48] Easier said than done, right? Well the first step is to realize we need to take a positive attitude about change. Let's face it, if we know we have to make a change, resisting it doesn't help—so accept it and move forward.

To make a change, we have to change our thoughts and habit, or make the change a habit to make it successful.[49] Recall that the three-step model for changing habits is: (1) develop a *clue*, (2) implement the *new behavior*, (3) *reward* the changed behavior.

/// **In the opening case,** if managers at NYCIC follow the guidelines for overcoming resistance to change and develop an effective plan using the change model, change can be implemented successfully at Rider. ///

WORK APPLICATION 11-6

Give a specific example of when a change model would be helpful to a specific manager.

ORGANIZATIONAL CULTURE

Organizational culture should be how the firm achieves its mission by living its values and belief on a daily basis,[50] and management needs to be specific about the values and behaviors it expects from its people.[51] **Organizational culture** consists of *the shared values and assumptions of how its members will behave.*

It's not easy to build a culture that's open and excited about change, rather than resistant to it.[52] But the culture should instill ethical standards[53] and cultivate people who care about each other and about their work.[54] In this section, we describe how people learn the organization's culture and the importance of having a strong positive culture.

Learning the Organization's Culture

When hiring, an important consideration is matching the person to the culture. Newcomers need to learn and be integrated into the organization's culture.[55] Culture is learned through observing and interacting with employees, events, and training.[56] Here are five ways that employees learn the organization's culture.

1. *Heroes*—such as founder **Tom Watson of IBM**, **Sam Walton** of **Walmart**, **Herb Kelleher** of **Southwest Airlines**, **Frederick Smith** of **FedEx**, and others who made outstanding contributions to their organizations.

2. *Stories*—often about founders and others who have made extraordinary efforts, such as **Sam Walton** visiting every **Walmart** store yearly or someone driving through a blizzard to deliver a product or service. Public statements and speeches can also be considered stories.

3. *Slogans*—such as "Quality is Job 1" at **Ford**; **McDonald's** Q, S, C, V—Quality, Service, Cleanliness, and Value; The **H-P Way**; **FedEx**'s People—Service—Profit philosophy.

WORK APPLICATION 11-7

Identify the cultural heroes, stories, slogans, symbols, and ceremonies for an organization you are or have been a member of.

4. *Symbols*—such as logos, plaques, pins, and jackets, or a **Mary Kay** pink **Cadillac**. Symbols are used to convey values.

5. *Ceremonies*—including rituals such as a chest bump and awards dinners for top achievers.

If you hear expressions such as, "That's not how we do things here," or "This is the way we do things here," you are learning the organization's culture.

Strong and Weak, Positive and Negative Cultures

The two dimensions of an organization's culture are strong and weak, and positive and negative.

Learning Outcome 11-4

Explain the two dimensions of an organization's culture.

Strong and Weak Cultures   Organizational cultural strength is characterized by a continuum from strong to weak. Organizations with clear values that are shared to the extent of similar behavior have strong cultures. In strong cultures norms are used to enforcing desired behavior.[57]

Organizations that have no stated values and do not enforce behavior have weak cultures. So the more alike the values and behavior, the stronger the culture, and vice versa. **Whole Foods, Southwest Airlines,** and **Starbucks** are recognized as having a strong culture.[58] "**IBM**ers value: (1) dedication to every client's success; (2) innovation that matters, for our company and for the world; and (3) trust and personal responsibility in all relationships. There is a sense of pride and of being able to distinguish yourself as an IBMer."[59]

Positive and Negative Cultures   An organizational culture is considered positive or *healthy* when it has norms that contribute to effective performance and productivity. A negative or *unhealthy* organizational culture is a source of resistance and turmoil that hinders effective performance.

The most effective organizational culture that leads to effective performance is strong and positive. Companies with strong positive cultures include **Apple, Google, J&J, P&G,** and **3M**. Although **IBM** has a strong culture, its CEO Virginia Rometty is changing one aspect. She wants IBMers to think fast and move faster with innovations.[60]

Negative unhealthy cultures can be costly. The **Wells Fargo Bank** culture of incentives to meet high quotes lead to employees creating accounts customers didn't want. **Volkswagen (VW)** said that its flawed culture of tolerance for rule-breaking lead to illegal lower emissions ratings.[61] **Uber**'s unhealthy macho culture of not punishing discrimination and sexual harassment led to good employees leaving the company, more than 20 managers were fired, and founder CEO **Travis Kalanick** was pressured by the board to step down as CEO.[62]

Before accepting a job with an organization, you may want to learn about its culture to determine if it is the kind of organization you will enjoy working in. For example, if you are not competitive, you probably will not enjoy working for **PepsiCo**.

/// **In the opening case,** Ronnie feels that NYCIC has a strong organizational culture, whereas Rider had a weak culture. NYCIC needs to develop the shared values and assumptions of how members should behave at Rider. Many firms experience difficulty merging cultures. The OD team-building program (discussed later in this chapter) would be an excellent way to develop the NYCIC culture at Rider. ///

Communication Skills
Refer to CS Question 4.

WORK APPLICATION 11-8

Describe the organizational culture at a firm for which you work or have worked. Does or did the organization strive to have a strong positive culture? If so, how?

ORGANIZATIONAL CLIMATE

Organizational climate is *the relatively enduring quality of the internal environment of the organization as perceived by its members.* Climate is employees' perception of the atmosphere of the internal environment, such as its rules, and how employees are treated, which is important to group and organizational success.[63] *Organizational climate* is a broader term than *culture*.[64] Its definition will be explained throughout this section.

The major difference between culture and climate is as follows: Culture is based on shared values and assumptions of "how" things should be done (ideal environment), while climate is based on shared perceptions of the "way" things really are done (intangibles of the actual internal environment). An organization can claim to have a strong culture and have a negative climate. Employees can know how things should be, while being dissatisfied with their perception of the way things actually are. Managers sometimes say that employees are its greatest asset, yet employees don't perceive that they are treated that way.

Job satisfaction, discussed in Chapter 3, is based primarily on organizational climate. Morale is also an important part of organizational climate. **Morale** is *a state of mind based on employees' attitudes and satisfaction with the organization.* Morale can be different at various levels within the organization. Morale is commonly measured on a continuum ranging from high to low morale, based on the seven dimensions of climate listed below.

Organizational Culture or Climate?   AS 11-3

Identify each statement as being associated with:

A. Organizational culture   B. Organizational climate

_____11. "Employees are talking about starting a union because they were not happy about not getting a raise this year."

_____12. "Department members please fill out this questionnaire and return it to the human resources department when you are done, but no later than Wednesday."

_____13. "There is no policy, and no one has ever said anything about it, but the dress code is a suit and tie for work."

_____14. "Department members, from now on, you will be the only one checking the quality of your work."

_____15. Rotary International's motto, "Service above Self."

Learning Outcome 11-5

Explain the seven dimensions of an organization's climate.

WORK APPLICATION 11-9

Describe the organizational climate at a firm for which you work or have worked, based on the seven dimensions of climate. Does or did the organization measure its climate? If so, how?

WORK APPLICATION 11-10

Describe the morale at the organization.

Communication Skills
Refer to CS Question 5.

Dimensions of Climate

Some of the common dimensions of climate are the following:

- *Structure.* The degree of constraint on members—the number of rules, regulations, and procedures.
- *Responsibility.* The degree of control over one's own job.
- *Rewards.* The degree of being rewarded for one's efforts and being punished appropriately.
- *Warmth.* The degree of satisfaction with human relations.
- *Support.* The degree of being helped by others and of experiencing cooperation.
- *Organizational identity and loyalty.* The degree to which employees identify with the organization and their loyalty to it.
- *Risk.* The degree to which risk-taking is encouraged.

Studies show that poor climate tends to result in lower levels of performance, but not always.[65] We seek a sense of belonging.[66] Like plants, employees require a proper climate to thrive. Working in a climate you enjoy will also affect your performance.

/// In the opening case, often, large companies such as NYCIC take over a smaller company such as Rider because they are successful. In too many situations, the larger company changes the flexible entrepreneurial climate to one of bureaucracy, resulting in the small company's becoming less productive. NYCIC needs to focus on these seven dimensions of climate. The Rider employees need to shift identity and loyalty to NYCIC.///

See Exhibit 11.6 for a list of the dimensions of climate.

ORGANIZATIONAL DEVELOPMENT

Learning Outcome 11-6

Describe five organizational development techniques.

So far we have discussed the importance of managing change and developing strong positive cultures and climates. Now we focus on these topics as an ongoing, organization wide process, commonly referred to as organizational development (OD).[67] **Organizational development** is *the ongoing planned process of change used as a means of improving the organization's effectiveness in solving problems and achieving its objectives.*

EXHIBIT 11.6 |
Dimensions of Climate

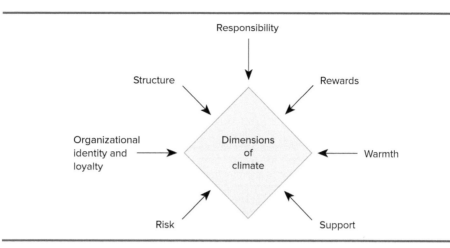

Managing and Changing Culture and Climate through OD

The first step in organizational development is to diagnose the problem(s). Indicators that problems exist, such as conflicts between diverse groups, the need for increased quality and productivity, low profits, and excessive absenteeism or turnover, lead management to call in a change agent to study the organization's problems and needs.[68] A *change agent* is the person responsible for the OD program. The change agent can use a variety of methods to diagnose problems.[69] Some methods are reviewing records, observing, interviewing individuals and work groups, holding meetings, and/or using questionnaires. After the problem has been diagnosed, OD techniques are used to solve it, as managers navigate the change.[70]

This section examines five OD techniques: training and development, performance appraisal, survey feedback, force field analysis, and team building. Training and development is presented first because the other four techniques usually include training.

Training and Development

After a position is staffed, there is usually a need to train the person to do the job. **Training** is *the process of developing the necessary skills to perform the present job.* **Development** is *the process of developing the ability to perform both present and future jobs.* Typically, training is used to develop technical skills of nonmanagers, while development is usually less technical and is designed for professional and managerial employees. The terms *training* and *development* are often used together; they are used interchangeably as well.

Communication Skills
Refer to CS Question 6.

The Training Cycle   Following the steps in the training cycle helps ensure that training is done in a systematic way. See Exhibit 11.7 for more details about each of the five steps in the training cycle. Model 11.1 summarizes the steps involved in conducting a job instructional training (JIT) session, which is part of steps 3 and 4 of the training cycle.

But much of what is taught through development isn't used on the job. Be honest. How many of the developmental skills you have learned through this course are you actually using in your personal and professional lives? It's tough to implement new skills because we don't like to change our habits.

/// **In the opening case,** management at NYCIC will have to determine the training needs of Rider employees, set objectives, prepare for training, conduct the training, and evaluate results so that the two units can work effectively as one organization. ///

Performance Appraisal

After employees are hired, and during and after their training, they must be evaluated so they know how they are performing.[71] **Performance appraisal** is *the ongoing process of evaluating employee job performance.* Performance appraisal is also called *performance job*

WORK APPLICATION 11-11

State how you were trained to perform a specific job. Explain how the training affected your job performance. How could training at this organization be used to increase performance?

EXHIBIT 11.7 | The Training Cycle

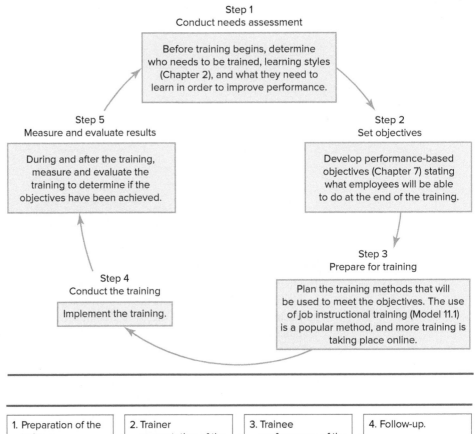

MODEL 11.1 | Job Instructional Training

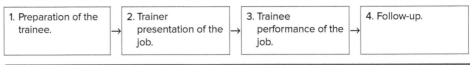

1. Preparation of the trainee. → 2. Trainer presentation of the job. → 3. Trainee performance of the job. → 4. Follow-up.

Communication Skills
Refer to CS Question 7.

Skill-Building Exercise 11-1 develops this skill.

WORK APPLICATION 11-12

Describe the performance standards for a job you hold or have held. How would you improve them?

Communication Skills
Refer to CS Question 8.

evaluation, performance review, and *performance audit.* Regardless of the name, performance appraisal is one of the manager's most important, and most difficult, functions.

The performance of employees is appraised according to two sets of objectives: (1) developmental and (2) evaluative. Developmental objectives are used as the basis of decisions to improve future performance. Evaluative objectives are used as the basis of administrative decisions to reward or punish past performance.[72]

The performance appraisal process has five steps. These are shown in Exhibit 11.8, and steps 2 and 3 are discussed below.

Developing Standards and Measurement Methods   After you determine what it takes to do the job, you should develop standards and methods for measuring performance. This is step (2) in the performance appraisal process. Poor standards are a major problem of performance appraisals.

To effectively assess performance, you need to have clear standards[73] and methods to objectively measure performance.[74] The term **standards** describes *performance levels in the areas of quantity, quality, time, and cost.* Sample standards for an administrative assistant could be to type 50 words (quantity) per minute (time) with two errors or less (quality) at a maximum salary of $15 per hour (cost).

Conducting Informal Performance Appraisals—Coaching   Performance appraisals should not merely be formal once-a-year, one-hour sessions. Employees need regular informal feedback

EXHIBIT 11.8 | Performance Appraisal Steps

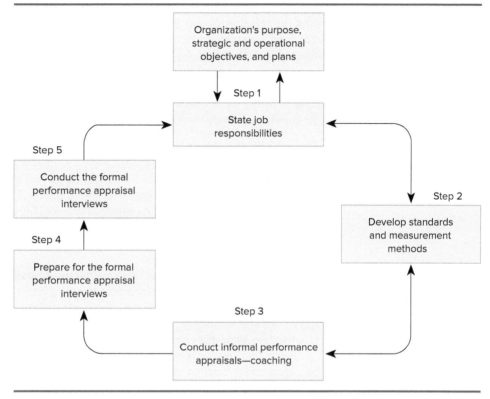

MODEL 11.2 | Coaching Model

on their performance—coaching.[75] The employee performing below standard may need daily or weekly coaching to reach increased productivity.

Learning Outcome 11-7

List the steps in the coaching model.

The coaching model is designed for use in improving ability and for dealing with motivation problems, as motivated employees are more productive and get better performance appraisals,[76] because coaching increases performance.[77] The **coaching model** involves *5 steps: (1) refer to past feedback; (2) describe current performance; (3) describe desired performance; (4) get a commitment to the change; and (5) follow up.*

Exhibit 11.8 lists the performance appraisal steps. Notice that steps 1 to 3 are double-looped (have two-headed arrows) because the development at one step may require the manager to backtrack and make changes. For example, during an informal appraisal, the manager may realize that environmental changes require a change in the employee's job and/or performance standards. Step 5 brings the manager back to step 1.

WORK APPLICATION 11-13

Identify the performance measurement method(s) used to evaluate your job performance. Describe how you would improve the method(s).

Survey Feedback

WORK APPLICATION 11-14

Describe a specific situation in which it would be appropriate to use the coaching model.

Companies want to know how their employees and customers feel about them,[78] and they agree they should conduct surveys more than once a year.[79] By waiting so long, feedback is often no longer relevant.[80] Companies including **Google** are conducting shorter frequent surveys to catch problems before they fester.[81] **Survey feedback** is *an OD technique that uses a questionnaire to gather data that are used as the basis for change.*

Measuring Climate   The survey feedback technique is commonly used to measure the organizational climate, or morale, which is a measure of job satisfaction.[82] Based on the results, the organization may set up training programs. Some of the signs that an organization may have a climate problem include high rates of tardiness, absenteeism, and turnover. When employees have many complaints, talk about unionization or striking, and lack pride in their work, the organization may have a climate problem that should be corrected.

Organizational climate is measured in the same way job satisfaction is (review Chapter 3). Survey feedback is the most common approach. But the dimensions included in the questionnaire vary from organization to organization.

Force Field Analysis

Force field analysis is *a technique that diagrams the current level of performance, the hindering forces against change, and the driving forces toward change.* The process begins by appraising the current level of performance. As shown in Exhibit 11.9, the present level of performance is shown in the middle of the diagram. The hindering forces holding back performance are listed in the top part of the diagram. The driving forces keeping performance at this level are listed on the bottom of the diagram.

After viewing the diagram, you develop strategies for maintaining or increasing the driving forces with simultaneous steps for decreasing hindering forces. For example, in Exhibit 11.9, the solution you select could be to have the salespeople go through a training program. You could spend more time working with the less productive salespeople. Speeding up delivery time could be worked on, while maintaining all the driving forces could lead to higher sales volume.

Force field analysis is particularly useful for group problem solving. After group members agree on the diagram, the solution often becomes clear to them.

Team Building

Team building is a widely used OD technique.[83] **Team building** is *an OD technique designed to help work groups operate more effectively.* Team building is used as a means of helping new or existing groups that are in need of improving effectiveness.

Team-Building Goals   The goals of team-building programs will vary considerably, depending on the group needs and the change agent's skills. Some of the typical goals are:

* To clarify the objectives of the team and the responsibilities of each team member.
* To identify problems preventing the team from accomplishing its objectives.
* To develop open, honest working relationships based on trust and an understanding of group members.

EXHIBIT 11.9 | Force Field Analysis

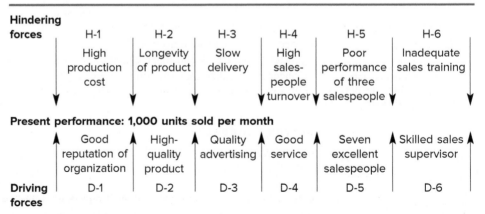

Team-Building Program Agenda   The team-building agendas vary with team needs and the change agent's skills.[84] Typical agenda topics include the following items:

1. *Climate building.* The program begins with the change agent trying to develop a climate of trust, support, and openness. He or she discusses the program's purpose and objectives. Team members learn more about each other and share what they would like to accomplish in the session.

2. *Process and structure evaluation.* The team evaluates the strengths and weaknesses of its process (team dynamics) (Chapter 9). The team explores and selects ideal norms.

3. *Problem identification.* The team identifies its strengths, then its weaknesses or areas where improvement is possible. The team first lists several areas where improvement is possible. Then it prioritizes them by importance in helping the team improve performance.

4. *Problem solving.* The team takes the top priority and develops a solution. It then moves to the second priority, followed by the third, the fourth, and so on.

5. *Training.* Team building often includes some form of training that addresses the problem(s) facing the group.

6. *Closure.* The program ends by summarizing what has been accomplished. Follow-up responsibility is assigned. Team members commit to improving performance.

Skill-Building Exercise 11-3 develops this skill.

Communication Skills
Refer to CS Question 9.

WORK APPLICATION 11-15

Identify an OD technique and explain how it is used by a specific organization, preferably one with which you have been associated.

/// **In the opening case,** at Rider, a good starting place for OD would be team-building sessions. In teams, Rider employees could be made aware of NYCIC's OD program and how Rider will be developed. Through team-building sessions, the planned changes of NYCIC could be implemented at Rider. After a period of months, NYCIC could use survey feedback to determine how the change program at Rider is perceived. The survey could serve as the basis for understanding the need for future change at Rider. As the teams develop at Rider, they can use force field analysis to work out any problems the new changes bring and to reach higher levels of performance as part of their team-building program. ///

APPLICATION SITUATIONS / / /

OD Techniques   **AS11-5**

Below are five situations in which an OD technique would be beneficial. Identify the most appropriate technique for each.

A. Force field analysis   D. Team building

B. Survey feedback   E. Performance appraisal

C. Training and development

_____ 16. "We need to teach our production department employees statistical process control techniques."

_____ 17. "We believe in developing our people. We'd like to give each employee better feedback to help them improve their performance."

_____ 18. "To improve productivity, we should identify the things that are holding us back and the things that are helping us be productive, too."

_____ 19. "We want an OD program that will enable us to better utilize the input of each manager."

_____ 20. "Morale and motivation are low in our organization. We'd like to know why and change."

GLOBAL DIFFERENCES

Change leadership skills are important globally, and MNC merge cultures. Here we discuss generalizations that may not apply to all companies. As stated, the Big Five personality types are global. Therefore, individuals in all cultures are more or less open to change. However, cultural values can influence openness to change. Countries including the United States value change, whereas other cultures, including some Arab countries, place less value on change and more on tradition and religious beliefs. The United States is known for creating urgency and for being time driven, setting deadlines for implementing change.[85] However, other cultures take a slower approach and are more patient, such as many Asian and Middle Eastern countries.

Collective (i.e., Japan, China, Mexico) versus individual (United States and much of Western Europe) societies do affect change. Collective societies tend to want to improve the team and organizations, so individuals are often more open to change to help others even when they personally may not gain and even lose, whereas those in individual societies are more concerned about helping themselves and are more willing to resist change that hurts them personally. The Japanese generate a lot more creative ideas for improvement than do U.S. workers. The Japanese tend to focus on small, incremental changes to improve processes and products, whereas Americans tends to focus on large, major changes. The baseball example used is that the Japanese try to get a hit, whereas Americans go for the home run.

Some cultures are more open to power and following orders for change without questioning authority, such as France, China, and India. However, other cultures are more willing to question and resist change, such as the U.S. and Scandinavian (Denmark, Sweden, and Norway) cultures, which can cause problems for companies trying to change. Participation in change also varies by culture and country development. For example, in the United States and Japan employees are highly trained and want to participate in planning and implementing change. However, in Third World countries employees are generally neither capable nor interested in being empowered to participate in the change process.

You will read more about global diversity in Chapter 12. Complete Self-Assessment Exercise 11-2 to determine how your personality affects your response to change and organizational culture.

Communication Skills
Refer to CS Question 10.

/ / / **Self-Assessment Exercise 11-2** / / /

Personality and Organizational Change and Culture

Let's determine how your personality relates to your ability to change and the type of culture you may prefer.

On the Big Five personality traits, if you are *open to new experiences,* you are willing to change and will do well in an adaptive-type culture. If you are closed to new experiences, you will tend to do well in a bureaucratic-type culture that changes slowly.

If you score high on *conscientiousness,* with a high need for achievement, you may tend to be a conformist and will most likely feel comfortable in an organization with a strong culture.

If you have a high *agreeableness* personality, with a high need for affiliation, you tend to get along well with people and can fit into a strong culture. You would do well in a cooperative-type culture that values teamwork and empowerment.

If you have *surgency* traits, with a high need for power,

you like to dominate and may not fit into a strong culture that does not reflect the values you have. You would tend to do well in a competitive-type culture that values individualism and high power.

Action plan: Would you like to work in an organization with a weak or a strong culture? What type of cultural values interest you?

_____

_____

_____

_____

Learning Outcome 11-8

Explain the relationship
between organizational
culture, climate, and
development.

THE RELATIONSHIP BETWEEN ORGANIZATIONAL CULTURE, CLIMATE, AND DEVELOPMENT

Organizational culture, climate, and development are all different, yet related. Climate refers to the shared values and assumptions of the *actual internal* environment, while culture refers to the values and assumptions of the *ideal* environment. Thus, culture informs climate. Often the concept of culture encompasses that of climate. However, in recent years, the concern with culture has increased, while research of the concept of climate has decreased.

Organizational development is commonly used as the vehicle to change culture or climate. Organizational development programs to improve performance tend to be wider in scope than culture or climate. Culture and climate changes can be a part of an extensive OD program addressing other issues as well.

/// **In the opening case,** NYCIC can overcome the resistance to change at Rider through a planned organizational development program involving team building. The OD program can be based on the change model. Through team building, NYCIC can change the culture and climate at Rider to be the same as that of NYCIC. ///

As we bring this chapter to a close, you should understand why people resist change and how to overcome it using a change model, know what organizational culture is and how we learn it, and be familiar with the dimensions of climate. You should also know five organizational development techniques and be able to improve performance through training people using the job instructional training model and the coaching model.

/ / / / R E V I E W / / / /

The chapter review is organized to help you master the nine learning outcomes for Chapter 11. First provide your own response to each learning outcome, and then check the summary provided to see how well you understand the material. Next, identify the final statement in each section as either true or false (T/F). Correct each false statement. Answers are given at the end of the chapter.

LO 11-1 Describe the four types of change.

The four types of changes are: (1) technology—machines and processes for creating products and services; (2) structure—organizational principles and departmentalization; (3) task—the way people perform their jobs; and (4) people—their knowledge and skill development.

Although automation is a technology change, it results in task and people changes. T F

LO 11-2 State why people resist change and how to overcome resistance.

Four major reasons people resist change are the desire to maintain the status quo, uncertainty, learning anxiety, and fear. To overcome resistance to change, one should first identify three major variables: (1) *intensity*—the strength of the intensity against change; (2) *source*—the source of resistance, whether facts, beliefs, or values; and (3) *focus*—the focus of resistance, which may be self, others, or the work environment. The 11 ways to overcome resistance to change include: (1) develop a positive climate for change; (2) encourage interest in improvement; (3) plan; (4) give facts; (5) clearly state why the change is needed and how it will affect employees; (6) create a win–win situation; (7) involve employees; (8) provide support; (9) stay calm; (10) avoid direct confrontation; and (11) use power and ethical politics.

The first reaction to rumors of change is resistance to the change. T F

LO 11-3 Explain how to use the Lussier change model when making changes.

To make a change, follow the steps in the Lussier change model: (1) define the change, (2) identify possible resistance to the change, (3) plan the change, (4) implement the change, and (5) control the change.

It is common to shorten the Lussier model to unfreezing, moving, and refreezing. T F

LO 11-4 Explain the two dimensions of an organization's culture.

The two dimensions of an organization's culture are strong and weak, and positive and negative. Organizations with strong cultures have clear values that are shared and enforced; those with weak cultures do not. Positive cultures contribute to effective performance; negative cultures hinder it.

Employees learn about the organization's culture through its heroes, stories, slogans, symbols, and ceremonies. T F

LO 11-5 Explain the seven dimensions of an organization's climate.

The seven dimensions of an organization's climate include: (1) structure—the degree of constraint on members; (2) responsibility—the degree of control over one's own job; (3) rewards—the degree of being rewarded for one's efforts and being punished appropriately; (4) warmth—the degree of satisfaction with human relations; (5) support—the degree of being helped by others and cooperation; (6) organizational identity and loyalty—the degree to which employees identify with the organization and feel loyalty toward it; and (7) risk—the degree to which risk-taking behavior is encouraged.

Morale is used to measure climate as being either high or low, based on the seven dimensions of climate. T F

LO 11-6 Describe five organizational development techniques.

Organizational development (OD) is the ongoing planned process of change to improve the organization's effectiveness in solving problems and achieving objectives. Five OD techniques are: (1) training and development, used to teach people their jobs; (2) performance appraisal, used to evaluate employee job performance; (3) survey feedback, which uses a questionnaire to gather data that are used as the basis for change; (4) force field analysis, used to diagram the current level of performance as well as the hindering and driving forces; and (5) team building, designed to help work groups operate more effectively.

Survey feedback can be part of other OD techniques, and it can also lead to the use of other techniques. T F

LO 11-7 List the steps in the coaching model.

The five steps of the coaching model are: (1) refer to past feedback, (2) describe current performance, (3) describe desired performance, (4) get a commitment to the change, and (5) follow up.

The coaching model is commonly used during the formal yearly performance review. T F

LO 11-8 Explain the relationship between organizational culture, climate, and development.

Climate refers to shared perceptions of intangible elements in the *actual internal* environment, while culture refers to the values and assumptions of the *ideal* environment. Often the concept of culture encompasses that of climate. Organizational development programs are commonly used to change culture and climate to improve performance.

As changes take place in the business environment, the organizational culture needs to change, and as culture changes, climate can deteriorate. T F

LO 11-9 Define the following 16 key terms.

Select one or more methods: (1) fill in the missing key terms for each definition given below from memory; (2) match the key terms from the end of the review with their definitions below; and/or (3) copy the key terms in order from the key terms list at the beginning of the chapter.

_____ are technological change, structural change, task change, and people change.

_____ are formal systems for collecting, processing, and disseminating the information necessary to aid managers in decision making.

_____ is the simplification or reduction of the human effort required to do a job.

_____ involves the variables of intensity, source, and focus and explains why people are reluctant to change.

_____ consists of the shared values and assumptions of how its members will behave.

_____ is the relatively enduring quality of the internal environment of the organization as perceived by its members.

_____ is a state of mind based on attitudes and satisfaction with the organization.

_____ is the ongoing planned process of change used as a means of improving the organization's effectiveness in solving problems and achieving its objectives.

_____ is the process of developing the necessary skills to perform the present job.

_____ is the process of developing the ability to perform both present and future jobs.

_____ refers to the ongoing process of evaluating employee job performance.

_____ is a term used to describe performance levels in the areas of quantity, quality, time, and cost.

The _____ involves these steps: (1) refer to past feedback, (2) describe current performance, (3) describe desired performance, (4) get a commitment to the change, and (5) follow up.

_____ is a technique that uses a questionnaire to gather data that are used as the basis for change.

_____ is a technique that diagrams the current level of performance, the hindering forces toward change, and the driving forces toward change.

_____ is a technique designed to help work groups operate more effectively.

KEY TERMS

automation   367
coaching model   379
development   377
force field analysis   380
management information
  systems (MIS)   367

morale   375
organizational climate   375
organizational
  culture   374
organizational development
  (OD)   376

performance
  appraisal   377
resistance to
  change   370
standards   378
survey feedback   379

team building   380
training   377
types of change   367

COMMUNICATION SKILLS

The following critical thinking questions can be used for class discussion and/or as written assignments to develop communication skills. Be sure to give complete explanations for all questions.

1. Which single technology change has had the largest effect on your behavior?

2. Of the four reasons people resist change, which one do you think is the most common?

3. Of the 11 methods for overcoming resistance to change, which one do you think is the best?

4. Describe your college's culture. Is it strong or weak? Are there any good slogans and/or symbols that help convey your college's culture? Give at least one new way (slogans/symbols, etc.) to promote your college's culture.

5. Using the seven dimensions of climate, describe your college's climate. Rate the morale of students as high or low, explaining your answer in detail.

6. One of the purposes of college is to train and develop students for future careers. How would you rate your overall college education?

7. A professor's job is to facilitate student learning, evaluate student performance, and assign grades. Do you believe your learning performance is evaluated effectively? How could it be improved?

8. Do your professors use consistent standards in terms of the work they require in their courses and the performance appraisal grades they give? Or do some professors require more work than others? Do some give lots of As while others give lots of lower grades? Is this diversity in work requirements and performance appraisal positive or negative? Why does it exist?

9. Which OD technique(s) can be used to improve consistency among professors in terms of work assignments and performance appraisals at your college? Which of the four reasons for resistance would be the dominant reason for faculty resistance to such a change? How would you rate the intensity, focus, and source of their resistance (see Exhibit 11.3, Resistance Matrix)?

10. Can a multinational company have one organizational culture, or does it need to have different cultures based on its business unit in each country?

CASE   / / /   **Elon Musk—Blazing New Frontiers**

Elon Musk is only the second person in Silicon Valley history to create three companies with the market capitalization of more than $1 billion: PayPal, SpaceX, and Tesla Motors. His visionary pursuits are in space and alternative energy technologies. He is a one-of-a-kind entrepreneur who plays by a different set of rules than the average individual. As Mathew DeBord of Business Insider describes him, "Musk is a survivalist and a strategic genius... he's on the offensive, defining Tesla's future before it can be defined by forces he can't control."[i]

The distinctive personality traits of Elon Musk are perseverance, high-risk orientation, creative thinker, self-belief, and hard work (he works 80–100 hours per week). [ii] He is not only an entrepreneur but also an inventor, innovator, and engineer. According to a *New York Times* review of his biography, "Mr. Musk is about as close as we have to early industrial titans like Henry Ford, Andrew Carnegie and John D. Rockefeller."[iii] He is truly an agent of change.

Elon Musk is a strategic visionary. At the center of his thought process is the question of what changes would have the greatest impact on the future of humanity. Musk zeroed in on two global trends: the transition to renewable energy sources and space exploration. A review of his portfolio of businesses shows that he prefers to invest in the projects that are aligned with these trends and that are changing how we live our lives. His vision is to make the planet cleaner and more sustainable for future generations using innovative technologies. He is also looking beyond earth to more distant planets like Mars, which he is aiming to explore and hopefully colonize someday.

In 2004, Musk along with his friend Martin Eberhard cofounded Tesla Motors, an electric car company. The first Tesla to hit the market in 2006 was priced at $100,000, and yet the interest from prospective buyers lining up to put in orders was unprecedented. In 2008, the U.S. economy was in a deep recession and Tesla nearly went bankrupt. Only a last-minute cash infusion saved the company from filing for Chapter 11 bankruptcy. Musk invested $40 million into Tesla and loaned the company another $40 million of his own money to save the company. He was also named CEO of Tesla that same year. He describes 2008 as the worst year of his life, as Tesla kept losing money and SpaceX was having trouble launching its Falcon 1 rocket. By 2009, Musk was living off personal loans just to survive.

In 2010, the Energy Department, in keeping with the Obama administration's efforts to support alternative energy related businesses, gave Tesla hundreds of millions in low-interest loans. Also, the company went public, becoming the first American automaker since Ford's debut in 1956 to do so. Tesla was soon generating positive headlines, including a glowing review for the Model S from *Consumer Reports*. The company's shares rose, and Tesla paid off the loans from the Energy Department. Musk has never forgotten what it was like to live on the edge of total collapse and an end to everything.

In early 2002, Musk founded Space Exploration Technologies or SpaceX. His long-term vision is to send people to Mars, which he regards as essential for the survival of humanity. In the immediate term, Musk's mission is to use SpaceX as the transport vehicle to supply the Space Station. SpaceX almost went out of business. The first three launchings of the company's small Falcon 1 rocket failed. One more failure, Mr. Musk said, and he would have run out of money. The fourth launch succeeded. In 2008, NASA awarded SpaceX a cargo contract, and in 2012, the company launched the first private spacecraft to dock with the International Space Station.

In 2015, SpaceX attracted new investors. Google along with Fidelity invested $1 billion in SpaceX. More good news came when the company landed a $1.5 billion NASA contract to fly astronauts to the space station. By the end of 2015, SpaceX had made 24 launches resupplying the International Space Station, setting many records along the way. Most recently, the SpaceX Falcon 9 made the first successful water landing of a reusable orbital rocket.[iv] SpaceX is aiming to land one of its capsules on the surface of Mars by 2018.

SolarCity Corporation is a provider of energy services. The company provides solar power systems for homes, businesses, and governments. SolarCity's value proposition of a cost efficient and environmentally friendly energy source aligns with Elon Musk's values. Elon Musk started at SolarCity as a shareholder. In 2003, he invested $10 million in the company. Skeptics and critiques questioned his decision. They argued that solar electric power will never turn into an efficient business model and thus not a good investment. However, Elon Musk saw it differently. He was taking the long view. In 2012, SolarCity went public and its shares jumped from $8 to $11.79. In 2014, Tesla's board approved a takeover bid for SolarCity. A year later (2015), the stock share price was $57.60 and the total market cap was $5.53 billion. Now Elon Musk owns 25 percent of SolarCity. This move by Elon and Tesla changed the perception of some of the same critiques who wanted nothing to do with Solarcity. There was a mind-set shift: "If the creator of SpaceX and Tesla Motors bets on that technology, then it means that there is truly something to it. The Wall Street community even came up with a term for this phenomenon and called it The Musk Effect."[v]

Between space rockets, electric cars, solar batteries, research into killer robots, and the billions he has made along the way, Musk is a real-life Tony Stark—which is why the studio used him as reference for the *Iron Man* movie.

Go to the Internet: To learn more about Elon Musk and his companies, visit his Web site at https://elonmusknews.org/ or conduct an Internet search for Elon Musk.

Support your answers to the following questions with specific information from the case and text or with information from the web or another source.

1. The chapter discusses four types of change that organizations typically encounter—technological, structural, task, and people change. Which of these is Elon Musk dealing with at his companies?

2. The case describes Elon Musk as a "change agent." Do you agree with this description? Explain.

3. Based on your reading from the text on the concept of organizational culture, in your opinion, what type of culture would you expect to find in any of Mr. Musk's companies, be it Tesla, SpaceX, or SolarCity?

4. According to the text, change can take one of two forms: incremental or discontinuous. In your opinion, are the changes pursued by Elon Musk incremental, discontinuous, or both? Explain your answer.

Cumulative Questions

5. Effective problem solving and decision-making are key traits of effective leaders (Chapter 10). Would you agree that these are traits that Elon Musk possesses? Explain your answer.

6. Being able to influence others' behavior is one of the cornerstones of effective leadership (Chapter 8). Effective leaders are able to influence followers and others to do or see things their way. In your opinion, how closely does this apply to Elon Musk?

Case Exercise and Role-Play

Preparation: In 2016, Tesla promised delivery of 80,000 cars and only managed to ship 76,230 to consumers. With the mass-market Model 3 just a year away, small production delays will have a more significant effect on sales figures. Assume that two of Tesla's VPs have been in conflict over who is to blame for the miss, each pointing the finger at the other. Elon Musk has decided to assign the task to your class for resolution. Chapter 5 discusses five conflict management styles: forcing, avoiding, accommodating, compromising, and collaborating. He wants your class to attempt to resolve this conflict using each of the conflict management styles.

In-Class Groups: The instructor organizes students into small teams and assigns each team one of the conflict management styles. Team members should not know in advance which style was assigned to the other teams. Each team should then develop a plan for resolving the conflict using their assigned style or approach. Each team is allowed to determine the exact nature of the conflict for their own purposes. Write out a script for dramatizing or playing out your plan.

Role Play: Each team presents a skit of their plan to the rest of the class. The class will determine which conflict management style the team is employing in its plan. A discussion should follow on the strengths and weaknesses of each style.

OBJECTIVE CASE / / / Supervisor Carl's Change

Carl was an employee at Benson's Corporation. He applied for a supervisor job at Hedges Inc. and got the job. Carl wanted to do a good job. He observed the employees at work to determine ways to improve productivity. Within a week Carl thought of a way.

On Friday afternoon he called the employees together. Carl told them that starting on Monday he wanted them to change the steps they followed when assembling the product. He demonstrated the new steps a few times and asked if everyone understood them. There were no questions. So Carl said, "Great. Start them on Monday, first thing."

On Monday Carl was in his office for about an hour doing the week's scheduling. When he came out to the shop floor, he realized that no one was following the new procedure he had shown them on Friday. Carl called the crew together and asked why no one was following the new steps.

LAMONT: We've done it this way for years and it works fine.

JENNIFER: We are all underpaid for this boring job. Why should we improve productivity? (*Several others nod.*)

LING: On Friday at the tavern we were talking about the change, and we agreed that we are not getting paid more, so why should we produce more?

Answer the following questions. Then in the space between the questions, state why you selected that answer.

_____ 1. The type of change Carl introduced was:

    a. task change   *c.* technological change

    b. structural change   *d.* people change

_____ 2. Using Exhibit 11.3, identify Jennifer's major resistance (box) to change.

    a. 1   *c.* 3   *e.* 5   *g.* 7   *i.* 9

    b. 2   *d.* 4   *f.* 6   *h.* 8

_____ 3. Using Exhibit 11.3, identify Ling's major resistance (box) to change.

    a. 1   *c.* 3   *e.* 5   *g.* 7   *i.* 9

    b. 2   *d.* 4   *f.* 6   *h.* 8

_____ 4. When implementing his change, Carl should have used which major step to overcome resistance to change?

    a. develop a positive climate   *e.* stay calm

    b. encourage interest in improvement   *f.* avoid direct confrontation

    c. plan   *g.* involve employees

    d. give facts   *h.* provide support

_____ 5. Lamont's response was a(n) _____ resistance statement.

    a. blocker   *d.* reverser   *g.* politician

    b. roller   *e.* sidestepper   *h.* traditionalist

    c. staller   *f.* threatener   *i.* assaulter

_____ 6. The best OD technique for Carl to have used for this change was:

    a. force field analysis   *d.* team building

    b. survey feedback   *e.* performance appraisal

    c. training

_____   7. Carl followed the Lussier change model steps.

        a. true   *b.* false

_____   8. Lamont's statement, assuming it is representative of the group, indicates a _____ organizational culture.

        a. positive   *b.* negative

_____   9. Based on Jennifer's response, it appears organizational climate and morale are:

        a. positive   *c.* in need of improvement

        b. neutral

_____   10. The conflict management style (Chapter 5) Carl should use in this situation (employees are not following the procedures) is:

        a. forcing   *c.* compromising   *e.* collaborating

        b. avoiding   *d.* accommodating

_____   11. Assume you had Carl's job. How would you have made the change?

Note: The meeting between Carl and the employees may be role-played in class.

SKILL-BUILDING EXERCISE 11-1

Coaching

Experience: In-class group exercise. You will coach, be coached, and observe coaching using the coaching model.

AACSB Competencies: Analytic skills, communication ability, and application of knowledge.

Objective: To develop your skill at improving performance through coaching.

Preparation: You should have read and understood the chapter.

Procedure 1 (2–4 minutes)

Break into groups of three. Make one or two groups of two, if necessary. Each member selects one of the three situations below in which to be the supervisor, and a different one in which to be the employee. You will role-play coaching and being coached.

BMV 11-1

1. Employee 1 is a clerical worker. He or she uses files, as do the other 10 employees. The employees all know that they are supposed to return the files when they are finished so that others can find them when they need them. Employees should have only one file out at a time. As the supervisor walks by, he or she notices that employee 1 has five files on his or her desk, and another employee is looking for one of the files. The supervisor thinks employee 1 will complain about the heavy workload as an excuse for having more than one file out at a time.

2. Employee 2 is a server in an ice cream shop. He or she knows that the tables should be cleaned up quickly after customers leave so that the new customers do not have to sit at a dirty table. It's a busy night. The supervisor looks at employee 2's tables and finds customers at two of them with dirty dishes. Employee 2 is socializing with some

friends at one of the tables. Employees are supposed to be friendly. Employee 2 will probably use this as an excuse for the dirty tables.

3. Employee 3 is an auto technician. All employees know that they are supposed to place a paper mat on the floor of each car to prevent the carpets from getting dirty. When the service supervisor got into a car employee 3 repaired, it did not have a mat, and there was grease on the carpet. Employee 3 does excellent work and will probably make reference to this fact when coached.

Procedure 2 (3–7 minutes)

Prepare for coaching to improve performance. Below, each group member writes a basic outline of what she or he will say when coaching employee 1, 2, or 3, following the steps in coaching below:

Step 1: Refer to past feedback.

Step 2: Describe current performance.

Step 3: Describe desired performance. (Don't forget to have the employee state why it is important.)

Step 4: Get a commitment to the change.

Step 5: Follow up.

Procedure 3 (5–8 minutes)

A. Role-play. The supervisor of employee 1, the clerical worker, coaches him or her (use the actual name of the group member role-playing employee 1) as planned. Talk; do not read your written plan. Employee 1, put yourself in the worker's position. You work hard; there is a lot of pressure to work fast. It's easier when you have more than one file. Refer to the workload while being coached. Both the supervisor and the employee will have to ad-lib.

The person not role-playing is the observer. He or she writes notes on the preparation steps in procedure 2 about what the supervisor did well and how he or she could improve.

B. Feedback. The observer leads a discussion on how well the supervisor coached the employee. It should be a discussion, not a lecture. Focus on what the supervisor did well and how he or she could improve. The employee should also give feedback on how he or she felt and what might have been more effective in getting him or her to change.

Do not go on to the next interview until told to do so. If you finish early, wait for the others to finish.

Procedure 4 (5-8 minutes)
Same as procedure 3, but change roles so that employee 2, the server, is coached. Employee 2 should make a comment about the importance of talking to customers to make them feel welcome. The job is not much fun if you can't talk to your friends.

Procedure 5 (5-8 minutes)
Same as procedure 3. But change roles so that employee 3, the auto technician, is coached. Employee 3 should comment on the excellent work he or she does.

Conclusion: The instructor leads a class discussion and/or makes concluding remarks.

Application (2-4 minutes):   What did I learn from this experience? How will I use this knowledge in the future?

Sharing: Volunteers give their answers to the application section.

/ / / SKILL-BUILDING EXERCISE 11-2 / / /

Improving the Quality of Student Life

Experience: Individual may share answers in groups or entire class, in class or online. You will experience being part of a quality circle to improve your college.

AACSB Competencies: Analytic skills, communication ability, teamwork, and application of knowledge.

Objective: To experience the quality circle approach to increasing the quality of student life at your college.

Preparation: Think of three things you would like to have improved at your college.

Procedure 1 (8-15 minutes)
Break into groups of five or six members, or as individuals or as a class. With groups, select a spokesperson. Your group is to come up with a list of the three to five most needed improvements at your college. Rank them in order of priority, from 1—most important to 5—least important. When you are finished, or the time is up, the spokesperson will write the ranking on the board.

Procedure 2 (3-10 minutes)
Options: A. The instructor determines the class's top three to five priorities for improvement.
            B. The class achieves consensus on the top three to five priorities for improvement.

Procedure 3 (5-10 minutes)
Each group selects a new spokesperson. The group develops solutions that will improve the quality of student life for the class's three to five priority areas.

Procedure 4 (5-20 minutes)
For the first-priority item, each spokesperson states the group's recommendation for improving the quality of student life. The class votes or comes to a consensus on the best way to solve the problem. Proceed to items 2 to 5 until you finish or time is up.

Discussion:

1. Are survey feedback and quality circles (as used in this exercise) effective ways to improve the quality of student life on campus?
2. Did the class consider that quality of student life is a balance between the college, the students, and society? Are your solutions going to benefit the college and society as well as the students?

Conclusion: The instructor may lead a class discussion and/or make concluding remarks.

Application (2–4 minutes):   What did I learn from this experience? How will I use this knowledge in the future?

Sharing: Volunteers give their answers to the application section.

/ / / SKILL-BUILDING EXERCISE 11-3 / / /

Team Building

Note: This exercise is designed for permanent class groups. Below is a survey feedback questionnaire. There are no right or wrong answers.

AACSB Competencies: Reflective thinking and analytic skills, communication ability, teamwork, and application of knowledge.

Objectives: To experience a team-building session and to improve your group's effectiveness.

Preparation: Check off the answer to each question as it applies to your class group. All questions have five choices.

Strongly Agree	Agree Somewhat	Neutral	Disagree Somewhat	Strongly Disagree

Conflict or Fight

1. Our group's atmosphere is friendly.

2. Our group has a relaxed (rather than tense) atmosphere.

3. Our group is very cooperative (rather than competitive).

4. Members feel free to say what they want.

5. There is much disagreement in our group.

6. Our group has problem people (silent member, talker, bored member, wanderer, arguer).

_____ | _____ | _____ | _____ | _____

Apathy

---

7. Our group is committed to its tasks (all members actively participate).

_____ | _____ | _____ | _____ | _____

8. Our group has good attendance.

_____ | _____ | _____ | _____ | _____

9. Group members come to class prepared (all assignments are complete).

_____ | _____ | _____ | _____ | _____

10. All members do their share of the work.

_____ | _____ | _____ | _____ | _____

11. Our group should consider firing a member for not attending and/or not doing his or her share of the work.

_____ | _____ | _____ | _____ | _____

Decision Making

---

12. Our group's decision-making ability is good.

_____ | _____ | _____ | _____ | _____

13. All members participate in making decisions.

_____ | _____ | _____ | _____ | _____

14. One or two members influence most decisions.

_____ | _____ | _____ | _____ | _____

15. Our group follows the five steps of the decision-making model (Chapter 10).
    Step 1: Define the problem.

_____ | _____ | _____ | _____ | _____

    Step 2: Set objectives and criteria.

_____ | _____ | _____ | _____ | _____

Step 3: Generate alternatives.

_____ | _____ | _____ | _____ | _____

Step 4: Analyze alternatives (rather than quickly agreeing on one) and select one.

_____ | _____ | _____ | _____ | _____

Step 5: Plan, implement the decision, and control.

_____ | _____ | _____ | _____ | _____

16. Our group uses the following ideas:

a. Members sit in a close circle.

_____ | _____ | _____ | _____ | _____

b. We determine the approach to the task before starting.

_____ | _____ | _____ | _____ | _____

c. Only one member speaks at a time, and everyone discusses the same question.

_____ | _____ | _____ | _____ | _____

d. Each person presents answers with specific reasons.

_____ | _____ | _____ | _____ | _____

e. We rotate order for presenting answers.

_____ | _____ | _____ | _____ | _____

f. We listen to others rather than rehearse our own answers.

_____ | _____ | _____ | _____ | _____

g. We eliminate choices not selected by group members.

_____ | _____ | _____ | _____ | _____

h. All members defend their answers (when they believe they are correct) rather than changing to avoid discussion or conflict, or to get the task over with.

_____ | _____ | _____ | _____ | _____

i. We identify the answers remaining and reach a consensus on one (no voting).

_____ | _____ | _____ | _____ | _____

j. We come back to controversial questions.

_____ | _____ | _____ | _____ | _____

17. We make a list of other relevant questions.

18. Our group uses the _____ conflict management style.

    a. forcing   *c.* avoiding   *e.* collaborating

    b. accommodating   *d.* compromising

19. Our group _____ resolve its conflicts in a manner that is satisfactory to all.

    a. does   *b.* does not

In-Class Exercise

This exercise is designed for groups that have worked together for some time.

Procedure 1-a (5–30 minutes)

Climate Building

To develop a climate of trust, support, and openness, group members will learn more about each other through a discussion based on asking questions.

Rules:

1. Rotate; take turns asking questions.

2. You may refuse to answer a question as long as you did not ask it (or plan to).

3. You do not have to ask the questions in the order listed below.

4. You may ask your own questions. (Add them to the list.)

As an individual and before meeting with your group, review the questions below and place the name of one or more *group members* to whom you want to ask the question next to it. If you prefer to ask the entire group, put *group* next to the question. When everyone is ready, begin asking the questions.

1. How do you feel about this course? _____

2. How do you feel about this group? _____

3. How do you feel about me? _____

4. How do you think I feel about you? _____

5. What were your first impressions of me? _____

6. What do you like to do? _____

7. How committed to the group are you? _____

8. What do you like most about this course? _____

9. What do you plan to do after you graduate? _____

10. What do you want out of this course? _____

11. How do you react to deadlines? _____

12. Which member in the group are you the closest to? _____

13. Which member in the group do you know the least? _____

Other _____

When the instructor tells you to do so, get together with your group members and ask each other your questions.

Procedure 1-b (2–4 minutes)

Participants determine what they would like to accomplish during the team-building session. Below are six major goals of team building; you may add to them. Rank them according to your preference.

_____ To clarify the team's objectives.

_____ To identify areas for improving group performance.

_____ To develop team skills.

_____ To determine and utilize a preferred team style.

_____ To fully utilize the resources of each group member.

_____ To develop working relationships based on trust, honesty, and understanding.

_____ Your own goals (list them).

Procedure 1-c (3–6 minutes)

Participants share their answers to procedure 1-b. The group can come to a consensus on its goal(s) if it wants to.

Procedure 2 (3–8 minutes)

Process and Structure:　As a team, discuss strengths and weaknesses in group process (how the group works and communicates). Below, list norms (do's and don'ts) for the group to abide by.

Procedure 3-a (10–15 minutes)

Problem Identification:　As a team, answer the survey feedback questionnaire. Place a *G* in the box to signify the team's answer. Don't rush; fully discuss the issues and how and why they affect the group.

Procedure 3-b (3–7 minutes)

Based on the above information, list 8 to 10 ways the team could improve its performance.

Procedure 3-c (3–6 minutes)

Prioritize the above list (1 = most important).

Procedure 4 (6–10 minutes)

Problem Solving:　Take the top-priority item. Then do the following:

1. Define the problem.

2. Set objectives and criteria.

3. Generate alternatives.

4. Analyze alternatives and select one.

5. Develop an action plan for its implementation.

Follow the same five steps for each area of improvement until time is up. Try to cover at least three areas.

Procedure 5 (1 minute)

Training:　Team building often includes training to address the problems facing the group. Because training takes place during most exercises, we will not do any now. Remember that the agendas for team building vary and usually last for one or more full days, rather than one hour.

Procedure 6-a (3 minutes)
Closure Application:

1. I intend to implement the team's solutions. Why?

2. What did I learn from this experience?

3. How can I apply this knowledge in my daily life?

4. How can I apply this knowledge as a manager?

Procedure 6-b (1–3 minutes)
Group members summarize what has been accomplished and state what they will do (commit to) to improve the group.

Sharing (4–7 minutes):   A spokesperson from each team tells the class the group's top three areas for improvement. The instructor records them on the board.

/ / / SKILL-BUILDING EXERCISE 11-4 / / /

Developing New Habits

Experience: Individual may share habits in groups or entire class, in-class or online.

AACSB Competencies: Analytic and application of knowledge.

Objective: To develop and share new habits.

Preparation: Select one or more topics from this chapter that will help you improve your human relations. Develop a new habit following the guideline from Chapter 1, section Habits and Skill-Building Exercise 1-4, on how to develop your cure, routine, and reward-change.

Procedure (5–30 minutes)
Follow the procedures from Skill Builder 1-4.

1. T.
2. F. The first stage of the change process is denial that the change will occur.
3. F. Unfreezing, moving, and refreezing are the steps of the Lewin change model.
4. T.
5. T.
6. T.
7. F. The coaching model is an informal performance appraisal method commonly used between formal evaluations.
8. T.

/ / / NOTES / / /

1. S.H. Harrison and D.T. Wagner, "Spilling Outside the Box: The Effects of Individuals' Creative Behaviors at Work on Time Spent With Their Spouses at Home," *Academy of Management Journal* 59(3) (2016): 841–859.
2. A. Murray, "Robots Need Not Apply," *Fortune* (August 1, 2015): 8.
3. D.J. Harmon, S.E. Green, G.T. Goodnight, "A Model of Rhetorical Legitimation: The Structure of Communication and Cognition Underlying Institutional Maintenance and Change," *Academy of Management Review* 40(1) (2015): 76–95.
4. Q.N. Huy, K.G. Corley, and M.S. Kraatz, "From Support to Mutiny: Shifting Legitimacy Judgments and Emotional Reactions Impacting the Implementation of Radical Change," *Academy of Management Journal* 57(6) (2014): 1650–1680.
5. E. Van Oosten and K.E. Kram, "Coaching for Change," *Academy of Management Learning & Education* 13(2) (2014): 295–298.
6. A. Lockett, G. Currie, R. Finn, G. Martin, and J. Waring, "The Influence of Social Position on Sensemaking About Organizational Change," *Academy of Management Journal* 57(4) (2014): 1102–1129.
7. R.C. Liden, S.J. Wayne, C. Liao, J.D. Meuser, "Servant Leadership and Serving Culture: Influence on Individual and Unit Performance," *Academy of Management Journal* 57(5) (2014): 1434–1452.
8. D.J. Harmon, S.E. Green, G.T. Goodnight, "A Model of Rhetorical Legitimation: The Structure of Communication and Cognition Underlying Institutional Maintenance and Change," *Academy of Management Review* 40(1) (2015): 76–95.
9. D. Eng, "Does Joy Help You Sell?" *Fortune* (January 2016): 30.
10. T. Monahan, "Revving Up Your Corporate RMPs," *Fortune* (February 1, 2016): 43–44.
11. G.B. Shaw, "Disrupt This," *Entrepreneur* (November 2015): 10.
12. A. Murray, "Lessons From the Fortune 500," *Fortune* (June 15, 2016): 14.
13. J. Ankeny, "20/20 Visions," *Entrepreneur* (January 2015): 32–36.
14. J. Rodkin and F. Levy, "Recruiting Preferred Skills," *BusinessWeek* (April 13–19, 2015): 43.
15. Y. Zhang, D.A. Waldman, U.L. Han, and X.B. Li, "Paradoxical Leaders Behaviors in People Management: Antecedents and Consequences," *Academy of Management Journal* 58(2) (2015): 538–566.
16. G. Colvin, "Four Things That Worry Business," *Fortune* (October 27, 2014): 32.
17. M.M. Moya and J.L.M. Aleman, "The Differential Effect of Development Speed and Launching Speed on New Product Performance: An Analysis in SMEs," *Journal of Small Business Management* 54 no. 2 (2016): 750–770.
18. A. Murray, "What Do Millennials Want?" *Fortune* (March 15, 2015): 14.
19. A. Murray, "Robots Need Not Apply," *Fortune* (August 1, 2015): 8.

20. A. Page, "Google Creates Parent in Shake-Up," *The Wall Street Journal* (August 11, 2015): A1, A2.

21. E. Van Oosten and K. E. Kram, "Coaching for Change," *Academy of Management Learning & Education* 13, no. 2 (2014): 295–298.

22. A. Murray, "Robots Need Not Apply," *Fortune* (August 1, 2015): 8.

23. Staff, "Self-Improvement Through Data," *Fortune* (March 15, 2016): 28.

24. G. Colvin, "Humans Are Underrated," *Fortune* (August 1, 2015): 100–113.

25. C. Sandler, "Business Lessons From the Art of War," *Costco Connection* (May 2014): 15.

26. Y. Zhang, D.A. Waldman, U.L. Han, and X.B. Li, "Paradoxical Leaders Behaviors in People Management: Antecedents and Consequences," *Academy of Management Journal* 58(2) (2015): 538–566; Q.N. Huy, K.G. Corley, and M.S. Kraatz, "From Support to Mutiny: Shifting Legitimacy Judgments and Emotional Reactions Impacting the Implementation of Radical Change," *Academy of Management Journal* 57(6) (2014): 1650–1680.

27. Y. Zhang, D.A. Waldman, Y.L. Han, and X Li, "Paradoxical Leader Behaviors in People Management: Antecedents and Consequences," *Academy of Management Journal* 58(2) (2015): 538–566.

28. Y. Zhang, D.A. Waldman, Y.L. Han, and X Li, "Paradoxical Leader Behaviors in People Management: Antecedents and Consequences," *Academy of Management Journal* 58(2) (2015): 538–566.

29. C. Fuzzell, "We're All Connected—And That Will Change Everything," *The Wall Street Journal* (February 28, 2015): R8.

30. G. Colvin, "A CEO's Plan to Defy Disruption," *Fortune* (November 17, 2014): 36.

31. Staff, "Shifting Gears," *BusinessWeek* (January 11–17, 2016): 19.

32. A. Murray, "Robots Need Not Apply," *Fortune* (August 1, 2015): 8.

33. M. Ulman, "Margin Quote," *Fortune* (December 1, 2015): 28.

34. M. Rosenwald, "Bound by Habit," *BusinessWeek* (March 19–25, 2012): 106–107.

35. S. Bing, "How to Kill a Good Idea," *Fortune* (April 1, 2016): 116.

36. E. Bernstein, "The Smart Path to a Transparent Workplace," *The Wall Street Journal* (February 23, 2015): R5.

37. Ken Hultman, *The Path of Least Resistance* (Austin, TX: Learning Concepts, 1979).

38. Q.N. Huy, K.G. Corley, and M.S. Kraatz, "From Support to Mutiny: Shifting Legitimacy Judgments and Emotional Reactions Impacting the Implementation of Radical Change," *Academy of Management Journal* 57(6) (2014): 1650-1680.

39. A. Lockett, G. Currie, R. Finn, G. Martin, and J. Waring, "The Influence of Social Position on Sensemaking About Organizational Change," *Academy of Management Journal* 57(4) (2014): 1102–1129.

40. A. Laffer, answer to "How Would You Classify the Laffer Curve Today," *BusinessWeek* (December 8–14, 2014): 71.

41. E. Van Oosten and K.E. Kram, "Coaching for Change," *Academy of Management Learning & Education* 13(2) (2014): 295–298.

42. L. Tomkins and E. Ulus, "Is Narcissism Undermining Critical Reflection in Our Business Schools?" *Academy of Management Learning & Education* 14(4) (2015): 595–606.

43. Q.N. Huy, K.G. Corley, and M.S. Kraatz, "From Support to Mutiny: Shifting Legitimacy Judgments and Emotional Reactions Impacting the Implementation of Radical Change," *Academy of Management Journal* 57(6) (2014): 1650-1680.

44. S. Shellenbarger, "Believers in the Project Beard and Other Office Rituals," *Wall Street Journal* (June 28, 2013): D1, D2.

45. S. Bing, "How to Kill a Good Idea," *Fortune* (April 1, 2016): 116.

46. M. Rosenwald, "Bound by Habit," *BusinessWeek* (March 19–25, 2012): 106–107.

47. "Disrupt This," Adapted from a quote from G.B. Shaw, *Entrepreneur* (November 19, 2015): 10.

48. A. Murray, "We Are All Technology Companies Now," *Fortune* (December 1, 2015): 8.

49. M. Rosenwald, "Bound by Habit," *BusinessWeek* (March 19–25, 2012): 106-107.

50. A. Murray, "The Pinnacles and Pitfalls of Corporate Culture," *Fortune* (March 15, 2016): 14.

51. E.Y. Zhao and T.Wry, "Not All Inequality is Equal: Deconstructing rhe Societal Logic of Patriarchy to Understand Microfinance Lending to Women," *Academy of Management Journal* 59(6) (2016): 1994-2020.

52. A. Murray, "Robots Need Not Apply," *Fortune* (August 1, 2015): 8.

53. G. Obrien, "Safety First?" *Entrepreneur* (September 2015): 36.

54. M.L. Stallard, "Building a Culture of Connections," *Costco Connection* (July 2015): 112.

55. E. Eng, "Does Joy Help You Sell?" *Fortune* (January 1, 2016): 30.

56. R.C. Liden, S.J. Wayne, C. Liao, J.D. Meuser, "Servant Leadership and Serving Culture: Influence on Individual and Unit Performance," *Academy of Management Journal* 57(5) (2014): 1434-1452.

57. R. Durand and P.A. Kremp, "Classical Deviation: Organizational and Individual Status as Antecedents of Conformity," *Academy of Management Journal* 59(1) (2016): 65-89.

58. P. Lencioni, "Being Smart is Overrated," *INC.* (October 2014): 128.

59. IBM website, http://www.ibm.com, retrieved on June 20, 2017.

60. IBM website, http://www.ibm.com, retrieved on June 20, 2017.

61. W. Boston, H. Varnholt, and S. Sloat, "VW Says 'Culture' Flaw Led to Crisis," *The Wall Street Journal* (December 11, 2015): B1.

62. G. Bensinger and M. Farrell, "Uber's Backers Force Out Leader," *The Wall Street Journal* (June 22, 2017): A1, A6.

63. M. Priesemuth, M. Schminke, M.L. Ambrose, and R. Folger, "Abusive Supervision Climate: A Multiple-Mediation Model of Its Impact on Group Outcomes," *Academy of Management Journal* 57(5) (2014): 1513-1534.

64. M. Brettel, C. Chomik, and T.C. Flatten, "How Organizational Culture Influences Innovativeness, Proactiveness, and Risk-Taking: Forstering Entrepreneurial Orientation in SMEs," *Journal of Small Business Management* 53(4) (2015): 868-885.

65. M. Priesemuth, M. Schminke, M.L. Ambrose, and R. Folger, "Abusive Supervision Climate: A Multiple-Mediation Model of Its Impact on Group Outcomes," *Academy of Management Journal* 57(5) (2014): 1513-1534.

66. D. Eng, "Does Joy Help You Sell?" *Fortune* (January 2016): 30.

67. Q.N. Huy, K.G. Corley, and M.S. Kraatz, "From Support to Mutiny: Shifting Legitimacy Judgments and Emotional Reactions Impacting the Implementation of Radical Change," *Academy of Management Journal* 57(6) (2014): 1650-1680.

68. A. Lockett, G. Currie, R. Finn, G. Martin, and J. Waring, "The Influence of Social Position on Sensemaking About Organizational Change," *Academy of Management Journal* 57(4) (2014): 1102-1129.

69. Q.N. Huy, K.G. Corley, and M.S. Kraatz, "From Support to Mutiny: Shifting Legitimacy Judgments and Emotional Reactions Impacting the Implementation of Radical Change," *Academy of Management Journal* 57(6) (2014): 1650-1680.

70. L. Tomkins and E. Ulus, "Is Narcissism Undermining Critical Reflection in Our Business Schools?" *Academy of Management Learning & Education* 14(4) (2015): 595-606.

71. E. Van Oosten and K. E. Kram, "Coaching for Change," *Academy of Management Learning & Education* 13(2) (2014): 295-298.

72. L. Weber, "Nowhere to Hide for Dead Wood Workers," *The Wall Street Journal* (August 22, 2016): A1, A10.

73. S. Marikar, "Tools for Your Remote Team," *INC.* (December 2015 / January 2016): 88-89.

74. P.B. Whyman and A.I. Petrescu, "Workplace Flexibility Practices in SMEs Relationship with Performance via Redundancies, Absenteeism, and Financial Turnaround," *Journal of Small Business Management* 53(4) (2015): 1097-1126.

75. A.L. Kenworthy, "Introduction: Coaching and Positive Emotions—Exploring a Collection of Resources in the Health and Wellness Domain," *Academy of Management Learning & Education* 13(2) (2014): 290-292.

76. J. Koopman, K. Lana, and B.A. Scott, "Integrating the Bright and Dark Sides of OCB: A Daily Investigation of the Benefits and Costs of Helping Others," *Academy of Management Journal* 59(2) (2016): 414-435.

77. E. Van Oosten and K.E. Kram, "Coaching for Change," *Academy of Management Learning & Education* 13(2) (2014): 295-298.

78. R. King, "Companies Want to Know: How Do Workers Feel?" *The Wall Street Journal* (November 14, 2015): R3.

79. Margin note, "98 Percent," *INC.* (June 2016): 107.

80. Staff, "Tracking the Mood of Your Employees," *INC.* (June 2016): 128.

81. R.E. Silverman, "Are You Happy in Your Job? Bosses Push Weekly Surveys," *The Wall Street Journal* (December 3, 2014): B1, B4.

82. R.E. Silverman, "Are You Happy in Your Job? Bosses Push Weekly Surveys," *The Wall Street Journal* (December 3, 2014): B1, B4.

83. A. Von Tobel, "Where Money Meets Morale," *INC.* (April 2014): 48–49.

84. A. Lockett, G. Currie, R. Finn, G. Martin, and J. Waring, "The Influence of Social Position on Sensemaking About Organizational Change," *Academy of Management Journal* 57(4) (2014): 1102–1129.

85. R.G. Lord, J.E. Dinh, E.L. Hoffman, "A Quantum Approach to Time and Organizational Change," *Academy of Management Review* 40(2) (2015): 263–290.

i. Elon Musk just made his smartest strategic move ever for Tesla by Matthew DeBord. Business Insider, Apr. 3, 2017 - (http://www.businessinsider.com/elon-musk-strategic-move-tesla-tencent-2017-3), accessed June 20, 2017.

ii. Elon Musk just made his smartest strategic move ever for Tesla by Matthew DeBord. *Business Insider*, Apr. 3, 2017 (http://www.businessinsider.com/elon-musk-strategic-move-tesla-tencent-2017-3), accessed June 20, 2017.

iii. Elon Musk, a Serial Entrepreneur. The New York Times, 2017 - https://www.nytimes.com/interactive/2016/07/25 /business/elon-musks-companies-spacex-telsa-solarcity.html?_r=0 , accessed June 20, 2017.

iv. The incredible story of Elon Musk, from getting bullied in school to the most interesting man in tech by Matt Weinberger, Business Insider Aug. 1, 2016 - (http://www.businessinsider.com/the-rise-of-elon-musk-2016-7), accessed June 20, 2017.

v. Elon Musk Biography: Success Story of The 21st Century Innovator. (2017). Astrum People website. Retrieved 1:29, Apr 21, 2017, from https://astrumpeople.com/elon-musk-biography/ accessed June 20, 2017.

Valuing Diversity and Inclusion Globally

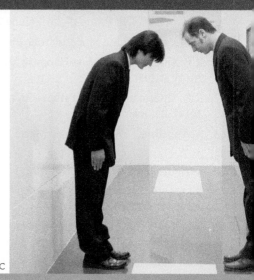

©Andersen Ross/Blend Images LLC

LEARNING OUTCOMES

After completing this chapter, you should be able to:

LO 12-1 Define prejudice and discrimination and state common areas of employment discrimination in organizations.

LO 12-2 State seven major diversity laws enforced by the Equal Employment Opportunity Commission (EEOC).

LO 12-3 Identify what diversity questions employers can and cannot ask job applicants.

LO 12-4 List the eight diversity groups that are legally protected by the EEOC.

LO 12-5 Explain sexism in organizations and ways to overcome it.

LO 12-6 Compare and contrast the Hofstede national culture dimensions with Project GLOBE.

LO 12-7 Define the following 11 key terms (in order of appearance in the chapter):

prejudice
discrimination
minority
bona fide occupational
    qualification (BFOQ)
disability
sexual harassment

affirmative action (AA)
    programs
sexism
multinational company
    (MNC)
expatriates
complaint model

OPENING CASE WORK SCENARIO

/ / / A small group of white women at We-Haul was standing around the water cooler talking. These were some of the statements they made: "There is a lot of prejudice and discrimination against women around here." "There are more nonwhite faces around all the time." "We even have workers with disabilities now, and it's uncomfortable to look at them and work with them." "There are plenty of women in this company, but very few of them hold professional or managerial positions." "We women here in the offices make only a fraction of what the men in the shop are paid, and with the cutbacks, women are not getting into the higher-paying jobs." "My male supervisor recently made sexual advances, and since I shot him down, he's been giving me all the lousy jobs to do." "I've complained to management about these inequities, but nothing seems to change for us white women."

At the same time, a group of white men were also talking. Some of their statements were these: "There are more nonwhites and women around all the time." "Why can't these minorities learn to speak English like the rest of us?" "These people are always complaining about not being treated fairly, when they are." "We've promoted a few to management, even though they are not qualified." "They don't make good managers anyway." "The way management positions are being eliminated, it's tough enough to compete against the men, let alone these others."

Are these statements, which may have been said in many organizations, based on fact or fiction? Do these attitudes help or hurt the individuals, others, and the organization? You will learn about these and other valuing-diversity issues in this chapter. / / /

HOW DIVERSITY AFFECTS BEHAVIOR, HUMAN RELATIONS, HAPPINESS, AND PERFORMANCE

Let's begin by defining diversity and inclusion and why they are important to you and organizations. *Diversity* refers to the degree to which differences exist among members of a group or an organization. *Inclusion* is a practice of ensuring that all employees feel they belong as valued members of the organization. In a later section we will expand the differences between the concepts of diversity and inclusion.

Diverse people behave differently and have different human relations in organizations. However, when groups develop and oppose each other (white people versus people of color, male versus female, management versus labor), behavior and human relations can suffer, leading to lower performance. Recall from Chapter 10 that groups and organizations that value diversity generally outperform those that do not.

As we have been discussing throughout the book, human relations skill are critical to career success, and so is your ability to work well with a diversity of people. So if you can behave effectively with a global diversity of people, you will have good relationships that make you happy, and you will have higher levels of performance.

Diversity in America?

We all know that there is diversity in cultures throughout the world. But do you realize that there are people from all over the globe living in America? The United States has cultural diversity at home as a country populated by immigrants. With the popularity of an American education and higher incomes, you will likely interact with people on campus and at work from other countries.[1]

According to the U.S. Census Bureau,[2] the U.S. population continues to grow slowly, with more than 325 million people, and it is rapidly diversifying. The Caucasian population in America is decreasing, as there are more deaths than births. The population growth is coming from minorities, and Hispanics are now the largest minority group. Today, minority births are now the majority. One in 12 children (8 percent) born in the United States is the offspring of illegal immigrants, making those children U.S. citizens. By counties, back in 2015, almost one-third of the population was of color, and in 370 counties across 36 states, less than half are Caucasian.[3] By around 2040, less than half of the total U.S. population will be Caucasian. By 2060, Caucasians are estimated to be 43 percent of the population, and one in three people will be Hispanic. Clearly the United States is currently a diversified country, and the trend will continue.

Global Diversity

There are 7.4 billion people in the world, and less than 5 percent live in the United States, with more than a billion people in both China (1.37 billion) and India (1.27 billion),[4] making up around 36 percent of the world population. Globalization is one of the most vital business trends of the past 50 years,[5] as large corporations have employee from, and conduct business, all over the globe.[6] It is important to realize that no matter where you are, you live in and are affected by the global environment. Globalization may require you to interact effectively with people from many different cultural backgrounds:[7] as an "employee" with coworkers, suppliers, and customers; as a "customer" in a local store; as a "student" in college; and as a "consumer" you use and buy products from other countries.

Is Diversity and Inclusion Really Important?

Yes! Discrimination is illegal, and promoting diversity and inclusion creates equal opportunities for all employees, so it is the right thing to do.[8] But it is also beneficial to business. Why? There is a wealth of evidence that diversity helps teams and organizations perform better in terms of creativity, innovation, revenue, and profits.[9] The global white population is decreasing, making diversity an important topic within the workplace.[10]

There is a good chance that during your career you will work for companies that compete with global corporations and/or do business with foreign companies. You may work for a foreign-owned corporation in the United States, and you may have the opportunity to go abroad to work. If you haven't already done so, you most likely will interact with people from other countries.

Like it or not, diversity is going to continue to grow. And again, the better you can work with diverse people, the greater are your chances of having a successful business career. Avoid ethnocentrism and develop your global mind-set.[11]

Are you willing to commit to offering inclusion to diverse people into your homogeneous groups? You can develop your human relations skills by collaborating and learning more about people who are different from you. That is what this chapter is all about.

PREJUDICE AND DISCRIMINATION

Learning Outcome 12-1

Define prejudice and discrimination and state common areas of employment discrimination in organizations.

Although progress has been made, prejudice and discrimination still exist in the United States and globally as people get differential or unfavorable treatment,[12] which has negative consequences.[13] Discrimination is usually based on prejudice.

Prejudice

Prejudice is *the prejudgment of a person or situation based on attitudes.* As stated in Chapter 3, an attitude is a strong belief or feeling. We tend to have developed biases as to whom we like and dislike, and we tend to like people who are like us. We are more attached to our agenda and biases than we realize, because it is often subconscious.[14] We tend to view the world from our own self-focused view with an *ethnocentric* view of our group being the best or right.[15] We need to break away from our prejudices that cloud our position.[16] Like organizations, we need to develop a global mind-set.[17]

If someone were to ask you, "Are you prejudiced?" you would probably say no. However, we all tend to prejudge people and situations. Recall that Chapter 2 discussed first impressions and the four-minute barrier. In four minutes you don't have time to get to know someone, yet you make assumptions that affect your behavior. Chapter 3 defined stereotyping as the process of generalizing the behavior of all members of a group.

Your prejudice is often based on your stereotype of the group.[18] To prejudge or stereotype a person or situation in and of itself is not harmful; we all tend to do this. Although prejudice is not always negative, if you discriminate based on your prejudice, you may cause harm to yourself and other parties.

Discrimination

Discrimination is *behavior for or against a person or situation.* To illustrate the difference between prejudice and discrimination, assume that Joan is a supervisor and is in the process of hiring a new employee. There are two qualified candidates: Dwane, an African American male, and Ted, a white male. Joan is white and has a more positive attitude toward whites. She stereotypes blacks as being not as productive on the job as whites. But she also believes that blacks deserve a break. Joan has a few options.

Joan can discriminate based on her prejudice and hire Ted. In the same manner, Joan could be prejudiced for Dwane and against Ted.

Joan can be aware of her prejudices, yet try not to let them influence her decision. She can interview both candidates and select the person who is best qualified for the job. Then there would be no discrimination. This option is legal and is the generally recommended approach because it is not discrimination.

/// **In the opening case,** the statements in the opening case reflect negative prejudice attitudes that can lead to discrimination. /// Discrimination has negative consequences at the individual, team, and organizational levels.[19]

WORK APPLICATION 12-1

Discuss a situation in which you were discriminated against for some reason.

Prejudice or Discrimination   AS 12-1

Identify each statement made by a white male as an example of:

A. Prejudice   B. Discrimination

_____ 1. "I select Latasha as my partner. Helen, you team up with Husain for this assignment."

_____ 2. "Kendra, what is wrong with you? Is it your time of the month?"

_____ 3. "I do not want to work the night shift. I refuse to, and you can't force me to change."

_____ 4. "Shawn hired a good-looking, blonde administrative assistant. I bet she's not very bright."

_____ 5. "Here comes that tall black Mookie; I'll bet he will talk about basketball."

Common Areas of Employment Discrimination

Historically, the five areas where discrimination in employment is most common are:

WORK APPLICATION 12-2

Cite an example of employment discrimination in recruitment, selection, compensation, upward mobility, or evaluation, preferably from an organization for which you work or have worked.

- *Recruitment.* People who hire employees fail to actively recruit people from certain groups to apply for jobs within their organization.

- *Selection.* People who select candidates from the recruited applicants fail to hire people from certain groups.

- *Compensation.* White males make more money than other groups.

- *Upward mobility.* Race and gender are significant influences on advancement.

- *Evaluation.* When organizations do not base evaluations on actual job performance, discrimination in compensation and upward mobility occur.

WORK APPLICATION 12-3

Have you, or has anyone you know, gone through diversity training? If yes, describe the program.

Be aware of the human tendency to prejudge and stereotype others, and avoid discriminating based on your prejudices. To help employees overcome prejudice and discrimination, organizations are providing diversity and inclusion training. Later in this chapter, we will discuss how organizations are helping their diverse workforces.

EQUAL EMPLOYMENT OPPORTUNITY FOR ALL

Because of discrimination, the government passed laws to make it illegal to discriminate against minorities and others, and to help them get jobs and advance. So, in this section, let's explain EEO and the laws it enforces,

Laws Affecting Employment Opportunity

Learning Outcome 12-2

State seven major diversity laws enforced by the Equal Employment Opportunity Commission (EEOC).

You are aware that an organization cannot discriminate against a minority. Who is legally considered a minority? The U.S. Equal Employment Opportunity Commission (EEOC) **minority** list includes *Hispanics, Asians, African Americans, Native Americans, and Alaska Natives.*

However, the EEOC protects more than minorities. "The EEOC is responsible for enforcing federal laws that make it illegal to discriminate against a job applicant or an employee because of the person's race, color, religion, sex (including pregnancy, gender identity, and sexual orientation), national origin, age (40 or older), disability or genetic information. It is also illegal to discriminate against a person because the person complained about discrimination, filed a charge of discrimination, or participated in an employment discrimination investigation or lawsuit."[20]

EXHIBIT 12.1 | Federal Employment Laws

Law	Description
Equal Pay Act of 1963	Requires men and women to be paid the same for equal work.
Title VII of the Civil Rights Act of 1964	Prohibits discrimination in all areas of the employment relationship. Enforced through the EEOC established 1972.
Age Discrimination in Employment Act of 1967	Prohibits age discrimination against people older than 40 and restricts mandatory retirement.
Pregnancy Discrimination Act of 1978	Prohibits discrimination against women because of pregnancy, childbirth, or related medical conditions.
Americans with Disabilities Act of 1990	Requires employers to provide "reasonable accommodations" to allow employees with disabilities to work.
Family and Medical Leave Act of 1993	Requires employers (with 50 or more employees) to provide up to 12 weeks unpaid leave for family (childbirth, adoption, eldercare) or medical reasons.
Genetic Information Act of 2008	Prohibits the use of genetic information in employment

Communication Skills
Refer to CS Question 2.

The EEOC has 53 offices across the nation. For more information visit its Web site (www.eeoc.gov) that provides information on employee rights. Some of the major laws and regulations affecting employment are presented in Exhibit 12.1 in chronological order.

Companies suspected of violating any of these laws may be investigated by the EEOC or become defendants in class-action or specific lawsuits. Clearly, it is important for you to be familiar with the laws that protect you from discrimination (your legal rights), and you should also know your organization's diversity guidelines.

Learning Outcome 12-3

Identify what diversity questions employers can and cannot ask job applicants.

Preemployment Inquiries

On the application blank and during interviews, no member of an organization can legally ask discriminatory questions. The two major rules of thumb to follow are:

1. Every question that is asked should be job related. When developing questions, you should have a purpose for using the information. Only ask legal questions you plan to use in your selection process.

2. Any general question that you ask should be asked of all candidates.

Below, we will discuss what you can (lawful information you can use to disqualify candidates) and cannot (prohibited information you cannot use to disqualify candidates) ask during a job interview. Prohibited information is information that does not relate to a bona fide occupational qualification for the job. A **bona fide occupational qualification (BFOQ)** *allows discrimination on the basis of religion, sex, or national origin where it is reasonably necessary to normal operation of a particular enterprise.* In an example of a BFOQ upheld by its supreme court, the state of Alabama required all guards in male maximum-security correctional facilities to be male. People believing that this requirement was sexual discrimination took it to court. The supreme court upheld the male sex requirement on the grounds that 20 percent of the inmates were convicted of sex offenses, and this creates an excessive threat to the security of female guards.

For a list of topics or questions that can and cannot be asked, see Exhibit 12.2.

WORK APPLICATION 12-4

Have you, or has anyone you know, been asked an illegal discriminatory question during the hiring process? If yes, identify the question(s).

EXHIBIT 12.2 | Preemployment Inquiries

Name

Can Ask: Current legal name and whether the candidate has ever worked under a different name.

Cannot Ask: Maiden name or whether the person has changed his or her name.

Address

Can Ask: Current residence and length of residence.

Cannot Ask: If the candidate owns or rents his or her home, unless it is a BFOQ.

Age

Can Ask: If the candidate is between specific age groups, 21 to 70, to meet job specifications. If hired, can you furnish proof of age? For example, an employee must be 21 to serve alcoholic beverages.

Cannot Ask: How old are you? Cannot ask to see a birth certificate. Do not ask an older person how much longer he or she plans to work before retiring.

Sex

Can Ask: Only if sex is a BFOQ.

Cannot Ask: If it is not a BFOQ. To be sure not to violate sexual harassment laws, do not ask questions or make comments remotely considered flirtatious.

Marital and Family Status

Can Ask: If the candidate can meet the work schedule and whether the candidate has activities, responsibilities, or commitments that may hinder meeting attendance requirements. The same question(s) should be asked of both sexes.

Cannot Ask: To state marital status. Do not ask any questions regarding children or other family issues.

National Origin, Citizenship, Race, or Color

Can Ask: If the candidate is legally eligible to work in the United States, and if this can be proved if hired.

Cannot Ask: To identify national origin, citizenship, race, or color (or that of parents and other relatives).

Language

Can Ask: To list languages the candidate speaks and/or writes fluently. Candidates may be asked if they speak and/or write a specific language if it is a BFOQ.

Cannot Ask: The language spoken off the job, or how the applicant learned the language.

Convictions

Can Ask: If the candidate has been convicted of a felony and other information if the felony is job related.

Cannot Ask: If the candidate has ever been arrested (an arrest does not prove guilt). Do not ask for information regarding a conviction that is not job related.

Height and Weight

Can Ask: If the candidate meets or exceeds BFOQ height and/or weight requirements, and if it can be proved if hired.

Cannot Ask: The candidate's height or weight if it is not a BFOQ.

Religion

Can Ask: If the candidate is of a specific religion when it is a BFOQ. Candidates can be asked whether they will be able to meet the work schedules or will have anticipated absences.

Cannot Ask: Religious preference, affiliations, or denominations.

Credit Ratings or Garnishments

Can Ask: If it is a BFOQ.

Cannot Ask: If it is not a BFOQ.

Education and Work Experience

Can Ask: For information that is job related.

Cannot Ask: For information that is not job related.

References

Can Ask: For the names of people willing to provide references or for the names of people who suggested the candidate apply for the job.

Cannot Ask: For a reference from a religious leader.

Military

Can Ask: For information on education and experience gained that relates to the job.

Cannot Ask: Dates and conditions of discharge. Do not ask about draft classification or other eligibility for military service, National Guard, or reserve units. Do not ask about experience in foreign armed services.

Organizations

Can Ask: To list membership in job-related organizations, such as union or professional or trade associations.

Cannot Ask: To identify membership in any non-job-related organization that would indicate race, religion, and so on.

Disabilities/AIDS

Can Ask: If the candidate has any disabilities that would prevent him or her from performing the specific job.

Cannot Ask: For information that is not job-related. In states where people with AIDS are protected under discrimination laws, you should not ask if the candidate has AIDS.

Legal Questions   AS 12-2

Identify the five questions below as:

A. Legal (can be asked)   B. Illegal (cannot be asked)

_____ 6. "Can you prove you are legally eligible to work?"

_____ 7. "What is your mother tongue or the major language you use?"

_____ 8. "Are you married or single?"

_____ 9. "Are you a member of the Teamsters Union?"

_____ 10. "Have you been arrested for stealing on the job?"

DIMENSIONS OF DIVERSITY AND INCLUSION

Learning Outcome 12-4

List the eight diversity groups that are legally protected by the EEOC.

The previous section presented the laws affecting minorities and other protected groups. This section discusses some of the legally protected in more detail, especially gender, and we discuss the progression going from affirmative action to valuing diversity to inclusion.

Diversity Types and Discrimination

Here is the EEO list of eight groups that can't be discriminated against in the sequence listed on the EEOC Web site with its definitions:[21]

- **Race** discrimination involves treating someone (applicants or employees) unfavorably because they are of a certain race or because of personal characteristics associated with race (such as hair texture, skin color, or certain facial features).

- **Color** discrimination involves treating someone unfavorably because of skin color complexion.

- **Religious** discrimination involves treating a person unfavorably because of his or her religious beliefs. The law protects not only people who belong to traditional, organized religions but also others who have sincerely held religious, ethical, or moral beliefs.

- **Sex** (including pregnancy, gender identity, and sexual orientation) discrimination involves treating someone unfavorably because of that person's sex. We will discuss sex in more detail in the gender, sexual orientation, and sexual harassment section.

- **National origin** discrimination involves treating people unfavorably because they are from a particular country or part of the world, because of ethnicity or accent, or because they appear to be of a certain ethnic background (even if they are not).

- **Age** discrimination involves treating some 40 or older less favorably because of his or her age.

- **Disability** discrimination involves unfavorable treatment because someone has a disability. People with a **disability** have *significant physical, mental, or emotional limitations.* The law requires an employer to provide "reasonable accommodation" to an employee or job applicant with a disability without undue hardship on the employer. For more information on the ADA, visit its Web site (www.ada.gov).

Communication Skills
Refer to CS Question 3.

- **Genetic information** discrimination prohibits getting and using information about a disability of an individual through genetic tests and the genetic tests of an individual's family members, as well as information about the manifestation of a disease or disorder in an individual's family members (i.e., family medical history).

Communication Skills
Refer to CS Question 4.

- **Others**. Although not listed by EEOC, there are many other types of diversity at work, and everyone should be included and treated fairly. Here are some of the other types of diversity: education, skills, personality, attractiveness, appearance, marital status, weight, height, family, socioeconomic status, and so on.

/ / / **Self-Assessment Exercise 12-1** / / /

Implicit Association Test (IAT)

To complete this diversity self-assessment, go to the Project Implicit website at https://implicit.harvard.edu/implicit/demo. From there, under "Project Impact Social Attitudes," you can select a "language/nation" and hit "Go"; then click "I wish to proceed" and select one of 14 tests to take, based on our diversity types with a breakdown of several races, and other tests; or your professor will select the one for you to complete. Simply follow the instructions at the site to complete a test and get interpretations of your attitudes and beliefs about the diversity group you selected. It's free, and you can take as many as you want to.

WORK APPLICATION 12-5

Have you or anyone you know been discriminated against? If so, explain the discrimination.

Gender, Sexual Orientation, and Sexual Harassment

Here we provide more detail related to diversity by sex and sexual harassment.

Gender   The terms *sex* and *gender* are often used interchangeably, but they are different. *Sex* distinguishes biological males and females. *Gender* does include sex, but it also includes common behavioral characteristics, language used to describe gender, clothes, and other things used to refer to the genders, which are learned through social interactions generalized by sex, often referred to as *masculine* (he's tough; he's good at math; he's a construction worker or doctor) and *feminine* (she's nurturing; she's good at English; she's a secretary or nurse). There are also negative terms used to pressure people into conforming to gender stereotypes (he's a sissy; she's a tomboy). We need to be aware of gender stereotypes and not judge others because they don't fit into our view of how males and females should look and act.

Sexual Orientation (LGBT+)   Sexual orientation is intended to emphasize a diversity of sexuality and gender identity-based cultures. LGBT refers to people who are lesbian, gay, bisexual, and transgender. There are other diversities including Q = for those who identify as Queer or are Questioning their sexual identity (LGBTQ); I = to include Intersex people (LBGTI); and A = A sexual (LBGTA). Putting them all together would be LGBTQIA. So, LGBT+ is becoming more common.

Many religions teach that we should not judge others. We need to include LGBT+ in our groups by avoiding homophobia (an aversion to homosexuals) and bias and discrimination based on a person's sexual orientation if we want to get along well with all people. The gender- and sexual orientation–neutral terms replacing *husband* or *wife* and *boyfriend* or *girlfriend* are *significant other* and *partner*. In some school systems, they no longer refer to the children as boys and girls.

Sexual Harassment   According to the EEOC, harassment and sexual harassment are sex discrimination that includes unwelcome sexual advances, requests for sexual favors, and other verbal or physical conduct of a sexual nature. This conduct constitutes sexual harassment when it explicitly or implicitly affects an individual's employment, unreasonably interferes with an individual's work performance, or creates an intimidating, hostile, or offensive work environment.[22]

To keep it simple, for our purposes, **sexual harassment** is *any unwelcomed behavior of a sexual nature*. There are two major types. *Quid pro quo* sexual harassment occurs when sexual consent affects job outcomes, such as getting a job or assignment or promotion, or keeping one's job. *Hostile work environment* sexual harassment occurs when unwelcomed sexual behavior creates an intimidating and offensive workplace for anyone. By far the most common offense is men sexually harassing women, but women also are the harasser, and same-sex harassment also takes place at work.

Dealing with Sexual Harassment   Most large firms have written policies defining sexual harassment and how to report violations.[23] When people find themselves in a sexual harassment situation, they often feel overwhelmed, confused, afraid, alone, and unable to find the words to confront the harasser. If the behavior is very serious, such as touching in private areas of the body, you may want to report the first offense. But if it is less obvious that sexual harassment was intentional, a warning may be given before reporting the offense. Some warning responses to the harasser, which can be revised to suit the offense, are as follows:

WORK APPLICATION 12-6

Have you, or has anyone you know, been sexually harassed? If so, describe the situation(s) (use language acceptable to everyone).

"I am uncomfortable when you touch me. Don't do it again or I will report you for sexual harassment."
"It is inappropriate for you to show me sexually graphic material. Don't do it again."
"I am uncomfortable with off-color jokes. Don't tell one to me again or I will report you for sexual harassment."

If the behavior is repeated, report the offense to your boss and/or some other authority in the organization. If the people in authority do not take suitable action to stop the harassment, you may take the complaint to the EEOC online at www.eeoc.gov.

/// **In the opening case,** a woman complained about a male supervisor making sexual advances. Do you think that was sexual harassment? ///

APPLICATION SITUATIONS / / /

Sexual Harassment   AS 12-3

Identify whether each behavior described below is:

A. Sexual harassment   B. Not sexual harassment

_____ 11. For the first time, Pete tells Kara she is sexy and he'd like to take her out on a date.

_____ 12. Jelena tells José he will have to go to a motel with her if he wants to get the job.

_____ 13. Latasha's legs are sticking out into the walkway. As Sam goes by, he steps over them and says, "Nice legs."

_____ 14. For the third time, after being politely told no, Aamir says to Jean, "You have a real nice (*fill in the missing sexual words for yourself*). Why don't you and I go out on a date?"

_____ 15. Antwan puts his hand on Lisa's shoulder as he talks to her and they are both comfortable.

Communication Skills
Refer to CS Question 6.

Dating Coworkers   Romance does change behavior and human relations at work. Sexuality at work detracts from productivity.[24] Employee dating is rarely a private matter, especially between a supervisor and subordinate. Romance can be disruptive to other employees, triggering questions about fairness and favoritism, and can disrupt team cohesiveness. A competent female can be stereotyped as simply the "boss's girlfriend."[25] Romance by both genders sometimes leads to sexual harassment once the relationship ends.[26] Inappropriate relationships can topple careers, and allegations of unwanted attention or favoritism can cost companies millions and land businesses in the headlines for all the wrong reasons, such as **Uber**.[27] To help avoid these problems, many companies have workplace-relationships policies.[27] If you work for a company with such policies, be sure to follow the rules, and you may want to think twice about a romantic relationship at work.

WORK APPLICATION 12-7

What are your views on dating coworkers? Have you dated coworkers, or will you date coworkers in the future?

Political Correctness   *Political correctness* is being careful not to offend or slight anyone with our behavior. Obviously, being politically incorrect hurts human relations, so we need to be careful how we behave. For example, you might think a joke about women, minorities, or any group of people is funny, but members of these groups can be offended in hearing the joke. Also, some people are very protective of political correctness, so even though the joke is not about an individual's group, he or she will still be offended and may report your behavior to management as being inappropriate. So you are better off not telling the joke, or other such behavior. Or at least ask the person if he or she wants to hear the joke before telling it. This also goes for texting and e-mailing words and pictures that could be considered offensive.

From Affirmative Action to Valuing Diversity to Inclusion

Communication Skills
Refer to CS Question 1.

Affirmative action (AA) as a concept was created in the 1960s through a series of policies at the presidential and legislative levels in the United States; but except in a few circumstances, AA does not have the effect of law.[28] For our purposes, **affirmative action (AA) programs** are *planned, special efforts to recruit, hire, and promote women and members of minority groups.* Over the years, support for AA declined as firms valued diversity.

Valuing diversity is broader in scope than AA as it doesn't focus simply on not discriminating against diverse groups and helping only some of them, sometimes at the expense of others through reverse discrimination. But valuing diversity still has a focus on accepting differences and on helping certain groups. as a means of improving organizational performance.

WORK APPLICATION 12-8

Describe affirmative action, valuing diversity, or inclusion at an organization, preferably one for which you work or have worked.

Most organizations have now moved from to valuing diversity to inclusion[29]—valuing all types of diversity, which includes integrating everyone to work together while maintaining their differences.[30] *Inclusion* is a practice of ensuring that all employees feel they belong as valued members of the organization: a feeling of being respected, being valued for who you are; feeling a level of supportive energy and commitment from others so that everyone can do their best work.[31] Many organizations are now using both terms or replacing the word *diversity* with the term *inclusion* to better reflect the shift.

SEXISM, RACISM, AND WORK AND FAMILY BALANCE

Learning Outcome 12-5

Explain sexism in organizations and ways to overcome it.

Sex and race are essential and pervasive sources of diversity at work, but there are inequalities.[32] **Sexism** refers to *discrimination based on sex. Racism* is discrimination based on race, which we also call minorities. Sexism and racism limit the opportunities of both women and men to choose the lifestyles and careers that best suit their abilities and interests. When women and minorities get stuck, so do organizations.[33]

This section examines women and minorities and advancement, overcoming sexism and racism, and changing gender roles and work and family balance. Before reading on, determine your attitude toward women and minorities at work by completing Self-Assessment Exercise 12-2.

/ / / **Self-Assessment Exercise 12-2** / / /

Attitudes about Women and Minorities Advancing

Be honest in this self-assessment, as your assessment will not be accurate if you aren't. Also, you should not be asked to share your score with others, and you may refuse to share your answers and score.

Answer the 10 questions below twice: once related to women and the other related to minorities. Place the number 1, 2, 3, 4, or 5 on the line before each statement for women and at the end of the statement for minorities.

Agree				Disagree
5	4	3	2	1

(*continued*)

/ / / **Self-Assessment Exercise 12-2** / / / (*continued*)

Women		Minorities
_____	1. Women/Minorities lack motivation to get ahead.	1. _____
_____	2. Women/Minorities lack the education necessary to get ahead.	2. _____
_____	3. Women/Minorities working has caused rising unemployment among white men.	3. _____
_____	4. Women/Minorities are not strong enough or emotionally stable enough to succeed in high-pressure jobs.	4. _____
_____	5. Women/Minorities have a lower commitment to work than white men.	5. _____
_____	6. Women/Minorities are too emotional to be effective managers.	6. _____
_____	7. Women/Minorities who are managers have difficulty in situations calling for quick and precise decisions.	7. _____
_____	8. Women/Minorities have a higher turnover rate than white men.	8. _____
_____	9. Women/Minorities are out of work more often than white men.	9. _____
_____	10. Women/Minorities have less interest in advancing than white men.	10. _____
_____ Total		Total _____

Women—To determine your attitude score toward women, add up the total of your 10 answers on the lines before each statement and place it on the total line and on the following continuum.

Positive attitude   10 -------- 20 -------- 30 -------- 40 -------- 50   Negative attitude

Minorities—To determine your attitude score toward minorities, add up the total of your 10 answers on the lines after each statement and place it on the total line and on the following continuum.

Positive attitude   10 -------- 20 -------- 30 -------- 40 -------- 50   Negative attitude

Each statement is a negative attitude about women and minorities at work. However, research has shown all of these statements to be false; they are considered myths. Such statements stereotype women and minorities unfairly and prevent them from getting jobs and advancing in organizations through gaining salary increases and promotions. Thus, part of managing diversity and diversity training is to help overcome these negative attitudes to provide equal opportunities for *all*.

Women and Minorities in the Workforce and Advancement

Let's define some terms and discuss the discrimination faced at work.

Sex, Minorities, and Discrimination   When we use the word *women*, we include minorities or females of color. When we use the word *minorities*, we include both sexes. Although both women and minorities face discrimination, minorities usually face even greater discrimination than white women.

We use *women in the workforce* as opposed to *working women*. Women who elect to work as homemakers make a great contribution to society. Unfortunately, these women are not commonly referred to as *working women* because they are not rewarded monetarily for their work. However, every female homemaker is a working woman.

Women make up about half of the U.S. workforce, but they are only paid 80 cents on the dollar compared to men.[34] Women make less than men in all but two of the occupations for which the United States publishes data,[35] and highly educated women fare worst of all.[36] In highly prestigious jobs, women perform equally but are rewarded significantly lower than men in terms of salary, bonuses, and promotions.[37]

The Glass Ceiling   Although research supports equality of the sexes, research also reports that it is more difficult for women and minorities to advance.[38] Despite modest progress, women are underrepresented at every management level, and it starts with entry level

Communication Skills
Refer to CS Question 7.

employees. Men are 30 percent more likely than women counterparts to be promoted into a managerial role.[39] Women are at a disadvantage when it comes to getting promoted to high-level management positions, especially women with children.[40]

The barriers to upward mobility in organizations are commonly called the *glass ceiling*—the invisible barrier that prevents women and minorities from advancing to the top jobs in organizations. Women CEOs face extra pressures and scrutiny as they must overcome the glass ceiling.[41] In the 2016 ***Fortune 500*** listing of the largest American corporations, only 21 CEOs (4 percent) were women, down from 24 in 2015.[42] At the current pace of progress, we are more than 100 years away from gender equality in the C-suite.[43]

WORK APPLICATION 12-9

How do you feel about having a female and/or a minority boss? Why?

Women   **AS 12-4**

Identify each of the following statements about women as:

A. Fact   B. Myth

_____ 16. "Men make better managers than women."

_____ 17. "Women generally work because they need the money and want to have a career."

_____ 18. "Male managers are generally more committed to their jobs than female managers."

_____ 19. "Female managers are generally viewed as more caring for the individual subordinate than male managers."

_____ 20. "About one out of every three managers is female."

Overcoming Sexism and Racism

Here we discuss reasons for sexism and racism and how to overcome them so that everyone has equal opportunity in inclusive organizations.

The Negative Effect of TV, Movies, Music, and Games   Culture promotes differences in males and females, and they will always be different, but their roles can and should be equal and promote positive self-concepts. Children learn these values and the media have an influence. Unfortunately, TV and movies promote sexism and depict for children a version of society in which females are stereotyped and hypersexualized.[44] Some songs and music videos also portray females as hypersexualized, and in some video games violence against females is part of the game: "The more hours of TV and other media a girl watches, the fewer options she believes she has in life. And the more hours a boy watches and plays sexist video games, the more sexist his views become."[45] Pornography in all forms also tends to degrade women and portray them as simply sex objections. How much time do you spend watching, listening to, and playing sexist and racist media?

WORK APPLICATION 12-10

Do you agree that the media contribute to negative sexist and racist stereotypes? Should the government do anything to help prevent it? If so, what?

Communication Skills
Refer to CS Question 8.

Sexist and Racist Language, Stereotype, and Behavior and Overcoming Them   Men and women should avoid using sexist and racist language. Sexist words such as *mailman* and *salesman* should be replaced with nonsexist terms such as *letter carrier* and *salesperson*. In written communication, the use of *he or she* is appropriate, but don't overuse it. Use neutral language and plurals—*supervisors* rather than *the supervisor*, which tends to end up needing a *he or she* as writing progresses. Avoid racist terms and jokes. Unfortunately, the media sometimes use sexist and racial stereotypes that affect attitudes toward sex and race.

Call people by name, rather than by sexist and racist terms. Working women are not girls and should not be called *girls* because this word is used to describe children, not grown women. Working men are not boys, so avoid such sexist terms.

Skill-Building Exercise 12-1 develops this skill.

Skill-Building Exercise 12-2 develops this skill.

Be wary of swearing in the workplace; it is preferable not to use such language. What is really gained through swearing? You can offend someone. Are you impressed by people who swear? Are people who do not swear pressured to do so at work?

If anyone uses language that offends you or others, assertively state your feelings about the words used. Many times, people do not use sexist and racist language intentionally and will not use it if they are requested not to. If it continues, however, report the harassment, as harassment is a form of EEOC discrimination.

Gender stereotypes about leadership tend to result in gender discrimination against women in management. Men are expected to possess qualities associated with leadership, such of assertiveness, confidence, and independence. Women are expected to be helpful, nurturing, and kind. Women who behave with aggressive male leadership characteristics are often penalized and criticized as being bossy.[46] **COO Sheryl Sandberg,** who is given much of the credit for growing **Facebook**, says that America and the world are not comfortable with women in leadership roles.[47] To get more women into management roles, we have to address our culture's discomfort with female and minority leadership.[48] How did you score on Self-Assessment 12-2?

Many working men are becoming more sensitive to sexism because they have wives and daughters in the workforce for whom they want equal opportunities. Exhibit 12.3 illustrates negative sexist stereotyping that needs to be eliminated. Such stereotypes and myths about women managers are a barrier to women's breaking the glass ceiling.

As discussed, women and minorities have biases and barriers to advancing that need to be overcome. One thing women and minorities can do is to be assertive (Chapter 5) and ask for raises and promotions. Having mentors and role models helps people advance, so women and minorities can be more assertive about asking for mentors. Effective networking also helps with advancement, so women and minorities can develop their networking skills (Chapter 9), and mentors can help get them into networks that can help them advance. Many organizations are developing programs to help women and minorities advance.

To be inclusive, we all need to *empathize* with everyone—put ourselves in their shoes and try to understand where they are coming from, and accept them for who they are rather than reject them or try to make them into who we want them to be—just like us.[49] One thing we should realize is that "our way" of interacting with others (or doing things) is not the only right style (or way of doing things). Are you truly open to letting people who are different from you at work be who they are? Recall that being happy is about relationships, and

EXHIBIT 12.3 | A Sexist (Stereotypical) Way to Tell a Businessman from a Businesswoman

Man	Woman
A businessman is aggressive.	A businesswoman is pushy.
He is careful about details.	She's picky.
He loses his temper because he's so involved in his job.	She's bitchy.
He's depressed (or hung over), so everyone tiptoes past his office.	She's moody, so it must be her time of the month.
He follows through.	She doesn't know when to quit.
He's firm.	She's stubborn.
He makes wise judgments.	She reveals her prejudices.
He is a man of the world.	She's been around.
He isn't afraid to say what he thinks.	She's opinionated.
He exercises authority.	She's tyrannical.
He's discreet.	She's secretive.
He's a stern taskmaster.	She's difficult to work for.

firms are placing a top priority on recruiting employees who can work with and manage a diversity of employees.[50]

/// **In the opening case,** there is negative sexist talk. Can these men and women change their attitudes and learn to value diversity and inclusion? ///

How Families and Sex Roles Are Changing

American Families Are Changing   American family households continue to change. The traditional family in which the husband works and the wife does not work outside the home is down to only 2 in 10 homes (20 percent).[51] In fact, just over half of adults are married.[52] Although single-parent families are much more likely to live in poverty and to rely on government assistance, more than 50 percent of babies are now born to unwed mothers[53] and one in three children (33 percent) live in a fatherless home (and the rate is much higher for African-American families).[54] Families are also changing as the number of same-sex marriages continues to grow, and the number of these couples that are raising children is increasing.

Recall the total person approach, which holds that our personal family life affects our work life. If we can have a happier family life, we can also have a happier work life. We will discuss some important family issues that may help improve your family life. For example, people yearn to better understand what makes a successful marriage. So, start with Self-Assessment Exercise 12-3 to check your knowledge of the facts about marriage.

Communication Skills
Refer to CS Question 9.

/ / / **Self-Assessment Exercise 12-3** / / /

Your Marriage Knowledge

Answer each question true or false by circling its letter.

T F   1. People prefer a mate who matches them in education, class, religious background, ethnicity, and age.

T F   2. About half of marriages end in divorce.

T F   3. Living together before marriage decreases the chances of getting divorced.

T F   4. Having a baby before marriage increases the chances of getting divorced.

T F   5. Getting married young (under 18 years old vs. 25) increases the chances of getting divorced.

T F   6. Compared to people with some college, high school dropouts have a higher divorce rate.

T F   7. Most divorces happen in the seventh year—the seven-year itch.

T F   8. Couples who are very unhappy should get divorced so they will be happier in future years.

T F   9. People who go through the stress of divorce and its aftermath have health effects that may not show up until years later.

T F 10. Compared to those who are happily married, people who get divorced have more health problems and symptoms of depression.

T F 11. Compared to those who are happily married, people who get divorced smoke and drink more.

T F 12. Workaholics have a higher divorce rate than nonworkaholics.

T F 13. Arguing is helpful to a marriage.

T F 14. Couples don't need to agree and solve all their problems.

T F 15. Couples that go to church/pray together have a lower divorce rate than those that don't—the family that prays together stays together.

To determine your marriage knowledge, count the number of correct answers, using the answer key below, and place your score here:

Knowledgeable   15 14 13 12 11 10 9 8 7 6 5 4 3 2 1   Not Knowledgeable

Answers[55]

1. True. The statement that "like attracts like" is factual.

(continued)

/ / / Self-Assessment Exercise 12-3 / / / (continued)

2. True. Since the mid-1960s, around half of marriages in any given year end in divorce.

3. False. Couples who live together are 50 percent more likely to get divorced. They tend to have a renter's agreement attitude that makes them less committed to sticking around through the hard times that just about all marriages go through.

4. True. People who have babies before marriage (compared to seven months or more afterward) have a 24 percent higher divorce rate.

5. True. The divorce rate is 24 percent higher for people under 18 than for those 25 or more years old.

6. True. High school dropouts have a 13 percent higher divorce rate than those with some college.

7. False. Most divorces occur in the fourth year.

8. False. Of couples that divorced, 50 percent were "happy" five years later. Of couples that were "very unhappy" but stayed together, 80 percent were "happy" five years later.

9. True. Research supports the fact that stress from divorce can show up years later.

10. True. Compared to those who get divorced, research supports the fact that people who are happily married say they are in better health, have fewer chronic health problems, and retain greater mobility in middle age.

11. True. Research supports the fact that divorced people smoke and drink more than happily married people.

12. True. According to Workaholics Anonymous, divorce is common.

13. True. Open-minded fair fighting often leads to resolving conflicts in any relationship. So use your conflict skills (Chapter 5) in your personal relationships.

14. True. Most successful couples never agree and solve all their problems—they outlast them through the marital endurance ethics. Have you heard the expression, "You don't want to go there" in discussions? Avoiding some less important issues helps couples stay together.

15. True. The divorce rate for church/praying couples is significantly lower, and they have better health than those who don't pray.

Marriage and Family Agreements   There are benefits to being married, and marrying young,[56] including being healthier, being more likely to live longer, being satisfied with your job, having more social support, having more wealth and income, and being involved in fewer unhealthy or risky behaviors.[57] Before entering marriage, it is helpful to discuss and agree on career and family plans and the distribution of household and child-care responsibilities. In fact, some couples are creating family plan prenuptial agreements. These agreements are not legal documents; they are simply written lists of items relating to future family and work issues.

For help preparing for marriage, most religious organizations offer courses. Two other sources include Engaged Encounter (www.engagedencounter.org) and Prep/Enrich (www.prep-enrich.com). For help making a good marriage even better, there is Worldwide Marriage Encounter (www.wwme.org).

Although dual-career couples generally agree to split the household and child-care responsibilities evenly, most husbands often spend less time than their wives do in these areas.[58] In fact, fathers spend half as many hours per week in child care (7 vs. 14) and about two-thirds the amount of hours doing housework (10 vs. 18) as mothers; but fathers do spend more hours doing paid work.[59]

Communication Skills
Refer to CS Question 10.

WORK APPLICATION 12-11

How do you feel about marriage and having a family agreement?

Fathers' Roles Are Changing   In the old days, most fathers worked long hours and spent little time with their children. Today, research has clearly found that fathers are important in child care.[60] Although there are many reasons people are criminals, one contributing factor is the father's influence—or lack thereof. Most males in jail don't know who their father is or have no relationship with him.

Many of today's fathers are slowly decreasing identifying themselves solely by their work,[61] as they want to have it all and spend more time with their children; some are curbing their own career goals. More fathers routinely spend time with their children, including staying home to care for them when they are sick and taking them to visit the doctor. More fathers are also supporting their wives' careers, as some move and take lower-level jobs, even to the point of quitting their jobs and staying home with the children,[62] which is called the "gender flip." However, the father needs a positive self-concept to overcome the stereotype of the man being the bread winner and put up with the potential peer pressure to be at work in a paid job.[63]

Mothers' Roles Are Changing   In the old days, most mothers stayed home and took care of the children. Today, in 8 out of 10 families, moms work outside the home.[64] Mothers who do leave the labor force tend to go back as the children get older.

Work at Home or in the Labor Force?   People taking time off from the job to focus on home and family often sacrifice career opportunities. Thus, the decision to take a leave from work is often heart-wrenching, and although more fathers are staying home, it is more often the mother. Women tend to have two potential tracks. Those who stay on the job are on the career track, and those who leave and plan to return are on the "mommy track." Unfortunately, many mothers, and fathers, who decide, for whatever reason, to stay home with the kids or to work outside the home get pressured and are made to feel guilty for the role they have chosen.[65]

Why can't we all just let moms and dads make their own decisions about where they work? Let's all make an effort to stop judgmental questions and to stop making moms and dads feel guilty. Let's congratulate them and make them feel good about their choices and about themselves! Remember, valuing diversity is about letting people live their own lives. So let's also not pressure people to get married, to have children, or to have more or fewer children than they want, and to stay at home or work for pay.

For the stay-at-home mom, two good resources are www.athomemothers.com for motherhood lifestyle and www.familyandhome.org for tips on transitioning from work to home. For the mom in the workforce, two good resources are www.momsrefuge.com for information on juggling work and family and www.workingmom.com for strategies to simplify parenting.

Family Leave   More mothers and fathers are taking maternity leave under the *Family and Medical Leave Act of 1993* to spend up to 12 weeks at home with their newborns and adopted children (or a child, spouse, or parents with a serious health condition), but almost half of all workers who are eligible are unable to take time off because the can't afford to go without income.[66] To know your legal rights, and for help getting leave, contact the Labor Department Wage and Hour Division at www.wageandhour.dol.gov and the Job Survival Hotline, operated from 9 to 5 by the **National Association of Working Women**, at 1-800-522-0925 or www.9to5.org.

Parenting   Men tend to be rewarded for being parents, but women tend to be punished.[67] Parenting can be stressful; many new parents experience a drop in marital satisfaction after the baby is born, and the stress can spill over onto the baby and the job. If we can avoid stressful parenting, we can better manage the stress at home and work. Children's basic personalities are developed during the first five years of life and affect them all their lives. Here are two simple guidelines to help develop a child's personality with a positive self-concept:

- *Engage in sensitive play.* Touch and hold children, and talk in a way they can understand. Stimulate and encourage them by making appealing suggestions for play. Refrain from unnecessary criticism; the "give more praise than criticism" rule is even more important for children than for employees. Remember that they are children—tell them they are smart and capable, help them when they need it, and praise their accomplishments.

- *Develop a warm, loving bond.* Children need to feel secure and know they are loved; sensitive play and dad's roughhousing helps.[68] Reading to children during these preschool years is a form of play that also helps academic performance in school; the more reading and less TV watching, the better the academic performance. Reading when putting children to bed and talking about their day is a great way to bond. It is much easier to bond and stay close when the child is young than to develop a relationship when they are school-age.

WORK APPLICATION 12-12

How do you feel about your parents and about being a parent? If you are or become a parent, how will you be different from your parents?

Work-Life Balance   In analyzing the needs of the workforce, work–life balance is high on the list of issues facing both employers and employees.[69] Thus, work-life balance is a perpetually hot topic, with 40 percent of full-time Americans workers logging more than 50 work hours a week.[70] Connectivity technology advances such as the smartphone have blurred the line between the workday and off hours.[71] People say these technologies help them do the job, but they end up working more hours, as some 44 percent of Internet users regularly perform some job tasks outside of work.[72]

Although some men are getting more involved in child care,[73] and both men and women say balancing work and family life difficulties deters them from seeking executive roles,[74] work-life balance is especially difficult for women because of gender family responsibility inequity.[75] Family-friendly practices, such as onsite child care, relate to low absenteeism.[76]

Trying to maintain a balance between work and family is stressful for many people. Unfortunately, the stress can lead to nagging, which is a relationship and marriage killer. Remember, when you are in conflict nagging doesn't help; use the resolving conflict model from Chapter 5 so you can successfully resolve the conflict without hurting the relationship. For more information and help, visit the **Families and Work Institute** Web site www .familiesandwork.org.

GLOBAL CULTURAL DIVERSITY AND RELATIONS

Employees from different countries do not see the world in quite the same way because they come from different national cultures.[77] Understanding national culture is important because it affects nearly every aspect of human behavior,[78] making cultural sensitivity an important skill.[79] For the MNC, all of the workplace diversity exists, plus national culture as well.[80] Therefore, capability to manage such cultural diversity has become one of the most important skills for global leaders.[81] In this section, we discuss Hofstede's cultural dimensions and Project GLOBE.

National Culture and GLOBE

Learning Outcome 12-6

Compare and contrast the Hofstede national culture dimensions with Project GLOBE.

Hofstede National Cultural Diversity   Back in the 1970s and 1980s, Geert Hofstede surveyed more than 116,000 **IBM** employees in 40 countries about their work-related values. He identified five cultural dimensions on a continuum in which employees differ (countries in parentheses are very high or low compared to other countries on the dimension).[82] These cultural dimensions continue to be studied.[83]

- *Power distance inequality versus power equality*—Power distance being distributed between levels of management down to employees can be more accepted (Russia and China) or rejected as employees want to participate in decisions that affect them (Denmark and Sweden).

- *Individual versus collectivism*—Individualist cultures believe individuals should be self-sufficient with loyalty to themselves first and the group and company second (United States and Netherlands), whereas collectivism places the group and company first (Indonesia and China).

- *Assertiveness versus nurturing*—Assertive cultures are more aggressive and competitive, with a focus on achievement and material possessions (Japan and Germany), whereas nurturing cultures emphasize the importance of relationships, modesty, caring, and quality of life (Netherlands and France).

- *Uncertainty avoidance or acceptance*—Uncertainty-avoidance cultures like structure and security and are less likely to take risks (Japan and West Africa), whereas uncertainty-acceptance cultures are more comfortable dealing with the unknown and change and taking more risk (Hong Kong).

- *Long-term versus short-term orientation*—Long-term cultures look to the future and value thrift (China and Hong Kong), whereas short-term cultures focus on the past and present and immediate gratification (United States and Germany).

Project GLOBE As Hofstede's research became dated, GLOBE confirmed his dimensions are still valid today and extended and expanded his five dimensions into nine, including hundreds of companies and more countries. Project GLOBE stands for **Global Leadership and Organizational Behavior Effectiveness**, which is an ongoing cross-cultural investigation of leadership and national culture. The GLOBE research team uses data from hundreds of organizations in more than 62 countries to identify nine dimensions in which national cultures are diverse. See Exhibit 12.4 for a list of the dimensions with examples of country ratings.[84] Notice that some of the GLOBE dimensions have the same or similar names as Hofstede's five dimensions. As shown through cross-cultural comparisons, there are differences,[85] especially between East and West cultures.[86]

EXHIBIT 12.4 | GLOBE Dimensions

DIMENSION	LOW	MODERATE	HIGH
Assertiveness People are tough, confrontational, and competitive.	Switzerland New Zealand	Ireland Philippines	Spain United States
Future Orientation People plan, delaying immediate gratification to invest in the future.	Russia Argentina	Slovenia India United States	Netherlands Canada
Gender Differences People have great gender role differences.	Sweden Denmark United States	Brazil Italy	Egypt China
Uncertainty Avoidance People are uncomfortable with the unknown/ambiguity.	Bolivia Hungary	Mexico United States	Austria Germany
Power Distance People accept power inequality differences.	South Africa Netherlands United States	England France	Spain Thailand
Societal Collectivism Teamwork is encouraged (vs. individualism).	Greece Germany	Hong Kong United States	Japan Singapore
In-Group Collectivism People take pride in membership (family, team, organization).	Denmark New Zealand	Israel Japan United States	China Morocco
Performance Orientation People strive for improvement and excellence.	Russia Venezuela	England Sweden	Taiwan United States
Humane Orientation People are fair, caring, and kind to others.	Singapore Spain	United States Hong Kong	Indonesia Iceland

Source: Adapted from Javidon, M., and House, R. J., "Cultural Acumen for the Global Manager: Lessons from Project GLOBE," Organizational Dynamics, vol. 29, no. 4, 2001, 289–305.

APPLICATION SITUATIONS / / /

GLOBE Dimensions   AS 12-5

Identify the dimension of cultural diversity exemplified by each statement.

A. assertiveness

B. future orientation

C. gender differences

D. uncertainty avoidance

E. power distance

F. societal collectivism

G. in-group collectivism

H. performance orientation

I. humane orientation

_____ 21. The people in this country have one of the highest savings rates in the world.

_____ 22. Managers throughout organizations in this country focus on getting the job done through teamwork.

_____ 23. People in this country are thought to be difficult to negotiate with.

_____ 24. In some companies in this country, the women get the coffee for the male managers.

_____ 25. The people in this country follow the football/soccer team closely as they take great satisfaction from watching their team in the World Cup.

_____ 26. Managers place great importance on status symbols such as having the executive dining room, reserved parking spaces, and big offices.

_____ 27. Managers don't seem to care about the safety of their employees and provide poor working conditions.

_____ 28. Employees get nervous and stressed when they even hear that changes are coming.

_____ 29. Employees focus on constant small changes to make the products and processes better.

Cross-Cultural Relations

As you read these seven cultural diversities, realize that you are being presented with stereotyped generalizations. Observations from one country or culture are not necessarily applicable to others. The examples are not meant to judge "right" and "wrong" behavior. They are intended to illustrate cross-cultural differences that do affect human relations, and they may help you avoid cultural bloopers.

Diversity in Customs   The Japanese and Chinese place a high priority on human relations and teamwork. If you try to be an individual star, you will not be successful in Japan and China. However, the French do not place high importance on team effort. If you are very outspoken, you will be considered impolite in Japan. If you refuse to be involved in receiving and giving gifts, you will offend Japanese people. However, don't wrap gifts in white paper because white is a sign of death. Also, don't place chopsticks straight up and down; doing so imitates an offering to the dead. Many Japanese companies start the day with exercises and company cheers. If you do not actively participate, you will be an outsider.

Americans prefer to speak face-to-face from a greater distance than people of most other countries. If you back away or turn to the side from others, they may follow you and create a dance, and you may be considered cold and standoffish. During face-to-face communication, Latinos tend to touch each other more than Americans. Jumping when unexpectedly touched could create an embarrassing situation.

Gestures vary from country to country. For example, Americans prefer eye contact. However, the Japanese tend to look at the knot in a Japanese colleague's tie, or at the neck, to show respect. In Australia, making the "V" sign with the hand is considered an obscenity rather than a sign for victory.

Diversity in Attitudes toward Time   Americans typically view time as a valuable resource that is not to be wasted, and socializing is often considered a waste of time. However, it would be considered impolite to start a business meeting with Hispanics without engaging in a certain amount of relaxed small talk. The Chinese are more long-term oriented than Americans, and it takes many meetings to get to the point where they can trust you and do business.

There is also a difference between respecting deadlines and being on time. American and Swiss businesspeople usually expect you to be precisely on time for an appointment. However, in several countries, you could find yourself going to an appointment on time, only to be kept waiting. In some countries, if you call a meeting, most members will be late. If you get angry and yell, you could harm human relations.

Diversity in Work Ethics   The work ethic, viewing work as a central life interest and a desirable goal in life, varies around the world. Generally, the Japanese have a stronger work ethic than Americans and Europeans. With a strong work ethic, and the acceptance of automation, many Japanese plants are the most productive in the world. Although there is not much difference in work ethics between Americans and Europeans, Americans work more hours than Europeans.

Diversity in Pay   Americans, in general, are no longer the world's highest-paid employees. The Japanese and Europeans have caught up and earn as much as Americans. However, employees in Third World countries continue to be paid much less than employees in developed countries. That is a major reason so much of manufacturing is outsourced.

Pay systems also vary to meet employee values. One of the pay trends in the United States is pay for performance. However, some cultures value being paid for loyalty and following orders. Paying a salary works well in some countries, but not in others.

Diversity in Laws and Politics   The legal and political environment becomes increasingly complex as multinationals do business all over the world. Employee health and safety laws are generally more protective in developed countries than in Third World countries. Labor laws also vary widely from country to country. Western European nations offer good benefits, including a required four- to six-week vacation, paid holidays, and sick and family leave. Such differences change the actual labor cost per hour. It is also easier to terminate employees in some countries than in others.

In some countries, government structure and politicians are more stable than in others. A change in government can mean changes in business practices overnight.

Diversity in Ethics   When conducting global business, you may need to rethink business ethics. In the United States and some other countries, it is illegal to take and give bribes for doing business. However, in some countries, bribing is a standard practice of doing business. For example, an American businessperson complained to a local telephone company manager that the service person showed up and asked for a bribe, which was refused, so the telephone worker left without installing the phone. The businessperson was told by the telephone company manager that the matter would be investigated, for a fee (bribe). MNCs are working to develop global ethics codes.

Diversity in Participative Management   In Third World nations, employees need basic skills training and may not be capable of participating in management decisions. Some cultures, like those of Japan and the United States, value participation in management whereas others do not. In some cultures, employees simply want to be told what to do and are not concerned with enriched jobs.

Communication Skills
Refer to CS Question 11.

WORK APPLICATION 12-13

Have you experienced any cultural differences in human relations with others? If so, explain.

Management–labor relations vary globally. In France relations are more polarized than in the United States, whereas in Japan they are more cooperative. You should realize that management and human relations become more complex as styles change from country to country.

MANAGING DIVERSITY GLOBALLY

Because globalization is a major challenge, we have been discussing it in every chapter. In this section, we discuss multinational corporations and expatriates and managing diversity through inclusion.

Multinational Companies and Expatriates

Today even most small local companies compete with large multinational companies and conduct business with them. A **multinational company (MNC)** *conducts a large part of its business outside the country of its headquarters.* We live and work in the global village, with multicultural workplaces being managed by MNCs. As we move from a domestic to a global environment, global diversity becomes more complex and challenging. So for the MNC, all of the workplace diversity exists, plus national culture as well.

One thing we should realize though is that the demands of corporate leadership are changing how leaders manage in the global village.[87] Managers can't use simple Western techniques in some countries, like China, because they don't work in some cultures.[88] In fact, U.S. concepts are no longer held up as the dominant models, especially because managing is different in countries with government state ownership of enterprise (SOEs) businesses.[89] **Panasonic** blends Japanese tradition with American resourcefulness.[90] With globalization come complex human exchanges, making interpersonal skills and problem solving increasingly important.[91]

MNCs operate in virtually every major country. Complete Self-Assessment Exercise 13-4 to determine if you know in which country each MNC is headquartered.

With increasing globalization and workforce mobility, there is a chance that you will be sent to another country to conduct business.[92] It may be a brief visit, or it can be an

/ / / **Self-Assessment Exercise 12-4** / / /

MNC Country of Ownership

For each item, select the country of ownership. If your answer is the United States, check the USA column. If it's another country, write in the name of that country.

Company/Brand Product	USA	Other; List Country
1. Shell gasoline	_____	_____
2. Nestlé candy	_____	_____
3. Unilever Dove soap	_____	_____
4. Volvo cars	_____	_____
5. Barclays banking	_____	_____
6. Anheuser-Busch ImBev beer	_____	_____
7. AMC Theaters	_____	_____
8. Bayer aspirin	_____	_____
9. Kia cars	_____	_____
10. L'Oréal facial products	_____	_____
11. Samsung cell phones	_____	_____
12. Burger King fast food	_____	_____

(continued)

/ / / **Self-Assessment Exercise 12-4** / / / (*continued*)

Answers:

1. The Netherlands (Royal Dutch/Shell)
2. Switzerland (Nestlé Swiss Chocolate)
3. England
4. China acquired it
5. England
6. Belgium
7. China

8. Germany
9. South Korea
10. France
11. South Korea
12. Brazil

How many did you get correct? Place your score here _____.

---

international assignment as an expatriate. **Expatriates** are *people who live and work in a country other than their native country.*

Expatriates often experience culture shock, a state of confusion, and anxiety when they are first exposed to an unfamiliar culture.[93] There are changes with any move, but the changes compound tremendously when the move is to another country, especially between East and West.[94] Grasping the language and culture is difficult. Even with a common language accurate communication can be difficult.[95]

U.S. managers using traditional American management styles often fail in an overseas business culture because it is not effective in some countries.[96] You need to remember that you are the foreigner with the different customs and culture. Companies need to train expatriates in language, local culture, and local business practices so they can be successful globally. Diversity and inclusion training, and other methods, for everyone is our next topic.

WORK APPLICATION 12-14

What experience do you have with MNCs, such as competition, employment, purchasing?

Managing Diversity Through Inclusion

As discussed, we need to become more culturally competent,[97] but unfortunately, this is a weakness of many college graduates.[98] One more time, you need to get along with others,[99] and to do so you need to have a global mind-set.[100] In fact, companies seek employees who have intercultural competences,[101] and those with multicultural backgrounds.[102] Although effective management of diversity remains an elusive goal,[103] as it is difficult to get a diversity to employees to get along at work, here we discuss how organizations and you can improve your global diversity competency.

Diversity and Inclusion Policies and Practices   *Inclusion* must be part of managers' jobs starting with the CEO down.[104] Companies need active policies and practices to promote diversity. The policies and practices should promote a diversity climate of inclusion that is part of the *organizational culture* (Chapter 11). Records of diverse group hiring and promoting should be kept, and efforts should be made to help these groups succeed in the workplace, often called a *diversity audit.*

In promoting diversity, organizations need to follow all EEO laws, and have high standards and hire and advance the most qualified candidates. But given equal qualifications for the job, the diverse candidate (who in some cases will be a white male, such as nursing) can be given the job to support diversity. Make sure diverse employees have access to the same job training and other practices at work to have equal opportunities to advance. Also, have diversity training for all employees. Three practices that promote diversity follow.

Diversity Training   *Diversity training* teaches people how to get along better with diverse workers through inclusion. It helps diverse people to talk about bias and better understand each other by becoming aware of and more empathetic toward people different from themselves.[105] Training breaks down negative stereotypes and builds acceptance of differences, viewing people as individuals, and realizing that diversity improves teamwork and organizational performance. Training can last for hours or days. Most large companies offer diversity training.

Mentoring   No one gets to the top alone.[106] *Mentors* are higher-level managers who prepare high-potential people for advancement. Mentoring is a process that enhances management skills, encourages diversity, and improves productivity. Having mentors who are willing to work with you to develop your knowledge, abilities, and skills can help you in both your professional and your personal life. Mentoring can be between people in different companies or at the same company, formal or informal. Most large corporations offer several internally developed formal mentoring programs for its employees.[107]

Mentoring is especially recommended for women and minorities who want to advance to top-level positions because it can help them break into the "good old boy" networks that often make the selections for these jobs.[108]

Some MNCs today, such as **IBM**, are turning to online mentoring programs for global employee mentoring. With *e-mentoring,* employees typically fill out a profile, and the program's software matches them up with a mentor. Instead of getting together in person, the two meet and communicate electronically, such as via e-mail and **Skype**.

WORK APPLICATION 12-15

Give examples of how an organization promotes diversity and inclusion, preferably one you work(ed) for.

Network Diversity Groups   *Network diversity groups* have employees throughout the organization form a diverse group whose members share information about how to succeed in the company and how to help the company succeed, including **Cadence**.[109] **American Express** has been using these groups for over 22 years. Network diversity groups promote equality.[110]

HANDLING COMPLAINTS

The EEOC's job is to handle complaints that are brought to it, many of which result in lawsuits. Effective management can be measured by the lack of complaints. We should all strive to meet the goal of human relations by creating a win–win situation for everyone. However, no matter how hard you try, complaints will arise covering a range of topics, which may include discrimination. Use the open-door policy and let people feel as though they can come to you with a complaint. It is much better to get complaints out in the open and try to resolve them than to have people complaining to everyone else about you.

You can use the complaint model to help you resolve employee complaints in either a union or nonunion organization. The **complaint model** involves these steps: *(1) listen to the complaint and paraphrase it; (2) have the complainer recommend a solution; (3) schedule time to get all the facts and/or make a decision; (4) develop and implement a plan, and follow up.* Each step is discussed below.

Step 1: Listen to the Complaint and Paraphrase It   You need to understand what the other person needs,[111] so when you handle a complaint, don't just quickly dismiss it,[112] you need to be responsive.[113] First, if you are talking, they are hearing you, and it's not about you.[114] You have to listen to their case.[115]

Listen to the full story without interruptions, and paraphrase it to ensure accuracy. When someone comes to you with a complaint, try not to take it personally; even the best supervisors have to deal with complaints. Do not become defensive. Never talk down to the complainer, minimize the complaint, or try to talk the person out of the complaint.

Step 2: Have the Complainer Recommend a Solution   Ask the complainer to recommend a solution that will resolve the complaint. Requesting a solution does not mean that you have to implement it. In some cases, the recommended solution may not solve the problem. Or the solution may not be fair to others. In such cases, you should let the person know that the solution is not possible and explain why.

Step 3: Schedule Time to Get All the Facts and/or Make a Decision   Since complaints often involve other people, you may find it necessary to check records or to talk to others. It is often

Skill-Building Exercises 12-3 develops this skill.

WORK APPLICATION 12-16

Identify a complaint you brought to a supervisor. If you have never complained, interview someone who has. State the complaint and identify the steps in the complaint model the supervisor did and/or did not follow.

helpful to talk to your boss or your peers, who may have had a similar complaint; they may be able to offer you some good advice on how best to resolve the complaint. Even when you have all the facts, it is usually advisable to take some time to weigh the facts before making a decision.

Generally, the more quickly a complaint is resolved, the fewer the negative side effects. Too many supervisors simply say, "I'll get back to you on this," without specifying a time period. This response is very frustrating to the employee. Some supervisors are purposely vague because they have no intention of getting back to the employee. They are hoping the employee will forget about the complaint. This tactic may get the employee to stop complaining, but it may also cause morale, productivity, and turnover problems.

Step 4: Develop and Implement a Plan, and Follow Up   After getting all the necessary facts and advice from others, you should develop a plan. The plan may be developed by simply using the complainer's recommended solution. Work with the employee to find an alternative or present their own plan. You need to address the current complaint, but you usually also need to take action so that it doesn't happen again.[116]

Model 12.1 lists the four steps in the complaint model.

/// **In the opening case,** both the men and the women are complaining to each other about each other. A woman states that she did complain to management, but nothing happened. The minorities are also complaining about not being treated fairly. For things to change, management has to work to resolve complaints. ///

Complete Self-Assessment Exercise 12-5 to determine how your personality affects your ability to deal with diversity in the workplace.

MODEL 12.1 | Complaint Model

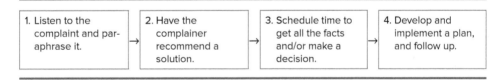

| 1. Listen to the complaint and paraphrase it. | 2. Have the complainer recommend a solution. | 3. Schedule time to get all the facts and/or make a decision. | 4. Develop and implement a plan, and follow up. |

/// **Self-Assessment Exercise 12-5** ///

Personality and Diversity

If you are *open to new experiences,* you are probably interested in learning about people who are different from you.

If you have a high *agreeableness* personality, with a high need for affiliation, you tend to get along well with diverse people. You most likely do not judge peoples' behavior negatively simply because it is different. But you may need to be assertive so that you are not taken advantage of.

If you scored high in *conscientiousness,* with a high need for achievement, you may tend to be a conformist and will most likely adjust to diverse situations.

If you have a high *surgency* personality, with a high need for power, you like to dominate and may not want to accept diversity. You may need to remember, as the conscientious may too, that your ways are not always correct and are not always the best ways of doing things.

Action plan: Based on your personality, what specific things can you do to improve your ability to value and manage diversity? If you are well adjusted, you are better at dealing with a diversity of people.

_____

_____

_____

_____

_____

_____

As we bring this chapter to a close, you should understand some of the major laws and areas of discrimination in employment and what sexual harassment is. You should also understand the importance of valuing and managing diversity at home and globally, and how to personally avoid discrimination against anyone. Last, you should be able to handle an employee complaint using the complaint model.

NOTE: If you don't plan to cover Appendix B, you may want to complete Skill Builder B-2 Course Learning, to reflect on the most important things you learned, or skills developed, through the course.

/ / / R E V I E W / / /

The chapter review is organized to help you master the 7 learning outcomes for Chapter 12. First provide your own response to each learning outcome, and then check the summary provided to see how well you understand the material. Next, identify the final statement in each section as either true or false (T/F). Correct each false statement. Answers are given at the end of the chapter.

LO 12-1 Define prejudice and discrimination and state common areas of employment discrimination in organizations.

Prejudice is a prejudgment of a person or situation based on attitudes. *Discrimination* is behavior for or against a person or situation. Common areas of employment discrimination include: recruitment, selection, compensation, upward mobility, and evaluation.

We all prejudge people and situations. T F

LO 12-2 State seven major diversity laws enforced by the Equal Employment Opportunity Commission (EEOC).

Seven of the major laws passed to protect against discrimination include: the Equal Pay Act of 1963, the Civil Rights Act of 1964, the Age Discrimination in Employment Act of 1967, the Pregnancy Discrimination Act of 1978, the Americans with Disabilities Act of 1990, the Family and Medical Leave Act of 1993, and the Genetic Information Act of 2008.

The Justice Enforcement Commission has the primary responsibility of making diversity laws. T F

LO 12-3 Identify what diversity questions employers can and cannot ask job applicants.

To avoid breaking the law, employers interviewing job applicants should follow two major rules of thumb: (1) Every question that is asked should be job related, and (2) any general question that is asked should be asked of all candidates.

An organization can discriminate as long as it can prove that it is reasonably necessary to normal operation of the enterprise. T F

LO 12-4 List the eight diversity groups that are legally protected by the EEOC.

The eight groups are: Race, Color, Religion, Sex, National origin, Age, Disability, Genetic information

The law states that the protected groups must be given special consideration in employment practices. T F

LO 12-5 Explain sexism in organizations and ways to overcome it.

Sexism is discrimination based on sex. To help overcome sexism, we should not use sexist language and behavior and we should discourage others from doing so.

Women who have been discriminated against based on gender can file a complaint with the EEOC. T F

LO 12-6 Compare and contrast the Hofstede national culture dimensions with Project GLOBE.

The two are similar because they both measure cultural diversity among countries. Back in the 1970s and 1980s, Hofstede identified five dimensions of diversity (power distance inequality vs. power equality, individuality vs. collectivism, assertiveness vs. nurturing, uncertainty avoidance vs. uncertainty acceptance, and long-term vs. short-term orientation) using employees of one company, IBM, in 40 countries. GLOBE confirmed that Hofstede's five dimensions are still valid today and extended and expanded his five dimensions into nine (assertiveness, future orientation, gender differences, uncertainty avoidance, power distance, societal collectivism, in-group collectivism, performance orientation, and humane orientation), and the sample includes hundreds of companies from more than 60 countries. GLOBE is also an ongoing study.

In general, Hofstede extended Project GLOBE from five to nine dimensions. T F

LO 12-7 Define the following 11 key terms.

Select one or more methods: (1) fill in the missing key terms for each definition given below from memory; (2) match the key terms from the end of the review with their definitions below; and/or (3) copy the key terms in order from the key terms list at the beginning of the chapter.

_____ is the prejudgment of a person or situation based on attitudes.

_____ is behavior for or against a person or situation.

The EEOC _____ list includes Hispanics, Asians, African Americans, Native Americans, and Alaska Natives.

A(n) _____ allows discrimination on the basis of religion, sex, or national origin where it is reasonably necessary to normal operation of a particular enterprise.

_____ are planned, special efforts to recruit, hire, and promote women and members of minority groups.

A(n) _____ refers to a significant physical, mental, or emotional limitation.

_____ is any unwelcomed behavior of a sexual nature.

_____ is discrimination based on sex.

A(n) _____ conducts a large part of its business outside the country of its headquarters.

_____ are people who live and work in a country other than their native country.

The _____ involves these steps: (1) listen to the complaint and paraphrase it; (2) have the complainer recommend a solution; (3) schedule time to get all the facts and/or make a decision; and (4) develop and implement a plan, and follow up.

/ / / KEY TERMS / / /

affirmative action (AA) programs   411
bona fide occupational qualification (BFOQ)   406

complaint model   424
disability   408
discrimination   404
expatriates   423

minority   405
multinational company (MNC)   422
prejudice   404

sexism   411
sexual harassment   409

/ / / COMMUNICATION SKILLS / / /

The following critical thinking questions can be used for class discussion and/or as written assignments to develop communication skills. Be sure to give complete explanations for all questions.

1. Clearly, women and minorities were held back from employment opportunities in the past. So shouldn't we give them special consideration today (like giving them jobs when they are qualified even though there are better qualified white males)? Should we be increasing or decreasing affirmative action programs?

2. Do we really need laws to get organizations to give equal opportunities to all? Should the current employment laws be changed? How?

3. Should religious people be given breaks and a special place to pray during their work time?

4. Some companies and jobs have a mandatory retirement age. Should the government pass a law stating a mandatory retirement age?

5. Do you feel comfortable being around people with disabilities? Should organizations make special efforts to hire individuals who are disabled? Are organizations that hire workers with disabilities just being socially responsible, or are the workers productive?

6. Do you agree that people who work together can date? How might dating lead to sexual harassment? Should organizations have policies about employee dating? If they have policies, what should the policies include?

7. Only a small percentage of *Fortune* 500 companies have female CEOs. One solution to increase the number of women CEOs would be to have co-CEOs, one male and one female. Do you think this would work?

Do you have any other ideas on how to break the glass ceiling?

8. Consider the statement, "Sexist and racist jokes are just meant to be funny and no one gets hurt anyway." Do you agree?

9. The traditional family hasn't been the norm for several years. Instead, it is being overtaken by dual-income earners and single parents. Are we better off today, or should we return to the traditional family?

10. The percentage of married people has declined over the years due to divorce and people living together. Also, male and female roles have changed. Do these trends help or hurt society?

11. Consider the statement, "With the global economy, people around the world are becoming more and more alike, so why be concerned about diversity?" Do you agree? Should organizations conduct diversity training?

CASE / / / Google's Diversity Progress Report

Led by founders Sergey Brin and Larry Page, Google has been one of the greatest technology companies in our time. With more than 60,000 employees in 50 different countries, Google makes hundreds of products used by billions of people across the globe, from **YouTube** and **Android** to **Smartbox** and, of course, **Google Search**. Google has revolutionized the way people research information and communicate globally. Unfortunately, Google's track record with diversity is not nearly as positive...and they admit it:[i] "We think Google's workforce should look more like the world. It is going to take time to get there, but we are on the road to increasing access to opportunity for everyone."[ii] Google is not the only tech company showing a lack of diversity in its workforce. Employment research at tech companies such as Google, **Apple**, **Facebook**, and others confirm what many already suspected: white men comprise the bulk of the workforce. African-Americans comprise about 7 percent and Latinos about 8 percent of the tech sector, in a nation where those numbers are 12 and 16 percent, respectively. Women comprise about 30 percent, despite being 51 percent of the population.[iii]

In 2014, Google took an unusual step to report its diversity data even though it wasn't positive. "We're not where we want to be when it comes to diversity. And it is hard to address these kinds of challenges if you're not prepared to discuss them openly, and with the facts," Google said in a report on its Web site. "All of our efforts, including going public with these numbers, are designed to help us recruit and develop the world's most talented and diverse people."[iv] In 2014, Google's demographic employment data looked as follows: in terms of race, 83 percent of Google's tech workers internationally were male. For non-tech jobs, the number was 52 percent. Its leadership was made up of 79 percent men. In terms of racial diversity, the company overall was 61 percent white, 30 percent Asian, 3 percent Hispanic, and 2 percent black. For tech positions, the numbers were similar: 60 percent were white, 34 percent

Asian, 2 percent Hispanic, and 1 percent black. In terms of management and leadership, the company was trending even more white; 72 percent of its leaders were white, 23 percent Asian, 2 percent black, and 1 percent Hispanic. [v]These numbers did not come close to reflecting U.S. demographics.[vi]

Therefore, the question is whether Google has lived up to its promise to change. According to January 2016 data, on gender diversity, 31 percent of Google employees globally are women and 69 percent are men. In terms of ethnic diversity in the United States, the company reported that in 2015, 4 percent of new hires were black, compared to 2 percent of their current population and 5 percent of new hires were Hispanic, compared to 3 percent of their current population. On gender hiring, Google reported that 21 percent of new hires were women in tech, compared to 19 percent of their current population and 24 percent of employees in leadership positions were women, a 2 percent increase from the previous year.[vii]

Many people feel that Google is being courageous in their openness about not meeting diversity goals. For example, **National Public Broadcasting (NPR)** feels that Google's willingness to be open will allow other technology companies to also be forthright.[viii]

The **Reverend Jesse Jackson** has asked for technology companies such as **Hewlett-Packard, eBay, Facebook,** and Google to improve diversity at their company annual shareholders meetings.[ix] In Google's case, they felt it was time to work with Jesse Jackson and publicly announce they were going to work on their unconscious diversity behavior. Google's goal is to become more conscious about diversity and knowingly improve. Google announced at their annual conference that they would be working with **Jackson's Rainbow Coalition** to increase the number of minorities in their company. As Reverend Jackson stated, "it's time to harness Google's moonshot thinking and innovation towards closing the gap when it comes to minorities and technology."[x]

Another positive step with regards to promoting more women to leadership positions is that Google's ad executive, **Susan Wojcicki**, was promoted to head **YouTube,** which is owned by Google. Mrs. Wojcicki has previously been in charge of Google's **AdWords, AdSense, Analytics,** and **DoubleClick**. She is the mother of four and originally rented her garage to Mr. Brin and Mr. Page in the search engine's early years.[xi] There is also evidence that Google is undertaking other diversity initiatives or programs. Examples include: **Wired Magazine** reported that **Google Lab** is building a legion of diverse coders; **USA Today** reported that Google has given $1 million to Latino groups, and **Essence Magazine** reported that Google hosted a "**Black Girls Code**" event to encourage careers in tech for young women. **Ebony.**

comconducted an interview with Google's **Director of Diversity and Inclusion, Ms. Yolanda Mangolini**, an African-American. It will be interesting to watch Mrs. Wojcicki's career and the changes taking place in Google's diversity programs. If Google is nearly as successful as they were with their search engine, then we can expect to see significant progress on its diversity landscape in the future.

Go to the Internet: You can watch a video and meet Susan Wojcicki at http://www.makers.com/susan-wojcicki. You can also listen to an NPR radio show that discusses Google's new diversity program at http://www.npr.org/2014/06/02/318209074/google-courageous-for-admitting-diversity-problem-so-what-now.

Support your answers to the following questions with specific information from the case and text or with information you get from the Web or another source.

1. What is the evidence from the case that Google values diversity or understands the importance of diversity?

2. The text identifies five areas where discrimination in employment is most common: recruitment, selection, compensation, upward mobility, and evaluation. In your opinion, how is Google doing in these areas?

3. The text discusses Affirmative Action (AA) and defines what it means: planned special efforts to recruit, hire, and promote women and members of minority groups. How would you assess or describe Google's AA programs?

4. In your opinion, is the glass ceiling still alive and well at Google or has Google satisfactorily addressed the issue?

Cumulative Case Questions

5. Chapter 6 discusses diversity and global leadership and the importance of not adopting a one-size-fits-all solution or leadership style. In your opinion, should Google be concerned about this? Explain.

6. Also, in Chapter 6, we discussed developing trust. The five dimensions of trust are integrity, competence, consistency, loyalty, and openness. Apply this concept to Google's decision to reveal its diversity data in 2014 even though it was not favorable to Google.

Case Exercise and Role-Play

Preparation: The instructor assigns one student in a pair to be CEO Larry Page and the other person in a pair to be a reporter from PBS New Hour. Assume that the two of you are meeting at a national shoe industry conference in Las Vegas. Prepare for the interview, during which you will be asking Larry about Google's lack of diversity. Write down a list of the specific diversity issues in the case and ask Larry how they are being addressed.

Role-Play: Matched pairs of Larry Page and the reporter will role-play. The role-play may be done in small groups, or two people may role-play before the entire class.

After the interview, the group or class discusses and critiques diversity at Google. Also, you should identify questions and diversity issues that were not discussed that would have been useful to learn about.

Hint: Google can be presented as being too busy making money to value diversity by the reporter. However, Google can reply they are being honest in their assessment and plan on doing a much better job of hiring a diverse workforce going forward.

OBJECTIVE CASE   / / /   Lilly's Promotion

The Carlson Mining and Manufacturing Company needs a new vice president of human resources. Its headquarters are in Detroit, but the company has mining and manufacturing plants in three states and five different countries. Foreign plants account for about 70 percent of total operations.

The president, Ron Carlson, is meeting with some of the vice presidents and the board of directors to decide who will be promoted to vice president. The following are excerpts from their discussion:

RON: As you know, we are meeting today to promote someone to vice president. Ted, tell us about the candidates.

TED: We have narrowed the list of candidates to two people. You all know the two candidates. They are Rich Martin and Lilly Jefferson. Rich is 38 and has been with us for 15 years, and he has worked in human resources for 10 years. He has an MBA from a leading business school. Lilly is 44 and has been with us for 10 years. She recently finished her BS in business going to school nights at the local state college.

JIM: Lilly is an African American female with older children. She is perfect for the job, fitting into two AA classifications. We can meet our AA quotas without promoting Lilly, but it would help. Besides, there are a lot of African Americans here in Detroit; we could get some great publicity.

ED: Wait a minute. We cannot have any girls at the VP level. You know they are emotional and cannot take the pressure of the job.

RON: Their performance records are about the same, but Rich has been with us longer, and is better educated.

The discussion ended in a vote. Lilly won by a large margin. Off the record: It was because she is a qualified African American female. If she were a white male, Rich would have been promoted.

Answer the following questions. Then in the space between questions, state why you selected that answer.

_____   1. Discrimination was used in the promotion process.
　　　　　　a. true　　　　　　　　　　*b.* false

_____   2. The primary area discussed in this case is:
　　　　　　a. recruitment　　　　*c.* compensation　　　　*e.* evaluation
　　　　　　b. selection　　　　　*d.* upward mobility

_____   3. Affirmative action affected the decision to promote Lilly.
　　　　　　a. true　　　　　　　　　　*b.* false

_____   4. Rich may have a case for reverse discrimination.
　　　　　　a. true　　　　　　　　　　*b.* false

_____   5. Sexism occurred in this case.
　　　　　　a. true　　　　　　　　　　*b.* false

_____   6. Ed's statement was:
　　　　　　a. factual　　　　　　　　　*b.* myth

_____   7. Ed used sexist language.

      a. true   *b.* false

_____   8. With Lilly being a minority member, she will most likely encounter cross-cultural relations problems.

      a. true   *b.* false

_____   9. Carlson is a multinational company.

      a. true   *b.* false

_____ 10. The most help Lilly got in getting to the vice president position was from:

      a. AAP   *c.* flexible work schedule   *e.* role models and mentors

      b. training   *d.* child care   *f.* wellness programs

11. Whom would you have voted for? Why?

12. How would you feel in Lilly's position, knowing that you are qualified for the job but that you have been selected because you are a minority? Lilly's response can be role-played.

/ / / SKILL-BUILDING EXERCISE 12-1 / / /

Sexism

Experience: Individual and group sharing in class or online. You will discuss sexist words and behavior.

AACSB Competencies: Reflexive thinking, diversity, and application of knowledge.

Objective: To better understand sexist language and behavior and how it affects human relations.

Procedure 1 (7–15 minutes)

Option A: Students give sample words and behaviors found in the workplace that are sexist (for example, words *foreman* and behaviors [a woman being required to get the coffee]). The instructor or a class member writes the headings "words" and "behaviors" on the board and records the class members' examples. Discuss how these sexist words and behaviors affect people's behavior in organizations.

Option B: Break into teams of five or six, making the number of males and females as even as possible. As in option A, develop a list of sexist words and behaviors and discuss how they affect people's behavior in organizations.

Procedure 2 (7–15 minutes)

Option A: As a class, select a few sexist words and behaviors. Discuss how to overcome this sexism.

Option B: As a group, select a few sexist words and behaviors. Discuss how to overcome this sexism.

Conclusion: The instructor may lead a class discussion and/or make concluding remarks.

Application (2–4 minutes):   What did I learn from this exercise? How will I use this knowledge in the future?

Sharing: Volunteers give their answers to the application section.

Male and Female Small-Group Behavior

Experience: In-class group exercise

AACSB Competencies: Analytic skills, reflexive thinking, diversity, and application of knowledge.

Objective: To see if there are any differences in male and female behavior in small groups.

Preparation: Some of the class members will need to bring smartphones to class to record small-group discussions.

Procedure 1 (15–20 minutes)

Experience: In a small group, you will make a decision that will be recorded, and then you will analyze the recording to determine if there are differences in male and female behavior.

Break into teams of five or six. Make the number of males and females as even as possible in each group. Be sure each group has a recorder. As a group, you will select a candidate for a job opening. As an individual, read the information below and think about whom you would hire in this situation. When all group members are ready, begin your discussion of whom to hire. *Be sure to record the conversation.* Discuss each candidate's qualifications fully, coming to a group consensus on whom to hire. Do not vote, unless the time is almost up. You must make a decision by the deadline stated by your instructor. Try not to finish very early, but if you do, wait for the rest of the class to finish before going on to the next procedure.

You are a member of the local school board. The board is making the decision on which candidate to hire for the open position of girls' high school tennis coach. The following is information on each candidate.

Kishana Jones: Kishana has been a history teacher at a nearby high school for 10 years. She was the tennis coach for one year. It has been five years since she coached the team. Kishana says she stopped coaching because it was too time-consuming with her young daughter, but she misses it and wants to return. Kishana's performance was rated as 3 on a scale of 1 to 5. She never played competitive tennis, but she says she plays regularly. You guess Kishana is about 35 years old.

Soren Hansen: Soren works as a supervisor on the 11 p.m. to 7 a.m. shift for a local business. He has never coached before. However, Soren was a star player in high school and college. He still plays in local tournaments, and you see his name in the paper now and then. You guess Soren is about 25 years old.

Chelsea Clark: Chelsea has been a basketball coach and a teacher of physical education classes for a nearby high school for the past five years. She has a bachelor's degree in physical education. Chelsea has never coached tennis, but she did play on the high school team. She says she plays tennis about once a week. You guess Chelsea is about 40 years old.

Lisa Williams: Lisa has been an English teacher at your school for the past two years. She has never coached, but she did take a course in college on how to coach tennis. She is popular with her students. Lisa plays tennis regularly, and you have heard she is a pretty good player. She is African American. You guess Lisa is about 24 years old.

Hank Chung: Hank has been teaching math at your school for seven years. He was a star player in high school in Japan, and he played tennis for a successful U.S. college team. He still plays for fun regularly. He has never coached or had any type of coaching courses. He applied for the job the last time it was open four years ago but was not selected. You guess Hank is about 30 years of age.

Sally Carson: Sally has taught physical education classes at your school for the past four years. She never played competitive tennis but has a master's degree in physical education and has had courses regarding how to coach tennis. Sally taught and coached field hockey at a high school for 15 years before moving to your city. You guess she is about 48 years old.

Procedure 2 (1–2 minutes)

As an individual, answer the following questions. Circle the letter of your response.

1. Who spoke more?

    a. males   *b.* females   *c.* equal time

2. The one individual with the most influence in the group was:

    a. male   *b.* female

3. The one individual with the least influence in the group was:

   a. male   *b.* female

4. Overall, who had the most influence on the group?

   a. males   *b.* females   *c.* equal influence

5. Interruptions came more frequently from:

   a. males interrupting females

   b. females interrupting males

   c. equal interruption from both

6. Of the total discussion time, I spoke for about _____ minutes.

Procedure 3 (2-4 minutes)

Total the group's answers to the six questions in procedure 2. All members should write the totals next to the questions above.

Procedure 4 (20-30 minutes)

Play back the recorded discussion. As it plays, write down who talks and for how long they talk. If one person interrupts another, note it as "male interrupts female," or vice versa. When the tape finishes, add up the number of minutes each person spoke. Total the male and female times. As a team, answer the six questions in procedure 2 above. Were the answers the same before and after listening to the recorded discussion?

Conclusion: The instructor may lead a class discussion and/or make concluding remarks.

Application (2-4 minutes):   What did I learn from this experience? How can I use this knowledge in the future?

Sharing: Volunteers give their answers to the application section.

Source: The idea to develop this exercise came from Susan Morse, University of Massachusetts at Amherst, in "Gender Differences in Behavior in Small Groups: A Look at the OB Class," paper presented at the 25th Annual Meeting of the Eastern Academy of Management, May 12, 1988.

/ / /   SKILL-BUILDING EXERCISE 12-3   / / /

Handling Complaints

Experience: In-class small group exercise. You will initiate, respond to, and observe a complaint role-play. Then you will evaluate the effectiveness of its resolution.

AACSB Competencies: Analytic skills, communication ability, and application of knowledge.

Objective: To experience and develop skills in resolving complaints.

Preparation

During class you will be given the opportunity to role-play handling a complaint. Select a complaint. It may be one you brought to a supervisor, one that was brought to you, one you heard about, or one you made up. Fill in the information below for the person who will role-play bringing you a complaint to resolve. Explain the situation and complaint.

List pertinent information about the other party that will help him or her play the role of the complainer (relationship with supervisor, knowledge, years of service, background, age, values, and so on).

Review Model 12.1 (complaint model) and think about what you will say and do when you handle this complaint.

Procedure 1 (2–3 minutes)

Break into as many groups of three as possible. (You do not have to be with members of your permanent team.) If there are any people not in a triad, make one or two groups of two. Each member selects a number 1, 2, or 3. Number 1 will be the first to initiate a complaint role-play, then 2, followed by 3.

Complaint Observer Form

During the role-play, observe the handling of the complaint. Determine whether the supervisor followed the steps below, and how well. Try to have both a positive and an improvement comment for each step in the complaint model. Be specific and descriptive. For all improvement comments, have an alternative positive behavior (APB). What could have been done or said that was not?

Step 1.   How well did the supervisor listen? Was the supervisor open to the complaint? Did the supervisor try to talk the employee out of the complaint? Was the supervisor defensive? Did the supervisor get the full story without interruptions? Did the supervisor paraphrase the complaint?

          (positive)   (improvement)

Step 2.   Did the supervisor have the complainer recommend a solution? How well did the supervisor react to the solution? If the solution could not be used, did the supervisor explain why?

          (positive)   (improvement)

Step 3.   Did the supervisor schedule time to get all the facts and/or make a decision? Was it a specific date? Was it a reasonable length of time?

          (positive)   (improvement)

Step 4.   Did the supervisor develop and implement a plan, and schedule a follow-up? (This step may not have been appropriate at this time.)

Preparation: You should have prepared to handle a complaint.

Procedure 2 (8–15 minutes)

A. Number 1 (the supervisor) gives his or her preparation complaint information to number 2 (the complainer) to read. Once number 2 understands, role-play the complaint (step B). Number 3 is the observer.

B. Role-play the complaint. Put yourself in this person's situation; ad-lib. Number 3, the observer, writes his or her observations on the complaint observer form.

C. Integration. When the role-play is over, the observer leads a discussion on the effectiveness of the conflict resolution. All three should discuss the effectiveness; number 3 is not a lecturer.

Do not go on until told to do so.

Procedure 3 (8-15 minutes)

Same as procedure 2, only number 2 is now the supervisor, number 3 is now the complainer, and number 1 is the observer.

Procedure 4 (8-15 minutes)

Same as procedure 2, only number 3 is now the supervisor, number 1 is now the complainer, and number 2 is the observer.

Conclusion: The instructor leads a class discussion and/or makes concluding remarks.

Application (2-4 minutes):   What did I learn from this experience? How will I use this knowledge in the future?

Sharing: Volunteers give their. answers to the application section.

/   /   /   SKILL-BUILDING EXERCISE 12-4   /   /   /

Periodical Articles

Experience: Individual written assignment, articles may be presented in class, or shared in small groups or online.

AACSB Competencies: Analytic skills, communication ability, and application of knowledge.

Objectives: To gain some specific knowledge regarding a topic of your choice, and the choices of other students in the class. You may be handing in the answers to your article, and/or making a 3–7 minute presentation of your article to the class. Your instructor will tell you the requirements.

Preparation: Select a human relations topic that you would like to learn more about. It can be any topic covered in this book or a topic not covered, if related to human relations.

   Now go to the library (a reference librarian can help you) or online (preferably to a college business periodical index such as ABI Inform or Premier Source) and find an article to read and report on.

   Write down the following information:

   Author's name(s): _____

   Title of article: _____

   Title of the periodical publication: _____

   Date of publication and page number(s) and or web link and date accessed: _____

Be sure to write neatly. You may be asked to report to the class or pass this assignment in to the instructor. Be prepared to give a three- to five-minute talk on your article.

1. What did the article say? (Give a summary of the most important information in the article.)

2. How does this information relate to me and/or my interests?

3. How will I use this information in the future?

Procedure 1 (5–50 minutes)

Option A: One at a time, students come to the front of the room and give a three- to seven-minute speech on the article they read.

Option B: Break into small groups and share the answers to your article.

Conclusion: The instructor leads a class discussion and/or makes concluding remarks.

Application (2–4 minutes):   What did I learn from this experience? How will I use this knowledge in the future?

When reading articles of interest to your career, always answer the three questions. Answering these questions will help you use the information rather than forget it and will develop your abilities and skills. To continue to improve on your human relations skills after the course is over, read more articles of interest to you.

Sharing: Volunteers give their answers to the application section.

/ / / SKILL-BUILDING EXERCISE 12-5 / / /

Developing New Habits

Experience: Individual may share habits in groups or entire class, in class or online.

AACSB Competencies: Analytic and application of knowledge.

Objective: To develop and share new habits.

Preparation: Select one or more topics from this chapter that will help you improve your human relations. Develop a new habit following the guideline from Chapter 1, section Habits and Skill-Building Exercise 1-4, on how to develop your cure, routine, and reward-change.

Procedure (5–30 minutes)

Follow the procedures from Skill Builder 1–4.

/ / ANSWERS TO TRUE/FALSE QUESTIONS / /

1. T.
2. F. The U.S. Congress writes the laws that must be signed into law by the president of the United States.
3. T. (It is called a bona fide occupational qualification [BFOQ].)
4. F. The law states that protected groups must not be *discriminated* against.
5. T.
6. F. It is the opposite; GLOBE extended Hofstede's research.

/ / / NOTES / / /

1. O.E. Varela and R.G. Watts, "The Development of the Global Manager: An Empirical Study on the Role of Academic International Sojourns," *Academy of Management Learning & Education* 13(2) (2014): 187–207.

2. U.S. Census Bureau website, www.census.gov, accessed June 27, 2017.

3. J. Adamy and P. Overberg, "Population of Nonwhites Grows," *The Wall Street Journal* (June 23, 2016): A3.

4. CIA website, https://www.cia.gov/library/publications/resources/the-world-factbook/rankorder/2119rank.html, accessed June 27, 2017.

5. A. Murray, "The Hard Truths of Globalization," *Fortune* (August 1, 2016): 6.

6. M.L. Turner, "Remote Control," *Entrepreneur* (January 2016): 75–79.

7. R.J. Reichard, S.A. Serrano, M. Condren, N. Wilder, M. Dollwet, and W. Wang, "Engaging in Cultural Trigger Events in the Development of Cultural Competence," *Academy of Management Learning & Education* 14(4) (2015): 461–481.

8. Call for papers, *Academy of Management Review* 40(4) (2015): 669–670.

9. S. Sandberg, "When Women Get Stuck, Corporate America Gets Stuck," *The Wall Street Journal* (September 30, 2015): R3.

10. Y.R.F. Guillaume, D. Van Knippenberg, and F.C. Brodbeck, "Nothing Succeeds Like Moderation: A Social Self-Regulation Perspective on Cultural Dissimilarity and Performance," *Academy of Management Journal* 57(5) (2014): 1284–1308.

11. O.E. Varela and R.G. Watts, "The Development of the Global Manager: An Empirical Study on the Role of Academic International Sojourns," *Academy of Management Learning & Education* 13(2) (2014): 187–207.

12. S.Y. Lee, M. Pitesa, S. Thau, and M.M. Pillutla, "Discrimination in Selection Decisions: Integrating Stereotype Fit and Interdependence Theories," *Academy of Management Journal* 58(3) (2015): 789–812.

13. A. Joshi, J. Son, and H. Roh, "When Can Women Close the Gap? A Meta-Analytic Test of Sex Differences in Performance and Rewards," *Academy of Management Journal* 58(5) (2015): 1516–1545.

14. S.Y. Lee, M. Pitesa, S. Thau, and M.M. Pillutla, "Discrimination in Selection Decisions: Integrating Stereotype Fit and Interdependence Theories," *Academy of Management Journal* 58(3) (2015): 789–812.

15. M. Kelly, *The Four Signs of a Dynamic Catholic* (New York: Beacon, 2012).

16. M. Kelly, *Rediscovering Catholicism* (New York: Beacon, 2010).

17. O.E. Varela and R.G. Watts, "The Development of the Global Manager: An Empirical Study on the Role of Academic International Sojourns," *Academy of Management Learning & Education* 13(2) (2014): 187–207.

18. A. Joshi, J. Son, and H. Roh, "When Can Women Close the Gap? A Meta-Analytic Test of Sex Differences in Performance and Rewards," *Academy of Management Journal* 58(5) (2015): 1516–1545.

19. A. Joshi, J. Son, and H. Roh, "When Can Women Close the Gap? A Meta-Analytic Test of Sex Differences in Performance and Rewards," *Academy of Management Journal* 58(5) (2015): 1516–1545.

20. EEOC website https://www.eeoc.gov/eeoc/index.cfm, accessed June 27, 2017.

21. EEOC website www.eeoc.gov, accessed June 27, 2017.

22. EEOC website https://www.eeoc.gov, accessed June 28, 2017.

23. L.A. Mainiero and K.J. Jones, "Sexual Harassment Versus Workplace Romance: Social Media Spillover and Textual Harassment in the Workplace," *Academy of Management Perspectives* 27(3) (2013): 187–203.

24. M.B. Watkins, A.N. Smith, and K. Aquino, "The Use and Consequences of Strategic Sexual Performance," *Academy of Management Perspectives* 27(3) (2013): 173–186.

25. G. O'Brien, "Dipping One's Pen in the Company Ink," *Entrepreneur* (May 2015): 28.

26. L.A. Mainiero and K. J. Jones, "Sexual Harassment Versus Workplace Romance: Social Media Spillover and Textual Harassment in the Workplace," *Academy of Management Perspectives* 27(3) (2013): 187–203.

27. J. Smith, "With Cupid at the Office, Rules Can Reduce Hazards," *The Wall Street Journal* (February 11, 2013): B1, B7.

28. Electronic Code of Federal Regulations www.ecfr.gov accessed June 28, 2017.

29. Call for papers, *Academy of Management Review* 40(4) (2015): 669–670.

30. M.L. Besharov, "The Relational Ecology of Identification: How Organizational Identification Emerges When Individual Hold Divergent Values," *Academy of Management Journal* 57(5) (2014): 1485–1512.

31. F.A. Miller and J.H. Katz. *The Inclusion Breakthrough: Unleashing the Real Power of Diversity* (San Francisco: Berrett-Koehler, 2002).

32. J. Bercovici, "Inside the Mind of Sheryl Sandberg," *INC.* (October 2015): 78–80.

33. S. Sandberg, "When Women Get Stuck, Corporate America Gets Stuck," *The Wall Street Journal* (September 30, 2015): R3.

34. U.S. Census data, www.census.gov, accessed June 28, 2017. Staff, "Mind the Gap," *BusinessWeek* (June 25, 2017): cover.

35. Staff, "The Gender Wage Gap," *Fortune* (September 15, 2015): 16.

36. J. Adamy and P. Overberg, "Pay Gap Widest for Elite Jobs," *The Wall Street Journal* (May 18, 2016): A1, A10.

37. A. Joshi, J. Son, and H. Roh, "When Can Women Close the Gap? A Meta-Analytic Test of Sex Differences in Performance and Rewards," *Academy of Management Journal* 58(5) (2015): 1516–1545.

38. C. Suddath, "Can Women Ever Win at Work?" *BusinessWeek* (July 28–August 3, 2014): 62.

39. L. Weber and R.L. Ensign, "Promoting Women Is Crucial," *The Wall Street Journal* (September 28, 2016): B1.

40. B. Waber, "Gender Bias by the Numbers," *BusinessWeek* (February 3–9, 2014): 8–9.

41. R. Feintzeg and J.S. Lublin, "Female CEOs, a Rarity, Face Extra Pressures," *The Wall Street Journal* (August 10, 2016): B1, B8.

42. A. Murray, "Lessons From the Fortune 500," *Fortune* (June 15, 2016): 14.

43. S. Sandberg, "When Women Get Stuck, Corporate America Gets Stuck," *The Wall Street Journal* (September 30, 2015): R3.

44. K.L. Ashcraft, "The Glass Slipper: Incorporating Occupational Identity in Management Studies," *Academy of Management Review* 38(1) (2013): 6–31.

45. B. Waber, "Gender Bias by the Numbers," *BusinessWeek* (February 3–9, 2014): 8–9.

46. K. Lanaj and J.R. Hollenbeck, "Leadership Over-Emergence in Self-Managing Teams: The Role of Gender and Countervailing Biases," *Academy of Management Journal* 58(5) (2015): 1476–1494.

47. J. Bercovici, "Inside the Mind of Sheryl Sandberg," *INC.* (October 2015): 78–80.

48. S. Sandberg, "When Women Get Stuck, Corporate America Gets Stuck," *The Wall Street Journal* (September 30, 2015): R3.

49. G. Colvin, "Humans are Underrated," *Fortune* (August 1, 2015), 100–113.

50. G. Colvin, "Humans are Underrated," *Fortune* (August 1, 2015), 100–113.

51. J.S. Lublin, "TI Battles a Gender Gap in Job Experience," *The Wall Street Journal* (June 13, 2012): B10.

52. G. Segal, "The New American Family," *AARP the Magazine* (June–July 2014): 34–40.

53. News Report, NPR, aired September 30, 2014.

54. Staff, "One in Three Children in Fatherless Home," http://www.washingtontimes.com (December 25, 2012).

55. Staff, "One in Three Children in Fatherless Home," http://www.washingtontimes.com (December 25, 2012).

56. C. Murry, "Rules for a Happy Life," *The Wall Street Journal* (March 29–30, 2014): C1, C2.

57. E. Vitagliano, "Happy, Healthy, Holy," *AFA Journal* (December 2013): 14–15.

58. E. Byron, "A Truce in the Chore Wars," *The Wall Street Journal* (December 2, 2012): D1, D2.

59. Pew Research Center, "How Mothers and Fathers Spend Their Workweeks," http://www.pewresearch.org, access June 29, 2017.

60. L. Weber and J.S. Lublin, "The Daddy Juggle: Work, Life, Family and Chaos," *The Wall Street Journal* (June 13, 2014): D1, D2.

61. L. Ramarajan and E. Reid, "Shattering the Myth of Separate Worlds: Negotiating Nonwork Identities at Work," *Academy of Management Review* 38(4) (2012): 621–644.

62. L. Weber and J.S. Lublin, "The Daddy Juggle: Work, Life, Family and Chaos," *The Wall Street Journal* (June 13, 2014): D1, D2.

63. L. Weber, "Why Dads Don't Take Paternity Leave," *The Wall Street Journal* (June 13, 2013): B1, B7.

64. C. Rose, "Charlie Rose talks to Kirsten Gillibrand," *BusinessWeek* (September 18, 2014): 36.

65. L. Weber, "Why Dads Don't Take Paternity Leave," *The Wall Street Journal* (June 13, 2013): B1, B7.

66. L. Sandler, "How to Love Paid Family Leave," *BusinessWeek* (July 21-27, 2014): 8-9.

67. B. Waber, "Gender Bias by the Numbers," *BusinessWeek* (February 3-9, 2014): 8-9.

68. S. Shillenbarger, "Dad's Roughhousing Lessons," *The Wall Street Journal* (June 11, 2014): D1, D3.

69. J.N. Reyt and B.M. Wiesenfeld, "Seeing the Forest for the Trees: Exploratory Learning, Mobile Technology, and Knowledge Workers' Role Integration Behaviors," *Academy of Management Journal* 58(3) (2015): 739-762.

70. J. Alsever, "Take It Easy. That's An Order!" *Fortune* (December 15, 2015): 46.

71. M.M. Butts, W.J. Becker, and W.R. Boswell, "Hot Buttons and Time Sinks: The Effects of Electronic Communication During Nonwork Time on Emotions and Work-Nonwork Conflict," *Academy of Management Journal* 58(3) (2015): 763-788.

72. L. Weber, "Overtime Pay for Answering Late-Night Emails," *The Wall Street Journal* (May 21, 2015): B1, B6.

73. J.J. Ladge, B.K. Humberd, M.B. Watkins, and B. Harrington, "Updating the Organization Man: An Examination of Involved Fathering in the Workplace," *Academy of Management Perspectives* 29(1) (2015): 152-171.

74. N. Waller and J. Lublin, "What's Holding Women Back in the Workplace?" *The Wall Street Journal* (September 30, 2015): C1, C2.

75. W. Mosseberg, "After Leaning In," *The Wall Street Journal* (June 3, 2013): D1.

76. P.B. Whyman and A.I. Petrescu, "Workplace Flexibility Practices in SMEs Relationship with Performance via Redundancies, Absenteeism, and Financial Turnaround," *Journal of Small Business Management* 53(4) (2015): 1097-1126.

77. A. Chuang, R. S. Hsu, A.C. Wang, and T.A. Judge, Does West Fit with East? In Search of a Chinese Model of Person-Environment Fit," *Academy of Management Journal* 58(2) (2015): 480-510.

78. C. Hardy and D. Tolhurst, "Epistemological Beliefs and Cultural Diversity Matters in Management Education and Learning," *Academy of Management Learning & Education* 13(2) (2014): 265-289.

79. Call for papers, *Academy of Management Review* 40(4) (2015): 669-670.

80. W.L. Bedwell, S. M. Fiore, and E. Salas, "Developing the Future Workforce: An Approach for Integrating Interpersonal Skills Into the MBA Classroom," *Academy of Management Learning & Education* 13(2) (2014): 171-186.

81. G. Colvin, "Humans Are Underrated," *Fortune* (August 1, 2015), 100-113.

82. G. Hofstede, "Motivation, Leadership, and Organizations: Do American Theories Apply Abroad?" *Organizational Dynamics* (Summer 1980): 42-63.

83. A. Engelen, T.C. Flatten, J. Thalmann, and M. Brettel, "The Effect of Organizational Culture on Entrepreneurial Orientation: A Comparison between Germany and Thailand," *Journal of Small Business Management* 52(4) (2014): 732-752.

84. Adapted from M. Javidon and R. J. House, "Cultural Acumen for the Global Manager: Lessons from Project GLOBE," *Organizational Dynamics* 29(4) (2001): 289-305.

85. D. Baden and M. Higgs, "Challenging the Perceived Wisdom of Management Theories and Practice," *Academy of Management Learning & Education* 14(4) (2015): 539-555.

86. H.G. Barkema, X.P. Chen, G. George, Y. Luo, and A.S. Tsut, "West Meets East: New Concepts and Theories," *Academy of Management Journal* 58(2) (2015): 460-479.

87. J. Bussey, "Leadership Lessons From the Generals," *The Wall Street Journal* (December 12, 2014): R10.

88. A. Wolfe, "Jack and Suzy Welch," *The Wall Street Journal* (February 21-22, 2015): C11.

89. R.M. Kanter, "Why Global Companies Will Behave More and More Alike," *The Wall Street Journal* (July 8, 2014): R8.

90. P. Elkind, "Panasonic's Power Play," *Fortune* (March 15, 2015): 67-68.

91. G. Colvin, "In the Future," *Fortune* (June 2, 2014): 193-202.

92. J.R. Ramsey and M.P. Lorenz, "Exploring the Impact of Cross-Cultural Management Education on Cultural Intelligence, Student Satisfaction, and Commitment," *Academy of Management Learning & Education* 15(1) (2016): 79–99.

93. R.J. Reichard, S.A. Serrano, M. Condren, N. Wilder, M. Dollwet, and W. Wang, "Engaging in Cultural Trigger Events in the Development of Cultural Competence," *Academy of Management Learning & Education* 14(4) (2015): 461–481.

94. H.G. Barkema, X.P. Chen, G. George, Y. Luo, and A.S. Tsut, "West Meets East: New Concepts and Theories," *Academy of Management Journal* 58(2) (2015): 460–479.

95. B.M. Cole, "Lessons From a Martial Arts Dojo: A Prolonged Process Model of High-Context Communication," *Academy of Management Journal* 58(2) (2015): 567–591.

96. A. Wolfe, "Jack and Suzy Welch," *The Wall Street Journal* (February 21–22, 2015): C11.

97. J. Eisenberg, H.J. Lee, F. Bruck, B. Brenner, M.T. Claes, J. Mironski, and R. Bell, "Can Business Schools Make Students Culturally Competent? Effects of Cross-Cultural Management Courses on Cultural Intelligence," *Academy of Management Education & Learning* 12(4) (2013): 603–621.

98. M.E. Mendenhall, A.A. Arnardottir, G.R. Oddou, and L.A. Burke, "Developing Cross-Cultural Competencies in Management Education via Cognitive-Behavior Therapy," *Academy of Management Education & Learning* 12(3) (2013): 436–451.

99. W.L. Bedwell, S.M. Fiore, and E. Salas, "Developing the Future Workforce: An Approach for Integrating Interpersonal Skills Into the MBA Classroom," *Academy of Management Learning & Education* 13(2) (2014): 171–186.

100. O.E. Varela and R.G. Watts, "The Development of the Global Manager: An Empirical Study on the Role of Academic International Sojourns," *Academy of Management Learning & Education* 13(2) (2014): 187–207.

101. R.J. Reichard, S.A. Serrano, M. Condren, N. Wilder, M. Dollwet, and W. Wang, "Engaging in Cultural Trigger Events in the Development of Cultural Competence," *Academy of Management Learning & Education* 14(4) (2015): 461–481.

102. P.C. Godart, W.W. Maddux, A.V. Shipilov, and A.D. Galinsky, "Fashion with a Foreign Flair: Professional Experiences Abroad Facilitate the Creative Innovations of Organizations," *Academy of Management Journal* 58(1) (2015): 195–220.

103. Y. Chung, H. Liao, S.E. Jackson, M. Subramony, S. Colakglu, and Y. Jiang, "Cracking but Not Breaking: Joint Effects of Faultline Strength and Diversity Climate on Loyal Behavior," *Academy of Management Journal* 58(5) (2015): 1495–1515.

104. Box item, "Three Diversity Strategies That Work," *Fortune*.com accessed July 1, 2017.

105. Box item, "Three Diversity Strategies That Work," Fortune.com accessed July 1, 2017.

106. Staff, "The Best Advice," *Fortune* (October 1, 2015): 109.

107. N. Waller and J. Lublin, "What's Holding Women Back in the Workplace?" *The Wall Street Journal* (September 30, 2015): C1, C2.

108. B. Waber, "Gender Bias by the Numbers," *BusinessWeek* (February 3–9, 2014): 8–9; M. L. McDonald and J. D. Westphal, "Access Denied: Low Mentoring of Women and Minority First-Time Directors and Its Negative Effects on Appointments to Additional Boards," *Academy of Management Journal* 56(4) (2013): 1169–1198.

109. Company Spotlight, Cadence, *Fortune* (December 1, 2015): 45.

110. S.Y. Yousafzai, S. Saeed, and M. Muffatto, "Institutional Theory and Contextual Embeddedness of Womens Entrepreneurial Leadership: Evidence from 92 Countries," *Journal of Small Business Management* 53(3) (2015): 587–604.

111. E. Bernstein, "You Can Do It! Be a Motivator," *The Wall Street Journal* (June 16, 2016): D1, D3.

112. R. McCammon, "So, Here's the Bad News ..." *Entrepreneur* (July 2015): 24–25.

113. S. Painter, "Scott Painter's Tips on Surviving Screwups," *INC.* (November 2014): 32.

114. R. McCammon, "The Worst of Times," *Entrepreneur* (February 2016): 15–16.

115. C. Hann, "Fair Pay," *Entrepreneur* (May 2016): 23.

116. S. Painter, "Scott Painter's Tips on Surviving Screwups," *INC.* (November 2014): 32.

i. http://www.google.com/diversity/at-google.html accessed July 1, 2017.

ii. https://www.google.com/about/working/diversity/ accessed July 1, 2017.

iii. https://www.wired.com/2016/10/google-lab-thats-building-legion-diverse-coders/ accessed July 1, 2017.

iv. http://www.cnn.com/2014/06/04/living/google-doodles-diversity/ accessed July 1, 2017.

v. http://www.usatoday.com/story/tech/2014/05/28/google-releases-employee-diversity-figures/9697049/ accessed July 1, 2017.

vi. http://www.npr.org/2014/06/02/318209074/google-courageous-for-admitting-diversity-problem-so-what-now accessed July 1, 2017.

vii. https://www.google.com/diversity/ accessed July 1, 2017.

viii. http://www.npr.org/2014/06/02/318209074/google-courageous-for-admitting-diversity-problem-so-what-now accessed July 1, 2017.

ix. http://www.washingtonpost.com/blogs/on-leadership/wp/2014/05/29/google-admits-it-has-a-diversity-problem accessed July 1, 2017.

x. http://www.usatoday.com/story/tech/2014/06/30/google-rainbow-push/11775067/ accessed July 1, 2017.

xi. http://articles.latimes.com/2014/feb/05/entertainment/la-et-ct-new-youtube-ceo-20140205 accessed July 1, 2017.

Time, Career, and Etiquette Management

©Ronnie Kaufman/Blend Images LLC

LEARNING OUTCOMES

After completing this chapter, you should be able to:

LO A-1 Explain how to analyze your use of time with a time log.

LO A-2 State the three priority determination questions and determine when an activity on the to-do list should be delegated or assigned a high, medium, or low priority.

LO A-3 List the three steps in the time management system.

LO A-4 Identify at least three time management techniques you currently do not use but will use in the future.

LO A-5 Describe the four career stages.

LO A-6 List the five steps in the career planning model.

LO A-7 Explain at least three tips to get ahead that you can use to improve your chances of getting a job, raises, and promotions.

LO A-8 State two classifications of business etiquette and how etiquette overlaps between the two classifications.

LO A-9 Define the following 11 key terms (in order of appearance in the chapter):

time management	career planning
time log	career development
priority	career planning model
priority determination	career path
questions	job shock
to-do list	business etiquette
time management steps	

OPENING CASE WORK SCENARIO

/ / / Whitney and Shane were talking during lunch hour in a Friendly's Restaurant. Whitney was complaining about all the tasks she had to get done. She had all kinds of deadlines to meet. Whitney was a nervous wreck as she listed the many tasks. After a while, Shane interrupted to say that he used to be in the same situation until he took a time management workshop that taught him to get more done in less time with better results. Shane gave Whitney the details so she could take the course. In return, Whitney told Shane about a career development course she took. It not only helped her to get the job she has now, but also to know what she wants to accomplish in the future, and she learned proper business etiquette.

Have you ever felt as though you have more to do than the time you have to do it in? Do you ever wonder about your career? Do you know proper business etiquette? If you answered yes to any of these three questions, this chapter can help you. / / /

HOW TIME, CAREER, AND ETIQUETTE SKILLS AFFECT BEHAVIOR, HUMAN RELATIONS, HAPPINESS AND PERFORMANCE

Some people may question whether time management belongs in a human relations textbook. It is here because one of the major reasons people and especially managers do not have better human relations is their lack of time.[1] If you manage your time better, you will have more time to spend developing effective human relations and be happier. Developing time management skills is also an effective way to better balance work–family life,[2] reduce stress (Chapter 2),[3] and increase personal productivity.[4] It is possible for you to gain control of your life by controlling your time. How well you manage your time will affect your career success.[5]

Many people are concerned about their careers. Career planning is not just about getting a job; it's also about continually developing yourself so that you can advance throughout your career.[6] Careers are based on good human relations, which lead to higher levels of performance, career success, and happiness.

People using proper business etiquette behave differently than those that don't.[7] Inappropriate and unethical behavior can hurt human relations. A lack of manners in what you say or do, which you may not realize you are doing, can offend someone and hurt relationships and performance. This chapter focuses on improving your time, career, and etiquette management skills.

TIME MANAGEMENT

Our time is valuable.[8] Do you ever feel like there is never enough time?[9] Or that you have so much to do, but so little time?[10] Time is measured objectively, but how we spend our time is subjective, as we tend to waste time.[11] The term **time management** *refers to techniques designed to enable people to get more done in less time with better results.*

Time management skills will have a direct effect on your productivity and career success.[12] The focus here is on improving your time management skills, as we can gain an hour a day.[13] In this section, we examine ways to analyze your present use of time, a priority determination system, ways to use a time management system, and time management techniques.

Analyzing Time Use with a Time Log

The first step to successful time management is to determine current time use.[14] People often do not realize how much time they waste until they analyze time use.[15] Are you satisfied with how you spend yours? An analysis of how you use your time will indicate areas for improvement.

Time Log   The **time log** *is a daily diary that tracks activities and enables a person to determine how time is used.* You use one time log for each day. See Exhibit A.1 for an example. It is recommended that you keep track of your daily time use for one or two typical weeks. You can also use an electronic time log with your PC, laptop, tablet or smart phone.[16] Try to keep the time log with you throughout the day. Fill in each 15-minute time slot, if possible. Try not to go for longer than one hour without filling in the log.

Analyzing Time Logs   After keeping time logs for 5 to 10 school or working days, you can analyze them by answering the following questions:

1. Review the time logs to determine how much time you are spending on your primary responsibilities. How do you spend most of your time?

2. Identify areas where you are spending too much time.

3. Identify areas where you are not spending enough time.

WORK APPLICATION A-1

Why are time management skills important? How can you benefit by using the time management information discussed in this chapter?

Learning Outcome A-1

Explain how to analyze your use of time with a time log.

EXHIBIT A.1 | Time Log

You may photocopy this page or use the electronic version at http://connect.mheducation.com

8:00	Date _____
8:15	
8:30	
8:45	
9:00	
9:15	
9:30	
9:45	
10:00	
10:15	
10:30	
10:45	
11:00	
11:15	
11:30	
11:45	
12:00	
12:15	
12:30	
12:45	
1:00	
1:15	
1:30	
1:45	
2:00	
2:15	
2:30	
2:45	
3:00	
3:15	
3:30	
3:45	
4:00	
4:15	
4:30	
4:45	
5:00	
5:15	
5:30	
5:45	

4. Identify major interruptions that keep you from doing what you want to get done. How can you eliminate them?

5. Identify tasks you are performing that you do not have to be involved with. If you are a manager, look for nonmanagement tasks. To whom can you delegate these tasks?

6. How much time is controlled by your boss? How much time is controlled by your employees? How much time is controlled by others outside your department? How much time do you actually control? How can you gain more control of your own time?

7. Look for crisis situations. Were they caused by something you did or did not do? Do you have recurring crises? How can you plan to eliminate recurring crises?

8. Look for habits, patterns, and tendencies. Do they help or hurt you in getting the job done? How can you change them to your advantage?

9. List three to five of your biggest time wasters. What can you do to eliminate them?

10. Determine how you can manage your time more efficiently.

The remainder of this section presents ideas to help you improve your time management.

Priority Determination

A **priority** *is the preference given to one activity over other activities.* There usually isn't enough time to do everything, but there is time to do the most important things. Employees confessed to wasting about 40% of their time at work doing unimportant or downright irrelevant things.[17] Don't confuse being busy doing lots of activities with making progress on the important priorities (objectives).[18] Focus on your most important priorities (which are often fewer than you think),[19] doing them well, and eliminating essentially everything else.[20] So assign a priority to each task objective, and do the most important thing first (without unnecessary interruptions)[21]—make it a rule. Try to get at least 90 minutes of uninterrupted time a day.[22]

Tasks that you must get done should be placed on a to-do list and then prioritized, ranking the order of performance. According to **Peter Drucker**, a few people seem to do an incredible number of things; however, their impressive versatility is based mainly on doing one thing at a time.

Priority Determination Questions   Set priorities by answering three priority determination questions. The three questions are[23]:

1. Do I need to be personally involved because of my unique knowledge or skills?

2. Is the task within my major area of responsibility or will it affect the performance or finances of my department? Managers must oversee the performance of their departments and keep the finances in line with the budget.

3. When is the deadline? Is quick action needed? Should I work on this activity right now, or can it wait? Time is a relative term. In one situation, taking months or even a year may be considered quick action, while in another situation a matter of minutes may be considered quick action.

To summarize, **priority determination questions** *ask (1) Do I need to be personally involved? (2) Is the task my responsibility or will it affect the performance or finances of my department? and (3) Is quick action needed?*

Assigning Priorities   Based on the answers to the three priority determination questions, a manager can delegate a task or assign it a high, medium, or low priority.

Delegate (D)   The task is delegated if the answer to question 1, Do I need to be personally involved?, is no. If the answer to question 1 is no, it is not necessary to answer

WORK APPLICATION A-2

Identify your three biggest time wasters, preferably with the use of a time log. How can you cut down or eliminate these time wasters?

Communication Skills
Refer to CS Question 1.

Learning Outcome A-2

State the three priority determination questions and determine when an activity on the to-do list should be delegated or assigned a high, medium, or low priority.

questions 2 and 3 because a priority has not been assigned to the task. However, planning the delegation and delegating the task are prioritized. Unfortunately, some managers micromanage and don't save time by delegating tasks.[24]

High (H) Priority   A high priority is assigned if you answer yes to all three questions. You need to be involved, it is your major responsibility, and quick action is needed. But try not to have too many *H*s because you will lose focus on what is really important.[25]

Medium (M) Priority   A medium priority is assigned if you answer yes to question 1 (you need to be involved) but no to either question 2 (it is not your major responsibility) or question 3 (quick action is not needed; it can wait).

Low (L) Priority   A low priority is assigned if you answer yes to question 1 (you need to be involved) but no to both questions 2 and 3. It is not your major responsibility, and quick action is not needed. You can leave low priority items for later, or another day.[26]

WORK APPLICATION A-3

Identify at least three high priorities related to your education.

WORK APPLICATION A-4

List at least five activities on your to-do list. Based on the three priority determination questions, prioritize each activity as H, M, L, or D.

The To-Do List   The to-do lists is an important part of time management. The three priority determination questions are on the to-do list in Exhibit A.2 (or use the electronic copy online) and also appear in Application Situation A-1 to help you develop your ability to assign priorities. The **to-do list** *is the written list of activities the individual has to complete.* Feel free to make copies of Exhibit A.2 (or use the electronic copy online) and use it on the job. In summary, decide what is really important, put it on your list, and find the time to do it.

When using the to-do list, write each activity you have to accomplish on one or more lines and assign a priority to it. Remember that priorities may change several times during the day as a result of unexpected tasks that must be added to your to-do list. Look at the high (H) priority activities and start by performing the most important one. When it's done, cross it off and select the next, until all high-priority activities are done. Then do the same with the medium (M) priorities, then the low (L) priorities. As deadlines come nearer or get changed, priorities will change. With time, low priorities often become high priorities.

EXHIBIT A.2 | To-Do List

D Delegate—no to 1 **H** High priority—yes to all three questions (YYY) **M** Medium priority—yes to 1 and 2 or 3 (YYN or YNY) **L** Low priority—yes to 1, no to 2 and 3 (YNN)	1	2	3		
Activity	Do I Need to Be Involved?	Is It My Responsibility/ Performance/ Finances?	Is Quick Action Needed?	Deadline?	Priority

APPLICATION SITUATIONS / / /

Prioritizing To-Do List Activities   AS A-1

Prioritize the following 10 activities on the to-do list of a supervisor of a production department in a large company.

Priority Determination	1 Do I Need to Be Involved?	2 Is It My Responsibility/ Performance/ Finances?	3 Is Quick Action Needed?	Deadline?	Priority
D Delegate—no to question 1					
H High priority—yes to all three questions (YYY)					
M Medium priority—yes to 1 and 2 or 3 (YYN or YNY)					
L Low priority—yes to 1, no to 2 and 3 (YNN)					
Activity					
1. Chen, the sales manager, told you that three customers stopped doing business with the company because your products have decreased in quality.					
2. Your secretary, Rita, told you that there is a salesperson waiting to see you. He does not have an appointment. You don't do any purchasing.					
3. Jan, a vice president, wants to see you to discuss a new product to be introduced in one month.					
4. Chen, the sales manager, sent you a memo stating that the sales forecast was incorrect. Sales are expected to increase by 20 percent starting next month. You have no extra inventory.					
5. Latoya, the personnel director, sent you a memo informing you that one of your employees has resigned. Your turnover rate is one of the highest in the company.					
6. Rita told you that a John Smith called while you were out. He asked you to return his call, but wouldn't state why he was calling. You don't know who he is or what he wants.					
7. Sherise, one of your best workers, wants an appointment to tell you about a situation that happened in the shop.					
8. Karl called and asked you to meet with him and a prospective customer for your product. The customer wants to meet you.					
9. Tom, your boss, called and said he wants to see you about the decrease in the quality of your product.					
10. In the mail you got a note from Frank, the president of your company, and an article from *The Wall Street Journal.* The note said FYI (for your information).					

Source: Adapted from Harbridge House Training Materials (Boston).

Time Management System

Learning Outcome A-3

List the three steps in the time management system.

We all have the same 24 hours a day—so its all about how to use your time to manage important activities. Make a plan,[27] and be sure to include prioritized objectives and schedule time to complete them.[28]

The time management system that is presented in this section has a proven record of success with thousands of managers. It can also be used by nonmanagers and students. You should try it for three weeks. After that time, you may adjust it to meet your own needs.

The four major parts to the time management system are priorities, objectives, plans, and schedules: *Priorities:* Setting priorities on a to-do list helps increase performance. *Objectives:* Objectives state *what* we want to accomplish within a given period of time. Set objectives following the guidelines stated in Chapter 7. *Plans:* Plans state *how* you will achieve your objectives. They list the necessary activities to be performed. *Schedules:* Schedules state *when* the activities planned will be carried out.

Time management techniques all boil down to making a plan and sticking to it as much as possible. The **time management steps** *are as follows: (1) plan each week, (2) schedule each week, and (3) schedule each day.*

Step 1: Plan Each Week On the last day of each week, plan the coming week. Using your to-do list and the previous week's plan and objectives, fill in the weekly planning sheet on paper or electronically (see Exhibit A.3). Start by listing the objectives you want to accomplish during the week. The objectives should not be routine tasks you perform weekly or daily. For example, if an employee's annual review is coming due, plan for it. Planning

EXHIBIT A.3 | Weekly Planning Sheet

Plan for the week of ____________________

Objectives: (What is to be done, by when) (To + action verb + singular behavior result + target date [Chapter 7, Model 7.2, page 234])

Activities	Priority	Time Needed	Day to Schedule
Total time for the week			

For an electronic version, go to http://connect.mheducation.com.

too much becomes frustrating when you cannot get it all done. On the other hand, if you do not plan enough activities, you will end up wasting time.

Step 2: Schedule Each Week   Scheduling your week gets you organized to achieve your important objectives. You may schedule the week at the same time you plan it, or after, whichever you prefer. Planning and scheduling the week should take about 30 minutes. See Exhibit A.4 for a weekly schedule. Make copies of Exhibits A.3 and A.4 for use on the job. When scheduling your plans for the week, select times when you do not have other time commitments, such as meetings. Schedule around 65 percent of your available weekly and

EXHIBIT A.4 | Weekly Schedule

Schedule for the week of _____

	Monday	Tuesday	Wednesday	Thursday	Friday
8:00 8:15 8:30 8:45					
9:00 9:15 9:30 9:45					
10:00 10:15 10:30 10:45					
11:00 11:15 11:30 11:45					
12:00 12:15 12:30 12:45					
1:00 1:15 1:30 1:45					
2:00 2:15 2:30 2:45					
3:00 3:15 3:30 3:45					
4:00 4:15 4:30 4:45					
5:00 5:15 5:30 5:45					

For an electronic version, go to http://connect.mheducation.com

daily time for unexpected events. With practice, you will perfect weekly planning and scheduling. Steven Covey says, *The key to success is not to prioritize your schedule, but to schedule your priorities weekly and daily.*

Step 3: Schedule Each Day   At the end of each day, you should schedule the next day. Or you can begin each day by scheduling it. This should take 15 minutes or less. Using your plan and schedule for the week, and your to-do list, schedule each day on the form in Exhibit A.5. Be sure to include your three or four top priority items.

Begin by scheduling the activities over which you have no control, such as meetings you must attend, and be punctual. But don't forget to leave time for unexpected events.

Skill-BuildingExercise A-1 develops this skill.

EXHIBIT A.5 | Daily Schedule

Day _____	Date _____
8:00 8:15 8:30 8:45	
9:00 9:15 9:30 9:45	
10:00 10:15 10:30 10:45	
11:00 11:15 11:30 11:45	
12:00 12:15 12:30 12:45	
1:00 1:15 1:30 1:45	
2:00 2:15 2:30 2:45	
3:00 3:15 3:30 3:45	
4:00 4:15 4:30 4:45	
5:00 5:15 5:30 5:45	

Time Management   AS A-2

Match each statement with its part in the time management system.

A. Priorities   B. Objectives   C. Plans

D. Weekly schedule   E. Daily schedule

_____11. "I've decided how to get the work done following this step-by-step procedure."

_____12. "I know my major responsibilities and the order for doing each one."

_____13. "I just finished planned my week; now my next step is to. . . ."

_____14. "I'm pretty booked up on June 15, what time do you want to meet?"

_____15. "I want to be clear on this task. What is the end result you want me to accomplish?"

Communication Skills
Refer to CS Question 2.

However, don't procrastinate; schedule the task and just do it. And again, turn off your digital devices.

Schedule your high-priority items during your prime time. Prime time is the period of time when you perform at your best. For most people this time is early in the morning. Determine your prime time and schedule the tasks that need your full attention then. Do routine things, like checking your mail, during non-prime-time hours, after high-priority items are done.

Do not perform an unscheduled task before a scheduled task without prioritizing it first. If you are working on a high-priority item and a medium-priority item is brought to you, let it wait. Often, the so-called urgent things can wait.

Multitasking, Interruptions, and Procrastination

These three topics are highly related as multitasking leads to interruptions and procrastination on high-priority tasks. Interruptions lead to multitasking. When procrastinating, you tend to use multitasking and interruptions to put off doing your high-priority tasks.

Multitasking   Are you constantly doing multiple thinking tasks at the same time—multitasking? People are multitasking more today than ever, but research has shown that most people, even those who think they are good at it, are not good at multitasking. "Simply put, multitasking is a fantasy."[29] Why?

Although you may not want to believe it, research has shown that the human brain is not actually capable of doing two thinking (cognitive) tasks at the same time.[30] Think of it as a single-screen TV. You can't watch two shows at once, but you can flip back and forth, missing some of each show; the more shows you watch, the more you miss of each one. Time is lost when switching between tasks, and the time loss increases with the complexity of the task. Managing multiple tasks at once reduces your working memory and concentration and increases stress.[31]

People who multitask are actually less efficient than those who focus on one "complex" project at a time. Errors go way up, and it takes far longer—often double the time or more—to get the jobs done than if they were done sequentially. So stop multitasking and get things done.[32]

How would you assess your use of multitasking? Complete Self-Assessment Exercise A-1 to help you determine whether you are multitasking too much.

/ / / **Self-Assessment Exercise A-1** / / /

Multitasking

Identify how frequently you experience each statement.

Not frequently				Frequently
1	2	3	4	5

_____ 1. I have a hard time paying attention; my mind wanders when I'm listening to someone or reading.

_____ 2. I have a hard time concentrating; I can't do just one work/homework task for an hour or longer.

_____ 3. I have short-term memory loss; I forget if I did something recently.

_____ 4. I'm easily bored, distracted, and interrupted while doing work/homework.

_____ 5. I continually check for text, phone, and e-mail messages and go online while doing work/homework.

Add up your score (5 to 25) and place it here _____ . On the continuum below, mark the point that represents your total score.

Multitasking not an issue   1 --- 5 --- 10 --- 15 --- 20 --- 25   Possible over-multitasking

The five statements are all warning signs of over-multitasking. However, other issues, such as fatigue, could also cause these signs. Can you improve your time management by cutting down on multitasking and focusing more on one task at a time? If you don't like to spend much time doing one thing or get bored easily, at least try to select a good stopping point so that when you return to a task, you don't lose too much time figuring out where you left off. You can also write notes to help you quickly get back to being productive at the task when you return to it.

Interruptions and Distractions   Constant interruptions reduce productivity and increase stress,[33] and distractions tend to lead to interruptions. With things binging and bonging and tweeting at you, you don't think.[34] Here are some facts: the average time working on a task before being interrupted is 13 minutes, and it takes close to a half hour to get back to the same task; once back to the task, it takes 15 minutes to get back into the same level of intense concentration, and errors increase.[35] How would you assess your ability to avoid interruptions and distractions?

Smartphones. Smartphones are supposed to increase our productivity, but they actually prove to do the opposite.[36] Why? Because they lead to wasting time multitasking. The average person looks at their smartphone 221 time per day, or over three hours—that's about every four minutes.[37] How long can you go without looking at your smartphone? Try it. If you really want to get those important priorities completed faster and better, avoid multitasking.[38] Shut off your phone and other distractions and do one important thing at a time.[39] Here are ways to improve. Doing one thing at a time helps you avoid disruptions. Stay focused on your high-priority tasks; when interrupted with a non-urgent task, let it wait until you complete the high-priority task. You can save time by shutting off these disruptions—yes, your smartphone. Stay on track for a set amount of time, such as a half or full hour. After that set time, you can check for text, e-mails, etc.[40]; you don't always need to respond, but when you do, be brief; calling often saves time. Music, and especially TV, are distracting and can overtax the brain.[41] If you need background sounds to overcome distracting noise, try music that you don't really like or dislike, so you can ignore it, like classical music or ocean sounds, and you can wear noise-canceling headphones. So stop zoning out and get things done.

Procrastination   Let's face it, just about all of us procrastinate at times, but 25% of us identify as chronic offenders,[42] and for college students it may be as high as 70 percent.[43] How bad of a procrastinator are you? Let's talk about the negative effects of procrastination and some ideas to help overcome it.

When you procrastinate, you prioritize badly and leave important things not done. Post-poning or not making decisions or not taking action can be costly. For college students, you may know that procrastination results in lower grades, but the bad habit predicts lower salaries and a higher likelihood of being unemployed.[44]

Here are some ways to help overcome procrastination.[45] Just get started. You can just do part of the task; break it up into smaller parts. Use positive affirmations, such as, "I can do this." and "Get it done on time." Think about the good feeling you will have if you stop procrastinating and finish the task, or the bad feeling you have when not doing it or the stress of rushing through a last-minute effort that is not your best work. The time management techniques discussed in the next section also provide ideas.

Time Management Techniques

Learning Outcome A-4

Identify at least three time management techniques you presently do not use but will use in the future.

Self-Assessment Exercise A-2 includes 68 time management techniques. They include major time wasters and ways to overcome them. Complete the exercise to determine which techniques you presently use and techniques that can help you get more done in less time with better results. Review and prioritize the items in the "Should" column. Select at least your top priority item now to work on each week. Write it on your to-do list, and schedule it, if appropriate. Once you have completed the "Should" column, do the same with the items in the "Could" and "Do" columns. Then review the "N/A" ("not applicable") column items to be sure they do not apply.

/ / / Self-Assessment Exercise A-2 / / /

Time Management Techniques	(1) Should	(2) Could	(3) Do	(4) N/A
This list of 68 ideas can be used to improve your time management skills. Check off the appropriate box for each item. (1) I *should* do this. (3) I *do* this now. (2) I *could* do this. (4) *Does not apply* to me. **Planning and Controlling**				
1. Set objectives—long- and short-term.				
2. Plan your week, how you will achieve your objectives.				
3. Use a to-do list; write all assignments on it.				
4. Prioritize the items on your to-do list. Do the important things rather than urgent things.				
5. Get an early, productive start on your top-priority items.				
6. During your best working hours—prime time—do only high-priority items.				
7. Don't spend time performing unproductive activities to avoid or escape job-related anxiety. It doesn't really work.				
8. Throughout the day ask yourself, "Should I be doing this now?"				
9. Plan before you act.				
10. Plan for recurring crises, and plan to eliminate crises.				
11. Make decisions. It is better to make a wrong decision than none at all.				
12. Have a schedule for the day. Don't let your day be planned by the unexpected.				
13. Schedule the next day before you leave work.				
14 Schedule unpleasant or difficult tasks during prime time.				
15. Schedule enough time to do the job right the first time. Don't be too optimistic on the length of time to do a job.				
16. Schedule a quiet hour(s). Be interrupted only by true emergencies. Have someone take a message, or ask people to call you back during scheduled unexpected event time.				
17. Establish a quiet time for the entire organization, department, or other group. The first hour of the day is usually the best time.				
18. Schedule large blocks of uninterrupted (emergencies only) time for projects, etc. If this doesn't work, hide somewhere.				

(*continued*)

/ / / **Self-Assessment Exercise A-2** / / / (*continued*)

	(1) Should	(2) Could	(3) Do	(4) N/A
19. Break large (long) projects into parts (time periods).				
20. If you don't follow your schedule, ask the priority question (is the unscheduled event more important than the scheduled event?).				
21. Schedule a time for doing similar activities (e.g., make and return calls, write letters and memos).				
22. Keep your schedule flexible—allow _____ % of time for unexpected events.				
23. Schedule unexpected event time and answer mail; do routine things in between events.				
24. Ask people to see or call you during your scheduled unexpected event time only, unless it's an emergency.				
25. If staff members ask to see you—"got a minute?"—tell them you're busy and ask if it can wait until X o'clock (scheduled unexpected time).				
26. Set a schedule time, agenda, and time limit for all visitors, and keep on topic.				
27. Control your time. Cut down on the time controlled by the boss, the organization, and your subordinates.				
Organizing				
28. Keep a clean desk.				
29. Rearrange your desk for increased productivity.				
30. All non-work-related or distracting objects should be removed from your desk.				
31. Do one task at a time.				
32. With paperwork, make a decision at once. Don't read it again later and decide.				
33. Keep files well arranged and labeled.				
34. Have an active and inactive file section.				
35. If you file an item, put a destruction date on it.				
36. Call rather than write, when appropriate.				
37. Have someone else (delegate) write letters, memos, etc.				
38. Dictate rather than write letters, memos, etc.				
39. Use form letters and/or form paragraphs.				
40. Answer letters or memos on the document itself.				
41. Have someone read things for you and summarize them for you.				
42. Divide reading requirements with others and share summaries.				
43. Have calls screened to be sure the right person handles them.				
44. Plan before calling. Have an agenda and all necessary information ready—take notes on the agenda.				
45. Ask people to call you back during your scheduled unexpected event time. Ask when is the best time to call them.				
46. Have a specific objective or purpose for every meeting.				
47. For meetings, invite only the necessary participants and keep them only for as long as they are needed.				
48. Always have an agenda for a meeting and stick to it. Start and end as scheduled.				

(*continued*)

/// Self-Assessment Exercise A-2 /// (continued)

	(1) Should	(2) Could	(3) Do	(4) N/A
49. Conclude each meeting with a summary, and get a commitment on who will do what by when.				
50. Call rather than visit, if possible.				
51. Set objectives for travel. List everyone you will meet with. Send them agendas and have a file folder for each person with all necessary data for your meeting.				
52. Combine and/or modify activities to save time.				
Leadership and Staffing				
53. Set clear objectives for subordinates with accountability—give them feedback and evaluate results often.				
54. Use your subordinates' time well. Don't make them wait idly for decisions, instructions, or materials, or in meetings.				
55. Communicate well. Wait for a convenient time, rather than interrupting your subordinates and wasting their time.				
56. Train your subordinates. Don't do their work for them.				
57. Delegate activities in which you personally do not need to be involved.				
58. Delegate nonmanagement functions.				
59. Set deadlines when delegating.				
60. Set deadlines that are earlier than the actual deadline.				
61. Use the input of your staff. Don't reinvent the wheel.				
62. Teach time management skills to your subordinates.				
63. Don't procrastinate; do it.				
64. Don't be a perfectionist; define acceptable and stop there.				
65. Learn to stay calm. Getting emotional only causes more problems.				
66. Reduce socializing without causing antisociality.				
67. Identify your time wasters and work to minimize them.				
68. If there are other ideas you have that are not listed above, add them here.				

Communication Skills
Refer to CS Question 3.

/// In the opening case, Whitney could benefit from implementing the time management system and techniques presented here. ///

WORK APPLICATION A-5

From the 68 time management techniques presented in Self-Assessment Exercise A-2, list the three most important ones you should be using. Explain how you will implement each technique.

Learning Outcome A-5

Describe the four career stages.

CAREER MANAGEMENT

You must take the responsibility for managing your career. If you expect others to give you jobs, raises, and promotions, they may never come your way. In this section, you will learn how to manage your career successfully. The topics covered are career stages, career planning and development, getting a job, resumes, getting raises and promotions, global careers, and apparel and grooming.

Career Stages

Before planning your career, you must consider your career stage. As people get older, they have different career stage needs.

The 20s   This is the time when you are just getting started. The challenge is to prove that you have what it takes to get the job done well—and on time. There is a lot of pressure to be the best. You must develop the job skills needed to do the present job and to prepare for advancement. Initiative is needed. Do you realize that you will need to work long, hard hours to get ahead?

The 30s   This decade is the time when people develop expertise. In their 30s people often question their careers: Where am I going? Should I be here? Am I secure in my position? People feel trapped by financial demands and are frightened of changing careers even when they are not happy, because a change in career often requires a cut in pay to start at a lower position.

The 40s and 50s   By age 45, most people have weathered a failure or two and know whether or not they have a shot at advancement. In the past, people at this stage would settle into a secure job. However, many organizations have cut back. People in their 40s and 50s are sometimes forced to seek new employers or new careers. This can be difficult when trying to cope with growing older.

The 60s and 70s   At this stage, people begin to prepare for retirement, or may transition to part-time work. They can pass along what they have learned and provide continuity. People at this stage make good role models and mentors.

Career Planning and Development

There is a difference between career planning and career development. **Career planning** is *the process of setting career objectives and determining how to accomplish them.* **Career development** *is the process of gaining skill, experience, and education to achieve career objectives.* You must take responsibility for your career and develop a career plan. As stated by Whitney in the opening case, career planning, as through taking a course, can help lead to career success.

Most colleges and large organizations offer career planning and development services. The career planning counselor's role is not to find people jobs but to help them set realistic career objectives and plans. Many colleges also offer career placement services designed to help students find jobs. But it is the students' responsibility to obtain the job offer.

The career planning model can help you develop your own career plan. In preparation for Skill-Building Exercise A-2, you will find working papers to guide you in the development of your own career plan. The **career planning model** *steps are these: (1) self-assessment, (2) career preferences and exploration, (3) set career objectives, (4) develop a plan, and (5) control.*

Step 1: Self-Assessment   The starting point in career planning is the self-assessment inventory. Who are you? What are your interests, values, needs, skills, and experience? What do you want to do during your career? If you don't have the answers to these questions, most college career services offer free or low-cost tests that can help.

The key to career success is to determine the following: What do you do well? What do you enjoy doing? How do you get a job that combines your interests and skills? To be successful, you need to view yourself as successful (Chapter 3).

Step 2: Career Preferences and Exploration   Based on your self-assessment, you must decide what you want from your job and career, and prioritize those wants. It is also important to determine why you want to do these things. What motivates you? How much do you want it? What is your commitment to your career? Without the appropriate motivation and commitment to career objectives and plans, you will not be successful in attaining them.

Some of the things you should consider are: (1) which industry you want to work for; (2) what size organization you want to work for; (3) what type of job(s) you want in your career, including which functional areas interest you (production/operations, marketing, finance, human resources, and so on) and, if you want to be a manager, what department(s) you want to manage; (4) what city, state, or country you want to work in (people who are willing to relocate often find more opportunities); and (5) how much income you expect to earn when you start your career, as well as 5 years and 10 years from then.

Once you have made these determinations, read about your primary career area. Conduct networking interviews. Talk to people in career planning and to people who hold the types of jobs you are interested in. People in these positions can help provide information that you can use in developing your career plan. Get their advice. Determine the requirements and qualifications you need to get a job in the career that interests you. Getting an internship, fieldwork position, cooperative job, part-time job, and/or summer job in your field of interest can help you land the job you want after graduation. In the long run, it is often more profitable to take a job that pays less but gives you experience that will help you in your career progression.

Step 3: Set Career Objectives   Set short- and long-range objectives using the guidelines from Chapter 7. Objectives should not simply be a listing for the next job(s). For example (assuming graduation from college in May 2017):

- To attain a sales position with a large insurance company by June 30, 2020.
- To attain my MBA by June 30, 2021.
- To become a sales manager in the insurance industry by June 30, 2022.

Step 4: Develop a Plan   Develop a plan that will enable you to attain your objectives. A college degree is becoming more important for developing skills and earning pay increases. This is where career development fits in. You must determine what skills, experience, and education you need to get where you want to go and plan to develop as needed. Talking to others can help you develop a career plan.

You should have a written career plan, but this does not mean that it cannot be changed. You should be open to unplanned opportunities and take advantage of them when it is in your best interest to do so.

WORK APPLICATION A-7

What career development efforts are you making?

Step 5: Control   It is your responsibility to achieve your objectives. You may have to take corrective action. Review your objectives, check your progress at least once a year, and change and develop new objectives and plans. Update your resume (to be discussed) at the same time.

Exhibit A.6 lists the steps in the career planning model.

Communication Skills
Refer to CS Question 5.

Getting a Job

It has been said that getting a good job is a job in itself. In attaining any good job, you need to develop a career plan; develop a resume and cover letter; conduct research; and prepare for the interview. Research shows that most jobs are filled through networking[46] (Chapter 9), which can be helpful at each stage.

EXHIBIT A.6 | Career Planning Model

Step 1. Self-assessment.
Step 2. Career preferences and exploration.
Step 3. Set career objectives.
Step 4. Develop a plan.
Step 5. Control.

APPLICATION SITUATIONS / / /

Career Planning Steps   AS A-3

Match each statement with its step in the career planning model.

A. 1   B. 2   C. 3   D. 4   E. 5

_____ 16. "Once a year, I sit down and assess my career progress."

_____ 17. "I'm not sure if I want to work in a bank, so I'm applying for internships to find out what it's like."

_____ 18. "I'm finishing my B.S. in Business Management and I'm looking forward to working."

_____ 19. "I'm very knowledgeable about sports and I write well."

_____ 20. "I want to be a partner in a law firm within ten years."

Career Plan   Interviewers are often turned off by candidates who have no idea of what they want in a job and career. On the other hand, they are usually impressed by candidates with realistic career plans. Having a good career plan gives you a competitive advantage over those who do not.

Resume and Cover Letter   A recruiting executive at Xerox once said that the resume is about 40 percent of getting a job. The cover letter and resume are your introduction to the organization you wish to work for. If the resume is not neat, has errors, or contains mistakes, you may not get an interview.

The cover letter should be short—one page or less, as some recruiters don't even read it. Its purpose is to introduce your resume and to request an interview. The standard cover letter states the job you are applying for and summarizes your qualifications, and end by asking for an interview.

The use of a resume for part-time and summer employment can also give a positive impression that makes you stand out from the competition. Give copies to friends and relatives who can help you get a job.

Communication Skills
Refer to CS Question 6.

Research   Research is required to determine where to send your resume. Many colleges offer seminars in job search strategies. There are also a number of articles and books on the subject. Most people today find jobs through networking. Help-wanted ads in newspapers and online are common places to research jobs.

Once you land an interview, but before you go to it, you should research the organization. You want to determine as much about the organization as you can. For example, you should know the products and/or services it offers, know about the industry and its trends, and know about the organization's profits and future plans; www.hoovers.com may have the company information. For organizations that are publicly owned, you can get an annual report that has much of this information; they are also online at most company Web sites. While Hoover's is a great source of information about larger organizations; it doesn't work well for local businesses. To gather information on local employers you can use the Internet, Web sites, social media, and friends/family. If you know people who work at the organization, talk to them about these issues.

You should also develop a list of questions you want to ask the interviewer during or at the end of the interview. Asking questions is a sign of intelligence and shows interest in the organization. Two good areas to ask questions about are job responsibilities and career opportunities.

EXHIBIT A.7 | Common Interview Questions

Answering these questions prior to going to a job interview is good preparation that will help you get the job; written answers are better than verbal.

- How would you describe yourself?
- What two or three things are most important to you in your job and career?
- Why did you choose this job and career?
- What do you consider to be your greatest strengths and weaknesses?
- What have you learned from your mistakes?
- What would your last boss say about your work performance?
- What motivates you to go the extra mile on a project or job?
- What have you accomplished that shows your initiative and willingness to work?
- What two or three accomplishments have given you the most satisfaction? Why?
- Why should I hire you?
- What skills do you have?
- What makes you qualified for this position?
- In what ways do you think you can make a contribution to our company?
- Do you consider yourself a leader?
- How do you work under pressure?
- Why did you decide to seek a position in this company?
- What can you tell us about our company?
- What are your expectations regarding promotions and salary increases?
- Are you willing to travel and relocate?
- What are your long-range and short-range goals and objectives?
- What do you see yourself doing five years from now? Ten years from now?
- What do you expect to be earning in five years?

Don't forget that the company will be doing research on you through social media,[47] so remove any inappropriate pictures and statements before you start your job search.

Communication Skills
Refer to CS Question 7.

Prepare for Questions   You should also prepare to answer possible questions that you could be asked during a job interview (see Exhibit A.7 for a list of common interview questions). If you are asked to state strengths and weaknesses, don't give direct weaknesses; they should be strengths in disguise. For example, don't say, "Sometimes I have trouble getting along with others." Instead say, "I'm very accomplishment-oriented, and sometimes I push people to work harder and cause some conflict."

The Interview   The interview is given the most weight in job decisions in most cases. It is vital to make a very positive first impression (Chapter 2). This means conveying a relaxed presence and an ability to convey accomplishments and to pique the interviewer's interest quickly. Be sure to follow job interview etiquette; discussed in the next section. You also want to dress for success, which we discuss at the end of this section.

Many college career placement services offer workshops on how to interview for a job. Some offer mock interviews on camera that allow you to see how you conduct yourself during an interview. If this service is available, take advantage of it. During the interview, smile, be pleasant and agreeable, and offer compliments to interviewers.

After the interview, evaluate how well you did. If you want the job, send a thank-you letter or e-mail, add anything you forgot to say, and state your interest in the job and the fact that you look forward to hearing from the interviewer. Enclose or attach a copy of your resume.

If you did not get the job, ask the interviewer how you can improve. An honest answer can be helpful in preparation for future interviews.

WORK APPLICATION A-8

Which specific idea(s) on getting a job do you plan to use?

Resumes   To begin, complete Self-Assessment Exercise A-3 to evaluate your resume, if you have one or resume knowledge to help you write one.

/ / / **Self-Assessment Exercise A-3** / / /

Your Resume Evaluation

Rate either your current resume or your resume knowledge for each question as:

Describes my resume   5   4   3   2   1   Doesn't describe my resume

——— 1. My resume is based on a good career plan.

——— 2. My resume is customized; it's not simply a copy of some format blueprint.

——— 3. My resume does not include the word "I," and it has incomplete sentences.

——— 4. My resume is customized for each individual job; one size doesn't fit all.

——— 5. My resume is neat, attractive, and free of errors.

——— 6. My resume is one page long, or two pages max for five or more years of experience.

——— 7. My resume has digital/Internet capabilities.

——— 8. My most important selling points are listed first and given the most space.

——— 9. My resume states the specific job I'm applying for; it's not a general statement.

——— 10. My job objective includes my personal qualities and skills with the job.

——— 11. My resume has a qualification summary, or in 10–15 seconds, the recruiter can understand the job I want and that I am qualified to do the job.

——— 12. My resume includes accomplishments that are quantified.

——— 13. My resume includes concrete examples of skills, not just fluff words like *communication skills, team player, driven, organization,* and *interpersonal skills.*

——— 14. My experience includes employment by months and years; plus employer, address, telephone, and supervisor, if they want a reference.

——— 15. My experience that is not directly related to a job applied for focuses on transferable skills related to the job.

——— Total. Add up the number of points and place it on the continuum below.

Effective resume   75   70   60   50   40   30   20   15   Ineffective resume

The higher your score, the better are the chances of getting the job you apply for.

Let's begin by stating some general guidelines to resume writing, followed by the major parts of the resume. Although there is no one right way to write a resume, most resumes do include these parts. Also, note that the advice is from experts, but you can find people who do not agree with everything presented here, or there may be exceptions to these rules. While reading about the resume, refer to Exhibit A.8, Sample Resume.

Communication Skills
Refer to CS Question 8.

General Resume Guidelines   It is fine to follow some resume format, but you have to customize your resume, and you should have a unique resume for each job you apply for. Resumes are written with incomplete sentences to keep them short and to the point, without stating "I." For people with less than five years of experience, a one-page resume is recommended, and two pages is the max. Today, many employers are using some form of digital/online resumes. Even if you send a print copy, many companies scan your resume. We will discuss the e-resume later in this section.

Your most important selling points should be the most visible. Thus, place the most job-relevant qualifications first and give them the most coverage. If you have professional full-time work experience related to the job you are applying for, list experience before education. If you are a recent college graduate with the degree as your major qualification, list

EXHIBIT A.8 | Sample Resume (but it should be a full page)

John Smith
10 Oak Street
Springfield, MA 01118
413-748-3000   jsmith@aol.com

Objective

Competitive team player with excellent sales and communication skills seeks sales position with Best Buy.

Qualification Summary

Degree in business with a concentration in marketing. Marketing internship and marketing research experience. Sales and customer relations experience. Increased sales by 5 percent for employer. Developed communications, sales, and leadership skills through a variety of courses and jobs. Captain of the basketball team.

Education

BS Business Administration/ Marketing	**Springfield College,** Springfield, MA 01109. Business major with a concentration in marketing. 3.0 GPA. Graduation May 2020.
Courses	Sales—developed communication skills through three class presentations.
	Sales skills developed through 10 sales role-playing exercises.
	Marketing research—developed a questionnaire and conducted survey research for a local business, developing a customer profile to be used to target market sales promotions.
Marketing Internship	**Big Y Supermarkets,** 1050 Roosevelt Ave., Springfield, MA 01117, 413-745-2395. Supervisor: VP of Marketing John Jefferson. Worked directly for the VP on a variety of tasks/projects. Helped with the weekly newspaper ad inserts. Suggested a layout change that is being used. Spring Semester 2019.
Basketball Team	Member of the varsity basketball team for four years, captain senior year.

Experience

Salesperson	**Eblens,** 100 Cooley St., Chicopee, MA 01020, 413-534-0927. Sold clothing and footwear to a diverse set of customers. Employee of the month in July for the highest sales volume. Supervisor: Susan Miller. May to August 2018.
Landscaper	**Eastern Landscaping,** 10 Front St., East Longmeadow, MA 01876, 413-980-7527. Helped attract two new customers, a 5% increase. Interacted with customers and resolved complaints. Supervisor: Owner Thomas Shea. May to August 2016 and 2017.

education first. For more information on resume writing, visit you college career center or do an online search.

The e-Resume: As you may know, many organizations are requesting that resumes be sent electronically via e-mail. Be sure to follow their instructions. Do develop your resume in a word processing file. However, save your resume in your word processing document as a PDF file. Your resume is now an e-resume. Before sending it to an employer, send it to yourself so that you can see what it looks like. If it's a mess, fix it; then resend it to yourself until it reads well and looks good. Send it to the employer.

Getting Raises and Promotions

This section discusses tips to help you get ahead, career paths, and job shock.

Tips to Help You Get Ahead   Below are 10 ways to enhance your chances of career advancement:

- Be a top performer at your present job. If you are not successful at your present job, you are not a likely candidate for a raise or promotion.
- Finish assignments early. When your boss delegates a task, finish it before the deadline. This shows initiative.

WORK APPLICATION A-9

Make a resume following the chapter guidelines. Bring your resume to class. Your professor may allow class time for you to see other students' resumes so that you can give and receive feedback.

Learning Outcome A-7

Explain at least three tips to get ahead that you can use to improve your chances of getting a job, raises, and promotions.

- Volunteer for extra assignments and responsibility. If you can handle additional work, you should get paid more, and you show your ability to take on a new position.

- Keep up with the latest technology. Request the opportunity for training. Take the time to learn to use the latest technology. Read publications that pertain to your field.

- Develop good human relations with the important people in the organization. (Follow the ideas throughout this book.)

- Know when to approach your boss. Make requests when your boss is in a good mood; stay clear when the boss is in a bad mood unless you can help resolve the reason for the bad mood.

- Be polite. Saying "please" and "thank you," "pardon me," and so on, shows concern for others.

- Never say anything negative about anyone. You never know who will find out what you've said. That "nobody" may be a good friend of an important person.

- Be approachable. Smile, and go out of your way to say hi to people. Take time to talk to people who want your help.

WORK APPLICATION A-10

Which of the 10 tips for getting ahead need the most and the least conscious effort on your part? Explain your answer.

Career Paths   A **career path** *is a sequence of job assignments that lead to more responsibility, with raises and promotions.* In organizations that have career paths, it is easier to develop a career plan, because in a sense that's what career paths are. In the fast-food industry, career paths are common. For example, management trainees start out by going to a formal training program for a few weeks; then they are assigned to a store as a trainee for six months; then they go to a different store as an assistant store manager for a year; then they become a store manager.

Preparation for Getting a Raise or Promotion   It is very important to understand your job responsibilities and how you are evaluated by your boss, both formally and informally. Know your boss's expectations and exceed them, or at least meet them. Do what needs to be done to get a high performance appraisal. If you don't get a good performance appraisal, your chances of getting a raise or promotion will be hurt.

If you want a raise or promotion, it's your responsibility to prove that you deserve one; prepare your case. The way to prove it is through self-documentation of your accomplishments.

WORK APPLICATION A-11

Which specific idea(s) do you plan to use to help you get raises and promotions?

If you plan to ask for a raise, state a specific amount. Check to find out what other people in similar jobs are getting for raises, and what other organizations pay their employees for similar jobs. Check Web sites (www.salaryexpert.com, www.indeed.com/salary, www.salary.com, www.payscale.com) for market rates for salaries, posted by occupation. If your boss is a negotiator, be sure to follow the negotiation advice in Chapter 9.

Job Shock   Few jobs, if any, meet all expectations. **Job shock** *occurs when the employee's expectations are not met.* Expectations that the workplace is fair and that good work will always be recognized and rewarded are the leading cause of job shock. People also find part or many of their day-to-day tasks boring. Job shock has no quick cure. Talk to other people to find out if your situation is unique. If it's not, you probably have unrealistic job expectations. People often change jobs only to find the same frustrations they hoped to leave behind. Learn to realize that your unhappiness often springs from unrealistic job expectations. Developing a positive attitude (Chapter 3) and focusing on the positive aspects of your job can help shield you from future shocks.

Through personal development, you can improve your human relations skills and time management skills and advance in your career. Good luck in doing so.

Global Careers

Globalization will affect your career in one way or another. You could end up like William Lussier by taking a job in Europe working for a Japanese company. To advance you may leave the country and work abroad for a year or more. You could take a job working in the

United States for a foreign-owned company, for example, **Shell** (Netherlands), **Nestlé** (Switzerland), **Nokia** (Finland), **Samsung** (South Korea), or **Columbia Records** (Japan). Even if you work in America for a U.S. company, there is a good chance that you will work with employees from other countries here and with employees in other countries. You will likely deal with customers or suppliers from other countries. At the least, in the corporate world, you will compete with foreign companies for business. What type of global career do you want? Regardless of your career goals, possessing good human relations skills with a diversity of people is critical to your career success (Chapter 12).

Apparel and Grooming

If you are thinking that it is unfair to be judged by your appearance rather than for who you really are and what you can do, you are correct. However, if you haven't found out yet, life is not always fair. Fair or not, in most organizations, your appearance will affect your career success. Remember that you are judged on your appearance and how you look affects the business's image and success. However, your appearance is something over which you have control.

Apparel and grooming play a major role in making a good first impression because they help you get and keep a job. They are also important in maintaining your image to help you get raises and promotions. Your clothes should be proper business apparel that is well coordinated, well tailored, and well maintained. Your hair should be neat, trimmed, clean, and away from your face. Clean teeth and fingernails and fresh breath are expected. Avoid tattoos, body-piercing jewelry, and flashy jewelry that shows at work.

There are hundreds of image consultants, and etiquette classes are popular. Here are some generally agreed-on suggestions if you want to dress for a successful career in most organizations. /// **In the opening case,** Whitney and Shane may benefit by following the guidelines in this section. ///

Communication Skills
Refer to CS Question 9.

Communication Skills
Refer to CS Question 10.

Dress for the Organization and Job   Dress and groom like the people in the organization and specific job that you want. If you are not sure of the dress style, call or visit the organization before the job interview to find out, or at least possibly overdress, as suggested for job interviews. Once you are on the job, at least dress like your peers. In most cases, casual doesn't include jeans and T-shirts for professional employees. Dress similar to others in the firm when you get the job.

Job Interview   As a general guide, during a job interview never underdress (such as jeans and T-shirts) and possibly overdress. As a college graduate seeking a professional job, wear a suit if managers do (tie for men), even if you will not need to wear one for the job. However, some companies, like Google, advise casual clothes so don't show up in a suit. Do some research so you know what to wear.

Wear Quality Clothes   Quality clothes project a quality image. Start with a quality suit for job interviews and important days at work, such as your first day, to develop a good first impression. Look for sales when buying apparel, but don't buy a suit, or anything else you will wear to work, unless you really like it. If you feel good about the way you look, you will generally project a more positive self-image of confidence, which will help your career. So don't buy anything you don't really like, even if it is on sale.

Suggestions for Men   Men may want to follow these guidelines:

- **Grooming.** If other men in the organization do not have facial hair, long hair, or wear earrings, you may consider shaving, getting a haircut, and leaving the earrings at home, at least for the job interview.
- **Suit.** The suit is still the most appropriate apparel in many organizations. A typical business suit is blue or gray, commonly dark, and stripes are acceptable.

- **Shirt.** The business shirt is a solid color and may have thin stripes, though not loud. The shirt has long sleeves, and they show about ½ inch from the suit sleeves when your arms are by your side.

- **Tie.** The wrong tie can hurt the quality image of your suit. The business tie is silk and usually has some conservative design—no animals, sayings, or cartoon characters.

- **Shoes.** Conservative dark leather business shoes, not sneakers, are worn with a suit. If in doubt about whether your shoes, or any other parts of your business attire, are properly conservative for business, ask a qualified sales rep.

- **Matching.** The suit, shirt, and tie all match. Be careful not to mix three sets of stripes. Generally, with a striped suit, wear a solid-color shirt. Match the color of the design in the tie to the suit and shirt. The color of the conservative belt (small, simple buckle) is the same color as your shoes. The color of the thin socks match the color of the pants (no heavy wool or white socks), and the socks are long enough so that your legs never show.

Suggestions for Women   Women may want to follow these guidelines:

- **Grooming and jewelry.** Wearing heavy makeup, such as very obvious eye shadow, dark outlined lips, and excessive-smelling perfumes, is not appropriate for business. Makeup should be subtle to the point that people don't think you are wearing any, and if worn, perfume should be light. Jewelry is simple and tasteful, never overdone. Avoid long, dangly earrings.

- **Skirted suit.** The professional skirted suit is most appropriate; however, the conservative business dress with coordinated jacket is also acceptable. The skirt matches the blazer-cut jacket, and it reaches to the middle of the knee. With proper business apparel, you are not trying to make a fashion statement. Women have more color choice, but black, dark blue, and gray are good for the first suit.

- **Blouse.** The business blouse is silk or cotton and free of frills, patterns, or unusual collars; it is not low-cut. Low necklines come across as seductive, and people usually assume the sexual innuendo is intentional. Do not show your cleavage, even at business socials, because the image set forth will be lasting. You want people talking about your accomplishments, not your figure. Solid colors are preferred, with a greater range of collars acceptable so long as they contrast and coordinate with the color of the suit. The top button should be open.

- **No tie, scarf optional.** Don't dress like the guys. It is generally agreed that a woman wearing a tie may appear as though she is trying to imitate male apparel. However, a conservative scarf is acceptable if you want to wear one.

- **Shoes.** Leather shoes match the suit and are conservative. Avoid open-toe shoes. Shoes are not a fashion statement—they are comfortable, with a moderate heel; plain pumps are a good choice.

Communication Skills
Refer to CS Question 11.

- **Matching, and attaché case.** All apparel matches. Neutral or skin-tone pantyhose are worn with your business suit. Businesswomen carry an attaché case, which replaces a purse or handbag, whenever feasible.

Remember that what you think about affects how you feel, and how you feel affects your behavior, human relations, and performance. So think happy, confident thoughts that you are a winner and you will act and be perceived as a winner and career success will follow. Complete Self-Assessment Exercise A-4 to determine how your personality affects your time and career management.

In addition to looking good, you also have to behave appropriately in the business environment. So let's turn to business etiquette.

Personality and Time and Career Management

If you are *open to new experiences,* you probably are time-conscious and seek improvements. Being open and flexible, you may be good at career development.

If you have a high *agreeableness* personality, with a high need for affiliation, you may not be too concerned about time management and may freely give your time to others. However, you may need to work at saying no to requests that you don't have to do, so that you don't spread yourself too thin, you can get your own work done, and you can keep your stress level down. You also may not be too concerned about career advancement, because relationships tend to be more important to you than being a manager and climbing the corporate ladder.

If you scored high on *conscientiousness,* with a high need for achievement, you may tend to be time-conscious to achieve

your goals by the dates you set. You are concerned about career success, but without a high surgency need, your concern may not be to advance in management.

If you have *surgency,* with a high need for power, you like to be in control and may need to work at trusting people and delegating to save time. You most likely have aspirations to climb the corporate ladder. But be sure to use ethical power and politics.

Action plan: Based on your personality, what specific things can you do to improve your time management and career skills?

_____

_____

ETIQUETTE MANAGEMENT

Our behavior should be ethical using proper business etiquette. **Business etiquette,** *often referred to as manners, is the code of behavior expected in work situations.* Many organizations weigh etiquette during the job interview as part of the selection criteria and then for advancement. You may be thinking that it is unfair to judge job candidates by their manners, and you may be right. However, the reality of the business world is that firms do not want employees representing their organization who do not project a favorable image for the organization. You are judged by the way you look and act.[48]

Learning Outcome A-8

State two classifications of business etiquette and how etiquette overlaps between the two classifications.

Unfortunately, recent college grads lack professionalism.[49] If you haven't been concerned with business etiquette, start now because it is important.[50] We'll give you some tips in this section regarding in-person, digital, a possible mixture of the two.

In-Person Etiquette

In this section we discuss in-person etiquette to be used during conversations, while dining, and hoteling.

Conversation Etiquette   When you first meet people, especially those at a higher level in the organization, don't assume they want to be called by their first name. Address them with *titles,* such as *Mr.* or *Ms., Dr.,* and so on followed by *last name* unless they tell you to call them by their first name. Use proper business vocabulary, and avoid using obscene language (this goes for digital communication as well). *Profanity* tends to offend some people, but not using such words never seems to offend anyone.

Introducing people using proper etiquette includes presenting the lower-ranking person to the higher-ranking person, stating the higher-ranking person's name first: "Mr. Jones (VP), this is our new sales rep, Carl Jones." When people are of equal rank, mention the older one first. When introducing one employee to a group, present the group to the person: "Carl Jones, these are the other sales reps in our department, Tom Smith, Julio Gonzalis, and Mary Washington." It is also good manners to say a few things about the person being introduced:

Shaking hands is common business etiquette during introductions. Give a firm, not too strong, handshake with the right hand, and establish eye contact as you greet the person. If the other person extends a fist to your hand, you can change to a fist. Other forms of *touching,* such as hugs, are not common business etiquette, but they can be a norm to follow in some organizations.

Dining Etiquette   Table manners are important for some jobs because business is sometimes transacted during a meal. In fact, some managers will take the job candidate out to eat and observe etiquette, including table manners. Candidates with poor etiquette are not offered the job, or the business deal. Common etiquette is for the person inviting the other party out to eat to pay the bill. **Nina Zagat**, co-founder of the **Zagat Survey** restaurant guide, says: "When ordering food, you are not trying to draw attention to yourself or what you are eating." So avoid food that is messy, such as ribs and lobster. As a general guide, follow the lead of the other person's etiquette.[51] For more details on table manners, see Exhibit A.9.

Hoteling, Telecommuting, and Cubicle Etiquette   *Hoteling* is the sharing of workspace and equipment, such as desks, computers, phones, fax machines, copiers, eating areas, refrigerators, coffee machines, water coolers, and so on. Hoteling is common for mobile organization.[52] Do follow the general rule to do unto others as you would have them do unto you, such as cleaning up after yourself and making sure the equipment is ready for the next

EXHIBIT A.9 | Table Manners

The following are a few simple tips in case you are taken out to eat during the job interview or business meeting. If you get the job and take others out to eat, you are in the interviewer role, even if it's not a job interview. Many of the tips also apply to eating with others during your lunch breaks.

- Don't be starving when you go out to eat. Pigging out is not appropriate behavior and will not make a good impression on the interviewer.

- Do follow the lead of the interviewer; don't take charge.

- Do let the interviewer sit first.

- Do place your napkin on your lap after the interviewer does.

- If the server asks if you want a drink, do wait for the interviewer to respond. Don't ask for alcohol if you are underage.

- Don't order alcohol unless asked if you want a drink by the interviewer. If asked, ask the interviewer if he or she will be having a drink. If the interviewer say yes, have one; if the answer is no, don't have a drink. However, don't have a drink if you will feel its effects. You want to be in top form for the interview questions and discussion, and you want to maintain your proper etiquette.

- Do expect to order an appetizer, main course, and dessert. However, you don't have to order them all, especially if the interviewer does not. For example, if the interviewer asks if you would like an appetizer or a dessert, ask the interviewer if he or she is having one. If the server asks, wait for the interviewer to answer.

- Don't begin to eat any serving until everyone at the table has been served and the interviewer has begun to eat, and pass things around the table to the right.

- Do try to eat at the same pace as the interviewer so that you are not eating each serving much faster or slower than the interviewer.

- Don't talk with food in your mouth. Take small bites to help avoid this problem.

- Don't take the last of anything that you are sharing. It is also polite to leave a little food on your plate, even if you are still hungry.

- Do start using the silverware from the outside in. Follow the interviewer's lead when in doubt.

- Do not offer to pay for part or all of the bill. The general rule is that whoever invites the other out to eat pays the bill, unless otherwise agreed before going to eat.

- Do thank the interviewer for the meal. Also, be polite (say "please" and "thank you") to the server.

person, paying your fair share of any expenses (coffee, bill for lunch, employee presents), not taking other people's food and drinks without permission (return the favor), and respecting others' privacy (don't read or look at things on their desk, computer screen, mail, messages, fax).

Telecommuting is working from off the business premises, usually at home and on the road. Telecommuters usually do at least occasionally go to the work site, so hoteling etiquette applies. The unassigned workspace is called "free address" or "non-territorial offices."[53] Do take advantage of the face-to-face time at work and over the phone to network, showing enthusiasm for the people and work.

Cubicle etiquette refers to working in an open area close to others who can observe your behavior (see and hear you working and your nonwork activities). Try not to bother others by doing things like talking too loud, displaying things (on walls, desks, computer screens) that can offend others, and doing personal things (letting your cell phone ring, applying makeup, clipping nails). Don't eavesdrop, limit chit-chat, and use headphones.[54] Do dress appropriately (end of the last section Appendix A for details),[55] and unless it is part of the organizational culture, don't wear hats (like sports baseball caps) indoors.

WORK APPLICATION A-12

Give a job example of when a coworker behaved with improper in-person etiquette.Place your text here...!Digital Etiquette

Digital Etiquette

As you know, people are communicating more electronically, but don't let screens distract you from your important priorities. Knowing how to use information technology (digital) is important to your career, but you also need to be able to do so with proper business etiquette.[56] So here we discuss using cell phones and texting, e-mail and instant messaging, and telecommuting.

Cell Phone Etiquette   The cell (or smart) phone makes it tempting to do personal things while on the job. Business etiquette says not to do personal things in your work area. Because it is a problem, some firms have cell phone rules. So make your personal calls, check **Facebook**, and surf the Web on your break time and move out of your work area. If you do have a business cell phone, use it only for business, and don't use it (or your personal cell) when you are driving (it is illegal in some states and you greatly increase the chances of getting into an accident). See Exhibit A.10 for cell phone etiquette, which generally applies to personal or business use.

EXHIBIT A.10 | Cell Phone Etiquette

- Do speak loudly and clearly enough and speak slowly.

- Do call the person back if you get disconnected; it's the caller's responsibility to call back.

- When you are with others, show sincere interest in them by not constantly looking at your cell phone; place it out of sight and shut it off, or at least put it on vibrate, and don't have a loud, unusual ringtone.

- Don't take a call interrupting a personal conversation, meeting, or other activity unless the message is a true emergency. If you are driving, shut off your cell, or at least pull over to use your cell if it is urgent and you can't wait until getting to your destination (don't check your cell during red lights; they are often too quick and you end up driving while on your cell).

- Don't disrupt others with your cell conversations, such as by talking in meetings and public places (while walking down the street, in a store, restaurant, elevator, or classroom). Do go to a private place, or at least 15 feet away from others.

- Don't eat or drink, talk to others, or talk in the bathroom on your cell phone.

- Don't take multiple calls at one time, keeping people on hold. Do let voice mail take a message and call the person back.

- Do leave a brief message if the person does not answer. But don't use voice mail for bad news, sensitive or confidential information, and complicated information and instructions.

- Do call people back within 24 hours.

EXHIBIT A.11 | E-Mail Etiquette

- Do use complete sentences that are not filled with acronyms people may not understand. Remember that an e-mail is different from a less formal text/IM, and don't use all CAPS.

- Do keep it short and to the point; the best e-mail replies involve one word—Yes. Remember to let the person know what type of response you want.

- Do proofread your e-mail and spell and grammar check it before sending. Remember that your mistakes are in writing for the world to see, so don't embarrass yourself with poor writing.

- Do use a good but brief description of what the e-mail is about in the subject line.

- Do use the recipient's name in the greeting and sign your name, and be polite (please and thank you).

- Don't send needless e-mails, including CCing others who don't need to know your message.

- Don't send e-mails when you are highly emotional, especially angry, as it is easy to write things you will regret later; employees have been reprimanded or fired over inappropriate e-mails. So criticize (Chapter 4) and resolve conflicts (Chapter 5) in person, when possible; if not, at least be calm.

- Do assume your e-mail will be forwarded, and that it could be read in court. It is generally better not to send confidential information in an e-mail to ensure that it is not forwarded to an unintended person. Hopefully, you will not be doing anything unethical or illegal, or at least not in writing. Also, remember that deleted e-mails can be retrieved.

E-Mail and Texting/Instant Messaging Etiquette   Select the most appropriate media to send your messages (Chapter 4), so do use the phone if there will be multiple rounds of responses to save time, and remember that not everyone (especially older people) wants to text.[57] Don't forget the need for human contact through conversation. E-mail should be business formal, with texting and instant messaging (IM) less so. Don't send a text/IM unless it has immediate job relevance to the person—e-mail instead. See Exhibit A.11 for e-mail etiquette.

WORK APPLICATION A-13

Give a job example of when a coworker behaved with improper digital etiquette.

Don't get addicted to constantly checking your phone, e-mail, and text/IM, unless it is required by your job. The typical office employee checks e-mails 50 times and uses instant messaging 77 times. Check at set times throughout the day. And when you have something important to get done, shut off all your digital distractions.[58]

In-Person or Digital Etiquette

In this section, we discuss etiquette that can be either in-person or digital: job interviews (by webcam), meetings (via videoconferences), networking (online), presentations (on video and **PowerPoint**).

Job Interview Etiquette   As discussed, the job interview is the major criterion for job selection. Proper dress for in-person and webcam interviews is important to make a good first impression (Chapter 2). The career service department at your college may offer job interview training, and you may be able to use its webcam (commonly **Skype**) during the actual interview. Take advantage of its services. See Exhibit A.12 for etiquette do's and don'ts of job interviewing.

Meeting and Presentation Etiquette   Do be on time and be properly prepared by having done any assignments. The big issue today is whether or not to use digital technology such as cell phones, laptops, and tablets during *meetings* (including during videoconferences). As a general guide, follow the organizational culture and do as the people running the meeting. However, it is considered poor manners to be talking, texting, or surfing the web while others are talking (this includes presentations); if it's an emergency, take it outside. Even while *videoconferencing,* it's best to dress for business, and don't smoke, eat, or chew gum.

Presentations today commonly use PowerPoint (or Mac Keynote) slides, but don't bore your audience by simply reading the slides to them—talk to them and connect on a personal

EXHIBIT A.12 | Job Interviewing Etiquette

In Person and Webcam Interviews

- Do research the organization before the interview so that you can talk intelligently about it.

- Do be sure to get there a little early. Allow plenty of time for traffic and parking. If you are more than 10 minutes early, you can relax and wait before going to the receptionist. For webcams, sign on early enough to start on time.

- Do get the last name and proper pronunciation of the person who will be interviewing you, and greet the interviewer by using her or his last name.

- Don't sit down until the interviewer invites you to sit, and wait for the interviewer to sit first. Not an issue for webcam, just be seated.

- Do be careful of your nonverbal communication (Chapter 4). Sit up straight, leaning a bit forward in the seat, and maintain adequate eye contact to show your interest.

- Do take a little time to think about your answers. Talk clearly and loud enough, while watching your vocabulary to include proper English; avoid street talk or jargon.

- Don't be the first one to bring up salary and benefits.

- Do thank the interviewer for his or her time at the close of the interview.

- Do send a short follow-up, thank-you letter including information discussed during the interview on how you are qualified for the job, or that you thought about after the interview, and send another copy of your resume.

- Do call back if you do not hear whether you got the job by the decision date given by the interviewer, but not before the given date.

Webcam Interviews
In addition to the previous guidelines, here are a few specifically for webcam interviews:

- Do make sure the lighting is even. Don't have a bright light behind you or on the computer to avoid glare and shadows.

- Do try to have the appearance of a professional area. Don't have personal things in view (pets, phone, TV).

- Do turn off all possible distractions (phone, IM, TV, radio) and tell everyone at the interview site to keep the noise down and not to interrupt you during the interview.

- Don't even think about looking at your turned-off phone during the interview.

- Do rehearse to make sure you get the previously mentioned tips right (your college career center may help).

---

level. Keeping the slides to an outline of what you are to present, rather than long detailed text, will help you talk instead of read to the audience.

WORK APPLICATION A-14

Give a job example of when a coworker behaved with improper meeting, presentation, or networking etiquette.

Networking Etiquette   We've already discussed political networking (Chapter 9); now we remind you to use proper etiquette during the process. Remember to be polite and when asking for help, say please; and after getting help, say thank you. Don't ask your boss or people of higher rank to be your **Facebook** friend or **LinkedIn** contact, but you may do so if they ask you. Again, don't do personal social networking on the job.

Online Reputation   You need to be concerned about your *online reputation*. You may not think it is fair to be judged at work for your personal life, but remember that companies don't want employees who will embarrass them. Today employers are doing searches before hiring job candidates, and if they find negative information and pictures of you, you may not get the job.

WORK APPLICATION A-15

Do an online search on yourself. What were the results?

If you are employed, be careful about what you post about your employer because people have been fired for providing confidential information and negative comments about their boss and company. So do an online search on yourself, and if you find anything that is not professional, take it down or ask whoever put it there to take it off.

WORK APPLICATION A-16

Which etiquette tips will you actually use to improve your human relations in your personal and professional lives?

As we bring this chapter to a close, you should realize that better *time management* leads to more effective behavior and performance, which in turn leaves more time for human relations making you happier. You should understand the importance of setting and sticking to priorities, how to set priorities, and how to use the time management system. to plan and schedule your week and each day. How well you manage your time will affect your *career management* success. You should know how to develop a career plan, get a job, write a resume, get raises and promotions, and how to dress for success. But looking good is not enough. You need to behave using proper manners through both in-person and digital *etiquette management*. And be sure to maintain a professional online reputation to help you manage your career successfully.

/ / / REVIEW / / /

The chapter review is organized to help you master the nine learning outcomes for Appendix A. First provide your own response to each learning outcome, and then check the summary provided to see how well you understand the material. Next, identify the final statement in each section as either true or false (T/F). Correct each false statement. Answers are given at the end of the chapter.

LO A-1 Explain how to analyze your use of time with a time log.

To analyze your time, keep a time log for one or two typical weeks. Then answer the 10 questions in the text to analyze areas where your time can be spent more effectively.

Multitasking complex tasks is a good time management technique. T F

LO A-2 State the three priority determination questions and determine when an activity on the to-do list should be delegated or assigned a high, medium, or low priority.

The three priority determination questions are: (1) Do I need to be personally involved? (2) Is the task my responsibility or will it affect the performance or finances of my department? and (3) Is quick action needed? An activity is high priority when you answer yes to all three questions. An activity is medium priority when you say yes to question 1 and no to either question 2 or 3. An activity is low priority when you say yes to question 1 and no to both questions 2 and 3. If the answer to question 1 is no, the activity should be delegated.

After answering the three priority determination questions, you rank order each task on your to-do list. T F

LO A-3 List the three steps in the time management system.

Following the time management system, step (1) is to plan each week, step (2) is to schedule each week, and step (3) is to schedule each day.

Begin scheduling by listing activities over which you have no control, such as meetings. T F

LO A-4 Identify at least three time management techniques you currently do not use but will use in the future.

Answers among students will vary.

Procrastination is a time waster that leads to stress. T F

LO A-5 Describe the four career stages.

The four career stages are characterized as follows. The 20s are a time for proving one's ability as one gets started. The 30s involve the development of expertise and often some questioning of one's career path. By the 40s and 50s, most individuals have reached their highest level of advancement. In the 60s and 70s people begin to prepare for retirement.

Younger people face a greater threat of being laid off; with age comes job security. T F

LO A-6 List the five steps in the career planning model.

The five steps in the career planning model are: (1) self-assessment, (2) career preferences and exploration, (3) set career objectives, (4) develop a plan, and (5) control.

Following graduation from college is a good time to begin determining career preferences and exploration. T F

LO A-7 Explain at least three tips to get ahead that you can use to improve your chances of getting a job, raises, and promotions.

Answers among students will vary.

When applying for a job, it is best not to specify a job title so that employers can match your talents to the jobs they have open. T F

LO A-8 State two classifications of business etiquette and how etiquette overlaps between the two classifications.

Two classifications are in-person (conversation, dining, hoteling, telecommuting, and cubicle etiquette) and digital (cell phone, e-mail, texting, and instant messaging). The two classifications overlap because some business etiquette (job interviewing, attending meetings and giving presentations, and networking) can be done in person and/or digitally.

It is proper etiquette to take personal calls while talking business with coworkers so long as you say excuse me. T F

LO A-9 Define the following 11 key terms.

Select one or more methods: (1) fill in the missing key terms for each definition given below from memory; (2) match the key terms from the end of the review with their definitions; and/or (3) copy the key terms in order from the key terms list at the beginning of the chapter.

_____ refers to techniques designed to enable people to get more done in less time with better results.

A(n) _____ is a daily diary that tracks activities, enabling you to determine how your time is used.

_____ is the preference given to one activity over other activities.

The _____ ask (1) Do I need to be personally involved? (2) Is the task my responsibility or will it affect the performance or finances of my department? and (3) Is quick action needed?

A(n) _____ is the written list of activities the individual has to complete.

The _____ are as follows: step (1) plan each week, step (2) schedule each week, and step (3) schedule each day.

_____ is the process of setting career objectives and determining how to accomplish them.

_____ is the process of gaining skill, experience, and education to achieve career objectives.

The _____ steps are these: step (1) self-assessment, step (2) career preferences and exploration, step (3) set career objectives, step (4) develop a plan, and step (5) control.

A(n) _____ is a sequence of job assignments that lead to more responsibility, with raises and promotions.

_____ occurs when the employee's expectations are not met.

_____, often referred to as manners, is the code of behavior expected in work situations.

/ / / KEY TERMS / / /

Business etiquette   465
career
  development   456
career path   462

career planning   456
career planning
  model   456
job shock   462

priority   445
priority determination
  questions   445
time log   443

time management   443
time management
  steps   448
to-do list   446

/ / / COMMUNICATION SKILLS / / /

The following critical thinking questions can be used for class discussion and/or as written assignments to develop communication skills. Be sure to give complete explanations for all questions.

1. Based on your experience or observation, list ways in which people in organizations waste time. How can these time-wasting activities be cut back or eliminated?

2. It takes time to follow a time management system. Is the time taken worth the benefits? Will you use a time management system? Why or why not?

3. Are you a procrastinator? Are you a perfectionist? What are the pros and cons to being a procrastinator and perfectionist?

4. Have you done a career self-assessment? Was it easy or difficult? Why? Do you believe you could benefit from taking a career test? Why or why not?

5. Select a job you are interested in getting. Go online to one or more of the following Web sites to determine the compensation for the job you want: www.salaryexpert.com, www.indeed.com/salary, www.salary.com, www.payscale.com.

6. Do a job search for the job you are interested in getting. Go online to one or more of the following Web sites (or others related to your field) to find job opportunities: www.collegejournal.com (jobs and tips for new college grads); www.collegerecruiter.com (internships, and entry-level jobs); www.careerbuilder.com (jobs and advice); and www.indeed.com and (www.monster.com (a listing of jobs)

7. From question 6, or based on other sources, select an organization you would like to work for. Research the company and develop some questions in preparation for a job interview.

8. Prepare or revise your resume, and then evaluate it using Self-Assessment Exercise A-3. How did you score? Based on your assessment, revise your resume.

9. How would you feel about working for a domestic company and competing against foreign companies? How would you feel about working for a foreign company at home? How would you feel about working in another country and, if you are interested, what countries would you be willing to work in?

10. Will your apparel and grooming really affect your career success? Why or why not?

11. What are your thoughts on women showing cleavage at work? Should cleavage be covered or shown? Why? In your opinion, is a low neckline meant to be seductive, with intentional sexual innuendo?

12. Review the list of etiquette tips. Which three tips don't you use often now that will help you in the future? How will you change your etiquette?

OBJECTIVE CASE   / / /   Overworked?

In the following discussion, Iris is a middle manager and Peggy is a first-line supervisor who reports to her.

IRIS: Peggy, I've called you into my office to speak to you again about the late report.

PEGGY: I know it's late again, but I'm so busy getting the work out that I don't have time to do it. I'm always the first to arrive for work and the last to go home. I push hard to get the job done. Sometimes I end up redoing employees' work because it's not done properly. I often get headaches and stomach cramps from working so intensely.

IRIS: I know you do. Maybe the problem lies in your time management ability. What do you usually do each day?

PEGGY: Most of each day is spent putting out fires. My employees constantly need me to help them with their work. The days just seem to speed by. Other than putting out fires, I don't do much.

IRIS: So you can't get the reports done on time because of the number of fires. What is your approach to getting the reports done on time?

PEGGY: I just wait until there are no fires to put out; then I do them. Sometimes it's after the deadline.

IRIS: You are going to have to make some definite changes if you are going to be a successful supervisor. Do you enjoy being a supervisor?

PEGGY: For the most part I do. I think I might like to move up the ladder some day. But I like the hands-on stuff; I'm not too thrilled about doing paperwork.

IRIS: If you develop your time management skills, I believe you will find that you can get the job done on time with less stress. On Monday the company is offering a time management workshop. I took the course myself; it's excellent. It really helped me a lot when I was in your position, and still does today. It teaches you a three-step approach. Do you want to attend?

PEGGY: Yes, but what about the work in my department?

IRIS: I'll cover for you. On Tuesday, I want you to come see me first thing in the morning so that we can discuss what you learned and how you are going to apply it on the job.

Answer the following questions. Then in the space between questions, state why you selected that answer.

_____ 1. Keeping a time log and using a to-do list would be helpful to Peggy.

    a. true   *b.* false

_____ 2. Peggy seems to be effective at setting priorities.

    a. true   *b.* false

_____ 3. Peggy seems to delegate _____ activities.

   _a._ many   _b._ few

_____ 4. Setting weekly objectives, plans, and schedules would help Peggy get the reports done on time.

   _a._ true   _b._ false

_____ 5. Peggy seems to have a Type _____ personality.

   _a._ A   _b._ B

_____ 6. Peggy appears to be in the _____ career stage.

   _a._ 20s   _b._ 30s   _b._ 40s and 50s   _b._ 60s and 70s

_____ 7. Peggy has a career plan.

   _a._ true   _b._ false

_____ 8. The time management workshop is best classified as:

   _a._ career planning   _c._ career development

   _b._ career planning model   _d._ career path

_____ 9. From the case information, we can assume that this company has career paths.

   _a._ true   _b._ false

_____ 10. It appears that Peggy will be a good candidate for raises and promotions.

   _a._ true   _b._ false

11. How would you conduct the Tuesday morning session with Peggy?

/ / / SKILL-BUILDING EXERCISE A-1 / / /

Time Management System

Experience: Individual may share answers in-class or online. You will develop and share and discuss your plans and schedules for the week and your daily schedules.

AACSB Competencies: Reflective thinking, analytic skills, and application of knowledge.

Objective: To understand how to use the time management system to enable you to get more done in less time with better results.

Preparation: You need your completed plans and schedules.

Before using the time management system, you will find it helpful to keep a time log for one or two typical weeks. It is strongly recommended that you keep a time log and analyze it.

Note: For this exercise you will need copies of Exhibits A.1, A.3, A.4, and A.5. You may make copies of the exhibits or make your own copies on sheets of paper or go to the text Web site at http://connect.mheducation.com. While performing the steps below, refer to the text guidelines.

Step 1: Plan Your Week.   Use Exhibit A.3 to develop a plan for the rest of this week. Begin with today.

Step 2: Schedule Your Week.   Use Exhibit A.4 to schedule the rest of this week. Be sure to schedule a 30-minute period to plan and schedule next week, preferably on the last day of the week.

Step 3: Schedule Your Day.   Schedule each day using Exhibit A.5. Do this each day, at least until the class period for which this exercise is assigned.

Be sure to bring your plans and schedules to class or online meeting.

Procedure 1 (5-10 minutes)

Break into groups of five or six, and share and discuss your plans and schedules. Pass them around so that you and others can make comparisons. The comparisons serve as a guide to improving future plans and schedules.

Conclusion: The instructor leads a class discussion and/or makes concluding remarks.

Application (2-4 minutes):   What did I learn from this experience? How will I use this knowledge in the future?

Sharing: Volunteers give their answers to the application section.

/ / / SKILL-BUILDING EXERCISE A-2 / / /

Career Planning

Experience: Individuals may share answers in-class or online.   You will share your career plan with classmates to help make improvements.

AACSB Competencies: Reflective thinking, analytic skills, and application of knowledge.

Objective: To experience career planning; to develop a career plan.

Preparation: You will need the completed preparation that serves as your career plan.Answering the following questions will help you develop a career plan. Use additional paper if needed. Do not reveal anything about yourself that you prefer not to share with classmates during the in-class exercise.

Step 1: Self-Assessment
  a. List two or three statements that answer the question, "Who am I?"

  b. Think about two or three of your major accomplishments. (They can be in school, work, sports, hobbies, etc.) List the skills it took to achieve each accomplishment.

  c. Identify skills and abilities you already possess that you can use in your career (for example, planning, organizing, communicating, leading).

Step 2: Career Preferences and Exploration

a. What type of industry would you like to work in? (You may list more than one.)

b. What type and size of organization do you want to work for?

c. List by priority the five factors that will most influence your job or career decisions (opportunity for advancement, challenge, security, salary, hours, location of job, travel involved, educational opportunities, recognition, prestige, environment, coworkers, boss, responsibility, variety of tasks, etc.).

d. Describe the perfect job.

e. What type of job(s) do you want during your career (marketing, finance, operations, personnel, and so forth)? After selecting a field, select a specific job—for example, salesperson, manager, accountant.

Step 3: Set Career Objectives

a. What are your short-range objectives for the first year after graduation?

b. What are your intermediate objectives for the second through fifth years after graduation?

c. What are your long-range objectives?

Step 4: Develop a Plan

Use the following form to develop an action plan to help you achieve your objectives.

Career Plan

Objective _____

Starting date _____   **Due date** _____

Steps (what, where, how, resources, etc.–subobjectives)	When	
	Start	End

Procedure 1 (10-20 minutes)
Break into teams of two or three, or as an entire class. One at a time, go through your career plans while the others ask questions and/or make recommendations to help you improve your career plan.

Conclusion: The instructor leads a class discussion and/or makes concluding remarks.

Application (2-4 minutes):   What did I learn from this experience? How will I use this knowledge in the future?

Sharing: Volunteers give their answers to the application section.

/ / / SKILL-BUILDING EXERCISE A-3 / / /

Developing New Habits

Experience: Individual may share Habits in groups or entire class, in class or online.

AACSB Competencies: Analytic and application of knowledge.

Objective: To develop and share new habits.

Preparation: Select one or more topics from this chapter that will help you improve your human relations. Develop a new habit following the guideline from Chapter 1, section Habits and Skill-Building Exercise 1-4, on how to develop your cure, routine, and reward-change.

Procedure (5-30 minutes)
Follow the procedures from Skill Builder 1-4.

/ / / ANSWERS TO TRUE/FALSE QUESTIONS / / /

1. F. Multitasking is effective for juggling simple, not complex, tasks.
2. F. You should not rank order tasks because you will waste time renumbering them as new ones are added.
3. T.
4. T.
5. F. In the global economy, people of all ages are being laid off.
6. F. Career preferences and explorations, such as internships, should take place during college.
7. F. Recruiters are filling jobs that have specific titles, not matching talents with jobs. Resumes without specific job titles are usually put in the reject pile.
8. F. It is not proper business etiquette to take personal calls during business.

/ / / NOTES / / /

1. S. Shellenbarger, "Too Busy? Or Just Right?" *The Wall Street Journal* (May 14, 2014): D1–D2.

2. B.S. Kwan, "Work-Life Balance: Illusive and Elusive," *Costco Connection* (June 2014): 13.

3. A. Dizik, "For Some Managers, Doing Less Is More," *The Wall Street Journal* (April 28, 2014): R2.

4. A. Cohen, "What's Your Time-Saving Strategy?" *BusinessWeek* (September 9–15, 2013): 65.

5. R. Burzan, "Procrastination vs. Productivity," *Costco Connection* (January 2014): 31.

6. V.L. Kidwell, T.J. Grosser, B.R. Dineen, and S.P. Borgatti, "What Matters When: A Multistage Model and Empirical Examination of Job Search Efforts," *Academy of Management Journal 56*(6) (2013): 1655–1678.

7. D.M. Cable and V.S. Kay, "Striving for Self-Verification During Organizational Entry," *Academy of Management Journal 55*(2) (2012): 360–380.

8. S. Shellengbarger, "Put a Dollar Value on Your Time, With Help From New Tools," *The Wall Street Journal* (July 22, 2015): D1, D2.

9. M. Adams, "There is Never Enough Time," *The Wall Street Journal* (October 26, 2015): R4.

10. S. Bing, "Productivity Now!" *Fortune* (January 1, 2016): 100.

11. R.G. Lord, J.E. Dinh, and E.L. Hoffman, "A Quantum Approach to Time and Organizational Change," *Academy of Management Review 40*(2) (2015): 263–290.

12. V. Harnish, "Five Ways to Get Organized," *Fortune* (September 1, 2014): 42.

13. R. Abrams, "Gain an Hour a Day," *Costco Connection* (September 2016): 14.

14. J. Bercovici, "How Dick Costolo Keeps His Focus," *INC.* (March 2015): 48–57.

15. R.E. Silverman, "Where's the Boss? Trapped in a Meeting," *The Wall Street Journal* (February 14, 2013): B1, B9.

16. NPR, "News," aired January 12, 2015.

17. J. Bercovici, "How Dick Costolo Keeps His Focus," *INC.* (March 2015): 48–57.

18. V. Shmidman, "Advise," *Fortune* (October 1, 2015): 111.

19. M. Whelan, "Productivity Hack," *Fortune* (October 1, 2015): 114.

20. J. Krasny, "The Latest Thinking About Time," *INC.* (March 2015): 44–45.

21. J. Robinson, "Pay Attention!" *Entrepreneur* (September 2014): 60–65.

22. V Harnish, "5 Crucial Performance Metrics," *Fortune* (August 1, 2016): 32.

23. These questions are adapted from Harbridge House training materials (Boston), which was acquired by Coopers & Lybrand in 2007.

24. S. Leibs, "The Micromanager's Guide to Delegation," *Inc.* (March 2014): 19.

25. L. Welch, "A CEOs Job," *INC.* (May 2015): 49–50.

26. S. Shellenbarger, "Too Busy? Or Just Right?" *The Wall Street Journal* (May 14, 2014): D1–D2.

27. J. Krasny, "The Latest Thinking About Time," *INC.* (March 2015): 44–45.

28. J. Wang, "A Delicate Balance," *Entrepreneur* (September 2015): 136.

29. Staff, "When Good Habits Go Bad," *AARP Magazine* (January 2015): 19.

30. M. Kelly, *Rediscovering Catholicism* (New York: Beacon, 2010).

31. S. Shellenbarger, "Too Busy? Or Just Right?" *The Wall Street Journal* (May 14, 2014): D1–D2.

32. S. Shellenbarger, "Help! I'm on a Conference Call" *The Wall Street Journal* (February 26, 2014): D1–D2.

33. A. Dizik, "For Some Managers, Doing Less Is More," *The Wall Street Journal* (April 28, 2014): R2.

34. J. Robinson, "E-Mail Is Making You Stupid," *Entrepreneur* (March 2010): 61–63.

35. S. Shellenbarger, "The Biggest Distraction in the Office Is Sitting Next to You," *The Wall Street Journal* (September 11, 2013): D1, D3.

36. D.K. Berman, "Why Aren't Smartphones Making Us More Productive?" *The Wall Street Journal* (May 1, 2013): B1–B2.

37. A.J. Lombardi, "Tech Neck," *Strength & Conditioning* online accessed January 27, 2017.

38. Staff, "Self-Improvement Through Data," *Fortune* (March 15, 2016): 28.

39. R. Abrams, "Gain an Hour a Day," *Costco Connection* (September 2016): 14.

40. S. Shellenberger, "How Productivity Tools Can Waste Your Time," *The Wall Street Journal* (January 30, 2013): D1, D5.

41. S. Shellenberger, "At Work, Do Headphones Really Help?" *The Wall Street Journal* (May 29, 2012): D1, D4.

42. R. Burzan, "Procrastination vs. Productivity," *Costco Connection* (January 2014): 31.

43. S. Shellenbarger, "To End Procrastination, Look to the Science of Mood Repair" *The Wall Street Journal* (January 8, 2014): D1-D2.

44. S. Shellenbarger, "To End Procrastination, Look to the Science of Mood Repair," *The Wall Street Journal* (January 8, 2014): D1, D2.

45. S. Shellenbarger, "To End Procrastination, Look to the Science of Mood Repair," *The Wall Street Journal* (January 8, 2014): D1, D2.

46. A. Gumbus and R. N. Lussier, "Career Development: Enhancing Your Networking Skill," *Clinical Leadership & Management Review* 17 (2003): 16-20.

47. M. Maltby, "Should Companies Monitor Their Employees' Social Media?" *The Wall Street Journal* (May 12, 2014): R1-R2.

48. D.M. Cable and V.S. Kay, "Striving for Self-Verification During Organizational Entry," *Academy of Management Journal 55*(2) (2012): 360-380.

49. R.E. Silverman, "Recent College Grads Lack Professionalism," *The Wall Street Journal* (March 20, 2013): B8.

50. B. Haislip, "It Pays to Be Polite," *The Wall Street Journal* (November 12, 2012): R6.

51. A. Dizik, "How to Charm and Do Business over Dinner," *The Wall Street Journal* (January 27, 2011): D2.

52. R.E. Silverman and R. Sidel, "Warming Up to the Officeless Office," *The Wall Street Journal* (April 18, 2012): B1, B8.

53. R.E. Silverman and R. Sidel, "Warming Up to the Officeless Office," *The Wall Street Journal* (April 18, 2012): B1, B8.

54. R.E. Silverman and R. Sidel, "Warming Up to the Officeless Office," *The Wall Street Journal* (April 18, 2012): B1, B8.

55. B. Haislip, "It Pays to Be Polite," *The Wall Street Journal* (November 12, 2012): R6.

56. R.E. Silverman, "Recent College Grads Lack Professionalism," *The Wall Street Journal* (March 20, 2013): B8.

57. R.E. Silverman, "Recent College Grads Lack Professionalism," *The Wall Street Journal* (March 20, 2013): B8.

58. J. Robinson, "E-Mail Is Making You Stupid," *Entrepreneur* (March 2010): 61-63.

Applying Human Relations Skills

After completing this chapter you should be able to:

LO B-1 State why human relations skills are important.

LO B-2 Identify the most important human relations concepts from the entire book.

LO B-3 Determine your strongest and weakest areas of human relations.

LO B-4 Compare your present skills assessment with the one you did in Chapter 1.

LO B-5 Explain three options in handling human relations problems.

LO B-6 Describe the four steps of changing behavior.

LO B-7 Develop your own human relations plan.

OPENING CASE WORK SCENARIO

/// **Pat O'Conner and David Fredrick, two students nearing the completion of a human relations course, were talking about the course:**

PAT: This course has a lot of good practical advice that can help me develop effective human relations.

DAVID: I agree. Have you been using the information on a regular basis in your daily life?

PAT: Some of it. I'm so busy that I don't always have time to think about and actually do these things, even though I know they will help me. Have you been using it?

DAVID: Most of it. I figure that if I use these skills now rather than wait until I get a full-time job, I'll be that much ahead of the game.

PAT: Is there a way to do this?

DAVID: Yes, I've already read the appendix. It explains how to develop a human relations plan that you can put into action immediately.

PAT: Guess I'll go read it now.

DAVID: Good luck, see you in class.

Whether you are more like Pat or David, this appendix will help you develop your own human relations plan. ///

A REVIEW OF SOME OF THE MOST IMPORTANT HUMAN RELATIONS CONCEPTS

Learning Outcome B-1

State why human relations skills are important.

Let's highlight some of the most important information from each chapter in the book to tie things all together. If you cannot recall the information covered in any of the chapters, please return to the chapter for a review of the material.

Learning Outcome A-2

Identify the most important human relations concepts from the entire book.

Part 1. Intrapersonal Skills: Behavior, Human Relations, and Performance Begin with You   Chapter 1 defined some of the important concepts used throughout the book. Can you define the following: human relations, the goal of human relations, behavior, levels of behavior, group behavior, organizational behavior, and performance? Do you know how to change habits?

Can you define and discuss personality, stress, intelligence, learning styles, perception, and first impressions? If not, return to Chapter 2.

Can you define and discuss attitudes, job satisfaction, self-concept, and values? If not, return to Chapter 3.

Part 2. Interpersonal Skills: The Foundation of Human Relations   Can you define and discuss the importance of communications; the communication process; and how to send, receive, and respond to messages; situational communications; and how to deal with emotions and give and receive criticism? If not, return to Chapter 4.

Can you define and discuss transactional analysis, assertiveness, conflict management styles, how to resolve conflict with the collaborating conflict style, and interpersonal dynamics? If not, return to Chapter 5.

Part 3. Leadership Skills: Influencing to Help Yourself and Others Succeed   Can you define and discuss trait leadership theory, behavioral leadership theories, contingency leadership theories, and situational supervision? If not, return to Chapter 6.

Can you define and discuss content motivation theories, process motivation theories, reinforcement theory, and motivation techniques? If not, return to Chapter 7.

Can you define and discuss power, organizational politics, vertical politics, horizontal politics? If not, return to Chapter 8.

Can you define and discuss networking and negotiating? If not, return to Chapter 9.

Part 4. Leadership Skills: Team and Organizational Behavior, Human Relations, and Performance   Can you define and discuss team dynamics, group development stages, and how to lead groups and meetings? Can you also define and discuss problem-solving and decision-making approaches and models, and creative group problem-solving and decision-making techniques? If not, return to Chapter 10.

Can you define and discuss resistance to change and how to overcome it; organizational culture and climate; and organizational development? If not, return to Chapter 11.

Learning Outcome B-3

Determine your strongest and weakest areas of human relations.

Can you define and discuss prejudice and discrimination, equal employment opportunity, diversity groups, sexual harassment, sexism in organizations, global diversity and cross-cultural relations, and how to handle complaints? If not, return to Chapter 12.

Can you define and discuss time management, career management, and proper business etiquette. If not, return to Appendix A.

ASSESSING YOUR HUMAN RELATIONS ABILITIES AND SKILLS

Learning Outcome A-4

Compare your present skills assessment with the one you did in Chapter 1.

For each of the 12 statements below, record in the blank the number from 1 to 7 that best describes your level of ability or skill. This assessment will give you a direct comparison to the score for the same assessment back in Chapter 1.

Chapter 1 Short Assessment

Low ability/skill   High ability/skill

1	2	3	4	5	6	7

_____   1. I understand my personality profile, preferred learning style, how to handle stress and my perception bias (Chapter 2).

_____   2. I know my attitudes and value, how to improve my self-concept, and guidelines to handling ethical dilemmas (Chapter 3).

_____   3. I understand the communications process, how to deal with emotions, and how to give and received criticism to improve performance (Chapter 4).

_____   4. I understand transactional analysis, how to be assertive, and how to resolve conflicts without hurting relationships (Chapter 5).

_____   5. I understand leadership theories, types of trust and how to develop trust (Chapter 6).

_____   6. I understand the motivation process and the difference among content, process, and reinforcement theories (Chapter 7).

_____   7. I know how to gain and use organizational power and politics (Chapter 8).

_____   8. I know the professional networking process and can negotiate deals that create a win-win situation (Chapter 9).

_____   9. I understand team dynamics and their stages of development, how to conduct a meeting, and how to follow steps in making effective decisions (Chapter 10).

_____   10. I know reasons why people resist change and how to overcome the resistance, and how employees learn the organization's culture, and how firms use organizational development techniques to make changes (Chapter 11).

_____   11. I understand how important diversity is and can identify legally protected groups, and define prejudice, discrimination, sexism, sexual harassment, and racism; and handle complaints (Chapter 12).

_____   12. I can effectively manage my time and career using proper etiquette (Appendix A).

Scoring: Add up the 12 numbers and divide it by 12 to get your average between 1–7. Place your average score on the line below.

From Chapter 1 assessment _____

Place you score on this line _____

How different are the pre- and post-assessment scores? How do you feel about the difference. Do you believe the difference reflects how much you learned through this course?

End of Course Longer Assessment

Below is a more extensive assessment of you course learning.
For each of the 36 statements that follow, record in the blank the number from 1 to 7 that best describes your level of ability or skill.

Low ability/skill   High ability/skill

1	2	3	4	5	6	7

_____   1. I understand how personality and perception affect people's behavior, human relations, and performance.

_____   2. I can describe several ways to handle stress effectively.

_____   3. I know my preferred learning style (accommodator, diverger, converger, assimilator) and how it affects my behavior, human relations, and performance.

_____   4. I understand how people acquire attitudes and how attitudes affect behavior, human relations, and performance.

_____   5. I can describe *self-concept* and *self-efficacy* and how they affect behavior, human relations, and performance.

_____ 6. I know my values and can use ethical guidelines when facing ethical dilemmas.

_____ 7. I can describe the communication process and barriers that negatively affect communications.

_____ 8. I can effectively deal with my emotions and work effectively with emotional people.

_____ 9. I can give and receive criticism to improve performance.

_____ 10. I can describe transactional analysis.

_____ 11. I can identify the differences between aggressive, passive, and assertive behavior. I am assertive.

_____ 12. I can identify different conflict resolution styles. I understand how to resolve conflicts in a way that does not hurt relationships.

_____ 13. I understand the differences among trait, behavioral, and contingency leadership theories and that you don't have to be a manager to be a leader.

_____ 14. I know my preferred leadership style and how to change it to meet the needs of the situation.

_____ 15. I understand how to develop trust in relationships.

_____ 16. I understand the motivation process.

_____ 17. I can state the differences among content, process, and reinforcement theories.

_____ 18. I can give a one-minute motivational praise.

_____ 19. I can identify bases and sources of power.

_____ 20. I know how to gain power in an organization.

_____ 21. I can list political techniques to increase success.

_____ 22. I know how to develop a professional network.

_____ 23. I know how to conduct a conversation to get people to give me career assistance.

_____ 24. I know how to a negotiation successfully to achieve a win-win situation.

_____ 25. I can identify components of group dynamics and how they affect behavior, human relations, and performance.

_____ 26. I understand how to plan and conduct effective meetings.

_____ 27. I know how to use employee participation in decision making.

_____ 28. I know reasons why people resist change and how to overcome the resistance.

_____ 29. I understand the importance of, and how to learn the organization's culture.

_____ 30. I know organizational development techniques used to make changes.

_____ 31. I understand equal employment opportunity (EEO) and the rights of legally protected groups.

_____ 32. I can define prejudice, discrimination, sexism and sexual harassment in organizations.

_____ 33. I can effectively handle employee and customer complaints.

_____ 34. I understand how to use a time management system and techniques to get more done.

_____ 35. I know how to develop a career plan and manage my career successfully.

_____ 36. I know proper business etiquette.

To use the profile form below, place an X in the box whose number corresponds to the score you gave each statement above. If you did not cover any of the chapters or Appendix B, do not include them in the scoring below.

Profile Form

	Your Score							Parts and Chapters in Which the Information Was Covered in the Book
	1	2	3	4	5	6	7	
								Part 1. Intrapersonal Skills: Behavior, Human Relations, and Performance Begin with You
1.								2. Personality, Stress, Learning, and Perception
2.								
3.								

(continued)

Profile Form (*continued*)

4.								3. Attitudes, Self-Concept, Values, and Ethics
5.								
6.								
								Part 2. Interpersonal Skills: The Foundation of Human Relations
7.								4. Communications, Emotions, and Criticism
8.								
9.								
10.								5. Dealing with Conflict
11.								
12.								
								Part 3. Leadership Skills: Influencing Others
13.								6. Leading and Trust
14.								
15.								
16.								7. Motivating Performance
17.								
18.								
19.								8. Ethical Power and Politics
20.								
21.								
22.								9. Networking and Negotiating
23.								
24.								
								Part 4. Leadership Skills: Team and Organizational Behavior, Human Relations, and Performance
25.								10. Team Dynamics, Creativity and Problem Solving, and Decision Making
26.								
27.								
28.								11. Organizational Change and Culture
29.								
30.								
31.								12. Valuing Diversity Globally
32.								
33.								
34.								Appendix B. Time, Career, and Etiquette Management
35.								
36.								

Scoring: Add up the total numbers between 1–7, not including any numbers for any chapter or appendix not covered. Divide the total by the number of questions to get the average. Place the number between 1–7 on the line below.

_____ Average score

Recall that in Chapter 1 and above you answered the same 12 questions. You can also compare by scores to this longer assessment total score and also by chapter. For example, Chapter 1 question 1 is based on the contents of Chapter 2. So you could get the average of the above questions 1–3 and compare it to Chapter 1 question 1. For Chapter 7 motivation, compare Chapter 1 question 6 to the average of questions 16–18 above. Chapter 1 question 12 is from Appendix B questions 34–36.

When you have finished, you will have your early and your present assessment of your human relations abilities and skills. This will allow you to comparison of your scores, which represent your strong and weak areas of human relations. You will be using your profile form in the next section.

HUMAN RELATIONS PLANNING

In this section, you will learn about handling human relations problems, changing one's behavior, and developing a human relations plan.

Handling Human Relations Problems

Learning Outcome B-5

Explain three options in handling human relations problems.

In any organization, there are bound to be times when you disagree with others. You may be assigned to work with a person you do not like. When you encounter these human relations problems, you have to choose either to avoid resolving the problem or to confront the person to solve it. In most cases, it is advisable to solve human relations problems, rather than to ignore them. Problems usually get worse rather than better, and they do not solve themselves. When you decide to resolve a human relations problem, you have at least three alternatives:

1. *Change the other person.* Whenever there is a human relations problem, it is easy to blame the other party and expect that person to make the necessary changes in behavior to meet our expectations. In reality, few human relations problems can be blamed entirely on one party. Both parties usually contribute to the human relations problem. Blaming the other party without taking some responsibility usually results in resentment and defensive behavior. The more we force people to change to meet our expectations, the more difficult it is to maintain effective human relations. If you do elect to try to change the other person, be sure to use tips throughout this book, and especially handling conflicts (Chapter 5).

2. *Change the situation.* If you have a problem getting along with the person or people you work with, you can try to change the situation by working with another person or people. You may tell your boss you cannot work with so-and-so because of a personality conflict and ask for a change in jobs. There are cases where this is the only solution; however, when you complain to your boss, the boss often figures that you are the problem, not the other party. Blaming the other party and trying to change the situation enables us to ignore our behavior, which may be the actual cause, or at least part, of the problem.

3. *Change yourself.* Throughout this book, particularly in Part I, the focus has been on personal behavior. In many situations, your own behavior is the only thing you can control. In most human relations problems, the best alternative is to examine others' behavior and try to understand why they are doing and saying the things they are, and then examine your own behavior to determine why you are behaving the way you are. In most cases, the logical choice is to change your behavior. We are not saying to simply do what other people request. In fact, you should be assertive, as discussed in Chapter 5. You are not being forced to change; you are changing your behavior because you elect to do so. When you change your behavior, the other party may also change. Remember to create a win–win situation for all stakeholders.

Changing One's Behavior

Learning Outcome A-6

Describe the four steps of changing behavior.

Improving human relations generally requires a change in one's behavior. It is hoped that over the time period of this course, you have made changes in your behavior that have improved your human relations abilities and skills. In changing behavior, it is helpful to follow a four-step approach that encompass developing new habits (Chapter 1): step (1) assess your abilities and skills; step (2) develop new skills; step (3) change your behavior; and step (4) get feedback and reward yourself.

Step 1: Assess Your Abilities and Skills   You should consistently be aware of your behavior and assess it. Without becoming aware of your behavior and being committed to changing it, you cannot improve. You may know someone who has annoying behavior. The person is aware of it, yet does nothing to change. Without that commitment, this person will not change. Think about your own behavior; others may find you annoying, but do you change? What can you gain from changing? Can you make the change successfully?

You assessed your human relations abilities and skills at the beginning of the course and at the present. To continue your assessment, answer the following questions, using your profile form.

1. Have your profile numbers (1 to 7) gotten higher compared to what they were at the beginning of the course? Why or why not?

2. Review your five objectives from Chapter 1, following your profile form. Did you meet them? Why or why not?

3. What are your strongest areas of human relations (highest numbers on your profile form)?

4. What human relations areas do you need to improve the most (lowest numbers on your profile form)?

5. What are the most important abilities and skills you have developed and/or things you have learned through this course?

Step 2. Develop New Skills   The development of new skills can come in a variety of ways. In this course, you had a text to read. This information gives you the basis for new skills. In life, when there is no textbook, you can refer to libraries for periodicals and books that can give you the knowledge you need to change your behavior. You can also refer to friends and experts in the areas in which you need to improve. There may be workshops, seminars, and courses in these areas as well. But you can't develop new skills without developing new habits (Chapter 1).

Step 3: Change Your Behavior   Try to find safe, nonthreatening situations to try out your new behavior. Friends are usually willing to help; try your new behavior on them to see how it works.

EXHIBIT B.1 | Changing Behavior Model

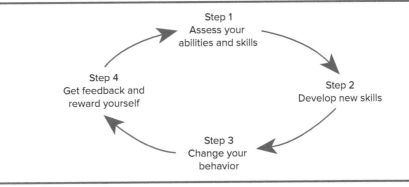

Step 1
Assess your
abilities and skills

Step 4
Get feedback and
reward yourself

Step 2
Develop new skills

Step 3
Change your
behavior

Progressively change your behavior as you develop skill and confidence. For example, if you want to develop your ability to speak in front of people, volunteer and speak in class when the instructor gives you the opportunity. Take a speech class or join Toastmasters.

As with anything else in life, developing new skills takes time and new habits. Try not to be discouraged. For example, if you want to develop more positive, or less emotional, behavior, be patient; it will not happen overnight. If you catch yourself acting emotionally, be aware of it and change to more controlled behavior. With time and persistence, you will have to catch yourself less often as you develop the habit of being patient.

Step 4: Get Feedback and Reward Yourself   Being aware of people's nonverbal communication will give you feedback on your behavior, as will their intentional behavior toward you. However, others' direct feedback requested by you is often more accurate and unbiased. After trying new behavior, ask people you trust if they have noticed any difference. Get their advice on what you can do to improve. For example, if you are trying to be more positive and to give less negative feedback to others, ask them if they have noticed any difference. Ask them to recall the last time they remember hearing you make a put-down statement. People are often willing to help you, especially when it benefits them. Recall that people like doing you favors.

You should also reward yourself for your efforts (step 3 developing a new habit). Notice we said efforts, not total success. Build on small successes; take one step at a time. As the saying goes, "Success by the yard is hard . . . but a cinch by the inch." Your rewards do not have to be big or expensive; you can treat yourself to a snack, take a walk, or do anything you enjoy. For example, say you want to stop putting people down, and you catch yourself in the act. Stop yourself in the middle and end by complimenting the person. Focus on the success, not the failure. Reward yourself rather than be disappointed in yourself.

Exhibit B.1 illustrates these four steps.

My Human Relations Plan

Learning Outcome B-7

Develop your own human relations plan.

Follow the changing behavior model and develop a plan to change your behavior. Write in the space provided.

Step 1: Assess Your Abilities and Skills   Select the one human relations area in most need of improvement. Write it below.

Step 2: Develop New Skills   Review the material in the text that will help you develop the skill to improve by using the behavior to develop new habits. You may also talk to others for ideas, and go to the library to find articles and books on the skill. You can even look into taking a workshop or course on the subject. Below, write down some helpful notes on these skills.

Step 3: Change Your Behavior   Describe what you will have to do to change your behavior. Try to be specific. What is the habit (Chapter 1) cue, changed behavior, and reward?

Step 4: Get Feedback and Reward Yourself   How will you get feedback on your changed behavior? How will you know if you have succeeded in changing your behavior? When will you reward yourself? How will you reward yourself?

Additional Plans   If you feel you can handle working on more than one change in human relations, follow the changing behavior steps and develop another plan. However, don't try to make too many changes too quickly.

/ / /   SKILL-BUILDING EXERCISE B-1   / / /

Human Relations Plan

Experience: Individuals may share human relations plans in groups in-class or online, or as an entire class

AACSB Competencies: Reflective thinking, analytic skills, communication abilities, and application of knowledge.

Objectives: To share your human relations plan with others in order to get feedback on it.

Preparation: You should have completed the human relations plan in the chapter.

Procedure 1 (5–15 minutes)
Break into groups of two to six persons (or as a class) and share your answers to the first four questions under step 1, assessing your abilities and skills. You may also look at and discuss each other's profiles, if you wish to do so. Share your human relations plans, offering each other positive feedback on your plans.

Conclusion: The instructor may lead a class discussion and/or make concluding remarks.

Application (2–4 minutes):   What did I learn from this experience? How will I use this knowledge in the future?

Sharing: Volunteers give their answers to the application situation.

/ / / SKILL-BUILDING EXERCISE B-2 / / /

Course Learning

Experience: Individuals may share course learning in groups, or as an entire class, in-class or online.

AACSB Competencies: Reflective thinking, analytic skills, communication abilities, and application of knowledge.

Objectives: To share your human relations abilities and skills developed through this course.

Preparation: You should answer the question,

"What are the most important abilities and skills you developed and/or things you learned through this course?"

Procedure 1 (5–30 minutes)
Break into small groups and discuss your learning, or volunteers tell the class the most important abilities and skills developed and/or things they learned through this course.

Conclusion: The instructor may lead a class discussion and/or make concluding remarks.

/ / / SKILL-BUILDING EXERCISE B-3 / / /

Developing New Habits

Experience: Individual may share Habits in groups or entire class, in-class or online.

AACSB Competencies: Analytic and application of knowledge.

Objective: To develop and share new habits.

Preparation: Select one or more topics from this chapter that will help you improve your human relations. Develop a new habit following the guideline from Chapter 1, section Habits and Skill-Building Exercise 1-4, on how to develop your cure, routine, and reward-change.

Procedure (5–30 minutes)
Follow the procedures from Skill Builder 1-4.

A

accommodating conflict style Type of conflict management style in which the user attempts to resolve the conflict by passively giving in to the other party.

affirmative action (AA) programs Planned, special efforts to recruit, hire, and promote women and members of minority groups.

assertiveness The process of expressing thoughts and feelings while asking for what one wants in an appropriate way.

attitude A strong belief or feeling toward people, things, and situations.

attribution A person's perception that the cause of behavior is either internal or external.

autocratic style (S-A) Supervisory style that involves high-directive–low-supportive (HD–LS) behavior and is appropriate when interacting with low-capability employees (C-1).

automation The simplification or reduction of human effort required to do a job.

avoiding conflict style Type of conflict management style in which the user attempts to passively ignore the conflict rather than resolve it.

B

bargaining Includes: (1) developing rapport and focusing on obstacles, not on the person; (2) letting the other party make the first offer; (3) listening and asking questions to focus on meeting the other party's needs; (4) not being too quick to give in; and (5) asking for something in return.

behavior What people do and say.

behavioral leadership theories Theories that assume that there are distinctive styles that effective leaders use consistently; that is, that good leadership is rooted in behavior.

Big Five Model of Personality Model that categorizes traits into the dimensions of urgency, agreeableness, adjustment, conscientiousness, and openness to experience.

bona fide occupational qualification (BFOQ) Allows discrimination on the basis of religion, sex, or national origin where it is reasonably necessary to normal operation of a particular enterprise.

brainstorming The process of suggesting many alternatives, without evaluation, to solve a problem.

burnout The constant lack of interest and motivation to perform one's job because of stress.

business etiquette The code of behavior expected in work situations (often referred to as manners).

C

career development The process of gaining skill, experience, and education to achieve career objectives.

career path A sequence of job assignments that lead to more responsibility, with raises and promotions.

career planning model A model that includes these five steps: (1) self-assessment; (2) career preferences and exploration; (3) set career objectives; (4) develop a plan; and (5) control.

career planning The process of setting career objectives and determining how to accomplish them.

coaching model Model that involves five steps: (1) refer to past feedback; (2) describe current performance; (3) describe desired performance; (4) get a commitment to the change; and (5) follow up.

coalition A short-term network used to meet an objective.

coercive power Power that involves threats and/or punishments to influence compliance.

collaborating conflict style Type of conflict management style in which the user assertively attempts to resolve the conflict with the best solution agreeable to all parties.

communication process Consists of a sender who encodes a message and transmits it through a channel to a receiver who decodes it and may give feedback.

complaint model A model that involves four steps: (1) listen to the complaint and paraphrase it; (2) have the complainer recommend a solution; (3) schedule time to get all the facts and/or make a decision; and (4) develop and implement a plan, and follow up.

compromising conflict style Type of conflict management style in which the user attempts to resolve the conflict through assertive give-and-take concessions.

conflict Exists whenever two or more parties are in disagreement.

connection power Power based on the user's relationship with influential people.

consultative style (S-C) Supervisory style that involves high-directive–high-supportive (HD–HS) behavior and is appropriate when interacting with moderate-capability employees (C-2).

content motivation theories Theories that focus on identifying people's needs in order to understand what motivates them.

contingency leadership theories Theories that assume that the appropriate leadership style varies from situation to situation.

contingency leadership theory A theory developed by Fiedler used to determine whether a person's leadership style is task- or relationship-oriented and if the situation matches the leader's style.

controlling stress plan Plan that includes: step (1), identify stressors; step (2), determine their causes and consequences; and step (3), plan to eliminate or decrease the stress.

creativity The ability to develop unique alternatives to solve problems.

D

decision making The process of selecting an alternative course of action that will solve a problem.

decoding The receiver's process of translating the message into a meaningful form.

development The process of developing the ability to perform both present and future jobs.

disability Significant physical, mental, or emotional limitation.

discrimination Behavior for or against a person or situation.

E

ego states Three states consisting of the parent, child, and adult.

Elton Mayo Called the "father of human relations"; he and his associates conducted research through the Hawthorne Studies from the mid-1920s to the early 1930s, known as the Hawthorne effect, that became a landmark in the human relations field. See also *Hawthorne effect*.

emotional labor Labor that requires the expression of feeling through desired behavior.

empathic listening The ability to understand and relate to another's situation and feelings.

encoding The sender's process of putting the message into a form that the receiver will understand.

equity theory A theory that is based on the comparison of perceived inputs and outputs; primarily Adams's motivation theory.

ethics The moral standards of right and wrong behavior.

expatriates People who live and work in a country other than their native country.

expectancy theory Vroom's theory that states that motivation depends on how much people want something and how likely they are to get it: Motivation = Expectancy × Valence.

expert power Power based on the user's skill and knowledge.

F

feedback The process of verifying messages.

force field analysis A technique that diagrams the current level of performance, the hindering forces against change, and the driving forces toward change.

forcing conflict style Type of conflict management style in which the user attempts to resolve the conflict by using aggressive behavior.

four-minute barrier The time people have to make a good impression (also called the four-minute sell).

G

giving praise Popularized by Blanchard and Johnson, the steps in giving praise are: (1) tell the person exactly what was done correctly; (2) tell the person why the behavior is important; (3) stop for a moment of silence; and (4) encourage repeat performance.

goal of human relations To create a win–win situation by satisfying employee needs while achieving organizational objectives.

grapevine The informal vehicle through which messages flow throughout the organization.

group behavior Things two or more people do and say as they interact.

group cohesiveness The attractiveness and closeness group members have for one another and for the group.

H

Hawthorne effect Refers to an increase in performance caused by the special attention given to employees, rather than tangible changes in the work. See also *Elton Mayo*.

horizontal communication The flow of information between colleagues and peers.

human relations (HR) Refers to interactions among people.

I

image Other people's attitudes toward an individual.

influencing process Process that begins with an objective; ethical leadership, power, politics, networking, and negotiating are used to motivate others to help reach the objective; and through trust and creating a win–win situation for all parties, the objective is met.

information power Power based on the user's information being desired by others.

initiating conflict resolution steps Three steps to follow when initiating a conflict resolution: (1) plan to maintain ownership of the problem using the XYZ model; (2) implement your plan persistently; and (3) make an agreement for change.

intelligence The level of an individual's capacity for new learning, problem solving, and decision making.

interpersonal skill The ability to work well with a diversity of people.

intrapersonal skills Skills that are within the individual and include characteristics such as personality, attitudes, self-concept, and integrity (also called self-management abilities).

J

job design The employee's system for transforming inputs into outputs.

job enrichment The process of building motivators into the job itself by making it more interesting and challenging; a means of getting job engagement.

job satisfaction survey A process of determining employee attitudes about the job and work environment.

job satisfaction A set of attitudes toward work.

job simplification The process of eliminating, combining, and/or changing the work sequence to increase performance.

L

laissez-faire style (S-L) Supervisory style that entails low-directive–low-supportive (LD–LS) behavior and is appropriate when interacting with outstanding employees (C-4).

leadership continuum A continuum developed by Tannenbaum and Schmidt that identifies seven leadership styles based on the use of boss-centered versus employee-centered leadership.

Leadership Grid Blake and Mouton's model identifying the ideal leadership style as having a high concern for both production and people.

leadership skill The ability to influence others and work well in teams.

leadership trait theory   Theory that assumes that there are distinctive physical and psychological characteristics accounting for leadership effectiveness.

leadership   The process of influencing employees to work toward the achievement of objectives.

legitimate power   Power based on the user's position power, which is given by the organization.

levels of behavior   Levels include individual, group, and organizational.

locus of control   A continuum representing a person's belief as to whether external or internal forces control his or her destiny.

M

maintenance roles   The things group members do and say to develop and sustain group dynamics.

management by objectives (MBO)   The process in which managers and their employees jointly set objectives for the employees, periodically evaluate the performance, and reward according to the results.

management information systems (MIS)   Formal systems for collecting, processing, and disseminating the information necessary to aid managers in decision making.

manifest needs theory   Theory of motivation that is primarily McClelland's classification of needs as achievement, power, and affiliation.

mediating conflict resolution steps   Four steps to follow when mediating a conflict resolution: (1) have each party state his or her complaint using the XYZ model; (2) agree on the problem(s); (3) develop alternative solutions; and (4) make an agreement for change, and follow up.

message   The physical form of the encoded information.

minority   Defined by the Equal Employment Opportunity Commission (EEOC) as Hispanics, Asians, African Americans, Native Americans, and Alaska Natives.

morale   A state of mind based on employees' attitudes and satisfaction with the organization.

motivation   The internal process leading to behavior to satisfy needs.

multinational company (MNC)   A company that conducts a large part of its business outside the country of its headquarters.

N

needs hierarchy   Maslow's theory of motivation, which is based on five needs: physiological, safety, social, esteem, and self-actualization.

negotiating planning   Includes researching the other parties, setting objectives, anticipating questions and objections and preparing answers, and developing options and trade-offs.

negotiating process   Process that has three, and possibly four, steps: (1) planning, (2) bargaining, (3) possibly a postponement, and (4) an agreement or no agreement.

negotiating   A process in which two or more parties have something the other wants and attempt to come to an exchange agreement (also called bargaining).

networking interview process   Process that includes these steps: (1) establish rapport—praise and read the person; (2) deliver the one-minute self-sell; (3) ask prepared questions; (4) get additional contacts for your network; (5) ask your contacts how you might help them; and (6) follow up with a thank-you note and status report.

networking process   Process that includes these tasks: (1) perform a self-assessment and set objectives, (2) create a one-minute self-sell, (3) develop a network, (4) conduct networking interviews, and (5) maintain the network.

networking   The ongoing process of building relationships for the purpose of politicking and socializing.

networks   Clusters of people joined by a variety of links.

normative leadership theory   A decision-tree model, developed by Vroom and Yetton, that enables the user to select from five leadership styles the one that is appropriate for the situation.

norms   The group's shared expectations of its members' behavior.

O

objectives   State what is to be accomplished within a given period of time.

one-minute self-sell   An opening statement used in networking that quickly summarizes your history and career plan and asks a question.

open-door policy   The practice of being available to employees.

organization   A group of people working to achieve one or more objectives.

organizational behavior (OB)   The collective behavior of an organization's individuals and groups.

organizational climate   The relatively enduring quality of the internal environment of the organization as perceived by its members.

organizational communication   The compounded interpersonal communication process across an organization.

organizational culture   Consists of the shared values and assumptions of how its members will behave.

organizational development (OD)   The ongoing planned process of change used as a means of improving the organization's effectiveness in solving problems and achieving its objectives.

organizational structure   The way managers design their firm to achieve the organization's mission and goals.

P

paraphrasing   The process of having the receiver restate the message in his or her own words.

participative style (S-P)   Supervisory style that is characterized by low-directive–high-supportive (LD–HS) behavior and is appropriate when interacting with employees with high capability (C-3).

perception   A person's interpretation of reality.

perceptual congruence   The degree to which people see things the same way.

performance appraisal The ongoing process of evaluating employee job performance.

performance formula The relationship between the three interdependent factors of ability, motivation, and resources, stated as: Performance = Ability × Motivation × Resources.

performance The extent to which expectations or objectives have been met.

personality A relatively stable set of traits that aids in explaining and predicting individual behavior.

politics The process of gaining and using power.

power A person's ability to influence others to do something they would not otherwise do.

prejudice The prejudgment of a person or situation based on attitudes.

primacy effect The way people perceive one another during their first impressions.

priority determination questions Questions that ask: (1) Do I need to be personally involved? (2) Is the task my responsibility or will it affect the performance or finances of my department? and (3) Is quick action needed?

priority The preference given to one activity over other activities.

problem solving The process of taking corrective action in order to meet objectives.

problem Exists whenever there is a difference between what is actually happening and what the individual or group wants to be happening.

process motivation theories Theories that attempt to understand how and why people are motivated.

Pygmalion effect States that supervisors' attitudes and expectations of employees and how they treat them largely determine their performance.

R

reciprocity Involves creating obligations and debts, developing alliances, and using them to accomplish objectives.

referent power Power based on the user's personal power.

reflecting statements Statements that paraphrase feelings back to the person.

reinforcement theory A theory that states that behavior can be controlled through the use of positive or negative consequences; primarily Skinner's motivation theory.

resistance to change Involves the variables of intensity, source, and focus, which together explain why people are reluctant to change.

responding to conflict resolution steps Four steps to follow when responding to a conflict resolution: (1) listen to and paraphrase the problem using the XYZ model; (2) agree with some aspect of the complaint; (3) ask for, and/or give, alternative solutions; and (4) make an agreement for change.

reward power Power based on the user's ability to influence others with something of value to them.

roles Shared expectations of how group members will fulfill the requirements of their position.

S

self-concept A person's overall attitude about himself or herself.

self-efficacy A person's belief in his or her capability to perform in a specific situation.

self-fulfilling prophecy Occurs when a person's expectations affect his or her success or failure.

self-interest roles The things group members do and say to meet their own needs or objectives at the expense of the team.

sexism Discrimination based on sex.

sexual harassment Any unwelcomed behavior of a sexual nature.

situational leadership A model, developed by Paul Hersey and Kenneth Blanchard, for selecting from four leadership styles the one that matches the employees' maturity level in a given situation.

stages in the creative process The four stages that include (1) preparation, (2) possible solutions, (3) incubation, and (4) evaluation.

standards Performance levels in the areas of quantity, quality, time, and cost.

status The perceived ranking of one member relative to other members of the group.

stereotyping The process of generalizing the behavior of all members of a group.

stress An emotional and/or physical reaction to environmental activities and events.

stressors Situations in which people feel anxiety, tension, and pressure.

survey feedback An organizational development (OD) technique that uses a questionnaire to gather data that are used as the basis for change.

systems effect When all people in the organization are affected by at least one other person, and each person affects the whole group or organization.

T

task roles The things group members do and say that directly aid in the accomplishment of its objective(s).

team building An organizational development (OD) technique designed to help work groups operate more effectively.

team dynamics Refers to the patterns of interactions that emerge as groups develop (these interactions are also called group process).

team performance model States that a team's performance is based on its structure, dynamics, and stage of development.

teamwork Involves working together to achieve something beyond the capabilities of individuals working alone.

Theory X Theory that holds that employees dislike work and must be closely supervised to get them to do their work.

Theory Y Theory that holds that employees like to work and do not need to be closely supervised to get them to do their work.

Theory Z   Theory that integrates common business practices in the United States and Japan into one middle-ground framework appropriate for use in the United States.

time log   A daily diary that tracks activities and enables a person to determine how time is used.

time management steps   The steps include: (1) plan each week, (2) schedule each week, and (3) schedule each day.

time management   Techniques designed to enable people to get more done in less time with better results.

to-do list   The written list of activities the individual has to complete.

total person approach   When an organization employs the whole person, not just his or her job skills.

training   The process of developing the necessary skills to perform the present job.

transactional analysis (TA)   A method of understanding behavior in interpersonal dynamics.

trust   The positive expectation that another will not take advantage of you.

two-factor theory   Theory consisting of Herzberg's classification of needs as hygienes and motivators.

Type A personality   The type of personality that is characterized as fast moving, hard driving, time conscious, competitive, impatient, and preoccupied with work.

types of changes   Types of changes include technical change, structural change, task change, and people change.

types of transactions   The three types include: complementary, crossed, and ulterior.

V

value system   The set of standards by which an individual lives.

values   The things that have worth for or are important to an individual.

vertical communication   The flow of information both up and down the chain of command.

W

win–win situation   Occurs when the organization and the employees both get what they want.

X

XYZ model   Model that describes a problem in terms of behavior, consequences, and feelings.